The Blackwell Guid

Continental Philosophy

—— Blackwell Philosophy Guides ——

Series Editor: Steven M. Cahn, City University of New York Graduate School

Written by an international assembly of distinguished philosophers, the *Blackwell Philosophy Guides* create a groundbreaking student resource – a complete critical survey of the central themes and issues of philosophy today. Focusing and advancing key arguments throughout, each essay incorporates essential background material serving to clarify the history and logic of the relevant topic. Accordingly, these volumes will be a valuable resource for a broad range of students and readers, including professional philosophers.

The Blackwell Guide to
Continental
Philosophy

Edited by

Robert C. Solomon
and
David Sherman

Blackwell
Publishing

© 2003 by Blackwell Publishing Ltd

350 Main Street, Malden, MA 02148-5018, USA
108 Cowley Road, Oxford OX4 1JF, UK
550 Swanston Street, Carlton South, Melbourne, Victoria 3053, Australia
Kurfürstendamm 57, 10707 Berlin, Germany

First published 2003 by Blackwell Publishing Ltd

Library of Congress Cataloging-in-Publication Data

The Blackwell guide to continental philosophy / edited by Robert C.
Solomon and David Sherman.
p. cm. – (Blackwell philosophy guides; 12)
Includes bibliographical references and index. ISBN 0-631-22124-7 (alk. paper) –
ISBN 0-631-22125-5 (pbk. : alk. paper)
1. Philosophy, European. I. Solomon, Robert C. II. Sherman, David
III. Series.
B803 .B57 2003
190 – dc21   2002006208

A catalogue record for this title is available from the British Library.

Set in 10/12½ Galliard
by Graphicraft Limited, Hong Kong
Printed and bound in the United Kingdom
by TJ International, Padstow, Cornwall

For further information on
Blackwell Publishing, visit our website:
http://www.blackwellpublishing.com

Contents

Notes on Contributors

Steven Best is Associate Professor of Philosophy at the University of Texas at El Paso. He is the author of *Postmodern Theory* and *The Postmodern Adventure* (both with Douglas Kellner) and other books.

Noël Carroll is Professor of Philosophy at the University of Wisconsin–Madison. He is the author of *The Philosophy of Horror*, *The Philosophy of Mass Art*, and *Beyond Aesthetics*.

John Coker is Associate Professor and Chair of Philosophy at the University of Southern Alabama. He is the author of several articles on Aristotle, Nietzsche, and Derrida.

David E. Cooper is Professor of Philosophy at the University of Durham. His several books include *Existentialism: A Reconstruction*, *World Philosophies: An Historical Introduction*, *Heidegger*, and *The Measure of Things: Humanism, Humility and Mystery*.

Stephen Houlgate is Professor of Philosophy at the University of Warwick. He is the author of *Hegel, Nietzsche and the Criticism of Metaphysics* (1986) and *Freedom, Truth and History: An Introduction to Hegel's Philosophy* (1991), and the editor of *The Hegel Reader* and *Hegel and the Philosophy of Nature* (both 1998). He was President of the Hegel Society of America from 1994 to 1996 and is currently editor of the *Bulletin of the Hegel Society of Great Britain*.

David Ingram is Professor of Philosophy at Loyola University of Chicago. He is the author of *Habermas and the Dialectic of Reason*, *Reason, History, and Politics*, *Group Rights: Reconciling Equality and Difference*, *Critical Theory and Philosophy*, and many other books.

Douglas Kellner is George Kneller Chair in the Philosophy of Education at UCLA and is the author of many books on social theory, politics, history, and culture, including *Critical Theory, Marxism, and Modernity*, *Jean Baudrillard*, *Postmodern Theory: Critical Interrogations*, *The Postmodern Turn*, and *The Postmodern Adventure* (with Steven Best).

Sean D. Kelly is Assistant Professor of Philosophy at Princeton University. His main publications are in phenomenology, philosophy of perception, and cognitive science.

Mary Beth Mader is Assistant Professor of Philosophy at the University of Memphis. She is the author of articles on Irigaray and Sarah Kofman, and is the translator of Irigaray's *The Forgetting of Air in Martin Heidegger*.

Jeff Malpas is Professor of Philosophy at the University of Tasmania, Hobart, Tasmania, Australia. He is the author of *Donald Davidson and the Mirror of Meaning* and *Place and Experience*, as well as many articles. He is also the editor of a number of collections.

Kelly Oliver is Chair and Professor of Philosophy at the State University of New York at Stony Brook and the author of *Womanizing Nietzsche, Subjectivity without Subjects*, and two books on Julia Kristeva, an original interpretation and a collection of essays, *Ethics, Politics and Difference in Julia Kristeva's Writing*.

David Sherman is Assistant Professor of Philosophy at the University of Montana at Missoula. He is the author of *Hegel's Phenomenology of Self-Consciousness* (with Leo Rauch) and of articles on critical theory, existentialism, and political theory.

Robert C. Solomon is Professor of Philosophy at the University of Texas at Austin. He is the author of *From Rationalism to Existentialism, In the Spirit of Hegel, From Hegel to Existentialism*, and *What Nietzsche Really Said* (with Kathleen M. Higgins), along with many other books.

Robert Wicks is Senior Lecturer in Philosophy at the University of Auckland, Auckland, New Zealand. He is the author of many articles on French and German philosophy and other topics.

Introduction

Robert C. Solomon

"Continental philosophy" is the curious name used to designate philosophy – or, rather, a large number of philosophies – on the continent of Europe over the past two centuries or so, roughly since the work of Immanuel Kant at the very end of the eighteenth century. Since it is a label that is more appropriate overseas than in Europe itself, it is bound to generate a certain amount of confusion. For instance, apart from such well-known names as Hegel, Nietzsche, Heidegger, and Sartre, there is no agreed-upon group of philosophers who form the continental canon. Nor does "continental philosophy" refer to any single identifiable kind of philosophy, style, concern, or tradition. Indeed, what is called "continental philosophy" includes a good number of literary theorists and writers, sociologists, social critics, psychoanalysts, and political activists, many of whom would not normally be considered (nor would they have considered themselves) philosophers. Much less does "continental philosophy" mark off a particular piece of territory. What goes on under that label is now being produced at a much more prodigious rate in the United Kingdom, the Americas, and Australasia than in Europe, where much of the philosophizing has turned to linguistic matters and more "analytic" issues. Nor does the label mark off any particular temperament or method. Hegel and Kierkegaard, just to name two of the earlier authors discussed in this *Guide*, share very little of either temperament or method other than a few fancy terms (most of them ironically adopted by Kierkegaard to mock the Hegelian project). The existentialists reject the idealists, and the postmodernists reject the existentialists. Indeed, it too often seems that the primary function of the phrase "continental philosophy" is to mark off an artificial battle line between so-called "analytic" and "continental" philosophers, where the only thing that is clear is that the two are hostile, suspicious, or at best merely tolerant of each other.

Let us begin this *Guide*, therefore, with the stipulation that no such antagonism is intended here. What will be discussed in this book cuts across continents and cultures and is concerned with epistemology, metaphysics, and the nature and structure of language (usually identified with analytic philosophy), as well as with sharp social criticism and "meaning of life" sorts of questions. Moreover, the tradition in which continental philosophy gets its bearings (and often rejects in turn) is the same "Western" philosophical tradition that motivates much of analytic philosophy. It begins with Socrates, Plato, and Aristotle and continues on to Kant. The language, the questions, and the concerns are for the most part shared, and even the much-touted differences in style tend to be caricatures. Obscure writing is neither defini-tive of nor exclusive to continental philosophers, nor is literary flair.

Within the recognized realm of continental philosophy, there is at least one divide that is as abysmal and sometimes as vicious as the more celebrated divide between "analytic" and "continental" philosophy. That is the polemical divide between "post-modern" and what one might call "pre-postmodern" or, some would say, "modern" European philosophers and philosophy. To be sure, one cannot intelligibly speak about the more notable philosophers of France in the latter part of the twentieth century without being steeped in the work of the German philosophers of the century or so preceding (though many do try). Nietzsche and Heidegger in particular are typically cited as important precursors of philosophical postmodernism, if not as postmodern themselves. Nevertheless, most of the philosophers and philosophies that (quite conscientiously) call themselves "postmodern" or "poststructuralist" are heavily indebted to those that precede them. In much more than a nominal sense, there could be no postmodern or poststructuralist philosophy if there were not first the rich legacy of modern philosophy.

Philosophically, these differences turn on the Enlightenment aspiration to develop a universal philosophy, including an all-embracing concept of knowledge, a univer-sal notion of human nature, and a "cosmopolitan" ethics and political philosophy. All of this might be clumsily summarized in terms of the traditional philosophical notion of "truth." G. W. F. Hegel, who in many ways epitomizes "pre-postmodern" or "modern" European philosophy, announced as the uncompromising goal of both his own work and philosophy through the ages "philosophical truth." This was not to be confused with more ordinary matters of truth (for example, the facts of history or the propositions of mathematics) but was an all-embracing, comprehensive, and "absolute" conception of truth peculiar to philosophy (and some would say, to *his* philosophy). But it was Hegel's "deconstruction" of the Cartesian tradition and the Kantian self that opened the door to poststructuralism.

Many of the postmoderns, by contrast, disparage and eschew the notion of truth altogether, often reaching back to Friedrich Nietzsche, the last great philosopher of the nineteenth century and arguably the first postmodern philosopher, who in some of his more outrageous pronouncements declared truth to be nothing more than "a mobile army of metaphors" and "the more useful errors of mankind." In Nietzsche's case, and in the case of many of the French postmodernists, the attack on truth is first of all an attack on dogmatism, an attack on the uncritical certainty that has been the goal of too much of philosophy and (especially) theology. This attack on truth, however, is much more than a skeptical response. At its most vehement, the attack on truth represents the rejection of the very idea of truth together with a rejection of the Enlightenment thinking that embodies it. It is also a rejection of traditional epistemology and a rejection of metaphysics (or, at least, a dogged resistance to meta-physics, which Jacques Derrida admits cannot be wholly overcome). It suggests, at least, a rejection of the very idea of "human nature," a rejection of any attempt to formulate a "totalizing" theory of ethics or politics, and a reconsideration (if not a rejection) of the very nature of philosophy.

The attack on truth leads, predictably, to a serious difference of style as well – or, rather, a difference in the very conception of what it is to "do" philosophy. Again, Nietzsche's style is often taken as a model. In contrast to the heavy academic writing of Kant and Hegel in particular, the buoyancy, the enthusiasm, and the excesses of Nietzsche's writings are taken as exemplary. He rarely pursues a topic for more than a few pages. Often his insights are captured in aphorisms, short pithy comments that are self-consciously ambiguous and "pregnant" with multiple interpretations. He can often be seen as taking up positions and making claims that are at odds with one another, or even in flat contradiction. He loves puns. He polemicizes. He makes exaggerated claims and uses extravagant language that is easily misunderstood. And, so too, in the late twentieth century, a generation of French philosophers and their Francophile acolytes thoroughly enjoyed themselves "outraging the philistines" (as the earlier French troublemaker Theophile Gautier once insisted), playing with and twisting language, engaging in extravagant and sometimes suspicious etymological investigations (here following Martin Heidegger as well as Nietzsche), occasionally basing a deep philosophical point on a pun, "deconstructing" virtually all foundational claims, and relegating a good many philosophical matters to the vicissitudes of politics and power.

As a matter of convenience, we might say that continental philosophy begins at the start of the nineteenth century, just before the death of Kant. ("Modern" continental philosophy, in its usual designation, begins with Descartes and covers the rich period up to and including Kant.) The dominant figure in early continental philosophy, as we said, was Hegel, but Hegel was immediately preceded and surrounded by an impressive array of "post-Kantian" philosophers who, like Kant, considered themselves "Idealists" of one kind or another. The names of Johann Fichte and Friedrich Schelling are particularly prominent, but there were many others besides. Arthur Schopenhauer, perhaps Hegel's most vocal nemesis, became the darling of the Romantics in mid-century. Other mid-century critics included the Danish philosopher Søren Kierkegaard and a promising student journalist at the University of Berlin, the young Karl Marx. The second half of the century was also remarkably rich with philosophical talent, typically spilling over into (and borrowing from) the social sciences. Psychologists such as Franz Brentano, biologically minded metaphysicians such as Edward Hartman and C. D. Lange, philosophy-minded physicists such as Ernst Mach, and "hermeneutical" philosophers such as Wilhelm Dilthey are exemplary. And then there was Nietzsche, perhaps the best known and currently most celebrated of all pre-postmodern philosophers – although, as I mentioned, he is often considered a postmodern as well.

The turn of the twentieth century was also marked by a rich variety of philosophical efforts, but perhaps the most definitive was the work of a Moravian mathematician, Edmund Husserl, who in his efforts to understand the nature of necessary truth and turn philosophy into a "rigorous science" established what came to be seen as an exciting new way of doing philosophy, *phenomenology*. He was followed and profoundly chastened by his student Martin Heidegger, who in turn inspired both a generation of Frenchmen, notably Jean-Paul Sartre and Maurice Merleau-Ponty, and latter-day hermeneutics, exemplified by Hans-Georg Gadamer. And that, with the war's end, started to bring the "Kant to phenomenology" phase of continental

4 Robert C. Solomon

philosophy to an end. But, of course, the history of ideas is never so neat, and what followed is even more difficult to summarize, if only because it is so recent and still, in many ways, undigested. What is clear is that German philosophy took a radical turn, or continued a radical turn it had taken with the rise to power of the Nazis in the early 1930s. Some of those philosophers, soon to be known as the "logical positivists," emigrated and set their mark on analytic philosophy, following an earlier refugee from the Continent, Ludwig Wittgenstein. Others, however, turned their philosophical talents to desperately needed social criticism, trying to find out how modern life and German culture had conspired to create Hitler and many other social ills.

Thus critical theory and the Frankfurt School were born. The Frankfurt School theorists, Max Horkheimer, Theodor Adorno, and Herbert Marcuse, for instance, challenged and questioned the whole of modern culture and problematized the Enlightenment (without ever completely rejecting it). They vigorously attacked Heidegger's flirtation with the Nazis as well as his philosophy, and made radical suggestions for the transformation of society. The next generation of Frankfurt School theorists, notably Jürgen Habermas, continued the critique, but with a more sympathetic eye to the Enlightenment. Habermas famously confronted the more conservative hermeneutics of Hans-Georg Gadamer, but then he in turn faced more contemporary dangers and opponents, particularly in the new postmodernists. Jacques Derrida and Michel Foucault, and many others besides, sky-rocketed into prominence in France and then throughout Europe and abroad. They turned on traditional philosophy in a radical new way and suggested that not just philosophy but modern culture itself were shot through with contradictions and insupportable pretensions. They were followed in turn by a new generation of feminist philosophers, deeply influenced but also deeply critical of Simone de Beauvoir, who deserves a great deal of credit for having more or less invented French feminism. The new French feminists provided a further radical twist to the ongoing critique of just about everything.

That is a brief history, grossly oversimplified, of the period and people we will be covering in this book. It could be written in many different ways, highlighting many different figures and movements. But in addition to that history, there is another, the history of the reception of these authors abroad. To understand what continental philosophy is, it is not only necessary to understand its internal tensions and "dialectic," but also the distortions wrought by its supposed antagonism with what is now called "mainstream philosophy" in the United States and the United Kingdom. Indeed, briefly considering the history of continental philosophy just in the USA, the UK, and Australasia, one can discern three rather distinctive periods.

First, beginning just after the Second World War and continuing well into the 1960s, European philosophers were mainly ignored and, when mentioned at all, treated as objects of suspicion and with considerable disdain. Jean-Paul Sartre and Albert Camus, who became famous as "existentialists" because of their novels and popular writings, were for the most part excluded from the philosophy curriculum as having little of philosophical interest to offer. (Sartre was the source of considerable amusement to English moral philosophers such as A. J. Ayer, who simply interpreted Sartre's admittedly polemical notion of "absolute freedom" as making the absurd and therefore instantly dismissible claim that one can do absolutely anything that one chooses.) Analytic icon Gilbert Ryle of Oxford once attended a conference with French phenomenologst Maurice Merleau-Ponty, who in the spirit of *détente* politely asked him whether he did not think that they were "after the same thing." Ryle responded, in a tone that expressed the general attitude of Anglo-American analytic philosophy toward the continental philosophy of the time, "I hope not!"

Hegel and Heidegger were quoted only as the butt of abuse. For instance, Hans Reichenbach quotes a few lines of Heidegger in his book, *The Rise of Scientific Philosophy*, as an example of impossibly obscure and "meaningless" philosophy. (As a dubious tribute to Hegel and his British followers, the leading British journal *Mind* once prefaced an issue with a bank page, identifying it as a picture of "the Absolute.") Continental philosophy – mainly Camus and Sartre – was increasingly taught in colleges and universities because of student demand. But it had virtually no philosophical respectability.

The second period, beginning somewhere in the 1970s, was commonly described as a period of "*rapprochment*" and mutual understanding. Books on the great European philosophers tried to explain their ideas in "analytic" terms (that is, clearly and straightforwardly). J. N. Findlay boldly tried to introduce Hegel to an analytic audience, and he was not (as he would have been) simply ignored or insulted. Arthur Danto, following Walter Kaufmann's artful de-Nazification of Nietzsche, wrote *Nietzsche as Philosopher*, making it very clear from the start that what he meant was Nietzsche as an *analytic* philosopher. Respectable books from respectable presses started to appear on Heidegger, Schopenhauer, and Husserl and on "phenomenology." Sartre was taken seriously. The links between Husserl and the great logician Gottlob Frege were appreciated and investigated. Articles started to appear on such topics as the similarities between G. W. F. Hegel and Harvard logician W. V. O. Quine. Graduate students started to write Ph.D. dissertations on prominent figures and topics in continental philosophy, and were not immediately relegated to the unemployment lines. Mainstream philosophers mentioned, quoted, and sometimes even wrote about those philosophers, who were no longer considered "on the other side," just a little bit exotic and obscure. It was a honeymoon period, and the label "continental philosophy" (as opposed to more specific topics, such as "phenomenology and existentialism") was rarely, if ever, used.

Then, in the 1980s, something new appeared. Jean-Paul Sartre had just died. He had been the great man (even Charles de Gaulle was quoted as saying, "Sartre, he *is* France"), but after his death he was quickly and oddly eclipsed in Paris. (In 1980, Vincent Descombes published a book on *Modern French Philosophy* that did not even give Sartre a chapter.) Overseas and across the channel, there was some interest in what would follow, but the rapidity with which philosophical fashions appeared and disappeared tried the patience of all but the very dedicated. For a brief period, "structuralism" was announced as the new way of thinking that would change the world. Some new names appeared: the anthropologist Claude Lévi-Strauss, a philosopher–historian named Michel Foucault, a peculiar psychoanalyst named Jacques Lacan, a mad Marxist named Louis Althusser, and a brilliant writer and literary critic named Roland Barthe. It was an odd assortment of characters and (as had happened with the "existentialist movement" several decades earlier) one by one the "structuralists" refused the title. As a movement, it quickly disappeared beneath the waves. What replaced it inevitably became known (more abroad than in France) as "poststructuralism." The new philosophical exports from France were bewildering in their variety, in their language, and in their posturing. It was also the age of the "tele-prof," ever new and more flamboyant philosophical stars, who burned brightly for a week – or sometimes a season – on television and then disappeared from the scene.

What finally emerged was the phenomenon of postmodernism. Its biggest star, soon eclipsed in Paris but enduring in the USA and elsewhere, was Jacques Derrida. "Deconstruction" became the coinage of the day. It was picked up with a vengeance by literary theorists, and with its Marxist underpinnings soon took on a lively role in politics as well, including, especially, academic politics. Deconstruction was picked up as a weapon by those who had an axe to grind with philosophy, and they were many. Whereas Derrida rightly prided himself on his extensive mastery of the Western philosophical tradition, many of his followers simply used him to attack that same tradition, knowing very little about it. Derrida may have questioned but he never wholly rejected metaphysics, noting that we are trapped in "the tradition" and we cannot escape it. At the same time, Michel Foucault was reborn as a star himself, no longer a philosophical or social historian or a structuralist, but now a powerful advocate of the neo-Nietzschean thesis that it is power that governs the success and failure of "discourses," and "truth" is but an illusion.

"Continental philosophy" was now set against traditional and "analytic" philosophy, but not as before, when European philosophy since Kant was for the most part simply unknown, unread, and therefore unappreciated. Now continental philosophy was often presented as the antidote to the disease of "mainstream" philosophy in Anglo-American philosophy. *Rapprochment* came to an end. Derrida was *denounced* when he came up for an award at the University of Cambridge. Some demagogic conservative philosophers have even found in continental philosophy a not so subtle substitute for now-defunct communism, a new and dangerous enemy to be eradicated, ignoring the fact that much of postmodernism is for the most part quietist and politically uncommitted.

This, unfortunately, is the environment in which we publish this *Guide*. It is our purpose, accordingly, to show students and other readers the enormous range and the fascinating variety of philosophical positions and philosophers who are all too often simply lumped together and dismissed without a sympathetic reading.

In what follows, we will try to present the highlights of what is now called "continental philosophy" by friend and foe alike. Needless to say, we have not been able to be all-inclusive. We apologize if one or another of a reader's favorite philosophers failed to make the cut. We might also note, to be frank, that despite the fact that the accepted rubric of our subject matter is "continental philosophy," the usual focus (and thus the focus in this *Guide*) is almost entirely on France and Germany. Denmark is usually mentioned only because of the existentialist philosopher Søren Kierkegaard. The Netherlands, despite the occasional reference to the great Spinoza in the seventeenth century, might never be mentioned at all: so, too, Belgium, the rest of Scandinavia, Portugal and Spain (despite the legacy of Unamuno and Ortega y Gassett), and Italy, despite the prominence of Vico and Croce, and a great many contemporary philosophers of note. Meanwhile, Eastern Europe is considered some other world, and while it must be admitted that the Balkans have had more than their fair share of troubles in the twentieth century, their philosophical exclusion is by no means therefore justified. Nevertheless, we have tended to be conservative rather than adventurous in our choice of figures to be covered, mainly due to space limitations. We have stuck for the most part with the rarely disputed French and German luminaries who have, for the most part, come to define what is intended by "continental philosophy." While we can imagine many other philosophers who might have been included, we cannot easily imagine the omission of any of the philosophers who we have included.

As for more current figures – that is, what is happening *now* – we can only say that we are in no position to make any judgments. Such pronouncements to the effect that one or another current philosopher is "the most important of his/her generation" is (in retrospect) much more likely to be laughable than plausible. (Sometimes it is the generation as a whole, and occasionally even the entire century, that after a time disappears from view.) If we had put together this *Guide* in the early 1970s, we might have made the mistake of making some (in retrospect) very foolish claims about the world-historical significance of structuralism. If we had put the *Guide* together in the early 1990s, we might have made some perhaps ultimately (in retrospect) foolish claims about the significance of postmodernism. (We might have even cited Baudrillard as a similacrum of some philosophical significance.)

What is in evidence now are some semblances of what might turn out to be a short-lived movement with the utterly predictable and not entirely serious name of "post-postmodernism." But who knows? The French dominated much of the late twentieth century in philosophy; or, at any rate, attracted the lion's share of attention and notoriety, just as the Germans did in the nineteenth century and in the last century, before two devastating and self-eviscerating wars. Perhaps it would be good if the focus were now to shift to some other part of Europe or, better, some other part of the world where philosophy remains as vibrant but is a little less used to the spotlight. Or, even better, the "transcendental pretense" of one small corner of the world projecting its prejudices on humanity as whole might come to an end. One of the virtues of continental philosophy and postmodernism in particular is its openness to multiculturalism and (at its best) its tolerance for other ways of thinking and doing philosophy. We can preserve cultural and ideological differences while nevertheless appreciating them, recognizing them for exactly what they are. They are differences within a single but pluralistic species whose greatest virtues as well as vices can be attributed to those swollen cerebral hemispheres that make philosophy not only possible but necessary.

──────────── Chapter 1 ────────────

G. W. F. Hegel: The Phenomenology of Spirit

Stephen Houlgate

Georg Wilhelm Friedrich Hegel (1770–1831) is one of the greatest (though also least studied) philosophers of the Western tradition. His thought spawned both Marxism and existentialism, and exercised considerable influence on many of the major philosophers of the twentieth century, including Dewey, Gadamer, Sartre, Derrida, and Habermas. It is true that many regard Hegel's work as too difficult and obscure to merit close scrutiny. Those who do take the trouble to study his work carefully, however, encounter a thinker whose richness and subtlety, in my view, is matched only by that of Plato, Aristotle and Kant.

Hegel was born in Stuttgart on August 27, 1770. He studied philosophy and theology at Tübingen, becoming friends there with Hölderlin and Schelling, and sharing their enthusiasm for Rousseau, Kant, and (initially at least) the French Revolution. From 1793 to 1800 he worked as a house tutor, first in Berne and then in Frankfurt-am-Main, and wrote several manuscripts on religion and love that remained unpublished until the early twentieth century. In 1801 he moved to Jena where, under the influence of Schelling, he began to develop his philosophical system. The distinctive introduction to that system, the *Phenomenology of Spirit*, which contains the famous analyses of the master/slave relation, the unhappy consciousness, and Sophocles' *Antigone*, was published in 1807. While he was rector of a school in Nuremberg, Hegel completed the first part of the system itself, the monumental *Science of Logic* (published in three volumes from 1812 to 1816).

In 1816 Hegel became professor of philosophy at Heidelberg and in 1817 published, under the title *Encyclopaedia of the Philosophical Sciences*, an outline of his whole system, including, in addition to logic, the philosophy of nature and the philosophy of mind or spirit (*Geist*). During his years in Berlin from 1818 to 1831, Hegel then published the works and delivered the lectures that would make him the most famous and influential philosopher in Germany. The *Elements of the Philosophy of Right* appeared in 1820, and two further, revised editions of the *Encyclopaedia* were published in 1827 and 1830. When he died on November 14, 1831, Hegel left behind not only his wife, Marie, and two sons, Karl and Immanuel, but also a body of thought that would inspire and provoke numerous philosophers, theologians, and social theorists right up to the present day (despite being neglected by much of the philosophical establishment in Britain and the USA).

Freedom and Mutual Recognition

Hegel has been treated by some philosophers not just with indifference, but with outright hostility and suspicion. Karl Popper, for example, famously counted him (with Plato and Marx) among the most potent enemies of the "open society." Such a judgment is, however, hard to sustain when one reads carefully what Hegel actually wrote and taught. His texts and lectures make it clear that he was in fact an unceasing advocate of freedom and rationality, and no friend of totalitarianism or obscurantism.

In the *Philosophy of Right*, Hegel argues that freedom entails exercising choice, owning property, and working to satisfy one's manifold needs. Freedom cannot, however, consist simply in doing what I want, because it is secured only when it is *recognized* by other individuals. I may insist that I am free to take possession of the objects of my desire, but I can do so in fact only when others acknowledge my right to own those objects.

For Hegel, rights are first established by the very concept of freedom itself, since that concept determines what freedom requires, and whatever *must* fall to me as a free being thereby constitutes my *right*. As a free being I have the right to own property or engage in work, whether or not others recognize that right. That is why I can demand of others that they respect my rights, whenever they fail to do so; if rights did not come first, they could not command recognition in this way. Yet the recognition afforded me by others is what allows me to *exercise* my rights. I may well have the inalienable right to own property, but I can become the rightful owner of this or that particular house only if others respect my right to do so. Accordingly, as Robert Williams puts it, "right is not actual or objective until it is recognized."[1]

For Hegel, therefore, concrete human freedom is inseparable from recognition. We demand that our freedom be recognized as our right, and we need the respect of others if our freedom is to be more than a dream. Furthermore, the very idea to which we appeal – that right commands recognition – requires of us that we respect the rights and freedoms of others in turn. To be free, therefore, we must be accorded recognition by those whose freedom we ourselves are bound to recognize: true freedom requires mutual respect and recognition between people. As Hegel states in the *Encyclopaedia Philosophy of Mind* (1830), "I am only truly free when the other is also free and is recognized by me as free."[2]

According to Hegel, human beings recognize and respect one another as free within communities, such as the estate or corporation in which they work and the state of which they are citizens. Hegel does, therefore, believe that human beings are born to live in the state, as many of his critics have charged. Yet this is not because he "worships" the state in any sinister, totalitarian manner. It is because he understands the state – at least when it is free and rational – to be the community in which mutual recognition is guaranteed both by the civic disposition of people and by the law. Hegel sets out the close connection between recognition, law and the state in these lines from the *Encyclopaedia Philosophy of Mind*:

> What dominates in the State is the spirit of the people, custom, and law. There man is recognized [*anerkannt*] and treated as a *rational* being, as free, as a person; and the individual, on his side, makes himself worthy of this recognition by overcoming the natural state of his self-consciousness and obeying a universal, the will that is in essence and actuality will, the *law*; he behaves, therefore, towards others in a manner that is universally valid, recognizing them – as he wishes others to recognize him – as free, as persons.[3]

States often fail to guarantee that citizens respect the law and one another, and often violate citizens' rights themselves. A rational state, however, is one that is held together precisely by a common respect for the law that requires people to show respect for one another.

Consciousness, Self-Consciousness, and Desire

Recognition may be found within society and the state, but is there anything to prevent our withdrawal from society, which would enable us to enjoy the untrammeled freedom of the hermit and so be relieved of the need to gain recognition? Physically, there may be nothing to prevent us; but in so doing, Hegel believes, we would deprive ourselves of the opportunity to acquire genuine *self-consciousness*. According to Hegel, I cannot fully understand who I am, if I remain alone by myself with only the objects of nature to attend to. I gain a proper consciousness of myself only when my self-understanding is recognized and confirmed by others.

This is not to say that in the absence of such recognition I would lack any self-awareness whatsoever. For Hegel, simple consciousness of an object, such as a house or tree, already incorporates the awareness that the object is distinct from *me*. Similarly, all perception brings with it the awareness that I, as perceiver, am capable of error. Yet such self-awareness falls short of articulated, objective self-consciousness and self-understanding: the latter, Hegel argues, requires the recognition by others of who we are. As Loewenberg (or, rather, his fictional creation, Hardith) puts it, Hegel thus "discover[s] an incipient social consciousness within the very bosom of self-consciousness."[4] A hermit's life is ultimately not for us: for we are born to understand who we are, and that means that we are born to be social and political beings. To learn precisely why this is the case, we must turn to Hegel's *Phenomenology*.

The *Phenomenology* describes, in prose both tortuous and elegant, the development of consciousness from its most primitive or naïve form – which Hegel names "sensuous certainty" – to its most mature form – self-knowing spirit or "absolute knowing." This development is to be understood not as historical, but as *logical*. The book does not examine how human consciousness has actually changed through time into modern self-understanding, but shows how certain general "shapes" of consciousness necessarily transform themselves, because of their very structure, into further shapes. The development traced by Hegel overlaps in certain parts with European history (for example, in the analysis of "Stoic" consciousness), but what gives Hegel's book its unity is the fact that it renders explicit what is logically entailed by being conscious.

Consciousness develops, according to Hegel, as it takes cognizance of what is implicit in its own experience, though initially hidden from view. Sensuous certainty, with which Hegel begins, is the form of consciousness that takes itself to be aware of the simple, immediate presence of things. It eschews all mediating categories and is quite certain in its own mind that what it has before it is nothing but *this, here, now* in all its simplicity. Its experience reveals, however, that what it is actually conscious of is not just simple immediacy after all, but a complex unity of different moments: a "now" that stretches back in time through other nows and a "here" that is spatially related to other heres. When sensuous consciousness accepts that its object is more complex than it initially thought, it transforms itself logically into a new shape: perception. This is not to say that every historical individual wedded to the immediate certainties of sensory experience will accept that he or she is actually conscious of complex objects of perception. It is to argue that the more developed standpoint of perception is *logically* implicit in that of sense certainty, and that those wedded to immediate sensuous certainty should acknowledge that the objects they relate to are more complex than they first think.

How does this process of logical development lead to self-consciousness? Hegel argues that perception grasps its object as a complex unity of many "nows" and many "heres," but that it cannot decide whether the true nature of the object lies more in its unity or in its multiplicity. Perception ends up distinguishing between the mani-fold character and the *inner* unity of the object. As soon as it regards its object as having an inner unity, however, it ceases to be mere perception and becomes under-standing. Understanding then learns that the inner unity of the thing actually con-sists in lawfulness, reason, and life. When this happens, Hegel claims, understanding proves to be not just consciousness of objects, but also *self*-consciousness – because it finds in its objects the very qualities that constitute its own nature. Prior to its mutation into self-consciousness, understanding already incorporates an element of self-understanding: it knows that it is precisely the *understanding*, rather than mere perception, of objects. Yet only when it encounters in the objects themselves nothing but qualities belonging to itself does it come to be self-consciousness in the full sense, that is, consciousness of itself *above all else*.

Hegel points out that understanding always takes itself to be conscious of what is other than it and does not realize that it is self-conscious. It is we phenomenologists, not understanding itself, who recognize that understanding is in fact conscious of itself. In Hegel's own words, "it is only *for us* that this truth exists, not yet for con-sciousness." Nevertheless, in understanding something else to be rational and law-like, understanding is, indeed, "communing directly with itself, enjoying only itself"; this, Hegel notes, is why understanding affords such satisfaction.[5] Self-consciousness is thus not merely an accident of nature, but is logically entailed by the structure of consciousness itself. Hegel's next task is to examine what is involved in being *explicitly* self-conscious, or "*what consciousness knows in knowing itself*."[6] We become explicitly self-conscious, in Hegel's view, when we make our selves and our own identity the explicit (and all-consuming) object of our concern, that is, when we become wholly and overtly absorbed by ourselves. As we shall see, such self-consciousness proves to be more complex and contradictory than it imagines.

The first thing to note is that consciousness comes to be wholly absorbed by itself while remaining conscious of what is *other* than it. Hegel's phenomenological method has shown that self-consciousness arises in our very consciousness of objects. When consciousness wakes up to the fact that it is primarily conscious of and concerned with itself, the objects of perception and understanding do not suddenly disappear from view. On the contrary, they remain before us as the external objects *in relation to which* we are principally conscious of ourselves. For Hegel, self-consciousness is thus not exclusively consciousness of oneself; it is a relation to something other than me in which I relate to myself above all.

This is not to deny that, like Descartes in the *Meditations*, I can "shut my eyes, stop my ears, withdraw all my senses" and "converse with myself" in total separation from things.[7] What can be reached through Cartesian doubt, however, is no more than *abstract* self-consciousness, because such doubt abstracts from the conditions under which alone concrete, all-embracing self-consciousness is possible: namely, consciousness of an external world in relation to which we find ourselves. As we shall see below, Hegel acknowledges that such abstract self-consciousness is possible and is an important moment of true, concrete self-consciousness. He claims, however, that true self-consciousness itself does not merely abstract from but (to borrow Kant's term) "accompanies" our consciousness of objects.

From Hegel's point of view, Descartes overlooks the moment of other-relatedness that is essential to true consciousness of oneself. Yet there is nevertheless something to be learned from Descartes about true self-consciousness: for in remaining conscious of real, external objects, self-consciousness must also seek to *negate* those objects. Consciousness finds itself in what is other than it; but the very otherness of the objects I encounter inevitably prevents me from relating wholly to myself. In order to achieve unalloyed self-consciousness, therefore, I must regard the object before me as something that is *not* essentially other than or independent of me after all, but there merely *for* me. I continue to consider the object to be real, and (unlike Descartes) do not declare it to be a figment of my imagination; but I deem it to offer no resistance to me and to yield to my ability to negate or consume it for my own satisfaction and self-enjoyment. Insofar as self-consciousness relates to itself through negating objects around it, it is, in Hegel's word, *desire* (*Begierde*). Self-consciousness necessarily takes the form of desire, therefore, because Descartes is half-right: consciousness does enhance its sense of itself by negating the objects around it, but it directs its activity of negation at a realm of objects whose reality is not in doubt and that, consequently, forever *remains* to be negated.

Note that desire arises at this point in the *Phenomenology* not (or, rather, not just) because we are organic, embodied beings, but because of the very nature of self-consciousness itself. Concrete self-consciousness is not immediate self-awareness, but self-awareness mediated by and inseparable from the awareness of what is other. Self-consciousness is interested in itself above all, and yet, as a complex form of *con-sciousness*, it is necessarily related to external things. If it is to attain an undiluted consciousness of *itself*, it must thus negate and destroy the other things it encounters. As this activity of negating what is other than itself, self-consciousness is desire. In Hegel's own words, the origin of desire is thus the fact that "self-consciousness is . . . essentially the return from *otherness*." Note that what we desire, in Hegel's view, is not the object as such, but rather, as Jean Hyppolite puts it, "the unity of the I with itself." If Hegel is right, in seeking to enjoy the object, we are in fact seeking to enjoy *ourselves*.[8]

The idea that desire is the practical activity of negating objects forms the cornerstone of the influential interpretation of Hegel's *Phenomenology* presented by Alexandre Kojève. Kojève lectured on Hegel's *Phenomenology* at the École des Hautes Études in Paris from 1933 to 1939 and counted in his audience many of the leading French intellectuals of the mid-twentieth century, including Merleau-Ponty, Bataille, Klossowski, Breton, and Queneau.[9] His lectures were published in 1947 and, together with the extensive commentary on the *Phenomenology* by Hyppolite which appeared in 1946, set the standard for reading Hegel in France (and beyond) for the following 50 years.

In my view, however, Kojève seriously distorts Hegel's account of self-consciousness in the *Phenomenology* by conflating the idea that desire is the activity of negation with the further idea that the subject of desire is essentially "empty." According to Kojève, the desiring subject is "an *emptiness* (*vide*) greedy for content; an emptiness that wants to be filled by what is full"; that is to say, "desire is *absence* of being" that seeks to fill itself "with a *natural*, biological content." To my mind, this distinctively Kojèvian conception of desire finds no place in Hegel's account. Desire does, indeed, negate the object. Yet it does so not to fill a void in the subject, but rather to confirm and enhance the subject's sense of self: desire, Hegel writes, is simply the movement of consciousness whereby its "identity of itself with itself becomes explicit for it." *Pace* Kojève, the desiring self in the *Phenomenology* does not lack a sense of its own being. If anything, it is rather too full of itself, for it regards everything around it as there for it alone. In so doing, desire considers the other to be nothing but an opportunity for desire itself to negate it. Desire is thus for Hegel "certain of the nothingness of this other," but it is by no means clear that desire takes itself to be sheer "absence" or "emptiness."[10]

From Desire to Mutual Recognition

Explicit self-consciousness must take the form of practical activity or desire. Hegel points out, however, that the self-certainty achieved in the satisfaction of desire is in fact not quite as unalloyed as it initially appears to be. This is because desire is satisfied only by negating and consuming something else. In the absence of other things, there is no satisfaction and no certainty of oneself. As Hegel writes, "desire and the self-certainty obtained in its gratification are conditioned by the object, for self-certainty comes from superseding this other." Consequently, "in order that this supersession (*Aufheben*) can take place, there must be this other."[11] Desire, for Hegel, is intrinsically contradictory: it needs the *other* so that it can enjoy itself *alone*.

Self-consciousness can therefore never revel undisturbed in its satisfaction and self-certainty. Whenever it is satisfied, it must once again seek out new objects that arouse its desire and enjoy itself in consuming them. As Hegel puts it, self-consciousness necessarily "produces the object again, and the desire as well," and it does so over and over again. This is why desire can never afford us the undiluted self-consciousness it promises: its certainty of itself is always interrupted by its renewed encounter with the other things it needs in order to enjoy itself. In Judith Butler's words, desire thus "affirms *itself as an impossible project*"; or, as Hegel himself states (in this somewhat ungainly sentence), "it is in fact something other than self-consciousness that is the essence of desire."[12] Yet Hegel does not conclude from this that genuine self-consciousness as such is impossible. Rather, he goes on to examine what is needed – beyond desire – for such self-consciousness to be achieved.

Desire fails to secure pure self-certainty because it always has to seek out new objects that are *other* than consciousness. In negating such objects, desire does find satisfaction and enjoys itself; but it ceases to be certain of itself as soon as it encounters the otherness and independence of things once again. A more secure self-consciousness would be achieved, however, if consciousness were able to preserve its certainty of itself in its very awareness of the independence of things. How might it do this?

Hegel's answer is clear: by turning its attention specifically toward things that in their very independence *negate themselves* and thereby allow consciousness to be certain only of itself. Simply eliminating all consciousness of other things is not an option for self-consciousness. Hegel has shown that self-consciousness first arises in our consciousness of other things, and that such consciousness of otherness remains an integral part of the consciousness that is explicitly concerned with itself. That is why self-consciousness must be desire. If consciousness is not to be restricted to being perennially renewed desire, therefore, the only logical alternative is for it to relate to something independent that negates itself for the sake of self-consciousness: "on account of the independence of the object, . . . it can achieve satisfaction only when the object itself effects the negation within itself."[13]

What kinds of objects perform such an independent negation of themselves? One possible candidate is the *living* object, or organism. In his account of understanding, Hegel argued that the objects of understanding include not just those that are law-governed but also those that are alive. Living beings thus belong among the objects that desire seeks to consume. Furthermore, as Hegel construes it, life is the explicit process of self-negation: death does not just descend on living organisms from the outside, but is immanent in life from the start, because "the simple substance of Life is the splitting up of itself into shapes and at the same time the dissolution of these existent differences."[14]

So, do living things afford us the opportunity of being conscious only of ourselves in being conscious of that which is independent of us? Almost, but not quite. The problem is that living things do not preserve their independence when they negate themselves: when they die, they simply cease to be. As Hegel puts it, "the differentiated, merely *living*, shape does indeed also supersede its independence in the process of Life, but it ceases with its distinctive difference to be what it is."[15] (The same is true of inorganic objects: insofar as they "negate themselves," they do so only by ceasing to be what they are.)

The logic of self-consciousness demands, however, that we achieve self-certainty in relating to objects that retain their independence from us. We can satisfy this demand only by relating to an object that negates itself but that is "equally independent in this negativity of itself." Such an object, Hegel maintains, cannot merely be a living thing (or an inorganic object), but must be another consciousness or self-consciousness. Consequently, "*self-consciousness achieves its satisfaction only in another self-consciousness.*"[16]

At this point Hegel appears no longer to be just a critic of Descartes, but to draw a positive lesson from the latter's meditations (though Hegel does not mention him by name). We do not learn from Descartes what it is to be concretely self-conscious; only phenomenology can teach us that. Nevertheless, in his *cogito* argument Descartes proves that consciousness retains an abstract awareness of its own independent identity and existence even when it calls into question and abstracts from every particular aspect of itself. The logic of self-consciousness demands that we achieve concrete self-certainty in relating to another thing that negates itself for our sake and that retains its independent identity in so doing. As Hans-Georg Gadamer writes, "only consciousness is able to . . . cancel itself in such a fashion that it does not cease to exist."[17] This fact, I would suggest, we learn from Descartes (as well, of course, as from Fichte).

It is important not to lose sight of the point at issue here. Descartes himself fails to see that concrete self-consciousness is to be gained in a relation to what is irreducibly *other* than consciousness. Yet he helps us to see that that very other cannot just take the form of an inanimate or animate thing, but must also take the form of another *self-consciousness*, for he shows that self-consciousness alone is able to negate every aspect of itself and preserve itself in so doing. Of course, to be genuinely and concretely self-conscious, that other self-consciousness must in turn be related to what is other than it, and so must itself be desire and relate to another self-consciousness. The specific point that Hegel is making here, however, is that the other, to which any concrete self-consciousness relates, must at least be capable of *abstract* self-consciousness: for only in this way can it thoroughly negate itself and at the same time retain its identity.

The desire to be certain of ourselves in our very relation to others is fulfilled not by consuming things, but by interacting with another self-consciousness – one that is not only capable of abstract self-awareness, but also takes the form of desire and relates to a self-consciousness other than itself. Self-consciousness is thus necessarily social or "spiritual": it is "'I' that is 'We' and 'We' that is 'I'." In this social relation, Hegel remarks, I find my own identity out there in an objective form: "just as much 'I' as 'object'." This is because I find my identity *recognized* by something other than and independent of me. This moment of recognition is built into the act of independent self-negation performed by the other self-consciousness: for by negating itself the other declares itself to be nothing in and for itself – it "posits its otherness . . . as a nothingness" – and so *makes way for me*. The other thus allows me to relate wholly to *myself* in relating to another, because all I see in the other is his or her recognition of my identity.[18]

If we are to enjoy full self-consciousness, the hermit's existence cannot be an option for us, for we can become properly self-conscious only in the society of others who recognize us. Of course, we could try to turn our backs on self-consciousness. Hegel would point out, however, that self-consciousness is logically entailed by consciousness itself. Insofar as we are conscious at all, we must therefore seek to become fully self-conscious. The hermit, it seems, lives at odds with the logic inherent in consciousness itself.

Kojève provides a very different explanation for the social character of self-consciousness. As noted above, Kojève understands desire to be "emptiness" or the "absence of being." Such emptiness is filled, we are told, by "destroying, transforming, and 'assimilating' the desired non-I." Kojève goes on to say that "the I created by the active satisfaction of such a Desire will have the same nature as the things toward which that Desire is directed." If it desires merely living things, it will thus become "a 'thingish' I, a merely living I, an animal I." In this way, however, desire cannot become explicitly conscious of its own essential emptiness; it cannot be, as it were, filled with non-being. Desire becomes explicitly and self-consciously "empty" and "negative" only when it negates and assimilates *another empty desire*. This is because the I that feeds on the desires of others comes to be nothing but desire and negativity through and through: there is nothing about it that is given, natural, and "thing-like." Furthermore, not only does desire seek to incorporate the desires of others; it also seeks to be *desired* and *recognized* by those others as free, negative desire. It is thus the "desire for 'recognition'." Society is human, therefore, "only as a set of Desires mutually desiring one another as Desires." Indeed, for Kojève, human history is nothing but the "history of desired Desires."[19]

Kojève's account of Hegelian desire is imaginative and influential (it impressed Sartre, especially), but it misses the crux of Hegel's argument. For Kojève, what drives desire to become social (through desiring another's desire) is the desire to be nothing but pure "*negating* Desire, and hence *Action* that *transforms* the given being," or the desire to be free from being determined by what is given.[20] In my view, this desire to be (and to be recognized as) *pure* negativity certainly plays a role later in Hegel's account; indeed, as Kojève himself points out, it is what gives rise to the life and death struggle. It does not, however, feature in the account of desire that we have been considering so far.

Hegel's own account shows not how desire seeks to become pure desire, freed from determination by independent objects, but how self-certainty is attained by a consciousness that considers independent otherness to be *irreducible*. Unlike Kojèvian desire, Hegelian desire learns that we are always conscious of what is other than and independent of us, and that we can never fulfill the desire to be purely free. For Hegel, if I am to be conscious of myself alone, I can thus do so only in relation to what is and remains independent of me. But how is this possible? Only if the other, in its very independence, negates itself and puts itself at my disposal. This in turn is possible only when another self-consciousness thinks of itself as nothing, recognizes me alone, and thereby enables me to find nothing but myself reflected in it. Gadamer puts the point perfectly: "if self-consciousness is to become true self-consciousness, then it must . . . find another self-consciousness that is willing to be 'for it'."[21]

To recapitulate: for Kojève, what drives self-consciousness to become social is its desire to *assimilate* (as well as be desired by) another's desire; for Hegel, by contrast, what renders self-consciousness social is its acceptance of the other as an *independ-*

ent source of recognition for itself. This significant difference between Kojève and Hegel leads them to very different views of what is implicit in and made necessary by social life.

According to Kojève, the direct consequence of desire's entrance into social relations is struggle and conflict. Each desire, Kojève insists, "wants to negate, to assimilate, to make its own, to subjugate, the other Desire as Desire." Furthermore, each seeks to have its exclusive right to satisfaction recognized by all other desires. "If . . . there is a *multiplicity* of these Desires for universal Recognition," Kojève concludes, "it is obvious that the Action that is born of these Desires can – at least in the beginning – be nothing but a life and death *Fight*."[22] This "fight" or struggle in turn leads to the creation of masters and slaves. Human social and historical existence is thus distinguished principally by fighting, slavery and work.

For Kojève (or, rather, for Kojève's Hegel), there is a point at which historical development stops: namely, when a community of mutual recognition is produced that puts an end to struggle and domination. (Kojève's Hegel identifies this "universal" state – somewhat bizarrely – with Napoleon's Empire.[23]) Nevertheless, what has prevailed throughout history prior to this point is nothing but struggle and domination, because these are generated by the very desire that gives rise to social interaction in the first place.

By placing struggle at the heart of social interaction (even though he believes it can be overcome), Kojève in my view paves the way (perhaps along with Nietzsche) for Sartre's bleak claim that "the essence of the relations between consciousnesses is . . . conflict." It is on the basis of this claim that Sartre then accuses Hegel of "optimism" for believing that genuinely mutual recognition is possible. Hegel is praised for his "brilliant intuition" that I "depend on the Other *in my being*"; but he is castigated for thinking "that an objective agreement can be realized between consciousnesses – by authority of the Other's recognition of me and of my recognition of the Other."[24]

Sartre's emphasis in *Being and Nothingness* on the inevitability of social conflict is notoriously uncompromising, but he is not alone in challenging what Jay Bernstein calls Hegel's "worrying 'reconciliations'."[25] Many post-Hegelians balk at Hegel's suggestion that mutual recognition is a real possibility in modern society (or perhaps even already achieved), and prefer to follow Kant in regarding recognition and respect as at most moral ideals in an essentially imperfect world. Some have even argued that the very idea of successful mutual recognition is unsustainable. Recently, for example, Alexander García Düttmann has claimed that "recognition is always embedded in a destabilizing tension . . . [and] is *always* an improper, dissimilar, one-sided recognition." Indeed, if one follows Hegel, Düttmann maintains, "recognition can become what is meant by its concept only in a struggle for life and death."[26] As we have seen, Kojève would not endorse such a definitive judgment. There is little doubt, however, that he opens the door to such judgments by claiming that the life and death struggle arises directly from the very nature of social interaction between self-consciousnesses.

In contrast to Kojève, Hegel argues that what is made necessary by the interaction between self-consciousnesses is mutual recognition rather than conflict. This does not mean that social and historical existence will in fact always be characterized by respect and love for one's fellow human beings; Hegel is not that naïve. It means that *logically*, when all that it entails has been rendered fully explicit, genuine social interaction turns out to require mutual recognition. Hegel does not deny that social conflict constantly arises. His claim, however, is that it arises not because we are social beings as such, but because we fail to understand properly what social interaction demands.

Note that, on this interpretation, there is nothing particularly "optimistic" about Hegel's belief that mutual recognition is a real possibility for human beings. That belief is grounded in a subtle comprehension of the form that genuine intersubjectivity logically must take: if social life is to fulfill its purpose and enable us to become conscious of ourselves in relation to what is other than us, there is nothing it can be *but* mutual recognition. For the Hegelian, it is actually Sartre who has lost sight of the truth: for the assertion that social life is in essence riven with conflict – the assertion on the basis of which Sartre accuses Hegel of "optimism" – can only be made by one who himself misunderstands what true intersubjectivity entails.

For Hegel, self-consciousness must be desire; but we achieve a fully objective sense of ourselves only by relating to something irreducibly independent in which we find our own identity reflected. Such a thing can only be another self-consciousness that *recognizes* us. Logically, therefore, concrete self-consciousness must be social and intersubjective. But why should the fact that I require recognition from another mean that our relation must be one of *mutual* recognition? Hegel's answer is to be found in §§178–84 of the *Phenomenology*.[27]

Genuine self-consciousness, Hegel writes, is faced by another self-consciousness by which it finds itself recognized. It has thus "come *out of itself*": it is not just enclosed within its own interiority, but sees its identity located, as it were, "over there." In such a relation, self-consciousness certainly gains a sense of self through being recognized. Yet at the same time, Hegel maintains, it feels that it has "lost itself," precisely because it finds its own identity over there in the eyes of the other. Equally, however, self-consciousness lacks any real sense that the other is genuinely *other* than it, since it sees in the other nothing but its own self. Insofar as self-consciousness does no more than find itself recognized by another, therefore, its consciousness of both itself and the other actually remains deficient.

To remedy this situation, Hegel argues, self-consciousness must "proceed to supersede (*aufheben*) the other independent being in order thereby to become certain of *itself* as the essential being." Self-consciousness does so by withdrawing itself from the other, locating its true identity within *itself* (as it were, "over here"), and thereby overcoming its previous sense of being what it is only in and through the *other*. In making this move, however, self-consciousness loses what has been shown to be a crucial ingredient of any concrete sense of self, and thus, as Hegel puts it, "proceeds to supersede its *own* self": for by insisting that its own identity resides wholly within itself, it abandons the idea that its identity is to be found reflected in another and so is something objective.

Yet all is not lost: for, as Hegel immediately points out, this withdrawal of self-consciousness out of the other into itself is in fact ambiguous. In withdrawing into itself, consciousness does indeed recover the certainty that it is what it is in itself. In Hegel's own words, "it receives back its own self . . . [and] again becomes equal to itself." At the same time, however, self-consciousness restores the other self-consciousness to its own proper otherness. It no longer sees the other merely as a mirror reflecting it, but "equally gives the other self-consciousness back again to itself . . . and thus lets the other again go free (*entläßt also das Andere wieder frei*)."[28] That is to say, self-consciousness *recognizes* the other as another free and independent self-consciousness. The action of self-consciousness is ambiguous for this reason: by withdrawing out of the other wholly into *itself*, self-consciousness lets the other go free, and thereby unwittingly affords itself for the first time the opportunity to be recognized by, and to find itself in, another that it knows to be genuinely *other* than it.

To begin with, self-consciousness did not "see the other as an essential being," because in the other it saw only itself. Yet it did not enjoy an unalloyed sense of self either, since it found itself "over there" in another (that it did not properly recognize). Now, by contrast, self-consciousness has a clear sense of its own identity and recognizes that the other is something wholly other than and independent of itself. Consequently, it can at last fulfill the condition required for concrete self-consciousness: for it can find *itself* recognized by and reflected in another that is known to be truly *other*.

Achieving self-consciousness, as we have seen, requires that I relate to myself in relating to that which is other than me. This means that I must relate to another self-consciousness that recognizes me alone. Self-consciousness must, therefore, be social and intersubjective. We now know that by itself recognition accorded to me by the other is not sufficient to enable me to be concretely self-conscious. To attain that end I must be recognized by another that I recognize in turn as a free and independent other. Genuine self-consciousness thus requires not just recognition of my identity by the other, but *mutual* recognition by each of us of the other. Self-consciousness must be a "double movement of the two self-consciousnesses" working freely together. In such a movement, Hegel writes, "each sees the *other* do the same as it does; each does itself what it demands of the other, and therefore also does what it does only in so far as the other does the same. Action by one side only would be useless because what is to happen can only be brought about by both."

Mutual recognition, for Hegel, requires the uncoerced cooperation of the two (or more) self-consciousnesses involved. Indeed, not only must the two self-consciousnesses freely recognize one another; in fact, they must both *recognize* that their mutual recognition and cooperation is needed for either to be concretely and objectively self-conscious. In Hegel's own words, they must "*recognize* themselves as *mutually recognizing* one another."

As Williams points out, genuine self-consciousness involves much more than mere desire (though it must also incorporate desire). Whereas desire "seiz[es] upon and negat[es] the object," genuine self-consciousness requires recognition from the other, which in turn entails "allowing the other to be what it is" and "letting the other go free." Self-consciousness would like to know only *itself* in the other and be the sole object of the other's recognition. Such self-certainty can be achieved, however, only "through membership or partnership with Other."[29] For one person to have a concrete and objective understanding of himself, he must join together with somebody else.

Note that, in the paragraphs we have been considering, Hegel is not merely setting out a moral ideal for humanity. He is unfolding with uncompromising rigor the necessary conditions for concrete self-consciousness. He shows that, as beings who are by necessity conscious of what is other than ourselves, we can achieve certainty of ourselves only when we are recognized by another whom we recognize as free in turn. This conception of mutual recognition, I contend, lies at the heart of Hegel's whole social and political philosophy.

The Dialectic of Master and Slave

According to Hegel, conflict is not produced by the logic that renders social interaction necessary in the first place. It is generated, however, by a primitive self-consciousness that fails to appreciate the importance of mutual recognition. Indeed, it is generated when self-consciousness is animated by a desire similar to that described by Kojève: the desire to be recognized as the activity of pure *negating*. Such desire is not sheer, self-absorbed desire as such, since it seeks recognition from another. Nevertheless, it wants to be recognized as "self-equal through the exclusion from itself of everything else" and thus as "the purely negative being of self-identical consciousness."[30] As Hegel demonstrates, this desire is profoundly contradictory.

Such self-consciousness wants to show that it is not bound to or limited by anything it is given to be by nature, that its identity is not tied to its sex, age, skin color, or anything to do with its body. Indeed, it wants to show that it is not even attached to life. It also wants to prove that it is not restricted by anything or anybody outside it. Such self-consciousness thus regards itself as absolutely free from determination or limitation by anything given to or other than itself. It tries to demonstrate this freedom in two ways: by seeking the death of the other and by ostentatiously risking its own life in the process. In this way, it shows that it values nothing except its own freedom or pure "being-for-self." Indeed, it shows that, in its own eyes, its own identity consists in nothing but the pure activity of *negating* anything given to or other than itself. Nowhere in his account does Hegel suggest that primitive self-consciousness thinks of itself as an "emptiness" that seeks to be "filled." Kojève is, however, right to say that it takes itself to be pure "negating-negativity." It is this desire to prove itself to be pure freedom and negativity by killing the other – a desire that animates each self-consciousness – that leads to the life and death struggle. This struggle is thus generated not by any scarcity of resources – or, as Paul Redding suggests, by the desire to "preserve life" – but, rather, by a primitive *idea* of freedom.[31]

Primitive self-consciousness not only wants to be free, it also wants to be recognized by the other as free. It wants the other to see that it is trying to kill the other and risking its own life in so doing. This desire for recognition is what plunges such self-consciousness into self-contradiction. Robert Solomon puts the point well: "insofar as one's identity arises and is defined only with other people, killing the others is self-defeating, for one loses precisely that source of recognition that one has come to require."[32] If either self-consciousness is to attain recognition, therefore, one of them must back down. This is not to say that in every such struggle one party will in fact back down, but that the *logic* of the situation requires that one capitulate. The one that does so shows thereby that it is not absolutely free after all. It is actually attached to life and afraid of death, and accepts that its identity is (at least in part) determined and limited by what is given to and other than it. This consciousness thus acknowledges that its identity *depends* on its own body and the realm of natural things around it, and in consciousness of this dependence it becomes the servant, bondsman, or slave of the other. The other self-consciousness, having succeeded in proving itself to be absolutely free and fearless, is recognized by the slave as his (or her) lord and master. The life and death struggle thus leads logically – if not always in fact – to the relation of master and slave.

This relation – Hegel's famous account of which profoundly influenced Marx – is not intrinsic to social life. It is not to be encountered, for example, where there is genuine mutual recognition. It is the result of a struggle for recognition by two (or more) *primitive* self-consciousnesses, one of which – the slave – finally accepts what Tom Rockmore rightly calls the "deep truth" that "life is as essential to it as pure self-consciousness" and thereby lets the other enjoy the feeling of unencumbered freedom.[33]

The relation between the master and the slave is complex. The master, Hegel says, dominates the slave indirectly, insofar as he exercises power over the very things in the world on which the slave acknowledges himself to be dependent. Yet the master also wields direct power over the slave and – both literally and figuratively – interposes the slave between himself and the things he plans to appropriate. This fact, that "the lord relates himself mediately to the thing through the bondsman," is especially important, because it explains why the master finds a level of satisfaction that eludes simple desire.[34]

Desire, we recall, negates and consumes things; but it also runs up against the independence of things, and so fails to "have done with the thing altogether" and thereby to achieve complete satisfaction. By interposing the slave between himself and things, the master succeeds in separating these two sides of desire from one another. He leaves the slave to deal with the independence and resistant "thereness" of the thing, and reserves for himself "the pure enjoyment of it." With the help of the slave, the master thus frees himself from the frustrations of desire and revels in the pure joy of consuming.[35]

By contrast, the slave faces what he regards as a world of unyielding independent objects. Yet the slave is still self-conscious desire himself and, as such, enjoys a degree of freedom to negate things. His activity of negation cannot, however, go so far as the consuming and destroying of things, but must restrict itself to transforming things that continue to be regarded as independent. This activity of transformative negation Hegel calls *work* or *labor*. (Hegel's point, by the way, is not that slaves may only ever work and never eat, but that they understand their distinctive activity *qua* slaves – rather than human beings as such – to be labor.) Labor, for Hegel, is thus desiring activity that meets resistance from things and so is "held in check" (*gehemmt*).[36] It does not negate the thing completely but reworks it – by, say, cooking it or giving it a new shape – into an object for the master's pleasure. The master is thus able to appropriate an object that is no longer regarded as wholly independent but looked upon merely as a means to his enjoyment. In the master/slave relation, therefore, desire is split into the distinct activities of production and consumption: one person labors and produces so that the other may consume and in so doing enjoy *himself* thoroughly.

A similar division between production and consumption is, of course, judged by Marx later in the nineteenth century to be inherent in capitalism. Whereas Marx, however, points to what he regards as an objective division in bourgeois society, Hegel – at least in the *Phenomenology* – is interested purely in the way in which certain forms of consciousness understand themselves. He is not claiming that the master is in fact free to do nothing but consume, but only that he takes himself to be free in this way (and that the slave reinforces this by taking himself to be bound to never-ending labor). Hegel immediately points out, however, that the master's own experience undermines the cosy conception that he has of himself.

The problem faced by the master is twofold. On the one hand, though he receives recognition from the slave, the master does not recognize the slave in turn, and so cannot find true value in the slave's recognition of him. The outcome, Hegel writes, "is a recognition that is one-sided and unequal."[37] On the other hand, the very relation that embodies for the master his absolute freedom – his dominance over the slave – also reminds him that in his freedom he is actually dependent on another. As Loewenberg's fictional characters, Hardith and Meredy, put it, the master's "need for recognition . . . is inimical to his self-sufficiency," and he "comes in the end to be haunted by a consciousness of dependence not dissimilar to that of the slave."[38] In this sense, the master sees the *truth* of his own situation expressed in the slave, and that truth proves to be uncomfortably double-edged: the absolute dominance of one person over another always *depends* on the subservience of the latter.

There is a further sense, however, in which "the *truth* of the independent consciousness" – the master – is to be found by looking to the slave: for in the slave we begin to see what the freedom and independence to which the master lays exclusive claim are *in truth*. "Just as lordship showed that its essential nature is the reverse of what it wants to be," Hegel writes, "so too servitude in its consummation will really turn into the opposite of what it immediately is . . . and be transformed into a truly independent consciousness." This does *not* mean, as Hyppolite famously suggests, that the master turns out to be "the slave of the slave, and that the slave is revealed to be the master of the master." It means, rather, as Solomon recognizes, that "the master becomes dependent on the slave; [and] the slave becomes *independent* of the master."[39]

How, then, does the slave prove to be free? First of all, through his labor: for, even though he is forced to work by the master, his labor is nonetheless his *own* activity. Furthermore, unlike the master's unchecked desire, which consumes the object and leaves nothing behind to mark its activity, labor enables the slave to give enduring objective expression to his freedom. The very independence of the thing for the slave preserves the work that the slave has done on it; so, "in fashioning the thing, the bondsman's own negativity, his being-for-self, becomes an object for him."[40] The slave may not find himself recognized by the other self-consciousness, but he does find his freedom *embodied* in the object of his labor.

Equally important to the slave's freedom is his fear of death. In the original life and death struggle, both self-consciousnesses seek recognition for themselves as "purely negative being" – being that is "self-identical" yet not tied to being anything in particular.[41] The master succeeds in gaining such recognition for himself, and gives expression to his sense of being "purely negative" in the unceasing consumption of objects around him. The slave, on the other hand, regards himself as bound to and defined by the given particularities of nature, and so appears to have no sense of being purely negative. Hegel points out, however, that in the fear of death the slave does in fact conceive of himself as sheer negativity after all: for in the moment of fear he envisages himself being *dead* and so being *nothing*. The slave does not merely register the fact that he will die at some time in the future; he thinks of himself as *being* dead and *being* nothing *now*. That, indeed, is what terrifies him: he sees everything about himself "inwardly dissolved" (*innerlich aufgelöst*) and "shaken to its foundations," and he trembles at the thought of actually being nothing whatsoever. Even though he shudders at it, the slave at this point entertains the thought of himself as *being*, yet being nothing in particular. He thus thinks of himself in a way that seemed to be reserved for the master alone, namely, as "pure negativity." As Kojève puts it, the slave in his fear catches "a glimpse of himself as nothingness."[42]

Fear by itself, Hegel remarks, is "inward and mute": it causes the slave to quake inside, but not to go out and actively negate the things around him.[43] Nevertheless, fear is not simply debilitating, for it deepens the sense of freedom that the slave gains through labor. Fear is sometimes understood by commentators merely to be that which forces the slave to labor in the service of the master in the first place. Hegel's point, however, is more subtle than that: it is that fear alters the slave's understanding of the meaning of labor itself.

The slave has to labor because he is subservient to the master. Through his labor, however, the slave discovers that he has the freedom to transform things himself and, indeed, to transform them according to his own will and intention. In working on things, he thus acquires what Hegel calls "a mind of his own" (*eigener Sinn*). The slave's freedom, however, is the freedom to transform the *particular* things that he encounters: to turn this piece of wood into a chair or these ingredients into bread. Accordingly, the slave develops *particular* skills, depending on what he is required to work on. The freedom that he exhibits in his labor is thus still a limited freedom: it consists in the *particular* ability to give new shape to these *particular* objects, and bears witness to the fact that the slave's consciousness is still mired in the world of given particularities (or, as Hegel puts it, that "determinate being still *in principle* attaches to it").

If the slave's freedom were to lie only in his ability to labor, then his identity would be defined solely by the particular skills that he possesses. They would be everything to him, and he would insist on being able to exercise them. The "mind of his own" that he acquires through his labor would thus slip into stubborn "self-will" or *Eigensinn*. Furthermore, he would show himself to be wholly dependent on – and slave to – his particular skills. His freedom would thus be "a freedom which is still enmeshed in servitude." He would evince "a skill which is master (*mächtig*) over some things, but not over . . . the whole of objective being."[44]

The character of the slave's labor is quite different, however, when it is preceded by the fear of death. In the fear of death, the slave quakes at the thought of being nothing at all; yet at the same time, Hegel suggests, the slave in his fear experiences his own "essential nature." The slave discovers that he retains a consciousness of *himself*, even when he understands everything about himself to have been "dissolved." He learns thereby that, ultimately, his being as a self-consciousness is not tied to being anything in particular. The slave thus realizes that the essential nature of self-consciousness is *"pure being for self"* (and in so doing somewhat resembles Descartes at the beginning of the second Meditation). It is this new understanding of himself, gained in the fear of death, that transforms the slave's understanding of his labor: for he can now understand his labor, not just as the exercise of a particular skill, but as the outward, active expression of the fact that his being as self-consciousness is *not tied to being anything in particular*. In other words, his labor can be regarded as a particular expression of his essential freedom *from* particularity and determinacy. Without the fear of death, the slave understands his labor to be nothing more than a particular skill; with the fear of death, however, he can understand his labor to be the work of his "negativity *per se*" or his "universal formative activity." He can thus see himself as master not just over some things, but over "the whole of objective being."[45]

Kojève recognizes that in the fear of death the slave confronts his own nothingness. Yet he does not appear to note Hegel's principal point: the slave's consciousness that his essence lies in being nothing in particular affords him a profound sense of freedom by allowing him to uncouple his identity from the particular labor he undertakes. The Hegelian slave does not regard his particular skills as defining who he is, but sees them as particular expressions of his *general* ability to negate and transform things. He is thus not just a one- (or two- or three-) dimensional being but, rather, a multidimensional being who knows that he can engage in all kinds of labor and is not tied to this or that particular job. Indeed, Hegel's slave may be said to share a similar vision to Marx. In the slave's world, as in communist society, no one is restricted to "one exclusive sphere of activity but each can become accomplished in any branch he wishes"; as a result, "there are no painters but at most people who engage in painting among other activities."[46] The significant difference between Hegel's slave and Marx, however, is that the slave acquires his sense of inner freedom through envisaging his own death, whereas Marx appears to neglect the topic of death altogether.

Death, Forgiveness, and Mutual Recognition

The master's claim to absolute self-sufficiency was vitiated by his sense of dependence; the slave, by contrast, turns out to enjoy a profound sense of freedom through his labor. The slave also feels himself to be pure negativity, though unlike the master he gives expression to this feeling in his labor rather than in consumption. The slave does not, however, attain complete freedom or self-consciousness, since he remains – outwardly, at least – subservient to his master and does not participate in a community of mutual recognition (which, by definition, requires the abolition of slavery). Nevertheless, there is much to be learned about true freedom from the slave.

Besides enjoying and conferring recognition (and having desires), the truly free self-consciousness must acknowledge that life and embodiment are essential to it and that it must engage in labor. It must also bring to mind its own death: for in envisaging itself being dead, it discovers that it retains a consciousness of itself, even in seeing everything about itself dissolved. It thus learns that its identity as a self-consciousness is not tied to being anything in particular, and that it does not need to cling on to its particularity in order to *be*. Bringing death to mind thus teaches us that we can let go of our particularity and still retain a consciousness of ourselves. We can give up this work or that and still retain the freedom to engage in other kinds of labor. This is not to deny that the particular identity we acquire in our chosen profession may be very important to us. It is simply to point out that that particular identity is not *absolutely* essential to our sense of selfhood, because it is always possible for us to find freedom in doing something else.

In a community of true freedom and mutual recognition, it will no longer be necessary to seek certainty of oneself through a struggle for recognition, or for some people to become slaves through fear of dying violently at the hands of another. Yet we will still need to be taught to let go of ourselves through being kept mindful of our mortality. The task of doing so, Hegel believes, falls to religion. An essential part of religious life, for Hegel, is thus keeping death in mind. This is not meant to lead to indifference, recklessness, or the actual desire to die. Religious faith trusts, rather, that we can be brought to a simple and honest acceptance of the fact that we are born to die, and that with that acceptance we will cease trying to cling on insistently to who we are. That in turn will afford us – within life – a sense of inner freedom, and will free us especially to love and forgive others.

In his 1821 manuscript for his *Lectures on the Philosophy of Religion*, Hegel maintains that the intimate connection between the acceptance of death and love for others is revealed supremely in the figure of Christ. "Love," Hegel writes, consists

> in giving up one's personality, all that is one's own, etc. [It is] a self-conscious activity, the supreme surrender [of oneself] in the other, even in this most extrinsic other-being of death . . . . The death of Christ [is] the vision of this love itself.[47]

The true religious life is thus one spent not in pursuit of other-worldly salvation, but in seeking to be infused here and now with the spirit of Christ – the spirit that lets death come and so lets itself be displaced, and in so doing shows love and forgiveness to others.

For the religious believer, therefore, death is not simply an object of fear (though the fear of death will never be completely removed); nor is it in any way an object of eager desire. Death is the utter negation of the self, the openness to and humble acceptance of which frees us to let go of ourselves and "forgive those who sin against us." In the *Phenomenology*, Hegel writes that forgiveness of others involves the "renunciation" of oneself: it entails ceasing to cling on to oneself and one's own "hard-hearted" judgment and giving the other a second chance. Forgiveness, for Hegel, thereby becomes the ground of reconciliation between individuals. Indeed, it makes possible the "reciprocal recognition which is *absolute* Spirit." In forgiving the other, I do not insist on subjecting the other to my own self-righteous judgment, but "let the other again go free"; I recognize thereby that, whatever he or she may have done, the other is always free to love, forgive and so recognize others in turn, including me. By making forgiveness possible, the open acceptance of death thus turns out to lead to the mutual recognition that is the condition of true freedom and self-consciousness.[48]

Mutual recognition must take the secular form of life in a state that guarantees rights under law. In Hegel's view, however, mutual recognition also requires a *religious* ground: for we need to know that it is compatible with the existential fact that we are born to die. Georges Bataille maintains that death or "dismemberment" is "not easily reconciled with the desire for recognition."[49] Religious faith, by contrast, knows that this is not unambiguously true. Death itself certainly destroys life and so removes the possibility of giving or receiving recognition (as the slave well understands). Yet an openness to and acceptance of death *within the very life we seek to preserve* makes possible forgiveness and with it mutual love and respect. For this reason, religion puts the acceptance of death at the heart of human life and understands such life (with all the labor and toil that it involves) to be renewed or "reborn" through it.

For Hegel, religion is thus integral to the community that is to be held together by loving, respectful unity with others, rather than by force and enslavement. It is in such a community that we find ourselves recognized as free and so gain genuine self-consciousness. Hegel's argument also suggests that such a community is the place in which genuine "life after death" is to be found. To my mind, this Hegelian idea that self-consciousness, recognition, and the acceptance of death are inseparably connected is one of the most profound in the history of Western philosophy, and it is one we would do well to pay heed to today.

Notes

1   Williams (1997), p. 101.
2   Hegel (1971), p. 171 (§431 Addition).
3   Hegel (1971), p. 172 (§432 Addition).
4   Loewenberg (1965), p. 83.
5   Hegel (1977), pp. 101–2 (§§163–4).
6   Hegel (1977), p. 103 (§165).
7   Descartes (1984), vol. 2, p. 24.
8   Hegel (1977), p. 105 (§167); Hyppolite (1974), p. 160.
9   Rosen (1998), p. 237.
10 Kojève (1980), pp. 38–40; Hegel (1977), pp. 105, 109 (§§167, 174).
11 Hegel (1977), p. 109 (§175).
12 Butler (1987), p. 91; Hegel (1977), p. 109 (§175).
13 Hegel (1977), p. 109 (§175). See also Lauer (1976, p. 99) and Pinkard (1994, p. 52).
14 Hegel (1977), p. 108 (§171).
15 Hegel (1977), p. 110 (§176).
16 Hegel (1977), p. 110 (§§175–6).
17 Gadamer (1976), p. 61.

18   Hegel (1977), p. 110 (§§176–7).
19   Kojève (1980), pp. 4, 6–7, 40.
20   Kojève (1980), p. 38.
21   Gadamer (1976), pp. 61–2.
22   Kojève (1980), p. 40.
23   Kojève (1980), pp. 58, 69.
24   Sartre (1958), pp. 237, 240, 429.
25   Bernstein (1984), p. 14.
26   Düttmann (2000), p. 191.
27   Hegel (1977), pp. 111–12.
28   Translation emended.
29   Williams (1992), p. 155.
30   Hegel (1977), p. 113 (§186).
31   Kojève (1980), pp. 4–5; Redding (1991), p. 182; Hegel (1977), pp. 113–14
     (§§186–7).
32   Solomon (1983), p. 450.
33   Rockmore (1997), p. 69; Hegel (1977), p. 115 (§189).
34   Hegel (1977), p. 115 (§190).
35   Hegel (1977), p. 116 (§190).
36   Hegel (1977), p. 118 (§195).
37   Hegel (1977), p. 116 (§191).
38   Loewenberg (1965), p. 88.
39   Hegel (1977), p. 117 (§193); Hyppolite (1974), p. 172; Solomon (1983), p. 451, my
     emphasis.
40   Hegel (1977), p. 118 (§196).
41   Hegel (1977), p. 113 (§186).
42   Kojève (1980), p. 47; Hegel (1977), p. 117 (§194). Miller translates "*innerlich aufgelöst*"
     as "quite unmanned."
43   Hegel (1977), p. 119 (§196).
44   Hegel (1977), p. 119 (§196).
45   Hegel (1977), pp. 117, 119 (§§194, 196).
46   Marx (1977), pp. 169, 190.
47   Hegel (1984–7), vol. 3, 125.
48   Hegel (1977), pp. 407–8 (§670).
49   Bataille (1997), p. 289.

References

Bataille, G. 1997: Hegel, death and sacrifice. In F. Botting and S. Wilson (eds.), *The Bataille Reader*. Oxford: Blackwell, 279–95.

Bernstein, J. 1984: From self-consciousness to community: act and recognition in the master–slave relationship. In Z. A. Pelczynski (ed.), *The State and Civil Society. Studies in Hegel's Political Philosophy*. Cambridge: Cambridge University Press, 14–39.

Butler, J. 1987: *Subjects of Desire. Hegelian Reflections in Twentieth-Century France*. New York: Columbia University Press.

Descartes, R. 1984: *The Philosophical Writings of Descartes*, 2 vols., trans. J. Cottingham, R. Stoothoff, and D. Murdoch. Cambridge: Cambridge University Press.

Düttmann, A. G. 2000: *Between Cultures. Tensions in the Struggle for Recognition*, trans. K. B. Woodgate. London: Verso.

Gadamer, H.-G. 1976: *Hegel's Dialectic. Five Hermeneutical Studies*, trans. P. C. Smith. New Haven, Conn.: Yale University Press (originally published 1971).

Hegel, G. W. F. 1971: *Philosophy of Mind. Being Part Three of the Encyclopaedia of the Philosophical Sciences (1830)*, trans. W. Wallace and A. V. Miller. Oxford: Clarendon Press (originally published 1830, 1845).

——1977: *Phenomenology of Spirit*, trans. A. V. Miller. Oxford: Oxford University Press (originally published 1807).

——1984–7: *Lectures on the Philosophy of Religion*, 3 vols., ed. P. C. Hodgson, trans. R. F. Brown, P. C. Hodgson, and J. M. Stewart. Berkeley, Calif.: University of California Press.

——1991: *Elements of the Philosophy of Right*, ed. A.W. Wood, trans. H. B. Nisbet. Cambridge: Cambridge University Press (originally published 1821).

Hyppolite, J. 1974: *Genesis and Structure of Hegel's Phenomenology of Spirit*, trans. S. Cherniak and J. Heckman. Evanston, Ill.: Northwestern University Press (originally published 1946).

Kojève, A. 1980: *Introduction to the Reading of Hegel. Lectures on the Phenomenology of Spirit*, ed. A. Bloom, trans. J. H. Nichols. Ithaca, NY: Cornell University Press (originally published 1947).

Lauer, Q. 1976: *A Reading of Hegel's Phenomenology of Spirit*. New York: Fordham University Press.

Loewenberg, J. 1965: *Hegel's Phenomenology. Dialogues on the Life of Mind*. LaSalle, Ill.: Open Court.

Marx, K. 1977: *Selected Writings*, ed. D. McLellan. Oxford: Oxford University Press.

Pinkard, T. 1994: *Hegel's Phenomenology. The Sociality of Reason*. Cambridge: Cambridge University Press.

Popper, K. R. 1966: *The Open Society and its Enemies*, 2 vols. London: Routledge (originally published 1945).

Redding, P. 1991: Hermeneutic or metaphysical Hegelianism? Kojève's Dilemma. *The Owl of Minerva*, 22(2), 175–89.

Rockmore, T. 1997: *Cognition. An Introduction to Hegel's Phenomenology of Spirit*. Berkeley, Calif.: University of California Press.

Rosen, S. 1998: Kojève. In S. Critchley and W. R. Schroeder (eds.), *A Companion to Continental Philosophy*. Oxford: Blackwell, 237–44.

Sartre, J.-P. 1958: *Being and Nothingness. An Essay on Phenomenological Ontology*, trans. H. E. Barnes. London: Methuen (originally published 1943).

Solomon, R. 1983: *In the Spirit of Hegel. A Study of G. W. F. Hegel's Phenomenology of Spirit*. New York: Oxford University Press.

Williams, R. 1992: *Recognition. Fichte and Hegel on the Other*. Albany, NY: State University of New York Press.

Williams, R. R. 1997: *Hegel's Ethics of Recognition*. Berkeley, Calif.: University of California Press.

Suggested further reading

Harris, H. S. 1997: *Hegel's Ladder*, 2 vols. Indianapolis, Ill.: Hackett.

Houlgate, S. 1991: *Freedom, Truth and History. An Introduction to Hegel's Philosophy*. London: Routledge.

——(ed.) 1998: *The Hegel Reader*. Oxford: Blackwell.

——2001: G. W. F. Hegel. In S. M. Emmanuel (ed.), *The Blackwell Guide to the Modern Philosophers from Descartes to Nietzsche*. Oxford: Blackwell, 278—305.

Lamb, D. (ed.) 1998: *Hegel*, 2 vols. Aldershot: Ashgate.

O'Neill, J. (ed.) 1996: *Hegel's Dialectic of Desire and Recognition. Texts and Commentary*. Albany, NY: State University of New York Press.

Pinkard, T. 2000: *Hegel. A Biography*. Cambridge: Cambridge University Press.

Pippin, R. 1989: *Hegel's Idealism. The Satisfactions of Self-Consciousness*. Cambridge: Cambridge University Press.

Stern, R. (ed.) 1993: *G. W. F. Hegel. Critical Assessments*, 4 vols. London: Routledge.

Stewart, J. (ed.) 1998: *The Phenomenology of Spirit Reader. Critical and Interpretive Essays*. Albany, NY: State University of New York Press.

Taylor, C. 1975: *Hegel*. Cambridge: Cambridge University Press.

Westphal, M. 1998: *History and Truth in Hegel's Phenomenology*. Bloomington, Ind.: Indiana University Press, 1998 (first published by Humanities Press, Atlantic Highlands, NJ, 1979).

Chapter 2

Arthur Schopenhauer

Noël Carroll

Arthur Schopenhauer (1788–1860) was born in Danzig (now Gdansk) to a prosperous German family. Educated initially for a life of business like his father's – a career not to Arthur's taste – Schopenhauer was freed to pursue other interests after his father's suicide in 1805. Studying at Gottingen and then Berlin, Schopenhauer completed his doctoral dissertation – "On the fourfold root of sufficient reason" – in 1812. Although he tried his hand at teaching, his inheritance was large enough so that he did not have to work for a living. In 1818, he published the first volume of his pessimistic masterwork, *The World as Will and Representation*. It was not an immediate success; however, after 1850, the book began to be widely read, not only because many regarded it as a user-friendly introduction to Kant, but also because of its high literary quality. Schopenhauer is undeniably an excellent writer, which is a major reason for the continuing popularity of his philosophy. He was also an important influence on the composer Richard Wagner and on the young Nietzsche.

Compared to most, Schopenhauer led an eminently comfortable life, daily replete with full meals, good conversation, and constant access to art. Though unlucky in love and embittered over being eclipsed in reputation by Hegel, Schopenhauer's own experience of suffering hardly seems commensurate with the dour and pessimistic view of human life that he is notorious for propounding, notably in *The World as Will and Representation*. Personally confronting little that any of us would count as extraordinary hardship, Schopenhauer argued that ours is the worst possible existence, stretched on a rack of unrelenting pain, unfulfilled desire, and boredom. Since these convictions seem scarcely motivated by Schopenhauer's personal experiences, it is to his metaphysics that we must turn for an account of his deep pessimism – his view of existence as perpetual suffering, relieved only on occasion for many of us by aesthetic experience and, for the very few, by the life of ascetic renunciation.

Schopenhauer's Metaphysics

For Schopenhauer, the philosophies of Kant and Plato, along with various Hindu and Buddhist writings, provide major sources of inspiration. Though critical of many of the details of Kant's philosophy, Schopenhauer accepts Kant's distinction between the phenomenal and the noumenal and uses it as the foundation of his philosophical system. That is, for Schopenhauer, the world can be comprehended under two aspects: the way it appears to us (the phenomenal aspect) and the way the world is in itself (the noumenal aspect). The world as it appears to us is the world as idea or representation; the world as it is in itself is the world as will. Just as we may perceive the well-known, reversible duck–rabbit figure as either a duck or a rabbit, so we may comprehend the world either as representation or as will. Let us take up these aspects one at a time.

What is it to comprehend the world as representation? It is to encounter the world, because of the structure of the human mind, in terms of certain categories: the categories of space, time, and causality (which Schopenhauer derives from Kant) and the category of the subject–object relation (which Schopenhauer introduces to supplement Kant's inventory). Schopenhauer calls these categories – these mental filters – the principle of sufficient reason. Because the mind is structured in terms of these categories, all ordinary experience and ordinary knowing falls under them and is organized by them.

The mind, so to speak, structures experience in terms of these categories insofar as it only accepts as intelligible input that which is amenable to these categories. Thus, in any experience, we organize the objects that we encounter in terms of space and time – we place them in space and time – and we see them as standing in causal relations to each other and also to us (where we fall under the category of the subject and they fall into the category of object). All ordinary experience is structured in terms of these categories. They are the categories in accordance with which we ordinarily cognize or come to know the world. Anything that eludes these filters – that fails to fall into these categories – would not be cognizable – not be knowable or capable of being experienced – in the ordinary sense (which includes scientific knowledge).

Why are these categories called the principle of sufficient reason? Because these categories supply the basic reasons or answers that we have to the questions that we ask about the objects of ordinary experience, such as "Where are they?" (space), "When are they?" (time), and "Why or wherefore are they?" (causality). It is because our minds organize or construct the world as representation in terms of these categories, moreover, that ordinary experience is of a plurality of individual things, separated in space and time, and as causes as distinct from effects and subjects as distinct from objects. Thus, the world as representation is governed by the principle of individuation (the *principium individuationis*); that is, in ordinary experience, phenomena appear to us as individual things – the horse over there, the tree next to me, the stone that crashes through the window.

The phenomenal world (the world of phenomena) is the world as representation, a world experienced as composed of individual things due to the fact that our minds are structured in terms of the principle of sufficient reason. It is the world as it is familiar to all of us. But, like Kant, Schopenhauer is not convinced that this is the whole story. The world as representation is the world as it appears to us. But how is the world in itself – apart from cognition in light of the principle of sufficient reason? We say that the mind constructs the world in virtue of the aforesaid categories. But what is it constructing? Upon what are these categories operating? What is the input that they are organizing? If these categories are being applied, it must be the case that they are being applied to something. There must be a way the world is in itself, a way apart from the manner in which our experience of it structures it categorically. Schopenhauer, along with Kant, thinks of this as the noumenal aspect of the world, in constrast to the phenomenal aspect, that is, in contrast to the world as it appears to us due to the nature of our minds.

For Kant, however, although we can know that there is this noumenal aspect to the world – that there is a way the world is in itself – we can know nothing specific about it. Why not? Because to know, in the ordinary sense, about the content of the noumenal realm would be to apply our categories of understanding – the principle of sufficient reason – to noumena in the way we treat phenomena. But if we proceed in that fashion, we will no longer be talking about the noumenal realm but about the phenomenal realm – the world as it appears to us given the structure of our minds. If to know is to apply the principle of sufficient reason, then we cannot cognize the noumenal realm, since, by definition, the noumenal realm is that which is inaccessible to the relevant categories. If anything is susceptible to cognition, understood in terms of the categories, then it is phenomena, not noumena. Consequently, for Kant, apart from knowing that there is something in itself, nothing else can be said of it. Subsequent philosophers, including Schopenhauer, found this conclusion frustrating. There is nothing more effective for provoking the philosophical imagination than telling a philosopher that something is impossible. Thus, Schopenhauer set out to discover a means for knowing about the way the world is in itself that could circumvent the epistemological obstacles that Kant had identified.

In a nutshell, Schopenhauer's challenge was this: all ordinary knowledge is connected to the categories. These categories individuate things in space and time and organize them in causal relations. Presumably, the way the world is in itself might not be like this – it might not be comprised of things that are individuated in space and time and organized causally. Perhaps it exists in some non-plural state, a state in which objects are not distinct from each other or from subjects, nor are causes and effects independent existents. But since space, time, and causality are our categories of knowledge – because anything we can be said to know must be cognized on their terms – how can we know anything about a realm where these categories are necessarily inapplicable?

Clearly, an important presupposition here is that the limits of our knowledge are co-extensive with what is cognizable in terms of the categories. But if there is some sort of knowledge that is independent of the categories, that might open the possibility that that sort of knowledge can be had of the way the world is in itself. This is the key to Schopenhauer's solution of the Kantian problematic.

Schopenhauer agrees that we organize and know of external experience – our experience of phenomena, of the world outside us – in terms of the categories. But there is another dimension of experience, an inner dimension, and our knowledge of this inner dimension does not seem organized in terms of the principle of sufficient reason.

When we experience ourselves, so to say, from the inside, our experience is not shaped by the categories. I do not experience my inner self as located in space, nor does the subject–object relation appropriately describe self-consciousness. As we experience ourselves inwardly, subject and object are one; we are not objects to our-selves as subjects. Nor are our motives experienced as alien causes. So, to an appre-ciable extent, our experience of ourselves falls outside the principle of sufficient reason. When we know ourselves from the inside, the principle of sufficient reason is far from fully operational.

But this then implies that we do have a degree of access to something outside the phenomenal – to something apart from the world as representation. We have access to ourselves from the inside, and this experience and knowledge appears in impor-tant ways to lie outside the categories (of space, causality, and the subject–object rela-tion, though arguably not time). That is, we have access to the things in themselves – albeit limited access – just because we are, in virtue of our inner lives, inhabitants of the world in itself, the world outside the categories. We can know about the world in itself because, in part, we live there – or, more technically, because we are noume-nal ourselves.

Ordinary knowledge of what we experience as outside ourselves – representational knowledge – is governed by the principle of sufficient reason. But there is another kind of knowledge, the knowledge to be had from the inside of ourselves. This knowl-edge is not altogether mediated by the principle of sufficient reason. We know ourselves inwardly through direct acquaintance. And to the extent that this self knowledge by direct acquaintance is not exclusively governed by the categories, we can have some knowledge of the way the world is in itself. Furthermore, Schopen-hauer suggests, we can use this epistemic foothold in the noumenal realm to extrap-olate generalizations about the world in itself. That is, we can extrapolate from what we discover about ourselves through introspection in order to say something about the nature of the world in itself, since, again, we are directly acquainted with it through self-consciousness.

Schopenhauer concedes that we cannot be absolutely certain that what we ex-trapolate about the nature of the world in itself from our inner experience of our-selves is a fully reliable guide to the world in itself, but he maintains that it is the best (perhaps it is the only) way that we can hope to learn anything about the world in itself. Schopenhauer's intellectual honesty is certainly admirable here, but given the confident tone in which he goes on to characterize the world in itself, one wonders whether he has not vastly overestimated what one could be entitled to say of the entire noumenal world on the basis of such a small sample of it, namely, our own self-consciousness.

Nevertheless, Schopenhauer plunges ahead with his program. Encouraging us to introspect along with him, he bids us to ask ourselves: What is the nature of our inner life? What is distinctive about it? What are our essential inner features? For if we can answer these questions, we can, he believes (probably with insufficient warrant), hypothesize fruitfully that those are also essential features, across the board, of the world in itself.

So, looking inward, what do we find? What are we? In a word, Schopenhauer says "will" – the will to live, to expand ourselves, to preserve ourselves, to appropriate things, to forestall our own deterioration and dissolution, to keep ourselves intact, and to multiply. Our inner life shows itself to be involved in incessant striving to acquire what we need to continue to go on, and then to acquire ever more in order to augment our dominion.

Reflecting on the only specimen of the world in itself to which we have access – namely ourselves – Schopenhauer invites us to conjecture that the world in itself is will: the will to be, the will to life, the will to self-preservation and expansion, a sort of cosmic life force, which, moreover, is indivisible, since it is not susceptible to the principle of sufficient reason (which accounts for the division of things into separate entities).

The world in itself is will. Furthermore, since the world in itself is not plural, not divided – since it is all will – and since it is the world in itself that provides the necessary ground for everything that appears in the world as representation, we can hypothesize that everything – every individual thing – has an aspect of will. Here Schopenhauer is not only thinking of living things, such as plants, animals, and people, but of inanimate things as well, such as rocks. For example, look at the suspension bridge resisting, as we are wont to say, the buffets of the hurricane; it resists breaking apart; it holds together, struggling to maintain itself, attempting to preserve its integrity. In this regard, it manifests the will to self-preservation. For Schopenhauer (though perhaps not for all of the rest of us), this is not merely a metaphor. Thus, on the basis of such thinking, he concludes that everything in the world as representation – every individual thing – is a manifestation of will.

What is the relation of the world as representation – the world of individual things – and the world as will – the world of relentless, indivisible striving? For Schopenhauer, each thing that appears to us phenomenally is an objectification of will. That is, every individual object that appears to us is, at ground, a configuration or objectification of will, a coalescence of will predicated on preserving itself. Here a simile may be useful: each individual thing that appears to us is like a temporary wave on the surface of the ocean of will, gathering itself momentarily together into a temporary form, and striving to sustain its integrity, before eventually dissolving and reuniting with the ocean of indivisible will, of which it is only a transitory manifestation.

These objectifications of will, moreover, come in different grades. The quotient of will in a stone is less than the quotient of will in an animal, which, in turn, is less than the will objectified in a human being. Higher grades of will involve greater amounts of will, more complexly organized. However, by taking the appearance of individual things, these objectifications of will must ultimately be thought of as illusions. The world as representation is a veil – Schopenhauer refers to it in the Hindu idiom of Maya – since it is not the way the world is in itself. In itself, the world must be conceived of as unitary willing, the pure force of striving. The principle of individuation that governs the world as representation is finally an illusion arising from the objectification or expression of different grades of the indissoluble world-will that constitutes the very nature of the world in itself.

Schopenhauer's Pessimism

So far, Schopenhauer's analysis has yielded a view of reality as possessing two aspects: the world as representation and the world as will. But, as yet, we have not encountered Schopenhauer's vaunted pessimism. How does that enter the picture? In short,

Schopenhauer believes that pessimism follows from an analysis of what is involved in willing as such. He writes:

> All willing springs from lack, from deficiency, and thus from suffering. Fulfillment brings this to an end; yet for one wish that is fulfilled there remain at least ten that are denied. Further, desiring lasts a long time, demands and requests go on to infinity; fulfillment is short and meted out sparingly. But even the final satisfaction itself is only apparent; the wish fulfilled at once makes way for a new one; the former is a known delusion, the latter a delusion not as yet known. No attained object of willing can give a satisfaction that lasts and no longer declines; but it is always like the alms thrown to a beggar, which reprieves him today so that his misery may be prolonged till tomorrow. Therefore, so long as our consciousness is filled by our will, so long as we are given up to the throng of desires with its constant hopes and fears, so long as we are the subject of willing, we never obtain lasting happiness or peace. (Schopenhauer, 1969, vol. I, §38)

Through introspection, Schopenhauer believes (perhaps overconfidently), that we can discover the nature of the world in itself. It is will. Now, by further introspection and analysis, Schopenhauer encourages us to ask "What is it to will?" To will, he argues, is to desire. To desire, in turn, is to be conscious of a lack or a privation, the object of desire. But consciousness of a lack is painful; it involves suffering. Therefore, all desire is a form of suffering. It is our essential nature to desire inasmuch as we are essentially creatures of will. Therefore, desire saturates every moment of our life. Therefore, our life, through and through, is bound up with suffering.

Moreover, through reflection on our inner nature, we can gain insight into the nature of reality in itself. Therefore, the world in itself is ultimately an ordeal of suffering. That much follows from the presupposition that the world as will is one of ceaseless striving (of ceaseless desire). Furthermore, since we are contemplating it from outside the protocols of the principle of sufficient reason, this relentless, indivisible striving and suffering is not explicable; since it cannot be rationalized in terms of the principle of causality, the world as will has no cause. Suffering just is the nature of the world in itself insofar as it is an incessant process of inexplicable (and, therefore, senseless) striving.

Suffering is a virtually inexpungible curse on human life. Why? Human life is a life of desiring. Desires are either fulfilled or they go unfulfilled. If they are not fulfilled, we continue to endure pain. If they are fulfilled, satisfaction is fleeting; it lasts for but a moment and is soon followed by more rampaging desires and, therefore, more pain.

Desires have a tendency to give birth to more desires, more desires than can ever be quenched, and even where desires are momentarily met, the pleasure of fulfillment (if it is not immediately disappointing) is small in comparison to the amount of pain suffered in the antecedent interval of time in which we anticipate the realization of our desires. Think of the child who awaits her Christmas presents for months (an interval of pain, by definition, according to Schopenhauer) and then plays with her new doll for a few minutes before lurching toward her next gift.

Moreover, the cessation of desire, when it ever occurs, is most likely to give rise to a state of boredom, itself an unhappy experience, which, in turn, prompts the production of new desires (including artificial ones, such as the craving after fashion) and, of course, these new desires bring with them more pain. Desire, pain, boredom, pain, more desire, more pain – human life is an inescapable circle of suffering. We are like rats on a treadmill, constantly striving, but always finding ourselves in the same place, the place of pain.

It is noteworthy that Schopenhauer attempts to convince us of our sorrowful plight primarily by deduction, rather than by an empirical review of all the horrible features of human existence (from war, famine, and earthquakes to competition, envy, and hatred). However, Schopenhauer's argument may not be as compelling as it appears at first glance. There may be several gaps in the deduction.

For example, Schopenhauer connects desire with privation; but surely we can desire things that we do not lack: I desire my wife, but I am already happily married. Likewise, Schopenhauer associates desire with pain. But, in ordinary language, desire need not be painful; it may be a source of pleasure. Desire is only always painful under a technical definition, such as Schopenhauer's, that stipulates that any desire, any consciousness of a lack, is painful. Thus, Schopenhauer's conclusion that all is suffering may ride on an equivocation: the pain and suffering he has in mind is merely stipulative and should not be regarded as a necessary, unpleasant concomitant of all desire in the ordinary sense.

Furthermore, although Schopenhauer correctly observes that desiring is a continuing feature of human life – that we rarely cease desiring – he forgets that there is a difference between the fact that the life of desire does not cease and the claim that desires (specific desires) are never satisfied. Although I will be thirsty again tomorrow, my thirst right now may be sated agreeably with a cool beer. For these and other reasons, Schopenhauer's argument may not be as conclusive as he presumes.

Nevertheless, even if human life is not as miserable as Schopenhauer contends, a reasonable case might still be made that things are pretty bad. And whether human life is consummately deplorable, as Schopenhauer alleges, or merely pretty bad, it raises the unavoidable question of whether there can be relief from all the suffering, solace from the senseless and painful striving. To this end, Schopenhauer makes two suggestions: that life can be palliated, at least temporarily, through aesthetic experience; and that entire lives, albeit the lives of the very few, can be substantially ameliorated through the path of ascetic renunciation.

Schopenhauer's Aesthetics

Since ascetic renunciation is such a demanding discipline, aesthetic experience is, for most of us, our primary avenue of release from the wheel of striving. Moreover, since art makes aesthetic experience particularly accessible, art is of singular importance in Schopenhauer's system. Perhaps no other major philosopher accords art as high a status as Schopenhauer does. For him, art is nothing less than a source of salvation, albeit temporary.

How can art perform this function? According to Schopenhauer, although ordinary knowledge is in the service of the will, there is nevertheless another kind of knowledge that can release us from our implacable striving. This is knowledge of

Platonic Ideas. Since Platonic Ideas exist timelessly, if we sink ourselves into contemplation of them to the point at which they fully occupy our consciousness, then we will lose ourselves in these Platonic Ideas, forget our individuality, and – like the Platonic Ideas that occupy our minds – transcend the bonds of time. Such aesthetic experiences can occur in response to natural beauty, but works of art are particularly effective conveyors of Platonic Ideas and, for that reason, they afford the opportunity to escape the principle of sufficient reason and the principle of individuation.

Illuminating this process with respect to natural beauty, Schopenhauer writes:

> Raised up by the power of the mind, we relinquish the ordinary way of considering things, and cease to follow merely their relations to one another, whose final goal is always the relation to our own will. Thus we no longer consider the where, the when, the why, and the whither in things, but simply and solely the what. Further, we do not let abstract thought, the concepts of reason, take possession of our consciousness, but instead of all this, devote the whole power of our mind to perception, sink ourselves completely therein, and let our whole consciousness be filled by the calm contemplation of the natural object, a crag, a building, or anything else. We lose ourselves entirely in this object, to use a pregnant expression; in other words, we forget our individuality, our will, and continue to exist as pure subject, as clear mirror of the object, so that it is as though the object alone existed without anyone to perceive it, and thus we are no longer able to separate the perceiver from the perception, but the two have become one, since the entire consciousness is filled and occupied by a single image of perception. (Schopenhauer, 1969, vol. I, §34)

The event described here has two sides: the side of the object, the Platonic Idea; and the side of the subject, the pure, will-less subject of knowledge. The Platonic Idea is not the idea of an individual thing, like a rose, but is rather an idea of "roseness." Platonic Ideas are said to have greater objectivity than ideas of individual things, because they are clearer manifestations (objectifications or expressions) of will than are individual things. They are also alleged to stand outside the framework of the principle of sufficient reason, since Platonic Ideas – unlike individual roses – do not inhabit a specific place or time. Rather, they are akin to the idea of a species and, like the species "rose," they exist in no one space or time. Nor can the idea of a species enter into causal relations; "roseness" is neither a cause nor an effect. So the knowing subject, by turning his or her consciousness over to the Platonic Idea, becomes like it, thereby exiting the principle of sufficient reason and its service to striving.

The subject may arrive at this state through two routes: the object, whether a work of art or a particularly exemplary instance of some natural species, may arrest me perceptually in a strikingly compelling way that suddenly puts this series of events in motion; or, as a result of my putting myself in a certain contemplative attitude, an aesthetic attitude, the object comes to fill my consciousness entirely. Then I lose myself in the object; I sink myself in it perceptually; I open myself fully to the object and effectively merge with it.

But since my object of attention here is a Platonic Idea, and since a Platonic Idea stands outside of space, time, and causality, the subject takes on this aspect of the Platonic Idea; and as that happens, the division between the subject and the object dissolves. I leave my individual identity behind, along with the rest of the framework of the principle of sufficient reason and, in shedding my individual identity, I transcend my individual will, becoming what Schopenhauer calls a pure will-less, timeless subject of knowledge. Through contemplating the Platonic Idea and fusing with it, I enjoy a kind of knowledge independent of the principle of sufficient reason, which framework, of course, serves the designs of the individual will. Thus, knowledge of the Platonic Idea releases me from the realm of individual willing and striving.

For Schopenhauer, there are different modes of knowledge. Ordinary knowledge is born of the needs of the will; it is governed by the principle of sufficient reason. Science is the systematization of this kind of knowledge. But there is also knowledge of Platonic Ideas. This can be had from nature, but for most of us it is more readily available from art. But how exactly does art put us in contact with Platonic Ideas?

Art is the product of genius. A genius is a person with the capacity of knowing the world independently of the principle of sufficient reason. This is why, Schopenhauer comments, artistic geniuses are impractical and so bad at math; they are closer to lunatics than to scientists. The genius is capable of deriving Platonic Ideas from nature by using his or her imagination to complete nature – to glean the essential features of a species from a particular, imperfect instance of it. All of us have this capacity to some extent, as is demonstrated by the fact that we can be responsive to the products of artistic genius. But only the very few are capable of doing this with consistency. These are the artistic geniuses who enable the rest of us to see the world through their eyes – eyes not governed by the principle of sufficient reason – thereby affording the opportunity for us to undergo temporary release from the endless cycle of striving.

This process of immersion in Platonic Ideas, as relayed to us through works of genius, is pleasurable. But it is important to note that it is pleasurable in two distinct ways. Just as the process has two sides – the subjective and the objective – the process yields two kinds of pleasure: (1) a species of objective pleasure that is cognitive and comes through contact with the Platonic Ideas, granting us special insight into the nature of the world as will; and (2) a species of subjective pleasure that is affective and involves the feeling of release from the striving and pain of human existence. Inasmuch as this second sort of pleasure involves freedom from practical concerns, it bears some relation to Kant's notion of disinterested pleasure; however, Schopenhauer's account differs from Kant's insofar as Kant regards disinterestedness as a condition for aesthetic experience, properly so called, whereas, for Schopenhauer, detachment from the practical is a central point of aesthetic experience.

That is, for Schopenhauer, being disinterested (free from practical concerns, free from willing) is itself a form of pleasure – it is a matter of relief from the importunings of the individual will, where relief itself is a type of pleasure. For Kant, on the other hand, "disinterest" merely modifies the term "pleasure"; disinterestedness is not a particular kind of pleasure at being lifted above the stream of everyday life, as it would appear to be for Schopenhauer.

That Schopenhauer holds that aesthetic experience affords cognitive pleasure through the apprehension of Platonic Ideas may seem diametrically opposed to Kant's view that pleasure taken in free beauty has nothing to do with determinate concepts.

However, the difference turns out to be not so stark when one realizes that Schopen-hauer's Platonic Ideas are not concepts, let alone determinate concepts. Rather, they are objects of perception. The domain of art is the senses; art gives us sensitive or sensuous knowledge via perception.

Like Aristotle, Schopenhauer believes that a major portion of the pleasure to be had from art is cognitive – that is, pleasure derived from learning about the world as will. However, although this knowledge reaches us through perception, it is a form of general knowledge or knowledge of types, rather than knowledge of particular things.

How is this possible? Perhaps here it is best to consider an analogy between the illustrations or diagrams in dictionaries and the Platonic Ideas. A dictionary illustration of a sparrow is an idealized depiction of a sparrow, not a picture of a specific sparrow. The dictionary illustration provides knowledge of the essential features of the type or the species, and it does this by addressing perception. Simi-larly, the Platonic Ideas give us knowledge of different grades of the objectification of will at the level of the type or the species through idealizations that engage perception.

For Schopenhauer, the cognitive pleasure available through art can be thought of in terms of beauty. Since this pleasure is connected to knowledge, beauty is a func-tion of the clarity with which the work of art presents the type or Platonic Idea to perception. This is a crucial determinant of the pleasure that the work of art yields, but it is not the only determinant. Since what works of art provide are idealizations of different grades of the objectification of the will, the pleasure that they offer will vary in direct proportion to the degree of will being manifested or expressed through the work of art in question. The higher degree of will manifested or presented by the work of art, the more pleasure it yields. So, since a stone has less will than a man, a picture of the Platonic Idea of a man will manifest a higher degree of objectified will than that of a stone and, therefore, the picture of the man, all things being equal, will elicit greater pleasure than the picture of the stone.

Schopenhauer provides us with several dimensions along which we may plot the pleasure afforded by a work of art. For example, of any work of art we can ask: (1) Is the pleasure it affords predominantly affective (the negative pleasure of release) or cognitive (the positive pleasure of knowledge)? (2) How high is the objectification of will embodied in the artwork (for the greater the level of objectification, the more pleasure it yields)? Moreover, with these distinctions in mind, Schopenhauer also proceeds to rank the various forms of art hierarchically.

Architecture makes manifest the lowest grade of the objectification of the will – the conflict between gravity and rigidity (where rigidity resists gravity). This is not a very high level of objectification; it is not deeply revelatory of the true nature of the world-will; so, the pleasure that architecture affords is primarily affective – a matter of feeling a release from striving. The same can be said of spectacles of moving water, such as fountains. Landscape painting and still lifes portray living things. In that respect, they present us with higher objectifications of will and, therefore, more cog-nitive pleasure than architecture, while animal painting and sculpture stand higher still, because animals involve a greater objectification of will than fruits, vegetables, and foliage. Since human beings express the lineaments of will more clearly and forcefully than any other animal, paintings and sculptures of people provide more cognitive pleasure than any other form of visual art.

Poetry, however, ranks higher than visual art because it can present more aspects of the human objectification of will than painting and sculpture, thereby providing more profound insight into the nature of the world as will. And of the various forms of poetry, tragedy is the highest, since it gives us, in perceptible form, the clearest image of the deepest truth about human existence – that it is, at root, suffering, a matter of unspeakable pain. In this way, tragedy cuts to the essence of will in a powerfully revelatory manner.

So far, Schopenhauer has regarded forms of art in terms of their capacity to imitate different grades of the objectification of the will. But this raises a question about where to place music in the hierarchy of the arts, since music – pure orchestral music – is not straightforwardly an imitative art. In Schopenhauer's language, it does not imitate this or that degree of objectification of the will. However, rather than cashiering music from the order of the arts for this reason, Schopenhauer uses this feature of music to its advantage. He writes:

> Thus music is as immediate an objectification and copy of the whole will as the world itself is, indeed as the Ideas are, the multiplied phenomenon of which constitutes the world of individual things. Therefore music is by no means like the other arts, namely a copy of the Ideas, but a copy of the will itself, the objectivity of which are the Ideas. For this reason the effect of music is so very much more powerful and penetrating than is that of any of the other arts, for these others speak only of the shadows, but music of the essence. (Schopenhauer, 1969, vol. I, §52)

Whereas the other arts give us cognitive access to the will at various levels of objectification, music, through its tempos and rhythms, permits insight into the whole nature of the will as such, tracing its very pulsations, in a manner of speaking, by means of its melodies, harmonies, dissonances, cadences, and the like. Music affords perceptual acquaintance with the pulse of the world as will, thereby not only lifting us out of the world as representation, but enabling us to know its inner dynamism directly. Schopenhauer admits that he cannot prove this, but thinks that if we reflect on this hypothesis, we will come to concur with him.

Asceticism

For the vast majority of humans, art – and most especially music – provides us with our only prospect of respite from the wheel of striving. But there is also another, far less traveled route, namely ascetic renunciation. The natural inclination of human beings is egoism, the pursuit of one's own interests and desires. But this, according to Schopenhauer, is the source of human suffering. In order to avoid suffering, then, one must attempt to deny desire, to deny the will: "[T]hose who have once attained to denial of the will, strive with all their might to keep to this path by self-imposed renunciations of every kind, by a penitent and hard way of life, and by looking for what is disagreeable to them . . . [Asceticism is] this deliberate breaking of the will by refusing the agreeable and looking for the disagreeable, the voluntarily chosen way of life of penance and self-chastisement, for the constant mortification of the will." (Schopenhauer, 1969, vol. I, §68)

However, practices of fasting, chastity, and other forms of self-denial alone will not bring release. Knowledge is also required. Recall that the release that constitutes aesthetic experience is in large measure a function of the transcendence of the principle of individuation, which also correlates with insight into the nature of will. Similarly, if an entire life is to approach this sort of salvation, it too must involve transcending the principle of individuation in such a way that one perceives the true nature of will – that it is indissoluble and unitary, and that the distinction between our individuality and that of others is an illusion. Moreover, once such a person – call her a saint – realizes this, the clamoring of her individual will after her own interests subsides, and she sacrifices herself to others inasmuch as she regards their lives as her own (for we are all indissolubly of the same world-will).

Schopenhauer writes:

> Now, if seeing through the *principium individuationis*, if this direct knowledge of the identity of the will in all its phenomena, is present in a high degree of distinctness, it will at once show an influence on the will which goes still farther. If that veil of Maya, the *principium individuationis*, is lifted from the eyes of a man to such an extent that he no longer makes the egotistical distinction between himself and the person of others, but takes as much interest in the suffering of other individuals as in his own, and thus is not only benevolent and charitable to the highest degree, but even ready to sacrifice his own individuality when several others can be saved thereby, then it follows automatically that such a man, recognizing in all beings his own true and innermost self, must also regard the endless suffering of all that lives as his own, and thus take upon himself the pain of the whole world. No suffering is any longer strange or foreign to him. . . . [T]hat knowledge of the whole, of the inner nature of the thing-in-itself, which has been described, becomes the quieter of all and every willing. The will now turns away from life; it shudders at the pleasures in which it recognizes the affirmation of life. Man attains to the state of voluntary renunciation, resignation, true composure, and complete will-lessness. (Schopenhauer, 1969, vol. 1, §38)

That is, once one sees through the principle of individuation, one accepts one's identity with all suffering, and this quiets the will and leads one to turn away from it, sacrificing for others insofar as one draws no distinction between oneself and others. Desires are renounced, once the saint has perceived the true face of suffering that inheres in them, and their energy is dissipated by acts of self-mortification and self-sacrifice. This provides a route to more enduring solace than occasional encounters with works of art. But it is clearly an option for the very, very few. The names of Jesus and Buddha spring to mind, perhaps along with other rare mystics and holy persons. But it is not a vocation that most can shoulder. For us, there is the life of desire and merciless pain, leavened only by soothing intervals of aesthetic experience.

Concluding Observations

Schopenhauer's metaphysics are very complex and often hard to fathom. Why is it that once the saint gives up desire, she is not stricken with boredom? And how exactly is one able to turn away from the world-will when one is disgusted by its ferocity? It is not clear that Schopenhauer's system can consistently support all of the various scenarios that he proposes.

Similarly, the mechanics of aesthetic experience that Schopenhauer advances are often hard to square with his metaphysics. Supposedly, an encounter with architecture will momentarily lift us out of the world of striving, since when submerged in Platonic Ideas of rigidity and gravity we are outside the principle of sufficient reason. But how can that be? Surely, these particular Platonic Ideas, supposing that there are such things, must have something to do with tensile strength. Thus, how can we contemplate the idea of rigidity versus gravity outside the framework of the principle of sufficient reason, since tensile strength involves causality. And comparable points can be made of other forms of art. Can there be narrative, let alone tragedy, without causality?

But not only the details of Schopenhauer's ontology are perplexing. As already noted, the derivation of the ultimate nature of being as suffering is flawed at several points. Thus, it is perhaps not surprising that Schopenhauer has few followers among contemporary philosophers. One area, however, where his influence is still felt is the philosophy of art. In addition to his suggestive comments about various forms of art, his notion that aesthetic experience is a release from practical striving has exerted a continuing effect on the tradition, and has been adapted by art theorists and philosophers such as Clive Bell and Monroe Beardsley. Yet, even here, questions about the cogency of Schopenhauer's philosophy must be raised, since his view allows no accommodation for the possibility that some art, properly so called, is about connecting us to the world, not divorcing us from it. And surely we have more reason to believe that this too can be a legitimate function of art than we have to believe that the world is finally nought but a single orb of throbbing pain.

Reference

Schopenhauer, A. 1969: *The World as Will and Representation*, trans. E. F. J. Payne. New York: Dover.

Chapter 3

Søren Kierkegaard

David E. Cooper

"The Category of my Whole Authorship"

For all his influence upon twentieth-century philosophy and theology, the ambition of Søren Kierkegaard (1813–55) recalls a much older tradition. It is less the centrality of religious concerns that relates him to Muslim and Jewish philosophers such as Averroes and Maimonides than the policy Kierkegaard shares with them to shape and measure an authorship by a religious purpose. "The category of my whole authorship," Kierkegaard explains in a retrospective essay of 1848, *The Point of View for my Work as an Author*, is to "*make aware* of the religious, the essentially Christian." While recognizing that he cannot "compel" a reader to "judge" in favor of Christianity – "Perhaps he judges the very opposite of what I desire" – Kierkegaard thinks not only that he can compel the reader "to become aware and judge," but that unless the reader's verdict goes as "I desire," something has gone wrong. For the intended "movement of the authorship" has been to "get hold of 'the single individual,' religiously understood," of "single individuals before God" (*PV*, p. 452ff. (E)).[1]

In the same essay, Kierkegaard explains that it is due to this religious purpose that many of his writings, such as *Either/Or*, take the form of an "indirect communication." These are the pseudonymously published "aesthetic" works in which, Kierkegaard warns, the views expressed by the "authors" are not to be equated with his own. The reason for this strategy, we are told, is that the "illusions" of some readers – for example, their mistaken conviction that they are *already* genuinely Christian – "can never be removed directly." Instead they "must be approached from behind" by an "author" who, like Socrates, seemingly identifies with their own position, but only to expose its inadequacy (*PV*, p. 459 (E)). For Averroes, philosophy, in order effectively to serve as the "friend and milk-sister" of religion, must sometimes disguise a truth that, delivered "straight," would at best remain unabsorbed and at worst be dangerously misunderstood by many readers (Averroes, 1974, p. 306). Kierkegaard would concur.

Some commentators hold that Kierkegaard's estimate of the "whole authorship" should be taken with a pinch of salt. Either he simply misconstrued the character of his earlier writings, or his estimate itself belongs to the "indirect communication" and should be read as ironically or "Socratically undermining his own authority" (see Rée and Chamberlain, 1998, p. 6). There is no reason to accept this view. It may be that Kierkegaard exaggerates the degree to which, five years earlier (when *Either/Or* appeared), his conception of "the movement of the authorship" had crystallized. One should note, too, that it is only with the appearance of his most important work, the unappetisingly titled "*Concluding Unscientific Postscript to* Philosophical Fragments," that the concern with "religiousness" gets explicitly focused on "becoming a Christian" (*PV*, p. 452 (E)). But, with those qualifications, I suggest that *The Point of View* offers an honest and reasonably accurate picture of Kierkegaard's purpose from 1843 to 1848 and beyond. More importantly, his own account encourages an understanding of the writings as embodying an original, challenging, and reasonably systematic philosophy. For all the seeming disparateness of the topics that Kierkegaard addresses and the opaque, "indirect" character of much of that address, a prolonged and unusual argument for religious faith informs his authorship. All or most of his main themes – epistemological, ethical, psychological – revolve around that movement of argument and purpose.

Those themes, and indeed that purpose, do not crystallize until the early 1840s. While Kierkegaard's religious convictions are well attested by his *Journals* during the 1830s, his reputation during most of that decade, when he was a theology student at the University of Copenhagen, was that of a man about town, more focused on the theatre and fine food and wine than upon his studies. Three events, however, helped to change and settle the direction of his life. First, the death in 1838 of his father – a wealthy but pious and brooding merchant – inspired in the son filial guilt at his failure, as yet, to make something serious of that life. Second, his engagement in 1840 to the daughter, Regine Olsen, of a distinguished Copenhagen family, followed a year later by his breaking off the engagement, helped convince Kierkegaard that his was a literary and religious destiny, not the more worldly one of a family man. (He never clearly explained, and perhaps did not himself fully understand, his reasons for the break, although it is something Kierkegaard is plainly attempting to come to terms with, in a suitably indirect way, in several of his writings.) Finally, a visit to the University of Berlin in 1841 did much to shape Kierkegaard's philosophical direction, not through what he learned at the feet of Schelling and other luminaries, but through the repugnance that their abstractions and system-building evoked in him. It was on returning from Germany that Kierkegaard embarked, frenetically, on both his "aesthetic" and "religious" authorship. An intention to give up writing and move to the country was scotched when, in 1845–6, Kierkegaard became the target of vicious lampoons in a Danish periodical. The response that he felt compelled to make escalated into a series of works that were bitterly critical of the political, cultural, and religious establishment of his country. These later works were written in parallel with ones of a less polemical kind in which Kierkegaard strives to instill in his fellow-citizens an awareness of the real, demanding nature of Christian faith. When, in 1855, he collapsed and after a few weeks died, Kierkegaard was a famous and controversial figure in his native city, from which he had rarely roamed.

Given my endorsement of Kierkegaard's own stated understanding of his authorship, my sympathies are with commentators who are optimistic about "making sense" of Kierkegaard's writings and providing a "unifying interpretation" that would explain why these writings deserve the attention of philosophers, and not just biographers, literary critics, and psychoanalysts. (These commentators include C. Stephen Evans (1992), David R. Law (1993), and Mark C. Taylor (1975), who detected "a singular intention of the authorship . . . to lead the reader to actualize genuine selfhood in his personal existence" (1975, p. 23).) Nowadays it is unnecessary to defend these sympathies against critics of an earlier period for whom no such interpretation is possible because, bluntly, Kierkegaard was just no good as a philosopher. This seems to have been the dismissive attitude, ironically, of many commentators in Kierkegaard's native Denmark, and it surely informed the image he had for postwar "Oxford philosophers" as the conveyor of clever *aperçus*, but not someone to figure on the philosophy curriculum (for an account of these and other twentieth-century receptions, see Poole, 1998).

Rather more needs to be said about a currently fashionable view, espoused by advocates of a "new Kierkegaard," on which the reason why it is "risible" to attempt to make systematic philosophical sense of Kierkegaard is certainly *not* that he was a philosophical bungler. Rather, it was Kierkegaard's "project," on this view, not to forge a "new philosophy," but to demonstrate "the nullity of all philosophy" (Josiah Thompson, quoted in Law, 1993, p. 6). Kierkegaard was a *writer*, not a philosopher or theologian, who employed literary devices – irony, pseudonymy, and so on – not in the service of advancing any philosophical position, but of "undermining" or "deconstructing" any such position. On more radical versions of this approach, indeed, it is a mistake even to ask what a Kierkegaardian text is *about*, let alone whether it states anything *true* about something: for, with amazing prescience, he anticipated Derridian and Lacanian insights into a fragile, inescapable "play of signifiers" that refer to nothing beyond themselves. These "insights" are not, of course, *argued* for in his texts, for that would, self-defeatingly, turn them into yet more philosophical theses. Rather, they "show through," or are "embodied in," the literary devices of the texts. (See Mackey (1971) and Poole (1993) for less and more radical versions, respectively, of this approach.)

Even the more sober treatments of Kierkegaard as an anti-philosophical ironist or prototypical deconstructivist, uncommitted to any "positive" position, are exaggerated and productive of identifiable misinterpretations. Consider the welcome extended by the editors of a recent collection of essays to a "new Kierkegaard" who "rejoiced not so much in Christ the redeemer as in Socrates the ironist," apparently because of the latter's alleged refusal to hold any opinions (Rée and Chamberlain, 1998, p. 5). Certainly Kierkegaard admired Socrates, and perhaps the editors are thinking of a passage in the *Postscript* where Socrates is congratulated on the "truth" of his self-proclaimed "ignorance" in the face of "objective uncertainty." If so, they should note that, six pages later, Socratic ignorance is unfavorably compared with the "truth" of a genuinely Christian faith in a God–man that, by any rational criteria, is "absurd": "Compared with the strenuousness of faith," Socratic ignorance is no more than a "witty jest" (*CUP*, pp. 204, 210).

It is Kierkegaard's "indirect communication," his pseudonymous works, that have inspired the emergence of the ironic, "new" Kierkegaard. But even when attention is restricted to these works, the image of an ever-playful, self-undermining *auteur* is a distorting one. Those works do not consist *only* of parables, jokes, ironies, and literary pyrotechnics, behind which only a risibly prosaic reader would look for anything like a philosophical thesis. They contain extended sections of what looks like – and *is* – "straight" philosophical argumentation. Consider, say, the many pages devoted, in both *Philosophical Fragments* and the *Postscript*, to criticism of the Hegelian view that there is a rational necessity to historical events, and to establishing, instead, that "all coming into existence occurs . . . not by way of necessity" (*PF*, p. 75). Nothing here suggests that Kierkegaard is doing other than what he seems to be doing: arguing against one philosophical thesis and in favor of another.

When attention shifts to Kierkegaard's "signed," "directly religious" works, which appeared concurrently with the pseudonymous ones, an obvious difficulty arises for champions of the "new Kierkegaard." He himself, in *The Point of View*, emphasized the publication of these works in order to scotch the impression that he had "changed" from being an "aesthetic" to a "religious" author. We can emphasize it in order to press the "new" Kierkegaardians on their understanding of these works. If they are not themselves ironic and self-undermining, it is hard to see why the pseudonymous writings should be viewed in that way, for the "signed" ones are, typically, consonant both with Kierkegaard's assessment of his "whole authorship" and with what readers – we prosaic, old-fashioned ones, at least – have for long taken the import of the "aesthetic" writings to be. For example, the stated thesis of one of the 1844 *Four Upbuilding Discourses* is that "To need God is a human being's highest perfection." Not only is this the thesis that, according to *The Point of View*, informs the whole corpus, but one which many readers of the pseudonymous *Fear and Trembling*, of 1843, take to be the "message" of the discussion of that "knight of faith" and "single individual," Abraham.

If, however, the "directly religious" works are *not* to be taken "straight," the question is "*why* not?" The main reason for the "new" reading of the "indirect communication" – its pseudonymous authorship – does not apply. The only answer I can think of would appeal to a general, prior commitment to deconstructive readings of texts. If all texts are self-undermining, and can never say or be about what they seem to, then Kierkegaard's "signed" works will be no exception. Nor, of course, will the writings of Aristotle and Kant, of Enid Blyton and Raymond Chandler, and of deconstructivist commentators on Kierkegaard. A "new" reading of Kierkegaard would be required only for the reason that a "new" reading of everyone who has put pen to paper would be.

Here is not the place to rehearse the peculiarities of a globally deconstructivist posture toward texts. It is enough to remark that its "insights" are no more applicable to most of Kierkegaard's writings than to those of anyone else. Nor is it the place to judge whether the treatment of a man with an evident sense of religious, indeed soteriological, purpose as a playful, self-undermining gadfly is a moral, as well as an intellectual, affront. There is more urgent business: to elucidate the "movement" of thought that aims to "get hold" of "single individuals before God."

"The Father of Existentialism"

During much of the last century, Kierkegaard was neither a philosopher *manqué* nor an ironic anti-philosopher. He could be securely "placed" as the main precursor, alongside Nietzsche, of existentialism. Even the name owes to Kierkegaard, for when Jaspers, Heidegger, and Sartre restrict the term "existence" to the distinctive kind of being enjoyed by humans, they follow his precedent in distinguishing "existing *qua* human being" from being in general (*CUP*, p. 85).

Despite their reticence to acknowledge debts, it is not in question that Heidegger and Sartre were inspired by Kierkegaardian themes, first and foremost that of the "single" or "existing individual" whom they, like the Dane, summon to "authenticity" – to "become aware and judge" each for himself, and to "venture wholly to be oneself, as . . . this definite individual" (*SUD*, p. 341 (B)). For them, as for him, "single individuals" must "shake off 'the crowd'" (*PV*, p. 452 (E)), extricate themselves from the dictatorship of that "leveling" "phantom" – at once a "monstrous abstraction" and "the most dangerous of all powers" (*TA*, pp. 261, 263 (E)) – which Kierkegaard called "the public" and Heidegger "*Das Man*" ("Them"). There are other, more specific debts. Heidegger's (1980, §40) and Sartre's (1957, ch. 1) respective talk of *Angst* (anxiety) – something quite different from ordinary fear – as a confrontation with nothingness and an awareness of one's freedom comes straight from Kierkegaard. He, too, describes it as "absolutely different from fear," as a "mood" whose "object . . . is nothing," and as a sense of "*being able*" (*CA*, pp. 139, 141 (E)).

For these and other reasons – a shared hostility, for example, to "naturalistic" accounts of human behavior – it is appropriate that Kierkegaard is included in anthologies of existentialist writings. The editors of one such anthology are right to insist that he, like other figures represented in the volume, "holds that the meaning we find in life is not something that simply comes to us, but is something we attain through struggle . . . choices and commitments" (Guignon and Pereboom, 1995, p. 2). It is surprising, therefore, to find Paul Ricoeur denouncing as "pure illusion" Kierkegaard's reputation as "the father of existentialism." The only support Ricoeur provides for this denunciation, however, is the wildly exaggerated claim that "the supposed family of 'existentialist' philosophies never really existed" – so there was nothing to father. (The sole argument advanced for that claim, incidentally, is neither relevant to nor consistent with it: namely, that the "family" soon "collapsed," with Sartre heading toward Marxism, Heidegger toward "archaizing, poetic meditation," and so on [see Ricoeur, 1998, p. 10].)

A more judicious case, however, can be made for resisting too close an assimilation of Kierkegaard's thought to characteristically existentialist positions. It might be summed up by saying that this assimilation ignores the centrality of religion in Kierkegaard's thought. He may exhort his reader to "venture wholly to be oneself," but in the same breath makes it clear that only when "alone before the face of God" can the venture succeed. He indeed laments that people are generally "lost" in that phantom, "the public," but at the same time insists that the sole alternative for a person is that he "finds himself religiously" (*TA*, p. 267 (E)).

This summary way of stating the case, however, only gestures at the distance between Kierkegaard and his existentialist admirers, and may misleadingly suggest that, as Sartre held, existentialist predilections are incompatible with any type of religious conviction. The case might be elaborated through considering a passage from Alasdair MacIntyre's *After Virtue* in which Kierkegaard, at least in *Either/Or*, is held to proclaim "the distinctively modern standpoint . . . [that] . . . commitment [is] the expression of criterionless choice . . . for which no rational justification can be given" (MacIntyre, 1982, p. 38). The standpoint identified here is one usually associated with existentialism, but it is not Kierkegaard's. I argue later that he does offer a rational justification, albeit an unusual one, for the "choice" of religious faith. For the moment, I simply stress that, for Kierkegaard, what is necessary if one is to succeed, through choice and commitment, "wholly to be oneself," is precisely a "criterion" or "measure" (*Maalestock*). "The criterion for the self is always: that directly before which it is a self" (*SUD*, p. 363 (E)) – which, Kierkegaard goes on to argue, is God.

While it is wrong to saddle Kierkegaard with the view that life-shaping choices and commitments must be "criterionless," it is not similarly mistaken to harp on the importance for him that these have in attaining "the meaning we find in life." But to do so in the manner of many champions of "the existentialist Kierkegaard," without reference to religion, is incomplete and sets the wrong "tone." The impression is given that "authentic" choice matters "for its own sake" or is, *per se*, the achievement of genuine individuality and selfhood. But, as already noted, there can, for Kierkegaard, be no such achievement unless the choice goes a certain way. In this respect, his position differs even from that of "religious existentialists," such as Gabriel Marcel, for whom it is not, so to speak, definitive of the authentic or "available" person that his or her "absolute commitment" must be toward God.

Kierkegaard's concern for a criterion or measure of choice indicates a significant difference from existentialist writers in philosophical orientation or temperament. Typically these writers were, in current jargon, "anti-realists" or "humanists" for whom, as William James put it, "you can't weed out the human contribution" to the nature of reality (James, 1977, p. 455). The world is "a human world" of whose existence, independent of human perspective and interest, no sense can be made. Whether or not Kierkegaard *should* have been an anti-realist, given some of his remarks about knowledge, the fact is that he wasn't. (For a convincing reply to those who treat him as an anti-realist, see Evans (1998). On the anti-realist tendency of existentialism, see Cooper (2000, 2001).) In modern jargon, he was a "metaphysical realist," for whom there is a reality, "a system of existence," that may be inaccessible to human beings. "Is there not such a system? That is not at all the case . . . Existence itself is a system – for God" (*CUP*, p. 118). Nature is not some human "construct," any conception of which must be relative to human perspective: rather, nature or "the totality of creation, is God's work" (*CUP*, p. 246). Nor is historical truth dependent upon "the human contribution." If we cannot acquire knowledge of historical processes, this is because of the "illusiveness" of the "leap" by which historical events come about (see *PF*, p. 72ff.). Kierkegaard is no less a realist in the area of moral discourse. It is a mistaken, "pagan" view of virtue that is "satisfied with a merely human criterion" of good and sin (*SUD*, p. 365 (E)).

Kierkegaard's requirement for a criterion or measure of moral and other commitments that is not "merely human" indicates his distance, over the issue of realism, from most existentialist thinkers. If the world is "a human world," it is senseless to ask for an extra-human measure of our general conception of it. This distance also explains the presence in Kierkegaard's writings of a concern, typically absent from existentialist ones, for "certitude." Although Kierkegaard was a "metaphysical realist," he rejected the "skepticism" he attributes to Kant for holding that reality as such, the *an sich*, is necessarily unknowable (*CUP*, p. 328). Like Schopenhauer, Kierkegaard tries, as we shall see, to open up an "inner" or "inward" route to knowledge of reality. Although Kierkegaard respected the Greek, Pyrrhonian form of skepticism, it is, he thinks, a posture that cannot be genuinely sustained, despite the easy lip-service philosophers often pay it (*CUP*, p. 318). Certainly it was a posture that Kierkegaard did not envision himself sustaining. In his *Journals*, many poignant passages testify to his need for certainty – an "anchorage," a "centre," a "true Archimedean point," an "unshakable thing in life," a "regulating weight," a "compulsion." Without the certitude of an "anchorage" or "unshakable thing" – which Kierkegaard will identify with God – our "mass of information" will be without system or focus, our life will not be "bound by anything higher than [it]self," and Kierkegaard's quest for "the idea for which I can live and die" will remain frustrated (*J*, pp. 44–5, 66, 181, 241).

This quest for an Archimedean point that "must lie outside the world" (*J*, p. 43) is, for the anti-realist, misconceived, for there is nothing "outside" the "human world." But even by writers of an existentialist hue who are not obviously anti-realist in outlook, the search for certainty is rejected. Albert Camus, for example, held that reality was bound to remain "silent" in the face of our demands to know it, so that we are left understanding only a world that has been "reduc[ed] to the human, stamp[ed] with our seal." That may make our situation "absurd," but is nothing to lament; for by accepting the situation, yet "creating" our own beliefs and meanings, we attain "majesty" and "dignity" (Camus, 1975, pp. 23, 54, 104). For Kierkegaard, on the contrary, any such dignity requires the certitude of a "criterion," an "anchorage," "outside" the "human world."

To appreciate the place of this requirement is to locate Kierkegaard's philosophy in a tradition older than and inimical to existentialism. However original Kierkegaard's pursuit of certitude, it places him in the company of a long line of philosophers for whom the issue of certainty has been central. To locate Kierkegaard in this way raises a problem, however, since philosophers belonging to that tradition usually speak of endeavoring to "discover" what is certain, of "finding out" what is truly real. What, one wonders, is Kierkegaard doing, in the company of existentialists, placing so much emphasis on "choice," "commitment," "venture," and "will"? The short answer is that it is only through these "existential" endeavors – and not through "objective" inquiry – that, for Kierkegaard, certitude can be attained and the Archimedean point seized. Only the person who "choose[s], . . . stake[s] [his] whole life . . . shall see" (*J*, p. 185). To elaborate that answer, and so to grasp the "movement" of Kierkegaard's authorship, we first need to consider his accounts of knowledge and truth.

"Truth is Subjectivity"

Emphasis on a search for certainty may seem misplaced, given Kierkegaard's many references to an uncertainty to which all beliefs are subject and to the need for belief in the face of that uncertainty. Typically, however, those references are to what he elsewhere qualifies as "objective uncertainty." That Kierkegaard does not intend to rule out certainty of some kind is shown by passages where, in paradoxical idiom, this is contrasted with objective certainty – for example, when he writes that "the certitude of faith that relates itself to an eternal happiness is defined by uncertainty" (*CUP*, p. 455).

To appreciate that contrast, a glance at Kierkegaard's epistemology, briefly sketched in *Philosophical Fragments*, is required. Beliefs which go beyond the immediate deliverances of sensation are not immune to error, for we may be "deceived" when "drawing conclusions" about the world from our sensations (*PF*, pp. 82–3). More seriously, we cannot assume a general identity between "thought and being," not only because our concepts radically abstract from a rich, concrete reality, but because the "knower is an existing person" (*CUP*, p. 196) whose concepts are as much the product of imagination and interest as of detached inquiry. Unless, like Hegel, therefore, we render the identity of thought and being a "tautology," by surreptitiously smuggling our conceptual scheme into the fabric of reality (*CUP*, p. 122ff.), we should regard our beliefs only as an "approximation" to reality.

Such arguments have led other philosophers, such as Nietzsche, to an "anti-realist" denial of a reality independent of human perspective. That, we have seen, was not the direction Kierkegaard took. Given that he didn't, one might expect that he would have drawn *skeptical* conclusions instead. We just cannot know anything. But, for an interesting reason, he did not do this either. In his view, the fallibility error of our claims leaves it open whether one should believe or doubt them. This is because both attitudes are "acts of freedom" or "will": they are "opposite passions," not judgments determined by weight of evidence (*PF*, pp. 82–4). Certainly "a will to believe" is at work in embracing a claim not secured by the evidence, but it is no less an exercise of will to withhold belief in the Pyrrhonian manner.

In the case of ordinary empirical beliefs, "leaps" in the face of objective uncertainty are no cause for great concern: we cannot avoid making some if we are to function as agents and it is hardly the end of the world when, sometimes, we leap in the wrong direction. Matters are different, however, when we turn to "essential" or "ethical-religious knowing" (*CUP*, p. 198). Here, in the area of ideas for which people can live and die, certainty is necessary, for it would be madness to stake one's life on an "approximation." Hence lack of historical certainty concerning the life of Christ, where every "iota is . . . of infinite importance" (*CUP*, p. 26), would and should be disastrous for Christian belief – *if*, that is, the certainty of this belief were of the type to which "objective" inquiry aspires. It is a crucial claim of Kierkegaard's that this cannot be the type of certainty involved, for in connection with "essential knowing" our "objective uncertainty" is almost total. (Indeed, in the specific case of Christianity, as we shall see, the object of belief is worse than "objectively uncertain": it is plain paradoxical.) It cannot be the kind of certainty involved for a further important reason. In connection with Christianity, Kierkegaard writes, objectivity is an "extremely unfortunate category": for if an objective "demonstration of the truth of Christianity" were forthcoming, this truth "would have ceased to exist as something present" (*CUP*, pp. 43, 32). Instead, it would stand there "cold and naked," incapable of inspiring "trusting devotion" and of being "taken up into my life" (*J*, p. 44).

These remarks call for clarification, but let us first consider the unsurprising feeling, among many critical readers of Kierkegaard, that the certainty or "essential" knowing he intends is simply some psychological state – an inner conviction, say – that is neutral with respect to truth: knowing in the sense that a xenophobic bigot, perhaps, "knows" that the French are all liars, rather than knowing in an epistemic sense that requires a relation of the knower to what is true. But can the certainty or knowledge Kierkegaard has in mind be thus "truth-neutral"? If it is, that would be disappointing: his calls to faith, "passionate inwardness," and so on would reduce to exhortations to induce certain psychological states of no more than therapeutic value. Moreover, it would apparently conflict with Kierkegaard's repeated insistence that "subjectivity" in the form of "passionate inwardness" is "in the truth," that "subjectivity is truth" (e.g., *CUP*, pp. 203–4).

Critics, however, will urge that this conflict is indeed only apparent, for what Kierkegaard means by "subjective truth" itself turns out to be truth-neutral – unconnected, that is, with what is truly, objectively the case. To ask about truth subjectively, he says, is to ask about "the individual's relation" to an "object" of "knowledge," and this individual may be "in [subjective] truth" even when related to objective "untruth." Two pages later, Kierkegaard seemingly confirms his critics' worry when he claims that a shallow Christian, although possessing a "true idea of God," has less subjective truth on his side than a "passionate" heathen who lacks that idea (*CUP*, pp. 199, 201). Kierkegaard's reference to what is embraced in "passionate inwardness" as "true for" an individual should not disguise the fact, his critics conclude, that he is not talking about truth in an epistemic sense at all.

Although this conclusion is wrong, it is an understandable one, for Kierkegaard's remarks on subjectivity and truth are, frankly, a mess. In different passages, he veers between holding that, with "essential" belief, subjectivity is "the final factor" and objectivity a "vanishing" one; that subjectivity is simply "superior" to objectivity; and that genuine knowledge must have "objective reality" (for a medley of such passages, see Law, 1993, pp. 118–9). He is, moreover, inattentive to an ambiguity in the notion of objectivity. When he writes of Christianity approached in a "purely objective way," Kierkegaard understands the notion in a methodological sense: to be objective is to "leave [one]self out" of the inquiry, to conduct it in a detached, impersonal manner (*CUP*, p. 21). But when he refers, for example, to "objective reality," an ontological sense is involved: the objective is that which anyway is, independent of human perspective or belief.

Had he been attentive to that distinction, critics would have been less prone to interpret Kierkegaardian subjectivity as truth-neutral. For while the subjective, passionately inward person is not, of course, objective in his approach or stance toward the truth, it does not follow that, for him to be "in the truth," the objective reality of what is believed is immaterial. Indeed, it will emerge in the following section that, for Kierkegaard, genuine subjectivity requires an appropriate relation to what is objectively real or true – God. But how, if that is so, does one explain the *Postscript* passages, quoted two paragraphs ago, where he seemingly denies this? A close reading of the "passionate heathen" passage supplies an answer. The heathen may lack "the true idea of God": nevertheless, when he prays, it is "in truth to God" that he prays, even though he has no proper understanding of what he prays to. The shallow, skin-deep Christian, on the other hand, is "in truth worshipping an idol," for "he prays in untruth." In other words, the heathen is in the greater truth, not only because of his inwardness and passion, but because, despite his theological misconception, he *is* appropriately related to the real God. Far from gainsaying the claim that objectivity, in the ontological sense, is immaterial to subjective truth, this passage confirms it. Notice, incidentally, that even if this reading is mistaken, there is no justification for treating the passage as a global endorsement of "passion" irrespective of objective truth. The heathen, after all, is a *religious* believer. Had the object of his "worship" been the victory of the proletariat or the Hegelian Idea, one cannot imagine Kierkegaard describing him, however "passionate," as "in the truth."

Although how matters objectively stand is not, therefore, irrelevant to being, subjectively, in the truth, a question remains: Why does Kierkegaard insist that the subjective quality of "essential knowing" – its "passion" and so on – is crucial to its status as truth-bearing knowledge? Granted that it is "better" for various reasons – therapeutic or otherwise – for belief or faith to be "passionate," why should that be germane to its credentials as knowledge? Granted that the shallow Christian cuts an ugly figure, why distinguish him from his more "passionate" co-religionist in terms of truth? Such questions force one, in effect, to consider Kierkegaard's view, cited earlier, that for the shallow, methodologically objective Christian – one who believes solely on the basis of historical evidence, say – religion does not "exist as something present."

Kierkegaard characterizes subjective "inwardness" as "appropriation," and "subjective truth" as "the truth of appropriation." "Appropriation is . . . the main point," he tells us, "wherever the subjective is of importance in knowledge" (*CUP*, pp. 366, 21, 79). The negative point here is the denial that "ethical-religious knowing" is ever a matter, simply, of assenting to true propositions, on however a reliable basis, such as authoritative testimony. On that basis, I might be said to know that Caesar was bald, but not that he was "great." "If I do not know it by myself," if I do not "see" it, "then I do not know it at all" (*CUP*, p. 324). Such truths cannot be "directly communicated" by one person to another. Genuinely to know such matters, to be "in the truth" with respect to them, a person must appropriate them for himself. Thus only "two kinds of person can know something about" Christianity: those who are "impassionedly . . . faith-bound to it," and those who, with an "opposite passion," reject it (*CUP*, p. 52). For everyone else, Christianity is "not something present."

Kierkegaard supports this attractive conception of "essential knowing" as appropriation in two related ways. First, someone who is not "impassionedly interested" has not internalized such knowledge, and does not even *understand* what he purports to know or believe. In the case of empirical beliefs, this understanding may not be necessary: perhaps I can believe that various scientific hypotheses are true without understanding them. But it is different, as the Caesar example suggests, with "ethical-religious knowing." Someone "objectively indifferent" to the ethical "cannot come to know anything whatever" concerning the greatness or pettiness of another person (*CUP*, p. 52). So appropriation *qua* inward passion is a precondition of understanding, hence of belief and knowing, hence of being "in the truth."

Second, despite Kierkegaard's emphasis on the "inward," "ethical-religious knowing" is something that must manifest itself in a person's *life*. As James Conant puts it, for Kierkegaard "a religious [or ethical] inflection of a concept is only able to have its sense within the context of a certain sort of life" (1995, p. 277). This is Kierkegaard's point when he writes that a person's "life is the proof that he believes" (*J*, p. 185) and that "the subjective *thinker* has . . . actuality in his own ethical existence" (*CUP*, p. 228; my emphasis). The persuasive point is this: whereas I can believe that something is square or white without this having any necessary bearing on my life, I cannot similarly believe that something is sinful or worthy of worship unless this belief is taken up in my life. To proclaim "Adultery is a sin!" and then nonchalantly to go on and commit it must call into question the sincerity of the proclamation. Appropriation *qua* the taking up of a belief in a life, *qua* a willed commitment, is a precondition of having that belief, hence of the believer's having anything that could be "in the truth."

"Becoming a Subject"

For Kierkegaard, then, subjectivity as inward and lived "appropriation" is necessary to being "in the truth." But he makes a more radical claim: subjectivity *requires* a proper relationship to what is objectively real, God. How, though, could "appropriation" require that relationship? An "impassioned" atheist might surely both inwardly and vitally appropriate his or her conviction. Just as Kierkegaard means more than one thing by "objectivity," however, so he does by "subjectivity," and it is in a sense different from appropriation that subjectivity requires the "God-relation."

David R. Law rightly notes that, in Kierkegaard's writings, a "second meaning of subjectivity is 'becoming a subject,' i.e. becoming a proper self or person" (1993, p. 115). While every human is a "subject of sorts," it is a "task" really to *be* or *become* a subject, and Christianity "teaches that the way to become subjective" is "truly to become a subject" (*CUP*, pp. 130–1). Nothing is lost by substituting "self" for "subject" in such passages. So it is subjectivity *qua* selfhood, not *qua* appropriation, that requires the "God-relation." (This does not mean that appropriation drops out of the picture: on the contrary, no one can "become a subject" who does not appropriate.)

That selfhood requires the "God-relation" is explicitly stated. Someone "without God . . . is never essentially himself (which one is only by being before God) and therefore is never satisfied with being himself" (*CD*, p. 317 (E)). These words indicate that in order to be a self, a person must achieve self-understanding, and that this is achieved when he sees himself to be "before God." That Kierkegaard's argument involves these two claims is made clear in the following remarks: "this view, that to need God is man's highest perfection . . . wants to view man according to his perfection and bring him to view himself in this way, because in and through this view *man learns to know himself*. And for the person who does not know himself, his life is . . . indeed a delusion" (*FUD*, p. 88 (E)). Someone who knows himself recognizes his need of God: otherwise his existence is a delusion and not that of a genuine individual or self.

Since, for Kierkegaard, self-knowledge is both possible and the way to recognition of what is truly real, there is some parallel with Schopenhauer's notion of "a way from within" to what exists *an sich* (Schopenhauer, 1969, vol. 2, p. 195). What is this "way," according to Kierkegaard? It misrepresents him to suppose that he offers an "objective proof" of God's existence that any rational mind must find compelling. This is so despite an apparent structural similarity between his "move" from self-understanding to God and a well-known argument of Descartes. The latter argued that we know by introspection that we possess the idea of perfection and that, from this, we may *infer* God's existence, since only He could have caused us to have this idea (Descartes, 1988, p. 166). Kierkegaard rejects such "proofs." One is "deluded" in "thinking that [one] could demonstrate that God exists" (*PF*, pp. 190–1). So whatever Kierkegaard's "way" from selfhood to God, it does not take the form:

> The self is Φ
> If the self is Φ, God exists
> ∴ God exists.

Kierkegaard's way is at once phenomenological and dialectical, an interpretation of what is meant by certain experiences through rehearsing a number of "stages" of self-understanding, each more adequate than the preceding one. Human beings who are not entirely sunk in "crowd life" – with barely a sense of their individuality and the possibilities open to them – have certain experiences or, better perhaps, *intimations* of a self-reflective kind that indicate, however inchoately, something about themselves. Kierkegaard's concern is not to identify the cause of such intimations – God or something in the genes – but to articulate what is meant or "intended" by them. Properly construed, they intimate that one is truly a self only in the "God-relation," when "rest[ing] transparently in the power that established it" (*SUD*, p. 352 (E)). Typically, a person will – like Kierkegaard himself, perhaps – pass through several "stages on life's way" before recognizing the full significance of the intimations. What is appreciated at an earlier stage, however, is not abandoned: indeed, it will be "taken up," in the manner of an Hegelian *Aufhebung*, in the final interpretation. So the phenomenological way is a dialectical one. As Alistair Hannay nicely remarks, Kierkegaard does not, like Marx, turn Hegel upside-down, but "outside-in" (Hannay, 1982,

p. 52): the dialectical odyssey is neither that of the Idea nor of human history, but of the individual self.

Kierkegaard's way is not a "proof" of God, for laying bare the meaning of experiences no more settles matters of actual existence than does analysis of the meaning of words. Only if it were first established that the experiences have "external reference" could their interpretation be a proof of what actually exists. Kierkegaard nowhere tries to establish that. Nevertheless, for people who find Kierkegaard's way persuasive, and who cannot but take their intimations seriously, something has been proved: either those experiences are, after all, illusory, or selfhood requires the "God-relation."

The intimations on which Kierkegaard focuses may, at a pinch, all be subsumed under the umbrella of *despair*, the "sickness unto death" that afflicts nearly all of us. He leaves no doubt as to the significance of despair, opaque as that might be to those who are in it. It intimates that "the self is [not] the merely human self but . . . the self directly before God," and it is only when "despair is completely rooted out" that the self "in willing to be itself . . . rests transparently" in God (*SUD*, pp. 363, 352 (E)). Nevertheless, Kierkegaard makes several remarks about despair that sound puzzling. We read, for example, that despair is a "choice" that we should make (*E/O* II, p. 215); that we are in despair whether we know it or not; and that "the formula for all despair" is "to will to be rid of oneself" (*SUD*, p. 356 (E)).

These remarks, however, are consistent with one another and with the main claim about the meaning of despair. We should "choose" despair rather than dismiss it, when it strikes, as an aberration, a "funny turn," signifying nothing. Indeed, to take despair seriously is a precondition for someone to appropriate, in the "deepest sense," the idea that "his self, exists before . . . God" (*SUD*, p. 360). People can unknowingly be in despair since they, too, are prone to experience it: they may "pass it off," or immunize themselves against it, but that is a different matter. That the despairing person "wills to be rid" of his self invites two interpretations. As intimating a "higher" or "theological self," despair may incorporate a desire to be rid of a "lower," mundane self. Equally, for those doggedly attached to their "merely human self," despair induces resistance to the prospect of a "higher" self, achievement of which calls for rigor and devotion (see Hannay, 1998).

Fully to understand the significance of despair, one naturally turns to Kierkegaard's account of the self, sketchy as it is. We are told that man has a "double nature," for he is a "synthesis" of contrasting aspects, "infinite and finite," "temporal and eternal," "freedom and necessity" (*SUD*, p. 351 (E)), or a "synthesis of psyche and body . . . constituted and sustained by spirit" (*CA*, p. 146 (E)). A self is not, however, just a combination of such elements, for it exists only when an appropriate relation between them has "established itself." Despair is a "misrelation in . . . [this] synthesis" of aspects or elements.

Kierkegaard nowhere provides much clarification of this account of selfhood, although what he does *not* have in mind is sometimes clear. He is not, for example, proclaiming a Cartesian view of a person as a pair of substances, material and immaterial, somehow welded together. By the "eternal" aspect, therefore, he does not intend the everlastingness of an immaterial soul. Nor should the sketchiness of Kierkegaard's account really cause disappointment. For one thing, its *gist* is relatively clear. To be a self, a person must achieve an integrity and unity among otherwise fragmented ingredients of human existence: while he or she remains "changeable, double-minded, and unstable" (*PH*, p. 53), the self has not yet "established itself." Second, it would conflict with Kierkegaard's strategy to build, *ab initio*, an understanding of selfhood appropriated at the final stage on life's way into what is only *intimated* by despair. Only when despair is "rooted out" is the notion of selfhood gestured at by talk of a "synthesizing spirit" grasped as the meaning of those earlier intimations. And since it is as the result of "conscious action," of choices and decisions, that I am finally able "to call myself 'I' in any deeper sense" (*J*, p. 47), it is only to others who have made the same journey that I can communicate this deeper sense, one that, Kierkegaard recognizes, is only gestured at by his characterizations of selfhood.

"Stages on Life's Way"

All except the first and last of Kierkegaard's famous "stages on life's way" are best construed in terms of the intimations experienced by people at these stages that they are not yet selves, that their lives therefore remain "far . . . from what a man's life ought to be" (*PH*, p. 54). At the final stage, of authentic Christian faith, a person has learned, with despair now "rooted out," both to know and be himself. At the first stage, whose implied presence in Kierkegaard's account is usefully noted by Anthony Rudd (1997, p. 24), someone is too unreflectively sunk in "crowd life" to be aware of himself as – and hence to *be* – an individual person at all. Such awareness begins at the second, "aesthetic" stage, where most of us are stuck.

None of the "aesthetic" figures described in *Either/Or* – not even that "sensuous–erotic spirit," Don Juan – are totally unreflective: indeed, the eponymous protagonist of "The Seducer's Diary" is positively scheming. What unites these figures is not a taste for the arts but, roughly, their pursuit of enjoyment, especially of sensuous pleasure. Whatever its precise form, "every aesthetic life view is despair" (*E/O* II, p. 229), and this because the aesthete has not "chosen *himself*." This, in turn, is because his life, lacking in real commitment, is led "constantly . . . in the moment": it "hinges upon a condition outside itself," subject to external stimuli and mood. It is the life of someone who is not *a* self, but a "multiplicity," without that "holiest thing," the "unifying power of personality" (*E/O* II, pp. 234ff, 164). Ever prone to these uncomfortable reflections, the aesthete, if he "chooses despair" instead of brushing it off, will appreciate that his is the half-life of a merely finite creature, bound to the transient and governed by necessity. Nothing in his life answers to the other half of our "double nature." The aesthete "develops by necessity not by freedom," makes "no infinite movement," and is blind to what he "eternally possesses" (*E/O* II, pp. 229, 236). The proper synthesis of selfhood is not "established in" the aesthete.

"Judge William", who hammers these points home to his young aesthete friend, knows how to achieve this synthesis – through living "ethically." Here "ethical" has a different sense from the one it sometimes bears in the *Postscript*, as a synonym for the "higher" reaches of human existence. In *Either/Or*, the ethical is the realm of what Hegel called *Sittlichkeit* (from *Sitte* = custom) – that of the established norms and principles of a society that regulate people's "stations in life," as citizens, parents, spouses, or whatever. In the Judge's view, through commitment to such norms a person finds freedom, is "infinitized," and becomes conscious of his "eternal nature" (*E/O* II, pp. 218, 274–5). Through shaping his life according to general principles, a person is no longer subject to external "conditions," sunk in "finite" hedonistic pursuits, and living "in the moment," for he achieves lifelong constancy of purpose. In short, he becomes a self, integrating the opposing poles of his "double nature." For at the ethical stage, one's "finite" nature is not ignored: a happy, faithful marriage, for example, yields greater erotic satisfaction than serial seduction.

For Kierkegaard, however, it is not at this ethical stage that despair is "rooted out" and selfhood achieved. This is intimated by at least three kinds of experience to which even the ethically unblemished are prone. For what is intimated is that human beings cannot remain satisfied with the "merely human criterion" that social *mores* provide. The first experience – "almost . . . despair" – is described in a letter sent to the Judge by a Pastor friend (*E/O* II, pp. 343–56). This is the sense that, however ethically assiduous, "as against God we are always in the wrong." It is not that we first establish the existence of an ever-righteous God, in comparison with whom we are indeed "frail creatures": rather, the sense of perpetual guilt intimates a "higher" measure beyond humanly devised ethical ones. In ethical life, there remains a "misrelation between the finite and the infinite" (*CUP*, p. 268). In recognizing that he remains "in the wrong," an ethically impeccable person appreciates a capacity to "raise himself above the finite into the infinite" that is something more than an ability to regulate and lend constancy to his life by commitment to universal principles.

There is an intimating despair, second, in awareness of being "double-minded" or "hav[ing] two wills" (*PH*, p. 53). For, as noted, one is then a "multiplicity," lacking a "unifying power of personality." The cure for this despair proposed in *Purity of Heart* is to "will one thing." But why should this not be the ethical? After all, Kierkegaard himself insists that it cannot simply be something "big, no matter whether it be good or bad," and that the person who opts for the bad will surely be assailed, and torn apart, by "agonizing longing for the Good" (*PH*, pp. 55–6). He then argues, however, that this Good is not ethical good, for it is essential that the "one thing" be genuinely *one*, a unity. Ethical good only "appears to be one thing," and the person dedicated to it remains "double-minded," a "multiplicity" (*PH*, p. 52). To be genuinely one, a *telos* must be changeless, absolute, unconditioned, and without inner conflict: a "worldly goal," like the ethical, meets none of these criteria. The person who "manag[es] with custom and tradition in the city where he lived" (*CUP*, p. 244) regulates his life by a motley of changing norms that are relative to and conditioned by circumstances, and between which there can be collisions. Once he appreciates this, the person recognizes the need, if he is genuinely to "will one thing," for a "relation to the absolute *telos*" which does not "exhaust itself in relative ends" and may even require "renunciation" of them (*CUP*, p. 405). In other words, he must "draw nigh to God," for God alone is "one thing" – changeless, unconditioned, and so on (*CG*, p. 485ff.). Only a person wholly focused on the God-relation, therefore, is held together, as a self, by a "unifying power."

The themes of moral conflict and an absolute *telos* are present as well in *Fear and Trembling*. There, moral conflict is personified by the "tragic hero" who is torn apart, without hope of rational resolution, by conflicting ethical duties – in Agamemnon's case, to his daughter and people respectively. The book focuses, however, not on conflicts "within the ethical," but on a collision between the ethical and a "*telos* outside it" (*FT*, pp. 87–8). This collision is primarily illustrated by Abraham, a "knight of faith," who must decide between, on the one hand, ethical duties – to family and nation alike – and, on the other, God's command that he sacrifice Isaac. As that story suggests, the *telos* "outside" the ethical is the absolute duty to God that a person has in virtue of his "private relationship" with Him (*FT*, pp. 108, 88).

It is important to recognize, however, that the movement of thought in *Fear and Trembling* is not *from* the existence of and relationship with God *to* "suspension of the ethical." The "author" of the book, Johannes De Silentio, while "admiring" Abraham, does not "understand" him (*FT*, pp. 85–6). He is not himself a "knight of faith" but, rather, someone at the ethical stage who nevertheless reflects on what is intimated by his admiration for Abraham. Why is he loathe simply to condemn Abraham as a murderer, as he thinks that Hegel, and others who regard the ethical as "absolute," should do? That God is the absolute *telos* is where such reflection leads, not a premise established in advance.

What Johannes realizes, first, is that admiration would only be warranted if "the single individual is higher than the universal" (*FT*, p. 84), that the demands of selfhood "trump" ethical norms. This does not mean that the "single individual" may just ignore the ethical: rather, he "determines his relation to the universal through his relation to the absolute," not vice versa (*FT*, pp. 97–8). Otherwise, a person is not "the particular," following his own "higher . . . lonely path," but "sectarian," a face in "the crowd." Without a willingness to "suspend the ethical" in the name of fidelity to one's self, a person lacks that "authentically human factor," *passion* (*FT*, pp. 108, 103, 106, 145). That this passion must take the form of religious faith requires further reflection, the appreciation that, without faith, a person will remain in despair or "sorrow," hence not an authentic self. Only in "the bliss of infinity," and with a sense of one's "eternal validity," is "sorrow" overcome (*FT*, pp. 70, 75): only then is justice done to the "higher" aspects of one's "double nature."

The various intimations afforded by despair and admiration take us, then, from the ethical stage to a "higher" one, the religious. Has Kierkegaard, therefore, reached the destination of the "movement of his authorship"? Not quite. Abraham, while a "knight of faith," was not a Christian, and nor is Christian belief an essential ingredient in Kierkegaard's portrait of another "knight of faith" in the same book, the so-called "shopman" (*FT*, pp. 68–70). These knights remain, in effect, at the stage of what, in the *Postscript*, is called "Religiousness A," and distinguished from a specifically Christian "Religiousness B." It is arguable, indeed, that a knight of faith need not be a person of religious, at any rate theistic, belief at all. Perhaps a knight's faith could be in "an absolute good or absolute *telos*" without that "*telos* being identified in religious terms" (Rudd, 1997, pp. 157–8). Certainly some of the attitudes associated with Religiousness B, such as a willingness to renounce one's "finite" concerns and "die to immediacy," are not the prerogative of theists. Be that as it may, Kierkegaard is clear that the final stage is the faith of Religiousness B: only when "the object of faith" is the God–man – an "individual human being," Jesus – is there complete faith, "in which there is no despair at all" and, at last, the self properly relates "itself to itself" and "rests transparently in the power that established it" (*CUP*, p. 326; *SUD*, p. 372 (E)).

Readers sympathetic, until this final step, to Kierkegaard's interpretation of what is intimated through despair and related experiences, may judge that this is a step too far. Kierkegaard, in this final move, registers his own particular religious commitment – one that no phenomenology of intimating experiences could induce. This judgment is warranted, for Kierkegaard is at his weakest, perhaps, when arguing that selfhood, the "rooting out" of despair, requires specifically Christian faith. One such argument, in the *Postscript*, is that Christianity alone has the resources to explain a person's sense that he is too "corrupt," too "sinful," too much a "nothing," to achieve selfhood through his own efforts, however resolute. But other religions, including Islam, would claim to have such resources too.

A further argument concerns the paradoxical character of Christian faith. Already, in *Fear and Trembling*, Kierkegaard has asserted that faith must be in the teeth of reason. "Faith begins precisely where thinking leaves off," and what made Abraham a knight of faith is that he "believed on the strength of the absurd," since be believed that he would both lose Isaac and "receive him back" (*FT*, pp. 82, 65). In comparison with this "absurdity," however, the paradox of Christianity is "absolute." "The God-man is . . . absolutely the paradox" on which "the understanding must come to a standstill" (*PC*, p. 375 (E)). This is the alleged paradox of the word made flesh, of the eternal and divine as a historically located human being. Kierkegaard now argues that, because the paradox is absolute, it uniquely requires absolute faith, the maximum "inwardness" of commitment. "The more risk, the more faith" (*CUP*, p. 176) – and what could be more "risky" than faith in what is, from the standpoint of reason, utterly impossible? The argument is a bad one. My faith that tomorrow will turn out fine need not be "less" than your faith that tomorrow will also be the day after tomorrow. That mine is a faith in something logically possible, while yours is not, is irrelevant to the depth, resilience, and "inwardness" of our respective convictions.

It was not, we saw at the outset, Kierkegaard's purpose to "compel" his reader to "become a Christian," and certainly not by propounding "proofs" that no rational mind could fault. Even if such proofs were available, the person who is convinced solely by them may become a member of "Christendom," but not an authentic Christian whose faith is in spite of reason. It was Kierkegaard's purpose, nevertheless, to make his readers aware that if they take seriously their intimations, through despair, of the possible selves they might, and surely want to, become, they must transcend their merely "finite," "relative" condition. They must "leap" toward the religious. It is difficult to judge how disappointed Kierkegaard would be to have won readers who, while following him thus far, find themselves not at all compelled to make a further leap over the hurdle of Christianity's "paradox."

Note

1   See under Bibliography below for the key to citations from Kierkegaard.

Bibliography

Anthologies of Kierkegaard's writings

Bretall, R. (ed.) 1973: *A Kierkegaard Anthology*. Princeton: Princeton University Press. (References in the text followed by (B) are to this book.)

Guignon, C. and Pereboom, D. (eds.) 1995: *Existentialism: Basic Writings*. Indianapolis, Ind.: Hackett.

Hong, H. and Hong, E. (eds.) 1997: *The Essential Kierkegaard*. Princeton: Princeton University Press. (References in the text followed by (E) are to this book.)

Individual works by Kierkegaard

The capital letters preceding the following titles are the abbreviations for them used in this chapter. Unless otherwise specified, the works are as translated by H. V. and E. H. Hong in *Kierkegaard's Writings* (*KW*), 26 vols., Princeton: Princeton University Press, 1978–2000.

CA   *The Concept of Anxiety* (*KW*8)

CD   *Christian Discourses* (*KW*17)

CG   *The Changelessness of God* (*KW*23)

CUP   *Concluding Unscientific Postscript to* Philosophical Fragments (*KW*12)

E/O   *Either/Or* (1971), vol. I trans. D. and L. Swenson, vol. II trans. W. Lowrie. Princeton, NJ: Princeton University Press.

FT   *Fear and Trembling* (1985), trans. A. Hannay. Harmondsworth: Penguin.

FUD   *Four Uplifting Discourses* (*KW*5)

J   *Journals of Kierkegaard* (1960), trans. A. Dru. London: Fontana.

PC   *Practice in Christianity* (*KW*20)

PF   *Philosophical Fragments* (*KW*7)

PH   *Purity of Heart (is to will one thing)* (1961), trans. D. Steere. London: Fontana.

PV   *The Point of View for my Work as an Author* (*KW*22)

SUD   *The Sickness Unto Death* (*KW*19)

TA   *Two Ages: The Age of Revolution and the Present Age* (*KW*14)

Writings on Kierkegaard

Conant, J. 1995: Putting two and two together: Kierkegaard, Wittgenstein and the point of view for their work as authors. In T. Tessin and M. von der Ruhr (eds.), *Philosophy and the Grammar of Religious Belief*. Basingstoke: Macmillan, 248–331.

Evans, C. S. 1992: *Passionate Reason: Making Sense of Kierkegaard's* Philosophical Fragments. Bloomington, Ind.: Indiana University Press.

——1998: Realism and antirealism in Kierkegaard's *Concluding Unscientific Postscript*. In Hannay and Marino (1998), op. cit., 154–76.

Hannay, A. 1982: *Kierkegaard*. London: Routledge.

——1998: Kierkegaard and the variety of despair. In Hannay and Marino (1998), op. cit., 329–48.

——and Marino, G. (eds.) 1998: *The Cambridge Companion to Kierkegaard*. Cambridge: Cambridge University Press.

Law, D. R. 1993: *Kierkegaard as Negative Theologian*. Oxford: Clarendon Press.

Mackey, L. 1971: *Kierkegaard: A Kind of Poet*. Philadelphia, Penn.: University of Pennsylvania Press.

Poole, R. 1993: *Kierkegaard: The Indirect Communication*. Charlottesville, Va.: University Press of Virginia.

——1998: The unknown Kierkegaard: twentieth-century receptions. In Hannay and G. Marino (1998), op. cit., 48–75.

Rée, J. and Chamberlain, J. (eds.) 1998: *Kierkegaard: A Critical Reader*. Oxford: Blackwell.

Ricoeur, P. 1998: Philosophy after Kierkegaard. In Rée and Chamberlain (1998), op. cit., 9–25.

Rudd, A. 1997: *Kierkegaard and the Limits of the Ethical*. Oxford: Clarendon Press.

Taylor, M. C. 1975: *Kierkegaard's Pseudonymous Authorship: A Study of Time and the Self*. Berkeley and Los Angeles, Calif.: University of California Press.

Other works cited

Averroes 1974: *The Decisive Treatise*. Reprinted in A. Hyman and J. Walsh (eds.), *Philosophy in the Middle Ages*. Indianapolis, Ind.: Hackett.

Camus, A. 1975: *The Myth of Sisyphus*, trans. J. O'Brien. Harmondsworth: Penguin.

Cooper, D. E. 2000: *Existentialism: A Reconstruction*, rev. edn. Oxford: Blackwell.

——2001: *Humanism, Humility and Mystery*. Oxford: Oxford University Press.

Descartes, R. 1988: *Selected Philosophical Writings*, trans. J. Cottingham et al. Cambridge: Cambridge University Press.

Heidegger, M. 1980: *Being and Time*, trans. J. Macquarrie and E. Robinson. Oxford: Blackwell.

James, W. 1977: *The Writings of William James*. Chicago, Ill.: University of Chicago Press.

MacIntyre, A. 1981: *After Virtue: A Study in Moral Theory*. London: Duckworth.

Sartre, J.-P. 1957: *Being and Nothingness*, trans. H. Barnes. London: Methuen.

Schopenhauer, A. 1969: *The World as Will and Representation*, 2 vols., trans. E. F. J. Payne. New York: Dover.

Chapter 4

Karl Marx

Douglas Kellner

The work of Karl Marx (1818–83) is typical of continental philosophy insofar as his writings combine philosophy with material from other disciplines to carry out a critique of the present age. Continental philosophers as disparate as Hegel, Kierkegaard, Nietzsche, Sartre, and Foucault developed original theoretical perspectives on their respective sociohistorical situations with imposing intellectual inquiry that often synthesized philosophy with history, social theory, literature, or the sciences. Marx, of course, goes well beyond the confines of traditional university philosophy. His thought is identified with Marxism, a socialist and revolutionary movement that has been a philosophical and politico-historical force since the 1860s, and he has often been embraced or vilified because of the embeddedness of his ideas within history.

In this chapter, I will argue that while Marxism as a political movement and force has been vitiated with the collapse of "actually existing socialism" in the late 1980s,[1] as a theory Marxism still has much to offer. I will situate Marx's thought within the epoch of modernity that he so acutely theorizes and the dialectic of continental philosophy, interpreted as transdisciplinary interrogation of the contemporary epoch. In this reading, the thought of Karl Marx emerges from the ashes of communism as one of the enduring continental philosophies. It provides a grand philosophical synthesis of existing knowledge of history, society, economy, politics, and culture and sharp critical perspectives on modern societies. From this vantage point, far from being an outmoded nineteenth-century philosophy and failed utopian project, Marxism provides dialectical methods of inquiry that contain new ways of seeing and thinking about the world, original philosophical perspectives, and a radical critique of modern society and culture.

The Life and Times of a Revolutionary Hegelian

Karl Marx was born in Trier, Germany, on May 5, 1818, in a provincial region of the Rhineland that was strongly influenced by the culture of nearby France. Marx's ancestors were Jewish, though his father Heinrich converted to Christianity in order to preserve his job as a lawyer and government official. Karl's upbringing was thoroughly secular and both his father and his schooling immersed young Marx in Enlightenment humanism, while Ludwig von Westphalen, the father of Karl's child-hood sweetheart and later wife, Jenny, introduced Marx to the radical ideas of the French Revolution and to French utopian thinkers.[2]

Thus, young Marx was exposed to modern ideas in a primarily premodern milieu. It was not until his entry into the University at Berlin in 1836 that Marx systemati-cally studied Hegel and, in the heated atmosphere of the Young Hegelian movement, became involved in contemporary philosophical debates. Marx's Ph.D. dissertation, "The difference between the Democritean and Epicurean philosophy of nature," was written between 1839 and 1841, and accepted in Jena in 1841. In a thundering conclusion, which anticipated his emerging philosophical–political project, Marx wrote:

> As in the history of philosophy there are nodal points which raise philosophy in itself to concretion, apprehend abstract principles in a totality, and thus break off the rectilinear process, so also there are moments when philosophy turns its eyes to the external world, and no longer apprehends it, but as a practical person, weaves, as it were, intrigues with the world, emerges from the transparent kingdom of Amenthes and throws itself on the breast of the worldly siren . . . as Prometheus, having stolen fire from heaven, begins to build houses and to settle upon the earth, so philosophy, expanded to be the whole world, turns against the world of appearance. The same now with the philosophy of Hegel. (*MER*, pp. 10–11)

From Hegel, Marx appropriated a mode of critical and reflexive thought that re-worked motifs from Enlightenment rationalism, attacking obsolete forms of thought and society, while developing his own mode of thought and critique. In several early essays, Marx called for, in Enlightenment fashion, the "realization of reason" and a "ruthless criticism" of everything existing (*CW3*, p. 142). For the young Marx, "*realizing* the thoughts of the past" meant fulfilling the Enlightenment ideas of freedom, reason, equality, and democracy (*CW3*, p. 144). When he spoke of the "realization of philosophy" in an essay on Hegel, he envisaged the consummation of the Enlightenment project (*CW3*, p. 187), translating Enlightenment ideas into sociopolitical reality.

Hegel, of course, believed that reason was already realized in the Prussian state, but Marx's early essays assert that conditions in Germany were extremely backward, debased, anachronistic, and irrational (*CW3*, p. 176ff.). Using an analogy concern-ing the role of the bourgeoisie in the French Revolution and the situation of the pro-letariat in the contemporary era, Marx argued that the proletariat was a universal class that represented general suffering and the need for revolution (*CW3*, p. 186f.). For Hegel, the monarch and bureaucracy represented the universal interests of the polity, while for Marx these were false universals, refuted by the suffering of the proletariat, whose interests were not incorporated into the bourgeois state. The proletariat, by contrast, represented for Marx universal interests in emancipation and its mission was to overthrow capitalism – an event that Marx concluded was necessary to fulfill the promises of the Enlightenment.

Marx also took up Hegel's concept of historical stages and expanded on Hegel's notion that the present age was distinctive and original, marking a rupture with the past. In his Preface to *The Phenomenology of Spirit*, Hegel wrote:

> It is surely not difficult to see that our time is a time of birth and transition to a new period. The spirit has broken with what was hitherto the world of its existence and imagination and is about to submerge all this in the past; it is at work giving itself a new form. To be sure, the spirit is never at rest but always engaged in ever progressing motion . . . the spirit that educates itself matures slowly and quietly toward the new form, dissolving one particle of the edifice of its previous world after the other, . . . This gradual crumbling . . . is interrupted by the break of day that, like lightning, all at once reveals the edifice of the new world. (Hegel, 1965 [1807], p. 380)

After Hegel's death, his followers in the 1830s and 1840s took up the theme of the uniqueness of the present age and considered the possibilities of ascent to a higher stage of history. It would be Marx's life-work to provide an historical account of the origins and trajectory of the modern world. Hegel, by contrast, never really delineated the features of modernity, nor produced a detailed sociological analysis of the present age. Marx replicated Hegel's prodigious research in his effort to depict the birth and genesis of modern societies and their key stages of historical development, but he primarily investigated political and economic history, rather than cultural history, which was Hegel's focus.

For the Young Hegelians, the key to individual and social emancipation was liberation from religion; thus Marx and the progressive students of his generation saw modern thought and the modern age as quintessentially secular.[3] They were deeply influenced by the 1835 biblical criticism of David Strauss and the anthropological critique of religion developed by Ludwig Feuerbach (1957 [1841]). Strauss put in question the divinity of the Gospels by detailed textual analysis of the contradictions in the life of Jesus in the various Gospels. Marx's close friend Bruno Bauer challenged their authenticity, claiming that the biblical stories were sheer myth. Feuerbach disclosed the anthropological origins of religion in the need to project idealized features of human beings onto a godhead who was worshipped and submitted to. Feuerbach's trenchant critique reduced theology to philosophical anthropology and claimed that humans worshipped their alienated human powers in religious devotion, fetishizing human powers as divine.

The early Marx followed the Young Hegelians in producing a critique of religion and the state. The American and French Revolutions spurred new theories of radical democracy, which inspired Marx and his cohorts to criticize the old autocratic order that still dominated most of Europe. These "bourgeois" revolutions produced discourses that labeled "forms of inequality as illegitimate and anti-natural," and thus called attention to historically produced "forms of oppression." Relations of subordination such as serf/lord, or capital/labor, were presented as relations of domination, which Marx denounced while calling for their elimination.

Association with the Young Hegelian group of philosophical radicals in Berlin meant that Marx could not attain a teaching position in Germany, and so with philosophy Ph.D. in hand, he traveled to Cologne in 1842 and got a job with the

Rheinische Zeitung, soon after becoming its editor at the age of 24. Young Marx discovered the importance of economic conditions and the impact of capitalism in his work with the newspaper, writing articles on freedom of trade debates, bourgeois agitation for extended railways, reduction of taxes, and common toll and custom duties (*CW*1, p. 224ff.). He also discovered the plight of the poor, covering the trial of Mosel valley peasants accused of stealing wood from what used to be common land, but which was now declared to be private property. In addition, Marx championed Enlightenment ideas by attacking new Prussian censorship regulations and restrictions on divorce law, and published some of the most striking articles ever penned on behalf of freedom of the press (*CW*1, pp. 109ff., 132ff.).

Yet until his move to Paris in 1843, Marx lived in a relatively provincial and premodern Germany and was not really exposed first-hand to the emerging industrial–capitalist society, or to the working-class movement. In Paris, Marx began studying the French Revolution and then the classics of bourgeois political economy. He intended to support himself as co-editor of a *German–French Yearbook,* which was terminated after one issue; it was seized by police on the German border. Marx's article declaring "war on Germany" and supporting proletarian revolution (*CW*3, p. 175ff.) caused him to lose his German citizenship rights, making him an exile, first in France and later in Belgium and England, where he would spend most of the rest of his life until his death in 1883.

The *German–French Yearbook* included some important early essays of Marx and "Critique of political economy" by Friedrich Engels, who was to become Marx's collaborator and lifelong friend.[4] Engels was born in the northern German industrial city of Barman in 1820. His father was a factory owner and Engels went to work in the family firm at 17. After several years of clerical labor in Barmen and Bremen, Engels spent a year in military service in Berlin in 1841–2, where he became involved with the Young Hegelians. Engels was then sent to England in 1842 to learn the business of factory production in his father's factory, which was situated in the industrial heart of the most advanced capitalist society of the day. In addition to studying industrial production, Engels explored the new working-class life in England, compiling materials for a book that he published in 1845, *The Condition of the Working Class in England* (*CW*4, p. 295ff.).

Marx began seriously studying economics in Paris in 1843–4 and after an encounter with Engels in Paris in 1844, he intensified his economic studies. Convinced that the rise of capitalism was the key to modern society and history, Marx sketched out his analysis in the *Economic and Philosophical Manuscripts* of 1844. This text, unpublished in his lifetime, presented his initial perspectives on modern societies in terms of a sketch of the alienation of labor under capitalism and its projected emancipation (*CW*3, p. 231ff.).[5] Marx's *Paris Manuscripts* revealed that he had intensely studied classical political economy, French theories of revolution and socialism, and German philosophy, the three key components of what would emerge as the distinctive Marxian synthesis. Marx's early theoretical optic viewed modern society as a product of industrial capitalism; it criticized alienation, oppression, and exploitation from the standpoint of the ideals of the Enlightenment and German philosophy, and called for revolution to realize the positive potential of modernity while eliminating its negative features.

Marx acknowledged Engels's "Contributions to a critique of political economy" in the Preface to his *Manuscripts* (*CW*3, p. 232) and proceeded to develop his own analysis of the class structure of capitalist society, providing an early vision of modernity as a catastrophe for the working class (*CW*3, p. 231ff.). For Marx, capitalism transformed the worker into a commodity who was forced to sell his or her labor power. The worker's labor power thus belonged to the capitalist and its productive activity was forced, coercive, and unfree. Since the product of labor belonged to the capitalist, the worker could not be satisfied that its activity produced something for itself, and thus felt alienated from its product, its labor activity, other workers, and its own human needs and potentialities.

Marx's vision reconstructed Hegel's master/slave dialectic and conceptualized the alienation of labor in terms of, first, the alienation of the worker from the object of labor. In the capitalist mode of production, the objects and system of labor appear as something "alien," a power independent over worker, as no doubt the early industrial factory system appeared to workers. Second, the alienation of labor involved loss of control over the labor process (and over life activity) in a form of "wage slavery" in which the worker existed in a state of "bondage" to the capitalist master. Humans under capitalism were thus alienated for Marx from "productive activity," which appeared external, non-essential, coerced, and unfree. Labor in the capitalist system was thus not only unpleasant but constituted an alienation from one's very humanity, defined by Marx as free and productive activity. For alienated labor yielded no self-realization or satisfaction, constituting an alienation from species being, other people, and nature.

Whereas Marx, with Hegel and Feuerbach, envisages species life as universal, free, and creative activity that differentiates humans from animals, labor under capitalism for Marx is fragmentary, one-sided, and unnatural. The capitalist labor system enslaves individuals in factories, using up their time, the very medium of life. Marx's critique of capitalism thus presupposes a concept of human nature and non-alienated labor in which labor is conceptualized as essential life-activity, an enterprise through which one satisfies distinctly human needs and develops human potentials – or fails to develop them. Non-alienated labor for Marx is defined as free and conscious activity that develops human potentialities and thus enables individuals to realize their "species-being" or humanity.

Consequently, for Marx capitalist production is the basis of human alienation, and its dehumanization of human beings requires revolution to overcome it. Marx had not yet envisaged how capitalism was to be overcome, though it is significant that even in his early manuscripts he polemicizes against a "crude communism" – that is "leveling," destructive of individuality, and failing to cultivate the full range of human powers (*MER*, p. 82). Marx does, however, call for elimination of the system of private property, which is to be replaced by a "truly human and social property," in which "objects of use and enjoyment" (*MER*, p. 102) will be provided to individuals in order to enable them to engage in free and creative productive activity.

Marx's philosophical accomplishment was to concretize the conceptions of alienation and humanity developed by philosophers such as Hegel and Feuerbach, transforming philosophical concepts into social terms, thus taking universal concepts and reconfiguring them into historically specific ones. For Marx, alienation is neither a subjective nor an ontological concept, but a sociohistorical normative category that points to a deplorable state of affairs that should be overcome. Delivery from the alienation of labor for Marx is therefore a critical-revolutionary project involving the transcendence of capitalism.

In *The Wealth of Nations*, Adam Smith conceived of humans as bartering animals, in which self-love or egotism was seen as the primary human trait, and competitiveness the natural condition (Smith, 1937 [1776]). For Marx, by contrast, humans were primarily social, cooperative, many-sided, and protean, capable of novel historical development and creativity. Whereas Smith described labor as "Jehovah's curse" and an ontological burden, while valorizing rest, leisure, and tranquility, Marx saw productive activity and labor as the distinctive human trait. For Smith, the division of labor is the source of wealth of nations, whereas for Marx it is a catastrophe for the working class. For Marx, humans are many-sided beings, who require a wealth of activities and free-conscious self-determination to realize their basic human powers. Since, for Marx, individuals are social and cooperative, capitalism is in contradiction with human nature, and a new social system is required to emancipate humanity and create a society worthy of human beings.[6]

While for Adam Smith the capitalist market society provides the proper framework for human beings and capitalism is compatible with human nature, for Marx they stand in contradiction, requiring a new human and social system. Marx, however, does not have an essentialist theory of human nature in which human being is conceived as fixed, unchanging, and invariant. Rather, Marx is a historicist who sees humans developing throughout history, with distinctive needs and potentialities, but no fixed essence. For Marx, human nature is constantly changing and evolving, in tandem with development of the forces and relations of production.

Thus Marx undercuts the essentialism/historicism dichotomy that plagued previous philosophy, suggesting in effect to philosophers that they need to combine anthropology, history, the social sciences, and philosophy to properly theorize human beings, their alienation and oppression, and their potential emancipation. Marx never fully developed his philosophical perspectives, turning to political economy as his major intellectual focus, although I would argue that a theory of human nature, its alienation under capitalism, and potential emancipation underlies Marx's entire work. Marx's philosophical reflections were, from his *Paris Manuscripts* on, connected with developing a critical theory of contemporary society that situated philosophical issues in the context of the contemporary historical situation. In his 1844 manuscripts, for instance, Marx posed with trenchant insight the key questions that the alienation of labor under capitalism raised:

(1) What in the evolution of mankind is the meaning of this reduction of the greater part of mankind to abstract labor? (2) What are the mistakes committed by the piecemeal reformers, who either want to *raise* wages and in this way to improve the situation of the working class, or regard *equality* of wages (as Proudhon does) as the goal of social revolution? (*CW3*, p. 241)

Marx's answer to the first question was that although labor was a universal activity through which individuals satisfy their needs and distinguish themselves from animals, under capitalism labor takes the specific form of wage labor in which the individual "alienates" his or her self by selling one's labor power to the capitalist, thus producing for another and submitting to coercive and unfree activity. Consequently, the emergence of a modern industrial order was a catastrophe for the working class, which Marx perceived as a qualitatively unique situation in history. Marx concluded that increased wages are only "higher wages for slaves," suggesting that wage slavery itself must be abolished in order to allow the full development and realization of individual human beings (*CW3*, p. 295f.).

Marx assumed that humans were subjects who could potentially control and enjoy objects. In the emerging industrial system, however, objects controlled subjects and individuals were thus dominated by the objects of labor. Even the bourgeoisie failed to control the capitalist mode of production that spiraled into periodic recessions and depressions. The capitalist economy was out of control, and Marx and Engels envisaged a condition in which individuals controlled the system and objects of their labor instead of being controlled by them. Their concept of socialism thus presupposed a modern concept of sovereignty in which associated individuals would control the conditions of their life and labor.

Dialectics, Philosophy, and Science

Marx's emerging project combined philosophy, history and what we now call the social sciences. It is perhaps Marx's "Theses on Feuerbach," penned in Brussels as he was working on *The German Ideology* in 1845, that provide the most concise summary of his distinctive philosophical perspectives. The famous Thesis Eleven articulates the activist thrust of Marx's concept of philosophy: "Philosophers have only *interpreted* the world in various ways; the point, however, is to change it" (*CW5*, p. 8). Thesis One articulates Marx's particular blending of idealism and materialism in a dialectical overcoming of one-sided positions: "The chief defect of all previous materialism – that of Feuerbach included – is that things, reality, sensuousness, are conceived only in the form of the *object*, or of *contemplation*, but not as *human sensuous activity*, *practice*, not subjectivity. Hence it happened that the *active* side, in contradistinction to materialism, was set forth by idealism – but only abstractly, since, of course, idealism does not know real, sensuous activity as such" (*CW5*, p. 6).

Marx affirms Feuerbach's materialism with its emphasis on the body and the senses, but also Hegel's emphasis on the reality of thought and subjectivity, thus aligning himself with Hegelian dialectics without the idealism, as well as a critical Enlightenment tradition that stresses the senses, critical practice, and materialism. Marx's twist on the Enlightenment is that he radicalizes Hegel's emphasis on critique and negation and conceptualizes transformative activity as "revolutionary practice" (*CW5*, pp. 6–8).

Appropriating Hegel's concept of negation, Marx asserted that the dialectic of negativity "is the moving and generative principle" in Hegel (*CW3*, p. 332), whereby thought criticizes partial and one-sided views, overcomes contradictions through negation, and attacks institutions and forces that oppress and alienate human beings. Marx followed Enlightenment critique and Hegel's dialectics in systematically negating one-sided or oppressive existing realities, while attempting to overcome all contradictions and conflicts in higher syntheses. He also followed Hegel in seeing conflicts overcome through breaks and ruptures characterized by suddenness and novelty – a distinctly modern way of seeing. Hegelian–Marxian dialectics rejects continuity theories of history, stressing discontinuities. Marx in particular also focused on the breaks in history, which produced upheavals that generated turbulence, violence, and suffering in distinctly modern forms.

"Critique" for Marx thus delineated one-sided, contradictory, and oppressive forms of thought and social conditions that were to be negated and overcome. Marx privileged the concept of critique, making it a central aspect of his theory and subtitling several of his major books "*A Critique of*. . ."[7] Ridding Hegel's dialectics of idealism and an uncritical positivity toward existing society, Marx transformed dialectics into a mode of materialist investigation and social critique. Dialectics for Marx was connective, showing the relationship between different sectors of society and phenomena usually seen apart (i.e., like culture and social conditions). His dialectic was also negative and revolutionary, analyzing contradictions as well as connections, and delineating conditions in need of transformation. The Marxian theory was historical and materialist as well. "Contradictions," for example, referred to real historical conditions of tension and inequality, which required resolution through social struggle (as opposed to mere oppositions in which opposites – such as up and down, or either/or – are mere linguistic constructs that are equal and symmetrical, without tension or explosive force). And, as I show in a later section, the Marxian vision also condemned existing modern societies from the perspective of a form of socialist society with more freedom, justice, and social wealth.

Marx's philosophical–dialectical perspectives, however, moved beyond Hegel in turning toward empirical science as the proper method of inquiry and source of knowledge. To be sure, "science" for Marx is always *Wissenschaft*, in the German sense, which implies a historical, normative, and broad comprehensive mode of theorizing, tempered by rigorous empirical research, the testing of ideas in practice, the modification of concepts and hypotheses based on research, and a constant refinement, development, and systemization of results. Hence, following his early work in philosophy, Marx championed science over philosophy, calling for investigation of real individuals "in their empirically perceptible process of development under definite conditions" (*CW*5, p. 37). Further: "Where speculation ends, where real life starts, there consequently begins real, positive science, the expounding of the practical activity, of the practical process of development of men" (*CW*6, p. 37). Philosophy thus loses its self-sufficient medium of existence: it is absorbed into real history and disappears as an autonomous discipline, thus producing a sublation, or *Aufhebung*, of philosophy into science. This move provides a model of an interdisciplinary space and method which investigates the interconnection of the economy, state, social institutions, and culture in the constitution of capitalist societies; it criticizes the institutions of modern societies from the normative perspectives of ideals of a better society and more human life under an alternative form of social organization.

From a methodological standpoint, Marx began a reconstruction of philosophy and science, and developed a critical social theory fusing a new epistemology (i.e., radical historicism and praxis) with broad historical perspectives and detailed empirical research. By decisively breaking with Smith and bourgeois political economy, Marxian theory broke with previous conceptions of social science and inaugurated a new form of critical social science that privileged practice as the criterion of truth and rejected all ideas that could not be confirmed in practice, that could not be experimentally validated.

Marx's turn toward science was influenced by Feuerbach, who defended perception and empirical knowledge against Hegelian idealism. In his *Economic and Philosophical Manuscripts*, Marx insisted that his results were attained by "wholly empirical analysis," and that his critique of capitalism proceeded "from an *actual* economic fact" – the alienation of the worker under capitalism (*CW3*, pp. 231, 271). Yet Marx never really distinguished between science and dialectics, arguing that: "Empirical observations must in each separate instance bring out empirically, and without any mystification and speculations, the connection of the social and political structure with production" (*CW5*, p. 35). This passage brings out the combination of empiricism and dialectics in the Marxian conception: following the model of empirical science, the investigator is supposed to describe the facts of experience without speculation or distortion, and to connect social and political phenomena with the structure of the economy. In turn ideas are to be tested in practice, as "Man must prove the truth, i.e., the reality and power, the this-worldliness of his thinking in practice" (*CW5*, p. 6).

But the facts that Marx described are always historical, always subject to change and development, and the Marxian optic focused on the structures and movement of history as well as modern societies. Marx developed his theory of history and critical theory of society through concrete empirical and historical study, although his framework for the presentation of his analyses was arguably Hegelian and dialectical. As he later put it in *Capital*, Hegelian dialectics "is in its essence critical and revolutionary" (*MER*, p. 302), showing societies as riven with contradictions and crises, which lead to their breaking-up and collapse and thus movement to a higher stage of society. Developing this view of history would occupy Marx for much of his life.

Historical Materialism and Modern Societies

The early Marx represents a synthesis of Hegel and Enlightenment critical rationalism, as influenced by the radical democratic wing of the French Revolution. While working on his economic studies, Marx was expelled from Paris in 1845 for publishing in a radical *émigré* newspaper, and he moved to Brussels where he began his collaboration with Engels. Together they traveled to England to observe the new factories and industrial living and working conditions. Upon their return, they began to develop their sketch of the genesis of the modern world and what became known as "historical materialism" in *The German Ideology* (*CW5*), written in 1845–6 and never published in their lifetimes. The text is important, for it articulates some of their first formulations of the differentiated structure of modern societies, and also sketches out their historical materialist perspectives on human beings and society. Marx and Engels (*CW4*) also published a joint attack, *The Holy Family* (1845), on Bruno Bauer and their former Young Hegelian associates, who they now considered pseudo-radical and idealist. Marx published in addition (*CW6*, p. 105ff.) a critique of the economics of Proudhon in *The Poverty of Philosophy* (1846), declaring the French writer to be trapped in the idealist verbiage of Hegel, thus mystifying the concrete economic phenomena that Marx and Engels were attempting to analyze.

In investigating the origins and genesis of modern societies, Marx and Engels developed a new materialist theory of history and society, introducing the concepts of the mode of production, forces and relations of production, division of labor, ideology, and class struggle as keys to understanding society and history. They also produced a conception of history as a succession of modes of production, leading to the emergence of modern bourgeois society and its future transition to a communist society. For Marx and Engels, the highly differentiated mode of production associated with modern bourgeois society makes its appearance "with the *increase of population*" and presupposes the "*intercourse* (*Verkehr*) of individuals with one another" (*CW5*, p. 32).[8] Every society on the Marxian theory is constituted by:

> definite social relations [which] are just as much produced by men as linen, flax, etc. Social relations are closely bound up with productive forces. In acquiring new productive forces men change their mode of production; and in changing their mode of production, in changing the way of earning their living, they change all their social relations. The hand-mill gives you society with the feudal lord; the steam-mill with the industrial capitalist. (*CW6*, pp. 165–6)

Although this passage is often taken as an example of an alleged technological determinism in Marx, one can also read it as stressing the importance of social relations and differentiation in the constitution of modern societies. Social differentiation is in turn connected to the division of labor that begins in the family, leading to a division between mental and material labor, and serving as the motor for further social differentiation (*CW5*, p. 46f.). Differentiation, however, takes the form of relations of subordination and domination, and Marx developed one of the first critical theories of modern bourgeois society, attacking oppression and exploitation.

Although Marxian theory is often accused of limiting domination and oppression to class and neglecting such forms of oppression as gender and race (Balbus, 1982), Marx and Engels argue that inequalities begin "in the family, where wife and children are the slaves of the husband" (*CW5*, p. 46). They also refer to the "latent slavery in the family" and constantly criticize "patriarchal" forces, thus providing the conceptual space for a critique of the oppression of women. Indeed, Marx and Engels frequently describe the production *and reproduction* of social life as the basis of society and history (*CW5*, pp. 42, 43, 46, *passim*), and thus attribute conceptual importance to the family and social reproduction. Of course, their main focus would be almost exclusively on production and the oppression of the working class, although Engels would eventually write a book on the family (1972 [1884]).

Marx's dialectical theory also articulated the relationships between the economy, polity, society, and culture in modern social formations. His critical theory of society thus unfolds in an interdisciplinary space connecting economy, social structure, state, and culture. "Political economy" for Marx referred to a structure that combined politics and economics, describing a mode of social organization that Marx delineated as the "base" (*Unterbau*) for the set of modern legal, political, social, and cultural institutions and practices that he designated "superstructures" (*Uberbau*).

For Marx, modern societies were highly differentiated ones, divided between state and civil society, classes, and an increasingly complex economy. Following Hegel, Marx distinguished between state and "civil society" (better: "bourgeois society"), whereby "bourgeois society" referred to the sphere of private life in the family and economic domain, while the "state" described the sphere of public life.[9] As a member of the state, one was a *citoyen* with universal rights in a realm of freedom and equality, whereas in the sphere of bourgeois society one was a mere private individual in a fragmented and competitive domain of self-interest and competition.

Whereas Hegel posited the Prussian state as the realization of reason, which harmonized the contradictions of the socioeconomic order, Marx developed a more critical optic on the organization of the modern world. In his view, the fragmentation and divisions that Hegel described were not overcome in the modern state. Rather, society was bifurcated into two distinct spheres in which the individual "leads a double life, a heavenly and an earthly life, not only in thought, in consciousness, but in *reality*, in *life*: life in the *political community* where one regards oneself as a *communal being*, and life in *civil society* where one is active as a *private individual*, treats other human beings as means, is oneself reduced to a means, and becomes the plaything of alien powers" (*CW3*, p. 154). For Marx, the socially differentiated bourgeois society was a conflicted one, characterized by a "sphere of egoism and of the *bellum omnium contra omnes*. It is no longer the essence of *community*, but the essence of *differentiation*. It has become the expression of man's *separation* from his *community*, from himself and from other men" (*CW3*, p. 155).

Marx was thus one of the first to describe the social contradictions engendered by the differentiation of the new bourgeois society and to anchor the state in its structure. He adopted the category of differentiation from Hegel, for whom it was mainly a concept of logic, of thought, while for Marx it was a category of social analysis. For Hegel, "differentiation" (*Differenzierung*) signified a process of the creation, division, and externalization of categories, first in the realm of thought (Hegel's logic) and then into the fields of nature and spirit. In analyzing the realm of spirit (*Geist*), Hegel describes differentiations in the social and political sphere, arguing that these differentiations are absorbed, harmonized, and thus overcome (*aufgehoben*) in his philosophy. For Marx, by contrast, the differentiations under analysis referred to the concrete social–historical development of a structurally articulated bourgeois society, state, and forms of culture and everyday life, which he described in the language of social theory, rather than philosophy, consequently inaugurating the classical social discourse of modernity.

In the new fragmented bourgeois civil society, individuals were split into egoistic atoms, opposed to each other and driven by class-based self-interest and greed. The "rights of man" established by the bourgeois revolutions guaranteed that each individual maintains a certain sovereignty and set of rights *vis-à-vis* the state and society. Individuals were thus split between their life in the state, where they were free and equal, and everyday life in society, where inequality and unfreedom reigned. While from the standpoint of the state, the individual was a *citoyen*, possessing universal rights and equality with all other citizens, within civil society the individual was a mere *bourgeois*, characterized by particular interests, posed in a competitive struggle for existence with others.

Marx always recognized that the individual was an important product of bourgeois society that socialism would preserve and develop.[10] Yet he also saw that bourgeois society produced an atomized, fragmented form of individualism, limited and ruled by the demons of private interest. In addition, he believed that modern civil society also destroyed the communal ties of feudalism, and that community needed to be reconstituted in the modern world. Therefore, "political emancipation" was but a partial and abstract individual emancipation from the limitations of feudalism, which Marx ironically described as the "democracy of unfreedom" (*CW*3 [1843], p. 32). By contrast, Marx called for "human emancipation," which involved transcending the egoism, private property, and religion of civil society and thus, ultimately, the liberation of society from capitalism (*CW*3, p. 170f.).

Marx's vision of history from the 1840s was presented in the "Communist Manifesto," which sketches in dramatic narrative form his and Engels's view of the origins and trajectory of modernity (*CW*6, p. 477ff.) and concretizes the stress on "revolutionary practice" in his previous works with conceptions of class struggle. The "Manifesto" appeared in early 1848, anticipating the sequence of revolutions that broke out throughout Europe shortly after its publication. It provides one of the first critical visions of capitalist globalization and a gripping narrative of the origins and unfolding of capitalism.

For Marx and Engels, the rise of a global system characterized by a world market and the imposition of similar relations of production, commodities, and ideas on areas throughout the world was crucial in creating modern capitalist societies: "Modern industry has established the world market, for which the discovery of America paved the way" (*CW*6, p. 486). In turn, the "need of a constantly expanding market for its products chases the bourgeoisie over the whole surface of the globe. It must nestle everywhere, settle everywhere, establish connections everywhere" (*CW*6, p. 487). As Marx once wrote in a letter, the railway, steamer, and telegraph "finally represented means of communication adequate to modern means of production" (cited in Hobsbawm, 1979, p. 32), thereby making possible a world market: "The bourgeoisie, by the rapid improvement of all instruments of production, by the immensely facilitated means of communication, draws all, even the most barbarian nations into civilization . . . In a word, it creates a world after its own image" (*CW*6, p. 488).

In the Marxian vision, the bourgeoisie constantly revolutionized the instruments of production and the world market generated immense forces of commerce, navigation and discovery, communications, and industry, creating a potentially new world of abundance, diversity, and prosperity. Marx and Engels also indicated how as "the intellectual creations of individual nations become common property," nationalist "one-sidedness and narrow-mindedness become more and more impossible" (*CW*6,

p. 488). Pointing to the resources and positive creations of the world market that provide the basis for a higher stage of social organization, Marx and Engels indicated that the world market also produced a new class of "*world-historical*, empirically universal individuals in place of local ones" (*CW*5, p. 49). This class of individuals – the industrial working class, the proletariat – was reduced to abstract labor power, rendered property-less, and stood in opposition to the "existing world of wealth and culture" (*CW*5, pp. 48–9). Having nothing but its chains to lose and a world to win, Marx and Engels believed that the industrial proletariat would organize as a revolutionary class to overthrow capitalism and produce a new socialist society that would abolish poverty, inequality, exploitation, and alienated labor, making possible the full development of individuals and social wealth (*CW*5, p. 48f.; *CW*6, p. 490f.).

The Marxian theory was thus one of the first to posit a complex market system that would encircle the world. Marx and Engels envisaged the possibility of world global crisis and revolution, which would envelop the Earth in a titanic struggle between capital and its opponents. Their working-class revolutionaries would be resolutely internationalist and cosmopolitan, seeing themselves as citizens of the world rather than members of specific nations. The Marxian theory thus shared the illusions of many market liberals that the development of a world system of free trade would generate prosperity and cosmopolitanism, with both downplaying the importance of nation–states, nationalism, national rivalries, and wars which had characterized previous centuries and would continue to be important forces through the present.

Capital and Counterrevolution

In the exciting revolutionary year of 1848, Marx and Engels traveled, first, from Brussels to Paris and then to Germany, where the turbulent situation had gained Marx an amnesty. Marx returned to Cologne, where he gathered support for a newspaper, the *Neue Rheinische Zeitung*, which he published for the next two years. Marx and Engels sided with the bourgeois democrats who were fighting the old feudal powers for a modern parliamentary system. They envisaged a two-stage theory of revolution in which the workers would initially ally themselves with the bourgeoisie and then fight for a socialist republic. The counterrevolution prevailed, however; Marx's newspaper was shut down, and he was once again forced into exile.

Following his participation in the German and European revolutions of 1848–9, Marx emigrated to England and Engels joined him. It was the fate of Engels to work for the next 25 years in his father's manufacturing firm in Manchester, while Marx studied and wrote in London. During the 1850s, Marx and Engels were embroiled intermittently in the quarrels of the radical exile community, and both wrote regularly for the *New York Tribune* and other newspapers, keeping abreast of international political affairs. But Marx was primarily devoted to his economic studies, in which he analyzed in minute detail the economic structure of capitalism, refining his arguments concerning capitalism as the foundation of modern societies. During the 1850s and 1860s, Marx spent much time poring over economic texts and documents. Convinced that the capitalist economy was the key to the structure and processes of modern societies, and that only a major crisis of capitalist society could lead to a higher form of socialist society, Marx diligently studied all the salient economic documents and literature of the day, carrying out a systematic critique of previous economic theory, while producing his own.

Marx carried out his economic studies during the period that Hobsbawm (1979) described as "the Age of Capital." From his London vantage point, Marx was in an excellent position to chart out the unprecedented economic expansion that took place from the 1850s until his death in 1883. This was the era of the proliferation of new modes of mechanization, in which machine production produced immense quantities of goods, and expanded trade generated a dynamic world market. In addition, science and technology grew rapidly, constantly revolutionizing production. It was an era of great wealth but also tremendous divisions between rich and poor, which generated intense class conflicts that Marx and Engels chronicled.

Marx charted these developments daily at the British Museum library, where he kept abreast of the economic and political vicissitudes of the epoch: he sketched out his system of economics in an unpublished *Grundrisse*, or "Fundamental Outline" (1857–8; *CW28*) and published an introduction to his economic theory in 1859 (*CW29*). After years of poverty and relative obscurity, Marx eventually achieved a certain renown and notoriety. He was elected President of the Working Men's International Association and gave its inaugural address in 1864. And after working on his economic studies for over 20 years, Marx finally published the first volume of his *magnum opus*, *Capital*, which provides a critical analysis of the structure of modern societies, in 1867 (*CW35*). *Capital* was translated into many languages and was eventually recognized as a classic text of modern economic theory.

Marx's *magnum opus* brought together decades of prodigious research into the origins, genesis, and structures of capitalism. Modern capitalist society for Marx is a commodity-producing society that is characterized by large-scale industry, an ever-proliferating division of labor, and contradictions rooted in capitalist relations of production – in particular, the relation between capital and labor, the bourgeoisie and workers. Beginning with an analysis of the commodity, Marx sought the secret of capitalist "surplus value" and profit in the unpaid labor time extracted from workers. This theory of exploitation was combined with minute analysis of the power of the capitalist industrial system over the worker. In some of the more powerful passages in *Capital*, Marx notes how the division of labor "seizes upon, not only the economic, but every other sphere of society, and everywhere lays the foundation of that all engrossing system of specialising and sorting men, that development in a human being of one single faculty at the expense of all other faculties, which caused A. Ferguson, the master of Adam Smith, to exclaim: 'We make a nation of Helots, and have no free citizens'" (*MER*, p. 394).[11]

By *Capital*, Marx has thus come to conceptualize the present age as a system of domination whereby the commodity form comes to dominate society in its totality, in which the worker is reduced to commodity status and production is geared toward commodity production in order to produce profit and surplus value. Thus, modern societies are those ruled by capital, by abstract social forces that impose a system of domination on contemporary individuals. For Marx, capitalism is fundamentally a commodity-producing society and modernity is an era in history organized around the production of commodities. Whereas in premodern societies, fetishes were made out of trees or other animate or inanimate objects, under capitalism commodity fetishism metamorphizes value into exchange value, whereby use value, or the development of human beings, is minimized, and value resides primarily in the possession and use of commodities, and the ascendancy of abstract exchange value in the form of money.

Within the history of civilization, capitalism thus constitutes a unique mode of social organization, structured by the production, exchange, distribution, and consumption of commodities. Modernity for Marx thus is bound up with the triumph of capitalism: his book *Capital* is a testament to the power of capitalism, and a sign of the extent to which the working class is held in thrall by the power of the industrial system and the hegemony of the capitalist class over labor. Itself a sign of the times, *Capital* was researched and published during an era of unprecedented economic expansion and before the working class had organized and provided a counterforce to the "juggernaut" of capital. Marx's treatise was thus an expression of the victory of capital in an era of counterrevolution when capital reigned triumphant and did not yet face a powerful countervailing oppositional force. Marx himself, of course, was involved with a nascent movement that would contest capitalism and would militate for an alternative economic system and mode of social organization.

Socialism and Revolution

For Marx, modern capitalist societies constitute a form of social organization in which individuals lack conscious control and mastery of their social relations and in which individuals are alienated from and subordinated to an oppressive social system. A communist society, by contrast, would overturn "the basis of all earlier relations of production and intercourse, and for the first time consciously treat all natural premises as the creations of hitherto existing men, strip them of their natural character and subjugate them to the power of the united individuals" (*CW*5, p. 81). Thus, against the individual monadic subject of modern theory from Descartes through the Enlightenment and Kant to positivism, Marx envisages a collective organization of society that will consciously control production and social life.

Marx accordingly analyzed the new forms of social cooperation and association, the new interdependencies, which bound individuals together in the emergent bourgeois social order and which produced the potentialities for better, more free, and egalitarian forms of social association. For Marx:

> the real intellectual wealth of the individual depends entirely on the wealth of his real connections. Only this will liberate the separate individuals from the various national and local barriers, bring them into practical connection with the production (including intellectual production) of the whole world and make it possible for them to acquire the capacity to enjoy this all-sided production of the whole earth (the creations of man). *All-round* dependence, this primary nature form of the *world-historical* cooperation of individuals, will be transformed by this communist revolution into the

control and conscious mastery of these powers, which, born of the action of men on one another, have till now overawed and ruled men as powers completely alien to them. (*CW*5, pp. 51–2)

The division of labor, system of property, and competitive market system of the modern economy thus separate individuals from each other and from control over their labor activity, producing alienation and oppression. Yet the modern economy also brings individuals together, producing an expanding "wealth of real connections," novel forms of cooperation, and innovative forms of association that will make possible control of economic and social conditions, and a higher stage of history in which associated individuals can master their economy and society. Voluntarily associated individuals under socialism will, Marx claims, come to control their social production and apply their social power and productive forces to satisfy their needs and develop their potentialities. Thus, the genesis of modern society produces not only alienation and oppression for the working class, but the preconditions of its emancipation. This is a major theme of *The German Ideology*, and Marx and Engels's analysis culminates in a vision of world revolution, in which capitalism will be replaced by communism. They characterize communism as "the real movement of history and revolution as "the driving force of history," producing an especially revolutionist view of history (*CW*5, pp. 54, 83).

Thus, in addition to conceptualizing new forms of class conflict and differentiation, Marx was also among the first to see that capitalism was engendering new modes of cooperation and solidarity at the same time as it was dividing society into classes. In the 1853 article "On Imperialism in India," Marx argued that: "The bourgeois period of history has to create the material basis of the new world – on the one hand the universal intercourse founded upon mutual dependency of humanity, and the means of that intercourse; on the other hand the development of the productive powers of humans and the transformation of material production into a scientific domination of natural agencies" (*MER*, pp. 663–4). Marx thus characterized "universal intercourse" and "mutual dependency," or interdependence, as defining features of modern societies, which produced new modes of association as well as differentiation and conflict.

In the *Grundrisse*, Marx described the immense emergent sources of social power (over nature) contained in accumulated "scientific labour" and "technological application of natural science" combined with "the general productive force arising from social combination" (*MER*, p. 282). Marx's special contribution was that he identified complex cooperation as the secret "social force" propelling capitalist development and the rise of modernity. In his famous chapters in *Capital* – "Cooperation," "The division of labor and manufacture," and "Machinery and modern industry" – Marx analyzes the powers of the capitalist mode of production as deriving from modes of cooperation and the new forms of association in the factory, which produce new social powers and the basis for a yet higher form of social organization. In the chapter on cooperation, Marx writes that "the starting point of capitalist production" is the bringing together of a "greater number of labourers working together, at the same time, in one place . . . in order to produce the same sort of commodity under the mastership of one capitalist" (*MER*, p. 384). The early forms

of capitalist cooperation involved "the conversion of numerous isolated and independent processes into one combined social process" (ibid.).

In the chapter on cooperation, however, Marx puts his emphasis on capitalist
command, its "directing authority," as "counterpressure" to working-class resistance,
and on the development of an "industrial army of workmen" under the control of
supervisors and managers. In Marx's vision of political emancipation, he envisaged
the workers themselves appropriating the social powers of cooperation for their own
purposes, eliminating the capitalist owner and retinue of supervisors and managers
and taking over the process of production themselves to develop their own potentials and to produce for their own needs.

In stressing the social powers of cooperation and the division of labor, Marx thus
describes at once the new potentialities generated by capitalism, the capitalist appropriation of these powers to exploit and dominate workers, and a vision in which the
workers themselves utilize the new powers of association and cooperation for their
own purposes. Hence, while Marx analyzed the productive and social power of the
new modes of cooperation and association produced by capitalism, he also pointed
to the alienating and despotic side of capitalist specialization in the same pages that
he praised its powers. For Marx, both the negative and positive features of modern
capitalist societies were driving modernity toward an inevitable break or rupture
with capitalism. On one hand, Marx believed that the inherent crisis tendencies
of capitalism were leading to upheaval, intensified crisis, and eventual collapse. On
the other hand, he believed that positive features of modernity, such as increased
cooperation among workers in the process of production, big firms that brought
associated producers together in the workplace (where they could be organized
and increase their social power), and, especially, the tendencies toward automation which would eliminate socially necessary labor, would increase the realm of
freedom, and thus provide the basis for a freer, more egalitarian, and more democratic social order. From the Marxian perspective, capitalism and socialism are thus
two forms of modernity, two developmental models within modernity. Socialism,
in Marx's view, represented a higher stage of modernity, the preconditions for its
fulfillment.

The Marxian theory of socialism is integrally connected with Enlightenment
modernity in its advocacy of democracy as the highest form of political organization.
In an early commentary on Hegel, Marx championed democracy as the highest form
of state: "democracy stands to the other constitutions as the genus stands to its
species; except that here the genus itself appears as an existent, and therefore as one
particular species over against the others whose existence does not correspond to
their essence. To democracy all other forms of state stand as its Old Testament. Man
does not exist for the law but the law for man – it is a *human manifestation*; whereas
in the other forms of state man is a *legal manifestation*. That is the fundamental distinction of democracy" (*MER*, p. 20). Moreover, Marx championed a form of radical democracy. For Marx, unlike Hegel, sovereignty lies with the people and not the
state or monarch. The constitution under democracy "is a free product of man" and
represents "the self-determination of the people" (ibid.). Popular sovereignty thus
involves the self-government of the people in all realms of social life.

Marx, "the Battle for Democracy," and the Realm of Freedom

In the "Communist Manifesto," Marx and Engels champion the modern form of state, urging the workers "to win the battle of democracy" and to fight for establishment of a democratic republic. It is in his speech on the Paris Commune, however, that Marx most fully developed his views on democracy. The Paris Commune lasted for two months after the Franco-Prussian war in 1871, before the combined German and French forces crushed it and killed thousands of its supporters. Marx wrote that "the Commune was the positive form" of the workers' "social Republic" and represented "the self-government of the producers," serving "as a model to all the great industrial centers of France" (*MER*, pp. 632–3). The Commune was constituted by popular assemblies and its representatives were workers who were "revocable at short terms" and who received the same wages as other workers. The Commune would create a people's militia and police force and an elected judiciary:

> In a rough sketch of national organization which the Commune had no time to develop, it states clearly that the Commune was to be the political form of even the smallest country hamlet, and that in the rural districts the standing army was to be replaced by a national militia, with an extremely short term of service. The rural communes of every district were to administer their common affairs by an assembly of delegates in the central town, and these district assemblies were again to send deputies to the National Delegation in Paris, each delegate to be at any time revocable and bound by the *mandat imperatif* (formal instructions) of his constituents. The few but important functions which still would remain for a central government were not to be suppressed, as has been intentionally mis-stated, but were to be discharged by Communal, and therefore strictly responsible agents. The unity of the nation was not to be broken, but, on the contrary, to be organized by the Communal Constitution and to become a reality by the destruction of the State power which claimed to be the embodiment of that unity independent of, and superior to, the nation itself, from which it was but a parasitic excrescence. (*MER*, p. 633)

Marx therefore advocated a radical form of popular sovereignty and democracy in which the people would govern themselves. In place of representative democracy, a form of popular sovereignty would represent the self-government of the people: "instead of deciding once in three or six years which member of the ruling class was to misrepresent the people in Parliament, universal suffrage was to serve the people" (*MER*, p. 633). A people's militia and police force would guarantee that no permanent state apparatus would stand above and over society. The Commune constituted "the political form at last discovered under which to work out the economic emancipation of labor" (*MER*, p. 635).

In his most advanced vision of an emancipated society, Marx envisaged a realm of freedom made possible by the developments of modern technology and industry. In the *Grundrisse*, he sketched a theory of a possible rupture between capitalist and post-capitalist societies that would be as radical as those between pre-capitalist and capitalist ones. On his account, capital generates factories, machine production, and eventually an automatic system of machinery (*MER*, p. 278ff.). In his famous analysis of automation, Marx sketches out an audacious vision of the development of a fully automated system of production under capitalism which brings capitalism to an end and which produces the basis for an entirely different social system. In Marx's vision, the "accumulation of knowledge and of skill, of the general productive forces of the social brain," are absorbed into capital and produce machinery which "develops with the accumulation of society's science, of the productive force generally" (*MER*, p. 280). As machinery and automation evolve, the worker becomes more and more superfluous, standing ever-more powerless alongside the growing power of machines and big industry. On the other hand, machines free the worker from arduous and back-breaking labor. In this situation: "Labour no longer appears so much to be included within the production process; rather, the human being comes to relate more as watchman and regulator to the production process itself . . . He steps to the side of the production process instead of being its chief actor" (*MER*, p. 284).

The capitalist system thus makes possible "*a large quantity of disposable time*" which furnishes the space for the development of the individual's full productive forces" (*MER*, p. 286). Free time allows for more education and development of the social individual who can then enter "in the direct production process as this different subject. This process is then both discipline, as regards the human being in the process of becoming; and, at the same time, practice [*Ausubung*], experimental science, materially creative and objectifying science, as regards the human being who has become, in whose head exists the accumulated knowledge of society" (*MER*, p. 290). Thus capitalism produces the basis for a new society of non-alienated labor in which individuals will possess the free time to fully develop their human capacities and labor itself will be a process of experimentation, creativity, and progress, in which the system of automation produces most of society's goods and individuals can thus enjoy leisure and the fruits of creative work.

Such a society would be a completely different social order from that of capitalist society, which is organized around work and the production of commodities. Marx acknowledges that the new society would have a totally "*changed* foundation of production, a new foundation first created by the process of history" (*MER*, p. 293). In the third volume of *Capital*, Marx described this radically new social order in terms of a "realm of freedom," writing: "Freedom in this field can only consist in socialized man, the associated producers, rationally regulating their interchange with Nature, bringing it under their common control, instead of being ruled by it as by the blind forces of Nature; and achieving this with the least expenditure of energy and under conditions most favourable to, and worthy of, their human nature" (*MER*, p. 441).

Marx's most distinctive vision of socialism thus envisages a system that would mark a break in history as dramatic as the rupture between pre-capitalist and capitalist societies that produced modernity. While capitalism is a commodity-producing society organized around work and production, socialism would be a social order organized around the full development of individual human beings. Marx formulated this radical vision of a new society in his late text *Critique of the Gotha Program*, as the product of a transition to a higher phase of communism. In the first phase, the "prolonged birth pangs from capitalist society" would limit the level of social and individual development, but:

> In a higher phase of communist society, after the enslaving subordination of the individual to the division of labour, and therewith also the antithesis between mental and physical labour, has vanished; after labour has become not only a means of life but life's prime want; after the productive forces have also increased with the all-round development of the individual, and all the springs of cooperative wealth flow more abundantly – only then can the narrow horizon of bourgeois right be crossed in its entirety and society inscribe on its banner: From each according to his ability, to each according to his needs! (*MER*, p. 531)

Crucially, Marx saw the potentials for socialism rooted in the very historical trajectory of modernity. Eschewing moralistic and utopian concepts, Marx theorized that just as historical forces had produced capitalist modernity, so too would history provide the possibilities of constructing a socialist society. Yet such a transition would involve political choice and struggle, and so much of Marx's attention was devoted to analyzing the class forces and material conditions that could produce socialism. Consequently, from the mid-1860s into his final years, Marx devoted much energy to nurturing a socialist political movement. He sought political strategies that could produce a socialist revolution and a new stage of history that as radically broke with the previous stage as capitalist modernity broke with previous precapitalist social formations.

Crisis, Revolutionary Historicism, and the Transition to Socialism

Of course, the big question was how a socialist revolution could occur. At times, Marx envisaged that only a radical crisis and collapse of the capitalist system would generate the possibility of a transition to socialism. In the *Grundrisse*, for instance, Marx posited the rupture in terms of a cataclysmic collapse of capitalism, leading to a violent upheaval:

> the highest development of productive power together with the greatest expansion of existing wealth will coincide with the depreciation of capital, degradation of the laborer, and a most straitened exhaustion of his vital powers. These contradictions lead to explosions, cataclysms, crises, in which by momentaneous suspension of labour and annihilation of a great portion of Capital the latter is violently reduced to the point where it can[not] go on. These contradictions, of course, lead to explosions, crises, in which momentary suspension of all labour and annihilation of a great part of the capital violently lead it back to the point where it is enabled [to go on] fully employing its productive powers without committing suicide. Yet, these regularly recurring catastrophes lead to their repetition on a higher scale, and finally to its violent overthrow. (*MER*, pp. 291–2)

Yet in an 1872 Address to a Congress of the First International, Marx suggested that a democratic road to socialism "where the workers can attain their goal by peaceful means" was also viable, in countries such as America, England, and Holland (*MER*, p. 523). To some extent, Marx's politics were always *ad hoc* and oriented toward existing political struggles and movements and, contrary to many attacks on him, were never fixed and dogmatic. In an 1843 contribution to *The German–French Year-book*, which established the political principles for that venture, Marx wrote: "We shall confront the world not as doctrinaires with a new principle: 'Here is the truth, bow down before it!' We develop new principles to the world out of its own principles. We do not say to the world: 'Stop fighting; your struggle is of no account. We want to shout the true slogan of the struggle at you.' We only show the world what it is fighting for, and consciousness is something that the world *must* acquire, like it or not" (*MER*, pp. 14–15).

To a large extent, Marx followed this principle throughout his life. His sketch of socialism in *The German Ideology* – where one would "hunt in the morning, fish in the afternoon, rear cattle in the evening, criticize after dinner, just as I have a mind, without ever becoming hunter, fisherman, shepherd or critic" (*CW5*, p. 47) – reflects the ideals of the utopian socialism which predated the concept of communism to which Marx would eventually adhere. Indeed, the principles and ideals of the "Communist Manifesto" summed up the program of the emerging communist movement and in the 1848 revolution, Marx joined the struggles of liberals and workers for a democratic republic, projecting communism as an ideal for the future. During the 1860s, Marx articulated the principles of the First International Working Men's Association, again putting his socialist ideals aside, while, as just noted, in his writing on the Paris Commune, he championed the Commune form of government.

Thus, Marx tried to connect his political theory with the most advanced political forces of the day and articulated his principles in accord with the most radical struggles and movements. This form of "revolutionary historicism" derives political ideals from existing forces and struggles, rather than projecting an *a priori* blueprint that is then imposed on diverse movements and contexts. Indeed, Marx saw that in distinct political circumstances different forms of struggle and different alternatives were necessary, and thus never advocated one single strategy of revolution or concept of socialism, instead developing his concepts in concordance with existing struggles and potentials.

On the whole, Marxian political theory was oriented toward actually existing struggles as the bearers of hopes for revolution, and on the whole he adopted a multiclass model and analysis of class blocs, rather than the "melting vision" that pitted the proletariat against the bourgeoisie as in the "Communist Manifesto." Despite different emphases in his political theory, it was class struggle and a coalition of classes that was a necessary condition of any revolution or transition to socialism. Much of Marx's focus in his post-1848 works was on class analysis, in which he explicated class differences, alliances, and conflicts. Indeed, his materialist theory of history suggested that the role of classes was crucial in history, and his theory of revolution indicated that class struggle was a primary vehicle of achieving socialism.

While Marx believed that capitalism had developed the forces of production in a more revolutionary fashion than any previous social formation, he believed that there comes a time, as he put it in *Capital*, when "the monopoly of capital becomes a fetter upon the mode of production, which has sprung up and flourished along with, and under it. Centralization of the means of production and socialization of labor at last reach a point where they become incompatible with their capitalist integument. This integument is burst asunder. The knell of capitalist private property sounds. The expropriators are expropriated" (*MER*, p. 438).

Ultimately, Marx believed that capitalist societies would continually revolutionize themselves as they developed their potentials further, but that capitalism's contradictions and crisis tendencies would produce the transition to what he saw as a higher mode of civilization. In the decades following Marx's death in 1883, capitalism underwent many crises and a revolutionary working-class movement emerged, a wing of which embraced Marx's ideas. In addition, revolutionary regimes erupted that carried out socialist revolutions using Marx's ideas to legitimate their policies, and the Soviet communism bloc that was a mainstay of Marxism collapsed. What, then, are the limitations and contributions of Marxist theory in the light of historical experience and theoretical critique of Marxism?

The Limitations of Classical Marxism

The limitations of classical Marxism are evident in the "Communist Manifesto" and its "melting vision," in which capitalist societies melt down to two classes facing each other in irreconcilable hostility, the bourgeoisie and proletariat. Only a class war and the victory of the proletariat could resolve this contradiction in the vision of classical Marxism. Yet the very tendencies of social differentiation and fragmentation, analyzed elsewhere in the Marxian classics, confounded this two-class model portending a simplified class war, thus rendering this version of classical Marxism obsolete, or at least highly problematic. However, in *The Eighteenth Brumaire of Louis Bonaparte* and his other historical writings, Marx deployed a more complex model of class differentiation in contemporary modern societies.

Thus, certain versions of Marxism are antiquated; in particular, Marxism as the theory and movement of the proletariat, of proletariat revolution. Consequently, Marxism as a purported unity of theory and practice, as a project to totally transform the world through proletarian revolution, appears to be historically outmoded and even falsified. For many critics, Marx was simply too uncritical toward the proletariat, which he and Engels always saw as a universal class that represented universal interests of emancipation and that was inherently revolutionary. By virtue of the fact that it was the largest, most oppressed, and most potentially militant class, Marx identified the proletariat as the force of revolution from the early 1840s. He believed that bringing the working class together in factories produced a material basis for organization and that the proletariat could disrupt the capitalist production process through strikes and revolutionary activity, thus producing conditions for the overthrow of capitalism. Yet it was not clear how the uneducated masses would be able to gain class consciousness, organize, and exhibit the will and resolve – and sacrifices – to overthrow capitalism.

For neo-Marxists such as Herbert Marcuse, Marx's concept of the proletariat was rooted in a concrete analysis of the industrial workers in the factory system of his day, and thus the concept "proletariat" should not be applied to postindustrial conditions that exhibit a fragmentation of the working class into different class sectors and manifest different types for labor (see Kellner, 1984). On this account, while Marx provided a penetrating empirical analysis of the industrial working class of his day and while his scheme of revolution was justified by the nature of the class antagonisms of his time, and was manifest in later socialist revolutions, new theories of socialism and revolution are needed for the contemporary era.

Moreover, in historical retrospect, the lack of a theory of subjectivity, of the development of revolutionary consciousness, in the classical Marxian theory also vitiates its theory and practice. Marx seemed to think that class and revolutionary consciousness would develop naturally, as a result of the workers' position in the process of production. Later Marxian theorists, however, engaged in a heated debate concerning whether class consciousness developed spontaneously (as Rosa Luxembourg claimed), or would have to be brought to the workers from outside (as Kautsky and Lenin argued). But subsequent neo-Marxian theorists and others, by contrast, would develop more sophisticated theories of consciousness, communication, and education whereby political subjectivities could be formed that would strive for democratic social change.

Later neo-Marxist theorists also argued that Marx underplayed the role of culture in shaping consciousness and behavior and, in particular, integrating the working class within bourgeois society.[12] From this perspective, Marx put too much faith in the working class as an inherently revolutionary class and did not anticipate its fragmentation and integration within the capitalist system, as well as its growing powerlessness and conservatism in later stages of capitalist development. Moreover, the emphasis on a unified proletarian working class contradicted the tendencies of modernity toward class differentiation and fragmentation, tendencies recognized in some, but not all, of Marx's own work.

Many of Marx's texts also seem to place too heavy an emphasis on labor as the distinctly human activity, as the key to the development of the human being. Overemphasis on production is accompanied by an inadequate concept of intersubjectivity, lacking a fully developed theory of individual consciousness and its development in communication, symbolic action, and culture. Unlike later social theorists such as Durkheim, Mead, and Dewey, Marx failed to perceive the importance of wider communication in the development of new forms of association and solidarity. He thus put too much emphasis on class struggle, on direct action, and not enough on communication and democracy.

Indeed, Marx never grasped the significance of the institutions of liberal democracy as an important heritage of modern societies that should be absorbed into socialism. Although he espoused a model of radical democratic self-government in his writings on the Paris Commune, and while he long championed democracy as an ideal, Marx never properly appreciated the separation of powers and system of rights, checks and balances, and democratic participation developed within bourgeois society. Thus, Marx had an inadequate theory of democracy and failed to develop an institutional theory of democracy, its constraints under capitalism, and how socialism would make possible fuller and richer types of it.

There are also certain methodological limitations to the Marxian theory having to do with a too uncritical acceptance of modern science. There are certain dogmatic and positivistic tendencies within Marxism having to do with Marx and Engels's failure to criticize modern science in a sufficiently radical fashion.[13] From the moment of *The German Ideology*, Marx and Engels always saw their theory as exhibiting the method, rigor, and other virtues of natural science. They described their theory as science and adopted the term "scientific socialism" to describe the specificity of their theory. In his later works, Marx wrote of "the natural laws of capitalist production" and of "tendencies working with iron necessity toward inevitable results" (*MER*, p. 296). Such determinist discourse runs against the voluntarism and emphasis on revolutionary practice in other Marxian texts and points to a too uncritical bias toward science that is typical of modern theory.

Other dogmatic elements in the Marxian theory include an excessively reductive focus on production and economic factors, which sometimes took the form of economic reductionism. Yet here the emphasis on social relations and a dialectical model of social analysis provides a more critical optic and method. Likewise, although there is a version of Marxism that is close to historical determinism, and a tendency to project the inevitable triumph of socialism in some Marxian discourse, there are other examples of historical analysis in the Marxian ouevre that contrast tendencies of capitalist crisis with those of stabilization and that delineate the possibilities of historical regression and working class defeat (as, for example, in Marx's *Eighteenth Brumaire of Louis Napoleon*). And while some Marxian narratives of history are rather grandiose and sweeping in their import and reach, there is also patient and detailed historical research that does not fit facts into the preconceptions of the theory.

Marx in the Present Age

Hence, there are tendencies within Marx's voluminous corpus that undercut some of the more reductive tendencies in his thought that often are grounds for dismissal. Moreover, despite the collapse of communism, Marx's ideas continue to be relevant for comprehending and criticizing the contemporary era. Marx is widely acknowledged as one of the first theorists and critics of capitalist globalization, and as capital continues to be the major organizing force in the world today, relentlessly destroying past forms of life as it creates new forms of economy, society, culture, and everyday life, Marx's critical optic on capitalism is as relevant as ever. Moreover, Marx's mode of dialectic helps avoid the twin forms of economic and technological determinism that are dominant modes of theorizing the new economic and technological forms of the current era (see Best and Kellner, 2001).

Indeed, Marx's intense focus on technology and social forms and relations provides a useful optic to theorize the new forms of economy, society, politics and culture. His dialectical thought articulates the interaction between the economy and other domains of life, providing a method and a mode of thought that continues to be pertinent during an era in which the global restructuring of capital is producing vast transformation, turmoil, and conflict that requires new theories and oppositional practices. Moreover, as a new millennium unfolds, anti-globalization movements are emerging that are reconfiguring and expanding Marxian ideas.

Arguably, growing divisions between the haves and the have-nots in the current constellations of global capitalism render Marx's critique of exploitation, poverty, and oppression a still-valuable legacy, and whether Marx's crisis theory and analysis of capitalist contradictions producing a new form of civilization will anticipate future development remains an open question. Marx's stress on democracy remains an important political legacy, and it should not be forgotten that Marx himself never posited a vanguard party, was critical of all forms of bureaucracy, and advocated radical democratic self-government and not party rule; thus, he cannot be held responsible for the failures of "really existing communism" (see Kellner, 1995).

From the vantage point of philosophy, Marx's great intellectual and political achievement was to develop a synthesis of existing knowledge linking economics, politics, history, and human nature, and to develop it in a comprehensive and critical fashion. Marx produced a body of writings that is still one of the most impressive and influential theoretical achievements of all times, and that presents us with one of the great bodies of thought in the Western philosophical tradition. A product of its time, some aspects of the Marxian theory are obviously obsolete, but since we continue to live in an era defined by capitalist globalization, growing divisions between the haves and have-nots, and political conflict, Karl Marx's thought continues to speak to our contemporary situation.

Notes

1   For my reading of the status of Marxism after the fall of communism, see Kellner (1995). For 25 years, I taught Marxist philosophy at the University of Texas at Austin, before circumstances and choice took me to California. I would like to dedicate this study to those students who took Phil360 over the years. I would also like to thank Bob Antonio for comments on earlier versions of this study and for many fruitful discussions of Marx, philosophy, and social theory. Finally, thanks to Bob Solomon and David Sherman for many years of discussion of Marxism and continental philosophy, and useful suggestions for revision of this study.

2   Two of Marx's earliest texts, preserved from high school, stress the importance of developing one's individuality to the utmost and working for the good of humanity. See *CW1* (pp. 3–9). On Marx's life and times, see Mehring (1962), McLellan (1973), Riazanov (1973), and Wheen (2000). I use the abbreviation "*CW*" to refer to the volumes in Karl Marx and Frederick Engels, *Collected Works*, published from 1975 into the 1990s, to refer to the texts cited. "*CW1*" thus refers to *Collected Works*, volume 1, with page numbers cited following the volume number. I use *MER* to refer to texts collected in *The Marx–Engels Reader* (Marx and Engels, 1978).

3   In 1843, for instance, Marx wrote that the "criticism of religion is the premise of all criticism" (*CW3*, pp. 175–6). After this analysis, Marx simply concluded that the

criticism of religion was finished and occupied himself henceforth with social and political critique.

4 For Marx's contributions to the *Yearbook*, see *CW3* (p. 131ff.); for Engels's contribution, see *CW3* (pp. 418–43). On Engels's life and times, see Marcus (1974), Hunley (1991), and Carver (1989). For my view of Engels's contribution to Marxism, see Kellner (1999).

5 These notebooks were never published during Marx's life and their printing in 1932 caused a sensation, presenting a vigorous philosophical and humanist Marx who was quite different from the economic theorist and "scientific socialist" championed by the official Marxian working-class movements. On the importance of the *Paris Manuscripts* for the interpretation of Marxism, see Marcuse (1972 [1932], pp. 3–48).

6 On the difference between Marx and Smith, see Kellner (1977), which also discusses the "Adam Smith problem," referring to the differences in Smith's thought between the individualistic *Wealth of Nations* (1937 [1776]) and *Theory of Moral Sentiments* (1999), which emphasizes the social and cooperative nature of human beings.

7 In an early 1843 manifesto to the *German–French Yearbook*, Marx called for a "ruthless criticism of all that exists" and always made critique an important part of his method (*CW3*, p. 142). On the several senses of critique in the Marxian theory, see Kellner (1981); and for an analysis of the critical and dogmatic strains in classical social theory, including Marx, see Antonio and Kellner (1992).

8 The term "intercourse," or *Verkehr*, was used by Marx and Engels to describe the mode of interaction of individuals in a social environment. The term was soon replaced by "relations of production," which became the primary focus of their analyses of modes of social interaction. Yet the concept of *Verkehr* is broader and is close to what Habermas later described as social "interaction." In any case, it is false to claim that Marx and Engels reduced everything to production, for at least in their early writings they utilized a concept of social interaction. See, for example, *The German Ideology*, where Marx and Engels write that communism would overturn "the basis of all earlier relations of production *and intercourse*" (*CW5*, p. 81; my emphasis). See also *The Poverty of Philosophy*, where Marx describes society as "the product of men's reciprocal interaction" (*CW6*, p. 87). Later, Marx and Engels made cooperation and communication key forces of production, so they never excluded the dimension of social interaction from their optic, as critics ranging from Habermas (1971, 1984) to Baudrillard (1975, 1981 [1973]) have claimed. On the rise of modern societies and social theory, see Mazlish (1989).

9 See Hegel (1942 [1821]) and Marx in *CW3* [1843] (pp. 146–74). It is relevant to note that the German term used by Hegel and Marx was "*bürgerlich Gesellschaft*," or "bourgeois society," thus linking the new modern society with the rise of the bourgeoisie. The standard English translation of the term as "civil society" covers over this linkage, as does the current use of the term to describe the institutions of what Habermas has termed "the public sphere," which in his formulation describes those institutions between civil society and the state.

10 See Marx's *Paris Manuscripts*, where he affirms individuality as inseparable from one's social being, and valorizes a "real *individual* social being" (*CW3*, p. 299), and *The German Ideology*, where Marx and Engels also describe the individual as a key component of modern societies and an ideal to realize (*CW5*, p. 75ff.).

11 Throughout both the *Grundrisse* and *Capital*, Marx repeats his early analysis of the alienation of labor under capitalism and the overcoming of alienation under socialism, so I reject the thesis of the "two Marxs," one a philosophical humanist with a problematic of alienation and disalienation and the other a scientific socialist. This model is advanced

both by partisans of the later Marx such as Althusser, as well as partisans of the early Marx such as Fromm, who champion the philosophical humanist over the economistic revolutionary. I see, by contrast, Marx as a critical theorist of capitalism and champion of socialist revolution from 1844 until his death, who blends philosophy and science.

12 Analysis of contemporary capitalist culture as a mode of integration of the working class was a key theme of the Frankfurt school; see the discussions in Kellner (1989) and Wiggershaus (1994). This was also a major theme of Gramsci, Lukács, Bloch, and other so-called Western Marxists.

13 In *The German Ideology*, Marx and Engels analogized philosophy and masturbation to science and sexual intercourse, referred to idealist philosophy as "rubbish," and limited philosophy to summing up general results (*CW5*, pp. 36–9, *passim*), and henceforth would present their work as science. Such cavalier dismissal of philosophy, however, opens the door to dogmatism and positivism.

References

Antonio, R. J. and Kellner, D. 1992: Metatheorizing historical rupture: classical theory and modernity. In G. Ritzer (ed.), *Metatheorizing*. New York: Sage, 88–106.

Balbus, I. 1982: *Marxism and Domination*. Princeton, NJ: Princeton University Press.

Baudrillard, J. 1975: *The Mirror of Production*. St. Louis, Miss.: Telos Press.

——1981 [1973]: *For a Critique of the Political Economy of the Sign*. St. Louis, Miss.: Telos Press.

Best, S. and Kellner, D. 2001: *The Postmodern Adventure*. New York: Guilford Press/London: Routledge.

Carver, T. 1989: *Friedrich Engels. His Life and Thought*. London: Macmillan.

Engels, F. 1972 [1884]: *The Origin of the Family, Private Property and the State: In the Light of the Researches of Lewis H. Morgan*, trans. A. West. London: Lawrence and Wishart.

Feuerbach, L. 1957 [1841]: *The Essence of Christianity*. New York: Harper & Row.

Habermas, J. 1971: *Theory and Practice*. Boston, Mass.: Beacon Press.

——1984: *Theory of Communicative Action*, vol. 1. Boston, Mass.: Beacon Press.

Hegel, G. W. F. 1942 [1821]: *The Philosophy of Right*. New York: Oxford University Press.

——1965 [1807]: *The Phenomenology of Mind*. New York: Harper & Row.

Hobsbawm, E. 1979: *The Age of Capital*. New York: Vintage.

Hunley, J. D. 1991: *The Life and Thought of Friedrich Engels. A Reinterpretation*. New Haven, Conn.: Yale University Press.

Kellner, D. 1977: Capitalism and human nature in Adam Smith and Karl Marx. In J. Schwartz (ed.), *The Subtle Anatomy of Capitalism*. Santa Monica, Calif.: Goodyear, 66–86.

——1981: Marxism, morality, and ideology. *Canadian Journal of Philosophy*, supplementary volume, VII, 93–120.

——1984: *Herbert Marcuse and the Crisis of Marxism*. Berkeley, Calif., and London: University of California Press and Macmillan Press.

——1989: *Critical Theory, Marxism, and Modernity*. Cambridge: Polity Press/Baltimore, Md.: The Johns Hopkins University Press.

——1995: The obsolescence of Marxism? In B. Magnus and S. Cullenberg (eds.), *Whither Marxism?* London and New York: Routledge, 3–30.

——1999: Engels and modernity. In M. B. Steger and T. Carver (eds.), *Engels after Marx*. University Park, Penn.: The Pennsylvania State University Press, 163–78.

Marcus, S. 1974: *Engels, Manchester, and the Working Class*. New York: Vintage.

Marcuse, H. 1972 [1932]: The foundations of historical materialism. In *Studies in Critical Philosophy*. Boston, Mass.: Beacon Press, 2–48.

Marx, K. and Engels, F. 1975–: *Collected Works*. New York: International Publishers/London: Lawrence and Wishart (referred to in the text as *CW* with volume number; i.e., *CW*5).

——and——1978: *The Marx–Engels Reader*, ed. R. Tucker. New York: Norton (referred to in the text as *MER*).

Mazlish, B. 1989: *A New Science. The Breakdown of Connections and the Birth of Sociology*. New York: Oxford University Press.

McLellan, D. 1973: *Karl Marx. His Life and Thought*. New York: Harper & Row.

Mehring, F. 1962: *Karl Marx*. New York.

Riazanov, D. 1973: *Karl Marx and Friedrich Engels*. New York: Monthly Review Press.

Smith, A. 1937 [1776]: *An Inquiry into the Nature and Causes of the Wealth of Nations*. New York: Modern Library.

——1999: *The Theory of Moral Sentiments*. New York: Regnary.

Wheen, F. 2000: *Karl Marx. A Life*. New York: Norton.

Wiggershaus, R. 1994: *The Frankfurt School: Its History, Theories, and Political Significance*, trans. M. Robertson. Cambridge: Polity Press.

Chapter 5

Friedrich Nietzsche

Robert C. Solomon[1]

Friedrich (Wilhelm) Nietzsche (1844–1900) advocated a radical "revaluation of values" at the end of the nineteenth century and became an "untimely" prophet for the twentieth. The themes of relativism and nihilism, "the death of God," the disappointments of modernity, and the loss of European confidence, combined with a growing sense of meaninglessness and foreboding, found an expression in his philosophy. What would follow, we know, were two world wars, a worldwide depression, fascism, and the Holocaust. But in Nietzsche's philosophy the horrors of the future were always tempered by an abstract hope and the concrete love of life.

Nietzsche was a brilliant and ferocious stylist, who rarely backed away from even the most outrageous overstatements and accusations. He consequently invited all sorts of wild interpretations that went far beyond what he could have conceived or proposed. It is evident that Nietzsche intended to shock and provoke us and jar us into critical self-examination. What is not so clear is how we should take the many outrageous things he seems to say. Quotations that are so often snatched out of context from Nietzsche's texts were often written into a hypothetical context ("What if . . ."), or suggested as a thought experiment, or expressed ironically, or put in the words of a fictional character. (A notorious example: Nietzsche is quoted as saying, "You are going to women. Take your whip." But this was quoted by Nietzsche's fictional character Zarathustra, as spoken by an old *woman* in his fictional epic *Thus Spake Zarathustra*, and its meaning and its seriousness is thus deeply in question.) Thus the primary problem in reading Nietzsche is not trying to understand what he means (as with so many other authors in this volume). His sentences are admirably clear and concrete, and colorful besides. The primary problem in reading Nietzsche is trying to figure out to what extent he really *means* what he seems to be saying.

For example, throughout his works he lampoons and attacks the sentiment of pity, suggesting that those who feel it are hypocrites at best and that the world would be much better without it. But we know both from his own letters and from the reports of those who knew him that Nietzsche himself was an extremely compassionate and sensitive man. So how should we understand the extreme things that he says? Nietzsche sometimes seems to make fun of weakness, poverty, and the poor. He traces back the origins of morality to the most impoverished conditions of the ancient world and suggests that our values reflect a "slave morality." What are we to make of this? He prides himself on his discovery of "the Will to Power." But what does this ominous-sounding phrase (*der Wille zur Macht*) mean? Is it – as it is often interpreted – an endorsement of the power politics that gripped Germany from Bismarck to Hitler?

By contrast, Nietzsche's images are often celebrated far beyond their textual basis. He has his semi-fictional character Zarathustra announce the coming of the "*Übermensch*," but then never discusses who or what this *Übermensch* might be. He also has Zarathustra announce what he occasionally claims to be his greatest idea, the "eternal recurrence" of one's life. But this too is restricted to a few short mentions in his works. Even the "Will to Power," one of Nietzsche's best-known and notorious ideas, appears only sporadically and mainly in his unpublished notes.

Sometimes, Nietzsche excitedly describes horror in such a way that he seems to revel in it rather than distance himself from it. For example, in his most self-consciously polemical book, *On the Genealogy of Morals*, Nietzsche describes in gory detail the delight we take in punishing wrong-doers and the festivals of cruelty that have punctuated "civilized" society since ancient times. He seems to glory in the cruel ways in which warriors have treated their enemies, without mercy or the barest humane considerations. Are we to take these as endorsements? As mere reminders of how people behave? As attempts to shock and provoke us? As ironical, covertly condemning what the text seems to be approving?

And what are we to make of the notorious fact that Nietzsche often contradicts himself, sometimes on succeeding pages? Is Nietzsche just trying to give us different perspectives or ways of seeing the same phenomena? If so, does he or can he endorse any one of them? If not, should we therefore dismiss all of what he says as hopelessly muddled or inconsistent? These are the problems that face every Nietzsche reader, whether he or she is a beginning student or an advanced scholar.

Fighting for Life: Nietzsche *ad hominem*

Nietzsche's life and personality cannot be wholly separated from his work. Many of the intemperate and harsh claims that have made Nietzsche so notorious might be better understood by understanding the man who wrote them. After all, it was Nietzsche, perhaps more than any philosopher since Socrates, who insisted that what one says and what one does as a philosopher are all of a piece. It is for this reason, too, that Nietzsche so often employs those scandalous *ad hominem* arguments, described in every introductory logic and rhetoric book as the fallacy of attacking the person rather than the argument or position. But Nietzsche often does this on the grounds that the one is an indication (if not also a kind of "proof") of the other. Compare Nietzsche's strategy to that of an attorney doing cross-examination, disclosing the interests and biases of a witness in order to show how these would have guided his or her testimony.

So he says, in one of his last books, that the problem with Socrates was that he was ugly and didn't like his life, and this explains what is most important in his philosophy. Accordingly, it is only right and proper that we consider Nietzsche, too, in this light. Who was this man that he could make such brash and outrageous pronouncements about morality, religion, and even human nature as such? This is not to say, of course, that Nietzsche's philosophy should be read as mere autobiography or mere projection. The ideas, like any philosopher's ideas, must stand (or fall) on their own. Nevertheless, it is important to appreciate both Nietzsche's *ad hominem* arguments against others and the ways in which such arguments can be turned against him. As he writes in *Beyond Good and Evil*:

> Gradually it has become clear to me what every great philosophy so far has been: namely, the personal confession of its author and a kind of involuntary and unconscious memoir.[2]

So who was Nietzsche, whose personal confession and memoir we find so intriguing? He was born in 1844 in a small town (Röcken) in what is now eastern Germany. His father and grandfather were preachers, and the young Nietzsche aspired to be a preacher too, which throws into a revealing perspective his later polemical attacks on Christianity in particular and religion in general. His father and his younger brother died when Nietzsche was only four and he was raised by his mother, grandmother, and two maiden aunts. He shared his childhood with his younger sister Elisabeth, who would turn out to be something of the villain in the Nietzsche story. But as children, and for many years, they adored one another. He went to school, excelled in music and literature, and attended Bonn University in theology and philology (classical languages and literature), moving increasingly toward the classics.

In 1867 during his military service, Nietzsche fell from a horse and suffered a serious chest injury. This was the beginning of his continuing battles with ill health. Nietzsche was frail and sickly all the rest of his life. This should help us to understand why Nietzsche, more than any other philosopher, so stresses the importance of health, strength, and "life." Health is treated not just as precondition for a well-lived life (as, say, Aristotle would have argued) but as metaphor (together with its contraries, sickness, illness, and decay). It is a diagnostic tool for ideas, ideologies, worldviews, religions, and philosophies.

In 1869, at the age of 24, with a Doctorate from the University of Leipzig, Nietzsche started to teach at the University of Basel in Switzerland. He would rarely return to Germany again until the final, tragic years of his life. He lectured on the classics and on Greek philosophy (Plato and Aristotle). He was evidently a successful teacher and colleague. He was even appointed Dean! But in 1870 he served as a medical orderly in the Franco-Prussian War, and in addition to being horrified at the realities of warfare he contracted several serious illnesses that made much worse his already poor health. In 1879 he quit his job in Basel, and from then on spent his life living on a small pension and wandering between some of the most beautiful spots in Europe. He spent his summers in the Alps in Sils Maria and his winters on the Mediterranean, in Venice and Nice, for example.

Despite a few intense friendships (mainly by mail) he was for the most part very much alone. He twice considered marriage, and abruptly and unsuccessfully proposed first to a music student named Mathilde Tramedach (in 1872) and then later to the devastatingly talented and beautiful Lou Andreas Salomé. Lou and Nietzsche were close friends for what must have been the happiest and most creative months of his life. But then she ran off with his best friend (Paul Reé) and Nietzsche resigned himself to a life of solitude (not quite to say "loneliness").

Between 1882 and 1889, Nietzsche wrote ferociously and published his greatest works. We know from his notes and letters that he had hopes and plans for a great deal more. But in January 1889, he suffered a total breakdown, reputedly while saving a horse from a beating in the streets of Turino. (So much for Nietzsche's reputation as a monster without an ounce of compassion.) He remained alive for another decade in an almost vegetative state and died in 1900, at the very beginning of the century he did so much to prefigure. But what a terrible irony for a man who had boldly written "Die at the right time!"

From this very brief biographical sketch, we can appreciate how the one passion that rules Nietzsche's philosophy might be summarized as "the love of life." In itself, this is not very informative. But it does go a long way toward explaining why health and sickness play such an important role in his thinking, and why he so vehemently opposed all ideas and ideologies that he saw as demeaning to life. Foremost among these was the Christianity in which he had been raised and which he knew so well. Thus Nietzsche's late self-appointed role as "Antichrist" was very much – as that religion so often warns – an "inside job."

Falling in Love: Schopenhauer, Music, and the Greeks

Philosophers typically consider themselves masters of reason. Nietzsche, by contrast, was moved by and identified with his passion. (In this, he resembled no one so much as Kierkegaard, as Karl Jaspers insightfully noted.) And Nietzsche was a man of intense passions, love included, but intense loathing and contempt as well. While he was in school, Nietzsche discovered the first true love of his life, the literature of the ancient Greeks. He read the *Iliad* and the *Odyssey*. He read Sophocles and the great Greek tragedians. He read Plato and Aristotle. And like many German intellectuals of his century, his conception of the good life was very much shaped by his reading.

Nietzsche was smitten again in 1865, when he casually picked up a book by Arthur Schopenhauer the great German pessimist, *The World as Will and Representation*. And he fell in love again, still as a student, with the music of Richard Wagner and later, when he met him (in 1868), with the composer himself, who became something of a father figure to the fatherless Nietzsche. (He also fell in love with Wagner's wife, Cosima, but that is a very different kind of story.) Wagner had been heavily influenced by Schopenhauer's philosophy, and this provided an ideal subject of discussion. But by 1876, after writing essays full of praise about Schopenhauer and Wagner, Nietzsche found himself turning away from both of them. In his last works, Nietzsche still links them together, no longer favorably but as symptoms of German decadence. In both cases, Nietzsche's love had turned to loathing. Nietzsche later insisted that the break with Wagner was the single most painful experience of his life. And throughout his career, Nietzsche continued to wrestle with Schopenhauer's pessimism, which ran so counter to the passion for life that was the primary drive of his own philosophy.

It may be hard for us to imagine that Nietzsche fancied his true talent to be as a composer rather than as a philosopher, but this is, perhaps, a fair warning that we should not always take what Nietzsche says and believes about himself all too seriously. He did in fact compose a small volume of pieces for chorus and for the piano, more ponderous than profound. (These are now readily available on CD.) But it is evident that Wagner in particular did not respect his music at all, and it is not hard to imagine that his uncensored ridicule soon provoked Nietzsche to reject not only Wagner and his music but (within the next decade) much of "modernity" as well. No doubt there was some virtue in Wagner's insensitivity insofar as it made Nietzsche focus on his philosophy. For that we are grateful. Nevertheless, music enters into Nietzsche's philosophy in all sorts of ways, from his Schopenhauerian celebration of music as nothing less than the expression of life as such to the self-consciously musical structure of his writing. It is music, above all, that gives life meaning, he often suggests, and one of his most famous metaphors, his conception of the Dionysian, makes this amply clear.

That conception, as well as a great many others that prefigure his entire philosophy, is introduced in his eagerly awaited first book, *The Birth of Tragedy out of the Spirit of Music*. The book itself, at least through the eyes of his philological colleagues, was an academic failure. There were no footnotes. There was little of the meticulous, nit-picking philology that was expected in academia (then as now). There were wild and outrageous claims. And Nietzsche contaminated the mandated purity of classical scholarship with what then would have been considered contemporary pop music, as well as excessive praise for his friend and mentor, Richard Wagner. But Nietzsche's dual conception of the Apollonian and the Dionysian also marked a radical break with traditional views of the classics and ancient Greek life.

The Apollonian captured the established view of the Greeks as rational, autonomous individuals with a concern for order, moderation, beauty, and clarity (to a degree then unknown in the ancient world). The Dionysian, by contrast, captured the wild side of Greek culture – excessive and cruel, as in the frenzied orgies of the mystery cults of Dionysus, the god of wine – and the extreme violence and cruelty of such Greek tragedies as *Oedipus Rex* and *Medea*. (Dionysus himself, so the legend goes, was torn to shreds by the Titans, acting on orders from Hera.) Nietzsche's dramatic thesis was that Greek tragedy and Greek life could only be understood in terms of a combination of the Apollonian and the Dionysian, the orderly and the "civilized," the disorderly and the frenzied.

Throughout the book, there is an unmistakable secular theme, that life is suffering, but that this suffering cannot be "redeemed" by anything outside of life. In saying this, Nietzsche is starting to reject not only his Christian background but also the powerful philosophical rationalism of Socrates and Plato. Even in this first work, Nietzsche's conflicted attitude toward Socrates – admiring, envious, and disdainful – is already obvious. Nietzsche agrees that Socrates marked an important turning point in the history of ideas, but he also accuses Socrates of misdirecting Western thought with an exaggerated emphasis on Apollonian rationality and, with it, an unhealthy yearning for the "other-worldly."

Summing up his own worldview at that time, Nietzsche writes, "only as an aesthetic phenomenon is the world eternally justified." And of the Greeks themselves he says, "How much they must have suffered to become so beautiful." The pessimistic and atheistic philosophy of Schopenhauer is much in evidence, but what is also evident is that Nietzsche is struggling to put a bright face on that first Noble Truth of Buddhism that had so transfixed Schopenhauer, which says that life is essentially suffering.

Nietzsche, Science, Truth, and Truthfulness

In some of his early essays, Nietzsche introduces a theme that would occasionally appear in his writings throughout his career, what some philosophers would summarize as "the Problem of Truth." Briefly stated, the problem is this: "Is there such a thing as truth ('the true world')? And (if so) can we know it?" Philosophers have emphasized this aspect of Nietzsche's writings because it is – in the epistemo-logical temper of our times – an indisputably philosophical question. But it would be an enormous mistake to read Nietzsche primarily through the eyes of his supposed "theory of knowledge." He wrote very little about truth and knowledge, what amounts to scattered comments, devoid of any general theory. His longest single treatment, in the form of a parable, is only a page long (in *Twilight of the Idols*, "How the 'true world' finally became a fable"). In his book *Beyond Good and Evil*, Nietzsche calls the obsession with epistemology in modern philosophy "a timid epochism" and "philosophy in its last throes."

Nevertheless, Nietzsche's constant insistence on honesty and truthfulness and his obvious obsession to get to the truth about things belies the view that takes him to be a skeptic or dismissive about truth. Although questions of knowledge were always secondary in his mind, his considerations were aimed at answering the practical ques-tion *how to live and live well*. Thus one would not go far wrong in calling Nietzsche a *pragmatist* and linking his thought with that of the American philosopher William James (his near contemporary). For instance, the reason why Nietzsche rejects the idea of a "true world" or a world "in-itself" that is beyond the bounds of knowledge is because we haven't a clue what to *do* with such an idea. Furthermore, insofar as the world in-itself is conceived of as *another* world, a *better* world, it would seem to diminish the worth of this one, and thus it violates the ruling passion of Nietzsche's philosophy, the love of life – *this* life. It is not that Nietzsche raises skeptical doubts about knowledge so much as that he sees knowledge as valuable just because it is practical. In his own life, he often expressed his love of knowledge as a way of giving his own life meaning.

The concise view of Nietzsche's theses about truth is that there isn't any; that is, "there is no truth." But what does this mean? In a striking phrase in an early, unpublished essay, Nietzsche suggests that truth is "a mobile army of metaphors." But in *The Gay Science*, which Nietzsche considered one of his definitive works, he rather suggests a straightforward empiricist–pragmatist sense of truth, namely, "Let us put it to the test!" ("I do not wish to hear anything more of things and questions which do not admit of being tested.") But he also suggests that what seems true and even necessary to us might nevertheless be false. "Error might be among the conditions of life." And again, "What after all are man's truths? – They are his irrefutable errors." In his notes, he repeats this claim that truth is "a kind of error without which a species could not live," and he occasionally equates truth (as he does almost everything) with the Will to Power. He insists that there are "many kinds of truth" (a recurrent theme in nineteenth-century philosophy) and consequently, "there is no truth." In his notes, too, he returns to his ruling theme, "The value for *life* is ultimately decisive."

How should we understand this mish-mash of contrasting aphorisms? I think that here (as always) Nietzsche should be read contextually, and the question should be: What is he reacting against? What thesis (or theses) is he rejecting? In all of this, it is clear that Nietzsche is rejecting the idea of a true world behind the mere appearances, thus opposing himself to two philosophical giants, Plato and Kant. The world that we experience *is* the real world. He is also rejecting, as any good empiricist would, the idea of truths that make no difference whatsoever in experience and that therefore cannot possibly be tested. And like any good empiricist he is also attacking the dogmatism of both religion and academic scholarship, where insistence on the literal truth eliminates any question of disagreement, imagination, or a plurality of legitimate views. Nietzsche's use of the word "error" to refer to matters that are not absolutely literally true is illustrative of his general tendency to dramatic overstatement. What runs through his various comments is a thesis that is derivative of his ruling passion for life; namely that what is worth believing (whether or not we want to honor it with the name "truth") is what supports and enhances life.

Moreover, there is no reason to think that what supports and enhances life should be a singular or even a consistent set of theses. Quite to the contrary, "there are many kinds of eyes" and so many kinds of truths. But it is another overstatement to infer from this that there is *no* truth. Rather, it leads directly to one of Nietzsche's most celebrated themes, and the method of much of his philosophy as well. It is called "perspectivism," and it follows from Nietzsche's idea that philosophy should be a kind of experimentalism, thinking about things in different ways and looking at things from different angles. Thus art and aesthetics provide some ways of looking and thinking about the world, while science and scholarship suggest others. Religion and morality are also worldviews, perspectives rather than the absolute truths their proponents often proclaim them to be. One might trace this perspectivism back to Kant's "two standpoints" view (of nature and of morality), but Nietzsche goes far beyond Kant's view in suggesting both that there are no "necessary truths" in either realm and that there are any number of such perspectives.

Nietzsche's concerns about truth raise questions about his complex relationship to science and scientific thinking. Sometimes, he praises science above all for its anti-dogmatism and its experimentalism ("Let us try it?"). At other times, he opposes science to aesthetics and accuses scientists (and scholars) of a kind of *asceticism*, that is, a practice of perverse self-denial. Again, what is clear is that when science can serve as his weapon against religious and moral dogmatism, Nietzsche could not be more enthusiastic about it. But when science itself becomes dogmatic or moralistic, he attacks it as ferociously as he attacks any small-minded, life-stultifying enterprise. All in all, Nietzsche is more sympathetic to science than not, but it is worth emphasizing that what Nietzsche admires most about science is its experimental method and its continuous self-criticism. And that is how philosophy should proceed as well.

The Campaign Against Morality

While he was still at Basel, Nietzsche initiated his "campaign against morality" in a series of striking books, beginning in 1878 with *Human, All Too Human, A Book for Free Spirits*, followed by a second volume, *All Too Human II, Assorted Opinions and Sayings*, and then *The Wanderer and his Shadow* in 1879–80. The books were written entirely in short bursts and aphorisms, one- or two-sentence *bon mots* which variously punctured the balloons of metaphysics, gave high praise to science, and (like Freud to follow) offered diagnoses of everyday moral lives. One persistent theme in these works is what is sometimes called "psychological egoism," the idea that there are no unselfish or "non-egoistic" actions. Even love and pity, to take two of his most frequent examples, are not selfless or unself-interested. But Nietzsche wavers between the strong claim that every action is self-interested and the considerably more modest claim that no action is entirely selfless or unself-interested. (With the latter, even Immanuel Kant would agree.)

After Nietzsche left Basel and the respectability of academic life forever, the two *Human, All Too Human* books were supplemented by two even more radically experimental and probing aphoristic volumes, *Daybreak: Thoughts on the Prejudices of Morality* and *The Gay Science*. Here Nietzsche found his mature voice, and consolidated his various prejudices and crusades in a spectacularly anti-dogmatic (which is not to say meek or humble) style. The designation "free spirit" was one that Nietzsche took quite seriously, and it would be repeated as an identifying catchphrase throughout his books. Not only was he personally free of the restrictions (both moral and institutional) of university life. In his own "wanderings" he felt free to experiment with ideas unconstrained and to challenge even the most pious dogmas of his culture.

The dangers of such independence are obvious, and Nietzsche was well aware of them. It never occurred to him that one could live without values (in a state of what is often called "nihilism"). The question was *which* values, for he did not assume that the values of bourgeois Christian society were the only values. (Thus one of his chief complaints about "morality" is that it pretends to be synonymous with values, or at least the "highest" values.) Nietzsche was raised with the values of his immediate culture, but through the classics he had come to appreciate (and to some extent internalize) a very different (and by no means "primitive") set of values. And through his reading of Schopenhauer, and of Schopenhauer's well-informed interest in biology (not to mention his own on-going concerns with his health), Nietzsche came to fully appreciate the power of another set of values neither cultivated nor imposed by society, namely, the natural demands of the body. To be a free spirit was not to be free of values but to reflect, reexamine, and shake free of one particularly dogmatic and restrictive set of values, the values of Judeo-Christian and petty bourgeois morality.

Nietzsche famously declared himself an "immoralist" (and at the end of his career "the Antichrist" as well). But his philosophy might better be viewed as an attempt to revive a more affirmative morality than the traditional "Thou shalt nots" that define so much of the Judeo-Christian tradition. In *Daybreak*, for instance, he exclaims, "How can we hate ourselves and expect others to love us?" Nietzsche would savagely attack ordinary morality as "herd" and as "slave" morality, respectively, suggesting that it was both mindless and cowardly. But in his earlier books he offers us not so much a global argument, much less a general normative theory, but rather piecemeal and often painfully insightful observations of moral life, its inconsistencies, and hypocrisies. In this, he is more like the French moralists La Bruyere and La Rochefoucauld than the great moral theorists of modern times, Kant and Mill. Like the French moralists, Nietzsche's main weapon is ridicule, seeing moral behavior as ridiculous. They knew that the best way to puncture hypocrisy and pretence was not by way of extended argument.

It is in the "experimental" series of books from *Human, All Too Human* to *The Gay Science* that Nietzsche begins to question the unquestionable (Is having pity really a virtue?), to suggest the unsuggestable (Could God be a projection of our most pathetic traits?), to moralize against his own religion ("We are appalled by physical torture, but we accept without criticism the torture of the soul in Christianity."), and to question rationality ("How did rationality arrive in the world? Irrationally, as one might have expected, by chance.") – and this culminates in his most dramatic announcement, of "the death of God," in *The Gay Science* (III). He sums up his view in a poignant proclamation in book I, section 95 of *Daybreak*: "In former times, one sought to prove that there is no God – today one indicates how the belief that there is a God could *arise* and how this belief acquired its weight and importance: a counter-proof that there is no God thereby becomes superfluous . . . In former times . . . atheists did not know how to make a clean sweep."

It is in these books that Nietzsche so emphasizes his perspectivism, not so much as a philosophical "theory" as an approach to philosophy and as a mode of analysis. Morality, in particular, is interpreted as just one of several perspectives, thus undermining its claim to "trump" or absolute status. Contrasting Christian and Greek morals, Nietzsche finds that the Greeks were vastly superior. These books also have a light-heartedness that marks Nietzsche's definitive break with Schopenhauer. The very title, *The Gay Science*, is a flamboyant announcement of the joys of free thinking, as are many of the passages in the book itself. Pessimism, it turns out, is just another version of "slave morality."

With *Daybreak*, Nietzsche's "campaign" is fully under way. Although eccentric in its style, the campaign might best be considered as a strategy of "moral psychology", that is, the psychological and motivational analysis of those who embrace the Christian moral perspective. Accordingly, *Daybreak* is rich in *ad hominem* comments, as Nietzsche asks: What kind of person would accept a perspective that places so much emphasis on sin and suffering and is only "compensated" in an afterlife? Why would one want to believe in eternal damnation, or accept the degradation of the body and the denial of its pleasures? Nietzsche thinks that such notions as sin and afterlife are delusional, but his main focus is not on the falseness of Christian doctrines. It is rather on the cruelty and life-denial that such beliefs invite, the negative emotions and vicious motivations and the hypocrisy of such notions as "universal love."

Nothing would be a bigger mistake in reading Nietzsche, however, than to think that his campaign against morality is purely negative, with nothing better to take its place. True, much of Nietzsche's writing is directed against morality and moralists (and the religion that sustains them), but always with the purpose of putting something else – another "morality," if you will – in their place. In what is probably his most famous (and most obscure) book, *Thus Spake Zarathustra* (published in sections from 1883 through 1885), Nietzsche presents his alternative worldview. Perhaps one could call it an alternative religion, since Nietzsche's spokesman Zarathustra is modeled after the ancient Persian prophet and inventor of Zoroastrianism. But what Zarathustra preaches is very "this-worldly," to be "true to the earth!" There is no room for a God in heaven or an afterlife here.

"God is dead" is one of the central themes of *Zarathustra*. I hope it need not be said that Nietzsche does not have in mind a peculiar metaphysical claim here but, rather, that he refers to people's *belief* in the Judeo-Christian God. His claim is that many people who think that they believe in God really do not believe. Their actions and their feelings betray them. In his meetings with a great many colorful and bizarre characters, Zarathustra keeps encountering what he elsewhere calls "the shadows of God," the many perversions and distortions in our views of ourselves that remain tied to the belief in the supernatural Almighty.

It is in *Zarathustra*, too, that Nietzsche introduces his best known (and least detailed) image, the figure of the *Übermensch*. Whatever else he may be (and this is by no means clear) the *Übermensch* seems to signify some sort of ideal, "the meaning of the earth," perhaps also a goal to aspire to (except that Nietzsche does not suggest that it is possible to get there). Man is "a rope between ape and *Übermensch*," a "bridge." Elsewhere, he ridicules the ideas of "the improvers of mankind." But then again, it is often supposed (and it is not entirely wrong) that the point of Nietzsche's philosophy is to promote and inspire future *Übermenschen*.

Nietzsche's campaign continues into his most mature and best-known works, *Beyond Good and Evil* (1886) and *On the Genealogy of Morals* (1887). There he fleshes out his many probing aphorisms into something that might almost be called a "theory," except that Nietzsche quite explicitly limits the first to a "prelude" and warns that the latter is a "polemic." There are several significant shifts in his positions, although it would be a mistake to treat Nietzsche as changing his views entirely. For one thing, he weakens considerably his earlier psychological egoism and instead asks just how seemingly selfless actions could get motivated (a question on which Kant has weighed in heavily, insisting that reason and the moral law supply their own motivation). More important for the standard view of Nietzsche, his concept of "the Will to Power" moves to center stage. By the time he writes *Beyond Good and Evil* (and many of his unpublished notes from the same period), it is clear that not egoism but Will to Power motivates our actions. (And not only human actions. Nietzsche sometimes suggests that *all of life* is Will to Power and occasionally, in notes he just as well abandoned, that *everything* is Will to Power, a poor echo of Schopenhauer's metaphysical notion of "Will.")

Taking on the World: Masters, Slaves, and Resentment

In *Beyond Good and Evil* and *On the Genealogy of Morals*, but also in a section added to the second edition of *The Gay Science* (published in 1887), Nietzsche fully develops his moral psychology and provides a general answer to the questions about motivation he had been asking for most of the past decade. That answer is the Will to Power. But that suggestive yet clumsy phrase disguises more than it illuminates the often subtle diagnoses that Nietzsche offers us. For one thing, his investigation is no longer so sporadic and piecemeal. Now he utilizes his training as a philologist to construct an elegant (if extremely controversial) theory of the origins of moral language, particularly those key terms "good," "bad," and "evil." He also embraces a historical method, *genealogy*, the attempt to trace the *origins* of different sets of values and perspectives on life. Once again, the telling thesis is that what we call "morality" is in fact *just* a perspective, not "true" or commanded by an uncontrovertible God. It also coexists with alternative perspectives, some of which may be preferable in terms of good mental or physical health. But now Nietzsche makes full use of a distinction that he had toyed with throughout his campaign, between masters and slaves, and "master morality" and "slave morality."

Nietzsche's *Genealogy*, together with *Beyond Good and Evil*, is one of the seminal works in secular ethical theory. Plato gives us the perfect society; Aristotle gives us a portrait of the happy, virtuous life; Kant provides an analysis of "moral worth" and practical reason; John Stuart Mill gives us the principle of utility, with its benign insistence on collective "quality" happiness. Nietzsche, by contrast, offers us a polemical diagnosis in which morality emerges as something mean-spirited and pathetic. What we know as "morality" is in fact slave morality, so named not only because of its historical origins but because of its continuing servile and inferior nature.

The basis of slave morality, Nietzsche tells us, is resentment, a bitter emotion based on a sense of inferiority and frustrated vindictiveness. (He employs the French "*ressentiment*," which suggests a more global sense of bitterness.) He contrasts slave morality with what he calls "master" morality, which he presents as noble and self-secure. Although this is an exemplary instance of Nietzsche's perspectivism – slave and master moralities are alternative perspectives on value and values – Nietzsche's descriptions leave little question as to which of these two "moral types" he (and consequently we) find more appealing. But he does not argue that master morality is right or slave morality wrong, nor does he invoke any shared standard by which the two might be measured. To be sure, the master is more powerful and the slave is relatively impotent, but Nietzsche does not invoke levels of power to suggest that one sort of morality is better than the other.

Nevertheless, Nietzsche's "genealogy" of morals is clearly designed to make the novice reader uncomfortable with his or her slavish attitudes, and it is also written to inspire a seductive sense of superiority, the urge to be (if not the confidence that one already is) a "master." These are dangerous attitudes, quite opposed to the edifying moral support that we usually expect from ethical treatises. They all too easily give way to the sophomoric arrogance that "anything goes."

But Nietzsche has no such view in mind. In an early aphorism in *Daybreak*, he comments, "One should distinguish well: whoever still wants to gain the consciousness of power will use any means . . . He, however, who has it, has become very choosy and noble in his tastes."[3] In a section "What is Noble" in *Beyond Good and Evil*, he makes it very clear that it is human *excellence* he is defending and not mere self-indulgence and licentiousness. In this sense, one might well say that Nietzsche defends an ancient paradigm of ethics – now often called "virtue ethics." Aristotle's *Nicomachean Ethics* is typically cited as the prime example, and Nietzsche and Aristotle have a great deal in common, not only in their ethics of virtue but in their shared focus on biology and naturalism. The Greek word *areté* means both "virtue" and "excellence," and it refers to the particular traits (both moral and non-moral) of an individual. It can thus be contrasted with distinctively moral language, which refers to impersonal rules and suprapersonal (if not supernatural) justification. (This includes the unfortunate term "virtue" as a singular moral property, as opposed to the plural and pluralistic "virtues.")

The core of virtue ethics is the importance of moral character. In the evaluation of character, a person's motives and emotions in acting are considered essential. An action performed out of noble sentiments is a noble action, even if the act itself is inconsequential or unfortunate. Alternatively, an action that expresses vicious resentful sentiments will be vicious, even if (through error in judgment, by chance, or with an overly subtle sense of irony) the act itself has benign consequences. In Nietzsche as in Aristotle, the content of ethics is partially constituted by "feelings" (what Kant called the "inclinations"). Indeed, one would not be wrong to classify Nietzsche as a "romantic" philosopher who celebrates *the passionate life* (despite his rejection of Romanticism as applied to Schopenhauer's and other German philosophies). What "Will to Power" suggests is not only a motive for action but a way of life, passionate and energetic. (Nietzsche described himself as "dynamite" on the brink of insanity, an extreme metaphor for what is otherwise a very sensible philosophy.) The important thing, according to Nietzsche, is to cultivate one's natural talents and virtues and use even one's weaknesses and vices to create a beautiful life. In *The Gay Science* Nietzsche tells us, "to give style to one's character. A great art." That, perhaps, is the keynote of Nietzsche's ethics.

It is thus worth looking at Nietzsche's master/slave analysis, in *Genealogy* in particular, as a grand collective *ad hominem* argument, an argument that traces back whole systems of ethics to the personalities of peoples. It is hard not to acknowledge that the content of ethical analysis should include the motives of those who practice or create an ethics. Indeed, Kant himself would insist that one cannot evaluate the "moral worth" of an action without considering as central the intentions (or the "will") behind it. And, as Kant also points out, the distinction between the formal intentions (or maxims) of an action and the motives behind it may in practice be indeterminable. The substance of ethics is not to be found only in the circumstances and consequences of acts and judgments, and of course we no longer expect to find it in mere maxims and their formal generalization. The locus of ethics, according to Nietzsche as well as Aristotle, lies in the admirable (or pathetic) individual. Masters are ultimately virtuous in that they envision themselves as virtuous. Slaves are ultimately pathetic because they consider themselves as pathetic.

Nietzsche's "genealogy" is a psychological diagnosis as well as a (very polemical) historical investigation. It includes a very condensed and rather mythic account of the history and evolution of morals, but the heart of that account is a psychological hypothesis concerning the motives and mechanisms underlying that history and evolution. "The slave revolt in morality begins," Nietzsche tells us, "when *ressentiment* itself becomes creative and gives birth to values."[4] Modern critics might well dismiss such speculation as yet another version of the genetic fallacy: the question is not the genealogy, genesis, or motivation of morals but only, in neo-Kantian terms, the *validity* of our current moral principles. Traditional moral theorists and Nietzsche expositors thus often talk past one another, the former focusing on arguments concerning the form and justification of moral precepts, the latter exposing the ulterior motives that underlie these supposedly moral, impersonal, and necessary ideals. It is a large and still hotly debated question – how genealogy and psychology can serve to legitimately criticize current morality and moral philosophy.

Resentment is a powerful motive, and it is one of the more subtle questions of Nietzsche interpretation why such power is demeaned by Nietzsche as symptomatic of weakness. To add to the seeming paradox, in *Genealogy* Nietzsche writes, "A race of such men of *ressentiment* is bound to become eventually cleverer than any noble race; it will also honor cleverness to a far greater degree" (*GM* I 11). Nietzsche also expresses a grudging admiration for the original slaves:

> "the act of *most spiritual revenge*." It was the Jews who, with awe-inspiring consistency, dared to invert the aristocratic value-equation (good = noble = powerful = beautiful = happy = beloved of God) and to hang onto this inversion with their teeth, the teeth of the most abysmal hatred (the hatred of impotence), saying, "the wretched alone are the good; the suffering, deprived, sick, ugly alone are pious, alone are blessed by God . . . and you, the powerful and noble, are on the contrary the evil, the cruel, the lustful, the insatiable, the godless to all eternity, and you shall be in all eternity the unblessed, the accursed, and damned!" (*GM* I 7)

This, in a formula, is the structure of the slave "revaluation of values" that Nietzsche would like to undo. By designating master values (Aristotle's excellences) as "evil," the slave can view himself as morally superior because of his abstinence (that is, his inability to achieve excellence and obtain the good life). But the slave does not deprive himself by choice. Rather, he rationalizes his not having what he cannot have by "forgetting" that he cannot have it. And, more generally, the slave's topsy-turvy revaluation must "forget" its own motives and its ingenious efforts to "save face" and think itself superior. Thus slave morality is prone to massive self-deception and hypocrisy. "While the noble man lives in trust and openness with himself . . . the man of *ressentiment* is neither upright nor naive nor honest and straightforward with himself. His soul squints . . ." (*GM* I 10).

Throughout his career, Nietzsche also describes morality as "herd" phenomenon ("herd morality"). This is not the same as slave morality. Herd morality might best be viewed as modern bourgeois morality, exemplified by utilitarianism with its emphasis on happiness, comfort, and well-being. The metaphor of the herd suggests mindless conformity, leaderlessness, a life of dull comfort without ambition or nobility. Thus utilitarianism speaks of "the greatest good for the greatest number," interpreted as a minimum of pain and a maximum of pleasure. Betraying a common German disdain (mixed with envy and respect) for the English, Nietzsche interprets this in the least flattering way, as a philosophy of cow-like comfort. But in several ways – for example, in its naturalism, its rejection of metaphysical and supernatural supports for morality, and its larger focus on the greater good – utilitarianism is quite compatible with Nietzsche's ethics. He in fact read John Stuart Mill with consider-able enthusiasm, but one would never know this from what Nietzsche writes about him.[5]

One of Nietzsche's nastier cracks is "Man does not live for pleasure. Only the Englishman does." The barbed comment underscores Nietzsche's main disagreement with Mill. The centrality of pleasure and happiness (the utilitarians did not carefully distinguish these) seemed to Nietzsche both banal and psychologically false. Pleasure and the avoidance of pain were not (by the time of Nietzsche's mature works) primary motives of human behavior, rather only "accompaniments" of success, defined by the Will to Power. (Pleasure as a mere "accompaniment" is also a very Aristotelian theme.) He also rejected utilitarianism's central egalitarianism. (Mill: "Everyone is to count for one and only one.") Moreover, Nietzsche's concept of "the greater good" was anything but bourgeois. The greater good was determined by "the great man," who might cause considerable turmoil and bring enormous unhappiness in his pursuit of a greater society and culture. Thus Nietzsche's fantasy of the *Übermensch*. But for the utilitarian (in Nietzsche's caricature), the greater good is nothing more than comfort and the lack of pain. Thus Nietzsche's less well-known character (also in *Thus Spake Zarathustra*) "the last man," who dully proclaims "we have invented happiness – and blinks."

Nietzsche also accuses morality of being "unnatural," even "anti-nature." Again this charge should be considered separately from both "slave morality" and "herd morality," and it is arguably incompatible with them. The charge (which reaches its fullest expression in one of Nietzsche's last and best books, *Twilight of the Idols*) is that morality is "anti-nature" both in its arrogant attempt to change human nature ("Some wretched loafer of a moralist comments, 'No! Man ought to be different'") and in its continuing effort to destroy the passions ("We no longer admire dentists who 'pluck out' teeth so that they will not hurt any more"). Nietzsche is a very strong believer in human nature (that is, the biological determination of both the species and individuals) and his morality is often summarized in the ancient Greek slogan "Become who you are!," suggesting that each of us is born with particular talents, virtues, and vices, and what we can be is already determined by our natures. But if this is so, then slaves are "by nature" slavish, another Aristotelian thesis that Nietzsche makes even more brutish (in the *Genealogy*) by comparing masters and slaves to eagles and lambs, "as if a bird of prey could choose to be a lamb," or vice versa. The message is that one cannot choose one's basic nature, and no matter how "bad" the eagle's behavior may be for the sheep, there is nothing "evil" about it. Moreover, sheep, too, are as natural as any other creature, and their herd behavior is part of their nature. Nietzsche agrees that this is the common lot of the vast herd of humanity as well, and the fatalistic upshot of this shocking passage is that people *cannot* change their lot in life.

Master morality – albeit in refined and more artistic form and not just as primordial brutishness – is not only self-consciously "good" but also natural. The slave revolt is thus a revolt against what is natural, that is, what is strong and healthy and full of life. It is clear what prejudices Nietzsche is bringing to this analysis (and, as an *ad hominem* argument, we can easily understand how a sickly, lonely philosopher would admire such virtues). In Nietzsche's crudest fantasies, it is as if noble human beings once ruled the world while today the world is ruled by resentful mediocrities. But even at his crudest, Nietzsche (like his moral predecessor Jean-Jacques Rousseau) insists that "we cannot go back," that more than 20 centuries have had their beneficial as well as deleterious effects.

In particular, we have become *more spiritual* as well as more refined, largely under the auspices of slave morality and Christianity. What we should aspire to, therefore, is no longer what he described as "master morality," but a new kind of "legislation" of morals for the future, "beyond good and evil" but with the cultivated sensitivity of the best of the modern age. Nietzsche most often mentions the great German poet Goethe as exemplary of such a "higher man." Slave morality may have had its costs but it also conveys some benefits: "with noble men cleverness can easily acquire a subtle flavor of luxury and subtlety – for here it is far less essential than the perfect functioning of the regulating unconscious instincts or even a certain imprudence, perhaps a bold recklessness . . . or that enthusiastic impulsiveness in anger, love, reverence, gratitude and revenge" (*GM* I 10).

The Will to Power, Life Affirmation, and Eternal Recurrence

The "Will to Power" is perhaps Nietzsche's most notorious coinage. Looking back through the twentieth century, the very phrase reeks of fascism, violence, and the trampling of human rights. It does not help that the very influential German philosopher Martin Heidegger, once a Nazi himself, insisted that the Will to Power was the very core of Nietzsche's metaphysics. The postmodern French philosopher Gilles Deleuze similarly interpreted the "play of forces" to be the heart of Nietzsche. There is surprisingly little in Nietzsche's writings to support these views. The phrase "Will to Power" recurs with considerable frequency in Nietzsche's writings, to be sure, and Nietzsche's hypothesis, that people usually act for the sake of power rather than for pleasure or out of a sense of duty, has a certain plausibility. One might well see it as a refinement of the psychological egoism thesis that he earlier defended.

Nietzsche talks as if the Will to Power is the cornerstone of his philosophy, and too many commentators have uncritically agreed with him. But most of the discussion of Will to Power is to be found in his unpublished notes, and even where it clearly appears in the published texts Nietzsche's endorsement is by no means clear or straightforward. Indeed, the Will to Power has little to do with that mysterious metaphysical entity called "the Will," which Nietzsche lampoons in Schopenhauer. Nor is the Will to Power a singular entity, as the phrase would suggest (and as Schopenhauer insisted). Moreover, "Power" refers not only to strength and power over others but, more importantly, to self-discipline, making it perhaps an unfortunate and misleading term.

Given his biological ("physiological") orientation, Nietzsche also talks about Will to Power in order to emphasize the importance of drives, instincts, and purposive but unthinking behavior, as Freud would after him. Nietzsche had a strong predilection for evolutionary explanations (although he rejected what he took to be the Darwinian notion of "fitness.") Nietzsche reminded us that we are still animals, part of nature, driven by impulses and instincts not of our choosing.

In his unpublished notes, Nietzsche says some pretty wild things about the Will to Power, for example, that it underlies *everything*. In his more sober publications, he uses the phrase mainly to suggest an under-appreciated motive of human behavior, one that we often refuse to acknowledge. But it diminishes its explanatory power if it is said to motivate *every* human action, and Nietzsche's best explanations work by contrasting and confronting Will to Power with other motives. True, Nietzsche comes to reject the hedonism assumed by the utilitarians (and which he himself defended in his earlier writings), and to express this turnabout the phrase "Will to Power" attracts our attention. But we should be cautious of giving it an exaggerated place in Nietzsche's philosophy.

Nietzsche is by no means consistent in his conception or his evaluation of the Will To Power. In his earlier writings he sometimes seems to be horrified by it. (In *Daybreak* he refers to it as "the demon of man.") In *Beyond Good and Evil* he occasionally seems to celebrate it, but most of the time, it is simply presented as psychological fact, without evaluation. The (reasonable) suggestion is that someone does something because he or she wants more power. But in *Beyond Good and Evil* he insists that "a living thing seeks above all to *discharge* its strength."[6] Elsewhere he insists that it is the *feeling* of power that we strive for, a very different claim than the desire for power as such. (Certain drugs and moods, with which Nietzsche was certainly familiar, evoke the feeling of power but in fact are quite enervating.) Nietzsche tells us, "What one did formerly 'for God's sake' one does now for the sake of money, which *now* gives the highest feeling of power."[7] Or is it that we now *believe* that money provides more power than faith? Of course the feeling of power is much more akin to the feeling of pleasure (and how could pleasure *not* be a feeling?). It thus more closely parallels the hedonistic–utilitarian position that Nietzsche rejects. But are the two in fact on a par? It would seem, even on Nietzsche's more modest hypotheses, that they are not.

What is most impressive are not Nietzsche's often intemperate statements about the Will to Power but his observational insights as to its workings in human motivation. In *The Gay Science*, for instance, he suggests that love may be an expression of the will to power: "Our love of neighbor – is it not a lust for new possessions?"[8] And speaking of pity and gratitude: "Benefiting and hurting others are ways of exercising one's power upon others; that is all one desires in such cases."[9] Thus the most obvious interpretation of the Will to Power is power over other people and power institutionalized as *Reich*. But Nietzsche speaks of "*Macht*," not "*Reich*," and this might be better understood as personal *strength* rather than political power or power over other people. Thus even ascetics manifest the Will to Power. "Indeed, happiness – taken as the most alive feeling of power – has perhaps nowhere on earth been greater than in the souls of superstitious ascetics."[10] Thus Will to Power means effective self-realization and expression, and this certainly better suits Nietzsche's aesthetic vision of life.

Thinking of Will to Power as self-mastery, including self-discipline, self-criticism, even self-denial, gives us a much better handle on Nietzsche's conception than the warrior metaphors that he often employs. But what it also means, which is not the same, is self-affirmation, and with it life-affirmation, which is the very opposite of the aggressive posture that Nietzsche seems to strike with "the Will to Power." I earlier suggested that "Will to Power" was a code phrase for Nietzsche's main theme, the love of life (contrasted with Schopenhauer's loveless Will to Live). But Nietzsche has much better phrases for summing up this, the central theme of his philosophy. Two of them are *"amor fati"* ("the love of fate") and "eternal recurrence," the endless repetition of one's life (a familiar theme in Eastern philosophy).

Nietzsche's *amor fati*, usually offered to us by way of an exclamation, can be understood in several different ways. But it is first of all an affirmation of one's life, of simply being alive, and accepting whatever it is that life has dealt one. It is easy enough (speaking *ad hominem* again) to appreciate how Nietzsche, fighting against his own sometimes excruciating ailments and Schopenhauer's pessimism besides, might struggle to maintain this acceptance of life, as opposed to falling into resentment (although no one doubts that Nietzsche often did so, fighting it all the way). For someone else, *amor fati* might suggest a free and easy "don't worry, be happy" attitude toward life. But for Nietzsche (and for many of us) the struggle is much more difficult.

Unlike most moral philosophers, who remain for the most part safely "above" the human soap opera that they both analyze and justify, Nietzsche is clearly a *moralist*. He moralizes. He scolds. He is as judgmental as any of the Old Testament prophets. And yet, it is not as if Nietzsche was oblivious to this tendency in himself, nor is it as if he simply accepted it. Like that "loafer of a moralist" he so roundly lampoons, Nietzsche too seems to always be saying, "No! Man ought to be different." Against this, he laments, "I do not want to wage war against what is ugly. I do not want to accuse; I do not want to accuse those who accuse. *Looking away* shall be my only negation."[11] It is doubtful that he ever succeeded in this. But even with regard to the philosopher who first and foremost insisted that the philosopher should be an example of his philosophy, we should read Nietzsche with a good deal of compassion.

Loving fate, according to what Nietzsche is insisting here, means accepting with equanimity and even enthusiasm whatever happens, whatever people do, and whatever happens to you: "One wants nothing to be different not forward, not backward, not in all eternity. Not merely bear what is necessary, . . . but *love* it"[12] This does not mean that we should sit back idly, like that loafer of a moralist, that we need not take responsibility for what is in our hands. But the affirmation of life, in this sense, is something that we can all quite readily understand, even if, like Nietzsche, it is an idea that is at times very difficult to swallow.

Embracing the idea of eternal recurrence – that the sequence of events recurs again and again and again – underscores Nietzsche's "affirmation of life." Being willing to endure one's life, with all of its pains as well as its pleasures, indicates a love of life.

Resentment, regret, and remorse, by contrast, suggest an unwillingness to live one's life again, exactly as it has been. There is a difference implied here between loving one's life because of its achievements and enjoyments and loving one's life for the sake of life itself. This is a theme that goes through Nietzsche's philosophy from its beginnings in Greek philology and tragedy to his last book, his quasi-autobiography *Ecce Homo*. Nietzsche asserts (with Schopenhauer and the Buddhists) that *Life is suffering*, but the proper response to this is not resentment or disengagement (as Schopenhauer proposed), nor is it redemption of any kind. It should be whole-hearted "Dionysian" acceptance.

Near the end of *The Gay Science*, Nietzsche gives us his best description of eternal recurrence:

> What if some day or night a demon were to steal after you into your loneliest loneliness and say to you: "This life as you now live it and have lived it, you will have to live once more and innumerable times more; and there will be nothing new in it, but every pain and every joy and every thought and sigh and everything unutterably small or great in your life will have to return to you, all in the same succession and sequence – even this spider and this moonlight between the trees, and even this moment and I myself. The eternal hourglass of existence is turned upside down again an again, and you with it, speck of dust!"
>
> Would you not throw yourself down and gnash your teeth and curse the demon who spoke thus? Or have you once experienced a tremendous moment when you would have answered him, "You are a god and never have I heard anything more divine." If this thought gained possession of you, it would change you as you are or perhaps crush you. The question in each and every thing, "Do you desire this once more and innumerable times more?" would lie upon your actions as the greatest weight. Or how well disposed would you have to become to yourself and to life *to crave nothing more fervently* than this ultimate confirmation and seal?[13]

The same proposition is repeated in *Zarathustra*: "*not* . . . a new life or a better life or a similar life" but "this same, selfsame life."[14] This phrase, "this same, selfsame life," can be interpreted in a variety of ways. It certainly seems to mean, *in every minute detail*. Indeed, we have all noticed, perhaps to our dismay, that changing even one small event in the past might have resulted in any number of dramatic alterations of the present. Indeed, if you had been born only five minutes earlier, so the argument goes, you would have been, in some significant sense, *a different person*. And so, needless to say, if you regret having gone to business school instead of pursuing your true love of literature, or you wish that you had never gotten married and had children so young, the sense of who you might be would be truly bewildering.

As presented, the eternal recurrence is not an archaic theory of time, but a psychological test: "How would you feel if . . . ?" To be sure, it is a model of time that has ancient and illustrious roots, back to the Indian Vedas and the pre-Hellenic Greeks, but there is little evidence that Nietzsche seriously intended to embrace the metaphysical systems of which this view of time is a part. The eternal recurrence is a thought experiment. Its significance lies not in the details but, rather, in the general affirmation of one's life. Maudemarie Clark gives a nice explanation of eternal recurrence: in a long marriage, would one be willing to do it again? In other words, was it worth it, all things considered? A few minor changes here or there would not affect your view. Rather, it is the whole of the marriage – the whole of your life for that considerable amount of time – that is in question. If you would gnash your teeth and curse the very suggestion, we would have to say that your married life has been a waste. If, on the other hand, you claim to have no regrets, all things considered, then that is what we would call a happy marriage. It is also what makes a happy life.

Naturalizing Spirituality: The Faith of an "Antichrist"

Because Nietzsche is so often considered an anti-Christian and so an anti-religious thinker, it is too readily assumed that he had no room in his thinking for spirituality. But is "the death of God" necessarily the death of spirituality? Or is the idea that spirituality is necessarily bound to Christianity (or Protestant Christianity) just another one of those "shadows of God" from which Nietzsche seeks to free us? Nietzsche is among the most spiritual of philosophers, and this is how he sometimes views himself. In order to understand this, however, we have to forego all tendencies to identify spirituality with unworldliness, or with submersion in one organized religion or another.

It is perhaps possible to get a good grasp of what Nietzsche understands by spirituality by considering that art which Nietzsche considered most uplifting, most in tune with the inner truth of things, and that is music. We are not speaking just metaphorically when we claim to have a spiritual experience listening to a great piece of music. Indeed, that is what spirituality is all about. It is neither selfless nor selfish – indeed, that contrast seems not to apply at all. This much Nietzsche retained from Schopenhauer's aesthetics. But Nietzsche vehemently rejected Schopenhauer's conclusion that aesthetic appreciation was ultimately "disinterested." On the contrary, nowhere else are we so thoroughly interested and engaged. That's what beauty is. Allowing ourselves to get "carried away" by a great piece of music also allows us to overcome our everyday conception of "self" and feel part of the cosmos – or at least a little part of it – but this is a cosmic enlargement of self, not an abandonment of it.

In other words, music is spiritual in that it is *Dionysian*, and it catches us up in a passion that is wholly unselfish (without therefore being self*less*), a passion ultimately called "life!" Nietzsche's naturalistic conception of spirituality thus embraces his main theme as well as his conception of Will to Power (insofar as Will to Power is construed as the passionate love of life) and being "faithful to the earth" (where this is not to be construed as something merely mundane). In his *The Gay Science*, Nietzsche thus describes an earthly happiness as powerful as any biblical image of heaven, and far more palpable:

> Anyone who manages to experience the history of humanity as a whole as *his own history* will feel in an enormously generalized way all the grief of an invalid who thinks of health. . . . But if one endured, if one could endure this immense sum of grief . . . if one could finally contain all this in one soul and crowd it into a single feeling – this would surely

have to result in a happiness that humanity has not known so far; the happiness of a god full of power and love, full of tears and laughter . . . [15]

Notes

1   Occasional passages have been adapted from *What Nietzsche Really Said*, which I co-authored with Kathleen M. Higgins, published in 2000 by Schocken Books and Knopf.
2   *BGE* I 6.
3   *D* 34.
4   Nietzsche, *On the Genealogy of Morals*, trans. W. Kaufmann. Random House (1967). All references to this work are parenthesized in the text; e.g., *GM* I 10 (book I, section 10).
5   Evidence from Nietzsche's library indicates that he read Mill at length and thoroughly, indicating agreement with many of his key ideas. I thank Thomas Brobjer of Uppsala University for this information.
6   *BGE* 13.
7   *D* 204.
8   *GS* 14, p. 88.
9   *GS* 13, p. 86.
10 *D* 113.
11 *GS* 276, p. 223.
12 *EH* II 10, p. 258.
13 *GS* 341, pp. 273–4; *KSA* 3, p. 570.
14 *TSZ* III 13, p. 333.
15 *GS* 337, pp. 268–9.

Bibliography

Original works by Nietzsche

The capital letters preceding some of the following titles are the abbreviations for them used in this chapter.

	The Birth of Tragedy, Out of the Spirit of Music*	1872
	Four Untimely Meditations	
	"David Strauss, the confessor and the writer"	1873
	"On the uses and disadvantage of history for life"	1874
	"Schopenhauer as educator"	1874
	"Richard Wagner in Bayreuth"	1876
	Human, All Too Human, A Book for Free Spirits	1878
	Human, All Too Human II (Assorted Opinions and Sayings)	1879
	The Wanderer and his Shadow	1880
D	*Daybreak, Thoughts on the Prejudices of Morality*	1881
GS	*The Gay Science*	1882
TSZ	*Thus Spake Zarathustra, A Book for All and None*	1883–5
BGE	*Beyond Good and Evil, Prelude to a Philosophy of the Future*	1886
GM	*On the Genealogy of Morals, A Polemic*	1887

The Case of Wagner, A Musician's Problem	1888
Twilight of the Idols Or, How One Philosophizes with a Hammer	1889
The Antichrist	1895†
Nietzsche contra Wagner, Out of the Files of a Psychologist	1895†
EH Ecce Homo, How One Becomes What One Is	1908†
The Will to Power	‡

*Title changed to *The Birth of Tragedy, Or: Hellenism and Pessimism* in the second edition, published in 1886.
†Publication date; written in 1888.
‡Edited by others and published posthumously.

Modern editions of Nietzsche's works

[1872]/[1888]: *The Birth of Tragedy/The Case of Wagner*, trans. W. Kaufmann. New York: Random House, 1966.

[1873–6]: *Untimely Meditations*, trans. R. J. Hollingdale. Cambridge: Cambridge University Press, 1983.

[1878–9]: *Human, All Too Human*, trans. R. J. Hollingdale. Cambridge: Cambridge University Press, 1986.

[1881]: *Daybreak: Thoughts on the Prejudices of Morality*, trans. R. J. Hollingdale. Cambridge: Cambridge University Press, 1982.

[1882]: *The Gay Science*, trans. W. Kaufmann. New York: Vintage, 1974.

[1886]: *Beyond Good and Evil*, trans. W. Kaufmann. New York: Random House, 1966.

[1887]: *On the Genealogy of Morals*, trans. W. Kaufmann and R. J. Hollingdale/[1908]: *Ecce Homo*, trans. W. Kaufmann. New York: Random House, 1967.

1954: *The Portable Nietzsche*, ed. W. Kaufmann. New York: Viking/Penguin.

1967: *The Will to Power*, trans. W. Kaufmann and R. J. Hollingdale. New York: Random House.

1969: *Selected Letters of Friedrich Nietzsche*, ed. and trans. C. Middleton. Chicago: University of Chicago Press.

Works about Nietzsche

Allison, D. B. (ed.) 1977: *The New Nietzsche: Contemporary Styles of Interpretation*. New York: Dell.

——2000: *Reading the New Nietzsche*. Lanham Md.: Rowman & Littlefield.

Chamberlain, L. 1996: *Nietzsche in Turin: An Intimate Biography*. New York: Picador.

Clark, M. 1990: *Nietzsche on Truth and Philosophy*. Cambridge: Cambridge University Press.

——1994: Nietzsche's misogyny. *International Studies in Philosophy*, 26(3), 3–12.

Danto, A. 1965: *Nietzsche as Philosopher*. New York: Macmillan.

Gillespie, M. A. and Strong, T. B. (eds.) 1988: *Nietzsche's New Seas: Explorations in Philosophy, Aesthetics, and Politics*. Chicago: University of Chicago Press.

Gilman, S. L. 1987: *Conversations with Nietzsche: A Life in the Words of His Contemporaries*, trans. D. J. Parent. New York: Oxford University Press.

Hayman, R. 1980: *Nietzsche: A Critical Life*. New York: Oxford University Press.

Higgins, K. M. 1986: *Nietzsche's Zarathustra*. Philadelphia: Temple University Press.

——2000: *Comic Relief: Nietzsche's Gay Science*. New York: Oxford University Press.

Kaufmann, W. 1968: *Nietzsche: Philosopher, Psychologist, Antichrist*, 3rd edn., rev. and enlarged. New York: Vintage.

Krell, D. F. and Bates, D. L. 1997: *The Good European: Nietzsche's Work Sites in Word and Image*. Chicago: University of Chicago Press.

Magnus, B. 1978: *Nietzsche's Existential Imperative*. Bloomington, Ind.: Indiana University Press.

——and Higgins, K. M. 1996: *The Cambridge Companion to Nietzsche*. New York: Cambridge University Press.

Nehamas, A. 1985: *Nietzsche: Life as Literature*. Cambridge, Mass.: Harvard University Press.

Parkes, G. 1994: *Composing the Soul*. Chicago, Ill.: University of Chicago Press.

Schacht, R. 1983: *Nietzsche*. London: Routledge and Kegan Paul.

——1994: *Nietzsche, Genealogy, Morality: Essays on Nietzsche's* On The Genealogy of Morals. Berkeley, Calif.: University of California Press.

Solomon, R. (ed.) 1980: *Nietzsche: A Collection of Critical Essays*. Notre Dame, Ind.: University of Notre Dame Press.

——and Higgins, K. M. (eds.) 1988: *Reading Nietzsche*. New York: Oxford University Press.

Young, J. 1992: *Nietzsche's Philosophy of Art*. Cambridge: Cambridge University Press.

Chapter 6

Edmund Husserl and Phenomenology[1]

Sean D. Kelly

Introduction

Phenomenology is a movement in French and German philosophy that flourished during the first half of the twentieth century (roughly 1900–50). It continues to be practiced in modified form today both in the United States and elsewhere. Phenomenology provides a foothold into philosophical problems of various sorts – from problems in philosophical logic, ontology, and metaphysics to problems about the nature of mind and the content of perception. But to a first approximation at least, phenomenology takes its start in the fundamental problem of describing accurately and completely the essential features of our everyday lived experience.

Phenomenology stands at the foundation of a wide range of twentieth-century philosophy as it was practiced on the European Continent. European philosophers as diverse as Derrida, Habermas, Foucault, Gadamer, Levinas, de Beauvoir, Marcel, and Sartre all worked, at some point in their careers, either within or in relation to the phenomenological tradition. But perhaps the three most important and influential phenomenologists, the philosophers who did most to define and develop the method and substance of phenomenology, were Edmund Husserl (1859–1938), Martin Heidegger (1889–1976), and Maurice Merleau-Ponty (1908–61).

Phenomenology is often contrasted with the form of philosophy generally practiced in English-speaking parts of the world in the twentieth century. This contrast is neither very informative nor very accurate. It is true that Anglo-American philosophers such as Russell, Ayer, C. I. Lewis, Strawson, Evans, and Davidson were not influenced by – nor in many cases even familiar with – work in the phenomenological tradition. Nevertheless, the founding concerns of phenomenology are less alien to those of the Anglo-American tradition than the typical caricature would suggest. It is no concern of the present essay to defend this claim, but its truth should become apparent to those in a position to judge.

What, then, is the concern of the present essay? I cannot hope, within the constraints of the essay form, to give a full discussion of even the major contributors to the phenomenological tradition. In place of completeness, however, I offer unity. The goal of this essay is to begin an interpretation of the phenomenological tradition that identifies both the founding contribution that Husserl made to it and the way in which this contribution was appropriated, refined, and finally in some ways rejected by his successors.

I say I will begin the interpretation; what I have to offer is incomplete in at least three respects. First, I do not discuss Heidegger's important contribution to phenomenology in any substantive way at all. The interpretation has a place for Heidegger's contribution, and indeed it has been strongly influenced by the way I see Heidegger's role in the phenomenological tradition. But the story I tell here will focus almost exclusively on the work of Husserl and Merleau-Ponty.

Second, in presenting the work of Husserl and Merleau-Ponty, I will not attempt to do justice to its development over time. This certainly goes against the main tendency of the secondary literature. Commentators, for instance, often identify three distinct periods in Husserl's phenomenological work, and it is common to differentiate between at least an early and a late Merleau-Ponty. In contrast, I will emphasize a unified strain of thought that I believe characterizes the general outlook of each of these philosophers over the course of their careers. No doubt there are particular passages from various periods that go against features of this general interpretation, but I will not attempt to defend it against them here.

Finally, a more comprehensive interpretation of the phenomenological tradition would attempt to place it in the larger context of twentieth-century philosophical work. In particular, it would discuss in some detail the relation between the concerns of the phenomenologists and those of the early twentieth-century Anglo-American philosophers. There is much to be gained from such a discussion, but it goes beyond the scope of my present ambition.

There is an important sense, then, in which my project is stiffly constrained. Despite its apparent modesty, however, I believe it is a real achievement to give even the start of a unified interpretation to the phenomenological tradition. Indeed, it is an achievement that the figures within the tradition notoriously failed to attain. Heidegger's efforts to distance himself philosophically from his mentor Husserl, for instance, are well documented. Their only attempt to work together – in producing an article on "Phenomenology" for the *Encyclopaedia Britannica* in 1928 – ended in a rupture that lasted the remainder of Husserl's life.[2] And although Merleau-Ponty, in contrast, attempted to align himself strictly with the work of Husserl, this effort provides one of the more notable failures in his corpus.[3] Nevertheless, it is not by chance that it was Husserl in relation to whom Heidegger and Merleau-Ponty chose to work. What advance Husserl made over his predecessors, then, is one of the guiding questions for this essay. What advance his successors made over him, of course, is the other.

The substance of phenomenology

I have said already that phenomenology takes its start in the fundamental problem of describing accurately and completely the essential features of everyday lived experience. By "everyday lived experience" I mean the kind of active, engaged experience we have of the world throughout the course of our everyday lives: hearing the toll of a campus bell, seeing the smile of a friendly face, grasping a coffee mug by the handle and bringing it to one's mouth to sip. These experiences present the world to us; they do not – at least not in the first instance – present our experience of it. By the "essential features" of everyday lived experience I mean those features that are necessary and sufficient for them to be experiences, and in particular for them to be the very experiences that they are. Phenomenology's most basic premise is that it is more difficult to capture the essence of everyday lived experience completely and accurately than one might have thought.

William James, a contemporary of Husserl's whom he admired very much, characterized this difficulty well.[4] James considered the example of hearing a bell toll. It sometimes happens, he said, that we realize all of a sudden both that the bell has been ringing for some time and that we've been counting the rings. Perhaps when this realization dawns on us we've already counted the first four rings and are in the process of counting the fifth. James then asked the difficult question: In what sense were we aware of the first four rings? What, in other words, were the essential features of our experience of them?

The question is difficult because the two obvious possibilities – full conscious awareness and complete unawareness – are ruled out of court. We can't say that we were aware of the first four rings in the same way as we were aware, fully consciously, of the fifth; for if we did there would be no substance to the sudden realization that distinguished the one from the others. But we can't say that we were completely unaware of the first four rings either, for otherwise we wouldn't have been able to keep track of them as distinct entities in a series. Counting is precisely the kind of conscious activity that seems to require awareness of entities as such. To account for the details of this experience, then, we need a new category that lies somewhere between full conscious awareness and complete lack of awareness. But how to characterize this kind of dim awareness is not immediately clear. Husserl thought that the experiences of everyday life are replete with various kinds of dim awareness of this sort, and that it is the most basic task of phenomenology to characterize them.

Husserl came upon this project in a roundabout way. A mathematician by training,[5] his first work in philosophy focused on the philosophy of arithmetic.[6] After a critical review of this work by Gottlob Frege,[7] however, in 1894, Husserl turned his attention more generally to foundational problems in philosophical logic. His goal was to develop a philosophical approach to logic that not only accounted properly for the formal relations allowable between propositions, but also for the content found within them.[8]

In order to get "philosophically clear"[9] about the contents of propositions, Husserl believed, one must think about the mental states that typically invoke them. In the first place, these are linguistic utterances. So Husserl began his phenomenological inquiry by asking how linguistic utterances come to be the kinds of *intentional* structures that they are; how they come to be, in other words, mental states that are characteristically of, about, or directed toward objects and states of affairs in the world.

The key to answering this question, according to Husserl, lies in an analysis of the experiences that, in the most basic cases, make our linguistic utterances about the world possible. This analysis reveals two important facts. In the first place, everyday experiences, like the linguistic utterances they make possible, are intentional: we hear *the toll of the campus bell*, we see *the smile of a friendly face*, we grasp *the coffee mug by the handle*. Of course we can sometimes have episodes of conscious awareness – like hallucinations or dreams, for instance – that aren't directed toward actually existing objects. Perhaps we can even imagine a free play of conscious awareness – a manifold sensation of color, shape, and texture, for instance, without any awareness of these *as* the things they are. But perception is in the most basic cases directed toward objects and properties *as such*, and these other non-intentional cases are the exception instead of the norm.

The second important fact about experiences, according to Husserl, is that they always reveal their object from a perspective. This perspectivism is natural for bodily perceivers like us who are restricted to spatiotemporal points of view on the world, although of course it would not apply to omniscient knowers who are capable of taking a so-called "view from nowhere." That we are not such omniscient knowers is a phenomenological insight that bears much fruit.

When we combine the perspectivism of experience with its intentionality, we come upon a phenomenologically fascinating problem. For although experience can only reveal its object from a perspective, it is the full three-dimensional object toward which we are intentionally directed when we have an experience of it. To capture this fact Husserl says that objects are presented in experience as transcending – or "going beyond" – the experience we have of them. But how can experience be essentially perspectival and at the same time present objects to us as transcending the perspective that we have on them? Phenomenology's founding problem is to account for this possibility.

Husserl's understanding of intentionality in terms of transcendence, and especially his understanding of transcendence in the context of perception, was a crucial breakthrough peculiar to phenomenology. Both Heidegger and Merleau-Ponty took their start from the basic orientation that it provided. To characterize the breakthrough in Heideggerean terms, we can say that Husserl had learned to ask (though not necessarily to answer) the question of the being of entities.[10] He had learned, in other words, to puzzle over the way in which entities are present to us in our experience of them. His was the first move beyond the blind Cartesian dogma that objects, even in our experience of them, can be no more than extended things.[11]

If Husserl's characterization of objects was a revelation, however, his understanding of intentional states generally, and of experiences in particular, was hampered by a much more traditional commitment. Intentional states, according to Husserl, are immanent instead of transcendent. In other words, instead of going beyond what we experience of them, our experiences, when we reflect upon them, are present to us all at once in their entirety.[12] The immanence of intentional states, according to Husserl, stands in stark contrast with the transcendence of the objects toward which they are directed.

Both Heidegger and Merleau-Ponty reject Husserl's claim that intentional states are immanent in this sense. In Heidegger's language, Husserl's commitment to this idea reflects his inability to ask the question of the being of intentional consciousness.[13] In other words, it reflects his inability to puzzle over the way in which experiences themselves are presented to us. By simply assuming that experiences are presented to us[14] all at once in their entirety, Husserl leaves out the possibility that we could discover facts about an experience that we weren't aware of explicitly when we were in the midst of it. He leaves out the Jamesian possibility, for instance, that there was more to our experience of the first four rings of the bell than what we noticed about it at the time. And perhaps there are other kinds of experience that are ruled out as well.

Merleau-Ponty, indeed, thought that many genuine phenomenological features of experience are excluded if we accept Husserl's assumption that intentional states are immanent. He pursued his work on this topic from an interdisciplinary perspective, both as Professor of Child Psychology at the Sorbonne and later as Chair in Philosophy at the Collége de France. This interdisciplinary perspective gave him a wide array of physiological, psychophysical, phenomenological, and philosophical data on the basis of which to evaluate Husserl's claim. In the end, though, Merleau-Ponty based his rejection of the immanence of intentional states largely on his analysis of the phenomenology of unreflective bodily experiences such as grasping and other skilled visuo-motor activities.[15] As we will see, he argued that these kinds of bodily activity represent the world in a way that goes beyond what we can capture of them upon reflection. This is so, according to Merleau-Ponty, because the way of representing the world that is manifest in our bodily activity depends intimately upon the situation in which that activity occurs. Once we step out of that situation to reflect upon the activity itself, we change the content of the representation that was manifest in it.

Merleau-Ponty rejects, therefore, the Husserlian principle that intentional states are immanent, because it leads to descriptively inaccurate claims about the nature of bodily experience. Nevertheless, Merleau-Ponty's rejection of this Husserlian thesis takes place against the background of the phenomenological advances that Husserl made over those who came before him. In the sections that follow, I will attempt to defend this claim in greater detail.

Husserl

Husserl's phenomenological account of intentionality is based on, but supersedes, the work of two influential predecessors. From the account of perception developed by the British empiricists, Husserl takes two ideas. The first is that perception is, in some sense, the most fundamental, and therefore the paradigmatic, mental state. The second is that perception is in essence perspectival. From his teacher Franz Brentano, on the other hand, Husserl inherits the idea that mental states in general are characterized by their intentionality. Combining these two views, Husserl attempts to develop a phenomenological account of intentionality that takes perception (rather than belief or judgment[16]) as the paradigmatic intentional state.

As we have seen, the central feature of Husserl's account is that objects are experienced as transcending the intentional states directed toward them. In this lies the principal advance of Husserl's theory. First, it encourages him to emphasize (against the empiricists) that perceptions are more than mere perspectival images of their objects. Second, it encourages him to emphasize (against Brentano) that intentional states nevertheless present their objects from a perspective. The goal of this section is first to characterize these advances, and then to show how Husserl's commitment to the immanence of intentional states constrains his phenomenological account of them.

Perception as the paradigmatic intentional state for Husserl

Husserl believes that experiences make it possible for our thoughts to be about the world. He inherits this belief from the empiricist tradition of Locke, Berkeley, and Hume.[17] In particular, Husserl believes both that experience is the "ultimate source" of thought, and that the perception of physical things is the paradigmatic kind of experience. That experience plays such a crucial role in the development of Husserl's phenomenology is not often stressed.[18] It is nevertheless, I believe, the key to understanding Husserl's central contributions.

Husserl focuses on perception because he believes, as he says in *Ideas I*, that perception is that "primal experience from which all other experiencing acts derive a major part of their grounding force,"[19] and because he believes experience generally conceived is the "ultimate source"[20] of intentional life. Further, he focuses on the perception of spatiotemporal objects in particular because he believes that "it is sufficient to treat perception of the physical thing as the representative of all other perceptions (of qualities, processes, and the like)."[21] These concerns with perception, and in particular with the perception of spatiotemporal objects, are apparent from the beginning of Husserl's phenomenological work.

It is commonly agreed that at the end of his career Husserl emphasizes the grounding role that perception plays in intentionality. For instance, in *Experience and Judgment*, an unfinished text from the last period of his life, Husserl claims that one of the central goals of phenomenology is to characterize the relation between judgments and the underlying "pre-linguistic" experiences that make them possible.[22] Likewise, the passages quoted in the paragraph above show that in *Ideas I*, the canonical middle-period text published in 1913, Husserl considers experience, and indeed the perception of spatiotemporal objects, to be a central concern. But it is interesting to notice that already in 1901, in the *Logical Investigations*, Husserl clearly states his belief in the importance of experience to the possibility of intentional life. He writes there:

> If we imagine a consciousness prior to all experience, it may very well have the same *sensations* as we have. But it will intuit no things, and no events pertaining to things, it will perceive no trees and no houses, no flight of birds nor any barking of dogs.[23]

In short, without experience our mental states are not directed toward objects in the world.

Furthermore, it is clear that the perception of physical objects in particular is central to Husserl's understanding of intentional objects generally. This is true even at the time of Husserl's early phenomenological work between the *Logical*

Investigations and the *Thing and Space* lectures of 1907. As we will see, the perception of physical objects provides a paradigmatic model for Husserl in his development of the idea that intentional states are directed toward objects that are transcendent to them. This notion of transcendence is central to Husserl's account of intentionality, and it is a feature of intentionality that is clearest in the perceptual case. Although I will not be able to discuss it much here, I believe that this makes Husserl's treatment of the problems of intentionality importantly different from the treatment that they are typically given by Anglo-American philosophers working in the tradition of Frege, a tradition that famously emphasizes the methodological priority of language over experience.

Husserl's argument against the empiricist image theory of perception

The empiricists believed, like Husserl, that perception is perspectival (using the word very generally for the time being). Something like this idea is already pre-figured in the work of the Rennaissance painters on the laws of perspective. Indeed, the empiricist image theory of perceptual representation builds on the work of the Rennaissance painters, since it is based on the idea that what we directly perceive is internal, perspectivally rendered *images* of objects. Perception is intentionally directed toward physical objects in the world, according to this view, in virtue of the similarity that obtains between the internal image and the physical thing it's an image of.[24] As Bishop Berkeley's character Philonous puts the point, aping the position of his antagonist Hylas in the *Three Dialogues*:

> It seems then, you will have our ideas, which alone are immediately perceived, to be pictures of external things: and that these also are perceived by sense, inasmuch as they have a conformity or resemblance to our ideas.[25]

The empiricist idea that we immediately perceive pictures or images, instead of full three-dimensional objects, emphasizes the perspectival nature of perception.

Husserl emphasizes his version of the perspectival nature of perception in the following passage from the Sixth Logical Investigation. In perception, he says,

> The object is not actually given, it is not given wholly and entirely as that which it itself is. It is only given "from the front," only "perspectivally foreshortened and projected," etc. . . . [T]he elements of the invisible rear side, the interior, and so on, . . . are not themselves part of the intuitive . . . content of the percept.[26]

Husserl goes beyond the empiricist theory, however, when he insists that the experience of an object is not properly characterized as the mere experience of a perspectival image of it. There is a distinction, Husserl insists, between the presentation of a visible side of an object, which is what the empiricist offers, and the presentation of the object from a side, which is what we get in genuine perception. As Husserl says in the Fifth Logical Investigation, it is an essential feature of perception that it enables us to go beyond the "image" which alone [according to the empiricists] is present in consciousness, and to relate to it *as* an image to a certain extraconscious object. . . . [R]elation to its [transcendent] object is part and parcel of the phenomenological essence of consciousness.[27]

Perhaps an example will make this claim clear. Suppose I see something that I take to be a coffee mug. Necessarily, I see it from some point of view. But that doesn't mean that my perception of what I take to be a coffee mug is the same as my perception of what I take to be the relevant coffee mug façade. It is not. It is true, of course, *ex hypothesi*, that the very same pattern of colors is projected onto my retina in both cases; for the empiricist the very same image is perceived. Nevertheless, in the first case I experience much more than a mere façade. I see *a coffee mug* presented from one perspective, and I see it as something that transcends the perspective I have on it. I see it as a full-fledged three-dimensional object – in other words, a thing that has various sides not now visible to me, and whose various hidden sides each have their own colors, shapes, sizes, textures, and so on. This is part of experiencing something as a coffee mug, and it distinguishes that from experiencing it as a coffee mug façade.

This phenomenological distinction, Husserl argues, is something that the empiricists cannot account for. As a result, their image theory of perception is wrong. The argument for this claim reappears later in Merleau-Ponty, but Husserl had the gist of it.[28] It goes like this: In order to account for my experiencing something as a coffee mug, the empiricist would have to argue that the image projected by the object I'm experiencing resembles a coffee mug more than it does a coffee mug façade. Since the mug and the mug façade present exactly the same image, however, it cannot by itself resemble either object more than the other; it is the image of both equally. For the empiricist, therefore, there can be no distinction between experiencing something as a coffee mug and experiencing it as a coffee mug façade. Since by hypothesis there is a distinction between these experiences, the image theory of perception is wrong.[29]

Husserl's improvement over the empiricists is to insist that we don't get raw, uninterpreted images in consciousness, but data that are already interpreted as images *of some object or another*.[30] In order to characterize this distinction, Husserl says that in perception we are presented not with mere images of the visible side of an object, but with adumbrations (*Abschattungen*) of the object itself. The adumbration of the object that is presented in perception is the visible side *interpreted as* a side of the transcendent object that goes beyond it. We will see later what this interpretation consists in for Husserl. What's important for the moment is to notice that the motivation for this view is Husserl's desire to account for the phenomenological fact that normal perception is intentionally directed toward objects rather than just toward perspectivally rendered images of them.

Husserl's advance over Brentano

Husserl's phenomenological account of intentionality represents an advance over Brentano as well. Brentano believed, like Husserl, that mental states are intentionally directed toward objects.[31] Indeed, for Brentano, intentionality – direct-edness toward an object – is the defining feature of the mental. In order to make sense of the possibility of intentionality, however, Brentano employed the medieval doctrine of mental in-existence – the doctrine that every mental state contains its object completely within itself.[32] In other words, the intentional object is immanent to the mental state.

A major motivation for this account of intentionality – as Brentano later makes clear – is that the object that the thought is about need not exist in reality for the thought to be intentionally directed toward an object. For instance, suppose I deny the existence of a certain golden mountain, and suppose that this denial is justified – no such mountain exists. Nevertheless, my thought has an intentional object – if it didn't, it wouldn't be a thought at all. The intentional object must therefore not be an object in the physical world. As Brentano puts it:

> If someone thinks of something, the one who is thinking must certainly exist, but the object of his thinking [i.e., what the thinker has as his object] need not exist at all. In fact, if he is denying something, the existence of the object is precisely what is excluded whenever his denial is correct. So the only thing which is required by mental reference is the person thinking. The terminus of the so-called relation does not need to exist *in reality* at all.[33]

Although the terminus of the relation need not exist *in reality*, however, it must have some kind of existence, according to Brentano, or else the mental state will not be directed toward anything; that is, it will not be a mental state. Brentano's sugges-tion, therefore, is that the intentional object exists immanently within the mental state directed toward it.

This said, Husserl's advance over Brentano should be clear. Although Brentano insists, like Husserl, that mental states are intentionally directed toward their objects, he has no room for the distinction between the extramental object presented and the perspectival presentation of it in experience.[34] If intentional objects are immanent to mental states – presented to them completely and all at once – then they cannot also go beyond what is presented in the mental states.[35] If Brentano's conception of inten-tionality were applied to the perceptual case, it would have the effect that we expe-rience something like a cubist presentation of all sides of the object simultaneously. Clearly this is not a phenomenologically adequate account of experience. As Husserl says,

> A three-dimensional intuition . . . one that would bring to presentation all at once the full content of the thing in each of its constitutive parts and moments, outer and inner, front and back, is impossible.[36]

This impossibility is what Brentano is incapable of accounting for. His linguistically focused motivation may be what misleads him in this regard.[37]

The empiricists and Brentano, therefore, make complementary mistakes. The empiricists fail to notice that objects, rather than visible sides of objects, are presented in experience. Since images are nothing more than perspectival renderings of the visible sides of an object, and since there is no way to account for the possibility that these renderings should actually be directed toward *the physical object* that exists outside the mind, the empiricist image theory of perception is incapable of accounting for intentionality at all (with respect to physical objects). Brentano's weakness is the complementary one. Although he saw the directedness of mental states as their defining feature, he failed to notice that perception does not grasp its object as a whole and all at once, but always comes at it from one side or another. His doctrine of the mental in-existence of objects is by definition a rejection of the extramental transcendence of objects to intentional states. In a word, then, the empiricists couldn't make sense of the idea that it is *objects* we're directed toward, while Brentano couldn't make sense of the idea that the extramental objects that we're directed toward *transcend our experience of them.* The great advance of Husserl's phenomenology is that it is predicated on making sense of both of these ideas at once.

On the immanence of intentional states

Husserl's distinction between the presentation of an object and the object presented, we have seen, is a central feature of the phenomenology of perception. Since neither the empiricist account of perception nor Brentano's account of intentionality preserves this distinction, the question naturally arises, "What account of our mental states can make sense of the fact that objects are presented to us as going beyond our experience of them?" In the next section I will examine Husserl's answer to this question. In this section, however, I will discuss Husserl's idea that intentional states are themselves immanent instead of transcendent. Husserl's commitment to this idea ultimately constrains the answer he can give to the question of object transcendence.

Although the idea that objects transcend intentional states is an important breakthrough for Husserl, the idea that mental states are themselves immanent is much more traditional. In Husserl's mature work this idea supports four related features of an intentional state: the indubitability of its existence, the incorrigibility of the subject's knowledge of its qualities, its metaphysically basic nature, and its structure as an essence.[38] Only the first two of these will be important here.

Both Descartes and the empiricists agreed that our knowledge of our own mental states is indubitable. Although I can doubt whether the thing that my thought is about exists, they believed, I cannot doubt whether the thought about it does. This kind of indubitability, Husserl also believes, is one of the defining features of our mental states. His view on this issue is perhaps most clearly expressed in *Ideas I.* Suppose I find, in reflecting upon it, that I now take myself to be perceiving a table. "It would be a countersense," Husserl claims, "to believe it possible that a mental process *given in that manner* does *not* in truth exist."[39]

More than that, however, the qualities I take the experience to have, in reflecting upon it, are certain to characterize the experience as it really is. My knowledge of them, in other words, is incorrigible.[40] This is perhaps the most important aspect of Husserl's claim that intentional states, and especially perceptions, are immanent. Because they do not present themselves perspectivally, as physical objects do, there is nothing to any given perception beyond what I see in it:

Everything which we have worked out about the givenness of the physical thing loses
its sense here, and one must make that fully clear to oneself in detail. A mental process
. . . is not adumbrated. If I look at it, I have something absolute; it has no sides that
could be presented sometimes in one mode and sometimes in another. . . . [W]hat I see
when I look at it is there, with its qualities, its intensity, etc., absolutely.[41]

In this way all intentional states are, for Husserl, a bit like qualia, at least as they are
understood by some recent writers in contemporary philosophy of mind: *if* I take
them to exist they do, and *as* I take them to be they are. The interesting thing about
qualia, however, is that they are not typically taken by themselves to have intentional
features. This is because there is something uncomfortable about the combination
of intentionality and incorrigibility, and, as we will see, Husserl's blind commitment
to the latter directs and in some ways invalidates his treatment of the former.

    Many criticisms of Husserl have focused on his commitment to the immanence of
intentional states, or on features of his phenomenology that arise out of it. It is this
principle, for instance, that leads to Husserl's famous, and famously controversial,
transcendental reduction. The transcendental reduction proceeds by "bracketing existence," that is to say, by looking at the features of our pure mental states independent of the things in the world toward which they are intentionally directed. Such a
procedure makes sense only on the assumption that intentional states form a purely
independent realm, an assumption that is justified by the claim of immanence.[42] Eventually, the claim of immanence leads Husserl to argue for the ontological priority of
transcendental subjectivity, and indeed for a kind of transcendental idealism. In my
discussion of Merleau-Ponty I will say more about criticisms that focus on this aspect
of Husserl's work.

    The central point that I wish to emphasize here, however, is that Husserl's com-
mitment to the immanence of perceptual states – and especially to the incorrigibility of the subject's knowledge about them – strongly constrains any account he can
give of how perceptual states represent their objects as transcending them. For if a
subject's knowledge about his perception is incorrigible, then there cannot be any
further question about the features he takes its object to have. Those features, in
other words, cannot but be presented to him as completely determined. Husserl's
trick, as we will see, is to allow for the possibility that the subject sees an object to
have a certain determinate *kind* of feature without now being presented with the
determinate feature itself. But every aspect of a subject's perception, according to
Husserl, must be either a determinate presentation or the kind of thing that could
later become a determinate presentation. As we will see in the Merleau-Ponty section,
this is a metaphysical constraint that is not justified by the phenomenological facts.

Husserl's answer to the question how intentional states can refer beyond themselves

What account of our mental states does Husserl give, then, that explains the phenomenological fact that objects are presented to us as going beyond our experience
of them? The central feature of Husserl's account is that the raw data of sensation

(what Husserl calls the "hylé") are not experienced as such in their raw, uninterpreted state. Rather, they are always *interpreted as* data that present some object or other. Further, the object they are interpreted as presenting is, in my perception of it *as that object*, understood to have features that are not presented determinately by the hylé themselves. In this section I will attempt to clarify just what form this interpreted presentation takes.

The hylé, under a given interpretation of them, are central to what Husserl comes to call, by the time of his middle-period works, a noema (or more particularly, a noematic *Sinn*).[43] Versions of the noema, though not under that name, can be found as early as the *Logical Investigations*. One basic job of the noema is to categorize the hylé as falling under a concept, or fitting, as Husserl says, into some conceptual "frame."[44] The outline of the idea is essentially Kantian. For instance, if I intend the object as a coffee mug, then the hylé for the front side of the coffee mug are interpreted as fitting into the conceptual frame for coffee mug. The frame for a coffee mug says what a typical mug is like: it has a front side and a back side, each of which has a color, a shape, a size, a texture, and so on. Further, it may say things about holding coffee, being made of ceramic, and having a handle – in general, it lists all the features of the prototypical mug. Think of the frame as a list of feature-slots that any given coffee mug is assumed to fill in some determinate way. The hylé, then, fill in some of these slots. They fill in, for instance, the slots for the color, shape, size, and texture of the front side of the mug. These features of the object, when they are presented in good light at the right distance (and so on), are "determinate" in my experience of them.

But not every feature of an object is clearly and determinately presented to me in every experience. Accordingly, there are some feature slots that are incompletely filled or, as Husserl says, "indeterminate":

> If I see a house in sunlight, when the air is clear, then the color of the side turned toward me appears in its determinateness. If I see the house in the dark or in fog, then its color appears more or less indeterminately.[45]

At the extreme, there are features of the house that I know it has, but for which I have no sensuous presentation at all. For instance, the slots for the color, shape, size, and texture of the back side of the mug are completely unfilled. Since I see the thing to be a house, I see it as having a back side that has a determinate color, shape, size, and texture. But how these features are manifested in this particular mug is indeterminate in my current experience of it. For this reason, Husserl insists that

> Indeterminateness is never absolute or complete. Complete indeterminateness is nonsense; the indeterminateness is always delimited in this or that way. I may not know exactly what sort of form the back side has, yet it precisely has some form; the body is a body. I may not know how matters stand with the color, the roughness or smoothness, the warmth or coldness, yet it pertains to the very sense of the apprehension of a thing that the thing possess a certain color, a certain surface determination, etc.[46]

For Husserl, then, there are, at the extreme, two very different kinds of features that make up my experience of an object: there are the features that are determinately presented by the hylé – like the features of the front side of the mug – and there are the features that I *take* the object to have in virtue of having interpreted it as some particular object, but which are not themselves *presented* to me at all – like the features of the back side of the mug. Husserl calls these features, respectively, the proper and improper features of the perceived object, or sometimes the full and empty intentions of it. It is important to emphasize that the improper features of the object in my experience of it are in no way presented to me. As Husserl says in *Thing and Space*:

> The clear result of these considerations is therefore that improperly appearing moments of the object are in no way presented. *Perception* is, as I also express it, a complex of full and empty intentions . . . The full intentions . . . are the properly presentational ones; the empty are precisely empty of any presentational material.[47]

Although the improper features of the object are in no way presented to me, however, they are nevertheless an essential part of my experience of the thing *as an object*. To emphasize this, Husserl sometimes says that the improper features are co-apprehended, as opposed to presented sensibly. By "co-apprehended," here, he means something like "seen in virtue of the interpretation given, but not in virtue of any sensible presence":

> The improperly appearing objective determinations are co-apprehended, but they are not "sensibilized," not presented through what is sensible, i.e., through the material of sensation. It is evident [however] that they are co-apprehended, for otherwise we would have no objects at all before our eyes, not even a side, since this can indeed be a side only through the object.[48]

The improper features of the perceived object, therefore, are what account for the possibility that I can see the object as transcending my experience of it. In taking the hylé to represent an object of a particular sort, I see the object as having features that are not now determinately presented to me. These improper features of the experienced object are, as Husserl says, indeterminate in my experience of it.

But having said this, a question arises immediately. In light of the immanence of mental states, as we discussed it in the last section, we might ask how it is possible for there to be "indeterminate" features of experience. Recall that to say that perception is immanent is to say, at least in part, that my knowledge of the features of my perceptual state is incorrigible – there cannot be anything in the state that I do not have certain and complete knowledge of. But it seems, at least on the face of it, that there is a tension between an object's presenting itself indeterminately to experience, and the experience itself being available to me completely and with certainty. For example, suppose my experience of the color of my coffee mug is indeterminate because a thick fog surrounds the mug. Naturally I may not be able to say, in this circumstance, what the color of the mug is. But it may be that in addition the experience itself is so foreign and unrecognizable that I cannot say what it is like either. Perhaps the problem is exacerbated when I try to think of how to characterize the experience I have of the even more indeterminate back side of the mug. At any rate, once we have insisted, as Husserl does, that I have an experience of the back side, it seems less clear that the features of my experience are all available to me completely and with certainty.

Whether it is possible for there to be "indeterminate" features of experience in this sense depends, not surprisingly, on what the meaning of "indeterminate" is. Husserl's commitment to the incorrigibility of my knowledge of my mental states forces him to understand the indeterminate features of experience in a very special way. To say that the improper features of the perceived object are indeterminate, for Husserl, is to say that they are, to coin a phrase, *hypothesized but sensibly absent* in my current experience of the object. They are *hypothesized* in the following sense. It is in virtue of my having *interpreted* the hylé as of a certain kind of object – as having hypothesized, for instance, that the object is a mug – that my experience represents its object as the kind that has a handle on it. Assuming I don't see the handle on the front side of the mug, the experience will represent its object as a mug that has a handle on the back. But this improper feature of the mug is *sensibly absent*. That means that the feature slot for the handle in my concept of the object is unfilled. In short, I experience the mug determinately as having some handle, but the experience of that feature is indeterminate in the sense that it prefers no one handle over any other. As Husserl puts the point:

> [I]n the case of an appearing physical thing-Object, it would again fall in the bounds of the description to say: a "front side" is thus and so *determined* with respect to color, shape, etc., its "rear side" has "a color" but a "not further determined' one; the appearing physical thing-Object is, in these and those respects, altogether "*undetermined*" as to whether it is thus or so.[49]

By "indeterminate," therefore, Husserl means something like "hypothesized by, but not yet determined sensuously in, the experience." This is the trick, then. In order to intend the object as going beyond the hylé I'm now presented with, the noema interprets these sense data as being directed toward some object that I know has specific kinds of further properties that have not been explicitly determined yet in my experience of it. The indeterminate features in my experience of the object, according to Husserl, are not indeterminate in any substantive metaphysical sense; they are not the kind of thing that in their nature resist a complete and determinate characterization.[50] Rather, the indeterminate features in my experience of the object are just those that I take the object to have, but that I have not yet had any determinate sensuous presentation of. These kinds of features pose no problem at all for the incorrigibility thesis, since they are just the kinds of features that I could attribute completely and with certainty to my experience.

Husserl is forced by his commitment to the immanence of mental states, therefore, to understand the indeterminate features in my experience of an object in a certain way: namely, to understand them as hypothesized but sensuously absent. The phenomenological question is whether this characterization is correct; whether there is phenomenological evidence, in other words, for the claim that the indeterminate features of my experience of an object are not presented to me in any way at all. Merleau-Ponty claims that the phenomenological evidence points rather in the direction of a positive presentation of the indeterminate. And it is a central project of his *Phenomenology of Perception*, as he says right at the beginning of that book, to recognize the indeterminate as a positive phenomenon. The role of the body in presenting objects to us, and in particular the role of the strange category that Merleau-Ponty calls "motor or bodily intentionality," is essential, as we shall see, to the completion of this project.

Merleau-Ponty

Merleau-Ponty gets from Husserl both the idea that we perceive objects as transcending what we determinately see about them, and also the idea that the project of phenomenology is to describe the details of this experience. He moves beyond Husserl, however, in his characterization of the features we experience as indeterminate. For Merleau-Ponty, the essentially bodily motor-intentional relation to an object gives our experience some of its essentially indeterminate features. This focus on the role of the body in perception makes Merleau-Ponty's account of object transcendence importantly different from the one proposed by Husserl. It also opens up the anti-Husserlian possibility, which Merleau-Ponty endorses, that perceptual states present the world to us in a way that transcends our capacity to reflect upon them.

Making the indeterminate a positive phenomenon

We have seen that on Husserl's account the indeterminate features of a perceived object are hypothesized by the perceiver but sensibly absent in his experience of them. According to Merleau-Ponty, however, "we must recognize the indeterminate as a positive phenomenon."[51] The indeterminate features of the object are not merely features that I have no current sensuous experience of at all. As he says, ". . . the perceived contains gaps which are not mere 'failures to perceive'."[52] Rather, the indeterminate features are those that I am now experiencing, though *not as determinate* features of the object:

> There occurs here an *indeterminate vision*, a *vision of I don't know what* (vision de je ne sais quoi[53]), . . . [which nevertheless] is not without some element of visual presence.[54]

The project, for Merleau-Ponty, is to say what this positive but indeterminate experience is.

In many cases the indeterminate features of our experience are present to us in our bodily engagement with the thing toward which we're directed. The phenomenon of size constancy in perception provides a helpful example of this. Size constancy is the phenomenon according to which we experience a given object to be a constant size throughout a wide variety of perceptual contexts. For instance, as I move closer to and further away from an object, it looks to me to be a constant size throughout. Merleau-Ponty's phenomenological analysis of size constancy invokes an essentially bodily relation to the object seen.

Many empiricist philosophers and psychologists have found it difficult to explain the phenomenon of size constancy. They tend to think about the problem somewhat as follows. When I move in relation to an object, the size of the image that it projects onto my retina varies accordingly. As I move closer, the object projects a larger image onto my retina; as I move further away the size of its image decreases. This change in the retinal stimulus is what makes the phenomenon of size constancy so puzzling. For it is natural to think, according to these empiricists, that there must be a constant correlation between the properties of the retinal stimulus and the features of the perceptual experience that the subject has of the object. This assumption is sometimes called the "constancy hypothesis." If the constancy hypothesis is correct, then the change in the retinal stimulus that occurs as I move in relation to the object should be accompanied by a correlative change in my perceptual experience of the object. As I move away from the object, and the size of its retinal image decreases, I should experience the object to be getting smaller – and conversely as I move toward it. The phenomenon of size constancy suggests, however, that no such correlative change occurs. For this reason, the phenomenon is hard to explain.

The empiricists, nevertheless, have a characteristic account of the mechanism of the phenomenon of size constancy. The details of their account, and of Merleau-Ponty's trenchant assessment of it,[55] provide an interesting example of phenomenological criticism; but I will not go into them here. Instead, I note only the lesson that Merleau-Ponty draws from this case. According to him, we must conclude against the constancy hypothesis that "the sensible [experience] cannot be defined as the immediate effect of an external stimulus."[56] We must give up on the "constancy hypothesis," according to Merleau-Ponty, for the most basic of phenomenological reasons: it "conflicts with the data of consciousness."[57]

Still, the question remains how to account for the phenomenon of size constancy. One natural thing to say is that the subject, in his experience of the size of the object, is somehow "taking into account" the distance from which the object is being perceived. If that's right, then every experience of the size of an object involves in some way an experience of the distance to it as well. But what kind of experience of the distance to the object does the subject have? One option is that the subject experiences the distance as a determinate amount – 20 feet, for instance. If this is right, then the theorist can attribute to the subject (or perhaps to the subject's brain) a simple geometric algorithm by means of which he can calculate the constant size of the object given the size of the retinal image it casts and the determinate distance to it. This kind of cognitivist view, which reduces perceptual experience to rational algorithmic performance, has become the orthodoxy in perceptual psychology, and has been championed in particular by the late Irvin Rock.[58] It is also the approach that Husserl prefers.[59]

But Merleau-Ponty argues against this kind of cognitivism too. It is right, he believes, that every experience of an object involves in some way an experience of the distance to it (as well as the experience of many other contextual features). But we do not experience the distance to an object as a determinate value. Anyone who has ever rented an apartment understands this already. It is one thing to know that the living room is 18 feet long; it is quite another to stand in it and see its size. Merleau-Ponty says, therefore, that it is wrong to think that distance and other contextual features "can be treated as variables or measurable sizes, and therefore that they are already determinate."[60] Rather, we experience the distance to an object in an essentially indeterminate way.

The indeterminate experience of distance to an object, according to Merleau-Ponty, is present to us in our bodily engagement with the thing:

> If I draw the object closer to me or turn it round in my fingers in order 'to see it better', this is because each attitude of my body is for me, immediately, the power of achieving a certain spectacle, and because each spectacle is what it is for me in a certain kinaesthetic situation.[61]

Further, this bodily engagement with the thing manifests an essentially normative relation to it:

> For each object, as for each picture in an art gallery, there is an optimum distance from which it requires to be seen, a direction viewed from which it vouchsafes most of itself: at a shorter or greater distance we have merely a perception blurred through excess or deficiency. We therefore tend towards the maximum of visibility, and seek a better focus as with a microscope. . . . The distance from me to the object is not a size which increases or decreases, but a tension which fluctuates round a norm.[62]

This normative feature of the experience of distance, which is manifest in our bodily engagement with things, is precisely what cannot be captured by the cognitivist account. For the cognitivist, 18 feet is a fixed, determinate value; it is the same no matter what the context. But for genuine perception, according to Merleau-Ponty, 18 feet may be perfect for viewing one thing, but awful for another. This perfection and awfulness, this sense of the appropriateness of the distance to the thing seen, is an essential part of the way I experience distance to an object. And it is presented to me in what can only be called an immediate bodily way. To spell this out more clearly, we must look at the relation between our body and the experience we have of space. Merleau-Ponty's work on this topic is groundbreaking. As we will see, it has received support, too, from recent research in cognitive neuroscience.

Body and space[63]

Merleau-Ponty often proceeds, in the *Phenomenology of Perception*, by considering cases of visual pathology. In these pathological cases, he believes, the subject has explicitly available to him features of experience that are hidden from normal perceivers in everyday life. By studying these pathological cases, therefore, we can more easily make explicit to ourselves those features of experience that are normally hidden from us. To this end, Merleau-Ponty describes a patient named Schneider, whose visual pathology stems from a traumatic injury to the brain incurred during trench warfare in the First World War. Schneider's case of morbid motility, according to

Merleau-Ponty, "clearly shows the fundamental relations between the body and space."[64] The following somewhat lengthy passage occurs near the beginning of Merleau-Ponty's discussion of Schneider:

> In the . . . patient . . . one notices a dissociation of the act of pointing from reactions of taking or grasping: the same subject who is unable to point to order to a part of his body, quickly moves his hand to the point where a mosquito is stinging him. . . . [A]sked to point to some part of his body, his nose for example, [he] can only manage to do so if he is allowed to take hold of it. If the patient is set the task of interrupting the movement before its completion . . . the action becomes impossible. It must therefore be concluded that "grasping". . . is different from "pointing." From the outset the grasping movement is magically at its completion; it can begin only by anticipating its end, since to disallow taking hold is sufficient to inhibit the action. And it has to be admitted that [even in the case of a normal subject] a point on my body can be present to me as one to be taken hold of without being given in this anticipated grasp as a point to be indicated. But how is this possible? If I know where my nose is when it is a question of holding it, how can I not know where it is when it is a matter of pointing to it?

"It is probably because," Merleau-Ponty concludes, "knowledge of where something is can be understood in a number of ways."[65]

The general point of Merleau-Ponty's discussion is that the understanding of space that informs my skillful, unreflective bodily activity – activity such as unreflectively grasping the coffee mug in order to drink from it, skillfully typing at the keyboard, or automatically walking closer to an object to see it better – is not the same as, nor can it be explained in terms of, the understanding of space that informs my reflective, cognitive or intellectual acts – acts such as pointing at the coffee mug in order to identify it. As Merleau-Ponty says, in skillful, unreflective bodily activity

> my body appears to me as an attitude directed towards a certain existing or possible task. And indeed its spatiality is not . . . a *spatiality of position*, but a *spatiality of situation*.[66]

To give a name to intentional activities that essentially involve our bodily, situational understanding of space and spatial features, Merleau-Ponty coins the phrase "motor intentionality." Grasping is the canonical motor-intentional activity.

As recently as 1992, perceptual psychologists were loathe to distinguish between the kind of spatial information available to the visual system for visuo-motor activities such as grasping and the kind available for perceptual judgments about location implicit in acts of pointing. In a forward-thinking paper of the day, one psychologist writes:

> We often do not differentiate between grasping and pointing when we generalize about how vision is used when generating limb movements. It is possible, that how individuals use vision may vary as a function of whether they are generating pointing or grasping movements, and that some principles of how vision is used during reaching and pointing is [*sic*] not generalizable to grasping.[67]

This was a maverick view in 1992. Since that time, however, the important work of neuroscientists A. David Milner and Melvyn Goodale has opened the way for acceptance of this basic Merleau-Pontean distinction – the distinction between essentially bodily understandings of space and spatial features, on the one hand, and essentially cognitive or reflective understandings of these on the other. Much of Milner and Goodale's work comes from an analysis of D.F., a patient who suffered carbon monoxide poisoning that resulted in a visual pathology strikingly similar to that of Schneider. Milner and Goodale describe her situation as follows:

> D.F.'s ability to recognize or discriminate between even simple geometric forms is grossly impaired. . . . [Her] pattern of visual deficits [however] . . . is largely restricted to deficits in form perception. D.F. . . . recovered, within weeks, the ability to reach out and grasp everyday objects with remarkable accuracy. We have discovered recently that she is very good at catching a ball or even a short wooden stick thrown towards her. . . . She negotiates obstacles in her path with ease . . . These various skills suggest that although D.F. is poor at perceptual report of object qualities such as size and orientation, she is much better at using those same qualities to guide her actions.[68]

In particular, Milner and Goodale report, D.F. is capable of responding differentially to spatial features of an object such as its size, shape, and orientation, even in cases in which she is incapable of visually identifying those very features. One test of this involved the identification of the orientation of a slot. Quoting again from Milner and Goodale:

> [We] used a vertically mounted disc in which a [rectangular] slot . . . was cut: on different test trials, the slot was randomly set at 0, 45, 90, or 135°. We found that D.F.'s attempts to make a perceptual report of the orientation of the slot showed little relationship to its actual orientation, and this was true whether her reports were made verbally or by manually setting a comparison slot. [Further examination revealed a large variety of other reporting methods for which her performance was equally bad.] Remarkably, however, when she was asked to insert her hand or a hand-held card into the slot from a starting position an arm's length away, she showed no particular difficulty, moving her hand (or the card) towards the slot in the correct orientation and inserting it quite accurately. Video recordings showed that her hand began to rotate in the appropriate direction as soon as it left the start position. [One is reminded here, by the way, of Merleau-Ponty's claim that "from the outset the grasping action is magically at its completion."] In short, although she could not report the orientation of the slot, she could "post" her hand or a card into it without difficulty.[69]

Milner and Goodale go on to suggest a neurophysiological basis for the dissociation between pointing and grasping. They claim that there are two different streams of visual information flow in the brain, one of which is geared to perceptual judgment, and the other of which is geared directly to action. D.F.'s case is one of the principal pieces of evidence that there is not one common understanding of orientation on the basis of which both judgment and action occur but, rather, two different ways of understanding spatial qualities such as orientation. Indeed, D.F.'s understanding of the orientation of the slot, unlike the more familiar cognitive understanding, is essentially in terms of her bodily capacities and dispositions to act with respect to it. In the terminology of Merleau-Ponty, she has a motor-intentional understanding of orientation.

Motor intentionality and the positive indeterminate

I said that motor intentionality provides us with an essentially bodily relation to the object. Let me try to spell this out a bit more clearly. After I do so, I will show that this essentially bodily relation to the object is just what we need to make sense of Merleau-Ponty's notion of a "positive indeterminate" understanding of the back side of our coffee mug.

It is clear that motor-intentional activities – such as unreflectively grasping the coffee mug to drink from it – succeed at least partly in virtue of facts about the object toward which they are directed. For instance, I will change my way of grasping the mug if someone moves it; I'll reach over there instead of over here. But I'll also conform my way of grasping an object to the kind of object it is. For instance, even if it's in the very same spot, I'll grasp the mug differently when it's full than when it's empty, or when the handle is broken than when it's not. The differences in my bodily relation to the object are pervasive. My grip forms itself differently, my hand opening scales itself differently, and my entire body may even prepare itself differently if the object is perceived to be, for instance, very heavy instead of very light. The upshot is that in identifying an object motor intentionally my body typically prepares itself to deal with the entire object, not just with some independently specifiable set of spatial features of it.

When I say that my body prepares itself to deal with the entire object, I mean also that my body prepares itself to deal with the actual existing object, not with some representation of it. Indeed, the perceived existence of the object is so important to the grasping act that without it the action is measurably distinct. This is clear from another interesting empirical result, this one reported by Goodale, Jakobson, and Keillor.[70] These authors have shown that there are measurable qualitative differences between natural grasping movements directed toward an actual object and "pantomimed" movements directed toward a remembered object. When an actual object is present to be grasped, the subjects typically scale their hand opening for object size and form their grip to correspond to the shape of the object. In pantomimed actions, on the other hand, when there is no object present, although the subjects continue to scale their hand opening, their grip formation differs significantly from that seen in normal target-directed actions. It seems that the actual perceived presence of a thing, and not just some independent representation of it (like a memory), is necessary for the motor-intentional activity directed toward it. This is why Merleau-Ponty insists that motor-intentional activity is directed toward the object itself in all its particularity. As he says,

> In the action of the hand which is raised towards an object is contained a reference to the object, not as an object represented, but as that *highly specific thing* towards which we project ourselves, near which we are, in anticipation, and which we haunt.[71]

This is not merely the kind of direct realism that is sometimes found in the philosophical literature nowadays; it is not just the rejection of representational intermediaries. It is in addition an embrace of the positive notion of a whole bodily understanding of the object.

The understanding of the entire object that I have when I am grasping it is not an understanding I can have independent of my bodily activity with respect to it. My bodily activity with respect to the object just is my way of understanding it. We saw this already in the case of D.F. – the understanding of the orientation of the slot that she has in posting a card through it is not an understanding she can have independent of the posting activity. In particular, hers is not the kind of understanding of orientation that she can report in any way other than by actually posting the card through the oriented slot. But this kind of bodily understanding of the world is familiar to normal subjects as well. Merleau-Ponty gives the example of a typist's bodily understanding of the keyboard:

> To know how to type is not, then, to know the place of each letter among the keys, nor even to have acquired a conditioned reflex for each one, which is set in motion by the letter as it comes before our eye. If [bodily skill] is neither a form of knowledge nor an involuntary action, what then is it? It is knowledge in the hands, which is forthcoming only when bodily effort is made, and cannot be formulated in detachment from that effort.[72]

That there is a peculiarly bodily type of understanding of objects is the central point of Merleau-Ponty's category of motor intentionality: motor-intentional activity is a way of being directed toward objects that essentially involves a motor or behavioral component. As Merleau-Ponty says in introducing the phrase:

> . . . we are brought to the recognition of something between [reflex] movement as a third person process and thought as a representation of movement – something which is an anticipation of, or arrival at, the objective and is ensured by the body itself as a motor power, a "motor project" (*Bewegungsentwurf*), a "motor intentionality". . . [73]

In motor-intentional activity, in other words, there is not an independent way that we have of understanding the object, on the basis of which we act differentially with respect to it. Rather, our bodily activity is itself a kind of understanding of the object. I believe that this kind of essentially bodily engagement with the world is substantially different from every other kind of intentional state.

The main difference between motor intentionality and cognitive intentionality lies in their logical structure.[74] Every cognitive intentional state – states such as believing, hoping, desiring, and so on – has two separable parts: the intentional content of the state and its propositional attitude.[75] For instance, when I have a belief that the sun is rising, the content of the belief is that the sun is rising, and the attitude I have toward that content is belief. I might have hoped that the sun is rising instead of having believed it; likewise, I might have believed that the sun is not rising instead of that it is. The content and the attitude of (cognitive) intentional states are logically separable from one another.

The logical structure of motor-intentional activities is different. For motor-intentional activities, there is no independently specifiable content toward which the subject can have an attitude. This is because motor-intentional activity identifies its object in such a highly specific and context-sensitive way that any attempt to take up that specification of the object as such changes it into something other than it was at the time it was had.[76] An example should make this clear.

When she is posting the block through a slot oriented at 45°, D.F. is motor-intentionally engaged with the orientation of the slot. But what is the content – the representation of the way the slot is – that is manifest in this motor-intentional activity? To specify this content, we need to use concepts – roughly words – that D.F. already possesses and can apply in a variety of contexts.[77] The problem is that there seems to be no concept that D.F. possesses in virtue of which she is capable of performing the posting activity.[78] If there were such a concept, it would have to apply to objects in the world that are oriented at 45°, and only to those objects. But D.F. doesn't seem to be able to apply any such concept to the oriented slot. Remember, she can't say of it that it is oriented at 45°, but she also can't draw the slope of the slot on a piece of paper or even rotate her hand into the correct orientation without at the same time moving it toward the slot. In other words, she seems not to be able to represent the orientation of the slot at all except by means of posting the card through it. This is another way of putting the claim that motor-intentional activities constitute essentially bodily understandings of their objects.

But still, why can't we think of this activity itself as a way of understanding the orientation of the slot toward which she can have the attitude of belief? Why can't she say, in other words, "I believe the slot is oriented *this* way [said while posting the card through the slot]"? Well, she can *say* such a thing of course – she can utter the words – but the question is whether in doing so she is invoking the representation of the orientation of the slot that constituted the understanding she had of it when she was posting the card through the slot. We can easily see she is not.

The reason is that when she tries to use the posting action to refer to the orientation it identifies, the thought she has seems to be not about the orientation of the slot but, rather, about whatever orientation her hand happens to be in. If you change the orientation of the slot after she stops moving her hand, for instance, and you don't let her begin the posting activity again, she will continue to say that the orientation of the slot is whatever orientation her hand ended up in.[79] What is revealed in the posting activity, however, is the actual orientation of the slot – it's that orientation itself that the activity is sensitive to. So even if she can have an attitude toward the activity that manifests an understanding of the orientation, this is not the same as having an attitude toward the understanding of the orientation that the activity manifests.

The understanding of the orientation of the slot that D.F. manifests in her motor-intentional activity, therefore, is of a peculiar sort. It contains no independently specifiable content toward which she can have an attitude. Instead of "representing" the orientation of the slot, therefore, we might say that her motor-intentional activity "discloses" the orientation to her directly, and cannot be captured in the process of doing so. This coheres with Schneider's report of his own experience, for he says

> I experience the movements as being a result of the situation, of the sequence of events themselves; myself and my movements are, so to speak, merely a link in the whole process and I am scarcely aware of any voluntary initiative. . . . It all happens independently of me.[80]

Because motor-intentional activity is called forth by the situation in this way, and is therefore to some degree independent of the autonomous will of the subject, it does not have at its heart the kind of autonomous representational content that a subject could have an attitude toward.

This account of motor intentionality gives us the tools that we need to understand Merleau-Ponty's notion of the "positive indeterminate" in experience. Recall that Merleau-Ponty's goal was to explain how our experience of the back side of the mug does not merely hypothesize the existence of a handle, but is somehow positively, though indeterminately, aware of the actual thing. Now we can see that the bodily relation to the mug gives us a positive awareness of it as a whole, including an awareness of the "hidden" features such as its back side. This positive awareness of the mug is manifest in our bodily set, by means of which we are prepared to deal with it as a highly specific thing. The preparation to deal with the handle on the back side manifests itself in various features of my motor-intentional activity: my grip forms itself in such a way as to take account of the shape of the handle, for instance, and my hand opening scales itself to account for its size. My body may get these features of the handle wrong, of course, and if it does my motor-intentional activity will reveal itself to have understood the object as something other than what it is. This has the real repercussion that I'll probably knock the mug over or drop it. But when things are going smoothly, the whole mug – back side and all – will be positively revealed to me in my motor-intentional activity toward it.

Motor-intentional engagement with an object is indeterminate in a clear sense as well. For the way of understanding an object that is manifest in our motor-intentional activity is not specifiable as a definite representational content. There are two reasons for this, as we have seen. First, motor-intentional activity depends on the perceived existence of the actual object, not just on some representation of it; in other words, motor-intentional activity discloses the world. Second, the motor-intentional understanding of the object is not specifiable independent of the motor-intentional activity itself; it is an essentially bodily engagement with the world. These two features of motor-intentional activity give it its essential indeterminateness. Therefore, any attempt to specify the motor-intentional understanding of the object as a determinate representational content is self-defeating: the very attempt to characterize the content determinately turns it into something other than the essentially indeterminate thing that it is.

Finally, when we understand the positive indeterminate aspects of experience in the way that Merleau-Ponty does, we are forced to deny Husserl's claim that intentional states are immanent. Recall that incorrigibility is one of the four features of immanence for Husserl. To say that the subject's knowledge of his intentional state is incorrigible is to say that the qualities he takes the state to have, in reflecting upon it, are certain to characterize it as it really is. But if Merleau-Ponty is right, then our understanding of the essential features of motor-intentional activity is very far from being incorrigible. Indeed, to say that motor-intentional activity is indeterminate, in Merleau-Ponty's sense, is to say that the disclosive understanding of the world that it manifests is not specifiable as such. If the subject cannot even specify the content of her motor-intentional activity, indeed cannot have any attitude toward it at all, then her knowledge of the features of that intentional state is certainly not incorrigible. Rather, motor-intentional activity gives us a relation to, or a bodily understanding of, the world that goes beyond the subject's capacity to characterize it. Motor intentionality is transcendent in precisely this sense.

Conclusion

Husserl's development of phenomenology made a genuine advance over those of his predecessors. By taking perception as the paradigmatic intentional state, Husserl was able to emphasize both the perspectival aspect of intentionality (against Brentano) and the intentional aspect of perception (against the empiricists). In doing so, he happened upon perhaps the most basic problem of phenomenology: to characterize in a descriptively accurate manner how perception represents its object as transcending what is presented in the perception of it. He tried to guarantee the possibility of descriptive accuracy, however, by claiming that the essential features of experience are available to us incorrigibly; that experience, like all intentional states, is immanent.[81] He hoped that phenomenology would be the study of the pure realm of immanent content that is produced by the transcendental reduction. But this commitment forced him to give a peculiar answer to the phenomenological question. For according to Husserl, the hidden aspects of an object – those that transcend our experience of them – are hypothesized but sensuously absent.

Merleau-Ponty took up Husserl's phenomenological problem, but argued that we must recognize the indeterminate in experience as a positive phenomenon. Merleau-Ponty's emphasis on our bodily engagement with the world gave him the tools to make this claim precise. Our motor-intentional relation to the hidden aspects of an object – like the handle on the back side of a coffee mug – is positive but indeterminate. It is positive in the sense that it gives me a bodily preparation for a very particular handle; I'll be very surprised by, and will probably deal ineptly with, the mug if the handle turns out to be something else. This preparation for a very particular handle is very unlike what we find in Husserl's account, according to which our experience prefers no handle over any other.

Motor-intentional activity, according to Merleau-Ponty, is indeterminate as well. That's because our bodily engagement with the mug isn't specifiable as a determinate representation toward which the subject could have an attitude. Any attempt to specify the content of motor-intentional activity in this way is self-defeating, since the very process of doing so turns the motor-intentional relation to the object into something else. This is also unlike Husserl, since it defines a kind of intentionality that transcends my capacity to reflect upon it. Merleau-Ponty, therefore, rejects Husserl's claim that perception is immanent, and he rejects it on the very grounds that descriptive accuracy requires us to do so. This is closely tied to his reevaluation of Husserl's phenomenological method, and in particular of the transcendental reduction to a pure realm of immanent content. As Merleau-Ponty says in the preface to the *Phenomenology of Perception*, "the most important lesson that the transcendental reduction teaches us is the impossibility of a complete reduction."[82]

Notes

1   I would like to thank Bob Solomon and Bert Dreyfus for helpful comments and discussion.

2   The drafts for the *Encyclopaedia Britannica* article, and the correspondence between Husserl and Heidegger about it, appear in *Psychological and Transcendental Phenomenology and the Confrontation with Heidegger: the Encyclopaedia Britannica article, the Amsterdam lectures "Phenomenology and Anthropology," and Husserl's Marginal Notes in Being and Time, and Kant and the Problem of Metaphysics*, trans. T. Sheehan and R. E. Palmer (Boston: Kluwer, 1997).

3   See, for instance, the passages on the phenomenological reduction in the preface to Merleau-Ponty's *Phenomenology of Perception*. It is not surprising that a left-wing French academic writing in 1945 should choose to align himself with Husserl (a persecuted Jew) instead of Heidegger (a Nazi). But this attempt depends upon an interpretation of the phenomenological reduction that bears little resemblance to Husserl's understanding of that technique.

4   I think this example occurs in the *Principles of Psychology*, but I haven't been able to track it down.

5   He did his doctoral work on the calculus of variations, working for a while under the famous German mathematician Karl Weierstrauss.

6   His *Philosophie der Arithmetik* was published in 1891.

7   For more on their relation, see the letters between Husserl and Frege published in Gottfried Gabriel et al., *Gottlob Frege: Philosophical and Mathematical Correspondence*, trans. H. Kaal (Chicago: University of Chicago Press, 1980).

8   Edmund Husserl, *Logical Investigations*, trans. J. N. Findlay (London: Routledge and Kegan Paul, 1970), p. 269. This is §1 of Investigation I. Hereafter I will abbreviate references to this text as *LI*, followed by the Investigation number and the page in the edition listed here.

9   *LI* I, p. 248.

10   Heidegger writes that in bracketing the entity in order to focus on our experience of it, "what really is at issue now is the determination of the being of the very entity." See *History of the Concept of Time*, trans. Th. Kisiel (Bloomington, Ind.: Indiana University Press, 1992), p. 99. Hereafter I will refer to this text as *HCT*.

11   Perhaps this is not fair, since Kant's system is obviously concerned to think about not just objects, but objects as they are understood through the pure concepts of understanding. But Husserl's project was not the same as Kant's. In particular, Kant's transcendental method is completely anathema to the descriptive procedures of phenomenology.

12   More accurately, our experiences present themselves *as being present* all at once in their entirety. But I will be sloppy about this point in the text.

13   See *HCT*, §11.

14   As present.

15   The embodied nature of all types of perceptual experience, however, was vital to Merleau-Ponty's phenomenological work.

16   Brentano, following the Scholastics, developed his account of intentionality primarily for the cases of belief and judgment.

17   See Locke's *Essay Concerning Human Understanding*, II,1.2: "Let us then suppose the Mind to be, as we say, white Paper, void of all Characters, without any *Ideas*; How comes it to be furnished? Whence comes it by that vast store, which the busy and boundless Fancy of Man has painted on it, with an almost endless variety? Whence has it all the materials of Reason and Knowledge? To this I answer, in one word, From *Experience*." Similarly, we read in Hume's *Enquiry Concerning Human Understanding*, §II: "Or, to express myself in philosophical language, all our ideas or more feeble perceptions are copies of our impressions or more lively ones."

18   David Bell's book *Husserl* (London: Routledge, 1990) is typical in this respect. By empha-sizing the idea that "Husserl's theory of intentionality is entirely general and, to a large extent, purely formal" (p. 115), Bell fails to do justice to the way perception motivates Husserl's broader understanding of intentionality. Aron Gurwitsch, in *The Field of Con-sciousness* (Pittsburgh, Penn.: Duquesne University Press, 1964), places perception at the center of his discussion of Husserl's phenomenology. But Hubert L. Dreyfus and Harri-son Hall, in *Husserl, Intentionality, and Cognitive Science* (Cambridge, Mass.: The MIT Press, 1982), argue convincingly that Gurwitsch's interpretation of the perceptual noema as a percept, rather than a concept, has little support in Husserl's texts. Dreyfus and Hall, therefore, follow Dagfinn Føllesdal ("Husserl's notion of noema," in Dreyfus and Hall, 1982), who shows definitively that Husserl's noema is a generalization of the Fregean *Sinn* to all mental states. However, Føllesdal's important and influential work has given rise to a school of interpretation that places the emphasis on the logical, rather than the properly phenomenological, aspects of Husserl's work; in other words, it focuses atten-tion on the linguistic rather than the pre-linguistic cases of intentionality. Although this emphasis is not apparent in Føllesdal's own work, selective attention to the Fregean fea-tures of his Husserl has given rise not only to this linguistic school of interpretation, but also to such misguided criticisms of Husserl as those found in Michael Dummett's *Frege: Philosophy of Language* (2nd edn, London, 1981).

There is some illuminating discussion of Husserl's account of perception in David Woodruff Smith and Ronald McIntyre's book *Husserl and Intentionality* (Dordrecht: D. Reidel, 1982), as well as in Kevin Mulligan's article "Perception," in B. Smith and D. W. Smith (eds.), *The Cambridge Companion to Husserl* (Cambridge: Cambridge University Press, 1995). In neither case, however, is perception presented as the paradigmatic inten-tional state. By contrast, I will argue that the perceptual case is central for Husserl, since it is the paradigm of an intentional relation to a transcendent object. That Husserl described this intentional relation in terms that were too Cartesian and cognitivist is what generates the phenomenological responses to Husserl by Heidegger and Merleau-Ponty. That he had the radical idea to characterize intentionality on the model of the *perceptual*, rather than the linguistic, relation to a transcendent object, however, is what made his studies in phenomenology relevant to these thinkers in the first place. It is also what dis-tinguishes the phenomenological approach from the traditional analytic approach to intentionality that is grounded in the seminal work of Frege.

19   Edmund Husserl, *Ideas Pertaining to a Pure Phenomenology and to a Phenomenological Philosophy, First Book*, trans. F. Kersten (Dordrecht: Kluwer, 1982), pp. 82–3/70. Here-after I will refer to this text as *Ideas I*.

20   *Ideas I*, p. 82/70.
21   Ibid., p. 83/71. We might disagree with Husserl about either of these claims. For instance, we might attempt to show that perception of a physical thing is not representative of perception generally by arguing that the perception of an event, like the presentation by Lincoln of his Second Inaugural Address, is not relevantly akin to the perception of an object, like a house. Similarly, we might attempt to show that experience is not the ultimate source of intentional life by arguing that zombies, who by definition have no experiential life at all, are nevertheless quite capable of intentionality. Whether these arguments have any merit is not a question that I will pursue here. Husserl himself seems not to have wondered whether these empiricist claims about experience are justified. By this I mean that he accepted without question the empiricist *emphasis on* perception as the ground of thought, although he did not, of course, accept the empiricist *account of* perception (see the next section). But that these kinds of experiences are the primary model for his phenomenological account of intentionality is crucial.
22   See, e.g., Edmund Husserl, *Experience and Judgment: Investigations in a genealogy of logic*, trans. J. Churchill and K. Ameriks (Evanston, Ill.: Northwestern University Press, 1973), pp. 50–1.
23   *LI* I, §23, p. 309. By a "consciousness prior to all experience," Husserl seems to mean a being who consciously senses colors, sounds, shapes, textures, and so on, but does not experience them *as* the red of an apple, the cry of a baby, the roundness of a billiard ball, the rough of a carpet. Roughly, this is a being who has sense-data but no interpretation of them. See the discussion in note 30 of Philonous's passage in Berkeley's *Three Dialogues of Hylas and Philonous.*
24   Locke is the empiricist to whom this view is most often attributed; it is sometimes labelled the "picture-original theory of perception" in the secondary literature on him. See, for instance, J. L. Mackie, "Locke and representative perception," in V. Chappell (ed.), *Locke* (Oxford: Oxford University Press, 1998), pp. 60–8. Whether Locke himself, or indeed any of the British empiricists, actually held such a view is not particularly important to my point. The common attribution of the view to them is sufficient to account for its influence on Husserl. Perhaps it is more fair to attribute the image theory to the early sense-datum theorists, but I know of no evidence that Husserl was familiar with their work.
25   George Berkeley, *Three Dialogues between Hylas and Philonous* (Indianapolis, Ind.: Hackett, 1979), p. 39. Berkeley, of course, sides with Philonous against the image theory on the grounds that something that is sensible (such as an idea) couldn't possibly be similar in any relevant sense to something that is insensible (such as a material object). See, e.g., Philonous's comment on p. 41 of the *Three Dialogues*: "In a word, can anything be like a sensation or idea, but another sensation or idea?" This argument against the image theory, of course, is different from the one against it that Husserl gives. Interestingly, however, Heidegger and Frege both use this kind of Berkeleian argument to inveigh against the correspondence theory of truth (see my *Relevance of Phenomenology to the Philosophy of Language and Mind* (New York: Garland, 2001), ch. 1), although both attempt to avoid the radical idealism to which Berkeley himself was led by the move.
26   *LI*, pp. 712–13.
27   Ibid., pp. 593–4. The complete passage in the original reads: "Woran liegt es also, daß wir über das im Bewußtsein allein gegebene 'Bild' hinauskommen und es als Bild auf ein gewisses bewußtseinsfremdes Objekt zu beziehen vermögen? . . . [I]m phänomenologischen Wesen des Bewusstseins in sich selbst alle Beziehung auf seine Gegenständlichkeit beschlossen ist" (pp. 436–7 in the Husserliana edition, vol. XIX/I).

28 Husserl's critique of the image theory of perception is presented in the Appendix to §§11 and 20 of the Fifth Logical Investigation (pp. 593–6). Also important to this critique is the section on perceptual adumbration in the Sixth Logical Investigation. This is §14, especially §14b, pp. 712–15. It can be difficult to divine Husserl's intent here by reading only the Findlay translation of *Logical Investigations*, since the crucial German term, *Abschattung*, is translated in a variety of ways in this section. Among the translations are "shadowing forth," "aspect," and "projection." Noticeably absent is the English word "adumbration," which is the preferred translation of the term in the Kersten translation of *Ideas I*.

29 The empiricist could attempt to add a story about the importance of associations and memories in distinguishing these experiences. (Thanks to Casey O'Callaghan for pushing this point.) Perhaps I see something to be a barn, the empiricist could argue, in virtue of the memories I have for dealing with barns and the associations I have with them; seeing it to be a barn façade would involve a separate set of associations and memories. It is in virtue of the difference in associations and memories, on such an account, that there is a difference in my experience of something as a barn and my experience of it as a barn façade. The problem with this account, Husserl would say, is that there is no reason for one set of associations to get triggered over the other. Since the image of the barn is exactly the same as the image of the barn façade, the associations and memories triggered by the two images must be exactly the same as well. This follows from the empiricist assumption that the only thing that I actually *see* is the image. I would have different associations and memories with different images, of course. But if two images are themselves exactly the same, then there's no reason to suppose that they could by themselves trigger distinct associations and memories. Husserl gets around this by assuming that the "image" is always already taken under an interpretation in my experience of the thing.

30 The empiricist view is again clearly stated in Berkeley's *Three Dialogues*, this time by Philonous: "For instance, when I hear a coach drive along the streets, immediately I perceive only the sound; but from the experience I have had that such a sound is connected with a coach, I am said to hear the coach. It is nevertheless evident, that in truth and strictness, nothing can be *heard* but *sound*: and the coach is not then properly perceived by sense . . ." (p. 39). This view is very much like the early sense-datum theory of Bertrand Russell.

31 The most important work of Brentano's for Husserl is the first edition of *Psychology from an Empirical Standpoint*, trans. A. Rancurello et al. (London: Routledge, 1973). The German original was published in 1874. Husserl studied under Brentano in Vienna from 1884 to 1886.

32 Cf., *Psychology from an Empirical Standpoint*, pp. 88–94. Brentano's commitment to this doctrine may have changed throughout his career, as is argued by many commentators. If so, there was good reason for it, since the doctrine has some strange consequences. Cf., Dagfinn Føllesdal, "Brentano and Husserl," in H. L. Dreyfus and H. Hall (eds.), *Husserl, Intentionality, and Cognitive Science* (Cambridge, Mass.: The MIT Press, 1982), pp. 31–41. But both the doctrine and Brentano's commitment to it are clear in the 1874 edition of *Psychology*. Cf., Barry Smith, *Austrian Philosophy: The Legacy of Franz Brentano* (Chicago, Ill.: Open Court), pp. 41–5.

33 From the Supplementary Remarks prepared for the 1911 edition of *Psychology from an Empirical Standpoint*, p. 272. My italics.

34 See especially Husserl's treatment of Brentano in both the *Logical Investigations* and in *Ideas I*. The relevant passages are at *LI* V, §11, pp. 557–60, and §23, esp. p. 598, as well as in *Ideas I*, §85, esp. p. 206/174–5. For a related treatment of Husserl's advance over

Brentano, see Theodore de Boer, *The Development of Husserl's Thought*, trans. Th. Planti-
nga (The Hague: Martinus Nijhoff, 1978), pp. 133–41. De Boer emphasizes Husserl's
rejection of the Brentanian thesis that perceived content is immanent, but fails to appreciate the important relation between the transcendence of the perceived object and the
necessarily perspectival presentation of it to perception.

35 Cf., Føllesdal's treatment of this issue in "Brentano and Husserl," esp. p. 35. Føllesdal
locates the distinction between Husserl and Brentano in Husserl's introduction of a
noema – that *by means of which* mental phenomena are directed toward their objects. This
seems exactly right, albeit a bit underspecified. What I will add below is a story about
what it means to say that the noema is that *by means of which* mental phenomena are
directed toward their objects.

36 *Thing and Space: Lectures of 1907*, trans. R. Rojcewicz (Dordrecht: Kluwer, 1997), p.
44/52.

37 I cannot spell out this thought completely here, but the basic idea is this. Even if we stick
with Brentano's concern about mental states directed toward non-existent objects (such
as golden mountains), it is not at all clear that the intuition that motivates him in the linguistic case is preserved in the perceptual case. His intuition was that the thought about
the golden mountain is completely indifferent to the question whether the mountain itself
exists. Whether or not the mountain exists, the thought about it is exactly the same. Even
if this is right for the linguistic case, it's much less clear in the case of perception. Because
perceptions seem to be so closely connected with their objects, it may be a conceptual
truth that veridical perception – which actually lands on an object – is a different kind of
thing than hallucination – which has no object at all. This "disjunctivist" view, that hallucination has nothing at all in common with veridical perception, has recently been
defended by McDowell and others. Cf., John McDowell, *Mind and World* (Cambridge,
Mass.: Harvard University Press, 1994). Husserl – and Merleau-Ponty as well – is trying
to give an account of the related phenomenological fact that perception normally takes
itself to be directed toward objects.

38 See *Ideas I*, §§44–50. See also §11 of Heidegger's *History of the Concept of Time*. Notice
that what is indubitable is the existence of the intentional state, and what is incorrigible
is the subject's knowledge of the features of the intentional state. Naturally, it is an essential feature of intentional states that they present objects as having certain features. But,
of course, neither the existence of the object nor of the features it is represented to have
are guaranteed.

39 *Ideas I*, p. 100/85.

40 Here, it seems, Husserl agrees with Descartes but not with the empiricists. About Locke,
for instance, Michael Ayers writes, "Another important difference from Descartes lies in
Locke's conception of our awareness of the 'operations of our minds,' which he calls
'reflection.' Traditionally, in Aristotelian as well as Cartesian philosophy, the mind's reflexive awareness of its own activity . . . is a function of intellect, not sense. . . . For Locke, in
contrast, 'reflection' is simply a part of 'experience'. . . An important implication is that
thought is not, as Descartes had held, transparent to itself. Just as the senses give us only
superficial, coarse knowledge of external objects, so 'reflection' keeps us aware of our
thinking, but not of the ultimate nature of thought." See Michael Ayers, *Locke* (New
York: Routledge, 1999), p. 7.

41 *Ideas I*, p. 96/81.

42 For important historical discussions of the transcendental reduction, see Jean-Paul Sartre,
The Transcendence of the Ego: an Existentialist Theory of Consciousness, tr. F. Williams and

R. Kirkpatrick (New York: Hill and Wang, 1989) and Roman Ingarden, *On the Motives which Led Husserl to Transcendental Idealism*, trans. A. Hannibalsson (The Hague: Martinus Hijhoff, 1975), among many others.

43 Husserl's noema has famously been interpreted as a generalized version of Frege's *Sinn* – the public entity in virtue of which my linguistic utterances come to be about the world. See Dagfinn Føllesdal's important and influential paper "Husserl's notion of noema," in H. L. Dreyfus and H. Hall (eds.), *Husserl, Intentionality, and Cognitive Science* (Cambridge, Mass.: The MIT Press, 1982) for the best characterization of this view. Føllesdal is certainly right that the noema is that in virtue of which mental states come to be about the world. But because the noema finds its paradigmatic application in the context of perception, the problems it has to solve – and the ways in which it goes about solving them – are somewhat distinct. Failure to appreciate this difference has led some appropriators of Føllesdal's work to see in it an implicit condemnation of the Husserlian project. See especially Michael Dummett's off-the-mark criticisms of Husserl in his *Origins of Analytical Philosophy* (London: Duckworth, 1993).

44 See *Experience and Judgment* §21c for discussion of the frame (translated as "framework" in the Churchill and Ameriks translation). The following owes much to the development of this material by David Woodruff Smith and Ronald McIntyre in their book *Husserl and Intentionality* (Dordrecht: Reidel, 1982).

45 *Thing and Space*, §18, p. 49/58.

46 Ibid., §18, pp. 49–50/59.

47 Ibid., §18, p. 48/57.

48 Ibid., §17, p. 46/55.

49 *Ideas I*, §130, p. 312/270. Cf., *Thing and Space*, §18, p. 50/59.

50 They are not, for instance, metaphysically vague and in that sense uncharacterizable.

51 Maurice Merleau-Ponty, *Phenomenology of Perception*, trans. C. Smith (London: Routledge and Kegan Paul, 1962), p. 6.

52 *Phenomenology of Perception*, p. 11.

53 Notice that the Smith translation of this phrase, "a vision of something or other," precisely covers up the difference between Merleau-Ponty and Husserl. According to Merleau-Ponty it is not a vision of some *thing* or another which is itself determinate but which I have not yet determined. It is, rather, a positive presentation of something indeterminate, of an "I don't know what." It's a scope difference. Husserl thinks that there exists some determinate thing with which I have not yet been presented. Merleau-Ponty thinks that there exists a presentation of something that is itself not a determinate entity (for me).

54 *Phenomenology of Perception*, p. 6.

55 See, for instance, pp. 299–300 in *Phenomenology of Perception*.

56 *Phenomenology of Perception*, p. 8.

57 Ibid., p. 7.

58 See, e.g., Irvin Rock, *Indirect Perception* (Cambridge, Mass.: The MIT Press, 1997).

59 See Kevin Mulligan's article "Perception," in B. Smith and D. W. Smith (eds.), *The Cambridge Companion to Husserl* (Cambridge: Cambridge University Press, 1995), especially §6.1, for some discussion of Husserl on the various phenomena of perceptual constancy.

60 *Phenomenology of Perception*, p. 301.

61 Ibid., p. 303.

62 Ibid., p. 302.

63 The following two sections draw substantially on my own "The logic of motor inten-
    tional activity" (forthcoming in *Ratio*).
64 *Phenomenology of Perception*, p. 103.
65 Ibid., pp. 103–4.
66 Ibid., p. 100.
67 See Heather Carnahan, "Eye, head and hand coordination during manual aiming," in L.
    Proteau and D. Elliott (eds.), *Advances in Psychology 85: Vision and Motor Control* (Ams-
    terdam: Elsevier, 1992), p. 188.
68 *The Visual Brain in Action*, pp. 126–8.
69 Ibid., p. 128.
70 M. A. Goodale, L. S. Jakobson, and J. M. Keillor, "Differences in the visual control of
    pantomimed and natural grasping movements," *Neuropsychologia*, 32 (10), 1159–78
    (1994).
71 *Phenomenology of Perception*, p. 138; italics in the original.
72 Ibid., p. 144.
73 Ibid., p. 110.
74 For a more detailed account of the argument here, see my own "The logic of motor
    intentional activity" (forthcoming in *Ratio*).
75 See, for instance, John Searle, *Intentionality* (Cambridge: Cambridge University Press,
    1983).
76 A helpful analogy exists in Frege's account of concepts. Frege says that concepts are unsat-
    urated in the sense that they need to have an object added to them in order to be speci-
    fiable entities at all. Because of this, any attempt to refer to them as such turns them into
    something other than what they originally were.
77 If we specify the content using concepts she doesn't possess, then there's little sense in
    saying we've characterized *her* understanding of the orientation. That she must be able
    to apply these concepts in a variety of contexts is what Gareth Evans calls the "general-
    ity constraint" on concept possession. See Gareth Evans, *The Varieties of Reference*,
    (Oxford: Oxford University Press, 1982), ch. 4.
78 This is not to say that she doesn't possess the perfectly good concept [oriented at 45°].
    She may very well possess that concept. But that is not the concept manifest in her motor-
    intentional activity, as we shall see.
79 Personal communication with Melvyn Goodale.
80 *Phenomenology of Perception*, p. 105.
81 No doubt Husserl's desire to develop phenomenology as a "rigorous science" encour-
    aged him in this respect.
82 *Phenomenology of Perception*, p. xiv.

Chapter 7

Martin Heidegger

Jeff Malpas

Martin Heidegger (1889–1976) is one of the most significant and influential philosophers of the twentieth century. Along with Edmund Husserl, with whom he worked
for a period in the early 1920s, Heidegger played a crucial role in the development
of phenomenology. Through his appropriation of Kierkegaardian ideas, Heidegger
was pivotal in the development of twentieth-century existentialism – indeed, only
Jean-Paul Sartre can claim a similar significance in this regard. Although hermeneutic theory, particularly as developed by Wilhelm Dilthey, was an important influence
on Heidegger's early thinking, Heidegger also brought about a reorientation and
transformation in hermeneutics that was continued in the work of his student, Hans-
Georg Gadamer. Among more recent philosophical developments, the "deconstruction" of Jacques Derrida has its origins in Heidegger's own "de-structive" readings
of the philosophical tradition, while Michel Foucault declared that, for him,
Heidegger was (together with Nietzsche) the decisive thinker in determining the
course of his own work. In contemporary English-speaking philosophy, Heidegger's
influence is increasingly felt, not only in environmental philosophy, as well as in the
pragmatic appropriation of Heidegger's thought in the writings of Richard Rorty,
but in the development of Heideggerian ideas in the work of a number of philosophers from within the so-called "analytic" tradition, such as Hubert Dreyfus, Charles
Taylor, and Stanley Cavell. At the same time, Heidegger's political entanglement with
Nazism during the 1930s has been an important focus for a searching examination,
not merely of the political and moral culpability of Heidegger himself, but of the
political and moral culpability of philosophy and of European thought and culture
in general.

Heidegger's Life

Martin Heidegger was born on September 26, 1889, in the village of Messkirch in
Baden, South Germany, and throughout his life he remained strongly attached to the
Black Forest region from which he came – apart from a five-year period in Marburg,

he lived and worked in Messkirch, Freiburg, and the cottage he built for himself at Todtnauberg. Heidegger's family was lower middle class and Catholic. His father was sexton at the village church of St. Martin, in Messkirch, while his mother, Johanna, came from a farming family in the nearby village of Göggingen.

The eldest of three children, Martin Heidegger was identified as a gifted child by the local priest, and at the age of 14 was sent to study at a gymnasium in Konstanz and later Freiburg. Heidegger began theological and philosophical studies in training for the priesthood in 1909, but two years later discontinued his clerical training to focus instead on philosophy, while also undertaking work in science and mathematics. He completed his doctorate in philosophy at the University of Freiburg, in 1913, with a dissertation on "The doctrine of judgment in psychologism," and his habilitation dissertation, in 1915, on "Duns Scotus' doctrine of categories and meaning." In 1915, Heidegger also met Elfride Petri, an economics student from a North German Protestant background and, in 1917, the two were married, with their first son, Jorg, being born in 1919, and their second, Hermann, in 1920.

After working, from 1915 onwards, in a military postal office in Freiburg – concerns about his health meant that he was classified as having only limited fitness – Heidegger was sent, in 1918, for military training, and posted to a meteorological station at Verdun. At the end of the First World War, he returned to Freiburg to work as Husserl's assistant and, in 1919, finally broke, both personally and philosophically, with the Catholic establishment. In 1923, Heidegger took up a junior chair at the University of Marburg, moving to the senior chair in 1927. The following year he succeeded Husserl at Freiburg, where, after a brief but notorious period as University Rector under the Nazis (1933–4), he continued teaching, with some interruptions, until the end of the Second World War. In the course of the de-Nazification proceedings at the end of the war, Heidegger's Nazi sympathies during the 1930s led to him being stripped of his professorship and banned from teaching until 1949. In 1951, however, the University of Freiburg granted him emeritus status and he was able to lecture once more, continuing to give addresses and seminars into the late 1960s. He died on May 26, 1976, and was buried in the village churchyard in Messkirch where his father had been sexton.

Philosophical Development

"The hidden king"

Heidegger's early reputation rested not on his writings – in fact, in the ten or so years following the appearance of his habilitation dissertation he published almost nothing of note – but on his ability as a teacher. A short, and, in his younger years, relatively slight man, speaking in a provincial accent, sometimes affecting a somewhat "countrified" mode of dress (on one occasion, he turned up to lecture in a ski-outfit), and with a piercing gaze, Heidegger had an enormously powerful effect on those who attended his classes. Hannah Arendt famously talks of Heidegger's reputation spreading across Germany, from 1919 onwards, like the "rumor of a hidden king"

(Arendt, 1978, p. 294), while another witness to Heidegger's early teaching compared his impact in the lecture hall with that reported of Fichte and even of Luther (Petzet, 1993, p. 10).

Heidegger's success as a teacher was not, however, just a matter of personal style or charisma, but was also due to the character of his teaching as such. Melding together the ideas and approaches of Diltheyan hermeneutics and Husserlian phenomenology, as well as a set of problems and concepts taken from Greek ontology and medieval mysticism and metaphysics, Heidegger fashioned a way of doing philosophy that was characteristically his own; a way of doing philosophy that involved a transformation in philosophical inquiry, and that opened up the entire philosophical tradition in a new and revolutionary way, bringing his students into close contact with familiar texts as if they read them for the very first time. As Arendt writes, "The rumour about Heidegger put it quite simply: Thinking has come to life again; the cultural treasures of the past, believed to be dead, are being made to speak, in the course of which it turns out that they propose things altogether different from the familiar worn-out trivialities they had been presumed to say. There exists a teacher; one can perhaps learn to think" (Arendt, 1978, p. 295).

"The Turning"

In those days, as now, being a brilliant teacher was not enough to get one very far in academic life, and Heidegger's lack of publications in his early years was a recurrent source of difficulty. In 1927, however, he published *Being and Time* – a work presented in an incomplete form in order to secure for Heidegger the senior Chair at Marburg. Even unfinished, the book established Heidegger's reputation as a major figure, and it is on the basis of this work that Heidegger's international fame was established.

Being and Time was never completed, however, since in the period after 1927 (more specifically, in the years between 1930 and 1936) Heidegger's thinking underwent a shift, turning or "reversal" (*die Kehre*). This turning was not, however, a turning *away* from the problems of the earlier work so much as a turn *back* to them from a new direction – and also, in some respects, a re-appropriation of ideas that were present, though perhaps undeveloped, in his thinking prior to *Being and Time*. Moreover, while "the Turning" is usually taken to designate the specific shift in Heidegger's thinking that was connected with his inability to bring *Being and Time* to completion, it seems that Heidegger's thought actually underwent a number of crucial turns – it was, indeed, always "on the way," or, as Arendt put it, continually returning to its point of origin, continually beginning anew (Arendt, 1978, p. 298).

There do seem, in fact, to be a number of important points at which Heidegger's thinking underwent certain crucial shifts: one such turning point is marked by his close engagement with Aristotle in the years from 1921 to 1923 (see Kisiel, 1993, pp. 227ff.); another seems to have occurred in the course of his reading of the German romantic poet Friedrich Hölderlin in the late 1930s and early 1940s. In this respect, the idea of "the Turning" can be understood as directing attention both to the specific shift in Heidegger's thinking that occurred in the 1930s – and that is closely tied to a problem that Heidegger encountered in *Being and Time* (of which more will be said below) – as well as to the dynamic character of Heidegger's thought as a turning and returning to the single question that seems always to have stood at the center of his thinking: what Heidegger termed "the question of being."

The Question of Being

The question of being is not a new question that appears only with Heidegger's work, but is as old as philosophy itself. Amongst Greek and medieval thinkers, the question of being appears in terms of the question as to what is the really real, what is "substance." For Plato, the answer to the question was to be found in the eternal Forms or Ideas; for Aristotle, in the individual essences of each thing; for medieval thinkers such as Thomas Aquinas, in God. More recently, some philosophers have doubted that the question has any meaning, but the increasing tendency within modern thought, from Descartes onwards, has been to view the question of the being or reality of things as settled by the physical sciences and to construe being in terms of materiality or physicality. Heidegger's thinking of the question of being acknowledges a continuity with this metaphysical tradition, but it also represents a rethinking of both the question and of the tradition within which it arises.

Being and "life"

Heidegger's early career, especially his early career as a teacher, provides a useful starting point for any attempt to gain a preliminary understanding of the overall framework within which his rethinking of the question of being takes place. Indeed, the way in which Heidegger brought thinking "to life," as Arendt put it, is an indication both of the way in which he was able to give new breath to old questions and well-known texts, and also of the way in which he saw philosophy not as something divorced from life or from the existence of the philosopher, but as intimately connected with it. Heidegger saw philosophical inquiry as always grounded in a concern with concrete human existence. Moreover, this grounding in human existence is not a relation to existence conceived in a sense remote from the philosopher, but involves the philosopher's own existence as such. What seems to have marked Heidegger's teaching was thus a radical, questioning approach to his subject matter coupled with an intense, personal involvement. Philosophy, in Heidegger's classes, was no dry, "academic" pursuit, but was a form of "passionate thinking" – a vital and demanding mode of inquiry in which the very character of philosophical inquiry (indeed, of academic life as such, and even of the university), along with the mode of being of the inquirer, was itself at issue.

The personal involvement of the thinker in the task of thinking does not imply, however, that one can learn thinking by looking to the biography of the thinker – thinking is always and only addressed to the matter of thinking itself (Heidegger once introduced a lecture on Aristotle with a summary of the philosopher's life that consisted simply in the comment "Aristotle was born, worked and died" (Arendt, 1978, p. 297). The point is rather that one cannot think without one's own life and existence being at stake in such thinking. In this respect, truly radical (that is, philosophical) questioning always encompasses the questioner herself. Grasping this point – that the question of being is one in which our own being is always, already implicated – is perhaps the crucial step in coming to understand what might be at issue in the Heideggerian "question of being." Yet given that our being is indeed implicated in the question of being in this way, exactly *how* is it implicated? This still requires clarification – moreover, providing such clarification should also help in making the question of being itself a little less obscure.

Being and "presence"

The idea that the question of being concerns our own being as well as being as such is already present in Heidegger's early work in medieval philosophy and theology. There, the mystical experience of the individual's relation to God is seen as the necessary background to an understanding of the formal ontological and epistemological inquiries of medieval thinkers – only through relating it to such a background can medieval philosophy be grasped in relation to the living, human context in which it arose. Moreover, the connection between medieval metaphysics and medieval mysticism is also indicative of the connection between the question of being and the question of our own being. Against the background of medieval mysticism, the question of being is inevitably understood as a question that concerns our relationship to that which is transcendent of our own individual existence – in this respect, the question of being does not concern our own being as it might be understood independently of the being of other things, but asks after our being understood as just that sort of being that always stands in a relation to other beings (although the exact nature of that relation has still to be clarified). Moreover, inasmuch as the question of being concerns just this sort of "relatedness," so it concerns the being of things understood, not in terms of their factual existence as mere "stuff," but in terms of their coming to appearance as the things they are – in terms of their presence or presencing – which always occurs in relation to beings like us.

Heidegger uses a number of terms, often drawn from Greek thought, to refer to this idea of "presence" in its different aspects, including, for instance: "physis," the Greek work for the natural "emergence" or coming into being of things, and, perhaps most importantly, "aletheia," often translated as "truth" (although Heidegger later comes to abandon this translation) or else, more literally, as "disclosedness" or "unconcealedness." As Heidegger sees it, being just is the presence or disclosedness of things, and it is thus that the question of being always involves our being, since we are always involved in such presence or disclosedness. In this light, the question of being can be seen as a question that is essentially directed toward, to use a Heideggerian turn of phrase, "the disclosing of disclosedness" or, as it might also be put, "the presencing of presence" – toward, that is, the uncovering of the essential structure of presence or disclosedness. Inasmuch as the possibility of questioning itself rests on the possibility of presence or disclosedness (for only insofar as things are present or disclosed can they be opened to questioning), so one might also say that the question of being concerns the very being of questionability itself.

"Presence" and world

Yet such talk of "presence" and "disclosedness" may be thought simply to replace one obscurity with another – and obscurity is a charge that has been levelled at Heidegger's work all too frequently. So what exactly is involved in the "presence" and "disclosedness" that is invoked here? One tempting possibility is to suppose that the disclosedness of things is just their being known. Yet this is definitely not what Heidegger intends. Knowledge, at least in the sense of knowledge *that* (rather than the practical knowledge associated with knowledge *how* – "know-how" or skill), is always directed toward some fact, toward something that is the case: we know "that the bill has been paid," "that Bucharest is the capital of Romania," "that the atomic structure of water is one part oxygen to two parts hydrogen," "that we will have eggplant for dinner." Knowledge of things in this sense, however, is not the same as the "disclosedness" of things, since such knowledge already presupposes that things have first been disclosed as knowable. Knowing that the bill has been paid presupposes that we have some familiarity with what bills are, with what it is for something to be paid, with the particular bill in question, and ultimately with a whole framework of practices and things – a whole "world" – that can never be completely specified and that cannot be construed purely in terms of any finite set of discrete items of knowledge.

It is the grasp of things in terms of the multiplicity of "aspects" and relations that they comprise, or, as we might better put it, in terms of their complex locatedness within a world, that is at issue in Heidegger's talk of presence or disclosedness. Such a "grasp" of things cannot be construed simply in terms of our "knowing" things, but must encompass the entire range of our worldly engagement with them – including our practical engagement – and so involves our engagement with things as things rather then merely as epistemic objects. Moreover, if we cannot understand the being of things simply on the basis of their being objects of knowledge, neither can we understand our own being on the basis merely of our being as knowers. Our own being must itself be understood in terms of our locatedness in the world, explicated in terms of the full range of our engagement with things and with others like ourselves. We might say, in fact, that when construed as a question concerning presence or disclosedness, the question of being, which is *both* a question about our being and a question about the being of things, is also a question about the being of the world, since for there to be a world is for things to presence or to be disclosed.

The "ontological difference"

Understood in this way, the question of being – understood as a question concerning the presence or disclosedness of things – directs our attention to what might be referred to as the "structural whole" within which any particular thing can be present or disclosed, and which includes both what is disclosed thereby as well as that to which it is disclosed. To ask about the being of some particular thing is thus to ask after the presence or disclosedness of that thing, but to ask after this is not to ask about any particular feature of the thing (not its color, not its shape, not its biochemical structure, not its causal properties), and neither is it answerable by reference to any such feature. Instead, it is to ask after that which "makes possible" the being present of any such feature and which "makes possible" the being present of the thing as such.

Presence or disclosedness is thus not to be identified with some particular feature or property of things – not their being of a certain character or type, not their being known, not their being visible, not their being able to be experienced, not their being capable of certain causal interactions – for not only does this reduce things to what is merely an aspect or part of what they are, but it also misidentifies that which is the presencing or disclosedness of things (that is, their being) with *what it is* that thereby comes to be present or be disclosed. There is a tendency, nevertheless, to understand presence or disclosedness in just this way, and so to take the presence or disclosedness of the thing as identical with, for instance, its being a thing of a certain color and shape, with its being of a certain biochemical nature, with its being of a certain physical constitution. This tendency to understand the presence of things in terms merely of what is present really amounts to identifying being with just some particular being or beings (it identifies being with some particular aspect or feature of the being of things) and, in this respect, it amounts to a forgetting of the difference – the ontological difference, as Heidegger calls it – between being and beings (between *das Sein* and *die Seiendes*). Such a forgetting of the difference between being and beings is also a forgetting of being as such (*Seinsvergessenheit*).

The critique of metaphysics

Although Heidegger's early work was largely undertaken within the framework of medieval philosophy and theology, by the early 1920s he had come to see traditional theology, and ontology and metaphysics more generally, as characterized by a forgetfulness of being and so as covering over the difference between being and beings, between presence and what is present. This tendency is evident in the various metaphysical understandings of being as identical with eternal Idea or with individual essence (both of which focus on certain intelligible aspects of things), as God, as materiality or physicality. Indeed, according to Heidegger, the history of philosophy is a history of such forgetting.

Moreover, inasmuch as philosophical thinking covers over the difference between presence and what is present, so too does it cover over the way in which the question of being is always a question in which our own being is at issue. Thus, in a lecture course in 1923, Heidegger told his students that traditional ontology "blocks access to that being which is decisive within philosophical problems: namely, Dasein, from out of which and for the sake of which, philosophy 'is'" (Heidegger, 1999, p. 2). Here Heidegger uses the term "Dasein" (which literally means "there-being" and is used in ordinary German to refer to the fact of something's existence – "the book 'is there' on the shelf") to refer to the sort of existence that is characteristic of beings like ourselves. When philosophy covers over presence in favor of what is present, and so looks away from being to beings, so it also covers over the way in which what is present can only be present in relation to beings like ourselves. The forgetfulness of being is thus also a forgetfulness of our own being.

In this fashion, ontology obscures the way in which the question of being arises out of our own – namely, Dasein's – situatedness in the world and so out of our relatedness to things within the world; it thereby also obscures the way in which the question of being encompasses both ourselves and the things around us. The result is a way of thinking that is removed from the concrete circumstances that originally give rise to it and that treats the being of things in a way that severs things from the world and detaches them from any involvement with beings such as ourselves; a way of thinking that does indeed reduce being to beings and presence to what is present. Such a way of thinking also tends toward an understanding of ourselves that views our own being in a similarly "de-worlded," detached fashion – we understand ourselves as mere instances of things present, as biochemical systems or complex material objects. According to Heidegger, such a detached, even alienated view of ourselves is characteristic of modernity.

Properly understood then, the modern preoccupation with epistemology does not constitute a reawakening of the question of being (viewed in terms of its relation to human being), but is itself a symptom of the forgetfulness of that question. Not only does epistemology treat our being in terms only of our being as knowers, but it also presupposes our prior separation and detachment from the world and the things within it – a presupposition that underlies the skeptical concerns that motivate much epistemological thinking. Epistemology thus already depends on having turned away from presence to what is present – on having turned away from being to beings – and as it thereby involves a forgetting of the question of being, so epistemology involves a forgetting of the question of our own being.

Inasmuch as reawakening the question of being means reawakening the sense in which that question is a question in which we are always implicated, so reawakening that question is indeed a matter of reawakening exactly the kind of "passionate" thinking that Arendt notes as characteristic of Heidegger himself – a thinking that understands the way in which the question of being arises out of our own situatedness in the world, and so out of the prior disclosedness of things, and that encompasses both our being and that of the things around us.

From meaning to place

Heidegger's "Turning" does not only designate a particular episode in his intellectual autobiography, but also refers us to the way in which any fundamental thinking must involve a constant "turning back" to the situatedness of thinking as such, a "turning back" from what is disclosed to disclosedness as such and to our own involvement in such disclosedness, a "turning back" from beings to being. It is partly for this reason that Heidegger characterized his own thought as always "on the way," rather than in terms of having "arrived," and himself as a "seeker," rather than one who has found.

Moreover, if the question of being is one that must always be reawakened and rearticulated, then so too is it a question that will always be open to more than one mode of articulation. In a famous seminar in 1969, Heidegger sets out three different ways in which the question of being may be taken up, presenting them also as representative of three different stages in his own thinking (Heidegger, 1986, p. 344). While Heidegger does not identify all these stages with specific works or periods, and they clearly overlap in various ways, they do provide a useful way of charting the development of his thinking from early to late. The three terms that Heidegger identifies as markers here can thus be viewed as three successive poles around which his own thought turns.

The first stage, which Heidegger himself presents as specifically related to *Being and Time*, focuses on the question of being understood as a question concerning the *meaning* of being. It seems that it is this way of understanding the question of being that characterizes Heidegger's thinking up to the Turning of the 1930s. The second and third stages are more characteristic of Heidegger's thinking during and after the Turning. The second stage focuses on the question of being understood as a question concerning the *truth* of being and this focus on truth is especially important in Heidegger's writings during the 1930s and into the 1940s. The third stage takes up the question of being understood as a question concerning the *place* (*topos*) of being. It may be argued that the idea of place was already apparent in Heidegger's writing prior to the 1930s, but it is really in his writings from the 1940s and 1950s on the nature of dwelling and the dangers of technology that it comes to prominence. Meaning, truth, and place thus mark out three stages in the path of Heidegger's thought and, as such, they can also be viewed as marking stages in the progressive unfolding of but a single question – that of being – in which all three terms are already contained.

The Meaning of Being: *Being and Time*

The understanding of the question of being in terms of the question of the *meaning* of being is evident from the very start of Heidegger's 1927 *magnum opus. Being and Time* begins with a quotation from Plato – "For manifestly you have long been aware of what you mean when you use the word 'being.' We, however, who used to think we understood it, have now become perplexed" (Heidegger, 1962, p. 1 [H1]) – and Heidegger goes on to tell us that his aim in *Being and Time* is "to work out the question of the meaning of being and to do so concretely" (Heidegger, 1962, p. 1 [H1]).

Being and the unity of meaning

The question at issue here is one that harks back to the book that Heidegger tells us was the first philosophical text through which he worked: Franz Brantano's dissertation of 1862, *The Several Senses of Being in Aristotle*. As it arises in Aristotle, the problem of the *meaning* of being is also a problem that concerns the *unity* of being. Aristotle insists that there are a number of senses in which things can be, and while these ways of being stand in certain relations to one another, they nevertheless cannot be reduced to any single more encompassing sense of being. In taking up the question concerning the meaning of being, Heidegger also takes up this question concerning the unity of being, while nevertheless agreeing with Aristotle that any such unity cannot consist in the reduction of being to a single idea or category.

In fact, Heidegger understands the question of meaning, and the unity of meaning, that is at issue here from within the framework that is provided by his own studies in hermeneutics and phenomenology. From within this framework, meaning, "sense" (*Sinn*) or "intelligibility" is not to be identified with just what is presented as meaningful, but rather with the structure that allows something to be present as meaningful or intelligible. In this respect, the inquiry into meaning can be seen as having the same form as the inquiry into being understood as presence or disclosedness – indeed, this question of meaning can be viewed as the same as the question of presence or disclosedness.

The question of the *meaning* of being is thus a question that asks after the structure by which things are able to be disclosed as beings; it asks after the *unity* of the meaning of being inasmuch as it is indeed a single structure that is at issue here, even though it is a structure made up of a diversity of elements. Phenomenology is presented by Heidegger as a method for the uncovering of the unitary structure of meaning or intelligibility that is at issue here. However, since that structure is one that is usually hidden by our ordinary modes of engaging with things, phenomenology must also be hermeneutical in that it must aim, not only to exhibit the basic structure of intelligibility, but also to recover that structure from its usual hidden-ness.

Dasein as "being-in-the-world"

Heidegger argues that since it is with beings such as ourselves – beings for whom their own being "is an issue" – that the question of being first arises, so the inquiry into the meaning of being must also proceed, at least initially, through an inquiry into our being, that is, through an inquiry into the being of Dasein. Since the being of Dasein is distinct from the being of other things in this respect, so Heidegger uses "existence" to refer to the particular kind of being that is proper to Dasein – the basic structures of Dasein's existence are thus referred to as *existentials*. There is nowhere for such an existential inquiry itself to begin, however, other than through Dasein's own everyday understanding – even though that understanding may itself prove to be mistaken. Consequently, Heidegger begins his analysis with Dasein as it finds itself already "in" the world, in its practical engagement with things (such being "already in" he terms "throw-ness" or "facticity"), while acknowledging the preliminary character of that understanding. Yet if this must indeed be our starting point, then Dasein cannot be assumed to be identical with consciousness, with the knowing subject, or with some material body. These all represent abstractions from the primary experience of Dasein (of ourselves) as already given over to involvement in the world – to speaking, walking, writing, holding, making, and so on. Dasein can only be understood, at least to begin with, as "being-in-the-world," and any analysis of the structure of Dasein must therefore involve an analysis of the structure of the world in which Dasein is always already involved – a structure into which Dasein finds itself already "thrown."

It is important to note, however, that the way in which Dasein is "in" its world is not the same as the way in which, for instance, water may be spatially contained "in" a glass. The "being-in" of Dasein is the "being-in" of involvement rather than spatial containment. Such involvement is itself tied to Dasein's primary relatedness to things in their being as "*equipment*," that is, as things that are available for use or are "ready-to-hand" (*Zuhanden*), rather than as merely "present-to-hand" (*Vorhanden*) in a way abstracted from practical activity. Thus when I pick up the chalk in order to write on the blackboard, I grasp the chalk as something available for use, but when I merely examine the chalk in my hand, attending to its texture, its color and so on, I grasp it as something merely present or *occurrent* before me. Grasping things in their equipmental or available character is typically to grasp them in terms of which they show up within a certain social or cultural context. Indeed, in order for me to use the chalk as something with which to write, I already need to have a prior understanding of the chalk as something available for writing, and thus I already need to have a grasp of the set of practices within which chalk can be available in that way. This is indicative both of the way in which understanding operates always on the basis of certain prior understandings, as well as of the way in which those prior understandings are themselves socially and historically determined.

Inasmuch as Dasein's being is primarily made what it is through its practical, socialized dealings with things – and so it is through those practical dealings that things are first "disclosed" as intelligible – so its being or existence is not something established on the basis of some purely "interior" mental life, but only on the basis of its worldly involvements. In this respect, Heidegger's account of the structure of Dasein can be viewed as providing an important precursor to the so-called "externalist" theories of mind that have been associated with the work of Donald Davidson, Tyler Burge, and others.

Yet if Dasein is indeed constituted in such an "externalized" fashion – that is, merely in terms of its various practical involvements – then it is also threatened with being lost in the diversity and multiplicity of those involvements and in the depersonalized generality of the social (of what Heidegger calls "the They" or "the One" – *Das Man*). Indeed, Dasein has an inherent tendency – which Heidegger calls "falling" – to understand itself in just such an externalized and depersonalized fashion. But this tendency, and the more general tendency for Dasein to become lost in its dispersed involvements, threatens the idea of Dasein or "being-in-the-world" as a unitary mode of being (and so, one might say, it threatens the idea of the unity of the meaning of being as such). Yet if Dasein is indeed just that sort of being for whom its own being is always an issue, and that can therefore have a sense of its *own* being – a sense of its being as, in each case, "mine" – then Dasein must have a unity that is proper to it and that is more than merely a concatenation of otherwise unrelated activities or involvements.

Care, death, and temporality

"Care" (*Sorge*) is the term Heidegger uses to describe that aspect of Dasein's existence that concerns the way in which its own being is an issue for it. Care is thus tied
directly to Dasein's sense of itself, and so to Dasein's "mine-ness" or "own-ness."
Care is important in enabling us to understand how Dasein can be "in" the world:
Dasein's worldly involvements arise on the basis of care – that is, on the basis of the
way in which Dasein's being always matters to it – and so it provides us with a characterization of the nature of the unity that is proper to Dasein, but it does not yet
provide any explanation of how that unity is itself grounded. It certainly provides no
account of how Dasein can have a sense of itself.

Heidegger argues that the structure of care – the way in which Dasein's being is
an issue for it – is determined by the way in which Dasein grasps its own future possibilities in relation to what it already is and has been. Dasein is continually "projecting" such possibilities into its future and understands itself, and its life, in terms
of the possibilities that are open to it. This means that Dasein is constituted in a way
that is essentially temporal – time provides the horizon within which Dasein understands itself, as well as its world, and so time is the horizon within which things are
disclosed or brought to presence. Yet if the range of possibilities open to Dasein were
endless, if there were no limit to Dasein's projection of possibilities for its life into
the future, then there would be no limit to the possibilities in terms of which Dasein
could understand itself. If that were the case, however, there would be no sense in
which any one set of possibilities mattered to Dasein, since every set of possibilities
would be open to it and this would mean that nothing would stand out for Dasein
as significant (Dasein would also lack any sense of its own temporal character).

It is because Dasein's future projection of possibilities cannot go on for ever that
it can matter to Dasein just what possibilities become actual for it, but since Dasein
is itself defined in terms of its possibilities, this also means that Dasein can only have
a sense of itself inasmuch as its possibilities are indeed finite. It is death that marks
the limit of our possibilities; it is also death that represents the one possibility that
no one else can take on for us – no one else can die our own death – and so death
represents that which is our "ownmost" possibility. It is in the face of death that we
are forced to "own up" to ourselves and to recognize that only we can take responsibility for our lives. It is thus only in the face of the certain possibility of death that
the unity and "own-ness" of our lives is established and that the world, and the things
within it, are opened up to us. The meaning of being is thus to be found in the structure of our own finite temporality according to which our being-in-the-world is seen
ultimately to be grounded in our being-toward-death.

From Dasein to being

As it was actually published, virtually the whole of *Being and Time* is taken up by the
analysis of Dasein, culminating in the analysis of finite temporality, yet Heidegger's
original intention was that the work should comprise more than just this. *Being and*

Time was planned as a two-part work, with each part being made up of three divisions. The first division of Part I was to have set out the basic structure of Dasein's existence; the second division was to have shown how that existential structure was grounded in Dasein's temporal character; and the third division was then to have shown how Dasein's temporality was grounded in the temporality of being. Part II was to have worked back through the history of philosophy, providing a "retrieval" of the meaning of being from its philosophical forgetting – a counterpart to the retrieval from everyday forgetfulness accomplished in Part I – through a "taking apart" of philosophical thinking about time in the work of Kant, Descartes, and Aristotle. The work that actually appeared, however, comprised only Divisions 1 and 2 of Part I, the analysis of Dasein; the third division of Part I and the whole of Part II were absent.

   Being and Time fell short of its intended mark at the most crucial point: the shift from the analysis of the being of Dasein to the analysis of being as such. As a result, the work seems unable to progress beyond a certain level – it remains focused on the being of Dasein even while it recognizes that the question of being goes beyond the being of any particular being or mode of being. Indeed, inasmuch as it remains focused on the being of Dasein, so it may be seen to fall prey to a certain form of subjectivism or even idealism (although Heidegger himself firmly rejected any such criticism). The "failure" of *Being and Time* at this point – and in particular, Heidegger's inability, within the framework established by that work, to make the shift, the "Turn," from Dasein back to being – can be seen as lying at the heart of the "Turning" that Heidegger's thinking itself underwent in the period during the early to mid-1930s. In this respect, the "Turning" is not just a movement in Heidegger's own thinking, no matter whether tied to the events of the 1930s or to his thought as a whole, but a movement that must be accomplished by any genuine attempt to think the question of being.

Truth and Place: The Later Writings

By 1930, it seemed clear that the original project envisaged in *Being and Time* could not be brought to completion in quite the terms set out in that work. As a result, Heidegger came to focus more directly on the phenomenon that seems to lie at the heart of the question of being – on presence or disclosedness as such – rather than on that phenomenon as articulated through the structure of Dasein. In focusing more directly on disclosedness, Heidegger also comes to focus more directly on the question of truth and, through truth, on the idea of place.

The two senses of truth

Already, in *Being and Time*, Heidegger had distinguished between two senses of truth (Heidegger, 1962, §44, 212–30): first, truth as a matter of the adequacy of a judgment to its object according to which the truth of the statement "the picture is on the wall" is a matter of the correct representation of the state of affairs with regard to the picture and its position in relation to the wall; second, truth as itself a matter of the original uncoveredness of things according to which the picture, the wall, and their relatedness are disclosed such that judgment about them is even possible. The former sense of truth is dependent on the latter – truth as correctness is possible only on the basis of the more originary sense of truth as uncoveredness or disclosedness. It is truth that is the main concern of Heidegger's seminal essay "The origin of the work of art" (Heidegger, 1993b, pp. 139–212, originally given in lecture form in 1935–6) and in that work Heidegger looks to the way in which truth – that is, the original uncoveredness of things – is established and worked out in relation to the work of art.

Truth, art, and world

Disclosedness, and so also truth, is always, for Heidegger, a matter of the coming to be of a world within which particular things, and even ourselves, can come to presence. The coming to be of a world – the "worlding of the world," to use a Heideggerian phrase – is essentially a cultural–historical matter. It happens, not just for, or in respect of, an individual, but only in relation to a culture, a history, a "people." The same must also hold for disclosedness and so for truth: truth does not happen just for me, but only inasmuch as I belong to a larger cultural–historical world.

Truth, then, is always historical, which does not mean that truth is somehow relativized (for truth here does not refer merely to the truth of statements, but to truth as that originary disclosedness on the basis of which particular statements can be true or false) but, rather, that it only emerges with the emergence of particular historical worlds – particular historical articulations (or "grantings") of being. Such worlds do not only find their *expression* in great works of art, but, according to Heidegger, great works of art themselves *define* and *found* the worlds that are expressed in them. As such, great works of art themselves constitute particular under-standings of being – one might say that they allow things to "show up" in particu-lar ways and as part of a particular mode of ordering.

The central example that Heidegger uses to illustrate the ideas at issue here is that of the Greek temple. The temple is a work of art, and as such it is a particular thing located in a particular place. Yet it would be a mistake to think that the character of the temple as a work of art consisted solely in its being a thing made of certain mate-rials, configured with a certain form. As a work of art, the temple is a setting-up of an ordering and relating of things that allows certain aspects to stand out as signifi-cant and lets others fall away.

The temple establishes a point of focus that brings what stands around it clearly into view: the rocky plain on which it stands is now evident as rock, as the support-ing, but also concealing earth; the sky that is open above it is now evident as sky, as the all-encompassing expanse of world. The setting of these apart from and coun-terposed to one another establishes the cleared space within which individual things can be disclosed: human beings take on their own character as mortals who stand before the god whose temple this is, who till the soil, who work the stone, who look up to the sky; similarly, animals and plants, rivers and oceans, mountains and valleys, take on a specific character in accord with the ordering of things established in and through the temple. As Heidegger writes: "The temple-work, standing there, opens up a world and at the same time sets this world back on earth, which itself only thus emerges as native ground . . . The temple, in its standing there, first gives to things their look and to men their outlook on themselves" (Heidegger, 1993a, p. 168).

We might add that the temple gives to human beings their being as human, inasmuch as it enables their humanity and mortality to be understood within a particular set of worldly possibilities – it provides a "concretization" of what it is to be human without which no human could be. The character of the temple as a work of art is thus found not in its portrayal or representation of some thing other than itself, but in its setting-up of a world, and this is characteristic, not merely of the temple, but of all art. All art – at least, all great art – is essentially disclosive and, as such, all great art stands in an essential relation to truth.

"The origin of the work of art" is often seen as a pivotal work in Heidegger's thought, occurring as it does around the time of the "Turning," and it has also been extremely influential on subsequent thinkers. Gadamer, for instance, gives the essay a central role in his own work (Gadamer, 1997, p. 47). The particular path of thinking that is taken by "The origin of the work of art" is nevertheless viewed by Heidegger as something of a side-track – rather like those paths through the woods (*Holzwege*) that take one nowhere in particular and do not lead to any final destination. Yet the general direction of that path is one that Heidegger continues to follow. Indeed, in his later writings he remains focused on the idea of disclosedness or presence as a matter of the establishing of a certain cleared yet unitary dimension – rather like the forest clearing (*die Lichtung*) that offers space and light for things to appear – that is always centered on some particular thing (though it need not be a work of art), and yet also opens up a world. In essays such as "Building dwelling thinking" (Heidegger, 1993b, pp. 343–64, originally given as a lecture in 1951), Heidegger describes just such an emergence of world, and of disclosedness, as also the establishing of a place for human dwelling.

Building and dwelling

"Dwelling" is the word that Heidegger comes increasingly to use – partly as a result of his reading of the German romantic poet Friedrich Hölderlin (although the term already appears in §12 of *Being and Time*) – as a way of designating the way of being of mortals like ourselves. The opening up of world is thus something that happens only in relation to human being, even though human being is itself made possible, and disclosed as human, only through the opening up of world. The focus for dwelling, and for the opening up of the world, is not, however, human being or human activity taken on its own, but rather the thing around, and in relation to which, such activity is itself organized – say, a bridge or a jug of wine or, to use an example from Heidegger's very early writing that seems to presage the ideas in the later, the table in the family home (see Heidegger, 1999, pp. 68–70). Such things are themselves brought into being through human activity, through what Heidegger calls "building" (which can mean cultivation and "caring for" as much as it means construction), but human activity itself takes form only in relation to the things with respect to which it is focused. Moreover, since building is an articulation of dwelling, and dwelling presupposes a world, so building is itself possible only inasmuch as there is a world in which we already dwell.

Place, thing, and the Fourfold

In "The origin of the work of art," world was counterposed to earth, but in essays such as "Building dwelling thinking," world is understood as the unity of what Heidegger calls "the Fourfold" (*das Geviert*). The Fourfold is made up of four contrasting elements – earth and sky, gods and mortals – each of which is necessary to the overall structure, but no one of which has any priority over the others. The earth is that on which we stand and which supports and nourishes us; the sky is that which arches above us and in which we find light and open-ness; the gods are those ideals, values, and images that define us even while they go beyond us; the mortals are the beings that we ourselves are – beings that die. Since any particular thing stands at the intersection of an inexhaustibly rich set of interconnections (something reflected in the infinity of ways in which any such thing can be described), so the old bridge, the jug of wine, the family table, each gathers together, in its own ways, these four elements, along with all that is included within them, thereby bringing into focus a world as well as the things that stand within that world. The structure of the world that is established and maintained in this way is thus a structure established and maintained through the mutual interrelation of its elements, while those elements are themselves constituted only through their worldly relatedness.

The gathering together of the elements of the Fourfold in relation to a particular thing is not only the establishing and opening up of a world, but also the establishing of a particular locale or place, a particular *topos*. It is only within and with respect to such places that human dwelling is possible – dwelling is precisely a way of being-in-place. Not only is this idea captured in Heidegger's own use of the image of the forest clearing as a way of describing the character of disclosedness and the emergence of world (the idea is also presaged in the "Da" – the "there" – of "Dasein"), but it is also reflected in his various accounts of the way in which the siting or locatedness of a thing in relation to the things around it enables the opening up and "freeing" of those things such that they can indeed come into a relationship with one another and with the thing that stands at the center of that freed and open region. Much of Heidegger's later thinking is concerned with articulating the structure of such a "place" or locale, and thus takes the form of what Heidegger calls a "topology" of being – a saying of the place of being (Heidegger, 1986, p. 344).

One might, of course, view this talk of gods and mortals, of place and dwelling, as providing no more than a poetized description of a certain aspect of the human experience of the world. But the original question of being that drives Heidegger's thinking is at work in these later writings no less than in *Being and Time*. As always, Heidegger's concern is to understand being, not in terms of the existence of mere "stuff," but rather in terms of the disclosedness, the presencing, of things in all their complex locatedness within the world. Heidegger aims to let the things themselves appear, not merely as the objects of science, nor as components in a process of causal interaction, nor even just as things available for human use, but as things that can be disclosed in all of these ways and more. In this respect, the "poetic" language of Heidegger's later writings is not a resort to some more obscure or esoteric mode of speech, but a way of returning to, of retrieving, of remembering, the breadth and richness of what is at issue in the disclosedness, the presencing, the *being* of things.

The critique of technology

Closely tied to Heidegger's analyses of truth, place and dwelling in the later writings is a detailed critique of technological modernity that receives perhaps its fullest development in the essay "The question concerning technology" (Heidegger, 1993b, pp. 307–42; originally presented as a lecture in 1949 and, in revised form, in 1953). Heidegger argues that the metaphysical "forgetting of being" that has its origins in Greek thinking has its culmination in the modern technological ordering of the world. Indeed, he argues that rather than technology being merely something that follows on from philosophical and scientific inquiry, as the practical application of more fundamental ideas, the technological drive to mastery and control is what drives Western philosophy and science from the very start.

Crucial to Heidegger's analysis of technology is his claim that technology cannot itself be understood technologically – technology is essentially a mode of disclosedness, but a mode of disclosedness that conceals its own character as disclosing and that also closes off any other such mode of disclosedness. The essence of technology, says Heidegger, is something that he terms "Enframing" (*Gestell*). The original German word that Heidegger uses here carries a number of connotations lost in the English translation that connect with notions of manufacture, production, representation, and setting-in-place. Enframing is a mode of ordering or assembling that unifies everything under a single aspect – as resource or "stock" (*Bestand*) – to be taken up as part of a continual process of production, manipulation, transformation, and utilization.

Taken up in this way, a river becomes a source of hydroelectric power, to be dammed, controlled, transformed, and transferred; a forest becomes a source of timber to be managed and processed; the countryside becomes a product to be packaged and sold as part of the tourism industry; and human beings appear as a "human resource." In reducing things in this way to mere "resource" or "stock" – to their role within some broader system of ordering – technological enframing discloses things, but only as they appear within a single "frame" and a single set of possibilities. Things are interconnected as part of the limitless ordering of resources, but the nature of that interconnection is also such as to obliterate difference and distinction – everything becomes transformable, interchangeable, homogenous.

Moreover, the scope of technological enframing is total: even human being is taken up as resource and the very possibility of human dwelling endangered. Yet although the danger posed by technological enframing is great, Heidegger insists that we cannot reject technology any more than we should simply give ourselves over to it. The modern world is a technological world and we cannot simply change the character of that world by an act of will. Indeed, to suppose that we can is to give expression to the very drive for mastery and control that itself lies at the heart of technology as such (in this respect, Heidegger sees technological enframing as closely tied to modern subjectivism). Heidegger's refusal to allow that technology can be responded to in such a way has led some to regard his position on this matter as passive and quietistic – we can do nothing but wait. Heidegger also, however, has a more positive message: we cannot ourselves determine the character of the world, but we can maintain a questioning attitude toward technology as such; we can hope to reawaken and maintain a capacity for thoughtfulness; and, in perhaps small and marginal ways, we can allow things to show up outside of a purely technological frame. "Letting things be" in this way is what seems at the heart of the late Heidegger's emphasis on "releasement" or "tranquility" (*Gelassenheit*).

Nazism and the University: Heidegger's Politics

One of the defining problems for German, and, perhaps more generally, for European thinking in the twentieth century was its relation to Nazism. That problem takes on a special significance in relation to Heidegger. In 1933 Heidegger took on the role of Rector at Freiburg University, becoming the first National Socialist University Rector in Germany. He remained as Rector only until 1934, yet he seems to have retained confidence in the leadership of the National Socialist leader, Adolf Hitler, until at least 1936; although in the later 1930s, and into the 1940s, much of Heidegger's writing seems to have taken the form of an implicit critique of Nazism through an engagement with the work of Nietzsche and the Nietzschean idea of the "will to power," he never formally resigned his party membership. After the war, Heidegger remained reticent about what he nevertheless acknowledged as his "mistake" of 1933, with much that he did say seeming to be, at the very least, self-serving. For many, even more disappointing, even more damning, was his apparent failure to offer any significant comment on the horror of the Nazis' "final solution."

The question of what we should make of these facts is a difficult one that has engendered a vast amount of literature and argument. Even the exact extent of Heidegger's political entanglement has been a source of controversy. One thing that does seem clear is that Heidegger's entry into politics in the 1930s was the culmination of a long-standing interest in the politics of the university, and in the question of the role of the university in German society and culture more generally. Heidegger was already writing and thinking about such matters from very early in his career, and he must have viewed the chance of taking on the Rectorship at Freiburg in 1933 as an opportunity to finally put into practice ideas that had preoccupied him, in one way or another, for many years. Equally, it seems clear that he was soon forced to recognize that his own ideas did not find favor with the powers in Berlin – if he was an opportunist, he also seems to have been politically somewhat naïve and unrealistic.

Perhaps the central question concerning Heidegger's association with Nazism, however, has been the question as to what extent Heidegger's philosophy must itself be seen as tainted by that association. Is Heidegger's philosophy to be viewed as a Nazi philosophy? Is his involvement with Nazism indicative of some problematic political tendency hidden in his philosophy as such – might it be indicative of a tendency for that philosophy to lead to some form of moral or political blindness?

We should be careful about such questions as these, and we should be careful not only because of the ambiguities that reside in them, but also because they are questions to which answers are all too readily assumed. Particular readings of Heidegger's involvement with Nazism have often been the basis for simple and superficial criticisms or rejections of his thinking. Yet there is no way of dealing either with the question of Heidegger's involvement with Nazism or the character of his thought as such other than by working through that thought and coming to an understanding of it in its own terms. And doing this means keeping open the possibility that, while Heidegger's involvement with Nazism represents a deep personal failure in a time of great trial, it need not compromise the philosophical worth or significance of his thought.

References

Arendt, H. 1978: Martin Heidegger at eighty (trans. A. Hofstadter). In M. Murray (ed.), *Heidegger and Modern Philosophy*. New Haven, Conn.: Yale University Press (original work published in German in 1969 and in English in 1971).

Gadamer, H.-G. 1985: Martin Heidegger. In H.-G. Gadamer, *Philosophical Apprenticeships*, trans. R. R. Sullivan. Cambridge, Mass.: The MIT Press, 45–54 (original work published 1977).

——1997: Reflections on my philosophical journey. In L. E. Hahn (ed.), *The Philosophy of Hans-Georg Gadamer*. Library of Living Philosophers 24. Chicago, Ill.: Open Court.

Heidegger, M. 1962: *Being and Time*, trans. J. Macquarrie and E. Robinson. New York: Harper & Row (original work published 1927). Alternative translation by J. Stambaugh (New York: State University of New York Press, 1996).

——1986: *Seminare*. Frankfurt: Vittorio Klostermann.

——1993a: *Basic Concepts*, trans. G. E. Aylesworth. Bloomington, Ind.: Indiana University Press (original work published 1981).

——1993b: *Basic Writings*, ed. D. F. Krell, 2nd edn. New York: HarperCollins (a collection of original works published between 1927 and 1966).

——1999: *The Hermeneutics of Facticity*, trans. J. van Buren. Bloomington, Ind.: Indiana University Press (original work published 1988).

Kisiel, Th. 1993: *The Genesis of Heidegger's* Being and Time. Berkeley, Calif.: University of California Press.

Petzet, H. W. 1993: *Encounters and Dialogues with Martin Heidegger 1929–1976*, trans. P. Emand and K. Maly. Chicago, Ill.: Chicago University Press (original work published 1983).

Further reading

Biemel, W. 1976: *Martin Heidegger. An Illustrated Study*, trans. J. L. Mehta. New York: Harcourt Brace Jovanovich (original work published 1973).

Dreyfus, H. L. 1991: *Being-in-the-World: A Commentary on Heidegger's* Being and time, *Division I*. Cambridge, Mass.: The MIT Press (a new edition of this work is scheduled to appear soon).

Guignon, C. (ed.) 1993: *The Cambridge Companion to Heidegger*. Cambridge: Cambridge University Press.

Parkes, G. (ed.) 1987: *Heidegger and Asian Thought*. Honolulu: University of Hawaii Press.

Wolin, R. (ed.) 1993: *The Heidegger Controversy*. Cambridge, Mass.: The MIT Press.

Wrathall, M. (ed.) 2000: *Appropriating Heidegger*. Cambridge: Cambridge University Press.

Young, J. 1997: *Heidegger, Philosophy, Nazism*. Cambridge: Cambridge University Press.

Chapter 8

Jean-Paul Sartre

David Sherman

All good philosophers dedicate themselves to only a few truly important philosophical problems, and then progressively plumb their depths within an existing theoretical framework, but it is the great philosopher who furnishes us with a new way of thinking about these problems altogether. One such "problem," in particular, consists of questions concerning the nature and scope of human freedom in its metaphysical, phenomenological, sociohistorical, and political senses. It is this constellation of questions that unifies the prodigious and otherwise varied output of Jean-Paul Sartre (1905–80). The last generation of continental philosophers was heavily influenced by Sartre's originative responses to these questions, and they are the unacknowledged specters that haunt the present generation.

"A philosophy whose sole dogma is the affirmation of human freedom" is the way in which Sartre described his thought in 1947,[1] and despite his subsequent turn toward Marxism in the 1950s, there is little reason to retrospectively change this assessment. To be sure, with the evolution of Sartre's idea of social relations, the focus of this "affirmation" changes over time, but this does not mean that he breaks with his earlier commitments. Instead, Sartre simply extends the abstract principles that underlie his phenomenological commitments to the social realm, where they are concretized. The individual's "absolute" freedom of choice, which is the hallmark of Sartre's existential phenomenology, is empty, he comes to realize, if the sociohistorical situation within which the individual must choose affords only bad options. Crucially, however, not only does Sartre remain committed to "the affirmation of human freedom" in his shift of emphasis from the freedom of the individual to an oppressive social realm, but he remains steadfastly committed to the foundational role of individual freedom after this shift of emphasis as well. More specifically, through the successive focal points of Sartre's philosophy – crudely, the unbridled freedom of consciousness in his early phenomenological works, the more nuanced "freedom-in-situation" of his existential phenomenology, freely adopted individual and collective practices in his revision of Hegelian–Marxist dialectics, and the psychoanalytic synthesis of these prior standpoints to grasp the concrete unfolding of a life (Gustave Flaubert's) – this commitment remains constant. As Sartre summarily puts it toward the end of his life: "We are free, but we have to free ourselves, and so freedom must revolt against all forms of alienation."[2]

Such a concern with freedom is not one that is currently taken to be particularly auspicious. Most philosophers consider the concept of freedom to be rather old-fashioned, the residuum of a washed-out metaphysical tradition. Of course, these philosophers would concede, as actors in the world we must think of ourselves as free, for the deep structures that underlie actual deliberation and action (rather than our thinking about deliberation and action) are essentially incompatible with viewing ourselves as determined. But, at the end of the day, this argument concludes, despite the practical necessity of proceeding *as if* we are free, determined is precisely what we are. Or, as the widely accepted "compatibilist" position puts it, "freedom" is nothing more than acting in accord with our determined characters. Since Newtonian physics, the natural sciences have certainly led to this conclusion (despite the indeterminacy of quantum mechanics, which, it is generally held, does little to rehabilitate the "free will" perspective). So, too, in the social sciences, Marxists and Freudians (if not actually Marx and Freud themselves) have undermined the idea of freedom from both without and within. Moreover, Sartre's own philosophical influences had less than robust ideas of freedom. They either reconstituted freedom to make it synonymous with reconciling oneself to the social institutions of one's world (Hegel), articulated it within a narrow epistemological framework (Husserl), or equated it with an abstract notion of authenticity (Heidegger). And, finally, for the structuralists and poststructuralists who supplanted Sartre in France, the very notion of a "subject," much less a free one, is discarded, and in its place the primacy of language (Derrida, Lacan) or systems of power (Foucault) is asserted. In the face of this nearly categorical renunciation, Sartre's vigorous account of individual freedom is hopelessly out of step. It seems to me, nevertheless, that his unique amalgam of existential phenomenology and Hegelian-Marxism constitutes a powerful philosophical theory, one that has the theoretical resources to make a substantial contribution to current debates in continental thought concerning the problem of agency.

Sartre's Life

A novelist, playwright, literary critic, political activist, and, of course, philosopher, Sartre was one of the most commanding intellectual figures of the twentieth century. Described (pejoratively) by Michel Foucault as the last "universal intellectual," Sartre came to be seen as the very embodiment of French culture, thus prompting Charles de Gaulle to declare, in response to those who sought Sartre's arrest for his political activities during the postwar period, that Sartre was France, and one does not jail France.

Born on June 21, 1905 in Paris, Sartre was raised by his mother and grandparents, studied at the École Normale Supérieure, where he met his lifelong companion and colleague Simone de Beavoir, and through the 1930s intermittently taught philosophy at a number of French *lycées* (high schools). During this decade, Sartre also studied for a year at the French Institute in Berlin, where he immersed himself in phenomenology (in particular, the philosophy of Husserl), and then published a variety of works – most notably, his first novel (*Nausea*), a phenomenological account of the imagination (*Imagination*), and a pivotal philosophical essay, *The Transcendence of the Ego*, which laid the groundwork for his existentialist masterpiece, *Being and Nothingness*. In 1939–40, he published *The Emotions: Outline of a Theory* and *The Psychology of Imagination*, was conscripted, and, soon thereafter, was captured by the Nazis. While confined to a prisoner-of-war camp, Sartre kept an extensive diary, continued to develop his evolving philosophy, and otherwise composed and produced plays for his fellow prisoners. After gaining his freedom by posing as a civilian, he joined the French Resistance. Between the years of 1943 and 1948, Sartre published *Being and Nothingness* and *Anti-Semite and Jew*, essays such as "Existentialism is a humanism" and "What is literature?," various plays (including "The Flies," "No Exit," and "Dirty Hands"), the novel *The Age of Reason*, and helped found the newspaper *Les temps modernes*.

Although always a leftist, Sartre's move toward a more explicitly Marxist position, which contributed to his breaks with Albert Camus and Maurice Merleau-Ponty, is foreshadowed in the early 1950s by *Saint Genet, Actor and Martyr* (a biography of the French poet Jean Genet) and *The Communists and the Peace* (which reflects his complicated stance toward the Soviet Union). It was only with Sartre's pivotal 1957 essay, "Search for a method," however, that his more developed amalgam of existential phenomenology and Marxism was theoretically articulated. "Search for a method" was meant to be the precursor to a much larger study on dialectical reason, and in 1960 the first volume of Sartre's *Critique of Dialectical Reason* was published. (The second, unfinished volume was published posthumously in 1985.) In 1964, Sartre was awarded the Nobel Prize for literature, which he refused on the ground that "a writer should not be an institution." By the late 1960s, he expanded his political activities, which included supporting the 1968 student uprisings, but also broke with the Soviet Union due to its interventions in Hungary and Czechoslovakia. Although Sartre's health began to decline in the early 1970s, he continued to engage in various political activities, and published the first three volumes of his projected five-volume analysis of Gustave Flaubert, which was titled *The Family Idiot*. In 1980, Sartre died, at which time more than 50,000 Parisians flooded the streets of the Left Bank to pay their respects.

Early Phenomenological Works

Sartre was concerned, first and foremost, with crafting a philosophy that was able to capture the particularities of existence in all their diversity. According to Simone de Beavoir, he first learned of Edmund Husserl's phenomenology, which itself was concerned with "getting back to the things themselves," over drinks with a group of friends. Among this group was Raymond Aron, who had studied at the Berlin Institute the year before Sartre, and had recently returned to Paris. According to de Beavoir, when Aron informed Sartre that Husserl's phenomenology could take as its object of inquiry something as seemingly mundane as the cocktail that Aron was at that moment holding in his hand, Sartre turned white and began to tremble with excitement. And, indeed, through the remainder of the 1930s, Sartre's works heavily reflect Husserl's influence. As Sartre himself emphasizes in his war diaries (February 1940 entry), "Husserl had gripped me. I saw everything through the perspectives of his philosophy – which was in any case more accessible to me [than Heidegger's thought], thanks to its semblance of Cartesianism."[3]

Drawing upon his own teacher, Franz Bretano, Husserl's phenomenology is based on the notion of "intentionality," which is the belief that all consciousness, or, more simply, awareness, is a "consciousness of" or "awareness of" some object. This seemingly mundane notion, which will come to form the cornerstone of Sartre's philosophy, is actually fraught with philosophical import. On the empiricist model of knowledge (and, ultimately, the Kantian one as well), the mind is cut off from the external world, and our experiences only refer back to internal mental states or "representations," not to the objective world itself. As a result, this "inside–outside" model runs aground in skepticism. The concept of intentionality circumvents this problem by putting us in an immediate relation to the objects of our perception, but, as far as Husserl is concerned, it does not put an end to the problem of knowledge. According to Husserl, to get to "the things themselves," it is necessary to ascertain the "essential" or "ideal" nature of the objects of our experience, and to accomplish this task, he relies upon various so-called "reductions." The "eidetic reduction," for example, involves the attempt to turn from the contingent facts of the object under consideration to its essence through the cultivation of "essential insight," which can take the form of creative imagining, thought experiments, or any other method for getting beyond the object's merely contingent aspects. But to experience objects in their ideality – that is, in a way that would be necessary for any experiencing consciousness, and not just the particular one that is performing the eidetic reduction – Husserlian phenomenology requires another reduction. This reduction, the "phenomenological reduction" or *epoché*, is one in which the "natural attitude" toward the world is suspended or "bracketed." By using the "phenomenological reduction" or *epoché*, we shift from a psychological or natural perception of "real" objects to a philosophical act that "intends" the object in a neutral way. For Husserl, this allows us to come to know not only the ideal nature of the object, but also the ideal nature of the self to whom the object appears.

Despite portraying himself as a devotee of Husserl's philosophy during the 1930s, the fact is that from the very beginning Sartre appropriated only certain aspects of it, and then reconstituted these aspects for his own particular ends. In *The Transcendence of the Ego*, published a scant two years after he was first exposed to Husserl's thought in Berlin, Sartre rejects the very existence of a transcendental ego, which is arguably the linchpin of Husserl's phenomenology. For Husserl, the transcendental ego is consciousness in its ideality, and is seemingly a necessary condition of the suspension of the natural attitude, for it allows consciousness to grasp the ideality of the object. According to Sartre, however, Husserl's positing of a transcendental ego that is either "in" or "behind" consciousness interferes with the basic aim of his phenomenological project, namely, "getting back to the things themselves." This is because the transcendental ego needs to have its relationship to the objects of its intuition mediated. To intuit the object, then, we would first have to grasp the transcendental ego, which does not get us back to the things themselves but, rather, precipitates a collapse back into the well worn "inside–outside" problem of classic epistemology. In effect, this would negate the huge strides that Husserl makes with his concept of intentionality. Thus, Sartre contends, the existence of a transcendental ego would be nothing less than the "death of consciousness," because objects in the world would no longer be transparent to it.[4] By purging consciousness's "transcendental field" of all egological structures that might muddy it, in other words, consciousness is positioned directly before the objects that it perceives, and can intuit them as they really are (*TE*, p. 93). But what of the ego?

Sartre's radical thesis in *The Transcendence of the Ego* is set forth in the opening paragraph: "the ego is neither formally nor materially in consciousness: it is outside, *in the world*. It is a being of the world, like the ego of another" (*TE*, p. 31). Before elaborating on what it means for the ego to be "in the world," however, Sartre differentiates between the notion of the ego as "I," which is what is meant when he states that the ego is not formally in consciousness, and the notion of the ego as "me," which is what is meant when he states that the ego is not materially in consciousness. The formal "I" with which Sartre is more or less preoccupied is the "I" of Kant, the "transcendental unity of apperception," which stands behind our experience and unifies our countless perceptions and actions, thus making them our own. According to Sartre, however, Kant's transcendental "I" is not necessary, for the "I" arises from the objects of which it is intentionally aware: the unity of consciousness is to be found in the object itself. In other words, the "I" does not stand behind experience but, rather, arises from it. As a result, in its most basic mode, which Sartre calls here "unreflected consciousness," consciousness is impersonal. And, indeed, the "I" generally does not enter into our consciousness when we are absorbed in our various tasks in the world. There is only a basic consciousness of our task. For example, my consciousness when I play basketball is not of the form, "*I* will now dribble the ball, *I* will now shoot a jump shot, *I* will now fall back to play defense," but, instead, the far more fluid "dribbling the ball, shooting a jump shot, falling back to play defense." The "I" comes into play only if I reflect upon what I am doing, which usually arises from my failure to do it well (and, at least in this context, often just exacerbates the problem). As I shall discuss later, Sartre believes that there is a consciousness of consciousness – that is, an awareness by consciousness of itself in its awareness of objects – that enables it to move to this reflective level. In the meantime, however, the crucial point is that reflective consciousness is a derivative phenomenon, not a primary one. In this way, Sartre breaks with Descartes, whom, he argues, mistakenly conflates the reflective consciousness that says "I think" with the prereflective consciousness that actually thinks (*TE*, p. 45).

Since the "I" arises from our experiences, it can never be purely formal, as is the case with the transcendental "I" of Kant and Husserl. Thus, in the example set forth above, my "I" is the bare self-reflective unity that is comprised of my perceptions and actions while playing basketball. But while I am playing, it should be recognized, I do not consider my "I" stretched across time, which would implicate my self-identity or empirical ego; instead, my self-reflection is (or, at least, should be) strictly confined to that particular place and time. As Sartre puts it, the "I" is "an infinite contraction of the material me" (*TE*, p. 54). Conversely, it is the expansion of this

"I," or one's thicker self-identity or empirical self, to which Sartre refers when he speaks of the material "me," which is composed of states, qualities, and actions. A "state" (an emotional state, for example) is a transcendent unity of consciousnesses over time, such as my love or hatred for a particular person, whereas a "quality" is simply a predisposition toward a state based upon a tendency evidenced in my actions. Sartre's crucial point, however, is that a quality or full blown state does not exist *in* consciousness; rather, the propensity to "love" or "hate," as well as its actualization, is simply an ideal unity of so many doting or angry consciousnesses in the past – an ideal unity that is currently brought about *by* consciousness. Accordingly, Sartre contends that the material "me," which is composed of these states, qualities, and actions, is an object that is apprehended and constituted by reflective consciousness (*TE*, pp. 80–1).

The importance of this move to Sartre's overall philosophy can scarcely be overstated. By making consciousness responsible for the production of the material "me" or empirical ego – as he puts it, "it is a relation on the order of poetic production, or, if you like, a relation of creation" (*TE*, p. 77) – Sartre lays the foundation for his claim in *Being and Nothingness* that we are "absolutely free." To be sure, the reflective "I," which is the outgrowth of consciousness moving to the self-reflective level, generally tends to see itself in terms of the material "me" or empirical ego that has congealed over time; thus, we declare, "I can't agree to this," or "I hate that," as if these positions make up our "essence." But the fact of the matter, Sartre contends, is that there is nothing about the empirical ego that mandates this response, since the spontaneity of consciousness is weighted down by the historical constitution of the ego only to the degree that it chooses to be. Indeed, although I stand in a somewhat more intimate relationship to it, my empirical ego is an object for me in the reflective mode of the "I" in much the same way that it is an object for other people, with one critical exception: since I stand in a more intimate relationship to my ego, "objective" methods for coming to know it, such as observation, approximation, anticipation, and experience, are more fallible, for the ego tends to accompany my move to the reflective level (*TE*, p. 86). Furthermore, when in the unreflective mode, we may simply tend to act in accordance with these ideal egological structures, although, strictly speaking, we are conscious of neither the "I" nor the "me" in this mode. As we shall see, it is for this reason that Sartre's conception of "absolute" freedom is far more equivocal than many caricatures of his philosophy suggest.

Throughout the remainder of the 1930s, Sartre brings his modified account of Husserl's phenomenology to bear upon two perennial philosophical problems, namely, the ontological status of the imagination and the emotions. As to the imagination, he published two works, *Imagination* and *The Psychology of Imagination*, both of which are well-grounded in Husserlian intentionality, but otherwise deviate from Husserl's own concerns. Specifically, Husserl himself never strictly sought to bring his phenomenological method to bear upon the imagination, but only perceptions, and he may have disagreed with Sartre's extension of his method to images. In any event, Sartre maintains that the typical conception of an image as an inert content of consciousness is incorrect.[5] In contrast to, say, the Humean position that images are only a fainter, residual form of perceptual impressions *in* consciousness, he contends that images are not actually *in* consciousness at all, but, instead, are a certain type or mode *of* consciousness. Of course, Sartre does not deny that images are generally analogues of perceptible objects, which they in some sense represent, but they are not merely passive registers of perceptible objects in some fainter form either. Images are an active intending by consciousness *of* something, or, in other words, a positing by consciousness of an object that is other than consciousness. By virtue of this active comportment, the image is a "transformation" of the perceptible object, and not just a "filling out" of it, as is the case with Husserl's intending of perceptible objects. This intending, transforming act, Sartre says near the end of *The Psychology of Imagination*, is a "negative" one that is made possible by the fact that consciousness is "able to escape from the world by its very nature . . . in a word it [is] free."[6]

For Husserl, it should be recalled, the application of the *epoché* to perceptions is motivated by epistemological considerations (which might be why he never brought his phenomenological method to bear on the messier domain of images), while, for Sartre, the ability of consciousness to bring about this "nihilating withdrawal" from reality has significant practical implications. These implications are more clearly brought out in *The Emotions: Outline of a Theory*, in which Sartre does nothing less than attack our standard account of the emotions – an account that goes back to the ancient Greeks. If consciousness has the ability to "transform" the perceptible object in its subsequent imagining of it, then it would also seem to have the ability to transform it while it is being perceived.[7] And, indeed, Sartre makes this very point in *The Psychology of Imagination*, in which he contends that "when knowledge combines with affectivity it undergoes a debasement which is precisely what permits it to fulfill itself." Sartre's language here is somewhat equivocal, however. On the one hand, he is saying that knowledge is "debased" when it becomes affective in nature, which implicitly holds out the prospect that there can be a superior, unaffected knowing, while, on the other hand, he seems to suggest that this very debasement is itself the price of having any knowledge whatsoever. This latter claim, the stronger one, is another way of saying that all knowing occurs within a particular affective context that is based upon our practical considerations. It stands in sharp contrast to Husserl's *epoché* (and is somewhat reminiscent of the practical turn that Fichte gave to Kant's epistemology). At least as far as *The Emotions* is concerned, however, Sartre refuses to make this more radical move.

Once again relying upon Husserl's all important notion of intentionality, Sartre begins *The Emotions* by attacking a number of classical theories of emotion. From the psychological theory of James, which holds that emotions are only the consciousness of physiologically induced feelings, to the behaviorism of Janet, Sartre argues that what has been lost is consciousness – or, to be more exact, the significance or purposiveness that emotions have for consciousness. Behaviorism does not get to the essence of the emotion, but merely describes its outward manifestations, while physiological theories are based upon what has been called "the hydraulic model," namely, a model which holds that the human psyche is merely a caldron of pressures that demand some sort of release.[8] (This view is captured by such everyday phrases as "blowing one's top" or "exploding in rage.") Moreover, Sartre argues, even Freud, who recognizes the meaningfulness of emotions, continues to view them in passive terms – in other words, as things that we passively "undergo." Sartre contends, to the contrary, that emotions are intentional in that they are *about* the world; they are both a response to the world and a certain way of apprehending it.[9] In the face of the world's difficulties, we bring about what he calls a "magical transformation of the world" to enable us to better cope. Thus, emotions are an "abrupt solution of a conflict, a way of cutting the Gordian Knot,"[10] as is the case with the fox in Aesop's fable, who decides that the grapes he desperately wanted but could not obtain are really too green anyway. In other words, we affectively transform the nature of reality so as to make it easier to negotiate, transform our belief systems accordingly, and then proceed to live the reality that we have established.

Two crucial points need to be made here. First, as suggested above, Sartre is arguing that emotional knowledge is a degraded form of knowledge, and thus cryptically asserts that "freedom has to come from a purifying reflection or a total disappearance of the affecting situation."[11] In other words, he seems to be holding out the idea that there is some unaffected form of knowing, which arguably presupposes Husserl's phenomenological reduction. Given his position in *The Transcendence of the Ego*, however, it is by no means clear that he is entitled to this reduction. In fact, although he once cryptically mentions the phenomenological reduction in *The Emotions*, his emphasis is clearly on the eidetic reduction – namely, getting to the essential nature of an emotion. But, as we already saw, the eidetic reduction is undertaken in the natural attitude. In short, then, the problem is locating the standpoint from which consciousness can bring about its own freedom through a "purifying reflection" – that is, a detached standpoint from which there is no affective knowing. This is a problem that will come into sharper focus in *Being and Nothingness*. Second, Sartre's analysis in *The Emotions*, as well as every other early work, is starkly asocial. This point is unintentionally brought home toward the end of *The Emotions*, where he abruptly mentions the appearance of "a grinning face flattened against the window pane," which defuses our own affective constitution of the world and reveals the world itself as always-already magical.[12] This face arguably signifies one of the first encroachments of sociality into Sartre's phenomenology, and is subsequently fleshed out in the phenomenon that he refers to as "the look," which constitutes the centerpiece of his analysis of interpersonal relations in *Being and Nothingness*.

Phenomenological Ontology: *Being and Nothingness*

Although Sartre's early works are asocial, and thus (at least tacitly) suggest a withdrawal from the everyday world of experience, his attack on Husserl's transcendental ego arises from his belief that consciousness's immersion in the everyday world of experience is inextricable. For this reason, he argues, Husserl's philosophy is idealistic. In *Being and Nothingness*, which is the culmination of his "early philosophy," Sartre retains his qualified appropriation of Husserl's phenomenology, but moves past it in at least one crucial way: he brings it into a productive tension with Heidegger's phenomenological ontology. More specifically, Sartre draws upon Heidegger's idea that a human being is first and foremost a "being-in-the-world" (as opposed to a detached, knowing subject) to enrich his previous account of consciousness by bringing it into a relation with the "being of the world," which essentially includes a relation with other people (or, as Heidegger calls it, a "being-with"). It was during the Second World War that Sartre studied Heidegger, and as Sartre later put it: "The great change in my thinking was the war: 1939–1940, the Occupation, the Resistance, the liberation of Paris. . . . My great discovery was that of the sociality during the war."[13] Still, unlike Heidegger, who ardently rejects the subject–object, consciousness–world duality that goes back at least as far as Descartes's inauguration of the modern project, Sartre retains the primacy of consciousness. In a fundamental sense, then, his project in *Being and Nothingness* is based on an extremely precarious balancing act, namely, synthesizing Husserl's Cartesian inspired phenomenology and Heidegger's anti-Cartesian phenomenological ontology.[14]

The Introduction to *Being and Nothingness*, entitled "The pursuit of being," is by far the most difficult part of the book. Sartre's basic intent here is to contrast the way in which he sees the relationship between consciousness and being with other thinkers in the philosophical tradition. Predictably, Sartre begins by crediting Husserl's phenomenology with abolishing the dualisms that had formerly plagued philosophy, such as inside–outside, potency–act, and appearance–reality, but suggests that there is another dualism that arises in their wake, namely, that of the finite–infinite. This is because there is a "being of the phenomenon" – that is, an objectivity of the perceptible object – that outstrips the object's appearance to consciousness (the "phenomenon of being") at any given point in time and space. In other words, the object can always be perceived from another point of view. This means that the "being of the phenomenon" would only appear over an infinite series. Thus, Sartre argues, Husserl's phenomenology is mistaken insofar as it purports to uncover some "meaning" or "essence" of the phenomenon through the snapshot-like phenomenological reduction. (So, too, while different in many ways, Heidegger's anti-Cartesian phenomenological ontology is mistaken insofar as it sets out to recover "the meaning of Being.") In fact, there is no "meaning" or "essence" of the phenomenon, because being is nothing more than the ground upon which objects can reveal themselves to consciousness. In other words, being is only brute, self-identical existence. When Sartre states that "being is, being is in-itself, being is what it is,"[15] therefore, he is not taking refuge in mysticism, but is saying, far more mundanely, that there is nothing to say about being in the absence of a consciousness to which it appears.

For Sartre, therefore, it is not being, but rather consciousness, that is the principal object of inquiry, and in the Introduction, he introduces the prereflective cogito, which is at the very heart of his account of consciousness. As we observed when considering *The Transcendence of the Ego*, Sartre believes that there is an omnipresent consciousness of consciousness – that is, an awareness by consciousness of itself in its awareness of objects. Consciousness's awareness of itself, which is made possible by the prereflective cogito, is "non-positional," whereas its awareness of objects is "positional." Crucially, according to Sartre, non-positional consciousness, which is one with the positional consciousness of which it is aware, is the very foundation of knowledge. To put it colloquially, you must know what you know to truly know it. Sartre does not argue in any great depth for this position. My belief, however, is that he

thinks that positional consciousness alone – that is, our immediate, intentional awareness of the object – would irretrievably lose itself in the perceptible object. It is non-
positional consciousness's immediate awareness of this awareness that, crudely,
retrieves this knowledge and makes it our own.

Thus, according to Sartre, "the condition for a knowing consciousness to be
knowledge *of* its object is that it be consciousness of itself as being that knowledge"
(*B&N*, p. 11). The "of" in this sentence, it should be noticed, is italicized, and this
is done for an important pedagogical reason. Sartre believes that *prereflective* knowledge, which is basically non-cognitive or intuitive in nature, exists prior to the
subject–object split that is the essence of reflective knowledge. In other words,
because non-positional consciousness is one with positional consciousness, and
positional consciousness is only the immediate awareness of an object, the duality
implied by the word "of" is improper within the framework of prereflective knowledge. (Within this framework, therefore, the "of" only functions grammatically,
which is why Sartre puts parentheses around it when he uses it in this way.) Moreover, Sartre (dubiously) contends, as our primary mode of knowing, prereflective
knowledge allows "being [to] be disclosed to us by some kind of immediate access
– boredom, nausea etc." (*B&N*, p. 7). Finally, as we saw earlier, the non-positional
consciousness of the preflective cogito is also what permits consciousness to rise to
the reflective level, and it is at this level, which is a secondary formation, that reflective knowledge arises. And, of course, one such object of reflective knowledge, as
The Transcendence of the Ego teaches, is the empirical self, which is "out in the world"
like other objects.

By the end of the Introduction, Sartre has rudimentarily considered the two fundamental constituents of his phenomenological ontology, namely, the full, undifferentiated oneness of being and the "nothingness" of consciousness (which exists only
in relation to being). Matters are much more complicated, however, and over the
course of the first three parts of the book, Sartre will elaborate upon this picture,
while in the fourth and final part he will flesh out the practical consequences of his
phenomenological ontology. Before proceeding, however, it should be pointed out
that Sartre's account of the relation between being and consciousness in the Introduction (which largely makes explicit what was implicit within his earlier phenomenological works) circumvents both Cartesian realism and idealism. Due to its status
as a "nothingness" that cannot exist independently of the material world, consciousness is not a substance, which cuts against Cartesianism. And, conversely, due
to the existence of the material world, which supports consciousness in its being,
Berkeleyan idealism (i.e., the claim that there is no material world, and that the existence of a thing depends upon its perception by a mind) is ruled out. Moreover, as
against Cartesian realism, Berkeleyan idealism, and, for that matter, all other stripes
of idealism (such as Kant's "transcendental idealism"), Sartre contends that due to
its non-substantive, intentional nature, consciousness is not limited to knowledge of
its own ideas or representations. Instead, as we observed earlier, it engages the things
themselves, however partially (given that the "being of the phenomenon" can never
fully appear, since it is invariably viewed from a distinct perspective in space and time).
Ultimately, then, Sartre is a naïve realist – that is, one who believes that there is a
material reality to which the mind has direct (albeit partial) access.

Now, according to Sartre, human beings are dispersed across what he takes to be the three essential structures of being, namely "being-in-itself," "being-for-itself," and "being-for-others," as well as the three temporal dimensions (past, present, and future). Being-in-itself, as we have seen, is that aspect of being that is self-identical, and is alternatively described by Sartre as "solid," "a synthesis of itself with itself," or "full positivity" (*B&N*, pp. 28–9). Beyond referring to the material world, which constitutes his first paradigm of being-in-itself, however, being-in-itself also refers to "facticity." This refers to the brute facts (i.e., one's age, the earth's diameter), and includes the past. Sartre thus asserts that the past, "like facticity, is the invulnerable contingency of the in-itself which I have to be, without any possibility of not being it. It is the inevitability of the necessity of fact, not by virtue of necessity, but by virtue of fact" (*B&N*, p. 173).

Sartre emphasizes fact in opposition to necessity in this confusing statement because being-for-itself, which is consciousness, is not determined by "the facts," although consciousness must live its factual context. In other words, my actions necessarily arise in, and respond to, a given factual context, but this factual context can never compel me to act in a certain way. According to Sartre, this is because consciousness does not *contain* the ego or any other substance that would cause it to be determined by the laws of nature; rather, it is essentially a "nothing" or "nothingness" that perpetually transcends itself in the process of remaking itself. This idea is captured by the (equally confusing) claim that, as a "transcendence," consciousness is a "nihilating nothingness" that produces "*negatités*." The nothingness that *is* consciousness is active – it can imagine, doubt, interrogate, and experience absence – and in accord with its specific project, it nihilates (negates) various aspects of the solidity that is being in-itself.[16] To use Sartre's example: Upon entering a crowded café in search of my friend, I nihilate the fullness of being that is the café, which then will constitute the undifferentiated ground upon which my friend will spring up for my consciousness. If my friend does not appear, however, I will experience the café as being haunted by a negation or *negatité* – that is, an absence – which is "an objective fact" (*B&N*, p. 40). Of course, I can choose to change my project at any time, in which case, despite the relative constancy of the factual situation, the undifferentiated ground of my experience will change. And it is in this capacity to change my projects – even my deepest, most self-orienting ones – that my freedom lies: "Conscious being must constitute itself in relation to its past as separated from its past by a nothingness . . . Freedom is the human being putting his past out of play by secreting his own nothingness" (*B&N*, p. 64). Once again, this points to the fact that while consciousness is not "the self" (empirical ego), it must still live this self that it is not because this self is the stuff from which it will freely reconstitute itself. Thus, unlike being-in-itself, which refers to the past, being-for-itself refers to the future: "There is in my consciousness no moment which is not defined by an internal relation to the future" (*B&N*, p. 181).

A human being, in sum, is essentially in tension, torn between the facticity of its given "self" (empirical ego), which is in the past, and the self that would transcend it (i.e., *some* self that it must project because consciousness is always beyond this factical "self"), which is in the future. What human beings evidently are not, then, is "self-present." Thus, Sartre claims, "the present" disperses in this process by which consciousness "temporalizes itself": "The present is not; it makes itself present in the form of flight" (*B&N*, p. 179). Indeed, as a result of this divided nature, human beings themselves are perpetually in "flight."

This flight, according to Sartre, is manifested in the seemingly ubiquitous phenomenon of "bad faith," namely, lying to oneself or self-deception. The consciousness that is in bad faith, paradoxically, must know in its capacity as deceiver the truth that it hides from itself in its capacity as the deceived. Such a consciousness neither wishes to coordinate its facticity and transcendence nor overcome them in a synthesis but, instead, seeks to overemphasize one at the expense of the other. In *Being and Nothingness*, Sartre furnishes many examples of persons who act in bad faith, but one example, in particular, which involves a homosexual and his interlocutor, the "champion of sincerity," captures its dual nature. The "champion of sincerity," who seeks to get the homosexual to admit that he is "a homosexual," is in bad faith because he overemphasizes his counterpart's (and, presumably, his own) facticity at the cost of his transcendence – that is, he would pin down the homosexual to his factical self, which our freedom invariably transcends. Conversely, the homosexual, who denies his homosexuality by viewing his previous sexual encounters as part of a "restless search," is in bad faith because he overemphasizes his transcendence at the cost of his facticity – that is, he denies the factical self altogether, unmindful that, whatever his transcendent possibilities, he is that self.

The way in which the phenomenon of bad faith manifests itself is bound up with a person's self-conceptions, and every person's possibilities arise within a hierarchical framework of projects and behaviors that constitute these self-conceptions. These projects and behaviors, in turn, testify to the existence of a more basic project that reflects a person's underlying existential choice – in other words, an initial choice of oneself in the world that will establish the parameters of one's self-identity. Although this "initial project" itself varies from person to person, it testifies, in turn, to the existence of a universal project, "the fundamental project," which Sartre portrays as follows: "God, value, and supreme end of transcendence, represents the permanent limit in terms of which man makes known to himself what he is. To be man means to reach toward being God" (*B&N*, p. 724). Put simply (and without the religious overtones), the fundamental project is the desire to be a "for-itself-in-itself," namely, to be both absolutely free and absolutely stable in our self-identity.

Whether the fundamental project, and, for that matter, bad faith itself, are necessary is unclear. Sartre seems to suggest here that the fundamental project is a necessary structure of our being. We can give up neither our freedom (transcendence of the for-itself) nor our striving for a personal identity (facticity of the in-itself), and because we can never actually reach the for-itself-in-itself, given our divided nature, the possibility of good faith and authenticity would seem to be precluded. In his ensuing ethical writings, however, Sartre speaks disparagingly of the fundamental project, and tries to give good faith and authenticity a run for their money. But Sartre chose not to publish these writings, and, I think, for good reason. It seems that we must strive toward the for-itself-in-itself, even while acknowledging our inability to attain this ideal. To claim that we must "live our freedom," as some Sartre scholars do, smacks of a bad faith overemphasis of our transcendence, and is to engage in a performative contradiction: Our actions invariably reflect certain "in-itself" commitments to both our egos and the world. Moreover, we cannot live our split nature – one moment free, the next determined – which would produce a schizoid ego. Ultimately, then, transcendence and facticity cannot be effectively coordinated, for this assumes that these properties are functionally discrete, which they are not. Transcendence is always-already mired in a factical "situation," and facticity means nothing at all outside of its meaning for our freely chosen projects. As parts of a synthetic whole, they interpenetrate one another.

This account is further complicated when, 300 pages into *Being and Nothingness* (and nearly 200 pages after his analysis of bad faith), Sartre broaches the third constituent of being, being-for-others. This formally begins his analysis of social relations. But, of course, in his portrayal of bad faith – as is revealed by the example of the homosexual and the champion of sincerity – social factors hover right beneath the surface. And, in fact, fundamental aspects of self-formation, which underlie the bad faith problematic, are attributable to our being-for-others. Sartre begins his analysis of being-for-others with the well-worn problem of the existence of other minds, and, toward this end, he famously uses the example of a voyeur who is apprehended in the act of peeping through a keyhole. When the voyeur realizes that another person is looking at (and judging) him, he experiences "shame-consciousness," which Sartre analogizes to the prereflective cogito's consciousness of the consciousness of objects. In other words, shame-consciousness is non-positional and immediate in nature. Sartre asserts that with this type of consciousness, there can be no doubt that the Other exists as a subject, for in being the object of the Other's "look," the voyeur "experiences the inapprehensible subjectivity of the Other directly and with his being" (*B&N*, p. 361). Sartre's position here, in other words, builds upon his previous distinction between the intuitive "knowledge" of immediate self-consciousness, which has a direct access to being, and the conceptual knowledge of mediated (i.e., reflective) self-consciousness, which is always at a remove from being. Certainty of the other person's existence, Sartre asserts, can only be based upon intuitive experience, not conceptual knowledge.

The voyeur's objectification by the "Other-as-subject" reflects one moment in Sartre's account of interpersonal relations. With the advent of "the look," he says, "essential modifications appear in a person's structure": the self not only "comes to haunt the unreflective consciousness" (*B&N*, p. 349), but also becomes contested, for one's self-conception no longer depends solely on oneself. Echoing Hegel's master/slave allegory, in which two nominal self-consciousnesses fight for supremacy over one another to achieve the other's unilateral recognition, Sartre argues that we are *for* (as opposed to *with*) others because each one of us wants to objectify the Other in such a way as to make the Other support our own self-conceptions. Interpersonal relations, therefore, are essentially inscribed with conflict. The "Other-as-subject," who has turned the voyeur into a "being-as-object," could just as easily have been objectified by the voyeur under different circumstances. So, too, even after being caught, the voyeur can always turn the tables so that he becomes the "being-as-subject," while his accuser becomes the "Other-as-object." These reversals can go on indefinitely. Indeed, "hell is other people," as one of Sartre's characters asserts in his play "No Exit," because these relations of domination and subordination can neither be overcome (as is the case in Hegel's dialectic) nor even stabilized: "there is no dialectic of relations with the Other but rather a circle" (*B&N*, p. 474). Thus, my empirical self, which is formed within the dynamic interaction of being-in-itself, being-for-itself, and being-for-others, is no less stable.

Having fleshed out the three constituents of being, Sartre spends the final part of *Being and Nothingness* developing his idea of freedom. It is here, in particular, that he famously argues for the view that human beings are "absolutely free" – a view that is often misinterpreted. Throughout *Being and Nothingness*, Sartre is clear on the difference between what he occasionally calls "ontological freedom," which is the freedom of choice, and "practical freedom," which entails the freedom to obtain what one desires. It is not Sartre's view, as some critics suggest, that our practical freedom is in any way absolute; rather, this claim applies only to our ontological freedom. When Sartre maintains that even a prisoner is free, therefore, his point is not that the prisoner has the freedom to escape but, rather, that he has the ineluctable freedom to choose how he will comport himself in the face of his imprisonment, which includes, among other things, the freedom to try to escape. This may seem to be a denigration of the notion of freedom, but there is an important point here: all talk of practical freedom, at least implicitly, presupposes that we are ontologically free, for only free beings can have their freedom restricted. Moreover, as Sartre points out in what he refers to as the "paradox of freedom," the very notion of freedom presupposes hurdles: "Human-reality everywhere encounters resistances and obstacles which it has not created, but these resistances and obstacles have meaning only in and through the free choice that human reality is" (*B&N*, p. 629).

If there is a problem in Sartre's account of freedom, it relates not to the "absolute freedom" claim, but instead to the nature of "free choice" itself – that is, whether ontological freedom is such that we can see ourselves as self-determining irrespective of our practical freedom. Specifically, as we observed earlier, Sartre believes that we are oriented toward the world on the basis of an "initial choice" of ourselves, which first gives rise to our projects. But, crucially, he thinks that while this initial choice furnishes reasons for the goals that we pursue, and "accessory reflection" helps us to bring these goals about, there are no reasons that underlie our initial choice of ourselves. Because the initial project, which is non-reflective, causes reasons to come into being, it cannot be based on reasons itself, but only the pure, contingent spontaneity of consciousness. Sartre contends that it is precisely because our reasons do not determine our initial choice of ourselves, but only arise from it, that we are free. Still, it seems to me, this is unsatisfying in terms of the sort of freedom (and hence) responsibility with which we are left. Sartre does hold out the notion of a "purifying reflection," a sort of recontextualized Husserlian *epoché* in which an "immediate reflection" intuits the unjustifiability of the initial project, but this notion is problematic; he can explain neither the impetus for this "katharsis" nor its practical consequence, because, as an orienting principle, the initial project seems to be ontologically unavoidable. Ultimately, I think, we can make better sense of the relation between a purifying reflection and the initial project if we reject Sartre's "spontaneity" argument for both. The initial choice of the fundamentally orienting "initial project" should be understood as the outgrowth of a highly differentiated, multilayered complex of social, historical, and psychological factors. And, in turn, the "purifying reflection" should be understood as arising from another standpoint within this kaleidoscopic complex that is a person's subjective constitution, not as a katharsis arising out of nowhere. With his move to phenomenological Marxism in the 1950s, Sartre himself seems to embrace this view.

Phenomenological Marxism

When asked toward the end of his life whether the *Critique of Dialectical Reason* represented, as Althusser would put it, an "epistemological break" with *Being and Nothingness*, Sartre replied that it did not. To the contrary, claiming (rightly, to my mind) that such a notion was even inapplicable to the relationship between Marx's early writings and *Capital* (the context within which Althusser first used the term), Sartre emphasized "that there is more continuity in [his own] thought," and that the attribution of such a break would be "mistaken." Acknowledging that "there are changes," however, Sartre contended that "*Being and Nothingness* is a general point of view, a fundamental point of view. And the *Critique of Dialectical Reason* is a point of view that on the contrary is social and concrete. The one is abstract, studies general truths, and the other . . . places itself upon the plane of the concrete."[17]

One of the structures that lays the groundwork for Sartre's turn from the "general truths" of *Being and Nothingness* to "the plane of the concrete" is the initial project, and the work that most clearly mediates this transition is *Saint Genet, Actor and Martyr*, his biography of the writer Jean Genet. In what is arguably the most important passage in the book, Sartre details how the young Genet was caught in the act of stealing by an adult, who "pinned" him as a "thief" – and a thief is exactly what Genet became. The point is that Genet's initial choice of himself did not occur within a vacuum; rather, the very stuff of this choice was constituted by his sociohistorical context. In some vague sense, therefore, we "choose" ourselves, but what comes to concern Sartre is not the freedom of this choice itself (our "ontological freedom"), which he has already exhaustively addressed in his phenomenological ontology, but the limited range within which this "choice" must be made. This evokes our "practical freedom." Still, it is the desire to do justice to our underlying ontological freedom, I believe, that convinces Sartre to shift to questions of practical freedom, and, ultimately, the Marxism of the *Critique of Dialectical Reason*. Sartre's particular brand of Marxism is by no means "orthodox," however. Both stylistically and substantively, it is based upon his prior work. The investigation remains unrepentantly phenomenological in nature, and the ontological foundation remains the freely chosen commitment of the individual.

Surprisingly, then, near the beginning of *Search for a Method* – an essay that was written before the *Critique of Dialectical Reason*, but was published (in revised fashion) as an appendage to it – Sartre denigrates existentialism. With respect to Marxism, he claims, existentialism is only an "ideology," a "parasitical system living on the margin of Knowledge, which at first it opposed but into which today it seeks to be integrated."[18] Such a claim hardly seems like a prelude to an attempt to mediate Marxism with the concerns of existentialism – but, ultimately, it is belied by much of what follows. Thus, at the end of the first section of this essay, titled "Marxism and existentialism," Sartre states that "as soon as there will exist *for everyone* a margin of *real* freedom beyond the production of life, Marxism will have lived out its span, [and] a philosophy of freedom will take its place" (*SM*, p. 34). This assertion suggests that Marxism is, ultimately, in the service of a true existentialism, whose preconditions have not yet arisen. And, in the second section, titled "The problem of mediations and auxiliary disciplines," Sartre assails the "metaphysical existence" that economic classes have for orthodox Marxism when he states that "there are only men and real relations between men . . . mean[ing] only that we must expect to find the support of collective objects in the concrete activity of individuals. We do not intend to deny the reality of these objects but we claim that it is *parasitical*" (*SM*, p. 77). For Sartre, then, it would seem that Marxism and existentialism are "parasitical" upon one another – or, better put, they ought to dialectically inform one another. In the context that prevailed at the time, however, existentialism was an "ideology" because it was used to justify the notion that human beings are "practically" free, and Marxism was an "ideology" because it blindly held that the ironclad laws of dialectical materialism would lead to the ascendance of the working class. Ideally, existentialism would break up the reified structures of Marxism, and an emancipated Marxism would facilitate a sociohistorical context within which it would wither away and existentialism would no longer be a mere ideology.

More specifically, with respect to the relation between being and knowledge, Sartre asserts that Marx transcends the one-sided positions of Hegel and Kierkegaard. With Hegel, Marx "takes concrete man in his objective reality," but rightly does not claim to have attained the standpoint of "absolute knowledge," and, with Kierkegaard, he speaks to the "primacy of human existence," but does not fall into "frozen paradoxes ultimately referring to an empty subjectivity" (*SM*, pp. 12–14). In stark contrast to Marx, however, Sartre's "orthodox" Marxist contemporaries had idealistically posited for themselves an already "totalized knowledge" through their mechanistic interpretation of history, and had lost the moment of individual subjectivity. Sartre's goal is to rectify this situation, and in *Search for a Method* he broaches what is arguably the most important concept in the *Critique of Dialectical Reason* – namely, the concept of "totalization." According to Sartre, if there is to be "Truth," "it must be a truth that is to become, and it must make itself a totalization" (*SM*, p. xxxiv). In other words, the fragments of our knowledge must be "totalized" – that is, synthesized – to be made intelligible, which is Hegel's crucial point. But in contrast to both Hegel *and* orthodox Marxism, totalization, for Sartre, is an active, ongoing process. Because existence outruns knowledge, there are no final totalities (such as Hegel's "absolute knowing" or the communist society vouchsafed by dialectical materialism), which means that all totalizations are merely "detotalized totalities." In this sense, totalization is *anti*-totalitarian. It is here, indeed, that the moment of subjectivity is revived, for it is only through the negativity of what Sartre now terms "praxis" – that is, the practices that arise from our freely chosen projects – that we advance from totalization to totalization: "The subjective contains within itself the objective, which it denies and which it surpasses [by totalization] toward a new objectivity; and this new objectivity by virtue of objectification externalizes the internality of the project as an objectified subjectivity" (*SM*, p. 98).

The title of the third essay in *Search for a Method*, "The progressive–regressive method," reflects the method that Sartre himself utilizes in the *Critique of Dialectical Reason*. Extending and transforming the work of the Marxist sociologist Henri Lefebvre, Sartre argues that there are three stages in the process of comprehending the movement of history. The first stage, which Lefebvre had termed "descriptive," is, for Sartre, a rigorous "phenomenological description" of the events under consideration. Although it might seem superfluous to even articulate such a step, it should be recalled that Sartre's attack on orthodox Marxism arises, in no small part, from its propensity to either distort or simply forget the particulars of phenomena in its drive to make reality conform to its prefabricated categories. As a committed phenomenologist, Sartre will have no part of this. At this point the method itself, which, sequentially, is actually "regressive–progressive," comes into play. The regressive moment (termed "analytico-regressive" by Lefebvre) involves working back through the successive layers of causes and explanations that constitute the phenomena, while the ensuing progressive moment (termed "historical–genetic" by Lefebvre) involves working forward from this juncture to understand how the unfolding situation appeared to those human beings who lived it, and whose totalizing activities in the face of it actually made it what it was.

In the very broadest sense, the *Critique of Dialectical Reason* itself is intended to reflect this method. The first volume reflects the "analytico-regressive" moment by virtue of a regress that is meant to uncover the very intelligibility of dialectical reason itself, while the second volume (which Sartre aborted, but was posthumously published in its incomplete form) is intended to "retrace the stages of the critical progression" through the unfolding of history.[19] These aims are suggestive of both Kant and Hegel, as is, of course, the title itself. Accordingly, like Hegel, Sartre is concerned with *dialectical* reason, and, like Hegel, he views the dialectic as "both a method and a movement in the object [that are] one and the same" (*CDR*, p. 20). Unlike Hegel, who reviews the movement of his dialectic from the summit of "absolute knowing," however, Sartre, as we know, rejects all ultimate totalities. Instead, he seeks to vindicate the intelligibility of a dialectical reason based upon a "totalization *without* a totalizer," which devalues his own standpoint, and thus calls into question the intelligibility of his dialectical approach. It is on this point, however, that Sartre's project in the *Critique of Dialectical Reason* can be understood in terms of Kant's project in the *Critique of Pure Reason*. Like Kant, who engages in a critique of pure reason by pure reason, Sartre engages in a critique of dialectical reason by dialectical reason "to ground itself and to develop itself as a free critique of itself" (*CDR*, p. 21). So, too, like Kant, who attacked the dogmatic metaphysicians for claiming to grasp totality through a reason unadulterated by experience, Sartre attacks orthodox Marxists for rationalistically claiming to grasp totality from an "end of history" perspective. (In both cases, however, the aim is to vindicate the commitments of their predecessors in a modified way: Kant seeks to do justice to the practico-moral commitments of the metaphysicians, Sartre to the sociohistorical commitments of the orthodox Marxists.) And, lastly, like Kant, Sartre initiates his own Copernican revolution in dialectical reason by reasserting the primacy of the individual: "if we do not wish the dialectic to become a divine law again, a metaphysical fate, it must proceed from individuals, and not from some kind of supra-individual ensemble" (*CDR*, p. 36).

After clearing the methodological ground, which includes attacks not only on "Hegelian dogmatism" and "modern Marxism," but also "analytic reason," "dialectical hyper-empiricism," and Engel's "dialectics of nature," Sartre commences his own dialectical analysis by maintaining that "everything is to be explained through need" (*CDR*, p. 80). Need, in other words, is the first "negation," for it reflects the fundamental "lack" that is innate to human beings as natural beings – that is, as beings who must transform their environment to materially sustain themselves. This transformation takes place through the "original" praxis of an individual's transforming labor. But "to consider an individual at work is a complete abstraction," Sartre quickly adds, "since in reality labor is as much a relation between men as a relation between man and the material world" (*CDR*, p. 91). The "original" praxis of individual labor, in other words, always already mediates and is mediated by other individuals, who are similarly engaged. Sartre goes on to explain this mediation by enriching a concept that he had employed in *Being and Nothingness* – namely, that individuals are unified by "the look" of a third party, which transforms them from "Other-as-object" to an "us-object." Thus, he once again holds, it is the third party that unifies. Sartre now asserts, however, that the third party may well be part of the relation that he unifies as "the Third," and that in some sense everyone who is a part of this three-way synthesis might (at least alternately) function as a third in the process of maintaining the set of social relations: "Reciprocal ternary relations are the basis of all relations between men" (*CDR*, p. 111). For Sartre, the crucial point is that each as a unifying third is an individual, and that it is individuals who sustain social relations.

Sartre contends that what will ultimately motivate the nature of these relations is scarcity, which he takes to be nothing less than the basic fact of human existence. Indeed, it is not only the driving force of our conflict-ridden history, but is "the basis of the possibility of human history" itself (*CDR*, p. 125). Accordingly, scarcity is not just what tears us apart (such as in the ultimate case of war, which is invariably fought over scarce resources), but is also what brings us together in the first place (if, for no other reason, than to combat it). Human beings working together thus attempt to remake a world inscribed by scarcity more hospitable to their needs – as is the case for Hegel, "the world" is made into a human world. Invariably, however, there are unanticipated, or, at least, undesired affects, which Sartre calls "counterfinalities" (in contrast to "finalities," which are in accordance with the original objectives). In turn, counterfinalities, which Sartre describes as "alienated objectifications" of our praxis, become part of what he called "being-in-itself" within the framework of *Being and Nothingness*, but now calls the "practico-inert." The counterfinalities that make up the practico-inert, in other words, are part and parcel of the unfolding dialectical process itself. The world thus becomes progressively sedimented with counterfinalities, which come to delineate the infrastructure (i.e., the practico-inert) on which free praxis is brought to bear. This is Sartre's point when he asserts that the "practico-inert can be treated as a process" that "presupposes the entire praxis . . . which it reabsorbs and transforms in the object" (*CDR*, p. 713). Indeed, the infrastructure of the practico-inert becomes sedimented in such a way that it produces an inversion of the relation between praxis and its product: human beings become products of their products. This link between human beings and their products, in turn, gives rise to an "interest," which Sartre describes as follows: "Interest is being-wholly-outside-oneself-in-a-thing in so far as it conditions praxis as a categorical imperative" (*CDR*, p. 197). But while putatively based on the link between the individual and those things with which he identifies, interests (broadly defined) are no less social in nature – indeed, what's more, they are "ideological." As such, they are to be understood in terms of those with whom the interest is shared and those whom are excluded by it. This leads to classes of individuals, and for the working class, which is limited by the world that it has created, it means living a "destiny in exteriority of freedom" (*CDR*, p. 227).

It is at this point in the *Critique* that Sartre shifts to a consideration of human collectives, which, ostensibly, provide the resources that will remedy this state of affairs. Before continuing, however, it is worth briefly stepping back to consider the relationship (to this point) between the *Critique* and *Being and Nothingness*. It should be recognized that Sartre is working with the same types of structures, although the names have been changed to account for his new philosophical commitment, which he terms "realist materialism." For instance, praxis and the practico-inert are the progeny of being-for-itself and being-in-itself, and the relationship between the two sets of terms are both determined by one's project. So, too, the inability to achieve "totality" despite the necessity of continuing to totalize is akin to the inability of consciousness to make itself into a thing due to its freedom despite the necessity of continuing to synthesize the in-itself. And, finally, despite his turn toward Marxism, Sartre rejects any notion of a collective subject, and continues to rely upon "the Third" to form collectives.

The first sort of collective with which Sartre deals, "the series," is, predictably, the loosest. A series is an assemblage of isolated individuals (each with his or her own project) who coalesce around a common object. Due to their isolated status, however, they are powerless to effect any change with respect to that object. People waiting in line for a bus and trading in the marketplace, Sartre asserts, are examples of seriality, which is unorganized and distinguished by otherness. In the face of need or a shared danger, however, seriality is surpassed when individuals band together into a group – or, to be more exact, become a "group-in-fusion." The exact moment at which this transformation occurs is an elusive one. As Sartre portrays with his example of the storming of the Bastille, however, it is usually induced by one person among the series who, as a seminal "Third," articulates the sentiments of the individuals in the series, such as when one person screamed that the Bastille should be stormed. From a theoretical standpoint, the group-in-fusion overcomes the otherness of seriality, and each participant comes to see other members of the group, which does not have a hierarchical structure, as other "myselves." Crucially, however, the common praxis of the group-in-fusion is sustained by individuals. "Everyone is a third party" who is "sovereign," and "becomes through the change of praxis, the organizer of common praxis" (*CDR*, p. 370). In this way, individual praxis becomes more effective. Still, due to its unorganized structure, which could be splintered by any contingent event, the common objectives of the group-in-fusion are always up for grabs, thus leading the individuals who make up the group to seek greater stability through a "pledge." The pledge does succeed in further unifying the group, but it does so at a price, namely, the limitation of its members' individual freedoms. This is because a pledge means something only if it can be enforced – ultimately by violence. According to Sartre, despite the implementation of "fraternity terror," the "pledged group" still manifests the common freedom of its members, for it is "the right of all through everyone and over everyone" (*CDR*, p. 438).

At this point, however, the turn toward privileging the needs of the group over the rights of its individual members has been made, and the disparity between the two will only continue to increase. With the adoption of a hierarchical structure and detailed set of rules, the pledged group becomes a "statutory group" or "organization," and with the introduction of membership requirements, which justifies purges, the organization becomes an "institution." Finally, when an institution can extend its sovereignty to the whole of society itself, it does so by setting itself up as "the state," which, for Sartre, as for Marxists of other ideological stripes, only reflects the relative (im)balance of power between the competing groups that subsist within the society. And, to administer its power, the state layers itself with a bureaucracy that is cemented by a "cult of personality." (The allusion here is, of course, to Stalinism, an analysis of which constitutes hundreds of pages within the "progressive" moment of Sartre's project, namely, the unfinished second volume of the *Critique*.) Ironically, at this juncture in the dialectic of group formation, seriality, the most undeveloped collective form, becomes pervasive. The majority of society is once again isolated and powerless with respect to a common object that conditions their lives, which, of course, is the very condition that the dominant groups seek to bring about. Still, as is the case throughout, Sartre maintains that "the dialectical rationality of common praxis does not transcend the rationality of individual praxis [which still] goes beyond it" (*CDR*, p. 538).

Sartre ends the first volume of the *Critique* by applying his analysis of group formation to historically specific working class struggles. This prefigures the second volume's consideration of the actual unfolding of history itself (with its extended analysis of what was nominally history's most ambitious working class struggle, namely, the attempt to create a worker's state by way of Bolshevism in early twentieth-century Russia). Along these lines, the last subsection of the first volume, "The intelligibility of history: totalization without a totalizer," helps bring into sharper focus the primary objective of the second volume, which, as was stated earlier, is to determine whether the various strands of history can be comprehended as one History – or, to put it more precisely, whether dialectical thought can be made intelligible in the absence of a totalizer. To be sure, Sartre's failure to complete this volume, despite its many insights, calls this ambitious project into question. Indeed, it might be argued that given Sartre's firm commitment to an overarching dialectical analysis grounded in neither the workings of nature (Engels, "orthodox" Marxism) nor a universal subject (Lukács, variants of Western Marxism), but in the free, non-totalizing praxis of the individual, it was misconceived at its inception. Still, I believe, the summary rejection of Sartre by recent French philosophers has had dire philosophical and practical consequences. Perhaps the best example of this would be Foucault, who, as was previously mentioned, dismissed Sartre as a "universal intellectual." Foucault's own works perform an invaluable function by richly detailing particular institutional histories, but by rejecting, on principle, both the individual subject as such and the idea of one History, he leaves us without the two poles that could help mediate, and thus further enrich, our understanding of the normative shortcomings of these institutions. Even more importantly, by failing to look at the one History that ties these institutions together, which in the modern period is circumscribed by late capitalism, he blunts the prospects for genuine change by leaving virtually untouched that which substantially informs the nature of the particular institutions that he would reform.

In sum, I am arguing, despite its past abuses and inherent potential for abuse, there is still a need for the "universal intellectual," who is well positioned to articulate these interconnections. Indeed, the weakness of the *Critique of Dialectical Reason*, to my mind, does not lie in Sartre's attempt to mediate these institutional relations from a "universal" standpoint, but in his failure to sufficiently carry through these mediations by beginning his phenomenological analysis from the standpoint of a subject who is not already a social being. After concluding the *Critique*, one feels the need to reread it, this time keeping in mind the always-already social nature of the individuals who produce progressively larger social collectives and their attendant counterfinalities.

Conclusion

At the start of this chapter, I asserted that Sartre is first and foremost a "philosopher of freedom," and, yet, from the determining nature of the "initial project" in *Being and Nothingness* through the unforgiving dialectic of group formation in the *Critique of Dialectical Reason*, Sartrean freedom looks to be tenuous at best. So, too, in his last major work, an immense biography of Flaubert, which incorporates and concretely synthesizes the philosophical structures that were articulated in his earlier works, it would appear that Flaubert was all but destined to become "Flaubert." And, indeed, Sartre's characterization of freedom in a 1969 interview, which has since been titled "The itinerary of a thought," reflects this "all but destined" concept of freedom: "This is the limit I would today accord to freedom: the small movement which makes of a totally conditioned social being someone who does not render back completely what his conditioning has given him."[20] Despite this progressively narrowing margin for freedom within Sartre's works, his multifaceted commitment to freedom remains, as does the truth of his philosophical insights with respect to it.

To fully appreciate Sartre's account of freedom, it must be understood that his steadfast refusal to fold the first-person perspective into the third should not be seen in metaphysical terms but, rather, in terms of Kant's contention in the *Foundations of the Metaphysics of Morals* that the first-person perspective is the perspective of freedom, regardless of the metaphysical "fact of the matter." Although, as we observed, Sartre speaks of our "ontological freedom," his conception of freedom is actually better understood in phenomenological terms. As is suggested by the subtitle of *Being and Nothingness*, "A phenomenological essay on ontology," we are not in a position to make ultimate claims about the being of the world (ontology) or, for that matter, the way that the world *really* is (metaphysics), but only about the way in which consciousness is constrained to experience it (phenomenology). It is for this reason that Sartre can coherently reject both the "free will" position and the scientifically inspired "determinist" one in *Being and Nothingness*, for by making ontological or metaphysical claims about the nature of the world, both positions run afoul of phenomenology. Sartre's argument for freedom, therefore, is neither precluded by the causal picture offered by the sciences nor a refutation of it. It is, instead, a different, albeit equally valid, perspective.

A major shortcoming in Sartre's early position on freedom, as I suggested earlier, is his commitment to seeing freedom in terms of a pure spontaneity of consciousness, which smacks of the sort of metaphysical claim that he otherwise wants to reject. To be sure, Sartre is right when he asserts that reasons do arise from our choice of a fundamentally self-orienting "initial project," although even the concept of an initial project – that is, one underlying orientation toward the world – is too reductive. More to the point, as my criticism of the *Critique of Dialectical Reason* implies, this wrongly presupposes that we aren't always-already oriented on the basis of social considerations. There are sociohistorical and psychological reasons for our choice of an initial project. Thus, the strength of Sartre's phenomenological account of freedom does not lie in consciousness's pure spontaneity with respect to the individual choice of an initial project but, rather, in the recognition that, phenomenologically speaking, we can always put ourselves at a distance from all so-called "determining" factors by reflecting upon them. The "distance" that affords the possibility of this "purifying reflection," as Sartre puts it, is not an "empty space" generated by a pure spontaneity of freedom, however. Just as the choice of an initial project is sociohistorically conditioned, the reflective stance that we take toward it is as well. Sartre's "purifying reflection" only manifests our ability to adopt other historically generated perspectives on our lives – historically generated perspectives that are themselves the result of prior sociohistorical possibilities and the (hopefully reflective) choices that we made among them. Accordingly, our historical experience itself affords the grounds for the possibility of freedom, which brings Sartre very close to Hegel – without, of course, losing the first-person standpoint of the individual, as Hegel arguably does in his subordination of the individual to the collective subject or Spirit. The spirit of the time may well move in a particular direction, but this does not mean that the individual must march with it. As Sartre says in the *Critique*, "man is 'mediated' by things to the same extent as things are 'mediated' by man" (*CDR*, p. 79). This self-understanding suggests not only that the idea of freedom is built into the deepest structures of practical action, but that the idea of freedom has practical effects in the very historical unfolding that supposedly belies it.

Notes

1 See Dagfinn Follesdal, "Sartre on freedom," in P. A. Schilpp (ed.), *The Philosophy of Jean-Paul Sartre* (LaSalle, Ill.: Open Court, 1981), p. 372, quoting "Le Processus historique," *La Gazette de Lausanne*, February 8, 1947.
2 Jean-Paul Sartre, "Self-portrait at seventy" (an interview with Michel Contat), in *Life/Situations*, trans. P. Auster and L. Davis (New York: Pantheon, 1977), p. 88.
3 Jean-Paul Sartre, *The War Diaries: November 1939–March 1940*, trans. Q. Hoare (New York: Pantheon, 1985), p. 183.

4   Jean-Paul Sartre, *The Transcendence of the Ego*, trans. F. Williams and R. Kirkpatrick (New York: Hill and Wang, 1990), p. 41. Further references to *The Transcendence of the Ego* will be contained in the text in the form "(*TE*, p. ••)."

5   Jean-Paul Sartre, *Imagination: A Psychological Critique*, trans. F. Williams (Ann Arbor, Michigan: Ann Arbor Paperbacks, The University of Michigan Press, 1972), p. 134.

6   Jean-Paul Sartre, *The Psychology of Imagination* (New York: Citadel, 1991), p. 267.

7   See Joseph P. Fell, *Emotion in the Thought of Sartre* (New York: Columbia University Press, 1965), pp. 35–44.

8   Robert C. Solomon, *The Passions* (Garden City, NY: Anchor Press/Doubleday, 1976), p. 143.

9   Jean-Paul Sartre, *The Emotions: Outline of a Theory*, trans. B. Frechtman (New York: Citadel, 1976), p. 52.

10 Ibid., p. 36.

11 Ibid., p. 79.

12 Ibid., p. 82.

13 Michel Rybalka and Oreste Pucciano, "An interview with Jean-Paul Sartre," in P. A. Schilpp (ed.), *The Philosophy of Jean-Paul Sartre* (La Salle, Ill.: Open Court, 1981), p. 12.

14 As Sartre himself puts it in his 1948 lecture to the *Société française de philosophie*, in which he summarizes the fundamental theses of *Being and Nothingness*, "it is necessary to arrange a synthesis of the contemplative and non-dialectical consciousness of Husserl . . . with the activity of the dialectical project – but without consciousness, and hence without foundation – that we find in Heidegger, where we see, on the contrary, that the first element is transcendence." See Jean-Paul Sartre, "Consciousness of self and knowledge of self" (trans. N. Lawrence and L. Lawrence), in N. Lawrence and D. O'Connor (eds.), *Readings in Existential Phenomenology* (Englewood Cliffs, NJ: Prentice-Hall, 1967), p. 132.

15 Jean-Paul Sartre, *Being and Nothingness: An Essay in Phenomenological Ontology*, trans. H. E. Barnes (New York: Washington Square Press, 1956), p. 29. Further references to *Being and Nothingness* will be contained in the text in the form "(*B&N*, p. ••)."

16 Even more fundamentally, the ability of consciousness to negate various aspects of the world may well be the very condition of perception, for without this ability, being-in-itself would just be an undifferentiated mass, or what has been called a "blooming, buzzing confusion." See David Detmer, *Freedom as a Value* (La Salle, Ill.: Open Court, 1986), pp. 29–30.

17 Leo Fretz, "An interview with Jean-Paul Sartre," in H. Silverman and F. Elliston (eds.), *Jean-Paul Sartre: Contemporary Approaches to His Philosophy* (Pittsburgh, Penn.: Duquesne University Press, 1980), pp. 225–6.

18 Jean-Paul Sartre, *Search for a Method*, trans. H. E. Barnes (New York: Random House 1968), p. 8. Further references to *Search for a Method* will be contained in the text in the form "(*SM*, p. ••)."

19 Jean-Paul Sartre, *Critique of Dialectical Reason, Volume I: Theory of Practical Ensembles*, trans. A. Sheridan-Smith (London: Verso, 1991), p. 69. Further references to *Critique of Dialectical Reason, Volume I* will be contained in the text in the form "(*CDR*, p. ••)."

20 Jean-Paul Sartre, "The itinerary of a thought," in *Between Existentialism and Marxism*, trans. J. Mathews (New York: Morrow, 1979), p. 34.

Selected bibliography

Works by Sartre

1955: *Literary and Philosophical Essays*, trans. A. Michelson. New York: Criterion Books.

1956: *Being and Nothingness: An Essay in Phenomenological Ontology*, trans. H. E. Barnes. New York: Washington Square Press.

1964: *Nausea*, trans. L. Alexander. New York: New Directions.

1968: *Search for a Method*, trans. H. E. Barnes. New York: Random House.

1972: *Imagination: A Psychological Critique*, trans. F. Williams. Ann Arbor, Mich.: Ann Arbor Paperbacks, The University of Michigan Press.

1974: *Anti-Semite and Jew*, trans. G. J. Becker. New York: Schocken.

1974: *Between Existentialism and Marxism* (articles and interviews), trans. J. Mathews. New York: Morrow Quill Paperbacks.

1975: *The Emotions: Outline of a Theory*, trans. B. Frechtman. New York: Citadel.

1975: *The Wall and Other Short Stories*, trans. L. Alexander. New York: New Directions.

1981–9: *The Idiot of the Family*, trans. C. Cosman. Chicago, Ill.: University of Chicago Press (vol. I, 1981; vol. II, 1987; vol. III, 1989).

1985: *The War Diaries: November 1939–March 1940*, trans. Q. Hoare. New York: Pantheon.

1988: *"What is Literature?" and Other Essays*, trans. B. Frechtman. Cambridge, Mass.: Harvard University Press.

1990: *The Transcendence of the Ego*, trans. F. Williams and R. Kirkpatrick. New York: Hill and Wang.

1991: *Critique of Dialectical Reason, Volume I: Theory of Practical Ensembles*, trans. A. Sheridan-Smith. London: Verso.

1991: *Critique of Dialectical Reason, Volume II: The Intelligibility of History*, trans. Q. Hoare. London: Verso.

1991: *The Psychology of Imagination*. New York: Citadel.

1992: *Notebook for an Ethics*, trans. D. Pellauer. Chicago, Ill.: University of Chicago Press.

Works on Sartre

Anderson, T. C. 1993: *Sartre's Two Ethics*. Chicago, Ill.: Open Court.

Aronson, R. 1980: *Jean-Paul Sartre: Philosophy in the World*. London: New Left Books.

——1980: *Sartre's Second Critique*. Chicago, Ill.: University of Chicago Press.

——and van den Hoven, A. (eds.) 1991: *Sartre Alive*. Detroit, Mich.: Wayne State University Press.

Barnes, H. 1973: *Sartre*. New York: J. B. Lippincott.

——1981: *Sartre and Flaubert*. Chicago, Ill.: University of Chicago Press.

Bell, L. 1989: *Sartre's Ethics of Authenticity*. Tuscaloosa, Ala.: University of Alabama Press.

Busch, T. W. 1980: *The Power of Consciousness and the Force of Circumstances in Sartre's Philosophy*. Bloomington, Ind.: Indiana University Press.

Caws, P. 1979: *Sartre*. London: Routledge & Kegan Paul.

Catalano, J. S. 1980: *A Commentary on Jean Paul Sartre's Being and Nothingness*. Chicago, Ill.: University of Chicago Press.

Danto, A. C. 1991: *Sartre*. London: Fontana.

Desan, W. 1954: *The Tragic Finale: An Essay on the Philosophy of Jean-Paul Sartre*. Cambridge, Mass.: Harvard University Press.

—— 1965: *The Marxism of Jean-Paul Sartre*. New York: Anchor.

Detmer, D. 1986: *Freedom as a Value*. La Salle, Ill.: Open Court.

Fell, J. P. 1965: *Emotion in the Thought of Sartre*. New York: Columbia University Press.

Flynn, T. 1984: *Sartre and Marxist Existentialism*. Chicago, Ill.: University of Chicago Press.

Grene, M. 1983: *Sartre*. Lanham, Md.: University Press of America.

Howells, C. 1988: *Sartre: The Necessity of Freedom*. Cambridge: Cambridge University Press.

—— (ed.) 1992: *The Cambridge Companion to Sartre*. New York: Cambridge University Press.

Jameson, F. 1961: *Sartre: The Origins of a Style*. New Haven, Conn.: Yale University Press.

Jeanson, F. 1980: *Sartre and the Problem of Morality*, trans. R. V. Stone. Bloomington, Ind.: Indiana University Press.

LaCapra, D. 1978: *A Preface to Sartre*. Ithaca, NY: Cornell University Press.

McBride, W. L. 1991: *Sartre's Political Theory*. Indianapolis, Ind.: Indiana University Press.

McCulloch, G. 1994: *Using Sartre*. London: Routledge.

Santoni, R. E. 1995: *Bad Faith, Good Faith, and Authenticity in Sartre's Early Philosophy*. Philadelphia, Penn.: Temple University.

Schilpp, P. A. (ed.) 1981: *The Philosophy of Jean-Paul Sartre*. La Salle, Ill.: Open Court.

Silverman, H. and Elliston, F. (eds.) 1980: *Jean-Paul Sartre: Contemporary Approaches to His Philosophy*. Pittsburgh, Penn.: Duquesne University Press.

Wilder, K. V. 1997: *The Bodily Nature of Consciousness: Sartre and Contemporary Philosophy of Mind*. Ithaca, NY: Cornell University Press.

Chapter 9

Critical Theory

David Sherman

Due to an expansion in its usage, the term "critical theory" has become increasingly ambiguous. Among other things, it currently refers to certain types of literary, race, and gender theory, what has come to be known as "cultural critique," more generally, and the body of work produced by those thinkers associated with Frankfurt University's Institute for Social Research, or what is more commonly known as "the Frankfurt School." It is critical theory in this last sense that is the subject of this chapter, and, more precisely, the critical theory of the so-called "first generation" of Frankfurt School theorists. Active, roughly, from the late 1920s through the early 1970s, the most influential members of this group included Max Horkheimer, Theodor W. Adorno, Herbert Marcuse, Walter Benjamin, Friedrich Pollock, Siegfried Kracauer, Erich Fromm, Leo Lowenthal, and Franz Neumann. Even when restricted to these thinkers, however, the term "critical theory" remains somewhat ambiguous. It misleadingly suggests that they shared the same interests and perspectives, when, in fact, it would be closer to the truth to say that what they shared was a loose set of methodological commitments, the most important of which was to a multidisciplinary approach for constructing a comprehensive, neo-Marxist theory of contemporary society.

At the risk of being somewhat simplistic, however, two basic positions can be drawn out.[1] One position, which predominated during the 1930s, finds its clearest expression in Horkheimer's early writings. It holds that critical theory is concerned with mediating the ideals of philosophy (which includes such notions as "freedom," "equality," "justice," and "reconciliation") and society's prevailing practices and underlying tendencies. What makes critical theory "critical," indeed, is its refusal to yield unilaterally to either one. Like Kant, whose self-styled "critical" philosophy was designed to steer a path between the Charybdis of empiricism and the Scylla of rationalism within traditional philosophy, critical theory is designed to steer a path between traditional (German) philosophy and the social sciences. As against the uncritical idealism of the philosophical tradition, whose utopianism tends to see human beings "essentially" (i.e., in abstract or ahistorical terms) and their history "teleologically" (i.e., as geared toward the realization of this human essence), critical theory juxtaposes the facts of the social sciences. And, as against the uncritical realism of the social sciences, which views any attempt to speculatively pose alternatives to the present society as "meaningless" (and thus has the practical affect of confirming it), critical theory juxtaposes the norms of the German philosophical tradition. Critical theory, in sum, brings the insights of both into a dynamic tension to produce a materialist social theory.

During the late 1920s and early 1930s, this position was based upon the belief that the possibility for human emancipation continued to inhere within the institutional dynamics of the advanced capitalist societies, such that there was no ultimate contradiction between the norms of philosophy and the facts of the social sciences: the ideals of the former would be vindicated by the underlying tendencies within the latter. But with the increasingly catastrophic turn of events during the late 1930s and early 1940s, this relation between the norms of philosophy and the facts of the social sciences, or, as it is put in the vernacular, between theory and practice, became increasingly disparate. In response, Horkheimer all but gave up this position, while Marcuse continued to embrace it, albeit in a much more tentative fashion. With the rise of Jürgen Habermas, the doyen of the second generation of Frankfurt School theorists, the attempt to ground the ideals of the philosophical tradition in the social sciences was taken up with a new fervency, but for Habermas, whose political commitments run toward social-democratic reformism, its grounds are no longer to be found in economics and history, but rather in sociolinguistics.

The other basic position, which, in no small part, originates with Benjamin, finds its most far-reaching expression in Adorno's works. Although Adorno also sought to mediate the relation between philosophy's ideals and the prevailing sociohistorical practices in the service of an emancipated society, he discerned a somewhat more problematical relation between them. As a result, he had less confidence in their ultimate convergence – or, to be more precise, he had less confidence in the fact that if they did ultimately converge, it would testify to the existence of an emancipated society. This is because idealist philosophies, according to Adorno, have a dual nature: they not only posit the ideals toward which society ostensibly strives but, by virtue of their very abstractness, tend to see these ideals as already embodied in society's regressive practices, thereby legitimating them. Idealist philosophies are, in other words, inherently ideological, and thus obscure sociohistorical truths no less than they illuminate them. Adorno believed, however, that these obscured truths could be glimpsed by probing these philosophies for their internal contradictions, which he took to be a manifestation of the contradictions that exist in the society that gives rise to them. Because these contradictions arise from idealism's conceptual abstractness, which reflects and supports the abstractness of (monetarily mediated) social relations in capitalist society, it is necessary to reintroduce the moment of materiality that is lost. This is one of the reasons why Adorno privileges aesthetics as a vehicle of emancipation, for it resurrects a sensitivity to the natural world, which is just what idealism's abstract conceptual categories leave behind. Thus, while Adorno relied upon, and contributed to, the Frankfurt School's research in the social sciences, he focused on philosophy and aesthetics, as opposed to Horkheimer, who focused on social practices and their tendencies to instantiate philosophy's abstract ideals.

In what follows, I shall first provide a brief historical background of the Frankfurt School. I shall then consider what are ordinarily taken to be the three principal periods of first-generation critical theory by considering the works that are most representative of the primary philosophical positions within each period.[2] Unfortunately, given space limitations, this means that many of the Frankfurt School's works cannot be considered in this chapter, including, most conspicuously, the wealth of material concerning cultural phenomena.

Historical Background

Endowed by Felix Weil, the son of a wealthy industrialist, the Institute for Social Research was founded in 1923 for the purpose of providing an institutional context within which Marxist theory could be freely pursued – that is, pursued in a way that would be unconstrained by either the ideological dogmatism of the Communist Party or the rigid disciplinary divisions and pedantic style of German academic life. Inaugurated in 1924, the Institute's first Director was Carl Grünberg, a Professor of Law and Political Science, who specialized in the history of the workers' movement. Although it is unlikely that Grünberg was ever actually aligned with the Communist Party, he retained a strong commitment to orthodox Marxist methodology and, in particular, its doctrine of "historical materialism." This commitment was disputed by the younger members of the Institute, who, led by Horkheimer, charged that such an approach smacked of an orthodox (albeit secular) religion. In 1929, Grünberg was forced to step down from the Institute's Directorship due to illness, and in 1930, Horkheimer, who was then only 35 years old, assumed the position.

The first-generation Frankfurt School theorists were from varied disciplinary backgrounds: Horkheimer and Marcuse were philosophers, as was Adorno, who was a musicologist as well; Pollock, who was charged with administering the Institute's financial affairs, was an economist; Lowenthal was a literary theorist; Neumann was a lawyer; and Fromm, who was the best known of the group during the early 1930s, was a trained psychoanalyst. What they did share, however, was the same Jewish upper middle class background, which, given the rise of the Nazis, prompted most of them to flee Germany in the late 1930s. Benjamin, however, chose not to leave Germany until 1940, and when he was not allowed to cross from occupied France into Spain, he committed suicide at the border. Despite varied and circuitous routes, the others members of the Frankfurt School ended up in the United States, where they operated in exile. After the war, Adorno and Horkheimer returned to Frankfurt, where, besides their theoretical labors, they were instrumental in placing the German educational system on a sounder pedagogical footing. Marcuse, in contrast, chose to remain in the United States, where he taught at Brandeis University and the University of California at San Diego, and became the leading intellectual inspiration for the New Left during the late 1960s. Adorno, Horkheimer, and Marcuse, the three figures with whom this chapter will primarily deal, died in 1969, 1973, and 1980, respectively. By the late 1960s, however, their philosophical commitments were in the process of being supplanted by the second generation of critical theorists, who, led by Habermas, gave critical theory a communicative turn.[3]

1930–7: Interdisciplinary Materialism and Disintegrative Dialectics

Interdisciplinary materialism

With his assumption of the Institute's Directorship in 1930, Horkheimer immediately elucidated its new orientation. Although he continued to adhere to a Marxist position of sorts – in fact, for Horkheimer, the term "materialism" itself operated as a covering concept for his particular brand of Marxism – he largely rejected the prevailing doctrines of "orthodox" Marxism, which had more or less continued to function as the centerpiece of Grünberg's worldview. Accordingly, in his inaugural address, "The State of Contemporary Social Philosophy and the Tasks of an Institute for Social Research," Horkheimer rejects the overly simplistic base–superstructure model that had theoretically informed orthodox Marxism. On this model, philosophy, psychology, law, art, and all other cultural products are wholly derivative phenomena, and it is just the economy, or material being, that constitutes the true underlying reality. Such an approach is idealistic, he claims, for it largely abstracts from the existing social situation, and therefore, like other versions of idealism, is "ultimately devoid of any type of verification procedure."[4] Horkheimer further asserts that this model, which misinterprets Marx, is simply the flip side of a common misinterpretation of Hegel, which privileges the life of the mind or spirit, while viewing material life as wholly derivative. In contrast, he argues, there is only "one question" around which social philosophy must non-reductively "crystallize": "the question of connection between the economic life of society, the psychological development of its individuals, and the changes within specific areas of culture to which belong not only the intellectual legacy of the sciences, art, and religion, but also law, customs, fashion, public opinion, sports, entertainments, lifestyles, and so on."[5]

Horkheimer further explicates his brand of Marxism in two important articles that appeared in the *Journal of Social Research* (the Institute's own publication) in 1933. The first of these articles deals with the relationship between Horkheimer's materialism and metaphysics, the second with the relationship between his materialism and morality. In "Materialism and metaphysics," Horkheimer argues that the advocacy of materialism by orthodox Marxists played into the hands of its idealist opponents because it amounted to a metaphysical thesis, and a poor one at that, namely, that "materialism" amounted to the claim "that only matter and its movements are real"[6] (which draws sustenance from Engel's mechanistic *The Dialectics of Nature*). According to Horkheimer, however, materialism, properly understood, precludes any sort of claim that purports to capture "the nature of total reality," for all knowledge arises within a social context that is shaped by a particular set of human practices and objectives. This has important ramifications in terms of the question of praxis – that is, the attempt to transform existing social practices in accordance with theoretical objectives. It returns the responsibility for both formulating and bringing about these changes to "particular men within a particular period of time" (*CT*, p. 32), who are constituted by society and constitute it in turn, as opposed to the "longer view" of a metaphysically based praxis, which tends to discount the particular truths of the present in favor of eternal verities based upon the divine or nature. More generally, it reflects what is a basic methodological commitment of the first-generation theorists, namely, a commitment to the subject–object paradigm (which is just what is rejected by the second generation of critical theorists): "the subject–object relation is not accurately described by the picture of two fixed realities which are conceptually fully transparent and move towards each other. Rather, in what we call objective, subjective factors are at work; and in what we call subjective, objective factors are at work" (*CT*, p. 29).

If, by positing universal statements of abstract principle, metaphysics seeks to overcome what Horkheimer takes to be the ineluctible tension that exists between our concepts and objects by valorizing the former (despite the finite, sociohistorically conditioned nature of human knowledge), science illicitly seeks to resolve the tension by valorizing the latter. While science's "concepts are certainly dependent on their objects," it is also the case, although generally unacknowledged, that these concepts are no less conditioned by "the subjective factors in research and by the methods used and direction taken by the theoretical interests of the scientist" (*CT*, p. 28). It is only when it is acknowledged that science is bound up with history, according to Horkheimer, that it can avoid a collapse into "positivism," which reduces knowledge to a mere collection of facts regarding empirically confirmable regularities. Despite the differences between positivism and idealist metaphysics, however, their unmediated approaches (to the object and concept, respectively) bring them together in a crucial way: both "presuppose a subject who is independent of time" (*CT*, pp. 37–8). Thus, the anti-metaphysical stance of positivism is ultimately no less metaphysical than the idealistic metaphysics to which it is a response.

The necessity for overcoming the lack of self-reflection inherent in a positivistic approach to the sciences is a theme that Horkheimer also takes up in another early work, "Notes on science and the crisis." In this 1932 piece, Horkheimer declares, more plainly, that science's greatest virtue – namely, its demand that every step in its inquiry have a critical basis – is missing with respect to its most significant step, the setting of its tasks, which is done arbitrarily. In contrast to certain variants of "critical theory" (broadly defined) as it is presently practiced, however, Horkheimer's demand that science become self-reflective so as to recognize its subjection to the dynamics of history, and thus put itself in a position to fulfill its social responsibility, is by no means tantamount to the claim that it should see itself as merely a "social construct" in the first instance: "It is not for social interests to decide what is or is not true; the criteria for truth have developed, rather, in connection with progress at the theoretical level."[7] Seeing science as merely a social construct, in other words, would break off the mediacy of the subject–object relation every bit as much as orthodox Marxism's "dialectic of nature," the difference being that the latter absolutizes nature by purging the subjective moment, while the former wholly subjectivizes it.

In "Materialism and morality," Horkheimer goes on to attack classical morality in much the same way that he attacks classical metaphysics, which, historically, has often been taken to ground it. Appropriately, then, toward the end of "Materialism and metaphysics," Horkheimer anticipates his upcoming analysis of classical morality when he contends that his materialist theory of society "rejects a metaphysically grounded morality" because humanity's "striving for happiness is to be recognized as a natural fact requiring no justification" (*CT*, p. 44). Horkheimer starts "Materialism and morality" by pointing out that all idealist moralities are based upon "axiomatic constructions" whose very formality serves both to justify their allegedly eternal nature and to afford the necessary flexibility for the vissicitudes of modern life, which is far too complex and ephemeral to admit of substantive moral rules.[8] In this respect, Kant's morality is exemplary, for it posits such formal, timeless conceptions as "the categorical imperative" ("Act only according to that maxim by which you can at the same time will that it should become a universal law"), and "the good will," both of which imply that the individual must abstract from her particular interests in the service of an indiscernible general interest to be moral. Ultimately, however, such conceptions are not only "idealist illusions," but effectively operate against Kant's own intentions, for from such self-abnegating conceptions there is "a direct path that leads to the modern mysticism of sacrifice and obedience."[9] In contrast, Horkheimer asserts, a materialist ethic, motivated by compassion, seeks to alleviate human suffering by attacking its sociohistorical causes. In the present epoch, this suffering arises from the subjugation of human needs to an economic system whose productive capacities no longer justify the privations that it fosters. To the moral demand that human beings do their duty by obeying a formal, eternal rule structure, he opposes the ethical requirement that compassionate human beings become politically engaged in the cause of constructing concrete social structures that enable all human beings to flourish.

Crucially, however, Horkheimer dismisses neither the moral tradition, generally, nor Kant, in particular. Instead, he emphasizes the essentially historical nature of the moral enterprise, and, more specifically, the historical nature of particular values, which do not so much pass away as gradually transform over time. "The battle cries of the Enlightenment and of the French Revolution are valid now more than ever," Horkheimer asserts, but while they have retained their "actuality" (i.e., continue to be cultural ideals toward which we should strive) they should not be understood in the same way: "Politics in accord with this goal [of a rational society] therefore must not abandon these demands, but realize them – not however by clinging in a utopian manner to definitions which are historically conditioned – but in conformity with their meaning."[10] Put simply, this means that such ideals must change with the heightened possibilities presented by changing times. Thus, the progressive realization in the 1700s that there must be "freedom" and "equality" before the law, despite the inequality of property, is no longer progressive if the demand for freedom and equality remains limited to the law. During the 1700s, capitalism was still in its early stages, its productive capacities barely tapped, and the sanctification of property was a protection against the monarchy. Contemporary society, however, is marked by the accelerating monopolization of a vastly more generative productive capacity, which could meet the material needs of human beings to a much greater extent than the present social forms permit: "Only today have the resources of humanity become great enough for their adequate realization as an immediate historical task. The intense struggle for their fulfillment marks our epoch of transition."[11] Thus, in the modern epoch, "freedom" and "equality" must be extended from the juridical realm to the economic realm in order to truly have an emancipatory meaning.

Horkheimer's claim that Enlightenment values "are valid now more than ever" suggests that there remains within capitalist society the economic and cultural pre-conditions for a genuinely democratic socialist society. Of course, in contrast with the doctrine of historical materialism as postulated by orthodox Marxism – namely, that the ascendance of the working class is guaranteed by the inner workings of history (if not nature itself) – Horkheimer asserts that the "materialist theory certainly does not afford to the political actor the solace that he will necessarily achieve his objective; it is not a metaphysics of history, but rather a changing image of the world, evolving in relation to the practical efforts toward its improvement."[12] Nevertheless, during this period, one gets the sense that even if it is understood that a genuinely democratic socialist society is not guaranteed, this strain of critical theory sees it as a real historical possibility, and, in any event, certainly not in conflict with the underlying historical tendencies of the time.

Although Horkheimer's works from this period are most philosophically representative of this strain of critical theory, as well as the Frankfurt School's orientation, more generally, other members also produced significant pieces during this time. Following Horkheimer's lead, the theme that unified their various works was the attempt to mediate the relation between their respective disciplines and a materialist theory of society. Representative, along these lines, were the following essays, all of which were published in the early editions of the *Journal of Social Research*: Lowenthal's "On the social position of literature," which demanded that literature be appraised in terms of both the underlying economic structures that informed it and its tendencies to ideologically reinforce these structures; Pollock's "The present state of capitalism and the prospects for a planned economy," which argued that although the economic preconditions for a socialist society existed, the capitalist class had the means to indefinitely forestall this possibility through planning; and, most notably, Fromm's "On the methods and tasks of an analytical social psychology" and "Psychoanalytic characterology and its significance for social psychology," both of which reflect his ambitious project of synthesizing Marx and Freud.[13]

Disintegrative dialectics

Unlike Horkheimer's theoretical commitments, which changed over time, Adorno's commitments, though ceaselessly refined, remained relatively constant. A comparison of such later works as *Dialectic of Enlightenment* and *Negative Dialectics* (considered below) with "The actuality of philosophy" and "The idea of natural history," two seminal essays from the early 1930s, bears this out.

In the opening sentences of "The actuality of philosophy," which was written in 1931 for his inaugural lecture at the University of Frankfurt, Adorno presages what will be nothing less than his lifelong philosophical aim, namely, the liquidation of idealism. Philosophy must reject the "illusion" that "the power of thought is sufficient to grasp the totality of reality," he begins, for such an approach, which is based on the thesis that "autonomous reason" is able to develop reality "from out of itself," only "veils reality and eternalizes its present condition."[14] All idealistic philosophies are misconceived, Adorno believes, because sociohistorical concepts invariably condition rational thought. When idealistic philosophies purport to get behind these concepts to grasp the "totality" or "essence" of reality through what they take to be the autonomy of rational thought, therefore, they project, albeit unwittingly, the existing sociohistorical factors that condition their thought onto what they falsely privilege as such a reality. The sociohistorical nature of idealism's projections thus remain "veiled," and since these projections purport to capture nothing less than the "totality" or "essence" of reality, the existing sociohistorical conditions that inform them are "eternalized." The idealist philosophies of the day, such as neo-Kantianism, Husserl's phenomenology, and Heidegger's nominally anti-rationalistic fundamental ontology, all fell into this trap, according to Adorno, but, paradoxically, so did the "scientistic philosophies," which wholly rejected the idealist question concerning the "totality of reality." By privileging the natural sciences as the model for philosophical inquiry and seeking to "possess secure ground in the given," such philosophies also abstracted from the sociohistorical nature of philosophical concepts. Ultimately, therefore, they also tended to "eternalize" the given sociohistorical reality.[15]

For Adorno, these failures give rise to the question that motivates the title of his essay, namely, whether philosophy is "actual," which means whether "there exists an adequacy between the philosophic questions and the possibility of their being answered at all"[16] – or, more simply, whether philosophy still has the capacity to get at the "truth," its historic task, or just bogs down in existing intellectual attitudes (which is another, more profane, sense of philosophy's "actuality"). Adorno responds to this question by offering his own idea of philosophy, or, more precisely, his own idea of epistemology, which is based on dialectical and materialist principles. Preliminarily, he argues, "philosophy is interpretation,"[17] but not the interpretation of a truer world that hangs behind appearances. It is, rather, the interpretation of a constantly changing sociohistorical reality that can offer up no eternal truths, but can provide glimpses of fleeting sociohistorical ones, provided that the philosopher inquires in the right way. Inspired by Benjamin, Adorno asserts that the right way to proceed is by constructing "constellations" or "trial combinations" out of various constituents of the existing sociohistorical reality that will "light up suddenly and momentarily" sociohistorical truths. In other words, in much the same way that one would play around with puzzles or riddles, one imaginatively juxtaposes and rearranges various constituents of the existing sociohistorical reality in thought experiments until one "sees" the answer, that is, a sociohistorical truth. Such a process is "materialist" because it does not begin with large conceptual categories that schematize reality, as does idealism, but rather begins with what is often the smallest material constituents of reality and builds toward concepts. And it is "dialectical" because it does not reify either the subject or its truths. The concrete subject pushes beyond its sociohistorical conditioning through the imaginative construction of constellations, and the truths it "lights up" are "consumed at the same time," for the sociohistorical reality, and thus its truths, are constantly changing.[18]

Ruminating on the possibilities of this interpretive model, Adorno suggests that a sufficient constellatory construction of the commodity structure, which, as Marx taught, underpins capitalist society, could have the affect of lighting up Kant's "thing-in-itself" problem (i.e., the unknowable reality behind the world of appearances), and thus make it disappear. This hypothesis draws upon the work of the Hungarian

Marxist Georg Lukács, whose pivotal 1923 book, *History and Class Consciousness*, signaled a movement away from the objectivistic tendencies of orthodox Marxism, and had a strong influence on the Frankfurt School theorists. Thus, in accordance with Lukács's insight that the contradictions inherent within philosophical problems reproduce the contradictions inherent within the commodity structure, Adorno is suggesting that the stilted subject–object split implied by the thing-in-itself problem reproduces the stilted subject–object split within commodity production. In other words, the worker's separation from his product, whose social mediations hang behind his comprehension, is mirrored in the philosopher's separation from the unknowable thing-in-itself. When the sociohistorical reality that hangs behind the commodity structure is unveiled, therefore, the distinction between phenomenal knowledge and knowledge of the thing-in-itself disappears, for it becomes historically obsolete. Crucially, however, while Adorno buys into Lukács's dialectical analysis, he rejects Lukács's claim that the working class is the "universal subject" to whom the ideological mystifications of the commodity structure will appear, and that it is only from its standpoint that the truths inherent within the existing sociohistorical constellation can be unriddled. In this way, Adorno also differs from the other critical theorists, for whom the working class retains a somewhat privileged epistemic status.

While in "The actuality of philosophy" Adorno offers a normative epistemological model in which a non-reified subject neither cognitively constitutes reality nor is abstractly split off from it, in "The idea of a natural history" he offers what will become his basic approach for dealing with the antinomies generated by the philosophical tradition. "The idea of a natural history" was motivated by the issue of historical relativism, and, in particular, the three basic positions that had crystallized around this issue: the ontological claim that there is an absolute realm of values that transcends what appears to be their historical relativity (Scheler); the historicist claim that values simply are relative (Mannheim); and, most of all, Heidegger's attempt to collapse this antithesis in his fundamental ontology, in which "history itself . . . has become the basic ontological structure."[19] According to Adorno, who sees the question of ontology as a question of the status of the natural world, the first two positions artificially split the world into nature and history, while Heidegger's position achieves the "concrete unity of nature and history," but miscarries insofar as this unity is abstractly posited – that is, it is an overarching unity achieved by autonomous reason at the expense of the natural element, which is purged from its synthesis. It is Adorno's position, in contrast, that while history and nature interweave, they do not form an "encompassing whole" in which real history is transmuted into the abstract category of "historicity" and subsumed under Being.

More specifically, for Adorno, "history" and "nature" – and, for that matter, the two sides of every antithesis or "binary opposition" generated by the philosophical tradition – stand in a non-hierarchical relation to one another, in which each has a "double character."[20] On the one hand, each is irreducibly "other." "History," he contends, is characterized by "the occurrence of the qualitatively new," while "nature" refers to "what has always been." Depending on the object under consideration, then, each is to be used as a counterbalance to an overemphasis upon the other. In response to historical relativity, for instance, Adorno would pose the natural element, or, to be more precise, seek to resuscitate a remembrance of both external and internal nature (i.e., the natural in the subject), while in response to, say, Heidegger's ontological claims, which absorbed "historicity" into the nature of Being, he would juxtapose the contingent facticity of a changing sociohistorical context. On the other hand, each term passes into the other. What seems most historical is comprised of what is irreducibly natural within it (such as the struggle for existence), while, as Lukács asserted, what seems most natural is actually just "second nature," which is historically produced (such as the claims of classical economists who see the insatiable desire for goods and competition under capitalism as "natural"). And, indeed, it is the constellation that provides the key for interpreting "this alienated, reified, dead world," for it yields the insight that what was taken to be "natural" is really historical, thus potentially unfreezing a petrified history.[21]

Ultimately, for Adorno, privileging one of the two terms in any of the antitheses or binary oppositions bequeathed by the philosophical tradition results in an undialectical oscillation between the two extremes. Thus, in *Kierkegaard: Construction of the Aesthetic*, which was published one year later, Adorno maintains that by privileging subject over object (and, likewise, internal history over external history and history over nature), Kierkegaard does not merely subjectify the object (externalize internal history and historicize nature), but also unwittingly hardens the subject into an object (internalizes external history and naturalizes history), thus effectively negating his vaunted subjectivity. This basic thesis, as we shall see, is taken up again in *Dialectic of Enlightenment*.

1937–1940: *Critical* Theory

While in 1934 Marcuse could still contend that "the fate of the labor movement . . . is clouded with uncertainty,"[22] by 1937 this uncertainty (at least for the near future) had disappeared. With the ascendance of fascism in Germany during the mid-1930s, which crushed the progressive elements of the German labor movement (and forced the Institute for Social Research into exile), as well as the barbaric policies of Stalinism in the Soviet Union, the historical tide had turned against what Marxism took to be history's emancipatory force, namely, the proletariat. Under these deteriorating conditions, it became increasingly difficult for the Frankfurt School theorists to reconcile their earlier project of "interdisciplinary materialism," which had more or less continued to rely upon Marxism's more optimistic prognostications, with the actual course of historical events. It is within this context that Horkheimer steps into the breach with what is undoubtedly one of the defining works produced by the Frankfurt School, "Traditional and critical theory," which is the first work that calls "critical theory" by its name.

"Traditional and critical theory" is chiefly concerned with explicating the relation between theory and practice at a time when the gap between the two is rapidly widening. It was no easy matter to formulate the new historical relation. To continue to privilege "traditional" Marxist theory despite the turn of events would be to collapse into idealism (of which orthodox Marxism, its self-understanding notwithstanding, is a variant), while to privilege the prevailing practices – that is, to go along with the course of history, which had swept along a considerable percentage of the working class – would be to collapse into an apologetic for fascism. Thus, Horkheimer attempts to cleave a middle position. Horkheimer begins "Traditional and critical theory" by emphasizing that "the traditional idea of theory" is based on the scientific model, which, in turn, is based on the sort of deductive processes that hold sway in mathematics. On this account, knowledge is hierarchically classified and manipulated in a supposedly "objective" fashion; in fact, however, it is precisely "objectivity" that is lost in this process insofar as the sociohistorical context, which generates the particular forms that theoretical inquiry first takes, is bracketed. This model, moreover, conforms to the theoretical model that underpins capitalist society: "The seeming self-sufficiency enjoyed by work processes whose course is supposedly determined by the very nature of the object corresponds to the seeming freedom of the economic subject in bourgeois society."[23] Given the pervasiveness of this model, Horkheimer argues that "what is needed is a radical reconsideration, not of the scientist alone, but of the knowing individual as such" (CT, p. 199). Thus, in contrast to his analyses of the drawbacks of science during the period of "interdisciplinary materialism," which were based upon an "external" critique of the improper uses of science within society, Horkheimer shifts to an "internal" critique of the ways in which all knowledge tends to presuppose and reinforce a distorted image of society.[24]

Horkheimer's "radical reconsideration" thus issues in a "critical" theory, namely, a theory that "has society itself for its object." A "critical" theoretical approach, he argues, is distinguished by a tension in which, on the one hand, economic categories such as work, value, and productivity are interpreted just as they exist in the prevailing order, while, on the other hand, this interpretation is implicitly subjected to criticism, for "the critical acceptance of the categories which rule social life contain simultaneously their condemnation" (CT, pp. 207–8). With this notion, Horkheimer is advancing the idea of an "immanent critique" – namely, a critique whose standpoint exists within the very structures that are being subjected to critique. In other words, capitalist society is based upon certain abstract concepts, such as freedom, equality, and the harmonization of particular interests, and when these concepts are fully articulated, it turns out that they are at odds with the very order from which they arise. In this way, the critical theorist can avoid a collapse into either the abstract normativity of idealism or a wholly descriptive conformism. Of course, since the basis for such a critique is parasitic upon the society being critiqued, critical theory is historically contingent, or, as Horkheimer states, "this knowledge guarantees only a contemporary, not a future community of transmitters" (CT, p. 241). Indeed, it is the very possibility of critique that is called into question once "first-generation" critical theory moves into its third period in the 1940s. At this juncture, however, the grounds of critical theory itself are not yet being called into question.

In "Traditional and critical theory," moreover, Horkheimer qualifiedly shifts the locus of emancipation from the proletariat to the intellectual, who, nevertheless, continues to speak on the proletariat's behalf. Although, as Horkheimer puts it, "the situation of the proletariat is, in this society, no guarantee of correct knowledge" (CT, p. 213), it continues to be the repository of emancipatory hopes by dint of both its central and inherently subversive position within capitalism. The intellectual is thus committed to speaking on behalf of this class even when he or she is at odds with it: "The sharpness of the conflict shows in the ever present possibility of tension between the theoretician and the class which his thinking is to serve" (*CT*, p. 215). Along these lines, he distinguishes his notion of the intellectual's role from the role that the intellectual plays in orthodox Marxism by asserting that orthodox Marxist theoreticians dogmatically identify with the proletariat, while critical thought "must at times isolate its subject and throw him back on himself" (*CT*, p. 214). Horkheimer's depiction of the orthodox Marxist theorist here is misleading, because his belief that the proletariat suffers from a "false consciousness" is one with which orthodox Marxists concurred – thus the need for a "vanguard party." Still, critical theory, as Horkheimer conceives it, does differ from orthodox Marxism in important respects. While orthodox Marxism privileges the economy, and otherwise views cultural matters as epiphenomenal, Horkheimer maintains that "the dependence of the cultural on the economic has changed" as a result of "ruling economic and political bureaucracies" (*CT*, p. 237). So, too, while orthodox Marxism privileges the proletariat as a collective subject whose historical ascendancy is assured, and traditional bourgeois theory privileges the individual, Horkheimer does not privilege either one, for both are abstract: "Critical thinking is the function neither of the isolated individual nor of a sum-total of individuals. Its subject is rather a definite individual in his real relation to other individuals and groups, in his conflict with a particular class, and finally, in the resultant web of relationships with the social totality and with nature" (*CT*, pp. 210–11). To the extent that they "absolutize" their respective theories, "as though they were grounded in the inner nature of knowledge as such or justified in some other ahistorical way," both orthodox Marxism and traditional bourgeois theory posit "reified, ideological categories" (*CT*, p. 194).

"True theory is more critical than affirmative" (*CT*, p. 242), Horkheimer states at the end of "Traditional and critical theory," and in "Philosophy and critical theory," which was written by Marcuse in response to the discussion generated by Horkheimer's essay, Marcuse fleshes out the relation between "critical" and "affirmative" thought. In certain respects "Philosophy and critical theory," which was also published in 1937, reflects Marcuse's relatively recent break with phenomenology, or, to be more exact, the project of amalgamating Heidegger's phenomenological ontology and Hegelian-Marxism. As late as 1932, Marcuse's thought remained in Heidegger's orbit, as is evidenced by the publication of what had been his intended *habilitationsschrift*, *Hegel's Ontology and the Theory of Historicity*. Still, as Adorno points out in a review of the book, Marcuse was beginning to strain against the limits of Heidegger's philosophy in his attempt to move "from historicity to history," which leads Adorno to ask: "Why indeed should the 'ontological' question precede that of real, historical facts since Marcuse himself would like to bridge the gap between ontology and facticity?"[25] Marcuse will soon come to agree, and by the mid-1930s he begins to speak in terms of historical tendencies and human potentialities instead of ontological structures.[26] Thus, in a thinly veiled slap at Heidegger, Marcuse states in "Philosophy and critical theory" that "the philosophical ideals of a better world and of true Being are incorporated into the practical aim of struggling mankind, where they take on human form."[27]

In "Philosophy and critical theory," Marcuse develops a number of points in "Traditional and critical theory," two of which I shall address here. First, he stresses the utopian component in critical theory, which Horkheimer had only touched upon. As Marcuse puts it, there are two basic elements in a critical social theory, namely, the "concern with human happiness" and the recognition that it "can be attained only through a transformation of the material conditions of existence."[28] This concern with human happiness is the "without which not" of critical theory: It is the source of critical theory's normative impulse. When Horkheimer states that "true theory is more critical than affirmative," therefore, he is only denigrating those theories that affirm either the prevailing socioeconomic conditions or their underlying tendencies notwithstanding the actual fact of the matter, not "the affirmative" as a regulative ideal. And in the service of this ideal, Marcuse asserts, fantasy must be enlisted, for it can span "the abyss between rational and present reality."[29] Second, while "the affirmative" as a regulative ideal is indispensable to a "critical" theory, critical theory, as Horkheimer had stated, must still be able to discern "the affirmative" somewhere within the existing so as to stay "critical," otherwise it lapses. Following Horkheimer's notion of "immanent critique," Marcuse asserts that "the affirmative" can still be discerned within the classical bourgeois ideals, which have a dual nature: critical theory "only makes explicit what was always the foundation of [bourgeois philosophy's] categories."[30] Indeed, more than Horkheimer and Adorno, Marcuse always believed in the emancipatory power of bourgeois philosophy's most basic category, namely, rational thought: "Reason represents the highest potentiality of man and of existence."[31] It is precisely this belief, however, that is made somewhat more problematical during the next period of critical theory.

1940–5: The Critique of Instrumental Reason

In "Traditional and critical theory," Horkheimer asserts that "the issue is not simply the theory of emancipation, but the practice of it as well" (*CT*, p. 233), and in "Philosophy and critical theory," Marcuse asserts that "reason is the fundamental category of philosophical thought, the only one by means of which it has bound itself to human destiny." Yet, in *Dialectic of Enlightenment*, which is generally taken to be the most representative work of the first generation of critical theorists, not only practice, but reason itself, and therefore theory, is called into question. Before examining this work, however, I shall briefly consider Pollock's important essay, "State capitalism: its possibilities and limitations," for the socioeconomic picture that it paints is arguably presupposed by *Dialectic of Enlightenment*, and contributes to its pessimistic nature.

State *capitalism or state* capitalism

By the early 1940s, the Second World War was in full swing, and while the sociopolitical commitments of the warring nations were relatively distinct, their economies, surprisingly enough, were not. In particular, neither the fascist nor liberal democratic economies seemed to bear an especially strong resemblance to the classic capitalist model, which is distinguished by a private market made up of profit-driven competitors and a government whose attitude toward the operation of this market is essentially *laissez-faire* in nature. From Keynesian economic policies to the command economy, state intervention in the economic sphere seemed to be the rule. Thus, Marx's critique of political economy, which was based upon the idea that capitalism would be plagued by increasingly intense crises due to a tendency for the rate of profit to fall, was called into question. Pollock's "State capitalism: its possibilities and limitations" called it into question more than most.

According to Pollock, although "nineteenth century free trade and free enterprise are on the way out," capitalism itself is not, but instead will transform into "state capitalism," which could assume either a totalitarian or democratic form.[32] The defining feature of "state capitalism," he contends, is the relative displacement of the market by the state, which develops a "general plan." This plan involves coordinating access to credit (banks are transformed into government agencies), capital investment, production and distibution, prices and wages, consumption, and research and development. As a result, the "economic," strictly speaking, is displaced by the "political." This means that while a "pseudo-market" continues to operate, and the profit motive, at least nominally, continues to exist, the capitalist, in effect, no longer manages the enterprise. Ultimately, then, "the profit motive is superseded by the power motive."[33] Moreover, according to Pollock, due to the rationalization of the economy, which supersedes the natural laws of the market and therefore forecloses "economic problems in the old sense," there are no limits on state capitalism. Thus, he asserts, "we are unable to discover any inherent economic forces, 'economic laws' of the old or new type, which could prevent the functioning of state capitalism."[34] For Pollock, this means that Marx's crisis theory becomes obsolete. With planning, the economic havoc caused by increasing rates of surplus value extraction could be averted by political determinations, which might take the form of a full employment policy.[35] To use an expression that Adorno will come to increasingly use, the economy, and, more generally, society, effectively becomes "administered."

Although Pollock's thesis is generally deemed to animate *Dialectic of Enlightenment*,[36] it is not one that all the Frankfurt School theorists accepted, and, arguably, is not even one that Adorno accepted – at least unequivocally. In *Behemoth*, for example, Neumann argues that while the state had begun to intervene in the operations of the free market, in both the fascist and liberal democratic economies the profit motive was still controlling. Referring to Nazi Germany's economy as "totalitarian monopoly capitalism," Neumann asserts that the new forms into which capitalism was evolving were essentially an outgrowth of trends that Marxism had already diagnosed within capitalism. Neumann's analysis, in fact, is less reductionistic than Pollock's, for he does not privilege the economic at the expense of the political in the way that Pollock privileged the political at the expense of the economic. Even Adorno is inclined to charge Pollock's thesis with being reductive: it is based on "the undialectical assumption that a non-antagonistic economy might be possible in an antagonistic society."[37] In the aftermath of *Dialectic of Enlightenment*, however, the question will become how antagonistic Adorno himself thinks society actually is.

Dialectic of Enlightenment

While Adorno's early works evidence a certain wariness of Enlightenment reason – or, to be more precise, a wariness of its unreflective employment (i.e., an employment that does not reflect upon Enlightenment reason's own grounds and assumptions) – it is doubtful that the same could be said of Horkheimer's "critical theory" period, much less his "interdisciplinary materialism" period. In 1941, however, Horkheimer moves closer to Adorno's position with the publication of "The end of reason," a short essay that prefigures various themes that will be taken up in *Dialectic of Enlightenment*. "The end of reason" is wide-ranging in scope. It surveys the fate of reason since the Middle Ages, namely, its increasing instrumentalization in the face of skepticism; it considers the "gangsterism" of fascism, which is emblematic of reason's decline; it considers the relation between the decline of reason and the decline of the individual ego, which is due to economic and cultural processes that circumvent family and school to directly condition the young for unqualified obedience; and, after a renewed attack upon fascism, it ends with the either/or to which reason has historically progressed: barbarism or freedom. What is most striking in this work, however, is Horkheimer's dawning recognition that reason is a two-edged sword. "The idea of reason, even in its nominalistic and purified form, has always justified sacrifice,"[38] he states, and "the age-old definition of reason in terms of self-preservation always implied the curtailment of reason itself."[39]

These themes are more fully developed in *Dialectic of Enlightenment*, which is often taken to be one of the first "deconstructions" of Enlightenment reason. In certain respects (but only in certain respects) the analysis of reason is reminiscent of Nietzsche's analyses, which are a primary source of inspiration for poststructuralist thought. Nevertheless, unlike Heidegger, whose uncompromising attacks on reason and subjectivity are an even greater source of inspiration for most (but not all) strains of poststructuralist thought, Adorno and Horkheimer hold on to these Enlightenment notions. Their commitment to Enlightenment reason, despite its dialectical reversals, is manifest, as is evidenced by the book's Introduction, in which this commitment is made explicit various times in statements such as the following: "We are wholly convinced – and therein lies our *petitio principii* – that social freedom is inseparable from enlightened thought . . . If enlightenment does not accommodate reflection on the recidivist element then it seals its own fate."[40] Ultimately, *Dialectic of Enlightenment* is a critique of reason by (dialectical) reason[41] (namely, a critique of *Verstehen* by *Vernunft*), and, as such, is reminiscent of no less an Enlightenment project than Kant's *Critique of Pure Reason*. Furthermore, as was the case for Kant, the very grounds of such an undertaking are problematical, which is implicitly acknowledged by Adorno and Horkheimer in the Introduction as well: "Thought has to forgo not only the affirmative use of scientific and everyday conceptual language, but just as much that of the opposition. There is no longer any available form of linguistic expression which has not tended toward accommodation to dominant currents of thought" (*DOE*, p. xii). Through its experimental style (interdisciplinary and fragmentary), as well as sheer density, *Dialectic of Enlightenment* seeks to overcome this problem. It requires of the reader not only a sustained effort, but a contribution as well, which is in keeping with a book that was initially titled *Philosophical Fragments*. As is the case with Kierkegaard's *Philosophical Fragments*, *Dialectic of Enlightenment* seeks to resurrect individual subjectivity in the face of mass society's attempt to level all thinking to the "dominant currents of thought," which afford ideological cover to dominant economic and political interests. Generally speaking, the book immanently critiques Enlightenment rationality and subjectivity as they have historically unfolded by examining, respectively, the link between myth and Enlightenment, the genesis of the Enlightenment subject through an interpretation of Homer's *Odyssey*, the ultimate logic of Enlightenment morality, mass culture, and (through a constellatory, multiperspectival approach) the phenomenon of anti-Semitism.

The central thesis of the first essay, "The concept of Enlightenment," is that "myth is already enlightenment, and enlightenment reverts to mythology" (*DOE*, p. xvi). "Myth is already enlightenment" to the extent that the ancients sought to control the natural world through abstract principles of equivalence, which are the very stuff of Enlightenment thinking. Through the mythic offering of sacrifices, for example, they would barter with the gods to gain control over them, and, thereby, a hostile and threatening nature. So, too, for the ancients, myth meant not only "report, naming, and the narration of the Beginning, but also presentation, confirmation, and explanation, [which] grew stronger with the recording and collection of myths" (*DOE*, p. 8). "Enlightenment reverts to mythology," conversely, to the extent that it fetishizes its own products. This second, more crucial, prong of the thesis draws upon the insights of Max Weber, the early twentieth-century German sociologist, and Lukács, whom Weber strongly influenced. It was Weber's thesis that in disenchanting the world, reason becomes "formal" or "purposive" in nature – that is, relegated to calculating the best means to the ends sought, but unable to determine the ends themselves. Reason, in other words, functions as an arch-bureaucrat. In one sense, it becomes an end in itself, an "iron cage" of rationality in a lifeless world, while, in another sense, it indiscriminately serves any pre-rational end, since it cannot determine substantive ends. Lukács extends Weber's thesis to the reifying effects of the commodity form under capitalism, in which abstract principles of equivalence like labor and exchange value prevail, and Adorno and Horkheimer, in turn, extend Lukács' thesis to the top-down administrative processes of "state capitalism," which they see as the dead end of this process. Through increasing abstraction, which is the underlying tendency of capitalism in its movement from competitive to state forms, they argue, the particularities of the natural world are increasingly effaced. Enlightened thought thus increasingly becomes unenlightened about itself, and turns on the very subject in whose interest it ostensibly operates: "In class history, the emnity of the self to sacrifice implied a sacrifice of the self, inasmuch as it was paid for by a denial of nature in man for the sake of domination over non-human nature and other men . . . Man's domination over himself, which grounds his selfhood, is almost always the destruction of the subject in whose service it is undertaken" (*DOE*, p. 54).

This dynamic is probed by Adorno and Horkheimer within the context of their discussion of subject formation in Homer's *Odyssey*. Much like myth and Enlightenment, they contend, self-denial and self-assertion are intertwined – a fact which can

be more easily glimpsed by looking at the relatively uncomplicated dynamics of subjectivity shortly after "the subject" has sprung from its undifferentiated oneness with
nature. Accordingly, with every adventure, Odysseus, who Adorno and Horkheimer
describe as "a prototype of the bourgeois individual" (*DOE*, p. 43), preserves his
newly won subjectivity at the expense of his own internal nature, external nature, or
other human beings. For example, in the episode with the Sirens, whose "call of
nature" is both the beckoning of natural happiness and the death of subjectivity,
Odysseus plugs the ears of his oarsmen so that they cannot hear the call of happiness, and has himself bound tightly to his ship's mast, where he can listen to its call,
but cannot act upon it. Such are the relative fortunes of the working class and bourgeoisie within modern society, in which myth, domination, and labor are entangled.
The idea of self-denial in the name of self-assertion is made even clearer, since it is
made more literal, when Odysseus confronts the Cyclops Polyphemus. Cunningly,
Odysseus escapes Polyphemus by referring to himself as *Udeis* – which rhymes with
Odysseus, and in Greek means, quite literally, "no one" – for when Polyphemus
screams that *Udeis* has blinded him, there is no reason for other Cyclops to come to
Polyphemus's aid. By renouncing himself as a self, in other words, Odysseus affirms
himself, a point that he egoistically pauses to make to Polyphemus while escaping,
which costs the lives of his oarsmen.

This same dynamic – self-denial is already self-assertion, and self-assertion reverts
to self-denial – is evidenced in Adorno and Horkheimer's critique of Enlightenment
morality, which they take to be intrinsically sadomasochistic. Along these lines, Kant's
moral philosophy is especially representative. According to Kant, the subject must
abstract from all natural and historical residues to act upon the moral law, which is
tantamount to being free, but since it is the natural and historical that constitutes
"the subject" (*qua* "empirical self," which Kant disparages as the stuff of anthropology), Kant's moral subject is abstract in nature. Although seemingly swallowed up
by the imperatives of a pure practical reason that operates in accordance with universal laws, however, the concrete subject that is denied unwittingly reproduces the
very stuff of its empirical context precisely because of the thoroughgoing formality
of it moral decision-making procedures: "So long as the identity of the user of reason
is disregarded, the affinity of reason is as much to force as to mediation . . . Since it
exposes substantial goals as the power of nature over mind, as the erosion of its self-
legislation, reason is – by virtue, too, of its very formality – at the service of *any*
natural interest" (*DOE*, p. 87). In this way, Adorno and Horkheimer argue, Kant's
morality (which, Kant had hoped, would make good Christian ends through formal
means) slips into the immorality of the Marquis de Sade, and, for that matter, the
Nazis, both of whose "systems" were organized in accordance with the hierarchical,
systematizing principles of formal rationality.

Finally, in their critique of contemporary culture, "The culture industry: Enlightenment as mass deception," Adorno and Horkheimer argue that culture, once viewed
as a retreat in an otherwise profane commercial world, has been entirely assimilated
by that world – hence the term "culture industry," which once would have been perceived as an oxymoron. Culture is no longer designed to perform the function of
enabling what must now be called its "consumers" to think against the dominant
currents of thought, but rather is designed to do its consumers' thinking for them,
thus precluding the possibility of potentially subversive ideas: "The need which

might resist central control has already been suppressed by the control of the individual consciousness" (*DOE*, p. 121). This type of control, they conclude, signifies the end of the individual subject of competitive capitalism while exalting a pseudo-individuality that is based on one's accidental traits or preferences as a consumer. It takes the form of a stultifying sameness that reproduces the subordination to capital in the economic sphere within the entertainment sphere so as to more thoroughly confirm it, thus giving the lie to the idea that culture is an escape from work life.

It has subsequently been argued that the "Culture industry" essay, and, more generally, Adorno's miscellaneous cultural writings, presuppose a static dualism of "high" modernist culture, which is valorized, and "mass," "low," or "popular" culture, which is disparaged as regressive. Despite Adorno's attacks on various aspects of popular culture (the most notorious of which are his pieces on jazz), however, this characterization is incorrect. Although one might reject Adorno's analyses of particular cultural phenomena, he did not reject popular culture *qua* "popular" culture; rather, he believed that popular culture itself is not "popular" because it does not arise from the classes that consume it. The essential point of the "Culture industry" essay and Adorno's works on culture, therefore, is not so much that "high" culture is being crowded out (or, better, absorbed) by "low" culture, but that both high and low culture are commodified in the first instance by commercial interests, which superimpose culture from above. Indeed, Adorno recognized that in a society riven by class interests, there would be different cultural expressions, and that, ideally, popular culture would be an expression of the interests and concerns of the working classes. As he states in a letter to Benjamin, high culture and popular culture are "torn halves of an integral freedom, to which however they do not add up."[42]

In any event, in the final analysis, *Dialectic of Enlightenment* would seem to leave little hope for breaking out of the administered world of late capitalism. Actually, however, we are left with some possibilities. Adorno and Horkheimer assert, for instance, that by the "remembrance of nature in the subject, in whose fulfillment the unacknowledged truth of all culture lies hidden, enlightenment is universally opposed to domination" (*DOE*, p. 40). In different ways, it is to this "remembrance of nature in the subject," which is the fount of human happiness, that Adorno and Marcuse will advert in later aesthetic and psychoanalytic works. So, too, Adorno and Horkheimer assert that the notion of "determinate negativity," which is the driving force in Hegel's dialectic, is a form of Enlightenment thinking that does not fetishize its products – although by positing "Absolute knowing" as a historical end realized in his own time, Hegel, too, ultimately succumbed to this inclination (*DOE*, p. 24). Adorno's *Negative Dialectics*, which draws upon his earlier works, reflects the attempt to make good Hegel's promise.

1945–70: Theory and Practice in a One-Dimensional Society

Philosophy and psychology

In the decade following the Second World War, the Frankfurt School turned much of its attention toward psychoanalytic issues to better grasp the penchant for fascism that had just been observed. This decade ends with the 1955 publication of *Eros and*

Civilization, which reflects Marcuse's attempt not only to explain in neo-Freudian terms the psychological bases for fascism, but also to reveal an emancipatory standpoint within Freud's theories that went unnoticed by Freud himself.

In fact, the Frankfurt School's attempt to explain the sociopsychological bases of fascism began even before the war ended, although it was undertaken by one who actually was no longer a member. Due to theoretical differences, Fromm broke with the Institute for Social Research in 1939, and in 1941 his most influential work, *Escape from Freedom*, was published. *Escape from Freedom* probes the social psychology of Germany's lower and middle classes. Drawing on Weber's *The Protestant Ethic and the Spirit of Capitalism*, Fromm argues that the psychological preconditions for fascism were already present in these classes due to the self-renunciation demanded by their predominant religious (Lutheranism and Calvinism) and economic (competitive capitalism) forms. In keeping with Weber, however, he argues that the existential meaning that religion could still effectively offer in the Middle Ages had been lost, thus leaving humanity without purpose: far from being seen as desirable, then, the freedom bequeathed by modernity is alienating. For Fromm, the way to approach this problem is to revisit humanity's existential situation in terms of the potential for love and spontaneity rather than focus upon what he increasingly came to reject in Freud's corpus, namely, a biologically rooted drive theory. It is this position, which the other members of the Frankfurt School saw as idealistic (and, ultimately, conformist), that facilitated the break.

In 1950, Adorno, in conjunction with a group of American psychologists, published *The Authoritarian Personality*, which was based on interviews and questionnaires constructed to identify individuals with latent fascistic biases, that is, individuals susceptible to anti-democratic propaganda. Based on the scores of 2099 respondents in nine general areas – conventionalism, authoritarian submission, authoritarian aggression, anti-intraception (hostility to the subjective and imaginative), superstition and stereotypy, power and toughness, destructiveness and cynicism, projectivity (the outward projection of base impulses), and sex – the researchers found a strong relation between anti-Semitic and anti-democratic tendencies, as well as both of these tendencies and a childhood marked by parents whose discipline was strict, but arbitrary. And the psychology of this family, the study implies, is itself the result of the family's attempt to steel itself against unfathomable social pressures, and then project its feelings of anxiety and inferiority onto groups that are even more marginalized, who then serve as scapegoats. This accounts for the authoritarian personality's hostility toward the unfathomable "other," which, as Adorno and Horkheimer state in *Dialectic of Enlightenment* ("Elements of anti-Semitism"), is personified by the Jew.

Adorno produced a number of important theoretical essays on psychology in the early 1950s, such as "Freudian theory and the pattern of fascist propaganda"[43] and "Sociology and psychology,"[44] but it is only with Marcuse's *Eros and Civilization* that the Frankfurt School, in some sense, returns to its early 1930s project, namely, finding the grounds for the emancipatory ideals of the philosophical tradition in the social sciences. At this historical juncture, however, such a project was far more problematical. Given the recent ascendance of fascism in Europe and McCarthyism in the United States, as well as the conservatism of the 1950s, history did not seem to be on the side of the working class. And, given the basic thesis of *Dialectic of Enlightenment*, to which Marcuse largely ascribed, capitalist society seemed to have all the ideological tools that it needed to impede the radicalization of consciousness, thus precluding radical political practice. In search of an alternative emancipatory standpoint, Marcuse thus pursues Adorno and Horkheimer's "remembrance of nature in the subject" by pursuing Freud's biologically rooted drive theory.

Although Marcuse defends Freud's biologically rooted drive theory against neo-Freudian theorists because it both resists attempts to "normalize" the ego (i.e., reconcile it to the prevailing social realities) and holds the key to human happiness, in at least one crucial respect he disagrees with Freud, and this disagreement is the basis for his underlying position in *Eros and Civilization*. Specifically, Marcuse disagrees with Freud's contention in *Civilization and its Discontents* that our unsubjugated drives cannot be reconciled with the requirements of society. According to Marcuse, while historically this was true, inasmuch as human beings were largely preoccupied with meeting basic needs, it is not necessarily true, as Freud had undialectically suggested. Given our present level of technological advancement, Marcuse argues, a rational organization of time and resources could translate into a liberated society in which our libidinal impulses would not be repressed, but would find expression in society itself. In Freudian terms, then, Marcuse contends that Freud had wrongly assumed that the "pleasure principle" (the desire for immediate instinctual satisfaction) and the "reality principle" (the need to repress the instincts in the face of environmental demands) must be at odds. So, too, he argues, the high levels of repression that continue unabated in society must be understood in terms of the margin separating "necessary repression" and "surplus repression," which is justified by a condition of artificially induced scarcity (i.e., a scarcity that is not justified by a given society's possibilities). Human beings toil under these conditions, Marcuse asserts, because the historically specific form that the reality principle assumes in modern capitalist society is the "performance principle," which psychologically reinforces capitalism's imperatives.

In addition to drawing on Freud's earlier drive theory, Marcuse draws on his controversial distinction between the life and death instincts, namely, between Eros and Thanatos. According to Marcuse, although the life instincts are geared toward reproducing life on ever-larger scales, while the death instinct seeks a dissolution into the inorganic, they are interrelated and, in fact, are alike insofar as both ultimately seek a relief from tension. At least theoretically, then, the life and death instincts should both be sublimated in work. In the context of contemporary society, however, "it seems that socially useful destructiveness is less sublimated than socially useful libido,"[45] and that this asymmetrical dialectic cashes out as follows: the more rationalized society becomes, the more that work life demands the repression of the life instincts. This means not only that our sensuality becomes increasingly restricted to procreation, but also that the death instinct becomes increasingly unbound by the life instincts that should mediate it. The death instinct thus finds increasing and unmediated expression in all aspects of life – that is, it becomes more widespread and destructive: "Increasing cultural wealth and knowledge provides the material for progressive destruction and the need for increasing instinctual repression."[46] This "dialectic of civilization," furthermore, is buttressed by Freud's two-tracked theoretical analysis of the development of the repressive mental apparatus – namely, an "ontogentic" analysis, which considers the individual's development from birth, and a "phylogenetic" analysis, which speculatively advances civilization's archetypal development from birth. At both of these levels – that is, the individual and the collective – which are interrelated, the very possibility for development arises from an original guilt-inducing act that plays out in increasingly virulent cycles of resistance, guilt, and repression.

Marcuse does not succumb to pessimism, however, and argues that there are emancipatory possibilities inherent within this bad dialectic. Phantasy "retains a high degree of freedom from the reality principle,"[47] and consequently provides uncolonized images of happiness; art manifests "the repressed harmony of sensuousness and reason";[48] and there remain archetypes in Western culture, such as Orpheus and Narcissus, who embody joy and fulfillment. Ultimately, Marcuse asserts, a society built upon a new relationship between the instincts and reason – that is, a "libidinal rationality" (which presupposes, among other things, the end of the performance principle, surplus repression, and therefore a reduction in the work day) – is indeed possible. There would not only be a re-eroticization of the body, but also of the entire personality, as well as society itself. Those who reductively attack Marcuse for merely valorizing polymorphous perversity, such as Fromm, therefore miss his more important point that in this new context "sexuality would tend to its own sublimation": "the libido would not simply reactivate precivilized and infantile stages, but would also transform the perverted content of these stages."[49]

Philosophical models

During the 1960s, Marcuse and Adorno were the most productive critical theorists, and, from a strictly philosophical standpoint, *One-Dimensional Man* and *Negative Dialectics*, respectively, were arguably their most significant works (although, admittedly, in Adorno's case, it is virtually impossible to make this sort of distinction between *Negative Dialectics* and his posthumously published *Aesthetic Theory*, which are not only homologous, but mutually reinforcing as well).

Published in 1964, *One Dimensional Man* echos the fears of *Dialectic of Enlightenment*, although Marcuse's target is not the totalitarian impulse of modernity, more generally, but rather its particular manifestation – 20 years later – in the phenomenon of advanced capitalist society. Like *Dialectic of Enlightenment*, however, the fundamental concern of *One-Dimensional Man*, as the title suggests, is modern society's ability to bring about irrational or pseudo-reconcilations in which forms of opposition that would otherwise transcend prevailing social theories and practices are preempted. In his Introduction to the book, Marcuse acknowledges that this state of affairs raises the question of whether critical theory has lost the ground of its own critique, but he argues that even if there are no agents or agencies of social change, "the distinction between true and false consciousness, real and immediate interest still is meaningful."[50] In other words, for Marcuse, there is, at least in principle, some standpoint from which one's "true" needs and interests can be distinguished from those "false" needs and interests with which the individual is instilled by the ideological apparatus of the social totality, and which internally reinforce his repression. The question of whether (due to this state of affairs) critical theory itself is in any position to make this distinction, however, is one that Marcuse ultimately leaves unanswered.

Marcuse begins *One-Dimensional Man* by asserting that democracy and freedom no longer go hand-in-hand. While advanced capitalist society retains the support of the majority due to its ability to deliver the goods, the rights and liberties that were basic to prior stages of entrepreneurial capitalism "lose their traditional rationale and content" (*ODM*, p. 1). Indeed, precisely because it delivers the goods, the tendency of advanced capitalism to undercut basic rights and liberties is exacerbated, for non-conformity appears to the majority as socially useless. Implicitly drawing on his analysis of artificial scarcity, surplus repression, and the performance principle in *Eros and Civilization*, moreover, Marcuse claims that the prospects for liberation are effectively undermined by the perpetual implantation of new material needs, which artificially perpetuate the struggle for existence, and that the distinction between true and false needs can be made on this basis. Making this distinction is problematical, however, for "the efficiency of the system blunts the individuals' recognition that it contains no facts that do not communicate the repressive power of the whole" (*ODM*, p. 11). This means that the system no longer appears as ideological because it is permeated by ideology – in other words, the backdrop against which ideology might be identified as such disappears, which reflects the fact that ideology permeates even the production process. Thus, even the subjectivity of the working class is flattened, which calls its emancipatory role into question. This phenomenon, Marcuse adds, is only worsened by technological advancement, for by diminishing the quantity and intensity of physical labor, it further tends to conceal capitalist domination. The consciousness of the working class thus changes, and it is more easily integrated into the workplace and society at large. And, finally, this process is reinforced by the system's ability to project itself as tolerant and reasonable: a "subdued pluralism" obscures the system's unfreedom, and the rationalization of means obscures the system's overall irrationality.

There are factors at play, moreover, that implicitly call into question the emancipatory role played by the instincts in *Eros and Civilization*. After suggesting that ideological indoctrination penetrates the very instincts of the individual, Marcuse asserts that the diminution in the quantity and intensity of work has not redounded to the benefit of emancipatory practices, but has had the opposite affect: "Desublimation is practiced from a 'position of strength' on the part of society, which can afford to grant more than before because its interests have become the innermost drives of its citizens, and because the joys which it grants promote social cohesion and contentment" (*ODM*, p. 72). Marcuse calls this phenomenon "repressive desublimation." At first blush, "repressive desublimation" would appear to be an oxymoron. It was Freud's position that "sublimation" is the compelled redirection of the drives away from their principal object, which suggests that desublimation would be emancipatory. Marcuse, however, takes a more nuanced approach. As we saw in *Eros and Civilization*, in an emancipated society "sexuality would tend to its own sublimation," which means that the individual personality, and thus the larger society, would be eroticized. Sublimation, in other words, is not always inconsistent with emancipatory practices. The position that Marcuse is taking in *One-Dimensional Man* is the converse, namely, that desublimation in a repressive society would not necessarily serve the interests of liberation. In late capitalist society, the process of desublimation is ideologically manipulated by the culture industry to reinforce the existing social relations in various ways. Titillating movies, television programs, and novels tacitly reinforce mindless consumerism, and sex is routinely used to advertise products. This produces what Marcuse calls a "happy consciousness" – that is, a facile consciousness that on the surface is satisfied, but whose impoverished inner life is a source of unhappiness.

Finally, Marcuse argues, ideology penetrates language (both semantically and syntactically) to its core, such that the possibility of *truly* "thinking outside the box" is veritably foreclosed. Concepts that would comprehend the given facts, and thus afford the basis for transcending them, are losing their linguistic representation. This is achieved by "a telescoping and abridgement of syntax which cuts off development of meaning by creating fixed images which impose themselves with an overwhelming and petrified concreteness" (*ODM*, p. 91). Further exacerbating this situation, according to Marcuse, is the character of Anglo-American philosophy itself, whose linguistic analyses discard the speculative moment, and therefore tacitly reaffirm the bad given. In other words, in contrast to classic philosophy, in which "the subversive power of reason" seeks to mediate dialectically the critical tension between metaphysical ideals and the given reality, Anglo-American philosophy dispels the tension by dispelling the ideals: "The empiricism of linguistic analysis moves within a framework which does not allow such contradiction – the self-imposed restriction to the prevalent behavioral universe makes for an intrinsically positive [i.e., conformist] attitude" (*ODM*, p. 171). What linguistic philosophy fails to grasp, Marcuse contends, is that language cannot be abstracted from its concrete sociohistorical context without reifying it, with all its contradictions. The aim of language, instead, is to push beyond the present stock of meanings by making "the established language itself speak what it conceals or excludes" (*ODM*, p. 195).

Despite Marcuse's characterization of society as "one-dimensional," he continues to hold out hope in the reconciling power of reason. Any "transcendent project," he declares, "must demonstrate its own higher rationality" by serving the "pacification of existence" through optimizing "the free development of human needs and faculties" – given, of course, the material limits of the existing sociohistorical context (*ODM*, p. 220). Although Marcuse warns against "technological fetishism," he thus remains firmly committed to the Enlightenment project: "If the completion of the technological project involves a break with the prevailing technological rationality, the break in turn depends on the continued existence of the technical base, for it is the base which has rendered possible the satisfaction of needs and the reduction of toil – it remains the very base of all forms of human freedom" (*ODM*, p. 231). Ultimately, it is Marcuse's belief that technology could be aestheticized, which would involve the free play of thought and imagination, and would ostensibly circumvent the repressive aspects of the dialectic of Enlightenment.

At first blush, Marcuse's alternatives are presumably ones that would, in some sense, resonate with Adorno. But given Marcuse's concession that there are no forces within one-dimensional society that have the ability to bring about the historical alternatives that he has posited, Adorno would argue that ahistorically identifying such alternatives could conceivably cause more harm than good: by "subjectively constituting" these goals, Marcuse might ultimately implicate himself in the very dialectic of Enlightenment from which he seeks to escape. (This is why Adorno never speculated upon the state of sociohistorical reconciliation.) Despite overlapping diagnoses and concerns, therefore, there are differences between Marcuse and Adorno that might be understood as arising from an underlying difference of perspective: Marcuse uses concrete sociohistorical analyses to project what are ostensibly still immanent substantive ideals into the future, which then serve as a basis for praxis, while Adorno uses the non-substantive regulative ideal of the reconciled society in the service of concrete sociohistorical analyses that seek to expose the false promises and contradictions of the past, which then (albeit more problematically) serve as a basis for praxis. With the intensification of the civil rights movement, the advent of anti-war protests, and the birth of the New Left in the mid-1960s, which raised anew the question of the relation between theory and practice, this "difference of perspective" becomes more conspicuous, for it leads Marcuse and Adorno in different directions, both theoretically and practically.

In the decade following the publication of *One-Dimensional Man*, Marcuse, in response to rapidly changing social conditions, produced a number of politically explosive theoretical works. In "Repressive tolerance," which appeared in a 1965 book titled *A Critique of Pure Tolerance*, he argues that intolerance, and, indeed, violence, is morally justified (if not required) in response to capitalist society's depredations. This position, which is arguably the product of his diagnosis of the limits of pluralism in *One-Dimensional Man*, theoretically justified the confrontational politics that were beginning to take shape. The radical days of 1968, in turn, led Marcuse to take a more expansive theoretical approach. In *An Essay on Liberation*, published in 1969, he argues that the increasing incidence of Third World revolutionary movements effectively undermines capitalist markets abroad, and that, coupled with the student movements in the advanced capitalist societies (which are not "revolutionary" in themselves), has the potential to engender capitalist crises. And, finally, in his 1972 book *Counterrevolution and Revolt*, Marcuse argues that large segments of advanced capitalist society itself are becoming increasingly alienated. The surface appearance of a pacified consumer society, he argues, is belied by a widening disparity between the expectations created by the system's promises and the (dispirited) lives that people actually lead as consumers and workers ("workers" broadly defined, i.e., not just limited to orthodox Marxism's factory workers). For Marcuse, who now stresses a longer historical view, the emphasis is upon political education, which serves to build a United Front within the advanced capitalist societies.[51]

Like Marcuse, who tacitly returns to Hegel's dialectical notion of "determinate negation" in *Counterrevolution and Revolt*,[52] Adorno also believes that determinate negation is the appropriate philosophical starting point. But, for Adorno, who had his doubts about the efficacy of the New Left, this meant a return to the intricacies of theory itself, as opposed to the attempt to theoretically shape (or, worse, retrospectively justify) practice, which, he believed, invariably debases theory, and, ultimately, practice as well. This philosophical commitment led Adorno to take a different tack in *Negative Dialectics*, which was published in 1966, three years before his death.

Thus, unlike Hegel, and, for that matter, Marcuse, Adorno does not think that dialectics can "achieve something positive by means of negation"[53] – hence, a *negative* dialectic. In effect, negative dialectics gives the Hegelian dialectic a turn from "identity" toward "non-identity," which Adorno characterizes as follows: negative dialectics "does not tend to the identity in the difference between each object and its concept; instead it is suspicious of all identity. Its logic is one of disintegration" (*ND*, p. 145). Although the language of "identity" is new, *Negative Dialectics* hearkens back not only to Adorno and Horkheimer's emphasis upon "determinate negation" in *Dialectic of Enlightenment*, but, even more directly, to "The actuality of philosophy," which was written 35 years earlier. As we observed in "The actuality of philosophy," Adorno thinks that the constellatory framework gives rise to fleeting sociohistorical truths. This is another way of saying that objects of knowledge cannot be conceptually pinned or identified once and for all, thus establishing their "identity," but are constantly changing, which requires our concepts to change as well if we are to do justice to them. Quite simply, then, "the hinge of negative dialectics" is to "change the direction of conceptuality" (*ND*, p. 12).

This "change of direction" resonates throughout Adorno's philosophy, and fundamentally alters Hegel's dialectic. Thus, although Hegel and Adorno agree that subject and object, universal and particular, cannot be properly understood apart from their dialectical interrelation, Hegel privileges the subject, while Adorno privileges the object, and Hegel privileges the universal, while Adorno privileges the particular. For Adorno, this "axial turn," which converts Hegel's idealistic dialectic into a materialist one, redeems the true Enlightenment impulse in dialectics. Privileging "the object" (which, as a part of nature, the subject always already is) and "the particular" (which is the individual subject within the context of the social whole) ultimately recurs to the benefit of the Enlightenment subject, while abstractly privileging "the subject" and "the universal," as *Dialectic of Enlightenment* teaches, strips both of their natural content, and does violence to them in equal measure. Thus, while Hegel states that "the whole is true," Adorno declares in *Minima Moralia*, a book of aphorisms written after the war, that "the whole is false."[54] Again, this does not mean that "the whole" – namely, the universal – is not an essential moment in comprehension, since it must factor into all (nonfetishized) knowledge of particulars, nor does it mean that it somehow lacks reality, for Adorno is not a nominalist. Instead, "the whole is false" means that, like the concept with respect to its objects, it must be understood as being driven by the sensuous particulars that comprise it. For Adorno, then, to privilege the whole, as Hegel does, is to hypostatize it (to think it identically), and thereby falsify it. In this way, Hegel's "system," which culminates in Absolute Knowing (*Phenomenology of Spirit*) and the State (*Philosophy of Right*), goes astray. Adorno thus declares: "No universal history leads from savagery to humanitarianism, but there is one leading from the slingshot to the megaton bomb" (*ND*, p. 320). Hegel's teleology, in other words, is inconsistent with the type of Enlightened (self-reflective) thought that would truly be in the service of humanitarianism, which is an uncoerced reconciliation of the particulars that comprise the whole, but it is consistent with the sort of unreflective instrumentalizing reason that is part and parcel of the dialectic of Enlightenment.

More broadly, *Negative Dialectics* is a historically specific philosophical constellation. The Introduction, which begins with the momentous line that "philosophy, which once seemed obsolete, lives on because the moment to realize it was missed" (*ND*, p. 3), grapples with the concept of philosophical experience, and how this concept, as it has historically unfolded, conspires with the bad turn of historical events that precluded philosophy's own realization. Part One, in turn, considers Heidegger's fundamental ontology (which was also the subject of a 1964 book by Adorno, *Jargon of Authenticity*). Adorno's consideration of Heidegger here is due less to the fact that Adorno puts Heidegger on the same footing as Kant and Hegel, the two other philosophers with whom the book extensively deals, than with the fact that, according to Adorno, "the ontologies in Germany, Heidegger's in particular, remain effective to this day" (*ND*, p. 61). Adorno immanently critiques this ontology, while simultaneously seeking to make sense of the sociohistorical need that motivated it. In Part Two, Adorno sets forth his own concept of negative dialectics, some of whose basic commitments were summarized above. And, finally, in Part Three, Adorno "elaborates models of negative dialectics . . . to make plain what negative dialectics is" (*ND*, p. xx) – that is, we see Adorno's *negative* dialectic in action. The first two models with which Adorno deals in this part – Kant's freedom model and Hegel's history model – reflect his attempt to show that each is informed by that which it represses. Crudely, Kant's freedom model is suffused by the social totality from which it seeks to abstract, while Hegel's history model presupposes the very individual subject to which it otherwise gives short shrift.

In the final analysis, moreover, both models lose "the object," or natural element, as is the wont of all idealistic philosophies, according to Adorno. Yet, the last model that Adorno proffers in Part Three involves his own questioning of the status and possibility of metaphysics in the wake of Auschwitz. "The indifference of [the modern] consciousness to metaphysical questions . . . [hides] a horror that would take men's breath away if they did not repress it" (*ND*, p. 395), he states, for to continue to ask the metaphysical question is no less a condition of the possibility of emancipation than a resurrection of the natural element that metaphysics represses. For Adorno, in sum, it is only by continuing to ask the metaphysical question that we might ever dare hope to break the spell of metaphysical thinking, and thus redeem a "full, unreduced experience in the medium of conceptual reflection" (*ND*, p. 13). The aim of negative dialectics, in sum, is nothing less than rich individual experience, which is the unfulfilled promise of the Enlightenment.

Conclusion

Adorno's negative dialectics is often taken to be the final legacy of first-generation critical theory, and, for many second-generation critical theorists, reflects its dead end. According to Habermas, by rejecting the 1930s project, which revolved around the attempt to ground the philosophical ideals of the Enlightenment tradition in the social sciences, Adorno leaves us with a purely negative conception of reason that is relegated to impotently critiquing the prevailing state of affairs. The way out of this aporia, Habermas argues, is a linguistic turn in which the subject–object paradigm of the first-generation critical theorists is replaced by a communicative paradigm, which is based on what he calls an "ego–alter-ego relation." By virtue of what he claims are universal pragmatic considerations that implicitly underlie our use of language (or, as it is called in the vernacular, our "speech-acts") – namely, truthfulness, rightness, sincerity, and comprehensibility – Habermas claims to have found the grounds for a discourse ethics. Ostensibly, then, by the very act of speaking, we are implicitly committing ourselves to the realization of an uncoerced consensus through the force of the better reasoned argument, or what he calls an ideal speech community.

The details of this turn, as well as its merits, are well beyond the scope of this chapter. In terms of the project of the first-generation critical theorists, however, it should be pointed out that Habermas's abandonment of the subject–object paradigm has entailed the abandonment of not only nature as a thing of concern, but also the utopian themes that depended upon it, and which were so crucial to first-generation critical theory. Under these circumstances, one must wonder whether Habermas's communicative paradigm is implicated in the very dialectic of Enlightenment that he takes it to have surmounted.

Notes

1 See Susan Buck-Morss, *The Origin of Negative Dialectics: Theodor W. Adorno, Walter Benjamin, and the Frankfurt Institute* (New York: The Free Press, 1977), pp. 65–9.

2 See, for example, Seyla Benhabib, *Critique, Norm, and Utopia: A Study of the Foundations of Critical Theory* (New York: Columbia University Press, 1986) and Helmut Dubiel, *Theory and Politics: Studies in the Development of Critical Theory*, trans. B. Gregg (Cambridge, Mass.: The MIT Press, 1985).

3 For intellectual histories of the Frankfurt School, see Rolf Wiggershaus, *The Frankfurt School: Its History, Theories, and Political Significance*, trans. M. Robertson (Cambridge, Mass.: The MIT Press, 1995) and Martin Jay, *The Dialectical Imagination: A History of the Frankfurt School and the Institute of Social Research*, 1923–1950 (Boston: Little Brown, 1973).

4 Max Horkheimer, "The state of contemporary social philosophy and the tasks of an Institute for Social Research" (trans. P. Wagner), in S. E. Bronner and D. M. Kellner (eds.), *Critical Theory and Society: A Reader* (New York: Routledge, 1989), p. 34.

5 Ibid., p. 33.

6 Max Horkheimer, "Materialism and metaphysics" (trans. M. J. O'Connell), in *Critical Theory: Selected Essays* (New York: Continuum, 1992), p. 14. Further references will be contained in the text in the form "(*CT*, p. ••)."

7 See Max Horkheimer, "Notes on science and the crisis," in *Critical Theory: Selected Essays*, p. 3.

8 Max Horkheimer, "Materialism and morality," *Telos* 69 (Fall 1986), pp. 87–8.

9 Ibid., p. 95.

10 Ibid., p. 108.

11 Ibid., p. 109.

12 Ibid., p. 114.

13 See Rolf Wiggershaus, *The Frankfurt School*, pp. 118–23.

14 Theodor W. Adorno, "The actuality of philosophy" (trans. B. Snow), *Telos* 31 (Spring 1977), pp. 120–1.

15 Ibid., p. 121.

16 Ibid., p. 124.

17 Ibid., p. 126.

18 Ibid., p. 127.

19 Theodor W. Adorno, "The idea of natural history" (trans. R. Hullot-Kentor), *Telos* 60 (1984), p. 114.

20 My analysis here draws upon Susan Buck-Morss, *The Origin of Negative Dialectics*, pp. 57–9.

21 Theodor W. Adorno, "The idea of natural history," pp. 118–19.

22 Herbert Marcuse, "The struggle against liberalism in the totalitarian view of the state" (trans. J. J. Shapiro), in *Negations: Essay in Critical Theory* (London: Free Association Books, 1988), p. 42.

23 Max Horkheimer, "Traditional and critical theory" (trans. M. J. O'Connell), in *Critical Theory: Selected Essays*, p. 197. Further references will be contained in the text in the form "(*CT*, p. ••)."

24 Seyla Benhabib, *Critique, Norm, and Utopia*, p. 153.

25 This review, which was published in the first volume of the *Journal for Social Research*, is reproduced, in part, in Seyla Benhabib's Introduction to Marcuse's *Hegel's Ontology and the Theory of Historicity*, trans. S. Benhabib (Cambridge, Mass.: The MIT Press, 1987), p. xxxi.

26 Douglas Kellner, *Herbert Marcuse and the Crisis of Marxism* (Los Angeles: University of California Press, 1984), p. 61.

27 Herbert Marcuse, "Philosophy and critical theory," in *Negations*, p. 142.

28 Ibid., p. 135.

29 Ibid., p. 154.

30 Ibid., p. 145.

31 Ibid., p. 136. Martin Jay says that "despite the consistent emphasis on negativity in his work and the pessimism often attributed to it, Marcuse's writings always contained an implicit faith in possible realization of *Vernunft* in the social world." Martin Jay, *The Dialectical Imagination*, p. 71. And, as Douglas Kellner says, "from the 1930s until his death, Marcuse was convinced that reason can judge between true and false needs, pseudo- and real happiness." But as Kellner also points out, Marcuse "never really addresses or works out the issue of the foundation of critical theory." See Douglas Kellner, *Herbert Marcuse and the Crisis of Marxism*, p. 125.

32 Friedrich Pollock, "State capitalism: its possibilities and limitations," in A. Arato and E. Gebhardt (eds.), *The Essential Frankfurt School Reader* (New York: Continuum, 1993), p. 72.

33 Ibid., p. 78.

34 Ibid., pp. 86–7.

35 See ibid., p. 175, n. 28.

36 See, for example, Helmut Dubiel, *Theory and Politics*, p. 81.

37 Rolf Wiggershaus, *The Frankfurt School*, p. 282.

38 Max Horkheimer, "The end of reason," in *The Essential Frankfurt School Reader*, p. 33.

39 Ibid., p. 47.

40 Max Horkheimer and Theodor W. Adorno, *Dialectic of Enlightenment*, trans. J. Cumming (New York: Continuum, 1991), p. xiii. Further references will be contained in the text in the form "(*DOE*, p. ••)."

41 For a vigorous defense of this position, see Robert Hullot-Kentor, "Back to Adorno," *Telos* 81 (Fall 1989).
42 See *Aesthetics and Politics*, ed. F. Jameson (London: New Left Books, 1977), p. 123.
43 Theodor W. Adorno, "Freudian theory and the pattern of fascist propaganda," in *The Essential Frankfurt School Reader*, p. 118.
44 Theodor W. Adorno, "Sociology and psychology, " *New Left Review* 46/47 (December 1967–January 1968).
45 Herbert Marcuse, *Eros and Civilization: A Philosophical Inquiry into Freud* (Boston: Beacon Press, 1966), p. 86.
46 Ibid., p. 87.
47 Ibid., p. 140.
48 Ibid., p. 144.
49 Ibid., p. 202.
50 Herbert Marcuse, *One-Dimensional Man* (Boston: Beacon Press, 1991), pp. xliv–xlv. Further references will be contained in the text in the form "(*ODM*, p. ●●)."
51 See Douglas Kellner, *Herbert Marcuse and the Crisis of Marxism*, ch. 9.
52 Ibid., p. 292.
53 Theodor W. Adorno, *Negative Dialectics*, trans. E. B. Ashton (New York: Continuum, 1992), p. xix. Further references will be contained in the text in the form "(*ND*, p. ●●)."
54 Theodor W. Adorno, *Minima Moralia: Reflections from Damaged Life*, trans. E. F. N. Jephcott (London: New Left Books, 1974), p. 50.

Selected bibliography

Works by the Frankfurt School

Theodor Adorno

1973: *Jargon of Authenticity*, trans. K. Tarnowski and F. Will. Evanston, Ill.: Northwestern University Press.
1974: *Minima Moralia*, trans. E. F. N. Jephcott. London: Verso.
1982: *Against Epistemology: A Metacritique: Studies in Husserl and the Phenomenological Antinomies*, trans. W. Domingo. Oxford: Blackwell.
1989: *Kierkegaard: Construction of the Aesthetic*, trans. R. Hullot-Kentor. Minneapolis, Minn.: University of Minnesota Press.
1992: *Negative Dialectics*, trans. E. B. Ashton. New York: Continuum.
1993: *Hegel: Three Studies*, trans. S. Weber Nicholsen. Cambridge, Mass.: The MIT Press.
1994: *Prisms*, trans. S. and S. Weber. Cambridge, Mass: The MIT Press.
1998: *Aesthetic Theory*, trans. R. Hullot-Kentor. Minneapolis, Minn.: University of Minnesota Press.

Walter Benjamin

1969: *Illuminations*, trans. H. Zohn. New York: Schocken.
1986: *Reflections: Essays, Aphorisms, Autobiographical Writings*, trans. E. F. N. Jephcott. New York: Schocken.

Max Horkheimer

1991 (with T. W. Adorno): *Dialectic of Enlightenment*, trans. J. Cumming. New York: Continuum.

1992: *Critical Theory: Selected Essays*, trans. M. J. O'Connell et al. New York: Continuum.

1992: *Eclipse of Reason*. New York: Continuum.

1995: *Between Philosophy and Social Science*, trans. G. F. Hunter, M. S. Kramer, and J. Torpey. Cambridge, Mass.: The MIT Press.

Herbert Marcuse

1966: *Eros and Civilization: A Philosophical Inquiry into Freud*. Boston: Beacon Press.

1972: *Counterrevolution and Revolt*. Boston: Beacon Press.

1973: *Studies in Critical Philosophy*. Boston: Beacon Press.

1978: *The Aesthetic Dimension: Toward a Critique of Marxist Aesthetics*. Boston: Beacon Press.

1988: *Negations: Essays in Critical Theory*. London: Free Association Books.

1991: *One-Dimensional Man*. Boston: Beacon Press.

1991: *Reason and Revolution*. Atlantic Heights, NJ: Humanities Press.

Works on the Frankfurt School (generally)

Benhabib, S. 1986: *Critique, Norm, and Utopia: A Study of the Foundations of Critical Theory*. New York: Columbia University Press.

Bernstein, R. J. 1995: *The New Constellation*. Cambridge, Mass.: The MIT Press.

Dubiel, H. 1985: *Theory and Politics: Studies in the Development of Critical Theory*, trans. B. Gregg. Cambridge, Mass.: The MIT Press.

Jay, M. 1973: *The Dialectical Imagination*. Boston: Little, Brown.

Kellner, D. M. 1989: *Critical Theory, Marxism, and Modernity*. Baltimore, Md.: The Johns Hopkins University Press.

Whitebook, J. 1995: *Perversion and Utopia: A Study in Psychoanalysis and Critical Theory*. Cambridge, Mass.: The MIT Press.

Wiggershaus, R. 1995: *The Frankfurt School: Its History, Theories and Political Significance*, trans. M. Robertson. Cambridge, Mass: The MIT Press.

Works on individual members of the Frankfurt School

Theodor Adorno

Buck-Morss, S. 1977: *The Origin of Negative Dialectics: Theodor W. Adorno, Walter Benjamin, and the Frankfurt Institute*. New York: The Free Press.

Hohehdahl, P. 1995: *Prismatic Thought: Theodor W. Adorno*. Lincoln, Neb.: University of Nebraska Press.

Jameson, F. 1990: *Late Marxism: Adorno, or, The Persistence of the Dialectic*. London: Verso.

Jarvis, S. 1998: *Adorno: A Critical Introduction*. New York: Routledge.

Zuidervaart, L. 1994: *Adorno's Aesthetic Theory: The Redemption of Illusion*. Cambridge, Mass.: The MIT Press.

Walter Benjamin

Buck-Morss, S. 1989: *The Dialectics of Seeing: Walter Benjamin and the Arcades Project.* Cambridge, Mass: The MIT Press.

Nagele, R. 1991: *Theater, Theory, Speculation: Walter Benjamin and the Scenes of Modernity.* Baltimore, Md.: The Johns Hopkins University Press.

Pensky, M. 1993: *Melancholy Dialectics.* Amherst, Mass.: University of Massachusetts Press.

Max Horkheimer

Benhabib, S., Bonss, W., and McCole, J. (eds.) 1993: *On Max Horkheimer: New Perspectives.* Cambridge, Mass.: The MIT Press.

Herbert Marcuse

Bokina, J. and Lukes, T. J. (eds.) 1994: *Marcuse: New Perspectives.* Lawrence, Kansas: University of Kansas Press.

Kellner, D. M. 1984: *Herbert Marcuse and the Crisis of Marxism.* Berkeley and Los Angeles, Calif.: University of California Press.

Pippin, R., Feenberg, A., and Webel, C. P. (eds.) 1988: *Marcuse, Critical Theory and the Promise of Utopia.* South Hadley, Mass.: Bergin & Garvey.

Chapter 10

Jürgen Habermas and Hans-Georg Gadamer

David Ingram

[E]very one that asketh receiveth . . . and to him that knocketh it shall be opened. (Matthew 7:8)

My brother and I strongly disagree about the meaning of the Gospels: I think they tell a story about a humble humanitarian who urged his disciples to surrender their material possessions to devote their lives to redeeming the suffering of the poor and meek; he thinks they tell a story about the Son of God, who admonishes rich and poor alike to believe in Him for the sake of gaining eternal life. Regardless of who has got it right, one thing seems patently clear: our conflicting interpretations lack the transparency of meaning we normally attribute to the printed word which, after all, appears on the page in all its indisputable objectivity. In this respect, our interpretations appear to be much like our subjective judgments of taste: we can agree that the large body of water facing us is the ocean, but we can't agree on whether it looks green or blue.

No doubt my interpretation of the Gospels is also colored by a biased perspective (unlike my brother, I'm an atheist, committed to furthering social justice in *this* world). However, this fact about personal bias ignores what Hans-Georg Gadamer (1900–2001) and Jürgen Habermas (1929–) – the two most influential German philosophers living at the turn of the twentieth-first century – take to be the inescapably interpretative nature of even our most objective knowledge. If they are right, knowledge is inherently relative to the perspective of the knower. But a perspective, they remind us, need not be merely personal. Indeed, a perspective that is shared can be as universally accessible as that afforded by a telescope – assuming, of course, that one adopts the posture requisite for telescopic viewing.

Indeed, what Gadamer dubs *philosophical hermeneutics* – the science of interpreting texts named after the Greek messenger God *Hermes* – ostensibly shows that knowledge is inconceivable apart from adopting some perspective, horizon of understanding, or interpretative standpoint. Gadamer and Habermas insist that experience is necessarily filtered through a familiar way of understanding things. We already have at our disposal a way of organizing experience – be it a conceptual grid, language, or way of seeing – that determines whether (for instance) the T-shaped patch of color in my field of vision will be seen by me as a plane, bird, angel of God, kite, or mysterious flying letter. This applies as well to scientific knowledge. Without the theoretical, methodological, and technological presuppositions that first generate the questions guiding research, objective reality would never reveal any of its truths. For what are such truths but responses elicited from a range (or *horizon*) of possibilities? And what is this latter horizon but a field of significant events originally opened up – framed as meaningful in this way rather than that – by prior methods and technologies of inquiry, that is to say, by prior questions?

The world reveals a sense to us only in response to our questions, so that our knowledge of it consists of specific answers to specific questions we have tacitly or expressly posed in our encounters with it. Once we concede that these questions, in turn, are reciprocally provoked by questions emanating from the world (including our very being-within-it, which is itself experienced as something indelibly personal, social, cultural, and concretely present), then the truth of philosophical hermeneutics seems scarcely unavoidable. But, as we have seen, conceding this truth – that all knowledge is interpretation – seems to generate more problems than it solves. In particular, it seems to have the paradoxical effect of reducing objective knowledge to subjective interpretation. If interpretation is inescapably biased by aspects of the interpreter's being that are inherently personal and historical, then how can it not be subjective? And if it is subjective, how can it not contradict the guiding presupposition underlying the most rigorous disciplines of scientific knowledge, namely, that objectivity in knowledge can only be had by methodically bracketing out the personal and historically contingent *prejudices* that limit and distort our understanding? If objective truth is what we're aiming for, should we not rather try to limit, if not eliminate, interpretation?

As we shall see, Gadamer and Habermas respond differently to these problems. While both insist upon the presupposition-laden nature of knowledge-as-interpretation, they do not agree in their assessments of the value of scientific method in checking distorting prejudices. Although neither denies the appropriateness of using scientific method in checking the interpretative license of the natural scientist, they disagree sharply about the appropriateness of doing so in the case of the social scientist.

In Gadamer's opinion, the use of "objectifying" method in natural science is justified because the dominant question orienting experimental knowledge revolves around how to generate abstract uniform laws for predicting and controlling causal processes that can be tested in standardized, controlled environments. However, in the human sciences of law, cultural anthropology and what we in English-speaking countries call the humanities (i.e., the disciplines of literature, art, history, theology, and philosophy) the use of such a method interferes with the achievement of objective understanding and truth. Practitioners of these disciplines are expressly involved in the interpretation of texts whose meaning must be extracted explicitly in the form of answers to prior questions. These questions – which have the status of unclarified, taken-for-granted prejudgments – must be allowed to engage the text freely in a kind of dialogue without being methodically suspended, or bracketed out, as distorting prejudices.

Gadamer repeats this argument against using objectifying methods in his discussion of social science. Knowledge of society must be mediated by a prior understanding of social groups, which necessarily involves communicating with specific social agents in the manner of question-answer dialogue. Dialogue, in turn, entails a commitment to two principles: a principle of reciprocity, which requires treating one's interlocutor with equal respect, and a related principle of charity, which requires regarding one's interlocutor as reasonable, or as communicating claims that merit a presumption of coherence and truth. The combined effect of these principles is to adopt a somewhat reverential – and in Habermas's opinion, uncritical – attitude toward the social agents whose behavior one is trying to understand. What if these agents are not behaving reasonably? What if their professed claims do not cohere with their actions? What if the normative conventions in terms of which they understand what is right and wrong, good and bad, are themselves incoherent or irrational?

In Habermas's opinion, social conventions sometimes lead people to misunder-stand themselves and act in ways contrary to the way they would if they could gain clearer insight into their needs and the deeper (but hidden) effects of coercive social conditioning that shapes them. This is because social convention, language, and vir-tually all the symbolic media that delimit possibilities for understanding self and world are themselves conditioned by economic and political domination. This bias is largely overlooked because the distorting effects of domination are never manifested in the symbolic media they affect. In order to show how such convention underwrites a false (or *ideological*) understanding of social reality that prevents persons from acting with full consciousness and freedom, it would seem that one would have to adopt a different – non-dialogical and non-reverential – attitude toward them. Accordingly, Habermas urges the social scientist to adopt a suspicious attitude with respect to con-vention, which in turn requires regarding her fellow citizens as partly deluded. In short, the social scientist must shed the role of sympathetic participant in favor of being critic and therapist.

Social behavior thus presents itself as an incoherent text in thrall to hidden, pathological compulsions that must be objectively observed and causally explained. Interpretation here follows the methodological canon exemplified by psychoanalysis, which, in bracketing the superficial, conventional self-understanding of agents, traces the real meaning and motives of their behavior back to repressed memories of earlier traumas. Interpreted against the background of law-like stages of human moral evo-lution (analogous in some ways to the stages of psychosexual development elabo-rated by Freud), the traumatic suppression of basic needs for freedom and fulfillment, which is in conformity with the alienated and exploitative labor demanded by capitalism, appears as a contradiction: freedom and individuality – the twin moral pillars on which capitalism is premised – disappear under capitalism's own insistence on compulsive adherence to mechanical routine and sadomasochistic deference to authority.

Predictably, Gadamer questioned Habermas's recommendation to extend the general insight of philosophical hermeneutics in the direction of psychoanalytic *depth-interpretation*. In his opinion, such interpretation relies on objectifying explanatory methods and developmental laws that are themselves taken for granted. In placing herself outside a relationship of mutual dialogue with the social agent, the psycho-analytic sociologist has placed herself outside of any relationship of real knowing in which her own methodological and theoretical presuppositions might be critically questioned. She has also adopted a morally questionable attitude with respect to that agent: the superior stance of the enlightened, would-be social engineer, who proposes to alter his consciousness and behavior by radically undermining the wisdom and authority of those traditional conventions upon which he rightly (and unavoidably) relies.

The questions raised by the debate between Gadamer and Habermas thus strike at the very heart of what it means to be a free and enlightened person. Is socialization into convention and tradition something that makes freedom and enlightenment possible, or is it a kind of "brainwashing" that "programs" persons to think and behave in ways that, unbeknownst to them, advance the interests of the powerful? Can we ever transcend the boundaries of thought and volition imposed upon us by our language and culture and gain direct, transparent insight, based upon reasons that can be made self-evident to each of us, independently of having to rely upon the authority of tradition and convention? Or is it impossible to be this rational and free – and perhaps even irrational to try to become so? If, in the final analysis, we must take some conventions for granted – in effect, accepting them as authoritative for reasoning – does doing so necessarily obstruct our ability to act with freedom and insight?

In the remainder of this essay, I will attempt to clarify these questions by examining the hermeneutical philosophies of Gadamer and Habermas in greater detail. However, before concluding this introduction, I would like to suggest that the debate between these philosophers be interpreted as a conflict between two strands of German philosophy, one devoted to the Enlightenment's faith in critical reason in furthering progress and liberation, the other devoted to the Counter-Enlightenment's faith in tradition and authority in furthering cultural preservation and social belonging.

Biographical Background to the Gadamer/Habermas Debate

Gadamer began his advanced studies at Marburg in 1919, where at the age of 22 he completed his first dissertation on Plato under Paul Natorp. His training in classical philology would later inform his conservative belief in the timeless truth and authority of the classical tradition. His exposure (under the tutelage of Nicolai Hartmann) to phenomenology – the philosophical approach pioneered by Edmund Husserl – was also formative for him, in that it demonstrated the sense in which all objects of consciousness are "intended" or interpreted as meaningful by consciousness. However, it was only after Martin Heidegger arrived in Marburg in 1923 that Gadamer, who assisted Heidegger and completed his second dissertation on Plato under him, discovered the ideas that would later inspire his own philosophical hermeneutics. According to Heidegger, human existence (Dasein) is defined by a questioning concern for its own being and the being of the world. The being of the world is defined in terms of the freely chosen projects of people, but these projects, in turn, are chosen from a pre-given repertory of possibilities that have been handed down in tradition. Indeed, Heidegger darkly suggests that one belongs, or is fate-fully delivered over, to a "destiny" rooted in the life and language of one's "people" – a notion that dangerously converged with the Fascist nationalism promoted by the Nazi Party to which he himself later belonged.

Although Gadamer himself was never an active member of the Nazi Party, he was, like most German academics during the first half of the twentieth century, politically reactionary – so much so that he even belonged to the *Nationalsozialistischer Lehrerbund* (The National Socialist Syndicate of Teachers and Professors) that actively supported Hitler on a number of issues. Seen from the perspective of his youthful anti-modernism, which was nowhere better exemplified than in his defense of the kind of elitist, anti-liberal, and anti-democratic state extolled by Plato in his *Repub-lic* (the topic of Gadamer's second dissertation), Gadamer's later justification of tra-ditional authority and prejudice against the Enlightenment's defense of a universal, reason-based morality seemed to resonate all too closely with the reactionary politi-cal views of his former mentor.

By contrast, Habermas's entire career can be understood as a vindication of a universal, reason-based morality against the ethnocentric (indeed racist) tradition-fetishism of Fascism. In a review published in 1953, Habermas criticized Heidegger's explicit attempt to link his philosophy to National Socialism. This repudiation of Heidegger's thought was followed by Habermas's decision to study with Theodor Adorno, who, along with Max Horkheimer and Herbert Marcuse, was one of the leading members of the Frankfurt Institute of Social Research. The Institute's seminal writings on fascism, authoritarianism, and anti-Semitism exerted a profound influ-ence on Habermas. Since its founding in 1923, the Institute had been a notorious bastion of Marxist social theory. By the 1930s, it had enlisted Freudian psychoanalysis in its critique of such hallowed bastions of traditional authority as the patriarchal family. Although the Institute later muted its critique of tradition in light of what it perceived to be the uncritical tendencies inherent in Enlightenment rationalism, it never abandoned its faith in the emancipatory power of critical reason. If anything, Habermas's faith in critical reason surpassed that of his predecessors, who seemed increasingly enamored with the redemptive and reconciliatory yearnings implicit in religion and art. Just as important, while Adorno and Horkheimer tried to steer the Institute away from politics during the turbulent 1960s (no doubt remembering the lessons of the 1930s), Habermas sought to politicize it, and to that end actively sup-ported students demanding democratic participation in university governance.

In Gadamer and Habermas we thus find exemplified two different views of knowl-edge, the one locating truth in the timeless authority of tradition, the other locating it in the highly politicized arena of democratic politics. Despite this contrast in styles, it would be stretching things considerably to suggest that Habermas finds nothing of universal permanence and nothing of value in tradition. Likewise, it would be highly misleading to portray Gadamer as an uncritical defender of hierarchy and the status quo. In fact, both philosophers ended up repudiating – implicitly if not explic-itly – much of their earlier social and political thinking (ever true to his rationalist bent, Habermas today identifies himself as a liberal social democrat rather than a fire-brand Marxist revolutionary, while Gadamer, by elevating openness and dialogue as first principles of understanding, has made clear his support of liberal democracy).

Hence what makes their debate so interesting is that each can affirm most (if not quite all) of what the other has to say. Nevertheless, what separates them is significant and, as I have just suggested, deeply rooted in their distinctive philosophical and ideological backgrounds.

Now that I have situated Gadamer and Habermas with respect to their respective intellectual milieus, let me return once again to the issue at hand, which concerns their vastly different takes on the interpretative nature of our knowledge. The first order of business is to understand how one might defend the view that knowing what is objectively true depends upon a process of interpretation that is itself guided by presuppositions. This position finds its most classical formulation in Gadamer's *magnum opus, Truth and Method* (1960).

Gadamer

Gadamer's defense of the necessary connection between truth and interpretation consists of two arguments. The first argument purports to show that any attempt to achieve truth by methodically suspending or putting out of play the knower's interpretative framework (i.e., her personal and cultural presuppositions) is both counterproductive – leading to both dogmatism and skepticism – and impossible. The second argument shows that allowing the knower's interpretative presuppositions free play need not bias or distort our understanding, and that the position advanced by philosophical hermeneutics still permits a meaningful distinction between true and false understanding.

Gadamer's first argument refutes the assumption that the meaning of a text, utterance, or other human event is identical to the intentions of its author. The assumption seems plausible for the following reason. In cases in which the author and the interpreter share the same cultural background, understanding the author's intentions on the basis of what he or she has said (or done) is usually straightforward, and no special act of interpretation is required. However, in cases in which the author and interpreter share very different backgrounds, a special act of interpretation is required. Because the author's intentional state of mind is presumed to be so different from that of the interpreter, it seems the interpreter cannot rely on her own familiar way of understanding things. Indeed, relying on her own, familiar way of understanding things would necessarily involve misunderstanding the author. Think, for example, of the Spanish missionaries who first encountered Incan, Mayan, and Aztec civilizations; they failed to understand the inhabitants of these civilizations on their own terms – as practitioners of cultural systems that were every bit as complex and advanced as the ones they were familiar with. By uncritically projecting their own cultural expectations onto them, these explorers could understand them only as stupid Europeans who had somehow fallen prey to witchcraft and Satan worship.

Someone who understood the problem of cross-cultural interpretation this way, as a problem of mistakenly projecting one's cultural biases onto others who share very different biases, might well endorse the methodical practice of bracketing one's biases – the practice famously endorsed by Edmund Husserl and Wilhelm Dilthey, the founders, respectively, of modern phenomenology and hermeneutical philosophy. For only by bracketing one's familiar understandings would one be able to correctly *identify* with the other's state of mind. Here the problem of objective knowing is framed in a manner that has much in common with the problem of knowing in the hard sciences: the only way to ensure that one's understanding truthfully *corresponds* with the object of one's understanding (in this case, the intentional state of the other) is to *methodically* bracket out all the distorting biases that emanate from one's parochial culture and personal standpoint. Once one has cleared one's head of every cultural bias, one can then transport oneself into the cultural horizon that informs one's object of study. To take our earlier example, our Spanish missionary would have gained a clearer understanding of the New World inhabitants had he left behind his Spanish identity (language, customs, etc.) entirely and immersed himself totally in their culture, assuming their identity, as it were.

The assumptions underlying the aforementioned methodological theory of interpretation can thus be summarized as follows. First, it is assumed that knowing something involves empathetically identifying with it (true knowledge = correspondence with the object known) (*TM*, pp. 220, 250).[1] Second, it is assumed that the knower (the subject of knowledge) and the known (the object of knowledge) are radically distinct from one another (*TM*, p. 220). Third, it follows from these two assumptions that knowing something (identifying with it) requires methodically clearing away all of one's biases or presuppositions, so that the object of one's knowledge can be received into one's understanding without distorting it (*TM*, p. 237).

Now, according to Gadamer, the theory of knowledge that corresponds to this model of interpretation has a decidedly unfortunate consequence: skepticism, or the view that there is no objective truth and no knowledge that can be shared across historically and geographically disparate cultures. In particular, it is the second assumption cited above that implies skepticism (*TM*, p. 237). For if it is true that the knower and known are radically distinct from one another – so that, for instance, the knower only directly perceives or experiences her own perceptions and experiences of the object, and never the object itself – then we can never know whether our "subjective" experiences and perceptions truly mirror or correspond to the object. For in order to know this, we would have to somehow get outside our experience altogether, which of course is impossible.

This line of thinking suggests that the method for achieving true correspondence with the object – clearing away one's biases or, if you will, one's horizon of experience – is doomed to failure. However, it is important to note that, even if (as an interpreter of a text from an alien culture) one could manage to shed one's cultural and personal identity and assume the identity of the author, one's knowledge would be limited to reproducing the mental states of the author. Total immersion in (identification with) the mental states of the author, however, would preclude any communication between these states and the corresponding states of the interpreter, since the interpreter would have had to efface or suspend her own mental states in assuming the identity of the other. In other words, given the radical gulf separating the author's cultural biases from those of the interpreter, it would be impossible for the interpreter to critically compare her beliefs about the world with those of the author. Since they are speaking radically different languages and experiencing radically different worlds, it would be impossible for them to agree on anything. And so they could not share beliefs about the world that would count as objective knowledge (true for both of them) which might serve as a common standard of critical comparison. (Indeed, the only standard of comparison that could exist between them would be those superficial commonalities of a formal and aesthetic nature that could never provide a method for criticizing substantive truth claims – *TM*, p. 233.)

Aside from its skeptical implications, there are at least four questionable assumptions implicit in the methodological (or presuppositionless) account of interpretation. First, the very idea of presuppositionless knowing is absurd (*TM*, p. 270). We cannot step outside our horizon of experience, because experience is our *only* access to the world. Furthermore, our present experiences are always filtered through the lens of our past experiences, including experiences emanating from cultural and linguistic socialization (*TM*, p. 301). These presuppositions, or prejudgments (*Vorurteile*) as Gadamer calls them, form a necessary background (or *horizon*) against which we foreground our understanding of things. Experiencing something without a background would be as meaningless as understanding a word, such as "here" or "now," without a (con)text.

Second, although the acquisition of objective knowledge requires that we be able to distinguish our merely subjective experiences and opinions (the presuppositions that distort our understanding of things) from experiences and opinions that are objectively valid, we cannot often do this on our own. In many instances, our distorting biases seem objectively valid to us. So in order for us to question their validity, we need to be exposed to different (or contrary) experiences and beliefs. Stated differently, our capacity to critically bracket our subjective prejudices cannot be methodically exercised on our own, prior to meaningful communication with others. To think otherwise would be tantamount to dogmatism: the assumption that one's own power of reasoning, unchecked by any external source, is invincible. But if critical reflection upon prejudices necessarily occurs within the dialogical context of mutual questioning, then it cannot be methodically exercised or even consciously controlled (*TM*, p. 299). Conversations are two-way streets: the "game" (or "play") of questions and answers has an unpredictable life of its own, independent of the conscious decisions of the "players"; the questions initiated by one participant are in some sense answers that have already been provoked by the questions of the other.

Third, the fact that communication with others is central to achieving critical insight into one's biases casts doubt upon two other assumptions implicit in the model of presuppositionless interpretation. That model assumes that the knower and the known are separated by such a radical gulf that no communication between them is possible. The interpreter of a text from an alien culture cannot really understand the text as conveying a meaningful, potentially true message to her. All that she could do (assuming it were possible) would be to divine the hidden, mysterious psychology of the author. In other words, she could at best approach the meaningless text-object as some kind of evidence for inferring something about the subjective mental state of the author. However, this fourth assumption – that texts (or text-analogues, such as behaviors) designate "symptoms" on the basis of which we infer another person's psychological states – is incoherent. Unless the text (behavior) itself directly conveyed (or communicated) the psychological intentions of the author (actor), no such inference would be possible. So understanding the intentions of an author or agent cannot mean inferring them from some utterly meaningless evidence; even less can it mean divining them by somehow transposing oneself into the author/agent's hidden thoughts (*TM*, pp. 187–91).

It might seem that equating true understanding with understanding the intentions of the author/agent, directly expressed in his or her productions (texts and actions), might suffice for explaining the kind of communication that transpires between the interpreter and the interpreted. After all, we are no longer talking about mysteriously entering the private mind of someone else, but about understanding that person's intentions as directly revealed in his public presentations. For instance, we do not infer that someone is experiencing angry feelings on the basis of his throwing a chair; rather, throwing a chair is itself anger (*TM*, p. 225).

However obvious this may be, it does not, according to Gadamer, suffice to account for the kind of communication that transpires between interpreter and inter-preted. For one thing, the meaning of an action or text is not necessarily identical to the agent/author's intentions. To take the above example, suppose a person who throws a chair after hearing some terrible news sincerely states that he did so in order to release energy and not to vent distress. To onlookers, throwing a chair under these circumstances means "I am in distress!" no less than if the chair-thrower had expressly said so out loud. Despite protestations to the contrary by the chair-thrower, it is social convention, not personal intention, that determines meaning, and that goes for behavior as well as for speech (*TM*, p. 246ff.).

It is easy to extrapolate other examples from this case that demonstrate the non-intentional nature of textual meaning. For example, authors of texts sometimes delib-erately conceal from the reader what they really want, expect, or hope the reader will understand or believe (*TM*, p. 193). Under pressure of censorship, authors some-times say what they don't believe, or say what they believe in an indirect or hidden manner that is belied by their overt language. Not only do authors sometimes have many conflicting intentions in saying what they do, but conflicting intentions are multiplied when several persons coauthor a text. There are many signatories to the American Declaration of Independence. Whose intentions are we to take as defini-tive of the Declaration's meaning? What if some of these intentions included the intention that future generations of jurists interpret the Declaration in light of their *own* evolving standards of science and morality? Judges today interpret the Declara-tion as condemning slavery; maybe that coincides with the intentions of Thomas Jefferson, the author of the document. But contrary to what we and Jefferson might have wanted the Declaration to mean, it was interpreted by Justice Roger Taney (author of the infamous ruling in the Dred Scott decision of 1857) and other *antebellum* judges to mean what most of the other signatories intended.

Only after we "depsychologize" meaning, by viewing it as a public event that conveys a message about how things are in the world, are we in a position to under-stand how interpretation must be conceived as a dialogue that can facilitate the critical exposure of subjective biases. Simply put, in order to gain true understand-ing of a text (or text analogue, such as an action or work of art), the interpreter must understand it as conveying a message about the world that implicitly questions the interpreter's prejudgments about the same. For Gadamer (somewhat ironically) the questioning of the interpreter by the text is possible only if the interpreter simultaneously questions the text, and that requires allowing her prejudgments free play in formulating questions (*TM*, pp. 269–77).

In order to see why, recall that textual interpretation is unavoidably circular: the meaning of the whole is only revealed through its parts and vice versa (i.e., the parts reveal their full significance and coherence only after the text in its entirety has been read) (*TM*, pp. 190–2). Most importantly, even before the entire text has been read the reader understands the parts she has read in terms of what she anticipates she is going to read. The *projection* of a completed and fully coherent understanding of the text, which guides her reading along the way, represents anticipated answers to questions that she poses to the text, questions that, in turn, emanate from her own familiar cultural background (or hermeneutical situation) (*TM*, p. 265ff.).

For Gadamer, the curious thing about the hermeneutical circle – reading the parts in terms of a projected whole and vice versa – is that it presupposes a prior circle (what he calls an *ontological* circle) linking interpreter and text. On one hand, the interpreter's projection of completed textual meaning constitutes the meaningful being of the text. For there is no access to the text's meaning apart from the interpreter's anticipatory projection of meaningfulness, and no access to possible answers apart from prior questioning. On the other hand, the kinds of questions posed by the interpreter, which emanate from her 'being,' or existential, cultural, and historical identity, do not simply drop out of the sky. Rather, they are questions that are provoked and suggested by the text. In other words, the text that the interpreter now reads is part of an ongoing process of education, and another addition to a cumulative inventory of cultural knowledge, that has shaped her self-understanding as well as her understanding of the world (*TM*, p. 265ff.).

At first glance, this ontological conception of understanding seems counterintuitive as a model of knowledge. Gadamer's tendency (following his mentor Martin Heidegger) to talk about understanding as a kind of projection of presuppositions (or, in Gadamer's words, as an *application* of the text's meaningfulness to concerns emanating from the interpreter's own historical situation) invites the mistaken impression that understanding is just an arbitrary imposition of subjective biases (*TM*, pp. 311ff., 329ff.). For Gadamer, nothing could be further from the truth. To begin with, the text is approached as if it were an interlocutor who had something true to say about the world that the interpreter might learn from. Hence it provides a kind of external resistance to our subjective biases. Of course, such an attitude of respect may seem alien to our rationalist assumption, inherited from the Enlightenment, that true knowledge must rest on foundations that each individual, exercising her own reason alone, can make evident to herself, apart from any outside authority (*TM*, p. 271ff.). In fact, this prejudice against authority overlooks the fact that all of our reasoning occurs against the backdrop of cultural assumptions (embedded in the texts we have read) that have withstood the test of time and for that reason alone are accepted by us as "authoritative" (*TM*, p. 277ff.).

This last point about the objective resistance of the text as a partner in dialogue indicates two other ways in which projective understanding can aspire to objectivity

(*TM*, p. 367ff.). First, our interpreter must also check her understanding against other interpretations of the text. The history of past interpretations can be conceived as a continuous dialogue in which past interpreters have checked their interpretations against one another. In other words, the weight (authority) of a tradition of interpretation must already be effective in the understanding of the interpreter who seeks to truly understand (*TM*, p. 300ff.). She may well discover meaning in the text never before revealed by her predecessors – indeed, this is scarcely unavoidable given the uniqueness of her hermeneutical situation – but whatever meaning she does discover will have to respond to (and in some sense fit with) that tradition. Of course, reliance upon traditional precedent need not preclude revolutionary insight; but even revolutionaries see themselves as providing new answers to old as well as new questions. Thus, eighteenth-century revolutionaries in America and France who took themselves to be overthrowing the divine right of kings in favor of the right of citizen self-governance still appealed to God in justifying this new right. Despite their rationalist rejection of the old regime and its appeal to religious tradition, they also had to appeal to that same authority in justifying their revolution to the masses, most of whom, after all, were religious.

Second, the achievement of objective understanding is never final. Objectivity grows with experience; it is by expanding our horizon of understanding in dialogue with the tradition (and perhaps with many traditions) that we learn to sort out productive, meaning-revealing presuppositions from unproductive, meaning distorting (-concealing) presuppositions. Indeed, the greater the temporal and geographic distance separating interpreter and text, the greater the potential for critical dialogue. Unfamiliar (ancient or foreign) texts check the interpreter's natural inclination to project prejudgments uncritically, thereby enabling the extraction of timeless and universal meaning from otherwise parochial contents (*TM*, p. 297ff.).

Stated somewhat paradoxically, what Gadamer calls "consciousness of effective history" (*Wirkungsgeschichtliches Bewusstsein*), or the critical awareness of bias in one's understanding, is only increased by acquiring more experience, growing into more traditions, and enriching one's stock of presuppositions (*TM*, p. 351ff.). Objectivity, or openness to new meaning, is thus the reverse side of entrenching oneself more deeply into tradition and culture, and entrenching the presuppositions of tradition more deeply into our canon of authoritative truth. For every successful interpretation of a text succeeds in *fusing* the text's understanding of the way the world is with the interpreter's own (*TM*, pp. 306–374). She demonstrates its continuing truth by applying it to her own situation; in effect, she understands the text's meaning only by showing that it can be understood as reasonable and true by her own (and her contemporaries') lights, even and especially if it expands her (and their) understanding of what is reasonable and true.

The astute reader will note that the theory of truth I have just propounded has nothing in the slightest to do with adequately representing, or correctly corresponding to, an objective reality existing independently of understanding. This impression is further reinforced when we catalog the myriad ways in which Gadamer characterizes truth. Sometimes, Gadamer seems to equate "truth" with having any meaningful experience whatsoever. This usage of "truth" is taken from Martin Heidegger, who in turn equates the notion with an ancient Greek concept of understanding that supposedly designates a primordial disclosure of meaningful being as such (*aletheia*) (*TM*, p. 457).

Disclosure of meaningful being is no doubt a necessary precondition for truth. But "truth" understood in this way bears no resemblance to our ordinary understanding of "truth," conceived as an attribute that we ascribe to only the most correct or genuine beliefs and experiences. Drug-induced experiences are no doubt meaningful, but they are not necessarily true in conveying a correct or insightful knowledge of things.

Because Gadamer wants to assert that understanding provides access to experiences of truth that are not only meaningful but insightful, he cannot be understood as equating understanding with mere disclosure in the Heideggerian sense. Indeed, he elsewhere equates understanding with a special type of experience that is coherent in its meaningfulness. Now, many philosophers have sought to define true beliefs and experiences in terms of coherence. Thus, the truth of a belief or experience on this account would just mean its coherence with other beliefs and experiences and, most importantly, its coherence with just those beliefs and experiences around which most people cohere (or upon which they agree) (*TM*, p. 291).

Coherence accounts of truth doubtless apply to some beliefs and experiences (most notably those in mathematics). But, as accounts of textual meaning, they fail to satisfy on two accounts. First, understanding the coherence and reasonableness of something need not incline one to accept its truth. To return to an earlier example, I appreciate the internal coherence of my brother's interpretation of the Gospels, and I even appreciate the reasonableness of that interpretation, given his undaunting need for transcendent meaning and purpose. But I am not thereby persuaded of its truth.

A second difficulty that attends equating coherence and reasonableness with truth is that, on this account, I would never be able to confirm that something was indeed false. My failure to understand the coherence and reasonableness of something could just as well be caused by some blindness on my part, so failure to understand would never confirm the falsehood of the object of understanding. In other words, on this account we could have meaningful (i.e., coherent) experiences of truth, but no meaningful experiences of falsehood.

We are left with two alternative notions of truth in Gadamer's text: the deepening of one's understanding – as when we say that one has reached the truth of the matter, or achieved true insight – and the elimination of error, or correspondence with the way things are. These notions of truth are distinct: an interpretation can be correct (not erroneous) and still be superficial and partial; and it can be incorrect – involve a misreading that does violence to the expressly written word of the text – and yet be highly insightful and penetrating, and in that sense closer to the spirit of the text than any literally correct interpretation.

A close reading of Gadamer in fact shows that he uses "truth" to refer to both correctness and insightfulness. Although all disclosure of meaningful being is partial and selective (i.e., there is no way of highlighting something without also concealing something), Gadamer and Heidegger seem to believe that certain ways of *artistically* disclosing worldly phenomena can be truer (more insightful and revealing) than more mundane, superficially correct ways, such as mere factual description or pictorial representation. Non-representational art, poetry, and certain forms of symbolic sculpture and architecture often disclose our world in ways that are more original, more authentic, more illuminating, or just plain deeper, than our scientific understanding of the same, which might well be unsurpassed in its correctness. (Then again, as we shall see below, science too is notorious for inventing fruitful and productive hypotheses that often turn out to be factually false.)

For Gadamer, good (truer) interpretations are likewise more insightful and productive than bad ones. But Gadamer also thinks that good interpretations are true in the mundane sense of being more correct and accurate. This is most apparent when he talks about how the text contradicts the merely subjective, "unproductive" prejudices of the interpreter. Here he seems to have in mind "truth" understood as "correctness"; for he argues that methodical interpretations are not only superficial – neglecting as they do the explicit message of the text – but also dogmatic and uncritical, and thus likely to lead to error. As he emphatically reminds us, "working out appropriate projections, anticipatory in nature, to be confirmed 'by the things themselves,' is the constant task of understanding" (*TM*, p. 267).

What are we to conclude from this admittedly complicated account of truth? First, regardless of which sense of truth we have in mind, gaining true understanding is not a once-and-for-all "getting it right." Because of the circular nature of interpretation, there is no end to our sifting out erroneous and unproductive presuppositions. Achieving correct and insightful understanding is, as Hegel taught, an ongoing process. Second, because of the ontological circle in which events of interpretation are inextricably embedded, there is no single true interpretation that completely and finally captures the meaning of anything (*TM*, p. 298). My interpretation of the Bible is not less accurate and less insightful than my brother's. It is just different. The same applies to our understanding of things and events. Our lived experience of nature may contradict scientific learning – as when I experience the sun rising and setting or the impenetrable solidity of material objects. But that in no way falsifies my experience, whose guiding points of reference are very different from theoretical science. And if the many true interpretations of texts and natural events are partially relative to the distinct historical and existential horizons of the interpreters who proffer them, they are not, for all that, true relative to just any subjective reference point that might be adopted. For "true" means less biased and less incomplete relative to superficial and narrow interpretations of the same kind that lack the critical depth of effective historical consciousness.

Habermas

Despite their radically different philosophical orientations, Habermas has repeatedly acknowledged his indebtedness to Gadamer, both as a friend who helped him acquire his first major academic appointment and as a mentor, whose philosophical hermeneutics opened him up to a new way of rethinking the critical theory tradition of Frankfurt School social philosophy. However, in his first major work, *Knowledge and Human Interests* (1968), Habermas argued against one of the central ideas underlying Gadamer's philosophical hermeneutics. In particular, he argued that some hermeneutical presuppositions – specifically, those guiding inquiry in the natural, human, and social sciences – could be known to be self-evidently true (necessary and universal) by reason alone, unaided by conventional wisdom.

More importantly, Habermas argued that all knowledge either directly or indirectly presupposed the achievement of *undistorted* understanding and communication. By this expression he meant *rational* understanding and communication, free from the unconscious authority of tradition. This view contradicts the thesis of philosophical hermeneutics. For if Gadamer is right that all understanding relies on such authority (in the form of a linguistic–cultural background or horizon), how is understanding based on rational self-evidence possible?

In order to answer this question, let us turn to *Knowledge and Human Interests*. The aim of this work is to show that:

(a)   all knowledge is guided by presuppositions that take the form of interests;
(b)   different types of knowledge are guided by different interests that imply different standards and methods for attaining objective truth;
(c)   moral knowledge – about right and wrong, good and bad – is guided by a practical interest in achieving mutual understanding and communication that is radically distinct from the technical interest in achieving control that guides scientific knowledge; and
(d)   all knowledge directly or indirectly presupposes (implies an interest in) the achievement of a community of equals based solely on rational consent, free from the distorting effects of external or internal (psychological) domination.

The first aim, which allies Habermas's project closely with Gadamer's philosophical hermeneutics, is directed against what Habermas regards as a false view of scientific knowledge: positivism. According to Habermas, positivism commits two errors: it wrongly identifies knowledge as such with the kind of knowledge achieved by the natural sciences, and it wrongly identifies this kind of knowledge with a correspondence of knower and known that comes about independently of any presuppositions (*KHI*, pp. 80–1). So understood, positivism holds that true beliefs must be derived from a combination of self-evident reasons (such as mathematical axioms like the law of non-contradiction) and self-evident sensory stimuli (such as sounds, sights, smells, etc.). This view, in turn, implies that moral judgments about right and wrong, good and bad, can be neither true nor false; for moral judgments about what *ought* to be desired, commanded, or forbidden do not purport to correspond with logical truths or the way the world actually *is*.

Citing the pioneering work of Thomas Kuhn and others (*KHI*, p. 336), Habermas argues that the second error committed by positivism of equating knowledge with presuppositionless knowing runs contrary to our real experience of the world. Our direct experience with the world does not consist of having meaningless sensory impressions but consists in directly perceiving entities that have already been pre-interpreted in some meaningful way (e.g., telescopes as distinct from tree-like sticks). Not only are the things we directly perceive identified in terms of the concepts of our spoken language, but the inventory of our scientific knowledge consists of the linguistic entities of factual propositions and assertions.

In the natural sciences, facts undergo at least three types of interpretation. Not only are they framed in terms of our natural object-language, but they are framed in terms of higher-order meta- and theoretical languages (e.g., what some eighteenth-century "electricians" perceived to be a fluid that flowed through conductive media and could be stored in Leyden jars was later perceived, thanks to Benjamin Franklin, as magnetic repulsion involving positive and negative charges). Finally, and most importantly, facts in natural science are framed in terms of standard, quantifiable measurements and mathematical equations. This is because the experimental method deployed in natural science requires that the same results be duplicated over and over again by different researchers working in different contexts (*KHI*, pp. 126–9).

The method of measurement and standardized testing assures this possibility by imposing experimental controls on observation that require researchers to bracket differences stemming from their particular (personal, cultural, and contextual) limitations. Unlike in the humanities, the methodical bracketing of personal and cultural biases here opens up the possibility of revealing nature in a certain way, namely, as a nexus of invariant, universal causal regularities. And *this* way of interpreting nature follows from our interest in gaining technical control over it. Only if we conceive nature as causally ordered does it make sense to predict and thereby control the effects of our interventions in it (*KHI*, pp. 175–6).

There are thus many ways to interpret nature. Prior to Galileo, it was still customary to view nature as an expression of divine purposes seeking to realize their inherent natures. Those writing in the Age of Faith still interpreted the falling of a stone the same way Aristotle did almost a thousand years earlier – as the stone's desire to realize its natural state of rest rather than as a product of impersonal causal forces. However, once the need to survive compelled people to want to predict and control nature, it became necessary to interpret it as if it were a spiritless mechanism operating under predictable causal laws. However, seen from another perspective, the human species (in contrast with most animal species) has always distinguished itself by procuring its survival through thoughtful intervention in nature. In Habermas's terms, the interest in gaining technical control over nature was there from the beginning, implicit in the simplest trial-and-error learning. Hence, this interest did not arise with Galilean science, but was universally present in the human species in an anthropologically deep-seated sense. More precisely, such an interest is rationally demonstrable as a necessary adaptive drive that arose through natural selection as compensation for our physiological and instinctual deficits.

Just as the "objectifying" methods of natural scientific knowledge can be traced back to a necessary "knowledge-constituting" interest, so the same can be said for the non-objectifying methods of knowing deployed in the humanities. Positivism's insistence that all knowledge imitate the methods of knowing favored in the natural sciences ignores the fact that knowledge in the humanities is guided by a fundamentally different interest: a practical interest in reaching mutual understanding. At some point in the evolution of the human species, the biological survival of the individual could only be reliably secured within extended families and communities. The community, in turn, could only be maintained on the basis of (a) mutually agreed upon rules for speaking and behaving and (b) an enduring locus of shared identity, consisting of shared stories about the group's relationship to the gods and its own past (*KHI*, p. 176ff.).

Now, both (a) and (b) involve mutual understanding that essentially arises in the course of communication, whether it be handing down stories or reaching agreement on common aims and regulations. As we have seen, literature, philosophy, history, and the humanities fulfill this same aim of reaching mutual understanding through somewhat more sophisticated means. The historical interpretation of texts possessing traditional canonical authority (such as the Bible or the Declaration of Independence) bridges the gap between past and present that must not be allowed to grow too much if present generations are to identify with past generations. Were it not for this intergenerational continuity, our very identity and sense of purpose would be rootless, thus depriving society of one of its essential bonds. Likewise, the philosophical elaboration of moral ideals, such as social justice, bridges the gap between persons with conflicting aims and interests by providing commonly accepted rules for voluntary cooperation among equals. The important thing to note here, as in the case of historical interpretation, is that mutual understanding is accomplished through the free dialogical exchange of questions and answers.

Habermas concludes that the proper method for achieving moral–practical knowledge in the humanities is expressly interpretative in the circular manner described by Gadamer, and so necessarily dispenses with what scientific method can scarcely do without, namely, the controlled bracketing-off of presuppositions (*KHI*, p. 193ff.). Most importantly, because interpretative methods set in motion a critical dialogue capable of exposing unproductive, falsifying prejudices, they enable us to see how truth and objectivity can be possible, in the moral disciplines no less than in the natural sciences, *without relying upon scientific methods*. Here we see Habermas rationally demonstrating what Gadamer can only conceive as historically contingent and conventional: the essential difference in interests and methods separating natural from human science. Although Habermas renews Gadamer's defense of moral truth against the skeptical implications of positivism, he jettisons his faith in the power of dialogue to secure it. While Gadamer thinks that the dialogical "method" of understanding can be extended to social sciences – which he along with Habermas considers to be a species of moral science – Habermas thinks that it can only with qualification.

Let me explain. Habermas agrees with Gadamer that social scientists cannot identify, let alone explain, social behavior without first understanding it as inherently meaningful. I cannot identify the physical behavior of hand waving as an exemplar of a meaningful social action (of greeting as distinct from signalling, for instance) without first understanding that, in this context, such a behavior comports with norms of appropriate greeting behavior. And I cannot understand the sense of appropriateness that attaches to these greeting rituals without knowing that such rituals are taken to be good and proper ways of expressing a sense of solidarity that rightly merits recognition. Of course, none of this understanding would be possible if the social scientist could not engage her subject in open dialogue, perhaps even questioning her subject's belief that there exists a social solidarity that rightly merits recognition (*LSS*, p. 67ff.).

Despite its potential for achieving mutual critical understanding, Habermas doubts whether such a dialogically facilitated understanding suffices to comprehend fully *and* critically the deeper, hidden meaning of social behavior. An important part of the meaning of conventional behavior consists in facts about coercive socialization and systemic (or structural) social constraints that are not directly expressed in it. In other words, what's missing from our conventional understanding of right and wrong, good and bad, is the fact that this understanding itself is inculcated in us coercively through the use of sanctions and the appeal to parental and pedagogical authority, and reflects constraints imposed by economic and political structures that do not benefit all persons equally (*LSS*, p. 172ff.). For example, it is conceivable that our greeting behavior has become an automatic reflex that compels us to feel solidarity with our bosses in a way that would not merit recognition if we could gain a critical distance from our shared participation in the life of the company, for instance, by seeing the company as an unjust organization incorporating capitalist wage exploitation and class domination.

For Habermas, then, in order to understand fully conventional beliefs and behaviors, we must learn to partially bracket our everyday faith in their complete meaningfulness and truth, and instead view them as pathological effects, at once revealing and concealing, of social domination. Here, knowledge of self and society would seem to require emancipating ourselves from the effects of traditional convention rather than, as Gadamer says, entrenching ourselves more deeply in it (*LSS*, p. 168ff.). Indeed, it suggests that the interest guiding the pursuit of knowledge in critical social science is neither that of controlling natural processes, nor of conserving traditional meaning and identity, but of *emancipating* oneself from domination. For, it is with the advent of social (or class) domination that the production of tradition ceases to be the outcome of a dialogue among equals and assumes instead the form of a kind of brainwashing which aims at programming persons into accepting the false notion that the status quo benefits everyone equally.

Because social domination distorts the cultural and linguistic medium in which *all* knowledge (including natural scientific knowledge) is formulated, Habermas rather surprisingly concludes that our interest in knowledge converges with our interest in emancipation. Taken in its most radical sense, this equation suggests that full knowledge must await the revolutionary creation of a classless, democratic society composed of free and equal speakers (*KHI*, p. 314). Although a society composed of fully rational speakers would not alter the most basic and deep-seated interests guiding scientific inquiry, it would likely alter its terms and purposes, so that, for instance, "efficient production" might come to mean production aimed at satisfying basic needs for all (including aesthetic and environmental needs) instead of increasing profits for a few. To take another example, although the logic of scientific and technological knowing necessarily implies some specialization and hierarchy – for technical expertise empowers those who possess it – it might permit more democratic control and accountability in a society in which everyone shared equally in the ownership and management of society's productive assets.

Because unfreedom consists in being compelled by unquestioned presuppositions to behave in ways that are contrary to one's true interests, the interest in achieving emancipation cannot be satisfied apart from a special kind of knowledge, which

Habermas calls *reflection* (*KHI*, p. 198). Reflection, by which Habermas means achieving rationally self-evident insight into how unquestioned presuppositions distort our understanding, effectively dissolves whatever power such presuppositions have over us. Once we have freed ourselves from their power, we can begin to talk to one another rationally, with greater transparency and less distortion, about what our interests really are.

To summarize: Although Habermas agrees with Gadamer that all knowledge is guided by presuppositions, he thinks that the only legitimate presuppositions are those that can be seen to be rationally self-evident. The three knowledge-constitutive interests guiding understanding in the natural, human, and social sciences are examples of such presuppositions, for they can be shown to be necessary for explaining the legitimate (if limited) aims and methods underlying each science. Were it not for the fact that the production of tradition is distorted by domination, Habermas would also agree that the presuppositions emanating from cultural tradition are legitimate. But tradition is distorted by domination. So, while it is sometimes acceptable for lawyers, clergy, and literary scholars to approach canonical texts (or texts that are authoritative for a tradition) as expressing binding truth, it is not acceptable for social scientists to do the same with respect to social convention. Instead of engaging the conventional beliefs of social agents in dialogue, social scientists must observe them with suspicion, questioning their presumed reasonableness and authority as masks for eliciting acceptance of social domination. Thus, the proper method for critical understanding in the social sciences would appear to have more in common with psychoanalysis: the social scientist engages her subjects not as fully responsible and rational equals with whom she can have a dialogue, but as patients suffering from compulsive delusions.

As compelling as Habermas's defense of social–psychoanalytic interpretation is, it seems oddly self-defeating. How critical and emancipatory can a method of interpretation be that requires the methodical objectification of moral agents? Doesn't substituting the authority of the critical theorist for the authority of social convention merely replace the domination of tradition with the domination of technical expertise? This question, which I address below, touches on what is perhaps the most fundamental issue dividing Habermas and Gadamer: whether one must approach one's interlocutor with suspicion or trust in trying to understand the real meaning and motive of her behavior.

Conclusion

Before deciding whether a "hermeneutics of suspicion" might play a legitimate role in social science, it is imperative that we first briefly evaluate the disadvantages and advantages of the kind of universal theory of interpretation put forward by Gadamer and Habermas, as well as the advantages and disadvantages of their respective views about it.

As I see it, the advantage of a universal theory of interpretation over any theory that equates knowledge with the potential capacity to derive beliefs from presuppositionless insight is that the former seems to constitute a more adequate description about how we in fact experience our world. We experience our world as meaningful in a way that is already familiar to us. Why this should be so is not hard to fathom; before we experience any particular thing we have already foregrounded it against a background of possible significance. I could not perceive this tree-like phenomenon standing before me now to be a telescope if I had not already anticipated the possibility of encountering a world of scientific objects. Thus, all of my education into the culture of modern science prepared me to see a telescope rather than a tree; had I been born an Australian Aborigine, educated into a prescientific, animistic world, I might have recognized, instead, a totemic tree-spirit.

Not only does this example illustrate the way in which our experience is guided by presuppositions, but it shows that no experience is absolutely presuppositionless. Of course, one might show how any random presupposition can be proven rationally self-evident; but what counts as rationally self-evident will depend on other presuppositions. Indeed, given the intimate connection between reasoning, conceiving, and understanding a natural language, it is virtually impossible to imagine any absolutely presuppositionless knowing (including mathematical knowing). For the meaning of any concept or expression is embedded in expanding contexts, or circles, of linguistic meaning – literally the totality of our linguistic being, the infinite complexity of which can never be raised to transparent self-evidence.

Gadamer and Habermas rightfully appeal to the dialogical model of questions and answers to capture the way in which all experience is a kind of inquiry, or probing of expectations. However, in my opinion, they overextend the dialogical model. Both of them equate understanding with dialogical agreement. In one sense this is right. I cannot adequately understand something if it strikes me as wholly crazy, implausible, and beyond my comprehension. Yet, as I noted above, I can understand a view that I find otherwise coherent and reasonable and still disagree with it. Again, both Gadamer and Habermas have at times said or implied that reasonable agreement is equivalent to true understanding. But this is obviously false. Given the fallibility of our knowing, there is no guarantee that even a rationally achieved, unanimous agreement about the way the world is would necessarily correspond to the way things really are. Universal, rational consensus might be good enough reason (evidence) for *claiming* something was true, but it would not suffice to *prove* that it was so; even less would it suffice to definitely capture what we mean by "truth."

Let me now turn to the Gadamer/Habermas debate. There are really two points at issue here: whether one can methodically bracket one's conventional understanding in striving to achieve something like transparent, self-evident insight into the genesis and functioning of conventional presuppositions; and whether one should adopt an attitude of suspicion toward the conventional self-understanding of one's contemporaries.

Much of the debate between Habermas and Gadamer revolves around the capacity of persons to gain transparent insight into the genesis of their conventional presuppositions. At first glance, Gadamer appears to come out on top in this exchange. After all, whatever understanding we hope to gain is going to be filtered through the lens of some taken-for-granted language, with our conventional, day-to-day language functioning as the background for all our other, more artificial (technical and theoretical) meta-languages.

However, I do not read Habermas as challenging this – the definitive – thesis of philosophical hermeneutics. His point is rather different, namely, that we can gain relatively transparent insight into the deep structure of natural language and the mechanism by which that structure is generated. Habermas agrees with Gadamer that it is only by *first* participating in language as a trusting member of a speech community composed of equals that we acquire a true understanding of that language and community. Normally, we rely upon taken-for-granted social conventions in understanding and interacting with others. However, as Gadamer himself concedes, there are times when relying upon these conventions in a taken-for-granted manner is not enough. For example, when trying to learn a foreign language, one must sometimes learn basic rules of grammar. Of course, one needn't learn these rules to master one's own language; but acquiring a first language through habit and imitation is different from acquiring a second language, which is a more deliberative – and typically more rule-guided – process. A more compelling example comes from speech pathology. Persons who have sustained damage to the language centers of the brain, or who have undergone other forms of psychological or psychophysical trauma, often reacquire their ability to speak and understand only by methodically relearning language. What they formerly understood intuitively, as a matter of practical know-how, they must now understand objectively, as a matter of theory. Speech pathologists must delve even deeper into the objective structure of language and acquire a formal understanding of its innate, transformational grammar (as Noam Chomsky puts it). Ultimately, they need to acquire an objective distance with respect to an aspect of our being that is too familiar to us, too much a part of our unconscious, embodied existence, to be understood theoretically, absent some methodical reconstruction of formal rules (or laws).

As Habermas rightly notes, reconstructing the intuitive linguistic competence that unconsciously grounds our participatory involvement in a speech community explains how we come to understand our world in a meaningful way. The rules governing grammatical transformations, substitutions, and speaker–listener roles are coordinate with the ability to grasp basic categories of substance, causality, and objectivity. Consequently, brain dysfunctions and learning disorders that prevent persons from experiencing the world in a causally coherent way (or from perceiving objects as unified and temporally and spatially constant substrates of distinct and changeable properties) also manifest themselves as speech pathologies – and vice versa. The same applies in lesser degree to neurotic compulsions and schizophrenic episodes, in which the fragmenting (or confusing) of units of speech accompanies the fragmenting and confusing of units of objective and social reality.

Habermas sees no reason why the theoretical linguistics that helps explain the deep structures underlying some forms of *individual* psychopathology can't also explain the deep structures underlying some forms of *social* psychopathology. If we assume that it is pathological for citizens of modern, enlightened nations to deny their moral agency by attributing the source of right and wrong to nature, destiny, or some other objective power – witness, for example, our general abhorrence of the kind of mass conformity and deference to authority that overtook the German population during the Third Reich – then ideology is indeed a kind of social psychopathology. More precisely, ideology is a pathology that can be understood and explained with reference to a basic linguistic dysfunction. Just as the nonsense uttered by schizophrenics reflects a confusion of objective, social, and subjective categories, so the nonsense uttered by those in thrall to ideological delusion reflects something similar. As Karl Marx once observed, what is ideology but the transformation of ideas – products of subjective and social creation – into objective forces of nature that have an independent life of their own? And what is this "category mistake," this confusion of imperative act with static thing, but a convenient ruse for the powers that be? Can anything be more delusional than to justify domination by appeal to ideologies of human nature, divine predestination, transcendent morality – metaphysical "facts" that impossibly masquerade as unconditional imperatives? Can anything be more disingenuous than to equate freedom with the unimpeded permission to buy and sell?

So, to return to my original point, the real disagreement between Gadamer and Habermas is not over whether we can gain a methodical distance for theoretically articulating, causally explaining, and critically evaluating linguistic pathology; nor is it over the unavoidability of relying upon our natural language as the ultimate background for understanding our world. Rather, it is over whether it is morally appropriate to extend the psychoanalytic therapist–patient relationship to our everyday social relations.

Surely, Habermas is right to point out (following Freud himself) that our use of natural language is often shot through with little (and for the most part, innocuous) "pathological" inconsistencies, elisions, and slips. Our speech and writing is not the ideal coherent text that we, out of hermeneutical charity, might expect it to be. Furthermore, Habermas is probably right to insist that, when these inconsistencies in meaning threaten the very possibility of open dialogue, it might be appropriate for us to exit it. For example, participating in a dialogue in which you and your partner disagree about the rules governing conversational civility can be very risky. The logic teacher's legalistic insistence on impartial reason and definitional univocity might run counter to the street cleaner's free-wheeling appeal to personal anecdotes and literary imagery. Indeed, it might not have much in common with the informal way of arguing engaged in by most non-logicians. But agreement on the rules of rational conversation is hardly the only condition for civil engagement. What about agreement on the terms of discourse? If you are a Native American lawyer trying to defend your tribe's right to its sacred land, you might well feel that the way in which the law defines your "property" forecloses an effective defense. Do you continue to negotiate, or do you question the ideology of property that constrains and distorts the terms of a just settlement?

Doubtless, many good reasons can be offered for not participating in civil conversations with others, especially if they are our adversaries. But none of the countless harmless ways in which we question the motives and self-understanding of others amounts to relating to them as patients. Gadamer is right that, with very few exceptions (for instance, mass hysteria and mass delusion), the psychoanalytic model of doctor–patient dialogue cannot be extended to our everyday relations with others; for the social scientist to invoke this model in most ordinary circumstances would be the height of incredible *hubris*. Having denigrated the conventional understanding of her fellow citizens, the social scientist would have deprived herself of the only standpoint capable of critically checking her own bias.

Since their heated exchange in the late 1960s and early 1970s, Habermas seems to have moved closer to Gadamer's position. Besides acknowledging the difficulty of transferring the psychoanalytic model of interpretation to the social arena, which lacks the dynamics of transference peculiar to the therapeutic relationship (*TP*, pp. 29–31), he now has more confidence in the capacity of average persons to acquire critical insight into the ideological nature of what passes for conventional wisdom. Indeed, as Brazilian educator Paulo Freire reminds us in *Pedagogy of the Oppressed*, dialogue alone can be a powerful tool for undermining authority and domination.

Today, what draws Gadamer and Habermas ever closer is the fear that conversational understanding in all its varieties is being eclipsed by forms of experience that have more in common with scientific–technological modes of understanding. I have in mind not only the way our ability to manipulate a mouse or joystick on a computer video game has replaced our ability to talk to one another face to face, but the way in which deference to authority and top-down social engineering have taken hold of our lives.

Along with a spreading government bureaucracy, a consumer- and advertising-driven market economy has increasingly "colonized," as Habermas puts it in *The Theory of Communicative Action*, dimensions of everyday life pertaining to family, education, culture, and political association that are especially well-equipped to foster capacities and opportunities for critical dialogue. While the inner sanctum of the household as a place for reading, discussing, and quiet meditating has been violated by the rank commercialism and mindless spectacle of television, which replaces active questioning with passive viewing, the public spheres traversed by news media, political parties, and the like have become little more than vehicles for manipulation.

In *Reason in the Age of Science* (1981) and *Hermeneutics versus Science* (1988), Gadamer detects a similar malaise, observing that government and corporate agencies set the political agenda and carefully monitor what gets broadcast, thereby truncating and distorting the range of public opinion. Sound-bites and propaganda offered up by "spin doctors" replace arguments and analysis; meanwhile issues get submerged in a "cult of personalities," so that a politician's sex life becomes more important than his or her policy positions. Habermas concurs in this assessment (see *Between Facts and Norms* [1996]), ranking political apathy among the poor and uneducated as a social sickness every bit as pernicious as the cynicism of the rich and educated, who regard the most pressing issues of moral justice as mere technical matters to be scientifically decided by appointed elites trained in law, economics, and management.

To conclude, if Gadamer and Habermas have anything to teach us, it is that each and every one of us must exercise his or her right to speak and be heard. As participants in a cooperative venture of meaning-making, everyone must learn to cherish and identify with others in solidarity. At the same time, each of us must take our rightful place as equals in dialogically opening up the world to responsible reinterpretation.

Note

1 See under Selected bibliography below for the key to text citations.

Selected bibliography

Primary sources

Hans-Georg Gadamer

1976: *Philosophical Hermeneutics.* Berkeley, Calif.: University of California Press.

1981: *Reason in the Age of Science.* Cambridge, Mass.: The MIT Press.

1988: *Hermeneutics versus Science? Three German Views. Essays.* Notre Dame, Ind.: University of Notre Dame Press.

1989: *Truth and Method*, 2nd rev. edn. New York: Continuum. (References to this book are abbreviated in the text to "*TM*, p. ••.")

1999: *Hermeneutics, Religion, Ethics.* New Haven, Conn.: Yale University Press.

Jürgen Habermas

1971: *Knowledge and Human Interests.* Boston, Mass.: Beacon Press. (References to this book are abbreviated in the text to "*KHI*, p. ••.")

1973: *Theory and Practice.* Boston, Mass.: Beacon Press. (References to this book are abbreviated in the text to "*TP*, p. ••.")

1984 & 1987: *The Theory of Communicative Action*, 2 vols. Boston, Mass.: Beacon Press.

1987: *The Philosophical Discourse of Modernity. Twelve Lectures.* Cambridge, Mass.: The MIT Press.

1991: *On the Logic of the Social Sciences.* Cambridge, Mass.: The MIT Press. (References to this book are abbreviated in the text to "*LSS*, p. ••.")

1996: *Between Facts and Norms. Contributions to a Discourse Theory of Law and Democracy.* Cambridge, Mass.: The MIT Press.

Secondary sources

Bleicher, J. 1980: *Contemporary Hermeneutics: Hermeneutics as Method, Philosophy, and Critique.* London: Routledge Kegan Paul.

Hoy, D. 1976: *The Critical Circle: Literature and History in Contemporary Hermeneutics.* Berkeley, Calif.: University of California Press.

Ingram, D. 1980: Truth, method, and understanding in the human sciences. The Gadamer/Habermas controversy. Dissertation, University of California, San Diego, 1980. Reprinted by University Microfilm, 1980.

——1987: *Habermas and the Dialectic of Reason.* New Haven, Conn.: Yale University Press.

McCarthy, T. 1979: *The Critical Theory of Jürgen Habermas.* Cambridge, Mass.: The MIT
  Press.
Teigas, D. 1995: *Knowledge and Hermeneutic Understanding. A Study of the
  Habermas/Gadamer Debate.* Lewisburg, Penn.: Bucknell University Press.
Warnke, G. 1989: *The Hermeneutics of Gadamer.* Palo Alto, Calif.: Stanford University Press.
Weinsheimer, J. C. 1985: *Gadamer's Hermeneutics. A Reading of "Truth and Method."* New
  Haven, Conn.: Yale University Press.

Chapter 11

Michel Foucault

Robert Wicks

Foucault's Life

It was a fateful coincidence that Paul-Michel Foucault (1926–84) shared with Friedrich Nietzsche (1844–1900) the same date of birth – October 15 – for Foucault reincarnated many of Nietzsche's ideas in the twentieth-century French style. Although Nietzsche's modest upbringing contrasted with Foucault's privileged family circumstances, both children grew up under the matter-of-fact assumption that they would continue the family heritage: Nietzsche's father and grandfather were Lutheran ministers, and during his childhood, Nietzsche was "the little pastor"; Foucault's father and grandfather were surgeons, and Foucault was accordingly steered toward the medical profession. Both fulfilled their families' expectations in oblique ways: after some early years in the comforting bosom of Christianity, Nietzsche became a hard-line anti-Christian; after working within the context of health-related organizations as a young man, Foucault became a trenchant critic of the medical, especially psychiatric, institutions, and of rigid institutional structures in general. In their own times and in their own ways, both men transformed into intellectual rebels and revolutionaries.

At age 20, Foucault entered the École Normale Supérieure in Paris – a school that was then, and that remains, one of the most honored educational institutions in France. Such prestige carried with it a tremendous pressure to "shine" and to be "brilliant," and Foucault worked diligently within this academic environment, suffering sometimes from serious bouts of depression. There were rumors of a suicide attempt when he was 22, and these support the reflection that a driving and unsettling tension marked Foucault's personality – one that was probably complicated by his homosexuality. As a promising scholar in the late 1940s, Foucault's sexual inclinations stood in a collision path with the relatively conservative and restrictive French academic world of which he was a part, and within which he desired to excel.

Foucault joined the French Communist Party at age 24, and although this membership was short-lived, a Marxist spirit endured within Foucault's later writings: just as Karl Marx (1818–83) campaigned forcefully against institutional powers that exploited the less economically privileged population, Foucault never lost his sympathy for the disadvantaged and marginalized members of society, directing many of his books and articles to the exposure of the mechanisms responsible for social oppression. It was Foucault's destiny to become the champion of the outsider.

By the time Foucault had reached his late twenties, he had completed a course in psychopathology, had attended clinical training sessions and lectures on psychoanalytic theory, and had become part of the Philosophy faculty at the University of Lille, where he taught philosophy and psychology. Commuting back and forth between Lille and Paris, he simultaneously taught the same subjects at the École Normale Supérieure, using the nearby Bibliothéque Nationale for his research. Foucault would visit the well-stocked Bibliothéque almost daily for the next 25 years, locating hitherto obscure documents and manuscripts, often to usher them into significance through extended, wide-ranging, historical and culture-critical studies.

Foucault's knowledge of mental illness was enhanced by his experiences at the Sainte-Anne mental hospital and the Centre National d'Orientation at Fresnes – a prison that housed the French penal system's chief medical facilities. At the latter institution, Foucault had access to all prisoners, ranging from juvenile delinquents to murderers, and this provided him with insight into the interface between criminology and psychology. At the Sainte-Anne mental hospital, Foucault drew up psychological–neurological profiles of the patients, administered specialized psychological tests, and attended lectures on psychoanalysis given by the philosopher–psychiatrist, Jacques Lacan (1901–81), who was a member of the medical staff. Foucault's position as an intermediary between doctor and patient allowed him to understand the perspectives of both, sometimes quite saddeningly in connection with some of the patients for whom he cared, and whose treatment, in his view, was nothing less than tragic.

With the above experiences and recollections in mind, Foucault prepared his doctoral thesis on the history of madness. As a preliminary psychological study, commissioned when he was 28, Foucault wrote a lengthy introduction to an essay by Ludwig Binswanger (1881–1966) – a Swiss psychiatrist whose existential approach was inspired by the writings of the German philosopher, Martin Heidegger (1889–1976). Foucault had been studying Heidegger's and Nietzsche's texts during the early 1950s, despite their relative unpopularity in France after the Second World War.

Up until 1954, when Foucault wrote the introduction to Binswanger's essay, his intellectual interests pointed in the direction of psychology, philosophy, and scientific subjects related to the life sciences. In 1955, at age 29, Foucault's life took a different turn with a move to Sweden and a position as French Assistant in the Department of Romance Studies in the University of Uppsala. Here, he taught classes in French language and French literature, such as "The Conception of Love in French Literature, from the Marquis de Sade to Jean Genet." After three years, Foucault left for Poland, where he became director of the University of Warsaw's Centre Français, similarly teaching courses in the French language and on contemporary theater. One year later, in 1958 – owing to an episode of what appeared to be sexual entrapment by a member of the Polish police – Foucault relocated to Germany, where he obtained a position as Director of the Institut Français in Hamburg. During these years, which were marked by increasing literary interests, Foucault completed his doctoral thesis, and submitted it for acceptance in 1959, at age 33. In 1961, this thesis – *Folie et déraison; histoire de la folie à l'âge classique* (*Madness and Civilization – A History of Insanity in the Age of Reason*) – was published, and with its positive reception Foucault established himself as a notable intellectual figure in France. From this point on, his career blossomed.

During the first half of the 1960s, Foucault was a Professor of Philosophy at the University of Clermont-Ferrand. Then for two years (1966–8) he lived abroad as a visiting professor at the University of Tunis – a position that kept him away from Paris during the turbulent and revolution-recalling May of 1968. Upon his return to France later in 1968, Foucault headed the Philosophy Department at the experimental university at Vincennes, and in 1969 he entered into the commanding-echelon of French academic life with an election to one of the world's finest research institutes, the Collège de France, founded in 1520. With this election, and choosing the title "Professor in the History of Systems of Thought," Foucault joined the elite circle of Collège academics, which included Henri Bergson (1859–1941), Claude Lévi-Strauss (1908–), Maurice Merleau-Ponty (1908–61), and Roland Barthes (1915–80).

The 1960s were productive years for Foucault, and they issued in some of his best-known and most influential writings. Soon after *Madness and Civilization*, which traced the birth of the mental asylum, Foucault published *Naissance de la clinique – Une archéologie du régard médical* (*The Birth of the Clinic – An Archaeology of Medical Perception* [1963]), which documented the rise of the mathematical, quantitative approach to medical problems and to human bodily functioning in general. 1966 was perhaps one of Foucault's best publication years, since *Les Mots and les Choses – Une archéologie des sciences humaines* (*The Order of Things – An Archaeology of the Human Sciences*), a book that examined the foundations of knowledge during the Renaissance, Enlightenment and Modern periods, became a bestseller. To cap the decade, Foucault published *L'Archéologie du savoir* (*The Archaeology of Knowledge* [1969]), bringing into explicit thematization the method of inquiry he had been adopting up until this point.

Foucault devoted the last 14 years of his life to teaching and writing, frequently punctuating his daily affairs with leftist political activism, public lectures, and mass media appearances. Among the latter is his November 1971 debate with the American linguist–philosopher Noam Chomsky (1928–), shown on Dutch television. Chomsky had already established a reputation as a hard-fisted critic of the United States' military involvement in Vietnam and as a voice of social conscience, but his rationality-respecting approach to political strategy stood in domesticated contrast to Foucault's more forcefully iconoclastic and confrontational stance. A few years later, as an intellectual and historical comment on contemporary prison conditions, Foucault wrote *Surveiller et punir – Naissance de la prison* (*Discipline and Punish – The Birth of the Prison* [1975]), an account of the development of European penal systems. This work addressed not only the history of penitentiaries; it intended to enhance his readers' awareness of the oppressive institutional treatment received by groups of all kinds that are defined, relative to the status quo, as residing outside of the social norm. Expanding on this theme, Foucault focused in his final years upon the historical construction of people's sexual identities, hoping to understand some of the more fundamental institutional forces that shape the more feral aspects of the human psyche.

As the end of his life drew near, Foucault lectured frequently in the United States, visiting institutions such as Stanford University (1979), The University of Southern California (1981), The University of Vermont (1982), and the University of California at Berkeley (1979–83, on various occasions), where he continued to develop his work on human sexuality and the construction of human subjectivity. At an uncertain point during this time, Foucault contracted an immunodeficiency disease, and his subsequent AIDS-related illness took his life on June 25, 1984, at age 57.

The Experience of Growth and Liberation

To comprehend the intricate and nuanced texture of Foucault's writings, it is useful to reflect upon the experience of being released from a condition of bondage. This could be as dramatic as the day of liberation at the end of a long imprisonment, or it could be the release from oppressive working conditions at the end of a drudging week, or it could be the feeling of bright anticipation at the beginning of a long-awaited retirement. More abstractly, it could be the experience of being released, or of releasing oneself, from a stifling set of social relationships, or from one's former patterns of narrow-minded thinking. Each of these cases typically involves a mental expansion, a sense of greater openness to new possibilities, and a distinct feeling of "stepping beyond one's former boundaries." Within Foucault's thought, the ecstasy of liberation flows as a steady thematic undercurrent.

Globally considered, Foucault's revolution-friendly thought focuses more on liberty than upon either equality or fraternity: most of his writings are understandable as parts of a multidimensional inquiry into the experience of liberation, undertaken by a powerful and complicated mind. On the constraint-related side of this experience, Foucault examined the various sorts of institutional cages that societies can impose upon people, along with the kinds of psychological cages within which people can suffer in isolation. Hence arose his interest in mental illness, both of the individual and the social sort. He investigated the historical construction of these enclosures, and implicitly revealed to his readers ways to unravel, deconstruct, or otherwise dissolve their oppressive quality. By understanding how a structure of social constraint has been constructed, one can understand how to deconstruct it, and perceive more distinctly how such a cage need not permanently endure. As they appear in Foucault's writings, such analyses embody a sophisticated revolutionary and carnivalesque tenor.

On the less-rule-governed, or more unlawful, side of the liberation experience, Foucault's interest was drawn to extraordinarily creative individuals, such as avant-garde artists and writers. He regarded such people, who are often dissenters, renegades, outcasts, and outlaws, as having the talent and courage to break apart one of the most invisible and most difficult-to-dissolve cages in which we live, namely, the cage of consciousness that is literally informed by the language we inherit.

Foucault was distinctly aware that if the very language a person inherits is sexist and racist, for example, the person is left with little choice but to formulate expressions through an atmosphere of sexist and racist values, implicitly present in even the simplest verbal communications. In such situations, the occasional need for the outright transgression of established values can be easily justified, and outrageous artists often exercise their freedom to this very end.

Some of Foucault's own inquiries intended, quite fundamentally, to undermine conceptions that have remained relatively unquestioned for centuries, and which have been so steadfast and "natural" that they have presented themselves as a second nature to most people. One of these – an idea that reaches back to ancient Greece, if not earlier – is the concept that there is an essence, or solid core, or basic "self," or "soul," to every human being, and that this core, moreover, is of a rational kind. Foucault also questioned the legitimacy of many entrenched social structures, challenging the idea that what a society labels "normal," or "sane," is of any everlasting validity. He tended to dispute such claims, maintaining that the structure of societies, and of individual selves, is far more arbitrary and malleable than most of us tend to imagine. Inspirational to Foucault in this regard were the "medical relativist" writings of Georges Canguilhem (1904–67), which argued that the concepts of "normal" and "pathological" were historically variable, value-steeped, and unavoidably charged with political, technological, and economic import.

Insofar as social structures are arbitrary, they are changeable. And insofar as they are changeable, less constraining possibilities remain open. So it might not follow that if a society defines a certain sexual practice – such as homosexuality – as "wrong," that it is necessarily, or is even reasonably, definable as such. Since socially dictated norms can nonetheless appear to be natural and written right into the fabric of daily life, Foucault devoted much of his energy to showing, in very specific cases, that what is often taken to be natural is, in fact, no more than an alterable social fabrication. Within the regularities of our social world, he discovered far more artistry than natural law.

Foucault was also intrigued by the constructive significance of asymmetrical social relationships, especially within the context of clearly power-related interactions. His writings considered the standpoint of those in control, and they explored the mechanisms through which social discipline is maintained. In his later years, owing to the influence of Friedrich Nietzsche, Foucault investigated the ideas of *self*-control and *self*-discipline, noting that the distancing and control mechanisms that operate socially to dominate and oppress people are of a piece with the kind of control one can exert over oneself, although the latter may be used in a more constructive, creative, and self-liberating manner.

Upon first encounter, the array of subjects that Foucault's writings encompass – medicine, madness, prisons, art, politics, sexuality, linguistics, history – forms a confusing and somewhat tangled fabric. Though diverse, Foucault addressed most of these topics in connection with the idea of liberation, either by bringing to light constraints that are socially operative, but are nonetheless dimly perceived, or by revealing alternative styles of positive release from existing constraints. Foucault's particular and often peculiar choice of topics and historical episodes – among which he includes an obscure story of a young man who mass-murdered his entire family in 1835, and an unforgettably bloody account of a public execution in 1750s France – is further explained in reference to his interest in telling the stories of marginalized groups and of value-shaking historical events.

The rationale behind Foucault's expository method also issued from psychoanalytic roots: as Sigmund Freud (1856–1939) convincingly showed, bringing to light what has been forcibly silenced, or exposing what lies at the peripheries of "normality," is often far more truth-revealing than what one obtains when keeping close to the sanitized surface, and resting content to inspect only what has been allowed to manifest itself with the social stamp of approval. Highlighting non-privileged phenomena can be a kind of emancipatory act: giving voice to those who have been muted by the loci of established power can liberate those people, or the ideas they represent, from institutional oppression, and indirectly reveal the issues that a society is too fearful to confront.

To appreciate the specific selection of topics upon which Foucault wrote, we can once again recall the influence of Friedrich Nietzsche, not only because the title of Nietzsche's first book, *The Birth of Tragedy* (1872), established a model for Foucault's studies of the birth of the mental institution, the birth of medical perception, and the birth of the prison, but because Nietzsche himself prescribed the very intellectual program of study that Foucault appears to have adopted. Nietzsche wrote in *The Gay Science* (1882):

> *Something for the industrious.* – Anyone who now wishes to make a study of moral matters opens up for himself an immense field for work. All kinds of individual passions have to be thought through and pursued through different ages, peoples, and great and small individuals; all their reason and all their evaluations and perspectives on things have to be brought into the light. So far, all that has given color to existence still lacks a history. Where could you find a history of love, of avarice, of envy, of conscience, of pious respect for tradition, or of cruelty? Even a comparative history of law or at least of punishment is so far lacking completely. Has anyone made a study of different ways of dividing up the day or of the consequences of a regular schedule of work, festivals and rest? What is known of the moral effects of different foods? Is there any philosophy of nutrition? (The constant revival of noisy agitation for and against vegetarianism proves that there is no such philosophy.) Has anyone collected men's experiences of living together – in monasteries, for example? Has the dialect of marriage and friendship even been explicated? Have the manners of scholars, of businessmen, artists, or artisans been studied and thought about? There is so much in them to think about.
>
> Whatever men have so far viewed as the condition of their existence – and all the reason, passion, and superstition involved in such a view – has this been researched exhaustively? The most industrious people will find that it involves too much work simply to observe how differently men's instincts have grown, and might yet grow, depending on different moral climates.[1]

It is striking to discover in this comment a listing of key research topics taken up by Foucault during his later years. For instance, Foucault's *Discipline and Punish* contains reflections on the history of cruelty and punishment, not to mention studies of regimentation and daily scheduling in connection with the development of the late eighteenth-century European soldier. In his *History of Sexuality*, Foucault also thought through the histories of monastery life, friendship and marriage relationships, and generally examined practices of self-care, which included nutritional practices and alternative styles of daily regimen. Inspirations from Nietzsche diffused even further into the details of Foucault's studies, as we shall see.

The Influence of Martin Heidegger

When Foucault gave his last interview in June of 1984, he mentioned that Martin Heidegger had always been for him "the essential philosopher." What especially sparked his enthusiasm, Foucault added, was Heidegger's thought in conjunction with Nietzsche's. As mentioned above, Foucault studied the work of both philosophers in the 1950s, and his first publication – an essay entitled "Dream, Imagination and Existence" – was clearly influenced by the Heideggerian outlook. To appreciate Foucault's intellectual development, it is important to remind ourselves of some themes in Heidegger's earlier and later philosophy.

At the beginning of *Sein und Zeit* (*Being and Time*, 1927), Heidegger described the human being as one whose condition is special: unlike other living things, the human is a self-questioning being, to whom its very existence presents itself as a problem. This ability to raise questions, as Foucault would say, amounts to a kind of power, for in questioning – especially in the questioning of authority – there resides a force of liberating change. And being able to question oneself involves an implicit power to free oneself from one's former condition. If one is essentially self-questioning, then one is essentially self-freeing. Heidegger's characterization of the human being – an account that seminally influenced the early twentieth-century French existentialist tradition in the figure of Jean-Paul Sartre (1905–80) – precipitates a lack of sympathy, not to mention a charge of unauthenticity, with views that have simply ceased to subject themselves to question. Quite unlike Socrates, who was famous for claiming "not to know" the ultimate truth, those who advocate positions that no longer put themselves into question often claim to know absolutely. Such manifestly dogmatic positions include those that essentialize, compartmentalize, and ossify the human being within a cage of rigid definitions.

According to Heidegger, much of "what is" – what he referred to as "Being" itself – remains hidden, undisclosed, and unthought of. Ever-new possibilities remain latent in what is in general, and to be authentically human involves being questioning, being creative, and maintaining an open mind and a receptive attitude to possibilities unseen and previously unrealized. As a complement, then, to the idea of the human being as a fundamentally questioning being whose own possibilities are virtually endless, Heidegger conjoined a conception of reality itself that is multidimensional and filled with possibility. His thought is thereby intended to be opposed to monolithic, determinate, authoritarian systems that aim to regiment all of reality, and it hoped to resist those outlooks that present themselves as an end-all or absolute view. Part and parcel of this open-minded attitude is Heidegger's worried observation that the scientific, quantitative approach to the world can take on a totalizing, absolutist quality, and he cautioned against adopting this approach in an exclusive way, such that it ends up constricting human potentialities.

Despite the freedom of thought that Heidegger's outlook promotes, he also remained fully aware that human beings are not phantoms, and do not dwell time-lessly in the cosmic air: we are living, breathing, historical beings who are thrown into a very concrete world at a specific time and place, and who are impressed and informed with a distinctive linguistic style. In this flesh-and-blood situatedness, Heidegger noted that whenever we understand anything, we cannot avoid resting our understanding upon tacit presuppositions that direct our questioning, and that provide our questions with an internal coherence and initial social meaning. In short, as much as we try to remain receptive to new possibilities, our questioning remains guided by the presuppositions we inherit, many of which remain opaque to our immediate reflection. As a way to reveal, or to open, new dimensions of Being, Heidegger emphasized the value of artistic expression, and poetic expression in particular. Foucault's thought followed closely along this line, recognizing especially that the literary arts can enlarge the often-cramped and routine compartments of language, which Heidegger sometimes more reverently referred to as the "house of Being." Foucault also recognized historical studies as another such means of libera-tion, and he engaged primarily in this style of outlook-expansion.

Many of Heidegger's ideas are implicit in Friedrich Nietzsche's texts, but Heidegger intensified, accentuated, and developed Nietzschean insights with a distinctive emphasis upon existential, historical, and, in his later period, linguistic expression. These were ideas with which Foucault naturally sympathized, and one can imagine how the Heidegger–Nietzsche amalgam doubly impressed itself upon Foucault. Similarly, Foucault believed that we are fundamentally historical beings, and that if we are to gain any self-understanding, it is crucial that we identify the often-constraining presuppositions that have been passed on to us by previous gen-erations. Only then can we experience increased freedom and growth in a controlled way, for Foucault held that it is imperative to question these historical inheritances, if only to allow ourselves, as individuals, the space to recreate ourselves and self-determine ourselves to a greater extent, in view of the necessities for some kind of social structuring that inevitably carries with it a certain degree of oppression.

Foucault as "Archaeologist"

Upon hearing that a person is an "archaeologist" – someone whose work is to recon-struct a cultural lifestyle from a set of physical artifacts – it is easy to conjure up images of ancient ruins, pottery, arrowheads, cave paintings, stone temples, or mysterious tombs. As opposed to historical studies that center upon written texts, archaeology becomes crucial when a cultural group has left no written records. Some even believe that archaeology is more scientific and objective than the study of old texts, because so many of these texts – especially the very ancient ones – express interests that are predominantly political or religious, as opposed to purely documentary. Describing one's work as "archaeological" as opposed to "historical," then, can lend it an authority that is associated with the recognized authority of science, even if one's work is independent of scientific inquiries proper.

In Foucault's writings of the 1960s, the word "archaeology" becomes increasingly more pronounced as the years pass. In 1963, Foucault published a book whose sub-title was "an archaeology of medical perception"; in 1966, he presented "an archaeology of the human sciences"; in 1969, he explored "the archaeology of knowledge" itself. With such works, Foucault came forth as a scholar on an "archaeological dig," searching for overlooked treasures among the dust-covered texts in the well-stocked French national library. His subtitles and titles also suggest that if we focus on the term "archaeology," we can gain a clear sense of the perspective from which Foucault was writing during this important segment of his career.

In *The Order of Things*, Foucault characterized his idea of "archaeology" as follows:

> Quite obviously, such an analysis does not belong to the history of ideas or of science: it is rather an inquiry whose aim is *to rediscover on what basis knowledge and theory become possible* [emphasis added]; within what space of order knowledge was constituted; on the basis of what historical *a priori*, and in the element of what positivity, ideas could appear, sciences be established, experience be reflected in philosophies, rationalities be formed, only perhaps, to dissolve and vanish soon afterwards. I am not concerned, there-fore, to describe the progress of knowledge towards an objectivity in which today's science can finally be recognized; what I am attempting to bring to light is the episte-mological field, the *episteme* in which knowledge, envisaged apart from all criteria having reference to its rational value or to its objective forms, grounds its positivity and thereby manifests a history which is not that of its growing perfection, but rather that of its con-ditions of possibility; in this account, what should appear are those configurations within the *space* of knowledge which have given rise to the diverse forms of empirical science. Such an enterprise is not so much a history, in the traditional meaning of that word, as an "archaeology."[2]

Rather than revealing a people's daily lifestyle, as is done by traditional archaeolo-gists, Foucault-as-archaeologist aimed to reveal a people's knowledge-style, bringing to light the guiding assumptions that operate prior to any assertions that this or that fact happens to be known. Those familiar with the philosophy of Immanuel Kant (1724–1804) will recognize the term "*a priori*" in Foucault's characterization of "archaeology" – a discipline that Foucault defined as belonging to neither history nor science in any straightforward way. Kant's inquiries, although they differed from Foucault's insofar as they professed to have a quality of universality and necessity for all human beings, were also neither historical nor scientific: already, in the late 1700s, Kant considered not bits and pieces of factual knowledge, but sought to unveil the underlying structures of the mind that constitute a network of conceptual presup-positions for human knowledge, against which, in terms of which, and by means of which, all contingent facts about the world could arise to begin with.

As much as Foucault was inspired by Kant, he gave Kant's search for the univer-sal and necessary *a priori* conditions of human knowledge a modern twist, for he spoke of a "historical" *a priori* to be uncovered by his archaeological investigations, rather than a traditionally universal and necessary one. This modification of Kant's terminology reveals Foucault's more unassuming view that there might not necessarily be a single, invariant knowledge-style that is common to all humans but, rather, only a multiplicity of knowledge-styles that vary according to the specific time and place. Foucault's coining of the term "historical *a priori*," in place of Kant's more timeless "*a priori*," displays both Foucault's Kantian roots, side-by-side with Foucault's departure from Kant – a departure partially derived from Martin Heidegger's historical sensitivity, and one that allowed Foucault to make later use of compatible insights from Nietzsche.

Specifically, as noted above, one of Heidegger's contributions to the theory of understanding and interpretation (also known as "hermeneutics") is the idea that whenever we understand something, or say that we "know" something, this understanding rests "always already" upon interpretive historical presuppositions. Owing to their generality and obviousness, these presuppositions tend to remain hidden from us, for Heidegger observed that our guiding presuppositions are often invisible, precisely because they are "too close" to us, just as a person's eyeglasses are typically "invisible" to the extent that they function silently and unnoticeably, and become objects of attention perhaps only when they happen to break. In a clear sense, then, these customarily overlooked presuppositions, or prejudgments (as they were later referred to by the philosopher Hans-Georg Gadamer [1900–2001]), can be said to constitute a significant portion of our "historical *a priori*." Foucault's work of the 1960s can be regarded as a Kantian–Heideggerian attempt to reveal in detail exactly what these presuppositions were for various fields of knowledge and time periods. His work during this time was Kantian, insofar as it aimed to establish the "*a priori*" conditions for understanding in various fields. It was also Heideggerian, insofar as he conceived of the conditions for understanding as being historically rooted. "Knowledge-styles," in effect, became "interpretation-styles" within Foucault's view.

In *Madness and Civilization*, Foucault embarked forcefully on an archaeological exploration of the historical conditions underlying the emergence of some key institutions within European culture, and especially in France. His focus was upon the various social definitions and attitudes toward a socially discredited group of outsiders, namely, those whom the prevailing society labeled as "mad." Depending upon the time period, Foucault observed, the group of individuals included within this category varied. During the Age of Enlightenment (also known as the "Age of Reason," or, for Foucault, the "Classical Age") this group included not only people who would today be classified as mentally ill; it included also the physically ill, the criminally active, the unemployed, and the aged. At a point that began roughly in the mid-1600s, all were confined together indiscriminately as "the mad."

That the Age of Reason was also the age of world-transforming scientific discovery is worthy of note, for Foucault draws our attention to the significant social fallout that issued from the very same mentality that led to indisputable, and truly amazing, advances in general knowledge and technological achievement. As the concept of "reason" reached a level of cultural hegemony – a conception characterized by an impartial, disinterested, personally detached, measurement-centered, order-focused, regimenting style of thought – those "unreasonable" people whose behavior did not measure up to this conception of reason were soon shouldered over to the peripheries of social legitimacy. Since humans were conceived of as "rational beings," it was short work to define such non-typical people as subhuman, or as near-animals. In the 1700s, they were literally confined in cages within which, through active manipulation, they would be reformed, if possible, into hard-working, reasonable, predictable, law-abiding citizens. The social role of "absolute outcast," which had been assigned to the lepers in earlier ages, was played by the "mad" in the Age of Enlightenment.

At the dawn of the 1800s, homestead-like mental asylums were born from an attitude that more discriminatingly distinguished the mentally ill from the criminals and from the physically ill. For Foucault, this change in general attitude did not imply any noticeably improved treatment for the mentally ill, since those confined were treated now as moral outcasts, even though they were no longer treated violently as subhumans. Rather than being manhandled into more socially conforming behavior through physical punishment, as had been the previous practice, the mentally ill were made to feel guilty and became the victims of more subtle techniques of psychological abuse, such as the "silent treatment."

Madness and Civilization documented the social tragedy that arose when the classical idea that humans are essentially rational animals was intensified to the point at which it became a tool of oppression and social exclusion. With this first book completed, and having described the position of those who were subjected to medical authority, Foucault then considered the flip side of this situation in *The Birth of the Clinic*. Here, he observed how the growing authority of medical doctors paralleled the rise of scientific thinking, showing how their adoption of a supposedly impartial and deeply knowing "medical gaze" provided them with an authority reminiscent of what was formerly held by the Christian priesthood.

In *The Order of Things – An Archaeology of the Human Sciences* (1966), Foucault extended his historical examinations to account for the birth of human sciences such as psychology and sociology, along with the analysis of literature and mythology. In this effort, he crystallized in greater detail the global knowledge-styles or "*epistemes*" of the respective Renaissance, Classical, and Modern periods, mainly to emphasize that if one is to understand history, social structures, and the individuals who operate within those social parameters, it is necessary to focus not on timeless and unchanging essences, but upon processes of emergence, transformation, and erosion.

Foucault would later reconsider the validity of his sweeping references to three different "ages," each with its own peculiar, and permeating, knowledge-style, but in the 1960s he did try to identify the global thought-categories relative to specific epochs – their respective "historical *a priori*" structures – just as Kant had tried to identify the *a priori* thought-categories relative to the human being in general. In particular, Foucault claimed that the knowledge-style of Western culture up until the end of the 1500s was based on the ability to discern "resemblances" among things. Within this mode of thought, one could, for instance, hope to ease a headache by eating walnuts, because the brain-like shape of walnuts suggested that they might be related to the head. Or, one could hope to inflict damage on an enemy, or bring good fortune upon a friend, by inflicting damage upon or by taking care of an effigy, because the negative or positive attention to the representation would be thought to carry over to the intended object, owing to the resemblance between the effigy and the object that it represented. According to Foucault, such an essentially anthropomorphic and quasi-magical knowledge-style was relatively unproductive, since resemblances can be perceived endlessly, and can be perceived in connection with the most practically unrelated things.

The Classical period of the 1600s–1700s was the setting for the physical sciences, and in knowledge-style, this period was distinguished by the manner of thought previously mentioned: the Classical mind was order-focused, measurement-centered, abstracting, universalizing, and fundamentally impartial in observation. A paragon example can be found in Galileo Galilei (1564–1642), whose theoretical understanding of nature sharply distinguished the directly measurable, relatively invariant qualities of physical objects (e.g., the weight of a cube of sugar) from their more variable subjective effects (e.g., the sweet taste of the sugar), and led to the effective development of mathematical, objective, expressions of physical laws. One of the ground-level assumptions of this knowledge-style is that the inquirer ought to, and can, remain completely disengaged from the object observed, such as to perceive the object as it is in itself, untouched and unaffected by the observer's presence. Within this scientific outlook, the observer turns into a ghost-like manipulator of situations and things, in an attempt to bring their material essence to measurable light. As the Classical period extended forward in time, this scientific mentality was pointed explicitly toward living things and to human beings, leading to the development of the biological, psychological, and sociological sciences.

The beginning of the nineteenth century marked the outset of the Modern Age – an age characterized by a more acute sense of history and, thereby, of a deeper sensitivity to the fluctuating features of human experience. With a more closely attuned awareness to the passing of time, Modern thinkers experienced the breakdown of the Classical quest for timeless universalities, and developed more provisional, conditional, and restrained outlooks that displayed a more pronounced awareness of the theoretician's own contingent existence and intrinsic finitude. Foucault himself often embodied this awareness, as he reflected on the status of his own writings as twentieth-century historical artifactual constructions, knowing full well how time would eventually wash them away.

Foucault's final book of the decade, *The Archaeology of Knowledge* (1969), expresses the underlying investigative procedure of his earlier books in a linguistically focused manner: he speaks in a more explicit and focused way about various "discourses" and "discourse formations" that are typical for different epochs, and refers to his search for the historical *a prioris* of different time periods as an inquiry into the underlying practices that constitute the prevailing discourses. What is distinctive about Foucault's description of his project at this stage is not only his more accentuated linguistic focus, but also his growing awareness that language has an inexhaustible, complicated, if not convoluted and incongruous, multidimensional texture, and that it will not suffice to identify particular spirits of the various time periods. He began to realize more exactly how historical situations are thoroughly complicated: many tensions, alternative and interweaving strands of development, complementary themes, and variable rates of cultural change all figure into any concrete understanding of a historical subject matter, and these tend to foil the quest for global generalities. This conviction that historical studies require an extremely discriminating awareness – an awareness not unlike that of a connoisseur or wine-taster – at this point began to develop a force in Foucault's work, and it led him to complement the Kant- and Heidegger-inspired search for the "historical *a priori*" with a more self-conscious attention to nuance and detail characteristic of the aesthete – the kind of mentality that he found exemplified in the theorist of the "will to power," Friedrich Nietzsche.

Genealogy, Power/Knowledge, and Surveillance

As should now be evident, Foucault had a discriminating and analytic mind coupled with a daring personality, and his lively awareness of the interweavings, incongruencies, tensions, and multivalences within linguistic phenomena was matched by a similar perception of cultural phenomena in general. For any historical subject – whether it concerned the notion of what an "author" happens to be, or whether it concerned the development of penal systems – Foucault was able to discover a complicated tissue of antecedent historical phenomena that could explain the emergence of that subject within some cultural context.

Such historical studies are comparable to tracing the blood-lineage of a person back for centuries into the ever complicated and increasingly tangled roots of a genealogical tree – not for the sake of unveiling some single, original pair of ancestors such as Adam and Eve, but to show that any individual existence stems from hundreds, if not thousands, of often unrelated and often widely divergent personal histories. And indeed, during the 1970s, Foucault described his style of intellectual inquiry as "genealogical" in this very sense. The terminological inspiration was from Friedrich Nietzsche, whose *On the Genealogy of Morals* (1887) stood, in terms of his corresponding historical method, as exemplary for Foucault. An antecedent to the Nietzschean idea of "genealogy" is that of a legal "deduction" – a term used philosophically by Kant in the 1780s. In the centuries preceding Kant's lifetime, legal "deductions" were official, sometimes book-length, inquiries into the history of a fought-over river or parcel of land; their purpose was to trace the object back to some past owner and establish a legal title thereby.

The most well known work of this period is Foucault's *Discipline and Punish – The Birth of the Prison* (*Surveiller et punir – Naissance de la prison* [1975]). This was a historical exposé and social critique of the French penal system, for among his many observations, Foucault noted that "prisons do not diminish the crime rate," and that the overall stance of those who institute prisons has remained relatively unenlightened, not having changed much since the early 1800s. In connection with Foucault's theoretical approach, *Discipline and Punish* is important insofar as the idea of "power" – another concept traceable to Nietzsche's influence – can be seen clearly to have moved into the heart of his thinking, such that the notions of "discourse formation" and "episteme," although not completely abandoned, faded into the background.

During this phase of his career, Foucault regarded the presence of "power" in society in a somewhat negative light, insofar as social power was understood to be fundamentally freedom-restricting and manipulative. It was not so much individuals, however, whose power was regarded as a force of domination; it was the power inherent in an institutional framework, constituted by a set of established social practices. It is these faceless social practices, deriving exclusively from no one in particular, and yet adopted by segments of the population in general – by "them," as Heidegger would say – that were seen as responsible for molding people into various types suitable for the well-functioning of the society.

A clear example of the social power that Foucault had in mind can be seen in the formation of soldiers in the late eighteenth century. Before this time, if a person happened to have, among other qualities, a strong body, natural agility, and an alert manner, that person was regarded as naturally suited to be a soldier. Soldiers were believed to be found, rather than made. In later years, when "the classical age discovered the body as the object and target of power," people were seen as more akin to objects that could be manipulated, shaped, trained, and generally subject to use, transformation, and improvement. Social disciplinary practices of soldier-making thus became the norm, as people were increasingly regarded as pieces of clay to be shaped. The practice of reforming prisoners by trying to reshape their mentalities was similar, and was also generalizable: in a broad way, many social institutions, including the most well-intentioned ones, such as educational systems, could be understood as employing the oppressive and manipulative techniques of the prison.

In accord with the thought that many social institutions have a carceral, or prison-like, quality to them, Foucault observed that one of the essential functions of a prison-keeper is that of keeping the prisoners under surveillance. Within this context, Foucault gave an extended discussion of a remarkable architectural design for a perfect prison by the English philosopher, Jeremy Bentham (1748–1832). This "panopticon" was a doughnut-shaped building at whose center was located an observation tower – one that allowed its occupant to keep simultaneous watch on all of the cells in the surrounding dormitories. Unlike the dark, private, dungeons of the old days, the prisoners' cells were to be completely illuminated for the purpose of perpetual monitoring – "like so many cages, so many small theatres, in which each actor is alone, perfectly individualized and constantly visible." The goal was "to induce in the inmate a state of conscious and permanent visibility that assures the automatic functioning of power." Here, the observational standpoint's power reaches toward an almost superhuman magnitude, since it aims to survey, record, control, and assess everyone's movements at once.

Foucault's insights into the ways in which institutional structures maintain and perpetuate their power can be extended quite easily beyond the prison setting. To appreciate the contemporary applicability of Foucault's analysis, one can reflect upon the feeling of surveillance generated by one-way glass windows in civilian settings – feelings generated quite independently of whether anyone happens to be behind the window – and the increasing technological advances that allow those with institutional authority to monitor telephone conversations and other kinds of electronic communications without detection. The principle is exactly the same: social institutions with power exert their power by instilling the idea that those under control can be monitored, or placed under invisible surveillance, at any time. In this respect, Foucault's analysis of "panopticism" – the principle of the all-seeing eye – continues to be of widespread relevance. Just as the Classical physicist aimed to observe material things in a way such that his or her presence remained "invisible" and without affecting any changes upon the objects observed, the perfect social monitor, or "technician of behavior," aims to observe people in a way such that his or her presence remains invisible to, and non-interacting with, those under surveillance.

It is important to note that in some situations the panoptic frame of mind can be put to morally good use. It would be desirable in a hospital setting, for instance, where constant electronic monitors on all of the patients' bodily conditions were fully centralized at a central location for efficiency, thus shortening the response time in the case of emergency. Panopticism becomes objectionable, though, when the surveillance style is used to control sectors of social activity where people have not chosen to sacrifice a major proportion of their autonomy.

Another one of Foucault's influential ideas that took form during the 1970s is that "power" and "knowledge" always arise in an interdependency, reciprocity, and experiential amalgam with one another, just as "color" always accompanies "shape" in a visual experience. Part of the motivation for Foucault's association between power and knowledge issued from his concern with the political status of scientific knowledge. He observed that not only does scientific knowledge provide a power over nature, but that it also provides an institutional power to those who develop, manage, and control it.

More significantly, the intellectual atmosphere of Foucault's approach is extremely down-to-earth, and he retained an "existentialist" focus, to speak broadly. His analyses of key philosophical concepts such as "truth," "power," "language," and "knowledge" are all grounded within the details of concrete historical contexts. Trying to detach some non-historical, timelessly true, completely literalistic, universal, and unalterable conceptual structure from the infinitely complicated network of real-life happenings was quite antagonistic to Foucault's understanding and, in this respect, he resisted theorizing about any absolute truths or about any knowledge that is thought to be completely detached from concrete circumstances. Since concrete circumstances unavoidably involve social, political, and cultural dimensions, he insisted that any concrete understanding of knowledge and truth must recognize that these ideas are inextricably enmeshed within, infiltrated, and modified by changing historical conditions. He even recognized that the concept of "power" – the central theme of his theorizing during the 1970s – is completely empty, if it is thought in the absence of articulating the specific kinds and circumstances of the power under consideration.

In 1977, in an interview on *The History of Sexuality*, Foucault made a remark that has often been quoted, and often misinterpreted: "I am well aware that I have never written anything but fictions." Standing by itself, this sentence suggests that Foucault did not believe in "truth," and that his outlook is nihilistic. His next sentence, however, revealed a very different standpoint: "I do not mean to say, however, that truth is therefore absent." Truth, that is, is expressible through fictional discourse or, stated differently, artistic, figurative, mythic, metaphoric, and literary expression can express truth equally as well, or perhaps even better, than purely literalistic language. If, indeed, the true state of affairs is multi-dimensional, allusive, fluctuating, and not exhaustibly expressible within any finite linguistic framework, then Foucault can be read as someone who would have received with congeniality the Daoist statement that "the Way that can be spoken of is not the constant Way" (Laozi, *Daodejing*, Book I). Less remotely, Foucault can be read as a person who believed, with Friedrich Nietzsche, that the truth cannot be fully attained from a head-on, literalistic approach, but must also be softly brought forth with quiet charm, using indirect, artistic, and even mythic language.

In 1970 and in 1978, Foucault visited Japan, motivated in part by his interest in Zen Buddhism. Foucault's interest in Zen had at least three aspects, the first of which is that, like Zen, some forms of Christianity advocate stringent disciplinary techniques for the purposes of spiritual advancement. From the standpoint of comparative cultural practices, Foucault found that the Zen Buddhist monastic regimen stood in a striking parallel to Christian monastic discipline. In Zen as well, one can see embodied the Latin dictum *laborare est orare*, "to work is to pray." Second, the Buddhistic position that all existence is conditioned or contingent, along with the Buddhistic denial of a substantial self – positions which are opposed to fixed conceptual definitions – are compatible with Foucault's anti-Cartesian, more nominalistic standpoint.

Third, that Zen is a way of life, and bears a close kinship to Foucault's understanding of philosophy as a spiritual exercise or "practice of freedom" – a practice to be grounded on the principle of self-detachment, or self-distancing – was another factor in Foucault's interest in Zen. Moreover, although the following point remains undocumented, one can also imagine that the specifically Zen Buddhist style of awareness – a "being clearly aware of everything now at once" – could have been a further point of interest for Foucault, especially in connection with his interest in panopticism. The Zen Master, in being open to all perceptual details in a kind of openness that is both child-like and wisdom-informed at once, can be regarded as a positive version of the panoptic mentality that preoccupied Foucault during this time period. In Zen, one aims to be absolutely observant for the purposes of apprehending the vivid, existentially fluctuating presence of the world; in panopticism, one aims to be absolutely observant for the purpose of maximizing one's control over what is observed. In the former case, one lets the world freely be; in the latter case, one leans on the world heavily. Since Foucault was pragmatic to the core, and since he knew that Zen Buddhism was the religion of many samurai, one could expect him to have been fascinated by a very practical kind of power that can stem from what is, on the face of things, an exceedingly spiritual mentality.

Self-Control and Self-Artistry

In the late 1970s and early 1980s, Foucault developed his understanding of "power" in a manner more consistent with his general assumption that the world is complicated, fluctuating, and multidimensional, rather than simple, static, and essentially definable. Although his historical investigations had embodied this idea well in their details, his guiding conception of power, as noted above, tended to be conceived somewhat monolithically as an oppressive force impressed upon individuals by established institutional practices. In volume 1 of *The History of Sexuality* (*La volenté du savoir* [*The Will to Knowledge*], 1976), however, Foucault explicitly advanced a theoretically more informative and more "positive" conception of power as a dynamic network of social forces. These were conceived of as diverse, overlapping, sometimes conflicting, and sometimes mutually supporting networks, operating in ever-changing "matrices of transformation." His view was that power, although everywhere, is not singular, and that one can never be "outside" of power, but always already enmeshed in specific power relationships.

The explicit theme for Foucault's final period – one that can be seen to have been implicit in his earlier work – can be expressed by the question, "How is self-knowledge possible?" This is a traditional question, but Foucault's way of understanding it involved a unique mix of historical inquiry and philosophical depth: he considered, in usually meticulous detail, how fluctuating historical conditions have formed people's self-conceptions and, with this knowledge, he reflected upon how people within such alternative historical constellations have self-examined themselves. For example, in his study of the scientifically centered qualities of the Modern period, he described how people were implicitly taught to regard themselves as potential objects of scientific inquiry, and how they thereby reproduced, of their own accord, forms of self-understanding consistent with the idea that they were objects that could be thoroughly measured, predicted, and controlled.

Foucault's method is distinctive not only in its attention to historical detail and its acute analysis of how self-images, or subjectivities, are constructed, but in its sensitivity to the self-reinforcing mechanisms of social-value perpetuation. Insofar as a person tends to reproduce the world in his or her own self-image, there arises the accompanying effect of the person's recreating, duplicating, and perpetuating the very social structures that significantly created that person's identity to begin with. This same kind of reciprocity relationship, at one remove, can be seen in Foucault's conception of "power-knowledge," for power and knowledge are mutually reinforcing in a similar way: "It is not possible for power to be exercised without knowledge, it is impossible for knowledge not to engender power."[3]

Foucault's attention to the historical factors underlying various styles of sexual self-awareness during his final years was illuminated by his wider endeavor to understand the construction of people's subjectivities in general. Since sexuality is such a major force within the human psyche, the study of sexual awareness can go a long way toward explaining how people variously understand themselves. Foucault also noticed that sexually related discourses arise within many spheres of daily life, so an investigation of sexual awareness can reveal the broad structure of existing social power-matrices to a significant extent.

Emerging from Foucault's focus upon the social construction of the subject was a more artistic and creative dimension to power, namely, the idea that people have a measure of self-control and can "self-create" themselves according to their own designs. Although social practices can often embody an implicit dominating force over the individual, power also flows through the individual, and this can be expressed as a power of self-conquest, self-monitoring, self-formation, and self-legislation. So just as Foucault had explored the "techniques of behavior" associated with the prison and the panoptic mentality, he later explored the "technologies of the self" in an effort to understand the more creative side of how subjects are constructed. In the year before he died, Foucault remarked: "But couldn't everyone's life become a work of art? Why should the lamp or the house be an art object but not our life?"[4]

In his final years, Foucault complemented his more austere, detached vocabularies of "strategies," "technologies," and "techniques" with the more graceful and freedom-inspiring idea of an "aesthetics of existence" or "art of life," where the main concern was to give one's life a self-determined, aesthetic appeal and unique style. Once again, Friedrich Nietzsche stands as the inspiration, for in the first section of *The Birth of Tragedy*, Nietzsche described how people themselves become works of art when engaged ecstatically in the musical activities of song and dance. A decade later, Nietzsche reiterated the same theme, providing a detailed articulation to the thought later expressed only in passing by Foucault. Nietzsche wrote in 1882:

> One thing is needful. – To "give style" to one's character – a great and rare art! It is practiced by those who survey all the strengths and weaknesses of their nature and then fit them into an artistic plan until every one of them appears as art and reason and even weaknesses delight the eye. Here a large mass of second nature has been added; there a piece of original nature has been removed – both times through long practice and daily work at it. Here the ugly that could not be removed is concealed; there it has been reinterpreted and made sublime. Much that is vague and resisted shaping has been saved and exploited for distant views; it is meant to beckon toward the far and immeasurable. In the end, when the work is finished, it becomes evident how the constraint of a single taste governed and formed everything large and small. Whether this taste was good or bad is less important than one might suppose, if only it was a single taste![5]

Nietzsche's personalized and individualistic rendition of the art of life contrasts revealingly with Foucault's more socially and historically centered version. Although Foucault was similarly interested in the care of the self, he understood the construction of personal identity by focusing primarily on group behaviors, in keeping with his general thought that people are molded significantly from prevailing social forces. In Foucault, one reads less about the daily regimens of specific individuals, and more about the techniques of self-mastery employed by groups such as monastic and philosophical orders, whose common goal was to establish a certain kind of shared hygiene and spirituality. In this respect, the idea of liberation that one encounters in Foucault's later works conveys far less of an anarchistic tone, for it is tempered by the idea that rule-governedness is a condition for, and a path toward, freedom. One can say that Foucault took seriously Cicero's observation that freedom is the participation in power, rather than a self-isolating disengagement from it.

Conclusion: Liberation and Social Self-Construction

Foucault's predominant intellectual style was masterfully discriminating. It could even be called "atomizing" or "disintegrating." And, as noted above, he had the ability to take virtually any, apparently clear, simply understandable and univocal concept, and, like an analytical chemist, reveal how its constitution was in fact quite complicated, not to mention changing and potentially unstable. In addition, Foucault was also an extremely reflective individual: as one surveys his writings, one can see his own powers of discrimination being applied to his previous work – almost in an act of self-overcoming – to reformulate his views in a way that relied less and less upon univocal and universalizing categories. He became more authentically nominalist as time went on.

We have also seen that Foucault's transformation of thematic emphasis from the 1960s to the early 1970s led to the emergence of the idea of power in his writings. But just as he initially conceived of time periods and knowledge-styles in a univocal and conceptually smoothed-out manner, Foucault would initially conceive of power in a noticeably monolithic way as well, namely, as an oppressive power that was fundamentally antagonistic to freedom. As he became more discerning and discriminating in his reflections on power, Foucault soon reexpressed his view to reveal that power is not only an active energy within individuals, and can be "productive," but that it also manifests itself in dynamic and entangled constellations whose embodiment is not a matter incidental to understanding what power is, but is constitutive of power itself.

Foucault made corresponding refinements in connection with the idea of "knowledge": he believed that one cannot speak meaningfully of a specific time period's knowledge-style "in the abstract," since an understanding of any knowledge-style must be located explicitly within a certain historical constellation of power. In the work characteristic of his final years, Foucault's discriminating outlook led him to speak not globally about "subjectivity" or about "sexuality," but about many different subjectivities and different sexualities, all of which were linked into broad-based historical studies of the time and place within which they originated.

Insofar as Foucault's thought can be centered around the concept of liberation, his discriminating attitude of the conceptual connoisseur – if this is described more pragmatically as a "disintegrationist" attitude – can be understood as a force directed toward revolutionary change. The disintegration of some given structure need not be construed as a purely destructive act, especially when the structure is as intangible as a conceptual structure, or is as malleable as a set of practices. To the extent that past forms can be kept in memory, Foucault's disintegrationist thought can expand our horizons, such that we can regard our previous conceptual structures as steps along the way to a more comprehensive awareness. Such a view need not entail a progressive, linear conception of human development, for myriad possibilities present themselves at each step of the way – artistic creation is by nature unpredictable – and increased comprehension can occur along many alternative routes.

A standing problem for Foucault's thought, however, concerns whether his perspective is itself significantly constraining. That is, we can ask whether Foucault's efforts to explain our present styles of subjectivity in reference to the social forces that constructed them actually succeeds in breaking away from the more self-centered Cartesian style of philosophizing that had been a continuing legacy in France. To be sure, Foucault had strong doubts about whether there is any invariant integrity to experiential subjects, and he also resisted exclusively analyzing the individual subject from the first-person, phenomenological, or "inside" viewpoint. He clearly preferred to comprehend the individual consciousness in reference to various styles of historically constituted group consciousnesses. The cluster of group consciousnesses that constituted Michel Foucault, though, themselves appear to have determined him to prefer a group-centered and linguistically centered, as opposed to individualistically centered, style of understanding. Whether or not the parameters of his socially centered orientation provide for the possibility of significant self-transcendence remains a question, because it remains debatable whether sociality is foundational in every instance.

To appreciate the significance of the problem of self-transcendence in Foucault's thought as alluded to above, we can reflect upon Foucault's intellectual style, the mood of which is captured in the two words "discipline" and "control." These words convey an assortment of resonances, but the thoughts of "manipulation," "technique," "domination," and perhaps also "strategy" and "tactics" – all words that figure prominently in Foucault's analyses – are close to the core. There is a distinct objectivity of temperament to be discerned here, arising even within Foucault's discussions of alternative attitudes toward oneself – discussions that center around the ideas of "self-control," "self-discipline," "technologies of the self," and "self-regimentation." In sum, the objectifying tone of cybernetic thinking can be seen to inhabit, and to inhibit, Foucault's discriminating and disintegrationist perspective, despite its emancipatory designs. Foucault was indeed reflective, but in his efforts to understand and to transcend the objectifying mentality, he ended up taking an objectifying view toward the objectifying style of mind.

Looking down upon the objectifying standpoint in an intellectually cool, distanced, and non-committal manner, however, does not allow one to escape it, for the stance of analytic detachment is itself objectifying, and it reiterates the style of mind from which one seeks to be detached. In his lifelong effort to achieve a balance between the structured discipline of science and the creative freedom of art, it would appear that discipline tended to prevail and that liberation remained only a more distant prescription. That Foucault was a true advocate of self-determination and practical self-mastery, though, will remain one of the inspirations of his legacy.

A constructive way to understand Foucault's attention to rule-governedness in connection with his interest in freedom, and a way to address some of Foucault's critics, who regard his most thoroughly considered position as an amoral "might makes right" variety, or as either anarchist, nihilist, or pessimist, is to regard his final work on the care of the self as an overture to a political philosophy, or "care of the group." The question has been often asked how Foucault can legitimate the political judgments that he frequently made. Consistent with Kant and Hegel, and consistent with those contemporary theorists who, inspired by the ideals of the Enlightenment, insist upon invoking a universal rationality as a guide to political judgment, Foucault's association between rule-governedness and self-artistry would put him squarely on the side of those who claim that purely arbitrary, essentially whimsical, decisions are, in fact, unjustified, if no commitment to some set of rules will follow.

But just as Foucault spoke of a historical *a priori* in connection with the knowledge-styles of a time period, one can say that political styles are also historically variable. Moreover, the general idea that one is only free if one acts consistently according to laws one has made oneself, or as a group, can be seen to be consistent with, and might even issue from, Foucault's thought's on self-artistry. The main difference between Foucault and the Enlightenment-style thinkers would be his insistence that it is only possible to formulate rules or institute legislation that is suitable to the times and situation within which one lives. Exercising freedom within such a situation would not, then, be the anarchistic freedom to do whatever one wants whenever one wants, nor, however, would it be a freedom in accord with a timeless pattern of rock-solid, self-evident, rationally grounded constancies. It would be the freedom to act in accord with the historically specific laws one has made for oneself – laws whose optimal formulation require a sense of taste, discrimination, and, most importantly, wisdom. That there are no determinate rules for either artistic genius or for political wisdom is a commonplace idea, and it remains part of Foucault's wisdom to insist that an allegiance to a mechanical and universalistic conception of reason reveals a distinct lack of wisdom, simply because circumstances change, and because changing circumstances make people who they are.

Notes

1 Friedrich Nietzsche, *The Gay Science*, trans. W. Kaufmann (New York: Vintage Books, 1974), §7, p. 82.
2 Michel Foucault, *The Order of Things* (New York: Vintage Books, 1994), pp. xxi–xxii.
3 Michel Foucault, "Prison talk" [1975], in C. Gordon (ed.), *Power/Knowledge: Selected Interviews & Other Writings 1972–1977* (New York: Pantheon, 1980), p. 52.
4 Michel Foucault, "On the genealogy of ethics" [1983], in P. Rabinow (ed.), *Michel Foucault – Ethics* (London: Penguin, 1997), p. 261.
5 Friedrich Nietzsche, *The Gay Science*, §290, p. 232.

Selected bibliography

Works by Michel Foucault

1972: *The Archaeology of Knowledge*, trans. A. M. Sheridan Smith. New York: Pantheon.
1988: *Madness and Civilization – A History of Insanity in the Age of Reason*, trans. R. Howard. New York: Vintage.
1988: *The Care of the Self, Volume 3 of* The History of Sexuality, trans. R. Hurley. New York: Vintage.
1990: *The History of Sexuality, Volume I: An Introduction*, trans. R. Hurley. New York: Vintage.
1990: *The Use of Pleasure, Volume 2 of* The History of Sexuality, trans. R. Hurley. New York: Vintage.
1991: *Discipline and Punish – The Birth of the Prison*, trans. A. Sheridan. London: Penguin.
1994: *The Birth of the Clinic – An Archaeology of Medical Perception*, trans. A. M. Sheridan Smith. New York: Vintage.
1994: *The Order of Things – An Archaeology of the Human Sciences*. New York: Vintage.

Works on Michel Foucault

Bouchard, D. F. (ed.) 1977: *Language, Counter-Memory, Practice – Selected Essays and Interviews by Michel Foucault*, trans. D. F. Bouchard and S. Simon. Ithaca, NY: Cornell University Press.

Carrette, J. R. (ed.) 1999: *Religion and Culture – Michel Foucault*. New York: Routledge.

Davidson, A. I. (ed.) 1996: *Foucault and his Interlocutors*. Chicago, Ill.: University of Chicago Press.

Dreyfus, H. L. and Rabinow, P. 1983: *Michel Foucault – Beyond Structuralism and Hermeneutics*, 2nd edn. Chicago, Ill.: University of Chicago Press.

Faubion, J. D. (ed.) 1998: *Michel Foucault – Aesthetics, Method, and Epistemology; Essential Works of Foucault 1954–1984*, vol. 2. New York: The New Press.

Gordon, C. (ed.) 1980: *Power/Knowledge – Selected Interviews & Other Writings 1972–1977 by Michel Foucault*. New York: Pantheon.

Gutting, G. 1989: *Michel Foucault's Archaeology of Scientific Reason*. Cambridge: Cambridge University Press.

——(ed.) 1994: *The Cambridge Companion to Foucault*. Cambridge: Cambridge University Press.

Kritzman, L. D. (ed.) 1988: *Michel Foucault – Politics, Philosophy, Culture; Interviews and Other Writings 1977–1984*, trans. A. Sheridan et al. New York and London: Routledge.

Macey, D. 1994: *The Lives of Michel Foucault*. London: Vintage.

Martin, L. H., Gutman, H., and Hutton, P. H. (eds.) 1988: *Technologies of the Self – A Seminar With Michel Foucault*. Amherst, Mass.: The University of Massachusetts Press.

Miller, J. 1994: *The Passion of Michel Foucault*. London: Flamingo.

Rabinow, P. (ed.) 1997: *Michel Foucault – Ethics; Subjectivity and Truth. The Essential Works of Michel Foucault 1954–1984*, vol. 1. London: Allen Lane, The Penguin Press.

Chapter 12

Jacques Derrida

John Coker

Introduction

Jacques Derrida (1930–) is a leading figure in French poststructuralist philosophy. His prolific writings treat both philosophical and literary works, and they do so in various ways that are often subsumed under the label of "deconstruction." However, "deconstruction" is not a term that designates some essence or methodology of Derrida's philosophy, although it can serve as a provisional label for grouping together the various ways in which philosophical and literary texts are read by Derrida. Some of these "exemplary" readings by Derrida will be discussed in later sections. Though resisting definition, some traits of deconstruction can be noted. Deconstruction contests the attempt on the part of philosophies to set themselves up as the first word (e.g., to lay the foundations, or to determine the first principles [*archai*], or to determine *the* privileged method), or as the end-all and be-all (e.g., to achieve the absolute, or to set the ultimate ends [*teloi*] to be sought), of ontology, epistemology, or methodology. One (though only one) trait of a deconstructive contestation of these various notions is to demonstrate that philosophies seeking to be the first or last word cannot ultimately set and control their own contexts. A deconstructive reading typically operates by showing that the text of the philosophical work is, even if not designed to be or designed not to be, open to being set (even, perhaps, to setting itself) in another context that undercuts its claim to be the first or last word. In self-consistency (i.e., in order not to be yet another avatar of the philosophies it contests), a deconstruction cannot claim to have finally discovered *the* (primordial, proper, ultimate, or absolute) context, no more than it could claim to be the first or last word, whether ontological or methodological, in philosophy. Instead, the context of deconstruction is "limitless," which is also to say interminable and indeterminable (or, "indecidable"); one is left with a *mise en abime* (abyss), or hall of mirrors, of contexts. Derrida has claimed that a trait of "deconstruction would be the effort to take this limitless context into account, to pay the sharpest and broadest attention possible to context, and thus to an incessant movement of recontextualization" (*LI*, p. 136).[1] Since each philosophical text will be open

to recontextualization in its own particular way, deconstruction will operate somewhat differently depending on text and context.

One of Derrida's most memorable remarks is that "there is nothing outside the
text [*il n'y a pas de hors-texte*]" (*OG*, p. 158), which he later claims to "mean nothing
else" than "there is nothing outside context [*il n'existe rien hors contexte*]" (*LI*, p.
136). These remarks may be charitably construed as claiming that neither the outside
nor, by implication, the inside of either text or context are simply given or hold *simpliciter*. If the difference between text and context – their "delimitation" – is not
simply given nor holds *simpliciter*, then text and context are in interplay and are interwoven with each other. Moreover, text and context are in some, even if miniscule,
ways altered or reconstituted, in a way recontextualized, by the readings given and
remarks made about them. For this reason also the various notions that Derrida
deploys in reading various texts in various contexts operate somewhat differently
from each other. This chapter will further illustrate and discuss some of Derrida's
variously deployed notions, especially those that are most philosophically pertinent,
such as "*différance*," "archi-writing," "trace," and "supplement," but it shall begin
with "deconstruction" itself.

The Topics of Deconstruction: An Overview

Derrida's early (1967–72) writings deconstruct the philosophy of presence, which
includes the metaphysics of presence and logocentric philosophy, which will be discussed in turn. The metaphysics of presence comprises a kind of ontology where
being (or truth) has been understood in terms of some *presence*. Grasping such alleged
presences validates grasping what is and is not the truth. For example, Descartes
asserts the fully transparent self-presence of one's own mental states and derives a
privileged epistemic access. Another example is the notion of the given, whether it
is the ontologically *a priori* given of innate ideas, or the empirical given (e.g., sense-
data). Yet other examples are the phenomenological notion of "adequation" as full
"presence in person," and a traditional philosophical notion of "essence" (which
derives, etymologically, from *essentia*, itself derived from the improper Latin *present*
participle *essent-*, being). To deconstruct a philosophy of presence involves demonstrating that its theory is constructed (and its text is composed) out of terms and distinctions which, though taken by the theory as given or fundamental, are themselves
constructs open to interrogation, and which are demonstrably unstable and lack
ultimate grounds. Such ultimate grounds have traditionally been sought in the
metaphysics of presence.

Logocentric philosophy constitutes itself as exemplary of the *logos*, a Greek word
whose meanings include reason, speech, rational discourse, and rational accounts
(e.g., philosophical and scientific theories). Even when not (though often it is) overtly
a metaphysics of presence, logocentric philosophy nonetheless models itself, its
methods, and its standard of rationality on presences, whether these are essences,
paradigms, ideas, or idealizations, or what it takes as its givens. Methodologically if
not ontologically, logocentric philosophy installs categorical distinctions that are

often hierarchic binary oppositions. Especially in earlier writings, Derrida interrogates (in a manner to be discussed below, in the third through fifth sections) the opposition (with the first term privileged) "speech/writing"; but other oppositions are no less important, such as "presence/absence," "identity/difference," "paradigm/instance," "form/matter," and "intelligible/sensible." The privileged term of such distinctions is taken, by philosophers holding the distinction, to be dominant and allocates the proper place or role of the subordinate term. Which distinction is challenged depends on the position being deconstructed; the deconstruction of such distinctions involves a scrupulously close reading of the sort exemplified in Derrida's writings.

"Philosophy of presence," "metaphysics of presence," and "logocentric philosophy" designate essential aspects of the philosophical tradition only insofar as such philosophical positions constitute themselves as having or lay claim to such essentiality. Ultimately, in the wake of deconstruction, such phrases designate assemblages or configurations, for a successful deconstruction of such a philosophical position shows how such a position contains the seeds of its own undoing. The phrase "philosophy of presence" serves to group together positions such as foundationalism, essentialism, rationalism, and representationism. However, the upshot of a deconstruction of such philosophical positions is not an *anti*foundationalism, *anti*essentialism, and so on, for such an "anti-" would reinstall the very sort of *simple* binary opposition or difference that deconstruction is designed to challenge: Derrida himself has remarked that "it has also always been clear and insistent that deconstruction is not an anti-philosophy or a critique of philosophy" (*Points*, p. 73).

Derrida rarely writes at length about traditional rationalists or empiricists, with the notable exceptions of Plato and Kant. Instead, he concentrates on philosophers, such as Hegel, Nietzsche, Husserl, Heidegger, Austin, and Levinas, who sought in various ways to radically challenge previous philosophies. In each of these cases, Derrida disputes unacknowledged residual assumptions of the philosophy of presence in question by emphasizing other, often suppressed, notions that are marked in the very texts of philosophies of presence and that either undercut or intractably complicate those assumptions.

In logocentric philosophies assuming the speech/writing distinction, speech, whether interpersonal or in silent soliloquy, has been understood as the primary medium or milieu of thought. It has been taken to be exemplary of language because of its presumed immediacy – one's thoughts are voiced, one's intended meaning can saturate one's utterances and be simultaneously expressed and presented to oneself and to one's interlocutor in a present determinate context. Writing has traditionally been accorded the role of a mere but necessary instrumental supplement to speech: writing is a step removed from speech and merely represents it, though preserving by recording it. Moreover, writing has potentially deleterious effects; for example, a reliance on written records can degrade living memory. Also, a text can potentially be removed from its "original" thought and context of utterance, set into other contexts, and thereby may signify at variance with intended meaning. Because of such potentially deleterious effects on both the thinking/speaking subject and meaning, philosophies of presence have relegated writing to a subordinate place and role.

Derrida questions the distinction between what is internal and belongs to the thinking/speaking subject and what is external to this subject. According to Derrida, the "immediacy" of speech is a kind of verbal illusion or a mere idealization, sustaining the myth of a full self-presence of meaning. Instead of being a self-signifying unit of meaning or a "transcendental signifier," even verbal meaning is not wholly self-present. Rather, like writing as traditionally conceived, verbal meaning depends on reference to other signifiers, whose meanings in turn are not self-present.

Derrida's works of 1967 – *Of Grammatology*, *Writing and Difference*, and *Speech and Phenomena* – along with later works, challenge the speech/writing distinction and explore the implications of abandoning the idealization of speech. Especially pronounced in these works is the deconstruction of structuralism (in *Of Grammatology* and *Writing and Difference*) and of phenomenology (in *Speech and Phenomena* and *Writing and Difference*). I will proceed in the next three sections by discussing the deconstruction of Saussure's structuralism, Husserl's phenomenology, and Rousseau's philosophy of language, respectively, all of which are to be found in and are exemplary of Derrida's 1967 works. After that, in subsequent sections, I will discuss Derrida's later deconstructions, especially of Heidegger, Hegel, and Plato. Then I will discuss some ways of responding to a deconstruction. After that I will discuss some parallels, though also some important differences, between Derrida and Rorty. I will end by discussing Derrida's deployment of some deconstructive ethical notions.

The Deconstruction of Structuralism

One of the positions that Derrida challenges in his 1967 works, especially in *Of Grammatology* and *Writing and Difference*, is structuralism, whether it be linguistic structuralism (Saussure), anthropological structuralism (Lévi-Strauss), or literary structuralism (Rousset). I will limit my discussion to Derrida's deconstruction of Saussure's structural linguistics. Saussure's formula for the sign is

$$\frac{\text{Signified}}{\text{Signifier}}$$

albeit with this formula enclosed by an ellipse signifying the unity of the sign (later structuralists, such as Lacan and Barthes, will invert this formula and delete the ellipse). The signifier is an audible sound or visible mark, and the signified is a concept, none of which are simply given. Instead, signifiers and correlatively signifieds are both distinguished owing to differentiation: "The concepts are purely differential and defined not by their positive content but negatively by their relations with the other terms of the system" (Saussure, 1966, p. 114). Moreover, the sign is arbitrary in that the signifier "is unmotivated" and "has no natural connection with the signified" (Saussure, 1966, pp. 67, 69). The deconstruction of linguistic structuralism is accomplished by a further radicalization of Saussure's theory of the differential constitution of signifiers and signifieds.

One way to approach Derrida's radicalization is to note that the ellipse enclosing Saussure's formula may misleadingly suggest semantic atomism. "Semantic atomism," as Fodor and Lepore define it, holds that "the meaning of an expression metaphysically depends on some punctate symbol/world [or, signifier/signified] relation, some relation that one thing [e.g., a signifier] could bear to the world [or, to a signified] even if nothing else did" (Fodore and Lepore, 1992, pp. 260–1). However, semantic atomism would be contrary to the thesis that both signifiers and signifieds are differentially constituted. Of course, the unity of the sign could nonetheless be constituted if the differences among signifiers and signifieds were given as totality-unities – for example, in a fixed total system of differences and interdependences. And Saussure does in fact claim such a total system exists, at least at a given time: "Language [*la langue*] is a system whose parts can and must all be considered in their synchronic solidarity" (Saussure, 1966, p. 87).

Derrida proceeds to challenge the notion of language as a fixed system of differences by further elaborating on what Saussure holds to be the relation between verbal and written signs. According to Saussure, a written sign is nothing but a sign of a spoken sign – the signified of, say, the written word "word" is the enunciated word "*word*." The notion that writing is a step removed from meaning, a mere sign of a (spoken) sign, is a hallmark of what Derrida dubs "phonocentrism" – that is, the privileging of the voice – which is a prominent feature of logocentrism. Writing is relegated by Saussure to a position of exteriority, and a merely representative or proxy role, in relation to the inner system of language that is phonic. But, as an example of the sort of passages where Saussure notes but rejects a possibly more important role for writing to play, consider the following: "the spoken word is so intimately bound to its written image that the latter manages to usurp the main role. People attach even more importance to the written image of a vocal sign than to the sign itself" (Saussure, 1966, p. 24). Moreover, according to Saussure, although some may mistakenly believe that writing can serve better than sound to account for the unity of language over time, writing, to the contrary, creates "a purely fictitious unity" (Saussure, 1966, p. 25). Passages such as these betray an attempt on Saussure's part to hold the significance of writing at bay, to keep it from usurping the "proper" role of speech – Saussure ends up offering a sort of axiological prescription (viz., writing is to be relegated to a secondary and subordinate status in relation to speech) in what purports to be a purely scientific theory of language.

Saussure's axiological axiomatics (of a sort that Derrida will later [*LI*, p. 236] call a "hierarchical axiology, [an] ethical–ontological distinction") prevents him from investigating, in a scientifically neutral manner, the very *usurpation* (a form of displacement) of speech by writing that Saussure himself noted and that, as Derrida remarks, "necessarily refers to a profound possibility of essence" (*OG*, p. 40). That is, the usurpation of speech by writing may be an essential possibility in the constitution of speech itself. Moreover, insofar as Saussure privileges speech over writing because the latter is only an *image* or *figure* of, hence is less natural than (spoken, natural) language proper, he betrays his own thesis about the arbitrariness of the sign. That is, if signs are "arbitrary" or "unmotivated," then there is no reason in principle to set up a hierarchy of signs that privilege spoken over written signs – Saussure must be assuming, *contra* the arbitrariness thesis, that the general relation between phonic signifiers and signifieds is not arbitrary but "natural." Hence, Saussure is confronted with the following dilemma. On the one hand, the thesis of the arbitrariness of the sign would seem in principle to preclude Saussure from privileging spoken over written signs (both being no more or less arbitrary than the other). On the other hand, suppose that Saussure were to claim that the general relation between signifiers and signifieds is non-arbitrary and "natural." If so, and if, as Saussure himself acknowledges, writing can usurp (supplement and replace) speech, and if there is no good reason not to view this usurpation as any less natural than the general relation between signifiers and signifieds, then writing is no less natural, no less properly or essentially language, than is speech. Moreover, since writing is no less essentially language than speech, and since writing seems to be at a greater temporal and spatial distance from its meaning and referent than spoken signs, and since written signs, like spoken signs, are constituted differentially, it would follow that it is an essential possibility of language that it be theorized on the model, albeit radicalized, of writing. Were this model to be articulated, language would be theorized as "archi-writing" (originary writing) and the sign as an "archi-trace" (both of which notions must be put under erasure), for then language would be constituted by a system of differentiated signs (traces) that no longer bear any immediate or ultimately fixed relation to their signifieds (whether concepts, senses, or referents). That is, language would be constituted out of *différance* (a neologism signifying both difference and deferral). A language so constituted would not be a closed system of signs but, rather, open to new differentially articulated signifiers, much as speech is open to the supplement of writing.

Stated emblematically, Derrida's deconstruction of Saussure's theory of language not only would remove the ellipse from around the formula (thereby signifying a no longer closed unity or totality of the sign), but it would also put emphasis on the *bar* between "signified" and "signifier." This bar, as an inscription, graphically marks a difference between signified and signifier; even if one verbalizes the bar as "over," it still may be emblematic of a spatial differentiation that is a facet of *différance*. In fact, the removal of the ellipse and the placing of emphasis on the bar is one way to mark the shift from structuralism to poststructuralism (on which topic, see Nancy and Lacoue-Labarthe, 1992); emphasis on the bar would allow for some slippage or play between (though not an utter divorcing of) signifier and signified. More precisely, for Derrida, the present visible graphic bar would not be the mark of some (simply given or *simpliciter*) difference between signifier and signified (and it definitely would not mark a merely external difference between punctate signifying or signified units); instead, the bar would be a *re*mark(ing) of that more "originary" internal relation of differentiation among and between signifiers and signifieds that Derrida dubs *différance*.

The Deconstruction of Phenomenology

Derrida's discussion in *Speech and Phenomena* of Husserl's phenomenology exemplifies the deconstructive criticism of the idealization of speech and meaning and of the philosophy of presence. Deconstructive criticism includes the strategies of (1) challenging the categorical distinctions of philosophies of presence by effecting a reversal in and then ultimately questioning the basis of the distinction, usually by (2) emphasizing what such philosophies suppress. According to Derrida, Husserlian phenomenology, while eschewing metaphysical assumptions, nonetheless remains a logocentric metaphysics of presence. Derrida disputes Husserl's categorical distinction between expressive and indicative signs. According to Husserl, expressive signs alone are meaningful, for they express, and in speech give voice to, meaningful self-present acts of conscious lived experience, which are in turn available to pure reflection and description. By contrast, indicative signs, such as written signs, are only meaningless marks unless ultimately referred back to expressive meaning. Although Husserl admits that expression and indication are *de facto* intertwined in actual communication, he nonetheless retains the distinction *de jure* and buttresses it by alleging that pure expression can occur in silent soliloquy in solitary mental life. Derrida disputes this distinction by arguing, *contra* Husserl, that the entanglement of expression with indication is there from the outset, and that ultimately pure expression remains a mere idealization. For in order not to be merely momentary and evanescent, even verbal or pre-linguistically experiential expressive meanings must, as Husserl's own philosophy requires even for silent soliloquy, be reiterable, identifiable, and recallable over time as having the same meaning, hence must be articulated indicatively (cf., Wittgenstein's "private language argument" in *Philosophical Investigations* [1958]). Even in silent soliloquy, thinking and speaking are like writing and revising on the fly; overlooking this fact creates the verbal illusion of presence. Hence, exemplifying the deconstructive phase of reversal (*POS*, p. 41), this very necessity of reiterability implies that expressive meaning must involve indication from the outset, and Husserl's distinction founders. This claim is further reinforced by Derrida's critique of Husserl's theory of temporality.

Derrida pursues the deconstruction of Husserl's philosophy by deploying the second phase of deconstruction, that of stressing what the philosopher suppresses. According to Husserl's own theory of temporality, the living present moment involves traces of both the retained past present and anticipated future. If so, and since according to Husserl the retained past present is continuous with the recollected past, then the "living" present moment is never purely present, but is constituted with traces of a "dead" past. The ideality of a fully present self-identical expressive meaning, and of a pure reflection on and description of meaningful lived experience, amounts to a mere idealization. The expressive sign and even ideal non-linguistic meaningful experience can no longer maintain a pure self-identity of meaning but, like indicative signs, are invested with meaning by reference to other signifiers from which they are differentiated. That is, indicative signs *supplement* (i.e., mark and make up for a lack in, replace and displace; for more on this notion, see the next section) expressive signs, which in turn supplement ideal meanings, such that "the 'presence' of sense and speech had already from the outset fallen short of itself." Ultimately, "what is supplementary is in reality *differance*, the operation of differing which at one and the same time both fissures and retards presence, submitting it simultaneously to primordial division and delay" (*SP*, pp. 87–8).

Derrida's deconstruction of Husserl is one of his most philosophically cogent, for its "classical philosophical architecture" (*POS*, p. 5) has the force of a philosophical critique involving internal criticism which radically questions Husserlian and other phenomenologies that allege to be able to achieve pure reflection and offer fully adequate descriptions of meaningful lived experience. By his remark that phenomenology is always a phenomenology of perception (*SP*, p. 12) and hence modeled on the presence of the perceptual *eidos* (*OG*, p. 12), Derrida can be read as implying that all phenomenology constitutes a logocentric philosophy of presence. But the relation between deconstruction and phenomenology is far more complicated. First, deconstruction does not dissolve experiential significance into linguistic meaning, but must respect their difference. Second, in writing about Levinas (*WD*, p. 121), Derrida even remarks that "phenomenology is respect itself," for phenomenology is a radically, perhaps uniquely, open philosophy that does not foreclose anything, but exists within open and indefinite horizons, and it in principle commands nothing and is foreign to hierarchies. For this reason, phenomenology is open even to what contests its own precarious dependency on presence. Deconstruction is not designed to destroy or reduce to silence phenomenology or any other philosophical position: "It remains, then, for us to *speak*, to make our voices *resonate* throughout the corridors in order to make up for [*suppléer*] the break up of presence" (*SP*, p. 104). Instead, deconstruction contests the closure of such philosophies – the claim to be the be-all and end-all or the last word in epistemology, ontology, methodology, or rationality – by interrogating the terms and distinctions by which such closure is sought.

Supplementarity in the Deconstruction of Rousseau

The notion of the *supplement*, already noted in the deconstruction of Husserl in the previous section, receives one of its most pervasive deployments in Derrida's deconstructive reading of Rousseau in Part II of *Of Grammatology*. (*Of Grammatolology* is a work whose two parts are, as it were, basted together, and in between which, as Derrida points out (*POS*, p. 4), one could staple *Writing and Difference*.) The words "supplement" ("*supplément*") and its cognates such as "supply" (*suppléer*) are notably marked in the texts of Rousseau, especially the *Essay on the Origin of Languages*, of which Derrida offers a close reading. Rousseau articulates a genetic constitutional theory of language, according to which the first and most natural language is that of gesture, which is in turn supplemented by speech, and which is in turn supplemented by writing. The languages of gesture and speech are equally natural, though the former depends less on convention; living speech gives voice to the desire of immediacy of presence. By contrast, at least *prima facie*, the artifice of writing supplements – marks and makes up for a lack in, but also serves to replace – living speech (*OG*, p. 144). Hence, binary oppositions, with the first term valorized, get installed in Rousseau's text on its own terms: speech/writing, presence/absence, natural/artificial, and living/dead. But, remarks Derrida, Rousseau alleges that accents in language get "replaced [*supplée*] by . . . new articulations" (*OG*, p. 244; cf., 241), so that already marked within speech itself are supplements. Moreover, even the putatively "natural" language of gesture is doubly marked by supplementarity, for gesture is both supplemented by speech (e.g., when distance makes gestural communication impossible) and yet remains a "natural" supplement to speech. The unacknowledged yet notable pervasiveness of supplementarity in the texts of Rousseau warrants the claim that supplementarity "precedes the opposition of nature and culture: the supplement can equally well be natural (gesture) as artificial (speech)" (*OG*, p. 235) – and, one may add, it can be as natural/artificial as writing. Ultimately, however, the "writing" that is the supplement of speech would be anterior to both speech and writing in their ordinary senses: it would be an "arche-writing, movement of differance" that constitutes, in the heart of speech, its "trace, its reserve, its interior and exterior differance: as its supplement," and it constitutes an "economy of differance or supplementarity" (*OG*, pp. 60, 315).

Although marked, and remarked by Derrida, in the texts of Rousseau, no particular privilege need be accorded the term "supplement," as if it were the key to deconstruction. After all, there are kindred terms, less often discussed and deployed in texts by and about Derrida, that also work according to what is sometimes called a "logic of supplementarity." One of those notions, deployed in Derrida's close reading of Philippe Soller's book *Numbers* in the essay "Dissemination" in *Dissemination*, is that of a *graft*. Derrida remarks that "to write means to graft. It's the same word" (*DS*, p. 355): this claim is underwritten by the etymology of the word "graft," which ultimately derives from Greek *graphion*, a variation of *grapheion*, stylus, itself from Greek *graphein*, to write (*DS*, p. 202). Since the notion of a "graft" is deployed in reading a "merely" literary text, and since Derrida has not offered an extended deployment of that notion, it has not received as much comment as has the notion of a supplement (but see Culler, 1982, pp. 134–56); it could perhaps be provisionally deployed as a way of thinking about how supplementarity works. A botanical or biological (e.g., skin) graft is both unnatural (a matter of artifice) yet also quite natural – it challenges the distinction natural/artificial. In a philosophy of presence such as Rousseau's, one may remark how natural living language, as speech, requires supplementation by the unnatural yet natural engrafting into itself of writing. Or, to change to a related notion sometimes deployed by Derrida, writing is the necessary prosthesis of speech. The notions of "supplement," "graft," and "prosthesis" operate in very similar ways, yet differ according to text and context. (For some passages remarking on the "graft" and "prosthesis," see, e.g., *Glas*, pp. 34b, 168b.) Moreover, no one of these notions, not even all of them, can serve as the key to Derrida's philosophy; even they are bound up together with other deconstructive notions.

The Deconstruction of Heidegger

Derrida's deconstructive readings of Heidegger may be viewed as advancing some of Heidegger's own ways of radically questioning and of searching for an alternative to the metaphysics of presence. Derrida's close readings of Heidegger, which bring him into a close proximity to Heidegger's thought, develop some motifs in Heidegger's work (e.g., the challenge to the metaphysics of presence, the trace, difference) that also serve to contest other motifs (e.g., residual assumptions of the metaphysics of

presence, such as an originary presencing [*Anwesenheit*], or the "properness" of
the "event of appropriation" [*Ereignis*]). For Heidegger, the history of metaphysics
has been a metaphysics of presence that has an "ontotheological constitution."
Heidegger, who seeks to reinitiate an interrogation of the "meaning of Being," discusses the difference (sometimes called the ontico-ontological difference) between
beings (things that *are*, in present presence, or that have been or will be, but are
nonetheless modeled on present presence) and "Being," which has in the mainstream
of the Western traditional also been modeled on present presence (e.g., "Being" as
eternal, occupying a timeless present, or "Being" as nothing more than a highest
genus of beings, etc.). As Derrida remarks, Heidegger's texts open themselves, in,
even if not by, design, to two readings: on one reading ". . . the displacements [of
the metaphysics of presence in Heidegger's texts] would remain within the metaphysics of presence in general," especially insofar as Heidegger seeks to think of Being
in terms of an originary presencing (*Anwesenheit*); the other reading is that given by
Derrida (*MP*, p. 65).

Derrida cites passages from Heidegger's essay, "The Anaximander Fragment," that
on the one hand claim that even the early *trace* of the difference between Being and
beings gets obliterated when presence is conceived in terms of being present, and
that on the other hand claim that some vestige of the trace of the difference between
Being and beings remains preserved (*MP*, pp. 23–5). Advancing Heidegger's own
project of taking a step back out of the metaphysics of presence and ontotheology,
Derrida remarks that the *trace* of (the ontico-ontological) difference must not be
simply present or absent (*MP*, p. 24). The "trace," since it does not designate some
present-presence (even one that has been or will be), designates no metaphysical
concept proper, yet it will have been inscribed within metaphysics as an erasure of
itself, and in relation to which the metaphysics of presence itself will have been the
trace of the erasure of the trace (*MP*, p. 65). The "trace," then, is a mark of a context
that exceeds and recontextualizes the conceptualizations of the metaphysics of presence: the trace never appears, never becomes a presence, as such, yet it remains
marked in the text of metaphysics (*MP*, p. 66). This trace "is" the trace of "*différance*": "Beyond Being and beings, this difference, ceaselessly differing from and
deferring (itself), would trace (itself) (by itself) – this *différance* would be the first or
last trace if one still could speak, here, of origin and end" (*MP*, p. 67). Ultimately,
"trace" and "*différance*" are not names for some being, or for Being, and they mark,
but do not name, the ontico-ontological difference; instead, they re-mark, within the
text of metaphysics, that which "unceasingly dislocates itself in a chain of differing
and deferring substitutions" (*MP*, p. 26).

Derrida's readings of Heidegger exemplify how a deconstructive reading develops
motifs already marked in the texts of the philosophy (or literature) being read.
Whether that further deconstructive development is taken to be a criticism, and if so
whether it is destructive or constructive criticism, or is instead a welcome supplement, is left open for the reader and respondent. Note, finally, that although "trace"
and "*différance*" are pertinent notions by which to address Heidegger's philosophy,
they are not limited to a Heideggerian context: they are also deployed by Derrida in
reading various other texts, such as those of Freud and Husserl.

Deconstructive Remarks about Hegel

In contrast with his readings of Saussure, Husserl, Rousseau, and Heidegger, wherein Derrida's deconstructive remarks are made about notions that operate centrally within the texts of those thinkers, his approach to Hegel has tended to be oblique. That is to say, although in one respect his readings address themselves to the central Hegelian notion of *Aufhebung* (in Derrida's French, *la relève*; i.e., sublation), they do so by reading passages in Hegel that, arguably, are not at the heart of Hegel's philosophy. Derrida has made remarks that seem at first glance to imply that deconstruction is anti-Hegelian – "If there were a definition of *différance*, it would be precisely the limit, the interruption, the destruction of the Hegelian *relève* [viz., *Aufhebung*, sublation] *wherever* it operates." Nonetheless, this rather bold-sounding remark gets qualified, for it is directed against only the *Aufhebung* as interpreted, in a traditional "Hegelian" manner, in terms of totalizing dialectical speculation (*POS*, pp. 40–1).

One of Derrida's readings of Hegel – "From restricted to general economy" in *Writing and Difference* – approaches his philosophy obliquely through a deconstructive reading of Bataille's reading of Hegel. Later, in "The pit and the pyramid" in *Margins of Philosophy*, Derrida offers deconstructive remarks about Hegel's "semiology" that serve to demonstrate the intractable complications that result from Hegel's privileging of speech and phonetic writing; since this topic is not at the forefront in Hegel's philosophy, Derrida's tack here also may be considered oblique. Later still, in *Glas*, Derrida offers a reading of Hegel while, and in the context of, reading Genet – *Glas* is set up in two columns (often with additional inserts) on each page, the left column devoted to Hegel and the right to Genet. Derrida's tack into Hegel's philosophy is to address the topic of the family, both human and Holy, but the deconstruction of Hegel's philosophy is not primarily effected thematically in the Hegel column but, rather, in the inaudible but remarkable repercussions between the two columns. Since, of all of Derrida's writings, *Glas* is the furthest removed from having a "classical philosophical architecture," and since the challenges it presents to a more or less traditional philosophical reader are very great, it is difficult to determine exactly what its explicit and implicit deconstructive remarks are and whether they are pertinent and successful.

Perhaps exemplary of Derrida's deconstructive remarks about Hegel's totalizing dialectical speculation, including their obliqueness, is to be found in " Outwork" in *Dissemination*. Derrida notes that Hegel himself, in the Preface to *The Phenomenology of Spirit*, warns the reader about the problematic, ultimately extraneous, status of a preface in a philosophical work. (This warning about prefaces in a preface risks generating a paradox in its own right, regardless of deconstruction.) But despite the extraneousness of prefaces, Hegel writes them and includes them as part of his works. Hence, Hegel's prefaces are in one (very literal) sense part of the text, yet they are, on Hegel's own terms, not part of the text proper that does the work of philosophy. Hegel's prefaces are, as it were, grafted into and supplement Hegel's philosophical texts proper, and as such are not readily subsumed by the triadic model of totalizing

dialectical speculation; instead, Hegel's prefaces, as "outworks," serve to complicate dialectical reflection with an unsublatable fourth term, one both inside and
outside the dialectic (*DS*, p. 25). Ultimately, Derrida's deconstructive remarks about
Hegel seem not to have the force of a standard criticism or critique, but instead
serve to introduce intractable complications for totalizing dialectical speculation.
Derrida himself has remarked that deconstructive notions such as "*différance*" are
not simply *anti*dialectical, and may even be viewed as the attempt to dialecticize the
non-dialecticizable (*TS*, pp. 33–4).

The Deconstruction of Khōra

As a final example of deconstructive reading, consider Derrida's reading of Plato's
Timaeus in "*Khōra*" from *On the Name*. This reading continues the deconstructive
interrogation of the distinction, with first term valorized, of "*logos/mythos*" (a distinction that had already been challenged, in conjunction with the speech/writing
distinction, in the texts of Lévi-Strauss in *Of Grammatology*, and of Plato in "Plato's
Pharmacy" in *Dissemination*). One of the pivotal points in Derrida's reading of Plato
is in the remarkable notion of and role played by "*khōra*." *Khōra* is a milieu between
the intelligible eternal Forms and the sensible world of becoming; it is a receptacle
in which imprints of the eternal Forms are received and in which sensible likenesses
of the Forms are engendered. Neither intelligible nor sensory, neither eternal nor
transitory, neither being nor becoming, *khōra* is a third genus; even Plato's discussion of *khōra* would involve a bastard reasoning (*logismō tini nothō*) – it would not
determinately be a discourse of *logos* rather than *mythos* (*ON*, pp. 89–90). "*Khōra*"
is neither a proper name nor (merely) a figure of speech; it may, however, allow the
engendering of names of it that are neither determinately literal or metaphorical,
rational or mythical, such as "mother," "nurse," "receptacle," and "imprint-bearer"
(*ON*, pp. 92–3). Plato's philosophical reflections are so open and far-reaching that
they are driven to that bastard reasoning about the *khōra* that does not fit neatly into
his philosophical categories. Such, Derrida suggests, would be the result of any open,
aporetic, and investigative philosophy.

   Although Derrida's deconstructive remarks about *khōra* are bound to the text of
Plato's *Timaeus*, he holds it as exemplary for philosophy in general. While much
further argument would be needed to support this stronger claim, perhaps some provisional support can be given to it. Plato's *khōra* plays a role in the *Timaeus* not
unlike that of the imagination in Kant's philosophy – it is a third term that mediates
between the intelligible and the sensible. One way to view what Derrida is doing is
to see him performing a deconstruction of an occurrence of what Davidson has criticized as "the dualism of scheme and content." This way of viewing it would be apt,
for an exemplary case of the dualism of scheme and content is that of Kant, for whom
the concepts of the understanding provide the conceptual scheme, the intuitions of
sensibility the sensory content, and the mediating third is the schematism of the
imagination. Although he has made some pertinent remarks – in, for example, *The
Truth in Painting* – Derrida has not offered us a fully developed deconstruction of

Kant's scheme/content dualism. (Were Derrida to offer such a reading, taking as its topic the schematism and imagination in Kant, it would not be unheard of for him to approach Kant indirectly, say, via a reading of Heidegger's *Kant and the Problem of Metaphysics*. Such a deconstructive reading would be a way to pay respect to both Heidegger and Kant.) Derrida gestures toward such a reading of Kant when he claims that while he accords no special privilege to the schematism as an example of the sort of third, mixed, intermediary terms that serve to deconstruct binary and hierarchizing oppositions (note that "*khōra*," in another text and context, has served as such a third term), it is nonetheless the case that the imagination tends to operate in the history of philosophy as such an intervening third term (*TS*, p. 75; see also pp. 99–101).

In a further clarification, when asked whether the "schematism" is language, Derrida disavows being part of the linguistic turn (the notion that the problems of philosophy are little else than problems of language). The notion of the trace or the "mark" is not merely intra-linguistic; rather, it is also pre-linguistic or what opens language up to its other (*TS*, pp. 75–6). Nonetheless, noting how a deconstruction of the scheme/content duality by Derrida might be effected, and noting that one possible effect may be to open up a more important role for the imagination in philosophy, then, perhaps, a more creative response to deconstruction may be limned (however provisionally). Derrida has remarked that "*différance* finds itself enmeshed in the work that pulls it through a chain of other 'concepts,' other 'words,' other textual configurations" (*POS*, p. 40). Deconstruction may open up the possibility of new (unheard of or unforeseen) *configurations*, where "configuration" can be understood to be a Latinate rendering of Greek "*schēmatismos*."

Responding to Deconstructions

The reader, having been offered these various examples of deconstruction, may wonder about how to respond, reflectively, thoughtfully, and critically, to a deconstructive reading. One response may be to ask how exemplary is both the text being read and the philosophy articulated therein *as* philosophy. Is that text or philosophy truly exemplary of, for example, the tradition, or even of a philosophy of presence? One might allege that Derrida's deconstructive reading of Rousseau, insofar as it is taken to be a sort of critique, holds good only for the specificities of Rousseau's text: such a response is analogous to limiting a case to its facts in law. Such a response would not be precluded by Derrida, given some implications of his remarks about exemplarity. For the example, to the contrary of being a mere instance of a universal, or a mere token of a type (e.g., deconstruction), each reading by Derrida would be singular (one may say, each reading is "signature Derrida"). Yet, insofar as his readings reiterate the texts being read, they also operate with some degree of generality owing not least to their reiteration of the generality of claims made in the texts being read. In general, one may ask how exemplary is some reading by Derrida to be taken; one's answer may range from the claim that the deconstructive reading is utterly singular and bound to the text being read to the claim that the text is so emblematic of a philosophical tradition that the deconstructive reading has a very general significance. Even when Derrida seems to write (as in the essay *"Différance"* in *Margins of Philosophy*) or speak (in interviews such as *Positions*) at a very high level of generality, nonetheless his remarks – for example, about *différance* – are underwritten by some reading that he has already given, or by a "program of reading" that sketches a possible reading that could be performed.

A typical adversarial response to Derrida, which is by no means precluded, is to challenge his readings by demonstrating, or at least alleging, that he has misinterpreted, misrepresented, misunderstood, misread, and so on the text being read or the philosophy being discussed. This is the sort of response given by Searle to Derrida's remarks about Austin in "Signature, Event, Context" (in *Margins of Philosophy*). The cogency of such responses depends in part on whether they also engage in a meticulously close reading not only of the text or philosophy under discussion but also of Derrida's reading thereof. Instead of assessing the respective merits of these adversarial responses, I will simply remark that some of the adversarial, sometimes polemical, responses to Derrida have been rather heavy-handed. Perhaps this is because such adversaries believe that Derrida or his philosophical *cum* textual practice either in fact or in principle, or perhaps owing to some putative lack of principle, so violate interpretative or philosophical standards that his philosophy or texts do not deserve to be handled with even minimal care or charity in interpretation. In contrast with some such adversaries, Derrida shows respect for what he styles "protocols of reading" and, at their best, his readings display an admirable meticulousness in the construal of texts.

A different sort of response, challenging though non-adversarial, is to show, by meticulously close reading, that Derrida himself has overlooked or failed to remark on some notions or motifs in a text that he has read that actually make that text far more self-deconstructive, hence less "logocentric" or the like, than Derrida makes it out to be. This is the response both of De Man to Derrida's reading of Rousseau (in *Allegories of Reading*) and Barbara Johnson to Derrida's reading of Lacan's reading of Poe's *The Purloined Letter* (in *The Critical Difference*). This sort of response can be taken to *supplement* (viz., compensate for a lack in, replace) Derrida's reading to some extent. Derrida's own readings, and his philosophy, might even be taken to invite such supplemental readings.

A final mode of response, one that Derrida's works seem to invite by offering a challenge, would be to concede, for the sake of argument, Derrida's various readings of and remarks about phenomenology, Hegel, or structuralism, and then to design either some type of phenomenological hyper-reflection, or some type of hyper-dialectic, or some type of super-structuralism that takes Derrida's readings and remarks into account by incorporating or superceding them. To my knowledge, no work of philosophy has yet been written that even seriously attempts such a response, and perhaps the task of making such a response would be Herculean. Nonetheless, such a response is not necessarily precluded by Derrida, who alleges, for example, that his deconstructive notions such as *différance*, though challenging the Hegelian notion of *Aufhebung* (sublation) as interpreted in terms of absolute totalizing dialectical speculation, nonetheless also have a close "proximity" to *Aufhebung*; indeed, they can even serve to demonstrate that Hegel's philosophy is not *simply* logocentric, and that one cannot *simply* refute or have done with it (*POS*, pp. 40–2, 77–8). It is worth noting that phenomenology and Hegelian dialectic may have been especially open (one may say, vulnerable) to deconstruction, since they are scrupulously reflective philosophies that try not to leave pertinent matters out of account.

Moreover, although Derrida's works, in their own distinctive way, can be situated in the line of critiques of traditional Western metaphysics that can be seen as beginning with Kant and developed by Nietzsche and Heidegger, they nonetheless cannot, as deconstructions, rigorously imply that logocentric philosophy, the metaphysics of presence, or the like are simply *bad* or ought to be eliminated. For although deconstruction may involve a moment of reversal, where what has traditionally been valorized (e.g., speech, presence, life et al.) is overturned by what has traditionally been suppressed or marginalized (e.g., writing, absence, death et al.), the ultimate point of a deconstruction is to make the opposition, and with it the valorization, founder. For this reason, even logocentric philosophy or the metaphysics of presence would not merit *simple* condemnation. Perhaps, however, somewhat like Heidegger's notions of authenticity and inauthenticity in *Being and Time*, which are avowedly put forward as non-evaluative notions but nonetheless forcibly strike the reader as evaluative, "logocentrism," "the metaphysics of presence," and so on, and their alternatives such as "deconstruction," which are not put forward by Derrida as simply bad or good, or for that matter as simply neutral, can strike the unwitting reader as being respectively condemned or valorized.

Radical Meaning Holism: Rorty and Derrida

Derrida's ultimate alternative to the philosophy of presence can be compared to Rorty's anti-essentialist semantic holism. Rorty maintains that the milieu of meaning, and the model of the mind, is that of a continually rewoven web of sentential attitudes (e.g., I believe (or desire) that *p*). This web is not secured at any fixed points; even the sentential attitudes in it are contextually individuated. But context itself is not given and determinate – instead "it is contexts all the way down," inducing a "hall of mirrors" effect wherein it is always possible to redescribe by recontextualizing a term of a relation by dissolving it into relations among other things, or vice versa (Rorty, 1991, p. 100), In this "hall of mirrors," a *mise en abîme* of contexts, sentences can be dissolved into patterns of words, but words have meaning only in the context of a sentence; the putatively real can be redescribed in terms of images, and vice versa, such that the distinction between the "real" and the "image" founders (Rorty, 1991, p. 100). Instead of a web of sentential attitudes, Derrida's semantic system is that of a web of traces. The notion of a "trace" is that of a signifier whose meaning is never present as such but, instead, depends on its being interwoven with other signifiers in a web of differentiated and changing relations. Since neither this web nor meaning is ever complete or fully present, and since neither intention nor context nor any semantic atom ultimately fixes meaning, the result is a theoretical indeterminacy, a hall of mirrors or *mise en abîme*, of meaning and context, allowing for interminable recontextualization. Deconstruction can even be defined (*LI*,

p. 136) as "the effort to take this limitless context into account" by attending to "an incessant movement of recontextualization," such that "there is nothing outside context." For example (*see* "White mythology" in *Margins of Philosophy*), putatively literal terms can be recontextualized and redescribed as metaphorical, and vice versa, thereby calling into question the privilege traditionally accorded to the literal over the metaphorical; likewise, the distinction between text and context is itself open to recontextualization. In claiming both that sentential attitudes are contextually individuated and that context is not ultimately determinate but instead a hall of mirrors, Rorty lends credence to the argument (see Fodore and Lepore, 1992) that once semantic atomism is abandoned in favor of a semantic holism – one eschewing the "dogmas" of the analytic/synthetic and scheme/content distinctions along with reductionism – such holistic theories fail to account for identity of or to offer a sufficiently robust notion of sameness of "intentional content" in sentential attitudes. Rephrased in a more Derridean manner: in lieu of a "transcendental signifier," functioning as a semantic atom, the "identity/difference" distinction and its ultimate basis are rendered problematic.

Although Rorty's semantic holism, like deconstruction, can serve to challenge representationalism and essentialism, its canon of rationality involves maintaining optimal order, regularity, and equilibrium in the web: depending on how constricting the web is in terms of what it marginalizes and excludes, it may constitute a new guise of logocentrism with a normative ideal of rationality. In contrast, deconstruction seeks to splice into the web threads that disturb the equilibrium and cannot readily be fixed in place: the point is to open it to alternative possibilities, perhaps alternative configurations, that might otherwise be precluded, not to merely unravel or to destroy the web.

Although in some respects Derrida and Rorty are comparable, they also radically differ from each other in at least one important, and surprising, respect. Whereas Rorty advocates an utterly deflated notion of "truth" and a pronounced *anti*metaphysical, *anti*essentialist stance (in this regard he is a faithful heir of both the positivists and ordinary language philosophers), Derrida states the following: "Truth is not a value that one can renounce. The deconstruction of philosophy does not renounce truth – any more, for that matter, than literature does. It is a question of thinking this other relation to truth" (*TS*, p. 10). While the Hegelian notion of "truth" as "the whole," or the Heideggerian notion of "truth" as *alētheia*, or the notion of truth as adequation may, along with the metaphysical assumptions they are interwoven with, be open to deconstruction, the conclusion to be drawn is not necessarily to stop philosophical interrogation and reflection on truth and being. That is, one *may* (it is not precluded), but one *need not*, take deconstruction to amount to a *reductio ad absurdum* of grand philosophical notions such as "truth," "being," and so on. This is one reason why Derrida disavows the notion that he is articulating or limning some "post-philosophy" (*TS*, p. 10). Insofar as deconstruction involves contesting philosophies that lay claim or aspire to be the final word in ontology, epistemology, or methodology, and insofar as it contests simple oppositions, it would also in principle contest various philosophical attempts to *simply* put an end to metaphysics and the discourse thereof. Deconstruction allows for the possibility that metaphysics can *survive* deconstruction and live on: such "survival," a "*sur-vie,* of living on in a life-after-life or a life-after-death" ("Living on," p. 91), would incorporate an unsublatable moment of death. Although metaphysics may die endless deaths, the flip side of this coin is that it may live endless lives, may have many avatars, and may have a future. Deconstruction does not preclude these possibilities.

Deconstruction and Questions of Ethics: Hospitality, Justice, and Friendship

In later writings, Derrida offers reflections on hospitality (*Of Hospitality*), on justice and law ("Force of law"), on friendship (*Politics of Friendship*), on the gift (*Given Time* and *The Gift of Death*), and on democracy (*The Other Heading*). These reflections delineate an ethical and political alternative to the normativeness of rationality and give an ethical point to deconstruction. All of these ethical notions are limit-case ideals that are alternatives to Kant's regulative ethical ideals and are set in an uneasy relation with their ordinary and traditional philosophical counterparts. The ensuing discussion of these ethical notions will focus on the notions of hospitality and justice, although some remarks about friendship will be made at the end.

Unconditional hospitality ideally involves welcoming, making a hospitable place for and genuinely sharing with others; however, unlike in ordinary hospitality, in relation to which it is both the point but likewise an impossible ideal, no one would any longer be master of the house who sets house rules. Although unconditional hospitality is unrealizable, not only like a Kantian regulatory idea but also for structural reasons, it nonetheless puts a demand of responsibility on us. Although the laws of conditional hospitality, which operates in specific conditions and involves specific notions such as rights, duties, and so on, are heterogeneous with the law of unconditional hospitality, the two notions and their respective laws are indissociable – each invokes and prescribes the other (*OH*, p. 147). Derrida remarks that, to the contrary of stymieing the desire to be hospitable and of destroying the requirements of hospitality, the heterogeneous laws of unconditional and conditional hospitality would be brought to bear on each other by "intermediate *schemas*" of hospitality, thereby allowing, in responsibility and responsiveness, each to be responsive to the other (*OH*, p. 147). (Although "schemas" and "schematizing" are Kantian notions, Derrida's application is decidedly non-Kantian, since Kant excludes schema(tizing) in the case of ethical concepts or ideals.) Derrida goes so far as even to remark that "the problem of hospitality" is "coextensive with the ethical problem" (*OH*, p. 149). Since hospitality concerns the relation to the "other" (i.e., the foreigner, the stranger, the heterogeneous, etc.), and since it involves the schematizing of the heterogeneous laws of unconditional and conditional hospitality, "hospitality" already operates as a deconstructive ethical notion.

What holds for "hospitality" also holds, *mutatis mutandis*, for "justice." In "Force of law" Derrida distinguishes between justice, by which is meant unconditional justice, and the (positive) law with its specific prescriptions, proscriptions, and enforcement. The relation between justice and (positive) law is not unlike that between unconditional and conditional hospitality: both put demands on us, despite their heterogeneity, and what is necessary is to figure out how to *schematize* them together in particular cases. Derrida puts the matter as follows: ". . . deconstruction takes place in the interval that separates the undeconstructibility of justice from the deconstructibility of *droit* (authority, legitimacy, and so on)" ("Force of law," p. 945). Derrida's legal theory is, in relation to an American context, rather singular. For on the one hand, like American Legal Realism and some Critical Legal Studies, it challenges mechanical jurisprudence – if the rules were to determine the outcome of a case, so that "the judge is a calculating machine," then such a judge has abrogated justice and responsibility – and emphasizes an undecidability (cf., "indeterminacy") of law ("Force of law," pp. 961–3). On the other hand, this very undecidability is what opens law up to the "infinite 'idea of justice'"; the invocation of justice is a hallmark of natural law theory. However, unlike in traditional natural law theory, Derrida emphasizes both the indissociability and the radical heterogeneity of justice and the positive law. "Justice," for Derrida, is "incalculable" yet also must be taken into account in judicial decisions that (though Derrida does not put it this way) provide a schematization of justice in relation to the letter and application of the positive law. (By the way, in light of the ethical notions of hospitality and justice, to interrogate whether a philosophy is logocentric might also involve asking how hospitable and just it is to (its) others.)

Politics of Friendship is a very rich and dense, albeit highly readable, work. It involves a close reading and discussion of canonical writings on friendship by, amongst others, Aristotle, Cicero, Montaigne, Kant, and Nietzsche, along with a deconstructive reading of Schmitt's *The Concept of the Political*. (Derrida offers here what is arguably his most extensive and meticulous reading of Nietzsche in remarking on numerous passages about friendship in Nietzsche's writings.) I will end by hazarding a few remarks that, although they cannot but fail to do justice to this work, at least might give the reader some idea of the issues and discussions in it. Friendship operates in a torsion of asymmetry between the singularity of friendship (perhaps best expressed by Montaigne, who wrote "If you press me to say why I loved him, I feel that it can only be expressed by replying: 'Because it was him: because it was me'") and the purported universality of friendship, whether ethical (in ideas or ideals of "perfect friendship" or "true friendship," involving obligations) or political (in ideas or ideals of "political friendship" or in the closely related notion of "fraternity"). Friendship, however, is neither purely singular nor purely universal, nor is it simply the opposition between them, but instead friendship is articulated in the *schema* between singular and universal (*PF*, pp. 276–7). The pivotal role played by the schema serves to explain why Derrida challenges the fraternal schema ("brotherhood" and "fraternity") and the masculinist schema (i.e., the ignoring or marginalizing of friendships between women and women and between men and women; *PF*, pp. 277–8). The deconstruction of the notion of friendship serves not to refute the idea or ideal of friendship, but instead to open up possibilities of rethinking and reconfiguring friendship.

Note

1   See under Selected bibliography below for the key to text citations.

Selected bibliography

Derrida's writings

1967: *Of Grammatology*, trans. G. Spivak. Baltimore, Md.: The Johns Hopkins University Press, 1976. (References to this book are abbreviated in the text to "*OG*, p. ••.")

1967: *Speech and Phenomena*, trans. D. Allison. Evanston, Ill.: Northwestern University Press, 1973. (References to this book are abbreviated in the text to "*SP*, p. ••.")

1967: *Writing and Difference*, trans. A. Bass. London: Routledge, 1978. (References to this book are abbreviated in the text to "*WD*, p. ••.")

1972: *Dissemination*, trans. B. Johnson. Chicago, Ill.: University of Chicago Press, 1981. (References to this book are abbreviated in the text to "*DS*, p. ••.")

1972: *Margins of Philosophy*, trans. A. Bass Brighton. Chicago, Ill.: University of Chicago Press, 1982. (References to this book are abbreviated in the text to "*MP*, p. ••.")

1972: *Positions*, trans. A. Bass. Chicago, Ill.: University of Chicago Press, 1981. (References to this book are abbreviated in the text to "*POS*, p. ••.")

1974: *Glas*, trans. J. Leavey and R. Rand. Lincoln, Neb.: University of Nebraska Press, 1986.

1977: *Limited Inc.*, trans. S. Weber and J. Mehlman, ed. G. Graff. Evanston, Ill.: Northwestern University Press, 1988. (References to this book are abbreviated in the text to "*LI*, p. ••.")

1979: Living on (trans. J. Hulbert). In H. Bloom et al., *Deconstruction and Criticism*. New York: The Seabury Press.

1990: Force of law: the "mystical foundations of authority" (trans. M. Quaintance). In *Deconstruction and the Possibility of Justice. Cardozo Law Review*, 11(5–6).

1991: *Given Time. 1. Counterfeit Money*, trans. P. Kamuf. Chicago, Ill.: University of Chicago Press, 1992.

1991: *The Other Heading*, trans. P. Brault and M. Naas. Bloomington and Indianapolis, Ind.: Indiana University Press, 1992.

1992: *Points*, trans. P. Kamuf et al., ed. E. Weber. Stanford, Calif.: Stanford University Press, 1995.

1992: *The Gift of Death*, trans. D. Willis. Chicago, Ill.: University of Chicago Press, 1995.

1993: *On the Name*, ed. T. Dutoit, trans. D. Wood, J. Leavey, and I. McLeod. Stanford, Calif.: Stanford University Press, 1995. (References to this book are abbreviated in the text to "*ON*, p. ••.")

1994: *Politics of Friendship*, trans. G. Collins. New York: Verso, 1997. (References to this book are abbreviated in the text to "*PF*, p. ••.")

1997: *A Taste for the Secret*, trans. G. Donis, ed. G. Donis and D. Webb. Cambridge: Polity Press, 2001. (References to this book are abbreviated in the text to "*TS*, p. ••.")

1997: *Of Hospitality*, trans. R. Bowlby. Stanford, Calif.: Stanford University Press, 1997. (References to this book are abbreviated in the text to "*OH*, p. ••.")

References and further reading

Culler, J. 1982: *On Deconstruction: Theory and Criticism after Structuralism*. Ithaca, NY: Cornell University Press (London and Melbourne: Routledge & Kegan Paul, 1983).

Fodor, J. and Lepore, E. 1992: *Holism: A Shopper's Guide*. Oxford: Blackwell.

Kamuf, P. (ed.) 1991: *A Derrida Reader: Between the Blinds*. New York: Columbia University Press (includes an extensive bibliography).

Nancy, J.-L. and Lacoue-Labarthe, P. 1992: *The Title of the Letter*, trans. F. Raffoul and D. Pettigrew. Albany, NY: State University of New York Press.

Rorty, R. 1991: *Objectivity, Relativism, Truth*. Cambridge: Cambridge University Press.

Saussure, F. 1966: *Course in General Linguistics*, trans. W. Baskin. New York: McGraw-Hill.

Schmitt, C. 1996: *The Concept of the Political*, trans. G. Schwab. Chicago, Ill.: University of Chicago Press.

Wittgenstein, L. 1958: *Philosophical Investigations*, 3rd edn., trans. G. E. M. Anscombe. Oxford: Blackwell.

Chapter 13

Postmodernism

Steven Best and Douglas Kellner

In the realm of philosophy and other theoretical discourses, there are many different paths to the turn from the modern to the postmodern, representing a complex genealogy of diverse and often divergent trails through different disciplines and cultural terrains. One pathway moves through an irrationalist tradition from romanticism to existentialism to French postmodernism via the figures of Nietzsche, Heidegger, and Bataille into the proliferation of French postmodern theory. This is the route charted by Jürgen Habermas in *The Philosophical Discourse of Modernity* (1987), a trajectory that ultimately leads for him to the dead end of irrationalism and the catastrophe of fascism.

More positive narratives of the genealogy of the postmodern turn in theory include Richard Kearney's journey through the progression of premodern, modern, and postmodern modes of thought to the triumph of a new postmodern imagination and vision (1988). Also deeply rooted in aesthetic theory, Ihab Hassan (1987) describes the outlines of a postmodern culture of "unmaking" that emerges out of modernism, pragmatism, and changes in modern science that, at its best, will help advance William James' vision of an "unfinished pluralistic universe." John McGowan (1991) in turn tells the story of the emergence of poststructuralist, neo-Marxist, and neo-pragmatist postmodern theories arising out of the tradition of Kant, Hegel, Marx, and Nietzsche, building on but overcoming the limitations of their predecessors. Many accounts of the postmodern turn privilege Nietzsche and Heidegger as key progenitors of the postmodern turn who generate innovative and critical modes of thought, novel forms of writing, and emancipatory values (Vattimo, 1988; Kolb, 1990), providing a positive spin on the postmodern turn in philosophy.

We show in this study how assessments of the basic assumptions of modern philosophy by Kierkegaard, Nietzsche, and Heidegger generated provocative postmodern modes of discourse, writing, and criticism. A group of French thinkers in the 1970s associated with poststructuralism radicalized the critique of modern philosophy and became labeled as "postmodern" theorists (Best and Kellner, 1991). Derrida, Foucault, Lyotard, Baudrillard, and others developed original and challenging modes of thought and writing, driving philosophy into novel arenas and topics. In the 1980s, postmodern theory spread throughout the world, and American thinker Richard

Rorty also became associated with the postmodern turn in philosophy. Rejecting totalizing dismissals of postmodern thought and fervent affirmations, we adopt a dialectical approach that mediates between modern and postmodern theory to develop critical theory and politics for the contemporary era. We argue that while postmodern theory carries out radical critiques and some productive reconstruction of modern theory and politics, it is vitiated by its too extreme rejection of normative perspectives and modern theory, and thus we call for mediation between modern and postmodern discourses.[1]

Modern Theory and Kierkegaard's Assault on Reason

Modern philosophy has been largely secular and humanistic, focusing on the abilities of human beings to discover natural and social truths and to construct their worlds accordingly. Modern theorists assume that there is order and laws in the cosmos and society that reason can discover in order to represent and control nature and social conditions. Reason is deemed the distinctive human faculty, the cognitive power that would enable humans to dominate nature and create moral and just societies. Faith in rationality was born in the Renaissance and the scientific revolutions of the sixteenth and seventeenth centuries, enthroned in the eighteenth-century Enlightenment, and triumphant, though challenged, by the nineteenth century. Key nineteenth-century thinkers such as Kierkegaard and Nietzsche, however, questioned the pretensions of reason and modern theory, thus clearing the way for a postmodern turn in philosophy.

Danish religious philosopher Søren Kierkegaard carried out a systematic critique of the pretensions of reason and an abstract rationalism which he believed that the modern age was nurturing. Condemning reflection as a "danger" that ensnares people in logical delays and machinations, Kierkegaard compared it to a prison. Reflection is for him a form of captivity, a bondage which "can only be broken by [passionate] religious inwardness" (1978, p. 81). Reflection seduces individuals into thinking that its possibilities are "much more magnificent than a paltry decision" (1978, p. 82). It leads them to act "on principle," to dwell on the deliberation of the context of their actions and the calculation of their worth or outcome. Kierkegaard argues that this drives away feeling, inspiration, and spontaneity, all of which are crucial for true inner being and a vital relation to God. For Kierkegaard, as Nietzsche would later agree, genuine inner being (and culture) is characterized by the tautness and tension of the soul which characterizes passionate existence. But the "coiled springs of life relationships . . . lose their resilience" in reflection (1978, p. 78) and "everything becomes meaningless externality, devoid of [internal] character" (1978, p. 62).

Kierkegaard thus contributes to the development of an irrationalist tradition that has echoes in some later postmodern thought. Kierkegaard might well have agreed with his contemporary Fyodor Dostoevsky, who wrote: "An intelligent [reflective] man cannot seriously become anything . . . excessive consciousness is a disease" (1974, p. 3, 5). In an age overtaken by rules and regulations, genuine action – which

Kierkegaard assumes to be subjective and spontaneous – is frustrated at every turn. Complaining that we are too "sober and serious" (1978, p. 71) even at banquets, Kierkegaard bemoans the fact that even suicides are premeditated (1978, p. 68)! "That a person stands or falls on his actions is becoming obsolete; instead, everybody sits around and does a brilliant job of bungling through with the aid of some reflection and also by declaring that they all know very well what has to be done" (1978, p. 73). Thus, it is passion, not reflection, that guarantees "a decent modesty between man and man [and] prevents crude aggressiveness" (1978, p. 62). "Take away the passion and the propriety also disappears" (1978, p. 64).

The ambiguity in the word "passion" may cause some confusion here. To say that the age and its individuals are "passionless" is not to say there are no emotions whatsoever but, rather, that there is no true spiritual inwardness and depth, no intensively motivated action and commitment. It suggests that passion exists only in a simulated, pseudo-form, "the rebirth of passion" through "talkativeness" (1978, p. 64). "Chattering" for Kierkegaard gets in the way of "essential speaking" and merely "reflects" inconsequential events (1978, pp. 89–99). Hence, in "the present age," emotions – which in fact are all too pronounced – have been transformed into negative forces.[2] Anticipating Nietzsche's genealogy of the "slave revolt" in morality, Kierkegaard claims that the "enthusiasm" of the prior age of Revolution, a "positively unifying principle," has become a vicious "envy," a *negatively unifying principle*" (1978, p. 81), a leveling force in its own right insofar as those lacking in talent and resources want to tear down those who have them.

Both Kierkegaard and Nietzsche reduce egalitarian politics to herd envy of the strong or noble. Yet Kierkegaard systematically champions passion over reason. For Kierkegaard, there are three stages of existence – the aesthetic, ethical, and religious. In each of these stages, passion and non-rational components are deemed superior to rationality. In the aesthetic stage, it is the sensual pleasures of culinary taste, art, and eroticism that provide the earthly delights of everyday life, and not the machinations of reason. In the ethical stage, Kierkegaard valorizes the passion of resolve, choice, and commitment over universal principles and the faculty of moral judgment. The religious stage, however, is the highest mode of existence for Kierkegaard, who champions the infinite passion of the choice of Christian belief, the absurd faith in the Christian mysteries and paradoxes, and the subjective yearning for salvation and redemption as the heart and soul of the religious life.

Moreover, "truth is subjectivity" for Kierkegaard, who acclaims the subjective passion and commitment whereby a Christian subject lives in the truth, making it the form and substance of everyday life. Such existential truths are of far more value for Kierkegaard than the claims of philosophy and science. In particular, Kierkegaard mocked Hegel with his pretensions of absolute and objective truth collected into a totalizing system of knowledge. Likewise, Kierkegaard ridiculed the guarantees of Enlightenment reason and modern science to provide infallible methods of securing objective knowledge. Such "truths," for Kierkegaard, were of little existential import in contrast to the pleasures and insights of art, the imperatives of ethical commitment, and the infinite and inexpressible value of religious redemption.

For Kierkegaard, the subject was a solipsistic monad, yearning for salvation and infinite happiness, plagued with anxiety and guilt, obsessed with God and religious transcendence. The social bonds, community, and forms of association which modern social theory would valorize as the distinctive achievements of modernity, with modes of social integration, interaction, and social norms, were volatilized into a ghostly aura of the phantom public, leaving the individual in fear and trembling, alone before God and the passion of religious choice. Hence, Kierkegaard carries out a critique of reason, reflection, objective knowledge, and modern thought that would influence the postmodern turn in philosophy.

Nietzsche and the Postmodern

Nietzsche shares Kierkegaard's belief that contemporary thought, morality, and religion are contributing to the leveling process, but unlike Kierkegaard, who has positive conceptions of morality and religion, Nietzsche tends to see all existing forms of morality and religion – and Christianity in particular – as repressive of vital life energies and inimical to individuality. Thus Nietzsche radicalizes the Enlightenment critique of ideology and, like Marx, advocates a relentlessly secular approach to values and theory. Nietzsche's philosophical critique mutated into modern existentialism and then postmodern theory, making him a master theorist of both traditions and a link from existentialism to the postmodern turn in philosophy. In particular, Nietzsche anticipated later postmodern theory in his critique of the subject and reason, his deconstruction of modern notions of truth, representation, and objectivity, his perspectivism, and his highly aestheticized philosophy and mode of writing.

Nietzsche's celebration of the Dionysian and his critiques of Socratic reason and later rationalist Greek tragedy present an attack on figures of Enlightenment rationality and modern science. Nietzsche later makes it clear that the Socratic, or "theoretic man," who was the target of his critique in *Birth of Tragedy*, stands for modern science and rationality, and in the section "Attempt at a self-criticism" of this earlier work, Nietzsche claims that "it was *the problem of science itself*, science considered for the first time as problematic, as questionable," which distinguishes his position (1967a, p. 18). Indeed, Nietzsche led the way in questioning the value of science for life, suggesting that the "will to truth" and scientific lust for objectivity are masks for a will to power and advancement of ascetic ideals (1968a). Moreover, although it is often not noted, Nietzsche was one of the first to attack the organization of modern society and to develop a critique of modernity.[3]

From his early writings on, Nietzsche, like Kierkegaard, rails against a life-denying rationalism and idealist philosophy which champions reason over the passions. Nietzsche interprets the "subject" as a mere construct, an idealized sublimation of bodily drives, experiences, and a multiplicity of thoughts and impulses. This "little changeling," on Nietzsche's view, this subject, "is believed in more firmly than anything else on earth," but is for him a simple illusion created out of modern desperation to have a well-grounded identity. Belief in the subject is promoted by the exigencies of grammar which utilize a subject/predicate form, giving rise to the fallacy that the "I" is a substance, whereas it is really only a convention of grammar (Nietzsche, 1968b, pp. 37–8). For Nietzsche, "the doer" is "merely a fiction added to the deed – the deed is everything" (1968b, p. 45). "The subject," he concludes, is thus but a shorthand expression for a multiplicity of drives, experiences, and ideas.

In the spirit of Enlightenment, Nietzsche also polemicizes against metaphysics, arguing that it illicitly generalizes from ideas in one historical epoch to the entirety of history. Against this form of philosophical universalism, Nietzsche argues "there are *no eternal facts*, just as there are no absolute truths. Consequently, what is needed from now on *is historical philosophizing*, and with it the virtue of modesty" (Nietzsche, 1986, p. 13). Castigating traditional philosophy and values from a critical Enlightenment perspective, Nietzsche anticipates later postmodern critiques of metaphysics, assailing the concept of enduring knowledge, the notion of a transcendental world, and presenting metaphysical thought as a thoroughly obsolete mode of thinking. He attributes the "metaphysical need," at the heart of philosophies such as that of Schopenhauer, to primitive yearnings for religious consolation for the sufferings of life, and he urges "free spirits" to liberate themselves and pursue thinking and living *experimentally* (1986, p. 8).

Nietzsche's attack on foundationalism, universalizing thought, and metaphysics thus undertakes a "postmodern" turn in philosophy through a radical deconstruction of modern theory. But while deconstructionist philosophies typically terminate in the No, merely seeking to unravel a positive modern value system into a heap of disconnected fragments, Nietzsche starts and finishes with a big Yes, a life-affirming value, deconstructing only to reconstruct. Moving far away from Schopenhauerian pessimism, back toward a Greek view of tragedy, toward a Dionysian view of existence, Nietzsche seeks "a *justification of life*, even at its most terrible, ambiguous, and mendacious" (1968a, p. 521), a justification found in art, creativity, independence, and the emergence of "higher types" of humanity.

Yet Nietzsche's perspectivism denies the possibility of affirming any absolute or universal values: all ideas, values, positions, and so on are posits of individual constructs of a will to power, which are to be judged according to the extent to which they do or do not serve the values of life, creativity, and strong individuality. For Nietzsche there are no facts, only interpretations, and he argues that all interpretation is constituted by the individual's perspectives and is thus inevitably laden with presuppositions, biases, and limitations. For Nietzsche, a perspective is thus an optic, a way of seeing, and the more perspectives one has at one's disposal, the more one can see, and the better one can understand and grasp specific phenomena. To avoid limited and partial vision one should learn "how to employ a *variety* of perspectives and interpretations in the service of knowledge" (Nietzsche, 1968a, p. 119).

The concepts of perspectival seeing and interpretation provide Nietzsche with a critical counter-concept to essentialism: objects do not have an inherent essence, but will appear differently according to the perspective from which they are viewed and interpreted and the context in which they appear. He describes his own "search for knowledge" as manifested in the dream of having the "hands and eyes" of many others and of being "reborn in a hundred beings" (1974, p. 215). Cultivating this approach requires *learning to see* and interpret – "habituating the eye to repose, to patience, to letting things come to it; learning to defer judgement, to investigate and comprehend the individual case in all its aspects" (Nietzsche, 1968b, p. 65).

This passage points to another virtue of a perspectival optic: learning to grasp the specificity and particularity of things. Nietzsche mistrusted the distorting function of language and concepts which are overly abstract and general, and he required perspectival seeing and interpretation to grasp the uniqueness of concrete phenomena. Perspectival seeing allows access to "a complex form of specificity" (Nietzsche, 1968a, p. 340), which makes possible a more concrete and complete grasp of the particularities of phenomena. Seeing from conflicting perspectives also opens people to appreciation of otherness and difference, and enables them to grasp the uncertain, provisional, hypothetical and "experimental" nature of all knowledge.

Nietzsche's Progeny and the Postmodern Turn: From Heidegger through Derrida

Nietzsche's legacy is highly complex and contradictory, and in retrospect he is one of the most important and enigmatic figures in the transition from modern to postmodern thought. His assault on Western rationalism profoundly influenced Heidegger, Derrida, Deleuze, Foucault, Lyotard, and other postmodern theorists who broke with modern theory and sought alternative theories. Martin Heidegger, for instance, combines Nietzsche's radical critique of modernity with nostalgia for premodern social forms and a hatred of modern technology, which he sees as producing powerful forms of domination. In *Being and Time* (1962 [1927]), Heidegger develops Kierkegaard's and Nietzsche's critique of the masses and mass society through his concept of *das Man*, the impersonal One, or They-Self, which dominates "average everyday" being. The They-Self for Heidegger is a form of tyranny that imposes the thought, tastes, language, and habits of the mass onto each individual, creating a leveling process, such that "authentic" individuality demands radical self-differentiation from others (see Kellner, 1973). The process is facilitated by meditation on death and the contingency and finitude of human existence, which lends an urgency to creative endeavors.

For the later Heidegger, the critical focus shifted from the existential structures of individual existence and modern society to modern technology, which generates a *Gestell*, a conceptual framework that reduces nature, human beings, and objects to "a standing reserve," as resources for technical exploitation. Heidegger renounces modern and technological modes of thought and values in favor of premodern forms of contemplation and "letting Being be," thus rejecting modernity in its totality (1977). Like Nietzsche, he ultimately harkens back to premodern values, and with Ernst Junger, Oswald Spengler, and others he furthers a German anti-rationalist tradition that ultimately helped to produce fascism, an anti-modern culture that Heidegger affirmed and promoted.

Heidegger's assault on modernity was developed by Foucault and assorted postmodern theorists, while his attacks on metaphysics and modern thought became central to Derrida. Heidegger argues that modern subjectivity sets itself up as a sovereign instrument of domination of the object and that its own forms of representing the world are taken as the measure of the real (1977). For Heidegger, the representational form of modern thought and subsequent subject–object metaphysics illicitly enthrones the subject as the Lord of Being and positions individuals into an inauthentic relation with Being. Derrida radicalizes Heidegger's strike against dualistic metaphysics, while Rorty (1980) develops Heidegger's account of representation into a critique of philosophy as the mirror of nature. These ideas would eventually coalesce into a radical negation of modern philosophy, leading many to call for novel modes of postmodern thought and writing.

In the 1960s, various post-humanist and anti-metaphysical discourses emerged under the rubric of poststructuralism and, later, postmodern theory. These movements were premised on attacks on the Cartesian subject, Enlightenment views of history, and systemic or "totalizing" modes of modern thought that sought overarching unities and continuities in society and history. Although a spate of interesting thinkers such as Gilles Deleuze, Roland Barthes, Jean Baudrillard, and Julia Kristeva grew out of this ferment, Jacques Derrida, Michel Foucault, Jean-François Lyotard, and Richard Rorty emerged as perhaps the major philosophical figures in the postmodern turn in philosophy.

These thinkers were resolute historicists who assailed timeless metaphysical notions such as "Being" and overturned the Cartesian view of the subject in different ways, each taking a version of "the linguistic turn" (Rorty) in philosophy and social theory. Derrida attacks notions such as center, totality, and structure (1973, 1976, 1981a,b). For Derrida, difference is at the heart of everything: language has meaning only through a linguistic chain of differentiations. There is no immediate access to reality, no "transcendental signified" not mediated through a socially constituted language. In a linguistically created world of human meaning, there is nothing but an endless chain of signifiers, or "intertextuality."

Central to Derrida's thought is the attack on metaphysics. From his perspective, the entire Western legacy of philosophical thinking is Platonic/metaphysical in that it seeks to erase time, history, difference, and contingency from the world. Western philosophy seeks flight to an imaginary realm of pure and timeless universals, as it attempts to discover foundations for truth and stable values. Philosophical concepts such as "Forms," "clear and distinct ideas," "Absolute Knowledge," and the "transcendental subject" all seek to stop the dissemination of meaning within a closed system of "truth." This repression of meaning inevitably leads the metaphysical texts of Western philosophy into paradoxes, contradictions, and incoherencies that are ripe for "deconstruction."

To "deconstruct" is not the same as to destroy. Deconstruction attempts to undo logical contradictions and overturn rigid conceptual oppositions, while releasing new concepts and meanings that could not be included in the old system. At the heart of Western metaphysics, for example, Derrida finds the opposition between "speech" and "writing." This binary logic functions in an illicit way to establish speech as the means of giving "presence" to the world, while writing is deemed derivative and inferior. In Derrida's sense of "grammatology," however, all production of meaning is writing and subject to the infinite play of signification. By taking away the transcendental signified and advancing the concept of "differance" (language organized around difference and deferred, or mediated, understandings), Derrida, like Nietzsche, wants to leave us without transcendental illusions, metaphysical unities, and foundations that constrain thought and creativity.

Western culture for Derrida is pervaded by philosophy; its binary modes of thought are constitutive of its literature, science, morality, and imperialist politics. Philosophy itself is contaminated by metaphysics and moves of exclusion; to undo the logic behind the exclusion, to challenge the metaphysical underpinnings of the culture, is to put in question the culture itself. Ideology relies on two key metaphysical strategies: it constructs dualisms and hierarchies, and it seeks an absolute grounding point to derive one thing from another. Thus, dualisms are not innocent: one term (white/male/Western) is always privileged over another (person of color/female/non-Western); the superior term is not possible without contrast to the inferior term. The thrust of deconstruction clearly is normative and political: it is a protest against marginalization, the violence that isolates and silences a plurality of voices in the name of a hegemonic power or authority, and it inverts the dominant and valorizes the suppressed.

In this light, Derrida has taken many positions as an "engaged intellectual." He has attacked apartheid, supported Nelson Mandela, helped start an open university in Paris, spoken out against human rights abuses, and addressed feminist issues. Derrida has publicly proclaimed himself a communist and has at times linked his work to Marxist concerns (which is not to say that he is a Marxist or that deconstruction is a Marxist method; see Derrida, 1994). He has lashed out against apolitical interpretations of his work. But from what position can deconstruction speak, if there is no ground, if everything is indeterminate? Like Foucault, Derrida has no cognitive means of supporting his own position and no positive evaluative norms. Rather, his emphasis is on skepticism, destabilization, uprooting, and overturning.

The deconstructive emphasis of Derrida, Foucault, Lyotard, Rorty and others underscores one of the main deficits of postmodern theory – the failure to provide normative resources for ethics and political critique. This creates a strange paradox, one that Habermas (1987) terms a "performative contradiction," whereby the postmodern theorist assails modern theories and societies, yet renounces the resources to justify the critique as better, superior, or even accurate. As we see in the following sections, this problem afflicts key postmodern theorists such as Foucault, Lyotard, and Rorty.

Foucault's Critique of Rationality and Modernity

Foucault's works have been extremely influential in all fields of contemporary criticism, inspiring not only the "new historicism," but also innovative research in the areas of the family, sexuality, social regulation, education, prisons, law, and the state.[4] In a series of historical studies on madness and psychiatry, illness and medicine, the human sciences, prisons and punishment, sexuality, and ethics, Foucault redefines the nature of social theory by calling into question conventional assumptions concerning the Enlightenment, Marxism, rationality, subjectivity, power, truth, history, and the political role of the intellectual. Foucault breaks with universalist, foundational-ist, dialectical, and normative standpoints and emphasizes principles of contingency, difference, and discontinuity. Adopting a nominalist stance, he dissolves abstract essences and universals such as Reason, History, Truth, or Right into a plurality of specific sociohistorical forms.

Foucault challenges traditional disciplinary boundaries between philosophy, history, psychology, and social and political theory, as well as conventional approaches to these disciplines. He does not do "theory" in the modern sense that aims at clarity, consistency, comprehensiveness, objectivity, and truth; rather, he offers fragments, "fictions," "truth-games," "heterotopias," "tools," and "experiments" that he hopes will prompt us to think and act in new ways. Trying to blaze new intellectual and political trails, Foucault abandons both liberalism and Marxism and seeks a new kind of critical theory and politics.

By theorizing the connections between knowledge, truth, and power, such as emerged in the domain of the human sciences and are bound up with constituting individuals as distinct kinds of subjects, Foucault transforms the history of science and reason into a political critique of modernity and its various modes of power, which assume the form of "normalization" or "subjectification." Foucault holds to the Nietzschean view that to be a "subject" – that is, to have a unified and coherent iden-tity – is to be "subjugated" by social powers. This occurs through a "deployment" of discourse that divides, excludes, classifies, creates hierarchies, confines, and nor-malizes thought and behavior. Hence, toward the end of his career, Foucault declares that his ultimate project has been not so much to study power but, rather, the subject itself: "the goal of my work . . . has been to create a history of the different modes by which, in our [Western] culture, human beings are made subjects" (1982, p. 208).

Yet this is a misleading distinction that signals merely a shift in emphasis rather than approach, since subjectification is the means through which modern power oper-ates in Foucault's later writings. In a series of historical studies, Foucault analyzes the formation of the modern subject from the perspectives of psychiatry, medicine, crim-inology, and sexuality, whereby limit-experiences are transformed into objects of knowledge. His works are strongly influenced by an anti-Enlightenment tradition that rejects the equation of reason, emancipation, and progress. Foucault argues that an interface between modern forms of power and knowledge served to create new forms of domination. With thinkers such as Sade, Nietzsche, and Bataille, Foucault valorizes transgressive forms of experience, such as madness, violence, or sexuality, that break from the prison of rationality. Where modern societies "problematize" forms of experience such as madness, illness, and sexuality – that is, turn them into governmental problems, into areas of life in need of control and regulation – Foucault in turn queries the social construction of "problems" by uncovering their political motivations and effects and by challenging their character as natural, neces-sary, or timeless. In what he calls a "diagnostic critique" that combines philosophy and history (1989, pp. 38–9, 73), Foucault attempts to clarify the nature of the present historical era, to underline its radical difference from preceding eras, and to show that contemporary forms of knowledge, rationality, social institutions, and sub-jectivity are contingent sociohistorical constructs of power and domination, and therefore are subject to change and modification.

Foucault's ultimate task, therefore, is "to produce a shift in thought so that things can really change" (quoted in O'Farrell, 1989, p. 39). The goal of Foucault's historico-philosophical studies, as he later came to define it, is to show how different domains of modern knowledge and practice constrain human action and how they can be transformed by alternative forms of knowledge and practice in the service of human freedom. Foucault is concerned to analyze various forms of the "limit-experience" whereby society attempts to define and circumscribe the boundaries of legitimate thought and action. The political vision informing Foucault's work foresees individuals liberated from coercive social norms, transgressing all limits to experience, and transvaluing values, going beyond good and evil, to promote their own creative lifestyles and affirm their bodies and pleasures, endlessly creating and recreating themselves.

Foucault denies there can be any basis for objective descriptive statements of social reality or universal normative statements that are not socially conditioned and locally bound. He tries to show that all norms, values, beliefs, and truth claims are relative to the discursive framework within which they originate. Any attempt to write or speak about the nature of things is made from within a rule-governed linguistic framework, an "episteme," that predetermines what kinds of statements are true or meaningful. All forms of consciousness, therefore, are sociohistorically determined and relative to specific discursive conditions. There is no absolute, unconditioned, transcendental stance from which to grasp what is good, right, or true. Foucault refuses to specify what is true because there are no objective grounds of knowledge; he does not state what is good or right because he believes there is no universal standpoint from which to speak. Universal statements merely disguise the will to power of specific interests; all knowledge is perspectival in character. For postmodern theorists such as Foucault, the appeal to foundations is necessarily metaphysical and assumes the fiction of an Archimedean point outside of language and social conditioning.

Habermas (1987) rightly finds perplexing an approach that raises truth claims while destroying a basis for belief in truth, that takes normative positions while suppressing the values to which they are committed. For critique to be justified and effective, it should preserve standards by which to judge and evaluate, but Foucault's total critique turns against itself and calls all rational standards into question.

In dissolving all social phenomena in the acid bath of power and domination, Foucault prevents critical theory from drawing crucial distinctions, such as those "between just and unjust social arrangements, legitimate and illegitimate uses of political power, strategic and cooperative interpersonal relations, coercive and consensual measures" (McCarthy, 1991, p. 54). One cannot say, for example, that one regime of power is any better or worse than another, only that they are different – "Another power, another knowledge" (Foucault, 1979, p. 226).

Since ruling powers attempt to erase such distinctions, or to present injustice as justice, falsehood as truth, and domination as freedom, Foucault's position unwittingly supports the mystifications of Orwellian doublespeak, now more rife than ever (see Kellner, 2001), and blocks the discriminations necessary for social critique. If there are no standards or right, then, with Thrasymacus and Hobbes, we can conclude might is as right as anything. There can be no ideology critique where there is no distinction between true and false, and no social or moral critique without a distinction between right and wrong. The evaluative character of Foucault's own work is not any less normative for his refusal to explicitly confront it. The problem becomes glaring in his later work, where he employs normative terms such as liberty and autonomy, but fails to state what we should be free *for*. Foucault's anti-normative stance therefore forces him into self-defeating value neutrality.

Foucault eschews normative positions in part because he wishes to renounce the role of the universal intellectual who legislates values. For Foucault, the task of the genealogist is to raise problems, not to give solutions; to shatter the old values, not to create new ones. Any stronger, more prescriptive role, Foucault argues, can only augment existing relations of power and reproduce hierarchical divisions between rulers and ruled. But Foucault's error is to confuse provisional normative statements with dogmatic ones, to conflate suggestions to be dialogically debated with finalized creeds to be imposed, to fail to see that universal values can be the products not only of power or ideology but also of consensual, rational, and free choice.[5] Consequently, like most postmodern thinkers, he fails to provide normative grounds for critique and positive ideals, a deficit addressed by Lyotard.

Lyotard's "Postmodern Condition": Polemics and Aporia

While the early works of Jean-François Lyotard were strongly influenced by phenomenology, Marxism, and Nietzsche, in the 1980s he carried through a resolute postmodern turn in theory. In many circles, Lyotard is celebrated as *the* postmodern theorist *par excellence*. His book *The Postmodern Condition* (1984 [1979]) introduced the term to a broad public and has been widely discussed in the postmodern debates of the last decade. During this period, Lyotard published a series of books that promote postmodern positions in theory, ethics, politics, and aesthetics. More than almost anyone, Lyotard has championed a break with modern theory and methods, while popularizing and disseminating postmodern alternatives. As a result, his work has sparked a series of intense controversies (see Best and Kellner, 1991).

Above all, Lyotard has emerged as the champion of difference and plurality in all theoretical realms and discourses, while energetically attacking totalizing and universalizing theories and methods. In *The Postmodern Condition, Just Gaming* (1985 [1979]), *The Differend* (1988 [1983]), and a series of other books and articles published in the 1980s, he has called attention to the differences among the plurality of "regimes of phrases" which have their own rules, criteria, and methods. Stressing the heterogeneity of discourses, Lyotard argues, following Kant, that such domains as theoretical, practical, and aesthetic judgment have their own autonomy, rules, and criteria. In this way, he rejects notions of universalist and foundationalist theory, as well as claims that one method or set of concepts has privileged status in such disparate domains as philosophy, social theory, or aesthetics. Arguing against what he calls "terroristic" and "totalitarian" theory, Lyotard thus resolutely champions a plurality of discourses and positions against unifying theory.

In *The Postmodern Condition*, Lyotard turns affirmatively to postmodern discourse and sharpens his polemical attack against the discourses of modernity while offering new postmodern positions. In particular, he attempts to develop a postmodern epistemology that will replace the philosophical perspectives dominated by Western rationalism and instrumentalism. Subtitled *A Report on Knowledge*, the text was commissioned by the Canadian government to study

> the condition of knowledge in the most highly developed societies. I have decided to use the word *postmodern* to describe that condition. The word is in current use on the American continent among sociologists and critics; it designates the state of our culture following the transformations which, since the end of the nineteenth century, have altered the game rules for science, literature, and the arts. (Lyotard, 1984, p. xxiii)

Following our distinctions between postmodernity as a sociohistorical epoch, postmodernism as a configuration of art after/against modernism, and postmodern knowledge as a critique of modern epistemology (Best and Kellner, 1991, 1997), it would be more accurate to read Lyotard's text as a study of the conditions of postmodern knowledge, rather than of the postmodern condition *tout court*, for the text does not provide an analysis of postmodernity but, rather, compares modern and postmodern knowledge. Indeed, like Foucault, Lyotard carries out a critique of modern knowledge and calls for new knowledges, rather than developing analyses of postmodern forms of society or culture.

Consistent with his postmodern epistemology, he never theorizes modernity as a historical process, limiting himself to providing a critique of modern knowledge. Thus modernity for Lyotard is identified with modern reason, Enlightenment, totalizing thought, and philosophies of history. Failing to develop analyses of modernity and postmodernity, these notions are undertheorized in his work and this shifts postmodern theory away from social analysis and critique to philosophy. Lyotard thus carries through a linguistic and philosophical turn that renders his theory more and more abstract and distanced from the social realities and problems of the present age.

For Lyotard, there are three conditions for modern knowledge: the appeal to metanarratives to legitimate foundationalist claims; the inevitable outgrowth of legitimation, delegitimation, and exclusion; and a desire for homogeneous epistemological and moral prescriptions. Postmodern knowledge, by contrast, is against metanarratives and foundationalism; it eschews grand schemes of legitimation; and it is for heterogeneity, plurality, constant innovation, and pragmatic construction of local rules and prescriptives agreed upon by participants. The postmodern condition therefore involves developing an alternative epistemology that responds to new conditions of knowledge. The main focus of the book accordingly concerns the differences between the grand narratives of traditional philosophy and social theory, and what Lyotard calls "postmodern knowledge," which he defends as preferable to modern forms of knowledge.

To legitimate their positions, Lyotard claims that modern discourses appeal to metadiscourses such as the narrative of progress and emancipation, the dialectics of history or spirit, or the inscription of meaning and truth. Modern science, for instance, legitimates itself in terms of an alleged liberation from ignorance and superstition, as well as the production of truth, wealth, and progress. From this perspective, the postmodern is defined by an "incredulity toward metanarratives," namely, the rejection of metaphysical philosophy, philosophies of history, and any form of totalizing thought – be it Hegelianism, liberalism, Marxism, or positivism.

Lyotard believes that the metanarratives of modernity tend toward exclusion and a desire for universal metaprescriptions. The scientist, for instance, provides a paradigmatic example of modernity's propensity toward exclusion, as he or she rules out in advance anything that does not conform to formalizable or quantifiable knowledge (1984, p. 80). Lyotard argues that the modern act of universalizing and homogenizing metaprescriptives violates what he considers the heterogeneity of language games. Furthermore, he claims that the act of consensus also stifles heterogeneity and imposes homogeneous criteria and a false universality.

By contrast, Lyotard champions dissensus over consensus, diversity and dissent over conformity and consensus, and heterogeneity and the incommensurable over homogeneity and universality. He writes: "Consensus does violence to the heterogeneity of language games. And invention is always born of dissension. Postmodern knowledge is not simply a tool of the authorities; it refines our sensitivity to differences and reinforces our ability to tolerate the incommensurable" (1984, p. 75).

Knowledge is produced, in Lyotard's view, by dissent, by putting into question existing paradigms, by inventing new ones, rather than assenting to universal truth or agreeing to a consensus. Although Lyotard's main focus is epistemological, he also implicitly presupposes a notion of the postmodern condition, writing: "Our working hypothesis is that the status of knowledge is altered as societies enter what is known as the postindustrial age and culture enters what is known as the postmodern age" (1984, p. 3). Like Baudrillard, Lyotard thus associates the postmodern with the trends of so-called "postindustrial society." Postmodern society is for Lyotard the society of computers, information, scientific knowledge, advanced technology, and rapid change due to new advances in science and technology. Indeed, he seems to agree with theorists of postindustrial society concerning the primacy of knowledge, information, and computerization – describing postmodern society as "the computerization of society."

Yet the concept of "the postmodern condition," we would argue, points to some fundamental aporia in Lyotard and other French postmodern theories. His "war on totality" rejects totalizing theories, which he describes as master narratives that are somehow reductionist, simplistic, and even "terroristic," because they provide legitimations for totalitarian terror and suppress differences in unifying schemes. Yet Lyotard himself is advancing the notion of a "postmodern condition" which presupposes a dramatic break from modernity. Indeed, does not the very concept of postmodernity, or a postmodern condition, presuppose a master narrative, a totalizing perspective, which envisages the transition from a previous stage of society to a new one? Doesn't such theorizing presuppose *both* a concept of modernity and a notion of a radical break, or rupture, within history, which leads to a totally new condition that justifies the term *post*modern? Therefore, does not the very concept "postmodern" seem to presuppose both a master narrative and some notion of totality, and thus periodizing and totalizing thought – precisely the sort of epistemological operation and theoretical hubris that Lyotard and others want to renounce?

Against Lyotard, we might want to distinguish between master narratives, which attempt to subsume every particular, every specific viewpoint, and every key point into one totalizing theory (as in Hegel, some versions of Marxism, or Talcott Parsons), and grand narratives, which attempt to tell a "Big Story" such as the rise of capital, patriarchy, or colonialism. Within grand narratives, we might want to distinguish as well between metanarratives that tell a story about the foundation of knowledge and the narratives of social theory that attempt to conceptualize and interpret a complex diversity of phenomena and their interrelations, such as male domination or the exploitation of the working class. We might also distinguish between synchronic narratives that tell a story about a specific society at a given point in history, and diachronic narratives that analyze historical change, discontinuities, and ruptures. Lyotard tends to lump all large narratives together and thus does violence to the diversity of narratives in our culture.

In fact, Lyotard is caught in another double bind *vis-à-vis* normative positions from which he can criticize opposing positions. His renunciation of general principles and universal criteria preclude normative critical positions, yet he condemns grand narratives, totalizing thought, and other features of modern knowledge. This move catches him in another aporia, whereby he wants to reject general epistemological and normological positions while his critical interventions presuppose precisely such critical positions (such as the war on totality).

In our view, a more promising venture would be to make explicit, critically discuss, take apart, and perhaps reconstruct and rewrite the grand narratives of social theory rather than to just prohibit them and exclude them from the terrain of narrative. It is likely – as Fredric Jameson argues (1981) – that we are condemned to narrative in that individuals and cultures organize, interpret, and make sense of their experience through story-telling modes (see also Ricoeur, 1984). Not even a scientistic culture could completely dispense with narratives and the narratives of social theory will no doubt continue to operate in social analysis and critique in any case (Jameson, 1984, p. xii). If this is so, it would seem preferable to bring to light the narratives of modernity so as to critically examine and dissect them, rather than to simply prohibit certain sorts of narratives by Lyotardian Thought Police.

It appears that when one does not specify and explicate the specific sort of narratives of contemporary society involved in one's language games, there is a tendency to make use of the established narratives at one's disposal. For example, in the absence of an alternative theory of contemporary society, Lyotard uncritically accepts theories of "postindustrial society" and "postmodern culture" as accounts of the present age (1984, pp. 3, 7, 37, *passim*). Yet he presupposes the validity of these narratives without adequately defending them and without developing a social theory that would employ political economy and critical social theory to delineate the transformations suggested by the "post" in "postindustrial" or "postmodern." Rejecting grand narratives, we believe, simply covers over the theoretical problem of providing a narrative of the contemporary historical situation and points to the undertheorized nature of Lyotard's account of the postmodern condition. This would require at least some sort of large narrative of the transition to postmodernity – a rather big and exciting story one would think (see Best and Kellner, 2001).

In a sense, Lyotard's celebration of plurality replays the moves of liberal pluralism and empiricism. His "justice of multiplicities" is similar to traditional liberalism, which posits a plurality of political subjects with multiple interests and organizations. He replays tropes of liberal tolerance by valorizing diverse modes of multiplicity, refusing to privilege any subjects or positions, or refusing to offer a standpoint from which one can choose between opposing political positions. Thus he comes close to falling into a political relativism, which robs him of the possibility of making political discriminations and choosing between substantively different political positions, institutions, and social systems.

Lyotard's emphasis on a multiplicity of language games and deriving rules from specific and local regions is similar in some respects to an empiricism which rejects macrotheory and an analysis of hegemonic structures of domination and oppression. Limiting discourse to small narratives would prevent critical theory from making broader claims about structures of domination or legitimating critical claims made about society as a whole. His "wonderment at the variety of language games" and exhortation to multiply discourses, to produce more local narratives and languages, also replicates the current trend in academia to multiply specialized languages, to produce a diversity of new jargons. In fact, postmodern discourses themselves can be interpreted as an effect of a proliferating intellectual specialization, with its imperative to produce ever new discourses for the academic market. Against such theoretical specializations, we advocate the production of a common, vernacular language for theory, critique, and radical politics that eschews the jargon and obscurity that usually accompanies the production of specialized languages. This position is also advanced by Richard Rorty, although in a form that ultimately rejects theory.

Richard Rorty, the Attack on Theory, and Renunciation of Radical Politics

In theorizing the postmodern, one inevitably encounters the postmodern assault on theory, such as Lyotard's and Foucault's rejection of modern theory for its alleged totalizing and essentializing character. The argument is ironic, of course, since it falsely homogenizes a heterogeneous "modern tradition" and since postmodern theorists such as Foucault, Lyotard, and Baudrillard are often as totalizing as any modern thinker (Kellner, 1989; Best, 1995). But where Lyotard seeks justification of theory within localized language games, arguing that no universal criteria are possible to ground objective truths or universal values, Foucault steadfastly resists any efforts, local or otherwise, to validate normative concepts and theoretical perspectives. For Foucault, justification ensnares one in metaphysical illusions such as "truth," and the only concern of the philosopher–critic is to dismantle old ways of thinking, to attack existing traditions and institutions, and to open up new horizons of experience for greater individual freedom. What matters, then, is results, and if actions bring greater freedom, the theoretical perspectives informing them are "justified." From this perspective, theoretical discourse is seen not so much as "correct" or "true," but as "efficacious," as producing positive effects.

Continuing along this path, postmodernists have attacked theory *per se* as at best irrelevant to practice and at worst a barrier to it. Rorty assails both metatheory – reflection on the status of theory itself, which often is concerned with epistemological and normative justifications of claims and values – and theory, which he critiques in three related ways that emerge through his own articulation of the "end of philosophy" thesis. Rigorously trained in analytic philosophy, Rorty became a turncoat and abandoned the professional dogma that philosophy was "queen of the sciences" or the universal arbiter of values whose task was to provide foundations for truth and value claims. Philosophy has no special knowledge or truth claims because it, like any other cultural phenomenon, is a thoroughly linguistic phenomenon. For Rorty, language is a poetic construction that creates worlds, not a mirror that reflects "reality," and there are no presuppositionless or neutral truths that evade the contingencies of historically shaped selfhood. Consequently, there is no non-circular Archimedean point for grounding theory. Language can only provide us with a "description" of the world that is thoroughly historical and contingent in nature.

Thus, the first move in Rorty's assault on theory is an attack on the idea that theory can provide objective foundations for knowledge and ethics. Alleged universal truths are merely local, time-bound perspectives and masks for a "Real" that cannot be known. The second critique immediately follows: if there are no universal or objective truths, no neutral language to arbitrate competing claims, then "theory" has no power to adjudicate among competing languages or descriptions, a task that inevitably transforms theory into metatheory once the conditions of argumentation themselves become sufficiently problematic.

Hence, Rorty denies that the theorist can definitively criticize, argue, evaluate, or even "deconstruct," since there is no fulcrum from which to push one claim as "right," "correct," or "better" than another. The theorist is replaced by the ironist, one who is aware of the ineliminable contingency of selfhood and discourse. Accepting the new limitations, the ironist can only "redescribe" the older theories in new languages and offer new descriptions for themselves and others. We adopt values and ideologies on emotive rather than rational grounds. Every vocabulary is incommensurable with another, and there is no "final vocabulary" with which one can arbitrate normative and epistemological claims. Thus, for Rorty:

> The method is to redescribe lots and lots of things in new ways, until you have created a pattern of linguistic behavior which will tempt the rising generation to adopt it . . . This sort of philosophy does not work piece by piece, analyzing concept after concept, or testing thesis after thesis. Rather it works holistically and pragmatically. It says things like "try thinking of it this way" – or more specifically, "try to ignore the apparently futile traditional questions by substituting the following new and possibly interesting questions." It does not pretend to have a better candidate for doing the same old things which we did when we spoke in the old way . . . Conforming to my own precepts, I am not going to offer arguments against the vocabulary I want to replace. Instead, I am going to try to make the vocabulary I favor look more attractive by showing how it may be used to describe a variety of topics. (1989, p. 9)

One would think that this replacement of epistemological criteria of "truth" with aesthetic values of "attractiveness" would commit Rorty to relativism, but he denies the term on the grounds that it belongs to a discredited foundationalist framework, as the term "blasphemy" makes no sense within an atheistic logic. Whether or not we can say that Rorty is a relativist in the sense of someone who cannot demonstrate that one viewpoint is more true than another, he is not a "relativist" in the sense of someone who thinks that all claims are equally good or viable. Clearly, Rorty is pushing for some descriptions – those that celebrate contingency, irony, solidarity, and liberal values – over others, but he claims that one cannot "argue" for the new descriptions. On this level, the attack on theory means simply that it is useless to provide arguments for one's positions; the only thing one can do is to offer new descriptions and hope others will find them appealing and more useful for (liberal) society. Dethroning philosophy, Rorty claims that literature is a far more powerful tool for interpreting the world and offering the descriptions needed for self-creation and social progress. Fiction takes the place of theory. Of course, Rorty cannot help but argue for his positions, and is himself still writing philosophy, not fiction.

From this step follows the third argument in Rorty's attack on theory. The "theorist" should abandon all attempts to radically criticize social institutions. First, as we have seen, "critique" has no force for Rorty and, ultimately, one description is as good as any other. But "theory" on this level also means for Rorty the attempt, classically inscribed in Plato's *Republic*, to merge public and private concerns, to unite the private quest for perfection with social justice. Here, Rorty is guided by the assumption that tradition and convention are far more powerful forces than reason in the social construction of life, in holding the "social glue" together.

Rorty holds that philosophical views on topics such as the nature of the self or the meaning of the good life are as irrelevant to politics as are arguments about the existence of God. He wants to revive liberal values without feeling the need to defend them on a philosophical level: "What is needed is a sort of intellectual analogue of civic virtue – tolerance, irony, and a willingness to let spheres of culture flourish without worrying too much about their 'common ground,' their unification, the 'intrinsic ideals' they suggest, or what picture of man they 'presuppose'" (1989, p. 168). Since philosophy can provide no shared or viable foundation for a political concept of justice, it should be abandoned, and replaced with historical narratives and poetic descriptions. Ultimately, Rorty's goal is to redescribe modern culture and the vocabulary of Enlightenment rationalism in strongly historicist and pragmatist terms.

In this vein, Rorty's recent *Achieving Our Country* (1998) provides a provocative critique of the academic/cultural studies of the Left in the United States. Seeking liberal politics without (metaphysical) liberal theory and a pragmatic oriented politics rooted in a strong vision of social reform without the need for theoretical justification, Rorty asks the Left to get over its obsession with theory and cultural politics. He demands that the Left "kick its philosophy habit," and return to the kind of politics practiced by an earlier Left, the one of the Great Depression period, which was concretely wedded to social reform. Until such concrete progressive reforms are attained, Rorty maintains, "our country remains unachieved" (1998).

Taking a giant leap to the right of Foucault, Rorty claims not only that philosophy provides no foundation for politics, but that it plays no political role whatsoever. Despite his assault on foundationalism, Foucault was a tireless militant and "engaged intellectual" who used theory as a weapon for political struggle. For Rorty, however, philosophy has no public or political role. Reviving the classic liberal distinction between the public and private, Rorty claims that philosophy should be reserved for private life, where it can be ironic at best, while leaving political and moral traditions to govern public life. Even Derrida, master of subversion and irony, insisted that deconstruction entails political commitments, and at least made public and political gestures, however vague or dilatory.

We agree with Rorty's initial premise that consciousness, language, and subjectivity are historical and contingent in nature, that our relation to the world is mediated many times over, but we reject most of his conclusions. First, although we too are against foundationalism, we hold that it is possible for theory to construct non-arbitrary grounds to assess competing factual and value claims. These grounds are not metaphysical or ahistorical: they are found in the criteria of logic and argumentation which are reasonable to hold, and in shared social values that are the assumptions of a liberal democracy which Rorty himself affirms. Rejecting the implication of Rorty's position, we do not find it arbitrary to say that racism is wrong, or that critiques of racism or sexism are merely good "descriptions" with which we hope others would agree. Rather, we find the arguments for racism far weaker than the arguments against racism, and counter to liberal values that enlightened citizens hold – or should hold. The assumptions of these anti-racist arguments are of course themselves historical; they stem from the modern liberal tradition that proclaims the right of all human beings to a life of freedom and dignity. Rorty would rightly see this as a "tradition," but it is one that was constituted with a strong rational component and has compelling force for those who wish – and clearly not all do – to play the "language game" of democratic argumentation.

Similarly, while we do not know what the nature of the universe ultimately is, we find that astronomy provides a better "description" than astrology, that evolutionary theory is more compelling than creationism. Our court of appeal is reason, facts, verified bodies of knowledge, and our experience of the world itself, which is not infinitely malleable to any and all descriptions, such as the one that says the earth is flat. Symptomatic of this problem, Rorty adopts a problematic consensus theory of truth that holds that "truth" emerges from free discussion; it is "whatever wins in a free and open encounter" (1989, p. 67). This ignores the fact that even the "freest" inquiry can still produce falsehood and that might often continues to make right. Needless to say, the defense of such claims will require the tools of theory – science or philosophy – rather than fiction. Abandoning these tools, the ironist is disburdened of the need to defend his claims and tries to evade argumentative responsibilities in ways we don't tolerate in our undergraduate students. For Rorty, "interesting philosophy is rarely an examination of the pros and cons of a thesis" (1989, p. 9). Admittedly, argumentation is difficult and not always sexy, especially to the mind of an impatient aestheticist who seeks beauty, novelty, and speed over rigor, fairness, and coherence. Rorty is only one step away from Baudrillard, the self-proclaimed "intellectual terrorist" who prefers simply to blow up ideas with unsubstantiated claims and outrageous exaggerations rather than attending to matters of evaluating truth or falsehood, or patient empirical demonstration of his claims (see Kellner, 1989).

Moreover, without some kind of metatheory, Rorty cannot plausibly claim that liberalism is good or convincingly show which practices are to be favored over others.

If politics is strictly an aesthetic affair, what standards do we use to judge success from failure, good from bad politics? With Lyotard, Rorty seeks to proliferate ever new descriptions of the self and the world. This has the value of overcoming stale assumptions and entrenched dogmas, but it represents a fetishism of novelty over concern for truth and justice. On this scheme, there can be no gradual progress toward greater insight and knowledge; there is only succeeding and random points of discontinuity that scatter inquiry and knowledge in fragmented directions. Put in Rorty's own terms, our claim is that foundationalism, rationalism, and progressivist narratives of Western theory can be "redescribed" in better ways that make them more effective tools for historical analysis and social critique.

From our denial that theory is powerless to seek grounds of justification for claims, or to effectively challenge, counter, refute, or argue for specific positions, we hold that a crucial role of theory is to step beyond the circumscribed boundaries of individuality to assess the ways in which the social world shapes subjectivity. For Rorty, by contrast, the personal is no longer political. The question, of course, is not whether or not one should be theoretical, since all critical, philosophical, or political orientations are theoretical, at least in their embedded assumptions, which guide thought and action. No one hoping to speak intelligibly about the world can hope to avoid theory; one can either simply assume the validity of one's theory, or become reflexive about the sources of one's theoretical position – their compatibility, their validity, and their effects. The potential weakness and triviality of a non-theoretical approach is evident, for example, in the anti-theoretical biases of many cultural studies that mindlessly celebrate media culture as interesting, fun, or meaningful, while ignoring its economic, sociopolitical, and ideological functions.

For Theory and Politics

Theory is necessary to the extent that the world is not completely and immediately transparent to consciousness. This is never the case, especially in our own hyper-capitalist culture where the shadows flickering on the walls of our caves stem principally from television sets, the corporate-dominated ideology machines that speak the language of deception and manipulation. As we show in our book *The Postmodern Adventure* (Best and Kellner, 2001), which contains studies of Thomas Pynchon, Michael Herr, Mary Shelley, H. G. Wells, Philip K. Dick, and other imaginative writers, Rorty is right that fiction can powerfully illuminate the conditions of our lives, often in more concrete and illuminating ways than theory. Ultimately, we need to grant power to both theory and fiction, and understand their different perspectives and roles. For just as novels such as Upton Sinclair's *The Jungle* had a dramatic social impact, so too has the discourse of the Enlightenment, which provided the philosophical inspiration for the American and French Revolutions, as well as numerous succeeding revolts in history.

Postmodern attacks on theory are part and parcel of contemporary misology – the hatred of reason – that also manifests itself in the mysticism pervading some versions of deep ecology and ecofeminism, in anti-humanist attacks from "biocentric" viewpoints that often see human beings as nothing more than a scourge on nature, in the layperson's rejection of philosophy for common sense, in the pragmatist celebration of the technological and practical, in the postmodern embrace of desire and spontaneity over reflection, and in the mindless "spiritualism" pervading our culture (see Boggs, 2000, pp. 166ff.). The positive value of pragmatic critiques of theory is to remind one to maintain a close relationship between theory and practice, to avoid excessively abstract analyses and becoming mired in a metatheory that becomes obsessed with the justification of theory over its application – a problem that frequently plagues Habermas's work (see Best, 1995). The pragmatic critique helps keep theory from becoming an esoteric, specialized discourse, manipulated and understood only by a cadre of academic experts. No doubt we are not alone in our dissatisfaction with the highly esoteric discourse that comes not only from modernists such as Habermas, but also – and more so – from poststructuralist and postmodern champions of the ineffable and unreadable, or the terminally obscure and pompous.

Operating in the tradition of critical theory, we believe that the role of theory is to provide weapons for social critique and change, to illuminate the sources of human unhappiness and to contribute to the goal of human emancipation. Against Rorty's very un-postmodern dichotomization of the public and private (a centerpiece of bourgeois ideology), we believe that the citizens of the "private realm" (itself a social and historical creation) have strong obligations to participate actively in the public realm through rational criticism and debate. With Rorty, we do not believe that the theorist must seek to construct a perfect bridge between the public and the private, for the range of action and choice on the part of the individual always exceeds the minimal requirements of order in a free society. Rather, the role of the theorist is to help analyze what the conditions of freedom and human well-being might be, to ask whether or not they are being fulfilled, and to expose the forces of domination and oppression.

We see public intellectuals as specialists in critical thinking who can employ their skills to counter the abuses of the public realm in order to help reconstitute society and the polity more democratically. This involves helping to ensure that the private realm and its liberties and pleasures are not effaced through the ever-growing penetration of mass media, state administration, electronic surveillance, the capitalist marketplace, and globalization. Indeed, new media and computer technologies have created novel public spheres and thus unique opportunities for public intellectuals to exercise their skills of critique and argumentation (Kellner, 1997).

In addition, we believe that theory can provide *social maps* and *historical narratives* that supply spatial and temporal contextualizations of the present age. Social maps study society holistically, moving from any point or mode of human experience into an ever-expanding macroscopic picture that may extend from the individual self to its network of everyday social relations, to its more encompassing regional environment, to its national setting, and finally to the international arena of global capitalism. Within this holistic framework, social maps shift from one level to another, articulating complex connections between economics, politics, the state, media culture, everyday life, and various ideologies and practices.

Historical narratives, similarly, contextualize the present by identifying both how the past has constituted the present and how the present opens up to alternative futures. As argued in the historicist tradition that began in the nineteenth century – in the work of Hegel, Dilthey, Marx, Weber, and others – all values, worldviews, traditions, social institutions, and individuals themselves must be understood historically as they change and evolve through time. As in the form of Foucault's genealogies or various popular histories, historical narratives chart the temporal trajectories of significant experiences and events, political movements, or the forces constituting subjectivities. Against the postmodern tendency to randomize history as a disconnected series of events, we believe that historical narratives should grasp both historical continuities and discontinuities, while analyzing how continuities embody developmental dynamics, such as moral and technical evolution, that have emancipatory possibilities and should be further developed in the future (Best and Kellner, 1991, 1997, 2001).

Together, social maps and historical narratives study the points of intersection between individuals and their cultures, between power and knowledge. To the fullest degree possible, they seek to lift the veils of ideology and expose the given as contingent and the present as historically constituted, while providing visions of alternative futures. Maps and narratives, then, are meant to overcome quietism and fatalism, to sharpen political vision, and to encourage translation of theory into practice in order to advance both personal freedom and social justice. Social maps and historical narratives should not be confused with the territories and times they analyze; they are approximations of a densely constituted human world that require theory and imagination. Nor should they ever be seen as final or complete, since they must be constantly rethought and revised in light of new information and changing situations. Finally, as we are suggesting, these maps can deploy the resources of either "theory" or "fiction," since both provide illuminations of social experience from different vantage points, each of which are useful and illuminating, and necessarily supplement each other.

The social maps called classical social theories are to some extent torn and tattered, in fragments, and in some cases outdated and obsolete. But we need to construct new ones from the sketches and fragments of the past to make sense of our current historical condition, dominated by media culture, information explosion, new technologies, and a global restructuring of capitalism. Maps and theories provide orientation, overviews, and show how parts relate to each other and to a larger whole. If something new appears on the horizon, a good map will chart it, including sketches of some future configurations. And while some old maps and authorities are discredited and obsolete, some traditional theories continue to provide guideposts for current thought and action, as we have attempted to demonstrate in our various books that marshal both modern and postmodern theories to map and narrativize our present moment (see Best and Kellner, 1997, 2001).

Yet we also need new sketches of society and culture, and part of the postmodern adventure is sailing forth into new domains without complete maps, or with maps that are fragmentary and torn. Journeys into the postmodern thus thrust us into novel worlds, making us explorers of uncharted, or poorly charted, domains. Our mappings can thus only be provisional reports back from our explorations that require further investigation, testing, and revision. Yet the brave new worlds of postmodern culture and society are of sufficient interest, importance, and novelty to justify taking chances, leaving the familiar behind, and trying out new ideas and approaches.

Critical theories require a standpoint for critique and thus normative dimensions. As we have argued elsewhere (Best and Kellner, 1991, 1997), normative concepts and values such as democracy, freedom, social justice, human rights, and other value heritages of modern society were themselves validated in theoretical discussions and political struggles and provide important standpoints of critique. Normative critique, therefore, does not necessarily involve foundational or universalist positions, nor is it merely subjective and arbitrary. Rather, cultures and societies over long periods of history have come to agree that certain values, institutions, and forms of social life are valuable enough to struggle and die for, and one of the tasks of critical theory is to explicate and defend which normative positions continue to be relevant and vital in the contemporary era.

Finally, we need new politics to deal with the problems of capitalist globalization, environmental crises, species extinction, terrorism, and the failure of conventional politics to provide social justice and well-being for all. We fear that just as Rorty's and other postmodernists' assaults on theory block attempts to map and critique the new social constellations of the present moment, so too do attacks on radical politics and defense of a reformist liberalism and pragmatism vitiate attempts to deal with the new global forces of technocapitalism. Demonstrations against the World Trade Organization meetings in Seattle in December 1999 and the subsequent anti-globalization movement (see Best and Kellner, 2001) suggest that the radical spirit is still very much alive. Indeed, we believe that it is new social movements and the forces of radical opposition that provide the most promising avenues of radical democratic social transformation in the present moment.[6]

Thus, while postmodern approaches offer much to the reconstruction of critical theory and democratic politics for the present age, theories that fail to engage the proliferating and intensifying problems of capitalist globalization, that do not articulate the continuities between the old and the new, and that renounce the normative resources of criticism are severely limiting. To provide justification (of a non-metaphysical kind), or a defense of critical theories and alternative visions of what history, social life, and our relation to the natural world could be, continues to be necessary to the project of understanding and changing the world. We are in a troubling and exciting twilight period, in the crossroads between modernity and postmodernity, and the task ahead is to forge reconstructed maps and politics adequate to the great challenges that we face.

Notes

1   For our own perspectives on the modern and the postmodern, see Best and Kellner (1991, 1997, 2001).
2   In his book *The Present Age*, a commentary on a popular novel with that title, Kierkegaard (1978) distinguishes between antiquity and modern society, and the previous Age of Revolution and the present age (i.e., the 1840s), by noting a precipitous decline in passion; see our detailed analysis of this text in Best and Kellner (1990, 1997).

3 On Nietzsche's critique of modernity, see Kellner (1991); on the neglect of Nietzsche in classical social theory, see Antonio (1995); and on Nietzsche and the postmodern, see Best and Kellner (1997).

4 For further discussions of our positions on Foucault, Lyotard, and postmodern theory, see Best and Kellner (1991, 1997).

5 In fact, there is evidence that Foucault holds a similar position, that his intention is not to renounce normative discourse in general, but only the normative pronouncements of *intellectuals*, or, more restrictively, of Foucault himself, in order to allow for individual and public choice and debate. Thus, while Foucault refuses to say whether or not democracy is "better than" totalitarianism, he does not prohibit this distinction from being made by others: "I do not wish, as an intellectual, to play the moralist or prophet. I don't want to say that the Western countries are better than the ones of the Eastern bloc, etc. The masses have come of age, politically and morally. They are the ones who've got to choose individually and collectively" (1991, p. 172). For further discussion of the normative problems in critical theory, and an extended comparison of Foucault and Habermas, see Best (1995).

6 See Best and Kellner (1997, 2001).

References

Antonio, R. J. 1995: Nietzsche and classical social theory. *American Journal of Sociology*, 101(1), 1–43.

Best, S. 1995: *The Politics of Historical Vision: Marx, Foucault, and Habermas*. New York: Guilford Press.

——and Kellner, D. 1990: Kierkegaard, mass media, and *The Corsair Affair*. In R. Perkins (ed.), *The Corsair Affair. International Kierkegaard Commentary 13*. Macon, Ga.: Mercer University Press, 23–62.

——and ——1991: *Postmodern Theory: Critical Interrogations*. London: Macmillan/New York: Guilford Press (Chinese translation 1995).

——and ——1997: *The Postmodern Turn*. New York: Guilford Press/London: Routledge.

——and ——2001: *The Postmodern Adventure*. New York: Guilford Press/London: Routledge.

Boggs, C. 2000: *The End of Politics*. New York: Guilford Press.

Derrida, J. 1973: *Speech and Phenomena, and Other Essays on Husserl's Theory of Signs*. Evanston, Ill.: Northwestern University Press.

——1976: *Of Grammatology*. Baltimore, Md.: The Johns Hopkins University Press.

——1981a: *Positions*. Chicago, Ill.: University of Chicago Press.

——1981b: *Margins of Philosophy*. Chicago, Ill.: University of Chicago Press.

——1994: *Specters of Marx*. London and New York: Routledge.

Dostoevsky, F. 1974: *Notes From Underground*. New York: Bantam.

Foucault, M. 1979: *Discipline and Punish*. New York: Vintage.

——1982: The subject and power. In H. L. Dreyfus and P. Rabinow (eds.), *Michel Foucault: Beyond Structuralism and Hermeneutics*. Chicago, Ill.: University of Chicago Press, 208–26.

——1989: *Foucault Live*. New York: Semiotext(e).

——1991: *Remarks on Marx*. New York: Semiotext(e).

Habermas, J. 1987: *Lectures on The Philosophical Discourse of Modernity*. Cambridge, Mass.: The MIT Press.

Hassan, I. 1987: *The Postmodern Turn: Essays in Postmodern Theory and Culture*. Columbus, Ohio: Ohio State University Press.

Heidegger, M. 1977: *The Question Concerning Technology*. New York: Harper & Row.

Jameson, F. 1981: *The Political Unconscious*. Ithaca, NY: Cornell University Press.

——1984: Postmodernism, or the cultural logic of late capitalism. *New Left Review*, no. 146, 53–93.

Kearney, R. 1988: *The Wake of Imagination*. Minneapolis, Minn.: University of Minnesota Press.

Kellner, D. 1973: Heidegger's concept of authenticity. Ph.D. dissertation, Columbia University.

——1989: *Jean Baudrillard: From Marxism to Post-Modernism and Beyond*. Cambridge: Polity Press/Palo Alto, Calif.: Stanford University Press.

——1991: Nietzsche and modernity: reflections on *Twilight of the Idols*. *International Studies in Philosophy*, XXIII(2), 3–17.

——1997: Intellectuals, the public sphere, and new technologies. *Research in Philosophy and Technology*, 16, 15–32.

——2001: *Grand Theft 2000*. Lanham, Md.: Rowman & Littlefield.

Kierkegaard, S. 1978: *Two Ages: The Age of Revolution and the Present Age*. Princeton, NJ: Princeton University Press.

Kolb, D. 1990: *Postmodern Sophistications*. Chicago, Ill.: University of Chicago Press.

Lyotard, J.-F. 1984: *The Postmodern Condition*. Minneapolis, Minn.: University of Minnesota Press.

——1988: *The Differend*. Minneapolis, Minn.: University of Minnesota Press.

——and Thebaud, J.-L. 1985: *Just Gaming*. Minneapolis, Minn.: University of Minnesota Press.

McCarthy, T. 1991: *Ideals and Illusions: On Reconstruction and Deconstruction in Contemporary Critical Theory*. Cambridge, Mass.: The MIT Press.

McGowan, J. 1991: *Postmodernism and its Critics*. Ithaca, NY, and London: Cornell University Press.

Nietzsche, F. W. 1967a: *The Birth of Tragedy*. New York: Random House.

——1967b: *The Genealogy of Morals*. New York: Random House.

——1968a: *The Will to Power*. New York: Vintage.

——1968b: *Twilight of the Idols*. New York: Penguin.

——1974: *The Gay Science*. New York: Vintage.

——1982: *Daybreak*. Cambridge: Cambridge University Press.

——1986: *Human, All Too Human*. Cambridge: Cambridge University Press.

——1990: *Unmodern Observations*. New Haven and London: Yale University Press.

O' Farrell, C. 1989: *Foucault: Historian or Philosopher*. New York: St. Martin's Press.

Ricoeur, P. 1984: *Time and Narrative*, vol. 1. Chicago, Ill.: University of Chicago Press.

Rorty, R. 1979: *Philosophy and the Mirror of Nature*. Oxford: Blackwell.

——1989: *Contingency, Irony, and Solidarity*. Cambridge: Cambridge University Press.

——1998: *Achieving Our Country: Leftist Thought in Twentieth-Century America*. Cambridge, Mass.: Harvard University Press.

Vattimo, G. 1988: *The End of Modernity*. London: Polity Press.

Chapter 14

French Feminism

Mary Beth Mader and Kelly Oliver

Feminism in twentieth-century France is defined by a history of controversies and antagonisms, especially those between materialist feminists and psychoanalytic feminists. In the early 1970s the women's movement in France coalesced, if briefly, into the Mouvement de Libération des Femmes (the Women's Liberation Movement), known as the MLF. In May of 1968 there were monumental protests, riots, and strikes on college campuses and elsewhere in France. Like the student movements in the United States at the same time, prompted by the Vietnam War, the student movements in France produced a sense of optimism about the possibility and necessity of change. Along with students, many intellectuals, faculty, and workers took part in the protests against the government. Although the political situation changed very little as a result of the protests of May 1968, the attitudes and politics of intellectuals changed. There was hope that populist movements could affect transformation. Although much of the writing after May 1968 reflects the dissolution of this optimism, it was in this spirit that the MLF was born.

The name "Mouvement de Libération des Femmes" was first used by the media reporting on a group of women who were arrested for putting a wreath on the Tomb of the Unknown Soldier at the Arc de Triomphe and dedicating it to one more unknown than he, his wife.[1] The right to legal abortions was the mobilizing issue of the MLF in the 1970s. On April 5, 1971 the weekly magazine *Le nouvel observateur* published a manifesto signed by 343 women who claimed to have had illegal abortions. Simone de Beauvoir was at the top of the list, and was followed by some of the most famous women in France.

The more women, and groups of women, who became part of the feminist movement in France, the more disagreements and factions there were in the movement. Affiliation with the MLF became problematic when in 1979 Antoinette Fouque registered the name Mouvement de Libération des Femmes as the trademark, and MLF as the logo, of the organization she led, Psych et Po (short for psychoanalysis and politics). Psych et Po, a group interested in Lacanian psychoanalysis, also started a press called *des femmes* and opened several *des femmes* bookstores in Paris. Psych et Po's takeover of the name of the women's liberation movement was a source of great controversy amongst feminists in France. The controversy over Psych et Po didn't stop there. In her 1986 book, Claire Duchen reports that "Hélène Cixous who has been closely associated with the group [Psych et Po] even asserted at a conference in New York that French women did not use the words lesbian or feminist and was angrily contradicted by other French women present."

Like their Anglo-American counterparts, feminists in France disagree on questions of equality versus difference, relations to men, the status and nature of femininity and masculinity, and the role of feminism and feminist theory themselves. Some of the writers discussed here (Cixous, Kristeva), whose ideas about women, language, and marginalization have been very influential on feminism in the Anglo-American context, have disassociated themselves from the feminist movement in France. Others criticize the feminist movement for its heterosexism (Wittig). Still others criticize what has been called "French feminism" by the English-speaking world (Delphy). In spite of their problematic relationship to "feminism," the work of these theorists has been useful for feminist theory in the Anglo-American context.

The theorists discussed here represent two main trends in French feminist theory that have had a significant influence on, and are in dialogue with, Anglo-American feminist theory: social theory and psychoanalytic theory. While some feminists in France are more concerned with patriarchal social institutions and material and economic conditions, others are more concerned with psychic structures and patriarchal colonization of the imaginary and culture. Both of these trends move away from any traditional discussions of Nature toward discussions of socially constructed notions of sex, sexuality, and gender roles. While feminists interested in social theory focus on the ways in which social institutions shape our notions of sex, sexuality, and gender roles, feminists interested in psychoanalytic theory focus on cultural representations of sex, sexuality, and gender roles and the ways in which they affect the psyche. These two trends come together in productive ways in some of the most exciting work by thinkers discussed below. This negotiation between social theory and psychoanalytic theory speaks to one of the most promising tensions in recent feminist theory in the English-speaking world.

Whether they identify themselves as materialists, Marxists, psychoanalysts, feminists, or post-feminists, many of the writers we discuss are concerned with the connection between the social and the psyche. What is the relationship between social transformation and individual transformation and vice versa? Does social change necessitate changes amongst individual attitudes, behaviors, and psychic identities? Does individual change necessitate change amongst social institutions and political systems? Or, does change implicate both the social and psychic realms at the same time?

Starting with Simone de Beauvoir's distinction between sex and gender, which points to the social construction of gender stereotypes, to Monique Wittig and Colette Guillaumin's more radical claims that sex and race are themselves socially constructed, the denaturalization of sex, gender, and race have been important to Anglo-American feminism. French feminists and American feminists alike have had varied reactions to Beauvoir's attempts to make women equal to men by denying marriage and motherhood, criticizing love relations, and rejecting stereotypical gender roles. Even amongst the theorists who favor difference over equality, there is much disagreement about what difference is and what difference it makes. While

Luce Irigaray argues that social change can only take place when our laws reflect sexual difference between men and women, Colette Guillaumin and Christine Delphy argue that historically the concept of difference, especially natural difference, has been used to keep women oppressed. In dialogue with the French debates over equality and difference, Anglo-American feminist theory continues to struggle with these same issues.

Simone de Beauvoir[2]

Simone de Beauvoir was born in 1908 in Paris, where she lived until her death in 1986. She received her doctorate in philosophy from the Sorbonne, with a dissertation on Liebniz. From 1929 until 1943, she taught at the French equivalent to high school (*lycée*) before a brief career in radio and a full time occupation with writing and political activism. In 1945, she co-founded (with Maurice Merleau-Ponty and Jean-Paul Sartre) the journal *Les temps modernes*, a forum for leftist political thought. She published many novels, essays, and her most famous philosophical work, *The Second Sex* (1949). Although *The Second Sex* is considered by many to be the birth of contemporary feminist theory, Beauvoir didn't positively identify herself as a feminist until she became active with the MLF in the early 1970s. In 1974 she became the president of the League for the Rights of Women, and in 1979 she co-founded the journal *Questions feministes* with Colette Guillaumin, Christine Delphy, and Monique Wittig, among others.

Beauvoir's existentialist feminism marks the start of the second wave of feminism and the beginning of the modern women's movement. A mere five years after the right to vote was obtained by French women, and three years after the French Constitution was amended to accord women equality in most areas of life subject to legal regulation, Beauvoir published *The Second Sex*, her sweeping examination of the history of women's oppression as women and a sustained existentialist argument for their eventual emancipation. The book's catalytic impact on the French reading public, and on nascent women's liberation movements in many nations, is insusceptible to exaggeration. In this work, Beauvoir employs the philosophical instruments devised and honed by Hegel and Sartre to analyze the historical and nearly universal subjugation of women. She advances several strategies for an end to such a condition, although the book is not primarily a detailed plan for the global or local liberation of women. In general, her argument is existentialist and socialist rather than legalistic, reformist, or liberal. It denies all the major contemporary explanations or justifications for women's subordination – biological, Freudian, Marxian – and proposes instead that the problem has its roots in a fundamental ontological propensity for conflict on the level of the very being of consciousness itself.

Every consciousness has a continual tendency to flee the burden of its equally constant and overwhelming liberty. This is the liberty that makes human being an ontological exception in a surrounding world of objects that simply are what they are. By contrast with these objects, human being, loaded with the dubious freight of awareness and inevitably oriented toward the future in light of its past, can never merely be the sum of its present tallied features: it is always what it is not – what it is not yet and is no longer. Moreover, it is through the dynamic power of negation that is the core of conscious being that the human being denies and directly refutes any possibility that it might be truly a mere object. Consciousness is the active distinguishing of itself from what it is not. At the same time, though, consciousness can identify itself as what it is not; that is, it can take itself to be the object over against itself, as well as distinguish itself from that object. It can know itself in contrast to the object and it can attempt to know itself as a thing in the world, like the identified object. Indeed, one of the deepest temptations for the human being is the impulse to see itself in the world as an object rather than as the subjectivity that it inescapably is. But the human being in a world populated by others is ambiguously both subject and object, and never simply either. Any human being has an objectual life in the experience of another subjectivity. This painful ambiguity is lived out in several forms of existential disequilibrium. Notable among these is the project to reduce another subject to the status of an object in a pre-emptive move to avoid suffering the same reduced fate in the eyes of the other. Also, since the subject cannot confirm its subjectivity of itself – even Descartes felt the necessity of (substantiating) the existence of another subjectivity, God, after the discovery of the *cogito* – the subject seeks recognition of itself as a consciousness by another consciousness. The problem is that, on the one hand, a mere object cannot provide such recognition and, on the other hand, another subject is likely to attempt to annihilate the first subject in its own project of seeking recognition. So, this precarious subject seeks an odd sort of being, one that is fundamentally object yet enough of a subject that it can perform the function of recognizing the subject as subject. Woman is this creature. She is the product of a "male will to power" (*SS*, p. 78),[3] an Other who is not a true subject but the paradoxical "object endowed with subjectivity." Mainly mired in the immanence, passivity, and dependence characteristic of an object, she has the minimal glimmer of consciousness and liberty that enables her freely to confirm the active, rational, self-defining position of man as Subject. She is Other to man's Self, a kind of being intermediate between man and nature. As such, she is pure passageway for man's way-making "from hope to frustration, from hate to love, from good to evil, from evil to good" (*SS*, p. 144).

Historically, men and women have constituted two castes, one of which, in the quest described above, has established the place of the Other as subordinate. This is a necessary historical fact and is the result of males using their "biological advantage" (*SS*, p. 77) to impose this situation upon women. This advantage is the alleged greater male freedom from bodily constraints and the demands of the flesh; men have a head start over women in the general human project of transcending nature and the limits of the species, since women are tied bodily to nature's "mysterious processes" throughout their development. Adolescence for girls is often a stupefying demotion from active subject to the socially required passivity and dependence of "femininity." Women's complicity in their own subordinate status occurs in the assumption of this feminine status, in becoming the Other for the male Subject. Indeed, the enduring conflict between the two castes will persist "as long as femininity is perpetuated as such" (*SS*, p. 719). But women's fault is that they incorporate into themselves the alien male perspective on them and on the world. To adopt femininity is to internalize one's status as Other, something women have often proven eager to do. This eagerness occurs because women, too, since they are in fact endowed with consciousness, have a desire to flee their freedom. Femininity, then, is another form of flight; it tries to abandon the necessity of living a life of one's own by living it, essentially, for another, for the male subject. Both men and women flee through each other, though they do so asymmetrically and in different manners. Men do so by trying to create a caste of objects, women. Women do so by trying to become those objects. Neither can succeed in these escapist projects. Men's superiority becomes, in a predictable reversal, frighteningly dependent on an inferior being. All the artifice, disguise, and denial that women must employ in their own project of becoming objects betrays itself all too evidently as instances of subjectivity. For both castes, each effort to become object or subject undermines itself.

The way out of these self-defeating projects and interdependent conflicts is women's accession to subjecthood, but to a new kind of subjecthood that seeks equality in freedom, opportunities, rewards, and rights for both men and women. For women, independence from men is of paramount importance. Women must above all achieve economic independence, but sexual and moral independence are likewise crucial. The "new woman" (SS, p. 725) will inhabit "an androgynous world and not a masculine world" (SS, p. 726). She will actively project herself into the future in undertakings that are not restricted by man's need for an Other. She will cast off femininity, and her situation as "parasite" (SS, p. 724), without becoming either a man or a monster. She will have no use for the limiting social roles of mother, wife, and career woman. Her full adoption of the status of subject will not come at the price of a suppression of men into the position of object, which would be no improvement over the contemporary situation. Men will have to face their loss of the servile woman and relinquish their seized prerogative to put women in that subordinate position. The meanings imparted to sexual relations will change once they no longer take place within a "system that in its entirety conspires to affirm male sovereignty" (SS, p. 727). Labor, intellectual work, and the establishment of socialism will be the kinds of action in and through which women's newfound autonomy can be made manifest and cultivated. Women and men as unequal castes were the product of social imposition; men compelled women to be a subjugated caste. At this point in history, this caste system can be undone. For justice's sake, it should be, for Beauvoir, granted her existentialist ontology of human being. On her view, if women were not, in fact, also subjects, they could not resist. More importantly, they could not have resisted. But they have, and often as a result of Beauvoir's enormously influential work of feminist philosophy.

Luce Irigaray

It is instructive to compare Simone de Beauvoir's work to that of Luce Irigaray, taking as a point of departure their very different views of how the sexes are two. Born in Belgium in 1930, Luce Irigaray is a psychoanalyst, linguist, philosopher, poet, and activist who has been published widely and in translation for the past three decades.

Her first great success came with the publication of one of her doctoral theses as the volume *Speculum: de l'autre femme*. This work, which is highly critical of many figures central to Western philosophical and psychological thinking, occasioned her repudiation by the major Lacanian professional association at the time of its publication in 1974. Her work has gained her a substantial international audience, however, especially among thinkers interested in feminist critiques of the history of Western philosophy.

Irigaray describes her position on sexual difference as "in some way the inverse" of Beauvoir's, even though she supports and admires the efforts and successes of Beauvoir to argue for and help institute liberal reforms in the area of economic and social justice and equality for women. Equality, however, is not a sufficient cultural goal for women, according to Irigaray, and to make it a goal constitutes a grave philosophical, ethical, and political error. For Beauvoir, women have occupied the position of Other; man has made woman the Other, though she makes clear that woman is also complicit in her secondary status. The solution to this subjection is to claim the status of subject, to emerge from the debased status of Other by becoming like the male subject. The inferiority of woman that is indicated by the term "second" in the title *The Second Sex* can be eliminated by assimilation to the male subject, and there are no necessarily insurmountable barriers to that assimilation. Although Irigaray understands the *prima facie* liberating appeal of Beauvoir's arguments, for Irigaray the solution to the problem of the exploitation of woman must take place in the terms of that exploitation, namely, in terms of difference, not sameness. Instead of rejecting the socially imposed category of the Other, Irigaray argues that women might instead work to realize a feminine subject that is truly irreducible to the masculine subject, that actually is the other kind (*l'autre genre*). The question of the Other in the Western tradition has never actually been thought out properly, nor have the cultures of the West ever adequately conceived of sexual difference or alterity. With regard to sexual difference, women have always been thought of relative to a male standard, but the reverse has not occurred.

Irigaray's critique is to identify what she takes to be a false difference: "At the level of sexual representatives or representations, this distribution of identifications results in there being nothing more than a double polarity inside the economy of a single and same sex." What is lacking, then, for Irigaray, is the development of a culture of two that are truly different, not merely inverse reflections of each other, opposites, negations, complements, declinations of each other – or, for Freud, as castrated. All of philosophy's construals of the dual nature of human sexedness until this point fit into one or more of those categories, on her view. The author describes her own culture, thus, as "monosubjectual, monosexed." To describe this cultural regime, she invents the term "*hommosexuel*," a neologism that plays off the French word for "man" (*homme*) in order to suggest that sexuality itself in this culture is organized around one sex only and the psychic needs of that one sex.

The term "*hommosexualité*" also refers to her argument that what is recognized as the culture in which she lives takes place primarily among and for the benefit of men. Recalling Lévi-Strauss' work on kinship and signification, she argues that women are exchanged among men, from father to husband, and are marshaled as the uncredited material support for the higher cerebral activities of this primarily male culture. Their purpose is to tend to the bodies and emotions of men and to reproduce for their husbands male offspring. Neither the law nor religion truly recognizes this unpaid debt to the maternal body; a specifically female genealogy and hence the mother–daughter relation remain obscured in an unthought naturalism or an unchallenged valorization of the mother–son and father–son relations, in the case of Christianity. The specific needs and interests of women exist apart from this culture, in an unarticulated and unsublimated manner; because of this, and because of how the very notions of appearing and existing have been understood in the male cultural imaginary, these needs and interests appear not to exist at all. Women suffer profoundly from this lack of articulation of themselves, from lack of a language that suits their particular concerns, from lack of a genealogy that accurately situates them in history, from lack of a god that would provide them a means of transcendence, from lack of cultural practices that would respect and spiritualize their bodily nature. Indeed, women presently lack subjectivity because they lack a subjectivity of their own.

Philosophy is centrally complicit in the Western sexual monoculture. Throughout Western philosophy a single subject has been imagined and constituted, a subject that is unaware that there even could be multiple subjects. There is one philosophical model of the subject, built around the Platonic notion of the priority of the one over the many. It conforms to one version of a human: male, adult, Western, reasonable, capable. These qualities are conceived of as valuable and all humans can be hierarchically ranked on the basis of this standard. Thus, the world of humans can be divided up into those that are this subject and those who are designated in light of this model as "not-man" or "not-subject." Philosophy's ignorance of a sexed otherness or of sex as an otherness is not only a failure on the level of truth; it is an injustice with real lived consequences.

Philosophy is just one cultural instance of man's tendency to cope with the "problem" of his origin in another sex by depicting himself as self-generated. Irigaray finds this move not only in the origin stories of Christianity but in the classic works of philosophical writing, in which what is coded as feminine functions as an unthinkable ground for the transcendent thoughts of the thinker who construes himself as self-made, as independent from his material sources in what he designates as the merely natural. This amounts to a denial of sexual difference *per se*, and hence of his own sexual difference. Irigaray stresses an intolerable debt to the mother for her gift of life, as well as a debt to nature itself. The association of nature and mother is constant in her work; this is because she is trying to work in and on a cultural imaginary in which she finds these terms already firmly linked. This debt is unpaid; matter, nature, and woman have supplied mind, culture, and man in the form of the male thinking body, yet mind, culture, and man have not reciprocated with a provision to their supplier. The alleged integrity, constancy, and independence of the male subject have been fashioned by him out of the metaphysically and physically demoted mere raw material of this supposed auto-generation. In addition, man can see himself as self-created due to his separation of the material and the ideal and due to his construal of language as immaterial.

The metaphysical projects of Western philosophy themselves have been a part of such a project of denial. Irigaray critiques the emphasis on a metaphysics of solids, of a philosophical preoccupation with man's relation to objects, with elaborating ontologies of substance, and with the asymmetrically evaluated binary oppositions between the material and the transcendental, the sensible and the intelligible. Irigaray argues that both the logic of the solid form and logic itself as a formalism serve an unrecognized or repressed need on the part of "man" to cope with the specific exigencies of his own sexual difference. Fluids, on the other hand, are overlooked in Western metaphysics, and indeed, not able to be handled in this metaphysics. Fluids confound individuation: Does the child being born enter the air or is the air entering the child? Is the child inside the mother, or is the mother, as fluids infusing the child, inside the child? Irigaray does not think this special relation of interpenetration holds only in this figure of a woman carrying a child. Instead, this figure is only exceptional in that it allows us to discern rather well what is generally and ubiquitously the case, although it is obscured by the metaphysics of our culture. Irigaray appeals to the notions of fluidity to articulate an identity that would break with the (solid) consistency and coherence of the logos and of the subjectivity of man it allegedly supports. Fluidity always exceeds reason and the rational, for Irigaray, but it also makes possible unified, individuated solids; it does so as forgotten surrounding, backdrop, or ground against which distinct substances stand out. Philosophers forget that "without fluid" their thought would not cohere, or have any unity; the fluid is between solid substances, allowing them to join or unite. But this fluid-supportive condition does not itself stand out, and to call attention to it is to risk revealing that a mobile, non-solid necessity is actually the "ground" for the "solid" formulations of the logos.

Irigaray frequently alludes to a yet-to-be-constructed specifically female subjectivity that would respect the particular needs and values of women, and so be the condition of possibility for the first true meeting, in both love and culture, of men and women. This does not mean that what is lacking is symmetry between men and women, that women simply ought to mimic men's institutions and practices. Indeed, she frequently warns against such a thing and holds that mere accession to male halls of power or the creation of roughly parallel practices is not a solution. In fact, this parallelism, if enacted, would only amount to a mirror form of injustice. Were women to create "man" as a decerebrated, raw material upon which to found an order of spiritual, deracinated production, this would be no improvement on the situation. She seeks a specific sexed subjectivity for women, which would amount to a kind of identity and to the identity of a kind. However, the kind of identity that women could construct and have not yet constructed could be one that is multiple and changing to a more profound degree than the kind of identity of the man created thus far.

Irigaray seeks cultural change conceived on the grandest scale. She views her own writing as part of an effort to bring about "a new cultural era: that of sexual difference." To open her discussion of sexual difference as constituting "the horizon of worlds more fecund than any known to date," she writes in *An Ethics of Sexual Difference*: "Sexual difference is one of the major philosophical issues, if not the issue, of our age. According to Heidegger, each age has one issue to think through, and one only. Sexual difference is probably the issue in our time which could be our 'salvation' if we thought it through." Some of her more recent writings include specific proposals for legal, artistic, medical, and political reforms aimed at the eventual creation of this new culture of two sexed subjectivities.

Colette Guillaumin

Colette Guillaumin was born in 1934 in France, and received a doctorate in sociology in 1969 from the University of Paris, Sorbonne. She co-founded the journal *Questions féministes* and served on its editorial board until 1980. She has taught at the University of Paris VII and at the National Center for Scientific Research (CNRS), and is an active member of the International Association for the Study of Racism and the National Association for the Study of Women.

Guillaumin develops the notion of *sexage* or women's labor to describe women's unpaid and domestic labor as a kind of sexual slavery. She argues that the physical appropriation of women's bodies and labor is analogous to slavery, and analyzes women's oppression as primarily the result of this physical appropriation. The end result is that women are treated as property within patriarchy. Like Delphy and other materialist feminists, Guillaumin looks to the economic and social conditions of women's oppression, and diagnoses power relations between men and women in terms of those material conditions. She insists that discourses of femininity, motherhood, and woman perpetuate women's oppression by naturalizing these categories, which serves to make oppression and appropriation invisible.

Guillaumin is probably best known for her arguments that it is not race hierarchies that lead to racism but, rather, that racism leads to race hierarchies and the very conception of race. She traces the history of the concept of race, which she maintains is solidified only through extreme racist regimes, which codify it – for example, when race became legally classifiable in Nazi Germany or when in 1945 South Africa adopted legal categories of race. Guillaumin argues against all legal classifications of race, and points out that scientists have discarded the notion of race as biologically meaningful. Still, although she insists that notions of race are racist constructions and never neutral, she also argues that simply rejecting the idea of race is not enough to overcome racism. She maintains that although race has no biological or psychological reality, it has a significant social reality because of the history of race and racism. Therefore, we must continue to work against racism and racist constructions of race even while we acknowledge their effects.

Hélène Cixous

Hélène Cixous was born on June 5, 1937 in Oran, Algeria. She grew up in a multilingual environment, exposed to French, German, Spanish, and Arabic. She went to Paris in 1955 to study English literature at the University of Paris IV, Sorbonne, where she received her doctorate in 1968 with a dissertation on James Joyce. In 1969 she co-founded the journal *Revue de Théorie et d'analyse littéraire poétique*. In 1974 she founded the Centre de Recherches en Études Féminines at the University of Paris VIII. Cixous has published novels, plays, and autobiographical and theoretical essays. She is the recipient of many prestigious awards including the Prix Médicis for her first novel *Dedans* ("*Inside*"), the Legion d'Honneur, the Prix des

Critiques, and the Southern Cross of Brazil. In the Anglo-American context, Cixous is best known for her early theoretical essays in which she develops the notion of *écriture féminine*, or feminine writing, and for her work on Brazilian novelist Clarice Lispector, whom she maintains employs feminine writing.

Cixous sets out to shock the philosophers who have been so squeamish about the female body by exposing/creating it in her texts. She says: "Let them tremble, those priests; we are going to *show* them our *sexts*! Too bad for them if they collapse on discovering that women aren't men, or that the mother doesn't have one. But doesn't this fear suit them fine? Wouldn't the worst thing be – isn't the worst thing that, really, woman is not castrated . . ." She refuses to play what she calls "the game of penis-check played by the imperialist superpowers of the triumvirate with the mean solemnity that makes history." And, while as she says, "the penis gets around in my text," she won't allow herself "to be threatened by the big dick." Her criticisms of traditional philosophy and psychoanalytic theory are filled with this kind of playful irreverence.

In addition to her wicked fun with the traditions of men, Cixous creates feminine myths by reclaiming the feminine from its abasement in the Western culture. She re-reads traditional myths and literature in order to throw off the masculine metaphors that have been forced onto the feminine. For example, she tells the story of Dora from Dora's perspective in her play *Portrait of Dora*, re-tells the stories of Electra and Cleopatra in *Sorties*, and identifies with Medusa, Electra, Antigone, and Cleopatra. She says that she has been them all. In this way, she reclaims these female characters and their myths, and brings them to life again. In her fiction, she tries to actualize her image of feminine writing. She creates new myths of femininity using a variety of shifting styles. In "Castration or Decapitation" she compares psycho-analysis to fairy-tales. There, she argues that in both psychoanalytic theory and the tales of "Little Red Riding Hood" and "Sleeping Beauty" woman is "laid" between two beds, "ever caught in her chain of metaphors, metaphors that organize culture."

In order to be free of these masculine metaphors in which women have been caught, Cixous maintains that women must write their bodies. She seems to suggest that women need to create their own metaphors, metaphors that do not operate within a metaphorical economy of substitution. In this regard, she comes close to Irigaray's inversion of metonymy/metaphor. For Cixous it is women's bodies, par-ticularly their sexuality, which has been left out of Western culture's "masculine" economy of the Same. And she tries to imagine this "feminine" writing, *écriture féminine*, which expresses/creates a feminine libidinal economy.

Freud maintains that the libido is masculine and Cixous argues that within his dis-course the very notion of the unconscious is a product of a masculine imaginary. She insists that we need a new unconscious, a feminine unconscious. And if, as she main-tains, the unconscious is a cultural product, then we can create this new unconscious through writing. "Things are starting to be written," says Cixous, "things that will constitute a feminine Imaginary, the site, that is, of identifications of an ego no longer given over to an image defined by the masculine . . ."

At the end of "Castration or Decapitation," Cixous describes how she would imagine this feminine writing. It is important that for Cixous feminine writing cannot be theorized and therefore her text should not be read as a theoretical description. She considers herself a poet who is trying to create a feminine writing and imagines a text that has neither origin or end, a text with several beginnings that goes on and on. This text "asks the question of giving – 'What does this writing give?' 'How does it give?'" It isn't predictable or knowable. It is a tactile text, "close to the voice, very close to the flesh." For Cixous, the relation between feminine writing, the feminine libido, and the body is crucial. Her texts are manifestos calling upon women to write their bodies because feminine writing derives from the body. This "body" of hers, however, is not merely the physical body. She is not proposing some kind of biologism. Rather, for Cixous, the body is a complex of social and biological processes.

Because femininity is a matter of representation, it is crucial for women to write their bodies, their imaginations, their libidos. What is at issue is creating a new economy of representation that is not built on the repression of the feminine. Cixous argues that the phallocracy of Western culture has insured that a phallic representational economy has suppressed any other. Cixous maintains that men too have lost their bodies and their sexuality to the phallic economy, which is premised on a logic of metaphorical substitution, and which always returns to the Phallus. And this phallic economy has been erected "in the face of this person [woman] who lacks lack [castration]." It is her lack of lack upon which "manhood" is constructed, "flaunting its metaphors like banners through history." With this contention, Cixous is alluding to Freud's theory that women are inferior to men – their superegos are underdeveloped – because they don't undergo the castration complex.

Resonant with Irigaray's notion of Western culture as *hommosexuel*, Cixous believes that the masculine economy of metaphors is an economy of the Same ("monosexuality") in which feminine elements are always appropriated for its purposes. The master has invented his own Other and this is why this Other can be domesticated. Cixous tries to imagine a bisexuality that does not deny difference. For Cixous, bisexuality means the location within oneself of difference, of two sexes. She maintains that we are all bisexual; our primary bisexuality is perverted by phallocentric culture. She imagines a bisexuality that is a process of exchange and not a struggle to the death. In "The Laugh of the Medusa" she claims that writing is not masculine or feminine but in between. It is bisexual. The between seems to exist within each of us, the presence of difference within. Cixous proposes the bisexual as a third alternative to the binary masculine and feminine.

She continues to develop this notion of bisexuality as between in her later writings. In *Rootprints* (1994), she proposes the notion of *entredeux*, or between-two, as a between the masculine and feminine. Reminiscent of Irigaray, Cixous imagines this between-two as a passage to and from an other who is not interchangeable or even knowable. Between-two is the space within which sexual difference emerges as a curiosity and love. Love brings the sexes together through what Cixous refers to as "the common sex," the heart. She insists that the joy that is possible to the human heart comes only through an encounter with difference.

Julia Kristeva

Julia Kristeva was born in 1941 in Bulgaria. She was educated by French nuns, studied literature, and worked as a journalist before going to Paris in 1966 to do graduate work with Lucien Goldmann and Roland Barthes. While in Paris she finished her doctorate in French literature, was appointed to the faculty of the Department of Texts and Documents at the University of Paris VI (Denis Diderot) and began psychoanalytic training. Currently, Kristeva is Director of the Department of Science of Texts and Documents at the University of Paris VII, where she teaches in the department of Literature and Humanities. In April 1997, she received one of France's highest honors, the *Chevaliére de la légion d'honneur*, for her 30 years of intellectual work, which has been translated into ten languages. In addition to her work as a practicing psychoanalyst and her theoretical writings, Kristeva has written three novels.

Kristeva's work reflects her diverse background. Her writing is an intersection between philosophy, psychoanalysis, linguistics, and cultural and literary theory. She developed the science of what she calls "semanalysis," which is a combination of Freud's psychoanalysis and Saussure's and Peirce's semiology. With this new science Kristeva challenges traditional psychoanalytic theory, linguistic theory, and philosophy. In most of her writing, Kristeva's goal is to bring the speaking body, complete with drives, back into philosophy and linguistics. In one of her most influential books, *Revolution in Poetic Language*, she criticizes both Husserlian phenomenology and Saussurean linguistics for formulating theories of the subject and language that cannot account for the processes through which a subject speaks. There are two ways in which Kristeva brings the speaking body back into theories of language. First, she proposes that bodily drives are discharged through language. Second, she maintains that the structure or logic of signification is already operating in the material body. On Kristeva's analysis, language is in the body and the body is in language.

Kristeva's most influential contribution to philosophy of language has been her distinction between the semiotic and the symbolic elements of signification. All signification is made up of these two elements in varying proportions. The semiotic element is the organization of drives in language. It is associated with rhythms and tones that are meaningful parts of language and yet do not represent or signify something. Rhythms and tones do not represent bodily drives; rather, bodily drives are discharged through rhythms and tones. The symbolic element of language, on the other hand, is the domain of position and judgment. It is associated with the grammar or structure of language that enables it to signify something.

The dialectical oscillation between the semiotic and the symbolic is what makes signification possible. Without the symbolic, we have only sounds or delirious babble. But without the semiotic, signification would be empty and we would not speak. The semiotic provides the motivation for engaging in signifying processes; we have a bodily need to communicate. The symbolic provides the structure necessary to communicate. Both elements are essential to signification. And it is the tension between them that makes signification dynamic. The semiotic both motivates signification and threatens the symbolic element. The semiotic provides the negativity and the symbolic provides the states or stability that keeps signification both dynamic and structured. The semiotic makes change, even structural change, possible.

Kristeva sees her theory of the semiotic, especially as it is related to the maternal body, as an alternative to the Lacanian model of language acquisition. Lacan's account of signification and self-consciousness begins with the mirror stage and the paternal metaphor's substitution of the law of the father for the desire of the mother. On the traditional psychoanalytic model of both Freud and Lacan the child enters the social or language out of fear of castration threats. The child experiences its separation from the maternal body as a tragic loss and consoles itself with words instead. Paternal threats make words the only, if inadequate, alternative to psychosis. Kristeva insists, however, that separation begins prior to the mirror stage or Oedipal situation, and that this separation is not only painful but also pleasurable. She insists that the child enters the social and language not just due to paternal threats but also because of paternal love.

At bottom, Kristeva criticizes the traditional account because it cannot adequately explain the child's move to signification. If the only thing that motivates the move to signification are threats and the pain of separation, then why would anyone make this move? Why not remain in the safe haven of the maternal body and refuse the social and signification with its threats? Kristeva suggests that if the accounts of Freud and Lacan were correct, then more people would be psychotic.

Kristeva's concern to bring the body with all of its dynamic processes back into theory explains the types of discourses on which she focuses. Because traditional philosophy has revolved around fixed notions of a unitary and autonomous subject that covers over the dynamic processes that produce such a subject position, Kristeva is concerned with discourses that break down the identity of the subject and expose what she calls the subject-in-process. She focuses on crises in identification, most poignantly the maternal body. In "Stabat Mater," she criticizes some of the traditional discourses of maternity in Western culture, specifically the myth of the Virgin Mary, because they do not present the mother as primarily a speaking being.

Still, Kristeva has an ambivalent, sometimes hostile, relation to feminism and some aspects of the feminist movement in France. She objects to what she calls "herd" feminism (1980a, p. 135). And she rejects Simone de Beauvoir's stigmatization of maternity as the ultimate exploitation of women (1987, pp. 201–24). She counters that "it is difficult to speak of motherhood without being accused of normativism. Yet it is precisely in this experience that woman's specific relation to meaning and to the other is achieved, refined, and differentiated: to an other who is the child, neither the object of erotic desire nor the object of psychological need, but another subject" (2000a, pp. 105–6). This is the love of difference that makes "love thy neighbor as thyself" imaginable. Not only are all women different and all mothers different, but also women as mothers make it possible to imagine loving difference.

Kristeva insists that women's movements should demand attention to individual differences, especially sexual differences. She suggests that there are as many sexualities as there are individuals. In "Women's time" (1979) she describes the women's movement and feminism in terms of a Hegelian dialectic: universal–particular–individual. The first wave of feminism argues that abstract universal rights, the rights of man, be extended to women. The second wave of feminism argues for women's particularity and difference from men. The third wave of feminism, a kind of post-feminism, argues for the singularity of each individual against both the universal and the particular. Kristeva's individualism takes us beyond equality to singularity. She describes her project in the trilogy *Female Genius* (2000) as "a call to the singularity of every woman." She argues that the genius of extraordinary women such as Hannah Arendt, Melanie Klein, and Colette help all women to see what is extraordinary in their own ordinary lives. Conversely, she maintains that the genius of everyday life is women's genius, particularly a mother's genius. In creating new human beings, mothers are each singular innovators, reinventing the child anew all the time. Kristeva suggests that mothers might represent the "only safeguard against the wholesale automation of human beings." Each mother, and each mother–child relation, is singular and unique.

Monique Wittig

In *The Straight Mind and Other Essays*, novelist and philosopher Monique Wittig works out a kind of "materialist lesbianism," an analysis of sex, gender, heterosexuality and language that employs the instruments of the Marxian analysis of political economy. The primary objects of her work in theory are (i) heterosexuality, (ii) the role of the universal, and (iii) language and literature. Her analysis of all three relies on the notion of a category and critiques the categories that operate to produce various kinds of oppressions – or dominant and subordinate groups – to urge the eventual elimination of such categories.

Wittig's analysis bears some resemblance to Shulamith Firestone's notion of sex class, construing sex class, on analogy with economic class, as the product of conflictual relations between men and women. It is also akin to Adrienne Rich's notion of compulsory heterosexuality, which stresses the normative nature of heterosexuality as a social institution. Wittig introduces the notion of discourse as a crucial component in the creation of women as dominated beings – that is, of women in a social sense. Discourse, on this view, is an effective force imprinting and forming some human beings into a class oppressed in part by what this discursive force creates: womanhood. The category of sex itself is the primary tool both in the conceptual and material realms for the creation of a class oppressed by sex. The category of sex cannot be salvaged from its history of oppressive effects; there is no possible category of sex apart from its use as an instrument of oppression. It came into existence for this purpose and cannot outlive this purpose. The ontology of the category of sex, for Wittig, follows a Marxian construal of the constitutive relations of economic class. That is, the relations constitute the relata: the relation of conflict institutes classes that oppose each other at each historical stage. So, in this case, the conflictual relation between men and women creates the social categories of "men" and "women" as dominant and subordinate. "Woman" has a mythological status, for Wittig, while "women" are the "product of a relation of exploitation." Further, the general term "woman," an ideal, operates to mask the real status of "women" as an exploited class. The category of sex is also one that women cannot escape. For Wittig, the obligatory nature of heterosexuality is located in the very category of sex itself rather than in the "institution of heterosexuality," or its particular normative power, as it is in Rich's analysis. The category of sex seizes women in particular with peculiar adhesive force, designating them as sexual beings. (One can note here that with the term "sexual being" Wittig does not distinguish between being sexed, or being a member of a sex, on the one hand, and sexuality, or possessing an erotic capacity or dimension, on the other hand. Nor, to invent a third hand, does she distinguish between those two senses of "sex" and a third sense that pertains to sexual as opposed to asexual reproduction.) To be precise, the category of sex designates women as heterosexual beings, who must ever display the insignia of their sexual destiny. She writes: "They must wear their yellow star, their constant smile, day and night" (*SM*, p. 7). The discourse of sex, in particular the "myth of woman," is the causal origin of women's oppression. Women are those who are oppressed by the sex class system, which institutes sex as the instrument of that oppression. It is not that women simply are, and then are oppressed as women. Rather, what we know as women already are the deformed results of a mythology that has bowed them to a subordinate type. This type is politically and economically expedient to the class of men; hence, it is an effect of power. Lesbians, escaping heterosexuality, thereby are not women.

But these opposing categories are just one instance of a larger erroneous way of thinking that Wittig attributes to "straight society." This society is riven by numerous relations of dominance and subordination: race, class, age, and so on. Its functioning depends on these multiple layers of "difference" or "otherness." These differences are not innocent but, instead, are forms of domination: the different *are* the dominated, in fact. Wittig argues that the institution of these differences has a history that is part of the history of philosophy. She asserts that "conceptual tools resting on division" (*SM*, p. 50) were at first "precious" "mathematical and instrumental categories" that underwent a transformation into "normative and metaphysical categories." Revisiting Aristotle's table of opposites, Wittig claims that it originated as a Pythagorean table with a "technical, instrumental" purpose: to be used with the gnomon, "a kind of carpenter's square." But this table took a moral, metaphysical, and abstract turn with Aristotle. The dissociation of these terms from the crucible of practice forged them into the weapons of a metaphysical campaign for the oppressive ordering of human life. The "common people, the females, the 'slaves of the poor,' the 'dark'" are identified with non-Being. The "good, the male, the straight, the one" are aligned with Being. The female falls on the side of "discord, unrest, dark, and bad." Although Wittig does not provide detailed accounts of the precise working of this, she does claim that "abstract philosophical categories act upon the real as social." Wittig does not exempt her work from this position of acting "upon the real as social." But she wishes to follow Marx's and Engels' "dynamization" of Hegel in regarding metaphysical terms that operate in the social and political world as conflicts, between people or groups of people, rather than as "essential oppositions" (*SM*, p. 47). She will not, however, advocate the elimination of all metaphysical terms that operate upon the real. She advocates retaining the terms "humanity," "human," and "man," *even though* they have been appropriated by men as instruments of domination over women for ages. So, although one possible direction might be to give up this universalizing aim, and to abandon the terms expressing it, Wittig rejects this direction, arguing instead for women's accession to the universal and for their re-appropriation of the discourses of humanity. The problem, of course, is that of what this universal will be like. Can it remain the same kind of thing when it is articulated by someone who is a member of a group that has been constituted – by the former use of the universal – as someone *different*, as, precisely, someone not capable of representing any human? For Wittig, it cannot remain the same; if one universalizes a "difference," this will change both the universal and the particular. It will "cancel out" the particular difference and rid the universal of its traditional false and unjust identification with the male, the straight, the bourgeois. Wittig cites as an example of shifting an excluded difference into the universal the writing of Djuna Barnes, arguing that she "universalized the feminine" and thereby nullifies "the genders, by making them obsolete" (*SM*, p. 61). Proust, likewise, situated the "homosexual" at the center of his fictive world. But this changes the center – or universal standpoint – itself, for, as Wittig writes, "the minority subject is not self-centered as is the straight subject." The point is discernible: the eccentric cannot be centered in the same way as that which has never been eccentric. It finds its center everywhere, as Wittig writes, like Pascal's circle with the ubiquitous center and non-locatable circumference (*SM*, p. 62). Wittig will take a position, then, on the trend of the 1960s and 1970s, among both male and female philosophers, of seeking solutions to the postwar impasses of both metaphysics and political and sexual economy in the thinking of Difference. To emphasize allegedly preexisting differences, which are nothing but the marks of various campaigns of oppression and institutions of servitude, is merely to embed people even further in the destructive relations that constitute these differences. Hence, her exhortation that "women should . . . never formulate this imposition of being different . . . as a 'right to be different'" (*SM*, p. 55). Instead, women should occupy and claim the territory traditionally off-limits to them: the realm of the universal. She singles out "feminine writing" or the *écriture féminine* championed and exemplified by Hélène Cixous for special criticism. It is, she charges, a term that naturalizes the calamitous history of "the domination of women" (*SM*, p. 59). It implies that the particular character of woman is naturally "secreted" by women when in fact the "woman"-ness allegedly to be expressed or invented in such writing is a deformation produced by exploitative practices.

This deformation is evident in language, as linguistic gender. The linguistic rule that requires the display of the feminine gender is an essentially social and political obligation to mark and self-mark the dominated sex class. The social and political norm of sex display for women is concealed as *such* – that is, as itself an *instance* of domination – in its guise as purely a rule of language. The sex display obligation is asymmetrical. Wittig holds that the masculine is not a gender; it is the unmarked category that functions as the general. Linguistic gender is "the unique lexical symbol that refers to an oppressed group" (*SM*, p. 88). But language is also the only domain of free exchange with others, beyond categories and oppression. Since anyone can innovate in language, and push it to express new meanings, language itself is a social contract binding people together as free and equal. More importantly, it is literature

– especially that of experimentalists such as Proust, Barnes, and Sarraute – that can act as the incubator of new social meanings for human beings that contest the commonplace oppressions of our everyday categories.

Sarah Kofman

A reader of texts *par excellence*, philosopher Sarah Kofman is known best for her scrupulous, deeply engaged interpretations of Nietzsche, Freud, and Derrida. Though she neither situated herself within the current of *écriture féminine*, nor attempted a specific positive re-imagining of the feminine, her psychoanalytic and deconstructive readings of many of the central texts in Western philosophy sought to show the degree to which the work of the male philosophers of this tradition is tied in many ways to particular sexual economies. One way that this is so is that the philosophical project of valuing and seeking transcendence and intelligibility over immanence, sensibility, and materiality actually relies upon a sexual economy that identifies the sensible and material with the feminine. This means that the unarticulated condition of possibility for the crafting and working out of many philosophical projects has been this realm coded as feminine. Kofman, then, brings into view or lets be heard the needs and desires of the philosopher as a particular version of a male subject whose self-constitution as both male and philosopher *requires* for his bounding and integrity both the feminine and non-philosophy. Through scrupulous readings of Comte, Kant, Rousseau, Plato, and Blanchot, among others, she raises to prominence the points in their texts that betray this reliance on what is construed as other or as a sexed other. She demonstrates the complicity of those construals in the construction of the alleged others, as well as showing and showing up the philosophers' psychic investments in such constructions: constructing an other to construct oneself without conscious awareness of this project of self-construction, and without an awareness of the fears and desires regarding women that move and charge such constructions/construals.

In *The Enigma of Woman* (French 1989, English 1985), Kofman reads Freud's texts on feminine sexuality with an altogether feline balance between challenge and sympathy, showing Freud's unknowing proximity to views that might have genuinely broken out of a traditional sexual economy whose positions are disposed by a fundamental bewilderment, anxiety, or even horror at the prospect of women. To Kofman, Freud is struck by women's profound silence or "reserve" and in psychoanalysis offers the place for and the prompting of women's eruption into speech and out of what is her specialty: herself as an enigma. However, the analytic scene cannot do justice to these emerging speakers; the talking cure is a treatment that "extorts" speech from women, as it invites it, and that ultimately speaks over it with the masculine discourse of truth emitted by the master, the male analyst. (The book can be profitably compared with another roughly contemporaneous French feminist interrogation of Freud, one that is arguably harsher, offered by Luce Irigaray in *Speculum: de l'autre femme* [*Speculum: of the Other Woman*].) Kofman writes:

> Thus, although psychoanalysis may inveigh against the sexual repression to which women are subject, although it may invite them to shed their inhibitions and restore their right to speech, the remedy it offers is at the same time a poison since it can cure women only by contaminating them, by forcing them to "collaborate," to espouse the viewpoint of the other, of men, who are supposed to possess truth. (*EW*, p. 48)

So, the curative "poison" of psychoanalytic treatment is at the same time a therapy in the service of the analyst's infirmity; namely, his inability to bear both the abominable silence of women and their self-sufficiency, which this silence has in part implied. This reading of Freud's vision for the relation of female sexuality to women's speech exemplifies a hermeneutic strategy Kofman deploys frequently: elicit from the text what it does, how it operates, within the entire context of its production and use, rather than simply drawing out what it purports to express.

Michèle Le Doeuff

Like Kofman, the philosopher Michèle Le Doeuff reads texts with a jeweler's eye, relentlessly revealing the internal fault lines of philosophical arguments or systems that make them both glitter and crack. A member of the generation at the barricades in May 1968, her work treats a wide array of topics including literature, political philosophy, classical philosophy, feminist philosophy, and philosophy of the history of the sciences. She has published translations of Francis Bacon's *New Atlantis* and Shakespeare's *Venus and Adonis*. Her most important philosophical works to date are *The Philosophical Imaginary* and *Hipparchia's Choice: An Essay Concerning Women, Philosophy, Etc.*

In *The Philosophical Imaginary*, Le Doeuff makes explicit the externalized conditions of possibility for the integrity and operation of classic texts in Western philosophy, including major works by Plato, Descartes, and Kant. She demonstrates that – and how – contrary to the philosopher's conception of philosophical writing as approaching truth precisely by escaping the language and realm of the image, philosophical writing cannot purify itself of the image. Although images are supposed to be exiled from the domain of philosophy, they reenter at "sensitive points" in a work and function, under tension, paradoxically to both support and undermine the text's status as a free-standing work of philosophy. Basically, an image crops up in a work at a point at which the argumentation itself cannot suffice to establish a proposition, doing hard but unseen labor to allow the proposition to pass. Yet, the image itself will never be supported from within the text itself; its plausibility and efficacy rely on its easy and familiar circulation in the culture beyond the domain of philosophy. Philosophy supposes that the argument is merely flavored with such imported images to sugarcoat the pill of difficult thinking for those unused to the bitter remedy of rigorous thought. But Le Doeuff, in a typical deconstructive move, demonstrates the force and centrality of these underestimated images; they are no mere embellishment or crutch, but are the ungrounded grounds of and for allegedly well-founded arguments.

Le Doeuff also addresses philosophical, legal, and everyday discourses pertaining to public policies and legal practices concerning women's issues. In *Hipparchia's Choice*, Le Doeuff mounts a dual critique of two major tendencies in second-wave feminism: the feminism of equality and the feminism of difference. Considering questions of women's health – such as abortion, rape, contraception, battery, and clitoridectomy – she finds fault with both strands of feminist thinking. Feminism of difference, in addition to being ineffectual relative to the genuine life problems of women, is doomed to failure by its own internal inconsistencies. It proposes that difference itself be valued, but then proceeds to elevate one difference, sexual difference, above all others. Le Doeuff proposes that: "The only consistent way to give value to the fact of difference is to uncover differences by the thousands, or better, as Albert Jacquard suggests, countless differences which defy all lists" (*HC*, p. 228). But the feminism of equality, despite its significant successes in the areas of legal reform, achieved by the extension of the principle of equality to women as citizens, has reached an impasse in the passages of its collective political imagination. For sexual disparities persist – in the family, in custom, in "civil society" – despite the seemingly full legal application of the principle of equality. A profoundly novel imagining – which would challenge the merely apparent independence of the family and civil society from the sphere of the law and the state – is required. It must be prompted by a sort of creative disorientation like that generated in the midst of the feminist movement struggles of the 1960s and 1970s. That the feminism of equality sees its task as virtually completed makes it an unlikely source of the newly imagined categories that further change will need.

Christine Delphy

Christine Delphy was born in 1941 in France. She studied sociology at the University of Paris IV, after which she traveled to the University of California at Berkeley, where she received the Eleanor Roosevelt Foundation for Human Relations Fellowship for her involvement in the civil rights movement. Delphy continued to be politically active after she returned to Paris in 1966. She was involved in the MLF, the Féministes Révolutionnaires, and founded the journal *Nouvelle questions feministes*. She has held teaching positions at the National Center for Scientific Research (CNRS) and the University of Paris X.

Delphy is best known for her materialist feminism, which grew out of her involvement with leftist and Marxist groups in France in the 1960s. Like Guillaumin and Wittig, Delphy analyzes the interlocking systems of capitalist and patriarchal oppression. Her work focuses on the material conditions of women's oppression, especially unpaid and domestic labor. Unlike Kristeva, Irigaray, or Cixous, Delphy does not begin with notions of the unconscious and imaginary in order to account for sexual difference. Rather, she looks to material, economic, and social conditions. She rejects most psychoanalytic theories, which she sees as naturalizing sexual difference. In addition to her materialist feminism, and her criticisms of psychoanalytic theory, Delphy is also known for her analysis of what she calls "the invention of French

Feminism" by feminists, primarily in the United States, who favor theorists who do not identify themselves as feminists and who are marginal to the women's movement in France. She argues that, as a result, Anglo-American feminists have a completely skewed notion of feminism in France.

Conclusion

It is true that in the last quarter century the anglophone world of feminist philosophy has taken special note of philosophical work that originates in the academic environs of the French hexagon on questions that pertain to women. Delphy is correct to point out that initial categorizations of feminist thought in France by anglophone readers elsewhere tended to highlight and group together three deconstructive and/or psychoanalytically inspired philosophers – Kristeva, Irigaray, and Cixous – as "French feminism," though these authors have had complicated relationships with the main currents of activist feminism in France. In their journeys abroad, texts by these authors have indeed been categorized, interpreted, and employed in ways other than those they enjoyed in their homeland. The question is whether the adjective designating their national origins – French – implies that these texts accurately represent feminist thought *as a whole* in contemporary France. If psychoanalytic, deconstructive feminist philosophers – in particular the Kristeva, Irigaray, Cixous triad – are taken to represent all of contemporary French feminist philosophy, or even the most politically influential or operative versions of feminist philosophy in France today, this indeed would be a mistake. In fact, this essay's brief survey of feminist thought originating in France demonstrates that the variety of such thinking extends well beyond the triad initially identified as the core of "French feminism." Moreover, the importance of Simone de Beauvoir and materialist feminist thinkers ought not be underestimated, especially if one's aim is to understand which feminist thinking has in fact been most influential on the French political and social scene. But this is not the only aim one might legitimately pursue in studying feminist philosophical work done in France. And the fact that such writings do not represent all of the feminist work done in France, or even the feminist work that has been most politically influential there, does not mean that it ought not to have a life that extends beyond its initial life on the home front. Like "French fried" potatoes (chips, *frites*), "French feminism" is now on the (philosophical) menu outside of the national boundaries of France. This should no more be taken to mean that all feminisms in France are "French" (psychoanalytic, deconstructive) than that all potatoes in France are "French fried."

Feminist work in France today takes up questions of women's economic status in the new high-technology economy of France, of women's participation in representative politics at all levels (the parity law), of new legal definitions of the social unit of the household (the Pacs law), of questions of access to new reproductive technologies, and of labor law regarding paternity and maternity, among other issues.

But feminist work in France today also addresses social issues that are of particular urgency for Europe as a whole, especially as Jean Monnet's 1950 plan for the eventual political and economic integration of Europe sees its gradual institution. Feminist theorists and political leaders are active in the legal and political construction of a unified European community and are especially interested in building into the foundations of the Union mechanisms to help eliminate the persisting profound political and economic inequalities between men and women in Europe. Issues of special concern include: women and the reemergence of war in Europe; women's economic and social status in the era following the Cold War; women and the family policy of states whose social welfare systems are threatened by the economic pressures of increasing globalization; the problem of the apparent increase in the sexual trade of women and children after the demise of the Soviet Union; women's roles in economies that are in great turmoil, if not transition; and women and the various dislocations and migrations that impact European nations.

Dealing with the advent of the mature European Union is by itself a substantial task. To add to that task, France, like some other European nations, is undergoing a period of national self-scrutiny of its very recent colonial past, especially in North Africa, as well as its relations to Arab nations and ex-colonies more generally. The injustices of French colonialism and its legacies are far from having been understood or resolved. Traditional self-conceptions of the nation of France are proving to be inadequate at best in a country that is increasingly multicultural, multi-faith, as well as linguistically and racially diverse. Feminist thinkers are at the center of debates about how best to conceive of the nation and the citizen in this increasingly diversified and globalized context. Like French philosophy in general, feminist philosophical work in France maintains a constant engagement with the major philosophers and social theorists of the French and European past. In the decades to come, French feminist thinkers will likely maintain those points of reference in their venturing further afield to address feminist issues from an even more explicitly internationalist perspective.

Notes

1 For a history of the MLF, see Claire Duchen, *Feminism in France* (London: Routledge, 1986). For more information about the feminist movement in France and its importation to the English-speaking world, see also Claire Duchen (ed.), *French Connections* (Amherst, Mass.: The University of Massachusetts Press, 1987); Sherry Turkle, *Psychoanalytic Politics* (New York: Basic Books, 1978); Dorothy Kaufmann-McCall, "Politics of difference: the Women's Movement in France from May 1968 to Mitterrand," *Signs*, 9(2) (Winter 1983); Elaine Marks and Isabelle de Courtivron's introduction to *New French Feminisms* (New York: Schocken, 1981); Gayatri Spivak, "French feminism in an international frame," *Yale French Studies*, 62 (1981); Alice Jardine, *Gynesis: Configurations of Woman and Modernity* (Ithaca, NY: Cornell University Press, 1981); Toril Moi, *Sexual/Textual Politics* (London: Methuen, 1985); "Feminist readings: French text/American contexts," *Yale French Studies*, 62 (1981); Eva Martin Sartori and Dorothy Wynne

Zimmerman (eds.), *French Women Writers* (Lincoln, Neb.: University of Nebraska Press, 1991); Christine Delphy, "The invention of French feminism: an essential move," *Yale French Studies*, 87 (1995).

2   Many of the entries on individual thinkers are based in part on research and writing done by Rita Alfonso and Jennifer Hansen for the *French Feminism Reader* edited by Kelly Oliver (New York: Rowman & Littlefield, 2000).

3   See under Bibliography below for the key to text citations.

Bibliography
Simone de Beauvoir
Selected primary sources

1948: *The Ethics of Ambiguity*, trans. B. Frechtman. New York: Philosophical Library (original work published 1947).

1952: *The Second Sex*, trans. H. M. Parshley. New York: Knopf (original work published 1949). (References to this book are abbreviated in the text to "*SS*, p. ••.")

1954: *She Came to Stay*, trans. Y. Moyse and R. Senhouse. Cleveland, Ohio: World Publishing (original work published 1943).

1956: *The Mandarins*, trans. L. M. Friedman. Cleveland, Ohio: World Publishing (original work published 1954).

1959: *Memoirs of a Dutiful Daughter*, trans. J. Kirkup. Cleveland, Ohio: World Publishing (original work published 1958).

1965: *Force of Circumstance*, trans. R. Howard. New York: Putnam (original work published 1963).

1966: *A Very Easy Death*, trans. P. O'Brian. New York: Putnam (original work published 1964).

1968: *Les belles images*, trans. P. O'Brian. New York: Putnam (original work published 1966).

1969: *The Woman Destroyed*, trans. P. O'Brian. New York: Putnam (original work published 1968).

1972: *Coming of Age*, trans. P. O'Brian. New York: Putnam (original work published 1970).

1974: *All Said and Done*, trans. P. O'Brian. New York: Putnam (original work published 1972).

1984: *Adieux: A Farewell to Sartre*, trans. P. O'Brian. New York: Pantheon (original work published 1981).

Selected secondary sources

Bair, D. 1990: *Simone de Beauvoir: A Biography*. London: Cape.

Bergoffen, D. B. 1997: *The Philosophy of Simone de Beauvoir: Gendered Phenomenologies, Erotic Generosities*. Albany, NY: State University of New York Press.

Moi, T. 1994: *Simone de Beauvoir: The Making of an Intellectual Woman*. Oxford: Blackwell.

Schwartzer, A. 1984: *After the Second Sex: Conversations with Simone de Beauvoir*. New York: Pantheon.

Simons, M. A. (ed.) 1995: *Feminist Interpretations of Simone de Beauvoir*. University Park, Penn.: Pennsylvania State University Press.

Luce Irigaray

Selected primary sources

1985: *Speculum of the Other Woman*, trans. G. C. Gill. Ithaca, NY: Cornell University Press (original work published 1974).

1985: *This Sex Which Is Not One*, trans. C. Porter. Ithaca, NY: Cornell University Press (original work published 1977).

1991: *Marine Lover*, trans. G. Gill. New York: Columbia University Press (original work published 1980).

1991: *The Irigaray Reader*, ed. M. Whitford. Oxford: Blackwell.

1992: *Elemental Passions*, trans. J. Collie and J. Still. New York: Routledge (original work published 1981).

1993: *An Ethics of Sexual Difference*, trans. C. Burke and G. C. Gill. Ithaca, NY: Cornell University Press (original work published 1984).

1993: *Je, tu, nous: Toward a Culture of Difference*, trans. A. Martin. New York: Routledge (original work published 1990).

1993: *Sexes and Genealogies*, trans. G. C. Gill. New York: Columbia University Press (original work published 1987).

1994: *Thinking the Difference: For a Peaceful Revolution*, trans. A. Martin. New York: Routledge (original work published 1989).

1995: La question de l'autre [The question of the other]. In M. De Manassein (ed.), *De l'égalité des sexes* [*On the Equality of the Sexes*]. Paris: Centre national de documentation pédagogique.

1996: *I Love to You*, trans. A. Martin. New York: Routledge (original work published 1992).

1997: *Etre deux*. Paris: Bernard Grasset.

1999: *The Forgetting of Air in Martin Heidegger*, trans. M. B. Mader. Austin, Texas: The University of Texas Press (original work published 1983).

2000: *To be Two*, trans. M. M. Rhodes and M. F. Cocito-Monoc. New York: Routledge.

2000: *To Speak is Never Neutral*, trans. G. Schwab. New York: Routledge (original work published 1985).

2001: *Democracy Begins Between Two*, trans. K. Anderson. New York: Routledge (original work published in Italian in 1994).

2002: *Between East and West: From Singularity to Community*, trans. S. Pluhácek. New York: Columbia University Press (original work published 1999).

Selected secondary sources

Burke, C., Schor, N., and Whitford, M. (eds.) 1994: *Engaging with Irigaray: Feminist Philosophy and Modern European Thought*. New York: Columbia University Press.

Chanter, T. 1995: *Ethics of Eros: Irigaray's Rewriting of the Philosophers*. London: Routledge.

De Lauretis, T. 1984: *Alice Doesn't: Feminism, Semiotics, Cinema*. Bloomington, Ind.: Indiana University Press.

Gallop, J. 1982: *The Daughter's Seduction: Feminism and Psychoanalysis*. Ithaca, NY: Cornell University Press.

Hirsh, E. and Olson, G. A. 1995: "Je – Luce Irigaray": a meeting with Luce Irigaray. In *Feminist Ethics and Social Policy, Part II. Hypatia* 10(2), special issue.

Whitford, M. 1991: *Luce Irigaray: Philosophy in the Feminine*. London and New York: Routledge.

Colette Guillaumin

Selected primary sources

1979: Women and cultural values, classes according to sex and their relationship to culture in industrial societies. *Cultures*, 6(1), 40–8.

1980: The idea of race and its elevation to autonomous scientific and legal status. In UNESCO (ed.), *Sociological Theories: Race and Colonialism*. Paris: UNESCO Press.

1981: The practice of power and belief in nature: Part I. The appropriation of women (trans. L. Murgatroyd). *Feminist Issues*, 1(2), 3–28.

1981: The practice of power and belief in nature: Part II. The naturalist discourse (trans. L. Murgatroyd). *Feminist Issues*, 1(3), 87–109.

1982: The question of difference (trans. H. V. Wenzel). *Feminist Issues*, 2(1), 33–52.

1983: Herrings and tigers: animal behavior and human society (trans. M. J. Lakeland). *Feminist Issues*, 3(1), 45–59.

1984: Women and theories about society: the effects on theory of the anger of the oppressed (trans. M. J. Lakeland). *Feminist Issues*, 4(1), 23–39 (original work published 1981).

1988: Race and nature: the system of marks (trans. M. J. Lakeland). *Feminist Issues*, 8(2), 25–43.

1988: Sexism, a right-wing constant of any discourse: a theoretical note (trans. C. Kunstenaar). In G. Seidel (ed.), *The Nature of Right: A Feminist Analysis of Order Patterns*. Amsterdam: John Benjamins.

1991: "Race" and discourse. In M. Silverman (ed.), *Race, Discourse and Power in France*. Aldershot: Avebury.

1993: The constructed body. In C. Burroughs and J. Ehrenreich (eds.), *Reading the Social Body*. Iowa City: University of Iowa Press.

1995: *Racism, Sexism, Power and Ideology*. New York: Routledge.

Selected secondary sources

Adkins, L. and Leonard, D. 1996: *Sex in Question: French Materialist Feminism*. Philadelphia, Penn.: Taylor & Francis.

Juteau-Lee, D. 1995: Introduction: (re)constructing the categories of "race" and "sex": the work of a precursor. In *Racism, Sexism, Power and Ideology*. New York: Routledge.

Kester-Shelton, P. 1996: Guillaumin, Colette. In *Feminist Writers*. Detroit, Mich.: St. James Press.

Hélène Cixous

Selected primary sources

1972: *The Exile of James Joyce or the Art of Replacement*, trans. S. Purcell. New York: David Lewis (original work published 1968).

1976: The laugh of Medusa. *Signs*, 1(4), 875–99 (original work published 1975).

1981: Castration or decapitation? *Signs*, 7(1), 41–55 (original work published 1976).

1986: *Inside*, trans. C. Barko. New York: Schocken (original work published 1969).

1986 (with Catherine Clément): *The Newly Born Woman*, trans. B. Wing. Minneapolis, Minn.: Minnesota University Press (original work published 1975).

1990: *Reading With Clarice Lispector*, trans. V. A. Conley. Minneapolis, Minn.: Minnesota University Press.

1991: *"Coming to Writing" and Other Essays*, trans. S. Cornell et al. Cambridge, Mass.: Harvard University Press.

1991: *The Book of Promethea*, trans. B. Wing. Lincoln, Neb.: University of Nebraska Press (original work published 1983).

1993: *Three Steps on the Ladder of Writing*, trans. S. Cornell and S. Sellers. New York: Columbia University Press.

1994: *The Hélène Cixous Reader*, ed. S. Sellers. New York: Routledge.

1997 (with Mireille Calle-Gruber): *Hélène Cixous Rootprints: Memory and Life Writing*, trans. E. Prenowitz. New York: Routledge (original work published 1994).

1998: *Stigmata: Surviving Texts*. New York: Routledge.

Selected secondary sources

Conley, V. A. 1992: *Hélène Cixous*. New York: Harvester Wheatsheaf.

Moi, T. 1985: Hélène Cixous. In *Sexual/Textual Politics: Feminist Literary Theory*. New York: Methuen.

Sellers, S. 1996: *Hélène Cixous: Authorship, Autobiography, and Love*. Cambridge, Mass.: Blackwell.

Shiach, M. 1991: *Hélène Cixous: A Politics of Writing*. New York: Routledge.

Wilcox, H., McWatters, K., Thomson, A., and Williams, L. R. (eds.) 1990: *The Body and the Text: Hélène Cixous, Reading and Teaching*. New York: St. Martin's Press.

Julia Kristeva

Selected primary sources

1977: *About Chinese Women*, trans. A. Barrows. New York: Marion Boyars (original work published 1974).

1980a: Interview with Kristeva. In E. Baruch and L. Srrano (eds.), *Women Analyze Women*. New York: NYU Press (1988).

1980b: *Desire in Language*, trans. T. Gora, A. Jardine, and L. Roudiez; ed. L. Roudiez. New York: Columbia University Press.

1982: *Powers of Horror*, trans. L. Roudiez. New York: Columbia University Press (original work published 1980).

1984: *Revolution in Poetic Language*, trans. M. Waller. New York: Columbia University Press (original work published 1974).

1986: *The Kristeva Reader*, ed. T. Moi. New York: Columbia Press.

1987: *Tales of Love*, trans. L. Roudiez. New York: Columbia University Press (original work published 1983).

1989: *Black Sun: Depression and Melancholy*, trans. L. Roudiez. New York: Columbia University Press (original work published 1987).

1991: *Strangers to Ourselves*, trans. L. Roudiez. New York: Columbia University Press (original work published 1989).

1995: *New Maladies of the Soul*, trans. R. Guberman. New York: Columbia University Press (original work published 1993).

1996: *Julia Kristeva Interviews*, ed. R. Guberman. New York: Columbia University Press.

1996: *Time and Sense: Proust and the Experience of Literature*, trans. R. Guberman. New York: Columbia University Press (original work published 1994).

1997: *La révolte intime: pouvoirs et limites de la psychanalyse II*. Paris: Fayard.

1998, 2002: *The Portable Kristeva*, ed. K. Oliver. New York: Columbia University Press.

2000a: *The Crisis of the European Subject*, trans. S. Fairfield. New York: The Other Press.

2000b: *The Sense and Nonsense of Revolt*, trans. J. Herman. New York: Columbia University Press (original work published 1996).

2001: *Hannah Arendt* (trans. R. Guberman). New York: Columbia University Press (original work published 1999).

2001: *Melanie Klein* (trans. R. Guberman). New York: Columbia University Press (original work published 2000).

Selected secondary sources

Benjamin, A. and Fletcher, J. (eds.) 1990: *Abjection, Melancholia and Love: The Work of Julia Kristeva*. London and New York: Routledge.

Crownfield, D. (ed.) 1992: *Body/text in Julia Kristeva: Religion, Women and Psychoanalysis*. Albany, NY: State University of New York Press.

Lechte, J. 1990: *Julia Kristeva*. London and New York: Routledge.

Oliver, K. 1993: *Reading Kristeva: Unraveling the Double-Bind*. Bloomington, Ind.: Indiana University Press.

——(ed.) 1993: *Ethics, Politics and Difference in Julia Kristeva's Writings*. New York: Routledge.

——1998: *Subjectivity without Subjects*. New York: Rowman & Littlefield.

Smith, A. 1996: *Julia Kristeva: Readings of Exile and Estrangement*. New York: St. Martins Press.

Smith, A.-M. 1998: *Julia Kristeva: Speaking the Unspeakable*. New York: Stylus Press.

Monique Wittig

Selected primary sources

1971: *Les guérillières*, trans. D. Le Vay. New York: Viking (original work published 1969).

1975: *The Lesbian Body*, trans. D. Le Vay. New York: Morrow (original work published 1973).

1979 (with Sande Zeig): *Lesbian Peoples: Material for a Dictionary*. New York: Avon (original work published 1975).

1980: La pensée straight. *Questions feministes*, 7, 21–6.

1980: The straight mind. *Feminist Issues*, 1(1), 103–12.

1981: One is not born a woman. *Feminist Issues*, 1(4), 47–54.

1982: The category of sex. *Feminist Issues*, 2(2), 63–8.

1983: The point of view: universal or particular? *Feminist Issues*, 3(2), 63–70.

1985: The mark of sex. *Feminist Issues*, 5(2), 3–12.

1987: *Across the Acheron*, trans. D. Le Vay. London: Peter Owen (original work published 1985).

1990: *Homo sum*. *Feminist Issues*, 10(1), 3–11.

1992: *The Straight Mind and Other Essays*. Boston: Beacon Press. (References to this book are abbreviated in the text to "*SM*, p. ••.")

1996: *The Opoponax*, trans. H. Weaver. New York: Simon and Schuster (original work published 1983).

Selected secondary sources

Butler, J. 1990: Monique Wittig: bodily disintegration and fictive sex. In *Gender Trouble: Feminism and the Subversion of Identity*. New York: Routledge.

Cowder, D. G. 1991: Monique Wittig. In E. M. Sartori and D. W. Zimmerman (eds.), *French Women Writers: A Bio-Bibliographical Source Book*. Westport, Conn.: Greenwood Press.

Ostrovsky, E. 1991: *A Constant Journey: The Fiction of Monique Wittig*. Carbondale and Edwardsville, Ill.: Southern Illinois University Press.

Sellers, S. 1991: Monique Wittig. In *Language and Sexual Difference: Feminist Writing in France*. New York: Macmillan.

Wenzel, H. V. 1981: The text as body/politics: an appreciation of Monique Wittig's writings in context. *Feminist Studies*, 7(2), 264–87.

Sarah Kofman

Selected primary sources

1982: *Le respect des femmes*. Paris: Galilée.

1983: *Un métier impossible*. Paris: Galilée.

1985: *Mélancolie de l'art*. Paris: Galilée.

1985: *The Enigma of Woman*, trans. C. Porter. Ithaca, NY: Cornell University Press. (References to this book are abbreviated in the text to "*EW*, p. ••.")

1986: *Nietzsche et la scène philosophique*. Paris: Éditions Galilée.

1988: *Childhood of Art: An Interpretation of Freud's Aesthetics*, trans. W. Woodhull. New York: Columbia University Press (original work published 1970).

1991: *Freud and Fiction*, trans. S. Wykes. Cambridge: Polity Press (original work published 1974).

1992: *Explosion I: de l' "Ecce Homo" de Nietzsche*. Paris: Galilée.

1993: *Nietzsche and Metaphor*, trans. D. Large. Stanford, Calif.: Stanford University Press (original work published 1972).

1996: *Rue Ordener, Rue Labat*, trans. A. Smock. Lincoln, Neb.: University of Nebraska Press (original work published 1996).

1998: *Smothered Words*, trans. M. Dobie. Evanston, Ill: Northwestern University Press (original work published 1987).

1998: *Socrates: Fictions of a Philosopher*, trans. C. Porter. Ithaca, NY: Cornell University Press (original work published 1989).

1999: *Camera obscura*, trans. W. Straw. Ithaca, NY: Cornell University Press (original work published 1973).

Selected secondary sources

Anonymous 1997: Sarah Kofman, special issue of *Les cahiers du grif*, 3.

Deutscher, P. and Oliver, K. (eds.) 1999: *Enigmas: Essays on Sarah Kofman*. Ithaca, NY: Cornell University Press.

Edwin, S. 2002: "Impossible" professions: Sarah Kofman, witnessing and the social depth of trauma. In K. Oliver and S. Edwin (eds.), *Between the Psyche and the Social*. New York: Rowman & Littlefield.

Smock, A. 1984: Disastrous responsibility. *L'ésprit créateur*, 24(3), 5–20.

Michèle Le Doeuff

Selected primary sources

1977: Women and philosophy. *Radical Philosophy*, 17; also in T. Moi (ed.) 1987: *French Feminist Thought*. Oxford: Blackwell.

1979: Operative philosophy: Simone de Beauvoir and existentialism. *Ideology & Consciousness*, 6.

1984: The public employer. *m/f*, 9.

1987: Ants and women, or philosophy without borders. In A. P. Griffiths (ed.), *Contemporary French Philosophy*. Cambridge: Cambridge University Press.

1989: *The Philosophical Imaginary*, trans. C. Gordon. London: Athlone (original work published 1980).

1990: Woman, reason, etc. *Differences*, 2(3).

1991: *Hipparchia's Choice: An Essay Concerning Women, Philosophy, etc.*, trans. T. Selous. Oxford: Blackwell (original work published 1989). (References to this book are abbreviated in the text to "*HC*, p. ••.")

Selected secondary sources

Deutscher, M. 1987: Stories, pictures, arguments. *Philosophy*, 62(240).

Gatens, M. 1986: Feminism, philosophy and riddles without answers. In C. Pateman and E. Grosz (eds.), *Feminist Challenges*. Boston, Mass.: Northeastern University Press.

Grimshaw, J. 1996: Philosophy, feminism and universalism. *Radical Philosophy*, 76.

Grosz, E. 1987: Feminist theory and the challenge to knowledges. *Women's Studies International Forum*, 10(5).

Morris, M. 1981–2: Operative reasoning: Michèle Le Doeuff, philosophy and feminism. *Ideology & Consciousness*, 9.

Christine Delphy

Selected primary sources

1977: *The Main Enemy*. London: Women's Research and Resources Center (original work published 1970).

1980: A materialist feminism is possible (trans. D. Leonard). *Feminist Review*, 4.

1981: For a materialist feminism. *Feminist Issues*, 1(2), 69–76.

1981: Women's liberation in France: the tenth year. *Feminist Issues*, 1(2), 103–12.

1984: *Close to Home: A Materialist Analysis of Women's Oppression*. Amherst, Mass.: University of Massachusetts Press.

1987: Proto-feminism and anti-feminism. In T. Moi (ed.), *French Feminist Thought*. Oxford: Blackwell (original work published 1976).

1988: Patriarchy, domestic mode of production, gender, and class. In C. Nelson and L. Grossberg (eds.), *Marxism and the Interpretation of Culture*. London: Macmillan.

1991: Is there marriage after divorce? In D. Leonard and S. Allen (eds.), *Sexual Divisions Revisited*. London: Macmillan.

1992 (with D. Leonard): *Familiar Exploitation: A New Analysis of Marriage in Contemporary Western Societies*. Oxford: Polity Press.

1992: Mother's union? *Trouble and Strife*, 24, 12–19.

1994: Changing women in a changing Europe: Is difference the future for feminism? *Women's Studies International Forum*, 27(2), 187–201.

1995: The invention of French feminism: an essential move. *Yale French Studies*, 87, 190–221.

Selected secondary sources

Adkins, L. and Leonard, D. 1996: *Sex in Question: French Materialist Feminism*. Philadelphia, Penn.: Taylor & Francis.

Barrett, M. and McIntosh, M. 1979: Christine Delphy: Towards a materialist feminism? *Feminist Review*, 1, 95–106.

Jackson, S. 1996: *Christine Delphy*. Thousand Oaks, Calif: Sage.

Conclusion: What Now for Continental Philosophy?

Robert C. Solomon

What now for continental philosophy? Well the first thing that must be hoped for is an end to the divisiveness. By this I do not mean that healthy dialectic that is the essence of all good philosophy, nor do I mean to suggest that philosophy should in any sense become "unified." This has been the dream of many a system-builder to be sure, but such systems have almost always turned out to be anything but total or final – even if occasionally (as in that rich period from Kant to Hegel) they have turned out to be fascinating failures. This is the most historically astute message of postmodernism, the attack on "master narratives" and "totalizing theories," but such theories and the postmodern challenge are themselves now part of our philosophical history, and there are already signs that the next round of such ambitious narratives and theories has begun. Perhaps the need for such narratives and theories is yet another remnant of that persistent insecurity in modern philosophy that idolizes and emulates science (although in the philosophy of science, too, reductionism and other attempts to unify not so much science as the philosophy of science have turned out to be eviscerating). Or else, perhaps, it is an even older holdover from the days when (Western) philosophy was not easily distinguishable from Judeo-Christian–Islamic theology and the certainty and all-embracing security that was always its promise and its premise. Nevertheless, it is an impulse not easily stifled, although there will always be another Kierkegaard or Nietzsche or Foucault or Derrida to remind us that it is an impulse that must itself be questioned and challenged.

What has always been best about philosophy is its disunity and diversity. What the twenty-first century promises is not so much a new unity in philosophy (despite its inevitable globalization) but a rich confluence and cross-fertilization not only between Anglo-American philosophy and the "Continent" but around the world, involving any number of traditions (and continents) that have hitherto been allowed only (at best) a passing glance or a dismissive gesture in "Western" "mainstream" philosophy. But, indeed, the "West" is no longer a privileged enclave, and the "mainstream" has now gone global. The Chunnel not only connects England and France but, via the Internet, the whole world.

What has always been most appealing and most valuable about "continental" philosophy has been its insistence on what are now called "interdisciplinary" concerns and sources. To be sure, its lesser practitioners have not always displayed such cross-disciplinary curiosity or taken advantage of its many resources. After all, learning other disciplines is hard work, and it distracts from the more urgent business of demonstrating one's cleverness and defending one's turf. But Kant did not restrict himself to what is now often referred to as the "core" of philosophy, "M&E" (metaphysics and epistemology). Indeed, his philosophy is enormously misunderstood if it is restricted to just those few (admittedly magnificent) arguments in the first *Critique*. Nor does it help matters much if we just add Kant's brief but obligatory work on ethics. To understand Kant and his pivotal place in philosophy it is necessary to take account of the fact that he was an avid amateur physicist and astronomer, an anthropologist, a geographer, a devotee of the (admittedly minor) arts, and a philosophical statesman.

So, too, Hegel tried to embrace all human disciplines under the single umbrella of his system (though in truth he rather used the system as a crude template to very eccentrically organize and to some extent distort the "development" of as many "forms of consciousness" as possible). Nietzsche was an enthusiastic science student as well as an ambitious musician, a theology student as well as a philologist, a self-help spiritual writer as well as the "Death of God" Antichrist. And, to be sure, he was the greatest philosophical stylist since Plato. Heidegger and Sartre stretched far beyond their philosophical disciplines, into politics in particular (disastrously for Heidegger; sometimes embarrassingly for Sartre) as well as into the arts and cultural and social criticism. The postmodernists have shown missionary zeal in their efforts to draw upon and then spread their influence throughout the academic, intellectual, and artistic worlds. And, of course, inspired by Marx, the philosophers of the Frankfurt School committed themselves to incorporating social research and cultural phenomena into their philosophical approach as a matter of principle.

Whatever one thinks of these various philosophers, philosophies, and their influences, one must admit that their interdisciplinary reach is what philosophy at its best has always been about. Kant called metaphysics the "Queen of the Sciences," but philosophy in general, both as he practiced it and as he inherited it from two and a half millennia of predecessors, was more than a Queen. It was the Mother of all disciplines, even the very essence of human thought (if, that is, we would allow thought to have an essence or to be distinctively "human"). Out of philosophy came physics and biology, Aristotle's wonder about the natural world. Out of philosophy came a rich self-referential language and literature and the great themes of art. Out of philosophy emerged the shared concerns and confusions of an increasingly diverse humanity.

Or maybe not. Maybe philosophy simply *followed* all of these things, as Hegel (in a less ecstatic mood) declared in his later *Philosophy of Right*: "the owl of Minerva flies only at dusk." Nevertheless, the conclusion is the same. Philosophy, at its best, embraces the human spirit as a whole and sharply divides itself off from nothing, except, perhaps, those dull, daily urgencies that sap our energy and attention while making impossible the minimally reflective thought that is necessary for us to consider our lives rather than simply be submerged in them. But, of course, one might argue that this too is philosophy, which simply means, again, that philosophy is or never should be absent from or foreign to anything human. And that is what the best of the philosophies we have covered in this book have to tell us, even when they polemicize for or against the reflective life. Hegel may tell us that truth emerges only with reflection, while Nietzsche tells us that much of reflective thought is a lie, but they are both exemplary in pointing out that philosophy lies implicit in everything that we do, and will continue to define and structure our thought.

Index